ANNALS OF
THE NEW YORK ACADEMY
OF SCIENCES

Volume 444

EDITORIAL STAFF

Executive Editor

BILL BOLAND

Managing Editor

JOYCE HITCHCOCK

Associate Editor

M.K. BRENNAN

The New York Academy of Sciences
2 East 63rd Street
New York, New York 10021

Memory Dysfunctions: An Integration of Animal and Human Research From Preclinical and Clinical Perspectives

ANNALS OF THE NEW YORK ACADEMY OF SCIENCES
Volume 444

Memory Dysfunctions: An Integration of Animal and Human Research From Preclinical and Clinical Perspectives

*Edited by David S. Olton, Elkan Gamzu,
and Suzanne Corkin*

*The New York Academy of Sciences
New York, New York
1985*

Library of Congress Cataloging in Publication Data

Main entry under title:

Memory dysfunctions.

(Annals of the New York Academy of Sciences, ISSN 0077-8923; v. 444)
Result of a conference held June 13–15, 1984 by the New York Academy of Sciences.
Includes bibliographies and index.
1. Amnesia—Congresses. 2. Memory, Disorders of—Congresses. 3. Memory, Disorders of—Animal models—Congresses. I. Olton, David S. II. Gamzu, Elkan, 1943– . III. Corkin, Suzanne. IV. New York Academy of Sciences. V. Series. [DNLM: 1. Memory Disorders—congresses.

W1 AN626YL v.444 / WM 173.7 M533 1984]
Q11.N5 vol. 444   500 s   85-11603
[RC394.A5]   [616.85'232]
ISBN 0-89766-282-2
ISBN 0-89766-283-0 (pbk.)

SP
Printed in the United States of America
ISBN 0-89766-282-2 (cloth)
ISBN 0-89766-283-0 (paper)
ISSN 0077-8923

ANNALS OF THE NEW YORK ACADEMY OF SCIENCES

Volume 444

May 30, 1985

Memory Dysfunctions:
An Integration of Animal and Human Research from Preclinical and Clinical Perspectives[a]

Editors

DAVID S. OLTON, ELKAN GAMZU, and SUZANNE CORKIN

CONTENTS

[a]The papers in this volume were presented at a conference entitled Memory Dysfunctions: An Integration of Animal and Human Research from Preclinical and Clinical Perspectives, which was held by the New York Academy of Sciences on June 13–15, 1984.

Poster Papers

Financial assistance received from:
- American Cyanamid Company (Lederle Laboratories)
- Bristol-Myers/Pharmaceutical Research and Development Division
- Burroughs Wellcome Co.
- CIBA-GEIGY/Pharmaceuticals Division
- E.I. du Pont de Nemours & Company/Biomedical Products Department
- Fidia Research Laboratories
- Glaxo Group
- Hoechst-Roussel Pharmaceuticals Inc.
- Hoffmann-La Roche Inc.
- Lilly Research Laboratories
- Merck Sharp & Dohme/Research Laboratories
- Office of Naval Research
- Pfizer/Central Research
- Sandoz Pharmaceuticals
- Schering-Plough Corporation
- Searle Research and Development/Division of G. D. Searle & Co.
- Stuart Pharmaceuticals/Division of ICI Americas Inc.
- Warner Lambert Company

Introduction

DAVID S. OLTON

Department of Psychology
The Johns Hopkins University
Baltimore, Maryland 21218

ELKAN GAMZU

Department of Pharmacology
Hoffmann-La Roche, Inc.
Nutley, New Jersey 07110

SUZANNE CORKIN

Department of Psychology
Massachusetts Institute of Technology
Cambridge, Massachusetts 02139

The ability to remember information is a prerequisite for effective functioning in daily life. This volume brings together research findings on characteristics of normal memory, brain mechanisms involved in it, characteristics of memory impairments, pathological changes that produce them, and pharmacological techniques to alleviate them. Each of these approaches embodies information that is relevant to the others, and together they help advance the development of therapeutic interventions. Consequently, the material in this volume has relevance both to investigators who carry out basic research in memory, and to those who seek a practical treatment for memory disorders.

Five important themes interrelate the chapters presented here: Each of these themes reflects significant progress in the past few years and suggests directions that should be productive for future research.

Memory is not a single homogeneous process, and memory impairments are often discrete: Even when some abilities are profoundly impaired, others can proceed normally. Sensitive and diagnostic tests for different memory functions have shown striking dissociations of performance in amnesic patients. These dissociations have influenced theories of memory and of the functional organization of the brain and have identified the types of impairments that therapeutic interventions should seek to resolve. Theoretical analyses of memory have also made significant progress, and examples of new approaches can be found in many of these chapters. The confluence of cognitive psychology, artificial intelligence, and information processing has produced working, computational models of memory processes. These new ideas about the organization of mnemonic capacities have helped to develop better behavioral analyses of memory impairments; they have begun to influence neuroanatomical and neurochemical investigations of the neural systems underlying memory functions.

Animal models of human memory and memory impairments are necessary to obtain discrete manipulations and accurate measurements of brain systems. The criteria for developing and evaluating effective models have been well articulated. The emphasis on cognitive processes and the representation of information in animals, a newly emerging area that may eventually choose the label "comparative cognition," are describing ways to ask animals very sophisticated questions about their memory processes. Consequently, the experiments with animals are becoming ever more accurate models of human memory systems. Information gained from these models is critical if we are to describe precisely the neuroanatomical and neurochemical bases of normal memory and the types of pathology that can produce amnesia. Discrete tests of different memory processes can also assist the search for pharmacological compounds that affect memory. People remember a great deal of information that is not dependent upon language. Nonetheless, the vast majority of tests for human memory have used verbal material. The principles and ideas guiding memory research in animals can help advance our understanding of human nonverbal memory capacities.

Improvements in biomedical engineering have increased the ways in which the structure and function of the nervous system can be altered and assessed. Not many years ago, the brain was little more than a black box—only its most obvious features could be described. Now, detailed analyses can examine many of its most molecular constituents. For example, these types of studies provide a better understanding of the neuroanatomical and neurochemical mechanisms that are involved in memory and will ultimately permit the bridge between the psychological and neural analyses of memory. The information gained from these approaches is particularly useful for diagnostic assessment of the neural consequences of pharmacological interventions in people, and for direct analysis of the neuroanatomical and neurochemical mechanisms involved in memory.

Pharmacological strategies for the treatment of memory impairments have been intensively examined. The costs of coping with untreated memory impairments are already substantial and growing greater every day. The potential benefits of a successful pharmacological intervention are therefore great and ever increasing. Approaches emphasizing treatment have combined two often mutually exclusive talents. One is a creative search for novel compounds (or groups of compounds) to alter memory. The other is a controlled, skeptical analysis of the results in order to determine whether these compounds have significant therapeutic effects. A comparison of the types of changes produced by different compounds has implications not only for the treatment of memory dysfunctions, but also for our understanding of the neurochemical organization of the nervous system and the psychological organization of memory.

Aging is an area that has involved all of the approaches illustrated in this conference. With increasing age, some humans and some animals incur increasingly severe impairments of memory and neurochemical function. Some of these changes reflect pathological processes, such as those seen in Alzheimer's disease; others reflect "normal" aging. Because individuals differ substantially in the extent to which aging affects their psychological and neurochemical functions, comparisons of individual differences can be a particularly powerful way of interrelating specific types of memory impairments with specific neural alterations. Thus, the results of experiments with aging subjects can provide important insights to those who conduct studies with young individuals as well. Aging is a phenomenon important in its own right; it is also an independent variable that can help our understanding of the characteristics of normal and impaired memory, and the neuroanatomical and neurochemical mechanisms underlying them. The changes seen in aging can suggest the types of therapeutic interventions that may be of most benefit.

In summary, the topics of memory and memory impairments bring together research enterprises that approach similar issues from different, yet related, perspectives. As is often the case with converging analyses, the results obtained from one perspective are useful not only in the same field, but also in the related fields. The chapters that follow provide many examples of such fruitful interactions.

Many people and organizations helped to organize this conference and produce this volume. We thank The New York Academy of Sciences for suggestions about the topics and structure of the conference, and for taking care of the innumerable details associated with its implementation; the organizations that provided financial support; and the speakers and other participants for their contributions.

Distributed Models of Cognitive Processes

Applications to Learning and Memory[a]

JAMES L. McCLELLAND

Department of Psychology
Carnegie-Mellon University
Pittsburgh, Pennsylvania 15213

Several researchers, coming from a number of different backgrounds and viewpoints, have recently begun to think in terms of models of information processing and memory in which processing takes place through the simultaneous interaction of a very large number of very simple, but highly interconnected processing elements. The present paper gives a general characterization of this approach, describes some of the reasons for its appeal, considers how it relates to underlying physiological mechanisms, and discusses the implications of this view for our understanding of amnesia.

First, I want to make it clear that this approach is based on the work of many people. Perhaps most important has been the work described in the volume edited by Hinton and Anderson entitled *Parallel Models of Associative Memory*.[1] My own work on these models has been the result of a collaboration with David E. Rumelhart; most of the fruit of that collaboration will appear in a forthcoming book, though some of it is summarized here. It is also important to bear in mind that the class of models I will be describing represents a family resemblance structure. They have no necessary or sufficient conditions, though they generally agree on a number of basic properties. Third, the development of models of this class, which I will simply call distributed models, is still in its infancy. The application of these ideas to the psychology of normal memory and amnesia is just getting under way.

BASIC CHARACTERISTICS OF DISTRIBUTED MODELS

Distributed models are abstract characterizations of processing systems. They are analogous to computer programs, in that they do not specify the detailed physical processes underlying information processing; rather they describe processing at a more abstract, computational level. They differ from computer programs, though, in three fundamental ways. (1) Processing is thought to emerge from the interactions of a large number of simple (abstract) computational elements called nodes, rather than through the activity of a single, central processing unit. (2) The knowledge that underlies processing in distributed models is thought to be stored in the strengths of the connections between the nodes, rather than in data structures or compiled computer code interpreted by the central processing unit. (3) Learning in distributed models amounts to changes in the strengths of connections between the nodes, rather than changing the contents of data structures or recompilation of the program.

[a]Supported by a grant from the Systems Development Foundation. The author is a recipient of a Research Scientist Career Development Award (MH 00385).

What Are the Models Models Of?

A major issue that we must be clear about is what these models are models of. A major problem with answering this question is that different people answer it in different ways. My own view is that distributed models provide nice descriptions of the microstructure both of information processing and of the physiological substrate that underlies it. However, they do not describe the macrostructure at either level. At the cognitive level, this means that they do not describe the overall organization of behavior, though they are assumed to describe the structure of the primitive operations out of which the overall structure of behavior is built. At the physiological level, they do not describe the architecture of the brain in terms of the functional roles of different regions of the brain.

The fact that distributed models can be used to provide descriptions at two different levels of description does not mean that one and the same model will provide a satisfactory description at both levels, but simply that members of the same general class of models can characterize both levels. The exact relation between the two levels is, of course, a subject about which one could only speculate at this time. The models also have implications for how we should think about the macrostructure at either level. However, the laws that characterize the macrostructure of human performance may best be cast at a higher level of description. This is analogous to the relation between the subatomic and the molecular levels in physics and chemistry. Presumably, all the properties of molecular behavior have their basis in subatomic processes, but there are lawful regularities of molecular behavior that are conveniently captured, without resorting to a description of subatomic processes. Similarly, a description of the functions of the different regions of the brain need not refer in detail to the fact that each region is composed of neurons and synapses; and a description of the functions of each member of a sequence of information-processing steps need not refer to the fact that each step is based on the interactions of a large number of simple processing units all operating concurrently.

The fact that distributed models may be used to capture two different levels of description requires us to be clear about which level we are describing at any given time. In the first part of what follows, I will be describing models cast at the more abstract level, though when we turn to a consideration of amnesia, we will examine the relevance of the assumption that the same general principles apply at the physiological, as well as the psychological levels.

The remainder of this paper considers the relevance of distributed models to psychological and physiological theories of memory. The first section relates the approach to basic concepts in the psychology of memory. The second section mentions several reasons why the approach may prove to be appealing to psychologists. The third discusses the relation between distributed models at the psychological level and the possible physiological substrate of memory. The fourth section considers the phenomena of amnesia from the point of view of the distributed approach.

BASIC CONCEPTS IN MEMORY

The study of the psychology of memory has lead to a number of basic concepts. These have arisen from a variety of different theoretical contexts. Some of these concepts map easily onto the distributed framework, others do not. Here space only allows us to consider a number of concepts that can be easily related to this framework.

Current Representation or Mental State as Pattern of Activation

In distributed models, we think of a mental state as a pattern of activation over the set of computational elements whose activity underlies processing. This state is evolving and changing all the time, of course.

Let us note that the pattern of activation at any one time will reflect both the content of particular recent inputs to the memory system, for example a sentence an experimenter has given a subject to memorize, and the context in which that input occurs. For conceptual clarity, it helps to assume that the units in the model can be subdivided into those whose state is directly influenced by the content of the particular stimulus and those influenced primarily by the context; with the proviso that these units are interconnected with each other, so that the content conditions the context and vice versa.

It is also important to note that the nodes in a distributed model play particular roles in the patterns of activation. For example, in a system for processing words, some of the nodes will stand for different aspects of the sounds of the words and some for different aspects of their meanings. Different sounds are represented by alternative patterns of activation over the same set of sound nodes and different meanings by alternative patterns of activation over the same set of meaning nodes. It may be simpler to understand the models if we simply think of each node as standing for a particular attribute the item represented may or may not have; if the node is active, the item currently represented has the attribute, or at least the representation stipulates that it does.

Processing as an Interactive Process

Processing in distributed models results from the interactions of the processing elements themselves. The result of the interactive activation process is the evolution of the patterns of activation through time.

The pattern of activation produced by any given input will be widely distributed over a large number of different parts of the overall cognitive system; for example, if the input is a written sentence, it will be distributed over primary and secondary visual areas, language areas, and areas specifically involved in mediating the connections between the two. Some of these processing areas can be thought of as playing a role in producing the higher levels of the representation; others can be thought of as being the ones in which those higher level representations are formed. However, viewed in another way, all the nodes in all of the different parts of the system play a role, both in the representation and in the processing that forms and maintains that representation. Fundamentally, the processing elements are the representational elements and the representational elements are the processing elements.

The Long-Term Memory Trace

Patterns of activation come and go, and are replaced by subsequent patterns of activation. What these patterns leave behind is not a copy of the pattern of activation itself, but changes in the strengths of interconnections among the basic processing elements. These changes have the property that they associate the different parts of the patterns of activation; that is, the set of changes to the connection strengths resulting from a particular mental state is such that the changes tend to permit different parts of the state, when they recur, to reinstate other parts of it.

Two essential properties of the long-term memory traces are that they are distributed and superimposed on each other. By distributed, we simply mean that the connection strengths that underlie a particular pattern are distributed widely in the connections between all of the units that represent the pattern when it is active. By superimposed, we simply mean that the traces of many different patterns are superimposed in the same set of connection strengths.

Learning as Incrementation of the Connection Strengths

Learning, then, amounts to making changes in the strengths of interconnections. Such changes are assumed to underlie all types of learning, as we shall see when we discuss amnesia below.

Retrieval as Reinstatement

Retrieval of a memory trace amounts to reinstatement of a prior pattern of activation, using part of the pattern as a cue. Note that the cue can be part of the pattern itself (the content), or of the context, or a mixture of the two.

Recognition as Reinstatement of Context

By recognition, I refer here to recognition of previous occurrence in a particular context. We assume that this kind of a recognition involves an act of reinstatement too—in this case, the subject must reinstate the context of an item from the item, rather than the item from the context.

Procedural and Declarative Knowledge

It is quite clear that some of what we know we can talk about and reason explicitly about, and some of what we know we cannot. Our view is that these different aspects of our knowledge are both encoded in the cognitive systems as changes in the connections between units. The distinction is simply this: some of these units serve the special purpose of providing the substrate for recreating representations accessible to report and reasoning processes, while others are more directly imbedded in the internal structure of the cognitive system. Changes in interconnections in the latter parts of the cognitive system would influence the details of stimulus processing, such as the effectiveness of formation of a representation of a stimulus from a fragmentary input, but would not give rise to changes in overt reports.

It should be emphasized that some of the relations between familiar concepts and aspects of distributed models are more clear-cut than others. However, the ideas outlined in this section should begin to suggest a link between the constructs typically used in cognitive psychology and constructs intrinsic to the theoretical framework of distributed models of memory.

REASONS FOR THE APPEAL OF DISTRIBUTED MODELS

One reason why distributed activation models are appealing is that their relation to physiology is much easier to visualize than it is for other information-processing models. However, their appeal stems not only from their "physiological realizability" but also from the fact that they provide very attractive models at the psychological level. The most important feature of distributed activation models is that they generalize spontaneously. Consider what happens when a number of different exemplars of the same concept are presented for processing, in conjunction with the appropriate label. For example, consider what happens when a young child sees different bagels, each of which he sees in the context of some adult saying "bagel" (obviously this oversimplifies the learning situation, but let us assume that the same principles would apply in a more realistic case). Let's suppose that the sight of the bagel gives rise to a pattern of activation over one set of units, and the sound of the word gives rise to a pattern of activation over another set of units. After each learning experience of the sight of a bagel paired with the sound of its name, the connections between the visual nodes and the auditory nodes are incremented so that, when this particular bagel recurs, it will tend to reproduce the sound of the word. But all bagels are different, and many of them get eaten, so that the exact same bagel rarely reoccurs. What happens, through learning about each bagel, is that a composite memory trace of the average bagel gets built up; the central tendency gets built up but the random variability gets cancelled out.

This property does not seem so surprising, but it coexists with another property that often does seem surprising: it turns out that multiple, unrelated associations (e.g., between the visual pattern for bagel and the sound bagel, and the visual pattern for cupcake and the sound cupcake) can coexist on the same set of connections. Experiences with different bagels and experiences with different cupcakes will all produce changes in the same set of interconnections. The resulting composite memory trace will contain the central tendencies of both associations. It is as if the traces of different exemplars of each of the different associations are averaged separately, in the sense that the mechanism allows the traces for each association to coexist. This is a very rough characterization of the state of affairs; for a fuller understanding, see McClelland and Rumelhart.[2]

Because of these properties of distributed activation models, they provide natural accounts of such things as how we learn prototypes of concepts from distorted exemplars, how we learn linguistic rules from examples that conform to them, and how semantic memories emerge from specific episodic experiences. The first point has been amply documented in the work of Anderson.[3,4] Rumelhart and I have shown how a distributed model can provide a detailed description of the acquisition of the past tense of English by young children.[5]

There are a number of other aspects of human memory data that are readily explained by distributed models. Rather than elaborate on these, however, I will consider the relations between distributed models and the brain.

RELATION TO PHYSIOLOGY

Distributed models of memory are, of course, strongly inspired by basic properties of the brain. However, it would be incorrect to imply that authors of distributed models generally mean to assume that the nodes in the models correspond exactly to real neurons, or that the connections correspond to individual physical synapses between neurons. Generally, the models should be seen as more abstract than the actual physiology, focusing instead on providing detailed accounts at the psychological level.

On the other hand, the basic tenets of distributed models seem to correspond rather closely to possible models about the physiological implementation of information processing and memory in the brain. Thus, we can hope that the basic psychological properties that emerge from distributed models will correctly characterize properties of the neural substrate of learning and memory. Further, we can hope that it will not be too difficult to specify how particular models might be mapped onto the neurophysiological substrate. This is a major advantage of distributed models over computational models based on the analogy with the traditional computer. While such models, at least in some cases, provide a detailed account for human behavior, they do not necessarily make it easy to see how the processes they specify might actually be implemented in the brain.

RELATION TO THE PHENOMENA OF AMNESIA

Assuming that we believe distributed models to provide a reasonable account of the physiological substrate of information processing and memory, the following question arises: How would we be led to think about amnesia from a distributed point of view? It is probably premature to try to give a full answer to this question, but the following three issues can be addressed. How can distributed models of memory be reconciled with basic aspects of amnesia? How can we account for the residual learning that is observed in those domains where amnesiacs show deficits? Why does this form of amnesia seem to affect some aspects of memory but not others? The following discussion considers these issues, restricting attention to those aspects of amnesia that Squire[6] has called bitemporal amnesia.

Basic Aspects of Amnesia

Bitemporal amnesia is defined by the four characteristics described below. (A fuller review is provided by Squire.[6]) (1) Insult to mesial temporal lobe structures results in correlated deficits of anterograde and retrograde amnesia. While there are some reports of dissociation of these two aspects of amnesia, it is well established in cases of amnesia due to electroconvulsive shock that anterograde and retrograde amnesia are correlated in severity; both develop gradually through repeated bouts of electroconvulsive shock.[7] (2) The anterograde amnesia consists of a deficit in the acquisition of new knowledge accessible to verbal report or other explicit indications that the subject is aware of any particular prior experience; somewhat more controversially, it also consists of a more rapid loss of information once it has been acquired to a level equal to normal levels of acquisition through repeated exposure.[8,9] (3) The retrograde amnesia consists of an inability to give evidence of access to previous experiences within a graded temporal window extending back over an extended period of time prior to the amnesic insult. The size of the window varies with the severity of the amnesia, and good evidence places it at up to three years' duration based on careful experimental tests. (4) Most strikingly, memories that appear to be lost after an insult may come back. As the ability to acquire new memories recovers, so does the ability to remember old ones that had previously been lost. The recovery is gradual and it is as if the temporal window of retrograde amnesia shrinks. There is generally a residual, permanent amnesia for events surrounding the insult that caused the amnesia, lasting variously from days to minutes.

At first, some of these findings seem to be difficult to reconcile with a distributed model of memory. If all memories, old and new, are stored in the same set of connections, why is it that an amnesic insult selectively disturbs the newer ones? And why is it that the older memories that at first seemed to be lost can later be retrieved? The phenomenon seems to beg for an interpretation in which what is lost is access to that part of the memory store in which recent memories are held, rather than one in which all memories are stored, superimposed in the same set of connections.

However, Rumelhart and I[2] were able to provide an interpretation of these phenomena, in the context of a distributed model, based on the following assumptions. We assumed that each processing experience resulted in chemical-structural change in a large number of synapses in which many other traces had already been laid down; but that each new change underwent a gradual consolidation process, as well as a natural tendency to decay or return to the prechange state. Thus, we assumed that the changes resulting from a particular experience were widely distributed at one level of analysis, but that, at a very fine grain, within each individual synapse each change in its efficacy has a separate consolidation history. We assumed that consolidation made the residual part of the change less susceptible to decay and less susceptible to disruption. These assumptions can explain not only the findings on the temporally graded nature of retrograde amnesia, but also the fact that memory appears to decay more rapidly at first, but later decays more slowly.

So far this explanation simply takes existing consolidation accounts of the amnesic syndrome[10] and stipulates that the changes are occurring in synapses that they share with other changes occurring at other points in time. However, we need to go beyond this existing account to explain two of the important characteristics of the bitemporal amnesic syndrome. First, the hypothesis does not explain recovery; second, it does not explain the coupling of anterograde and retrograde amnesia.

To capture these two important aspects of the syndrome, we proposed that there exists a factor that we called gamma (which might be some kind of molecule) that is depleted by insult to the mesial temporal lobes. Gamma serves two functions in our model: it is necessary for consolidation (without gamma, new memory traces do not consolidate) and it is necessary for expression (without gamma, recent changes in the synapse do not alter the efficacy of the synapse, they are just ineffectual addenda, rather than effective pieces of new machinery). Implicit in these assumptions is the idea that gamma is only necessary during consolidation. Fully consolidated memories no longer need it for expression.

One helpful analogy for understanding this model is to think of a synaptic change as a new piece of functional structure, and consolidation as the glue that, when set, will hold it together and allow it to function. In this analogy, gamma is simply the clamp that holds the structure together. Without the clamp, the structure will fall apart before the glue is set; but once the setting is done, the clamp is no longer needed.

In this view, bitemporal amnesia simply amounts to taking away the clamps. Old fully consolidated synaptic changes no longer require them; new ones cannot function without them and will rapidly decay; but what of memories in an intermediate stage of consolidation? Here, we assume that the consolidation process has gone far enough so that the structures will not break up rapidly without gamma, but that it has not gone so far that they actually function effectively without it. When gamma returns, after a period for recovery, they may still be there, so they will be able to function again, and even continue to consolidate.

Space prevents a fuller discussion of this model here; suffice it to say that Rumelhart and I have completed a computer simulation of this model,[2] and we have shown how it can account for all of the aspects of bitemporal amnesia described above, simply by assuming that the amnesic insult depletes gamma, and recovery amounts to its gradual return to pre-traumatic levels. With a single parameter—gamma—that varies as a function of the amnesic insult, it accounts for phenomena ranging over a wide range of time scales; the rapid decay of information just presented to an amnesic subject over seconds and minutes, and the very extended backward reach of retrograde amnesia, over months and years.

So far I have said little about the fact that amnesiac's inability to acquire new material is not by any means completely uniform. There is now a very large literature on these spared learning effects.[6] The following summary seems to capture the basic characteristics of what is spared and what is not; a number of the papers in this volume provide reviews and viewpoints on these effects.

At one extreme, amnesiacs seem to be highly deficient in the ability to form accessible traces of particular individual episodic experiences; at another extreme, they seem to be completely spared in their ability to learn certain types of skills that require no explicit access to the previous processing episodes in which the skill was acquired. In addition, they show repetition priming effects as large as those exhibited by normal subjects in a variety of perceptual and association tasks. Within the domains where learning is impaired, even the densest amnesiacs seem to learn, however gradually, from repeated experience.[11] As an everyday example if this, H.M. is clearly aware that he has a memory deficit[10] though he can recount no particular episode in which the deficit was manifest.

Residual Learning in Domains Showing Deficits

Distributed models provide a natural way of explaining why there should be residual ability to learn gradually from repeated experience even within those domains where amnesiacs are grossly deficient in their memory for particular episodic experiences. For if we imagine that the effective size of the increments to the changes in synaptic connections is reduced in amnesiacs, then the general properties of distributed models—the fact that they automatically extract the central tendency from a set of similar experiences and build up a trace of the prototype from a series of repeated exemplars—automatically provide an account of the gradual accumulation of repeated information in the face of a profound deficit in remembering any specific episode in which that information was presented. Distributed models are naturally incremental learning models, and thus they provide a very nice account of how learning could occur through the gradual accumulation of small traces.

Spared Learning of Skills

However, distributed models do not account directly for the fact that certain kinds of learning are completely spared in amnesiacs, while others are not. It seems instead that the brain maintains a distinction between those synaptic connections underlying explicitly accessible episodic and semantic information on the one hand and those underlying priming phenomena and the acquisition of certain kinds of cognitive skills.[12,13] From a distributed memory point of view, we can speculate briefly on just why this might be. One conjecture is that one-trial learning of the contents of particular episodes and of specific propositions describing facts that can be explicitly accessed and considered requires very large changes in connection strengths; while the tuning of the networks that underlie cognitive skills is best carried out through very gradual modulation of connections, or at least does not require massive changes in a single trial. From this point of view, we would see the hippocampus and the consolidation processes it supports as providing a special booster to the strengths of synaptic connections in those parts of the brain over which the distributed patterns that stand for the accessible aspects of previous experience are represented.

CONCLUSION

The distributed approach to memory is exciting because it seems to do several desirable things at once. First, it provides a natural account of many aspects of information processing, learning, and memory. Second, unlike many other information-processing frameworks, it has more or less direct ties with possible neurophysiological implementations of the mechanisms it proposes. Third, it provides a relatively staightforward framework for interpreting much of what we know about certain neurophysiological deficits, such as amnesia. The approach has also been applied to account for aspects of deep dyslexia, semantic confusions of Wernicke's aphasics, and other aspects of degradation of function through brain damage.[3,14]

Work on distributed models of memory and learning is just beginning, and there is a lot more work to be done. But the models appear to provide a much more natural framework for integrating our knowledge of the neuropsychology, neurophysiology, and neurochemistry of memory with an understanding at a level closer to observable behavior.

REFERENCES

1. HINTON, G. E. & J. A. ANDERSON. 1981. Parallel Models of Associative Memory. Erlbaum Press. Hillsdale, NJ.
2. MCCLELLAND, J. L. & D. E. RUMELHART. 1985. Distributed memory and the representation of general and specific information. J. Exp. Psychol.: Gen. (In press.)
3. ANDERSON, J. A. 1983. Cognitive and psychological computation with neural models. IEEE Transactions on Systems, Man, and Cybernetics SMC-13: 799–815.
4. KNAPP, A. & J. A. ANDERSON. 1985. A signal averaging model for concept formation. J. Exp. Psychol.: Human, Learning & Memory. (In press.)
5. RUMELHART, D. E. & J. L. MCCLELLAND. 1985. Acquisition of a linguistic rule by a parallel distributed processing system. In Parallel Distributed Processing: Explorations in the microstructure of cognition. J. L. McClelland & D. E. Rumelhart, Eds. Bradford Books. Cambridge, MA. (In press.)
6. SQUIRE, L. R. 1982. The neuropsychology of human memory. Annu. Rev. Neurosci. 5: 241–273.
7. SQUIRE, L. R., P. C. SLATER & P. CHACE. 1975. Retrograde amnesia: temporal gradient in very long-term memory following electro-convulsive therapy. Science 187: 77–79.
8. HUPPERT, F. A. & M. PIERCY. 1978. Dissociation between learning and remembering in organic amnesia. Nature 275: 317–318.
9. SQUIRE, L. 1981. Two forms of amnesia: an analysis of forgetting. J. Neurosci. 1: 635–640.
10. MILNER, B. 1966. Amnesia following operation on the temporal lobes. In Amnesia. C. M. W. Whitty & O. L. Zangwill, Eds.:109–133. Butterworth & Co. London.
11. SCHACTER, D. 1985. Priming of old and new knowledge in amnesic patients and normal subjects. Ann. N.Y. Acad. Sci. (This volume.)
12. COHEN, N. 1985. Different memory systems underlying acquisition of procedural and declarative knowledge. Ann. N.Y. Acad. Sci. (This volume.)
13. SQUIRE, L. R. & S. ZOLA-MORGAN. 1985. The neuropsychology of memory: Humans and non-human primates. Ann. N.Y. Acad. Sci. (This volume.)
14. WOOD, C. 1978. Variations on a theme by Lashley: Lesion experiments on the neural models of Anderson, Silverstein, Ritz and Jones. Psych. Rev. 85: 582–591.

Analyses of Global Memory Impairments of Different Etiologies[a]

SUZANNE CORKIN, NEAL J. COHEN,[b]

EDITH V. SULLIVAN, RAE ANN CLEGG, T. JOHN ROSEN

Department of Psychology and Clinical Research Center
Massachusetts Institute of Technology
Cambridge, Massachusetts 02139

ROBERT H. ACKERMAN

Departments of Neurology and Neuroradiology
Massachusetts General Hospital
Boston, Massachusetts 02114

Chronic global amnesia is a clinically significant deficit in new learning of verbal and nonverbal material irrespective of stimulus modality; the deficit is disproportionate to other cognitive impairment and should be distinguished from the preservation of skill learning and repetition priming effects in global amnesia.[1-5] The purity and severity of the fact-learning impairment may vary from patient to patient.[6] Between-subject variability in the deficits of amnesic patients is not surprising because of the number of different etiologies of amnesia. Each etiology has its own neuropathological hallmark, and within an etiology the extent of damage to the affected anatomical and chemical systems may vary.[7] Etiologies also may differ in the severity of the acute phase of the illness and in the particular brain structures that are compromised, but different etiologies may be associated with common lesion sites. These sources of variation may account for the differences in memory capacities among amnesic patients. There are two possible explanations for such differences: The first is that a single anatomical or chemical system subserves fact-learning capacities, and thus interference with this system results in a single form of amnesia. The amnesia would have a variety of presentations that would reflect the interaction between insults to this memory system and insults outside this memory system; the latter may cause ancillary cognitive and noncognitive deficits that influence memory-test performance. The second possibility is that there exist multiple fact-learning systems, each specialized for different aspects of memory function. In this case, interference with the different anatomical or chemical systems would produce fundamentally different types of amnesia.

One approach to evaluating these alternative explanations proceeds by characterizing the precise nature of the behavioral variation among patients whose amnesias stem from different etiologies and from involvement of different brain regions. If global amnesia is a unitary disorder, then any differences in the memory deficits related to lesion site should be either quantitative (i.e., patients would differ primarily in the magnitude of mnemonic deficits rather than in terms of the pattern of deficits) or fully accounted for by the influence of nonmnemonic deficits. Alternatively, if global amnesia comprises different types of memory disorders affecting different neural

[a]Supported by National Institute of Mental Health grants MH24433, MH32724, MH06401, and MH08280.
[b]Dr. Cohen is now in the Department of Psychology, Johns Hopkins University.

systems responsible for different aspects of memory function, then there should be qualitative differences among patients in the nature of their impairment on tests of memory function, i.e., differences in the pattern of deficits across memory tests.

In order to address the issue of quantitative versus qualitative differences more fully, our laboratory has conducted evaluations of neurological and neuropsychological status in 21 patients with global amnesias of seven different etiologies affecting various brain regions. This paper reviews the neuropathological changes that characterize each etiology, presents the computed tomographic (CT) brain scans of illustrative cases, describes and compares patterns of cognitive deficit within and among groups, and reaches the tentative conclusion that the etiologies of amnesia that we studied differ quantitatively but not qualitatively with respect to mnemonic capabilities involved in fact learning.

METHOD

Subjects

The subjects included eight patients with anterior communicating artery (ACoA) aneurysms that ruptured, five with closed head injuries, three with anoxia, two with herpes simplex encephalitis, one with Korsakoff's syndrome, one with bilateral stroke, and one with bilateral medial temporal-lobe resection (case H.M.) (TABLE 1). On clinical assessment, all appeared to have normal language comprehension and perceptual processing abilities. In addition, all had intact knowledge about the world acquired early in life, though all had some retrograde amnesia. Other patients with certain classes of memory disorder were excluded from the study, such as those whose memory loss was restricted to particular domains or who were demented. The severity of amnesia on clinical observation ranged from mild to severe.

The patients whom we have examined in each etiologic group may not be representative of the populations of patients with those diseases who survive the acute phase of the illness. In order to participate in our research, patients had to be relatively healthy, able to travel to MIT, be globally amnesic upon clinical observation, and able to perform sophisticated neuropsychological tests. These sampling limitations and the small number of cases affect the generality of the conclusions in this paper.

Etiologies of Global Amnesia

Ruptured Saccular Aneurysm of the ACoA

The pathogenesis of saccular (also called berry) intracranial arterial aneurysms is believed to be congenital with contributions from acquired factors, such as atherosclerosis and arterial hypertension. Intracranial arterial aneurysms are focal saccular dilatations of an artery.[8] The aneurysmal sac is usually linked to the artery by a narrow segment, or neck. The arterial wall lacks normal muscular and elastic properties. As the sac formed by fibrous connective tissue enlarges, the wall thins and the aneurysm may rupture. Saccular aneurysms are located mainly on the vessels that form the circle of Willis, at the sites of arterial forking. About 30% of all cerebral aneurysms occur at the ACoA and the adjacent segments of the anterior cerebral arteries; aneurysms often exist multiply. Rupture results in bleeding into the subarachnoid space, and after some days may produce spasm of the arteries, which can result in infarction in the underlying cortex. Subarachnoid hemorrhage increases intracranial pressure acutely.

TABLE 1. Characteristics of Patients with Global Amnesia ($N = 21$)

Etiology of Global Amnesia[a]	Number of Cases		Education (Years)	Age at Onset of Amnesia (Years)	Duration of Amnesia (Years)	Age at First Test (Years)
	M	F				
Ruptured anterior communicating artery aneurysm	7	1	15.3	45.1	3.6	49.3
Closed head injury	3	2	12.7	27.2	2.4	29.8
Anoxia	3	0	15.3	41.7	1.4	43.0
Herpes simplex encephalitis	2	0	14.5	30.0	7.7	46.0
Korsakoff's syndrome	0	1	12	47	3	50
Stroke	0	1	12	58	.06	58
Bilateral medial temporal-lobe resection	1	0	12	27	30	27

[a] All lesions are presumed to be bilateral, though not necessarily symmetrical.

Mortality is high, and recurrent bleeding is frequent. Intracranial aneurysms are often treated surgically. The current procedure of choice is ligation of the neck of the aneurysm by means of a subfrontal approach using a surgical microscope.[9]

Global amnesia is not a necessary consequence of rupture of an ACoA aneurysm. When amnesia does occur, it may be due to involvement of posterior inferior medial

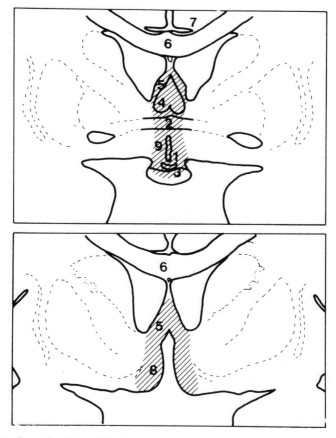

FIGURE 1. Coronal sections of the brain at the level of the anterior commissure (above) and septal nuclei (below). The areas of supply from perforating branches of the anterior communicating artery, as determined by infusion of contrast agent, are indicated by crosshatching and are identified by numbers: (1) lamina terminalis; (2) mesial anterior commissure; (3) optic chiasm; (4) columns of the fornix; (5) septum; (6) corpus callosum; (7) cingulum; (8) subcallosal area; and (9) anterior hypothalamus. The supply is limited to midline structure. (From Gade.[9] With permission from *Surgical Neurology*.)

frontal areas[10] or to interruption of small penetrating branches of the ACoA, causing infarction in one or more of the areas supplied: the septal region and anterior portions of the fornix, corpus callosum, and cingulum[9,11] (FIGURE 1). Two recent studies using CT scans implicate a basal forebrain lesion as critical for the occurrence of enduring global amnesia after rupture of an ACoA aneurysm.[12,13]

Among our cases, a CT brain scan of a 63-year-old man who had had an ACoA aneurysm clipped three years earlier revealed a widespread area of tissue loss in both frontal lobes, greater on the right than on the left, and extending back to the insula (FIGURE 2, A and B). Central areas of tissue loss included portions of the anterior cingulum, basal forebrain, and probably the anterior hypothalamus (FIGURE 2, A). Tissue changes were also seen in subcortical white matter outlining the frontal gyri (FIGURE 2, B, C, and D). These abnormalities on CT scan are consistent with typical postmortem findings in such cases.

Closed-head Injury

The pathophysiology of closed head injury is complex and varies widely from case to case. When head injury is severe, tissue changes may occur in the cerebrum, midbrain, and brainstem as a result of several different primary and secondary

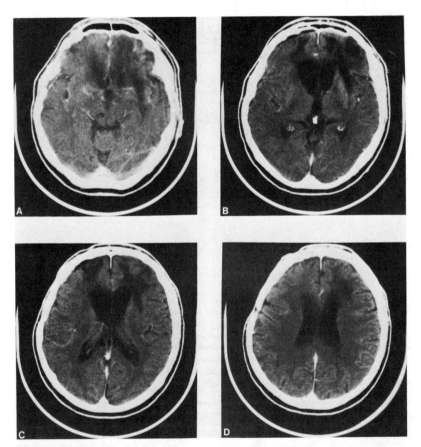

FIGURE 2. CT brain scan from a patient with rupture and clipping of an ACoA aneurysm (left side of brain is shown on the left).

TABLE 2. Pathophysiology of Closed Head Injury

Primary (Immediate on Impact) Brain Injury
A. Macroscopic lesions
   1. Contusions underlying site of impact (coup)
   2. Contrecoup contusion frequently in the undersurfaces of the frontal lobes and the tips of the temporal lobes
   3. Laceration of the brain from depressed skull fracture
B. Microscopic lesions
   1. Widespread shearing/stretching of nerve fibers
Secondary Mechanisms of Brain Injury
A. Intracranial hemorrhage
B. Edema in white matter adjacent to focal mass lesions
C. Diffuse brain swelling—hyperemia
D. Ischemic brain damage
E. Raised intracranial pressure
F. Brain shift and herniation
Secondary Insults from Extracerebral Events
A. Effects of multiple/systemic injury
   1. Hypoxia
   2. Fat embolism
Delayed Effects
A. Degeneration of white matter
B. Disturbed flow of cerebrospinal fluid—hydrocephalus

After Levin, Benton & Grossman.[17]

mechanisms[14–17] (TABLE 2). Even in cases of concussion, which by definition are said to occur without detectable pathology, permanent damage to the brain may be seen on histological examination.[18] CT brain scans reveal focal lesions when they occur, but they usually fail to show the widespread microscopic injury to nerve fibers,[19] which may be the major factor limiting recovery.[14–16] Injury to the cerebral white matter is disproportionately severe in the corpus callosum, where damage is attributable to stretching and shearing forces.[20]

One of the more common complaints after closed head injury is memory impairment, which may range from mild to severe.[21] Severe closed head injury, characterized by post-traumatic amnesia of several weeks, may result in marked and persistent global amnesia.[22] For neither mild nor severe impairments is the pathophysiology well understood. The memory disorder could result from mechanically induced strain on medial temporal-lobe structures, diencephalic structures, or both.

Cerebral Anoxia

Anoxia due to asphyxia or to cardiac arrest produces a systematic distribution of bilateral lesions involving parts of the cerebral cortex, particularly the hippocampus, globus pallidus, caudate nucleus, putamen, Purkinje cells of the cerebellum, dentate nucleus, and inferior olives. White matter is relatively well preserved. Localized abnormalities may be difficult to identify on CT scan.

One of the patients in the present series was a 29-year-old man who seven years previously had had an episode of anoxia secondary to cardiac arrest. The CT scan showed no specific lateralizing or localizing abnormalities (FIGURE 3). There was, however, indirect evidence of mild, diffuse neuronal loss, consisting of enlargement of the third and fourth ventricles (FIGURE 3, A and B), bodies of the lateral ventricles (FIGURE 3, C), Sylvian fissures (FIGURE 3, A and B), and cortical sulci (FIGURE 3, D). In addition, the superior cerebellar vermis was atrophied (FIGURE 3, B).

Herpes Simplex Encephalitis

Herpes simplex encephalitis is an uncommon viral infection. The airborne virus attains access to medial temporal-lobe structures by way of olfactory connections.[23] A

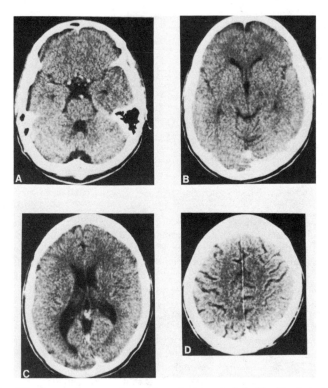

FIGURE 3. CT brain scan from a patient with cerebral anoxia (left side of brain is shown on the left).

definitive diagnosis is established by microscopic examination of biopsied brain tissue.[24] If treatment with an antiviral agent is begun early in the course of disease, necrosis can be minimized. The number and severity of neurological signs and symptoms vary from case to case.[25] According to Adams and Victor,[26] the initial symptoms evolve over several days and may include fever, headache, seizures, confusion, stupor, and coma. Focal neurological signs, such as aphasia and hemiparesis, may appear later in the disease. Other symptoms reflect the characteristic involvement of the inferomedial portions of the frontal and temporal lobes: olfactory or gustatory hallucinations, anosmia, temporal-lobe seizures, and bizarre or psychotic behavior. Memory impairment, presumably due to bilateral though often asymmetric involvement of the limbic system, usually becomes apparent in the convalescent stage of the illness and is a common residual deficit.[27]

After the resolution of encephalitis, a patient in the present sample received a craniotomy for drainage of a porencephalic cyst and implantation of a ventricular shunt (FIGURE 4). The CT scan performed 27 years after the onset of disease showed dilatation of the ventricular system, with the left temporal horn larger than the right (FIGURE 4, A), and the body of the right lateral ventricle larger than the body of the left (FIGURE 4, C). Tissue loss was seen in the posterior, inferior aspect of the left temporal lobe, which corresponds to the left medial temporal-lobe region. There was cortical atrophy in the interhemispheric fissure (FIGURE 4, B and C) and on the convexity.

Korsakoff's Syndrome

The cause of Korsakoff's syndrome is thiamin deficiency, usually secondary to poor nutrition associated with chronic alcoholism; the toxic effects of alcohol itself may also contribute to the pathology.[28,29] The brain lesions are distributed around the lateral, third, and fourth ventricles (FIGURE 5). Maximally affected areas include the dorsomedial nucleus of the thalamus, massa intermedia, floor of the third ventricle (especially the mammillary bodies), the periaqueductal region at the level of the third cranial nerve nuclei, the midbrain reticular formation, and the posterior colliculi. Although some investigators conclude that the neuropathology can be restricted to the mammillary bodies of the hypothalamus and the peritineum (an area just medial to the dorsomedial nucleus of the thalamus[30,31]), multiple lesions in other areas and frontal-lobe atrophy are often seen in chronic alcoholics at autopsy,[32] and must be kept in mind in understanding the behavioral correlates of Korsakoff's syndrome.

Bilateral Stroke

Minimal strokes producing bilateral focal lesions occasionally result in pure amnesic syndromes. The lesions may be in the thalamus[33] or in medial temporal-lobe structures.[34-36] The stroke patient in our study was a 60-year-old woman who became amnesic in 1982 during an arteriogram, which included vertebral-basilar and bilateral carotid studies. The arteriogram report describes possible emboli at the origin of both posterior cerebral arteries following the vertebral-basilar injection. The CT scan obtained 1.5 years after the onset of global amnesia showed tissue loss along the inferomedial aspect of the left temporal lobe (FIGURE 6, A–D), extending as far forward as the anterior horn of the left temporal lobe. Focal tissue loss was not seen on the right, but the temporal horn was enlarged, which is consistent with some diffuse neuronal dropout (FIGURE 6, A). In addition, there was considerable cortical tissue loss both prefrontally and in the high parietal regions (FIGURE 6, D–F). Atrophy of the superior cerebellar vermis was also noted (FIGURE 6, C).

Bilateral Medial Temporal-lobe Resection

This experimental operation was performed for a short period of time on several psychiatric patients who have been lost to follow-up, and on one patient with

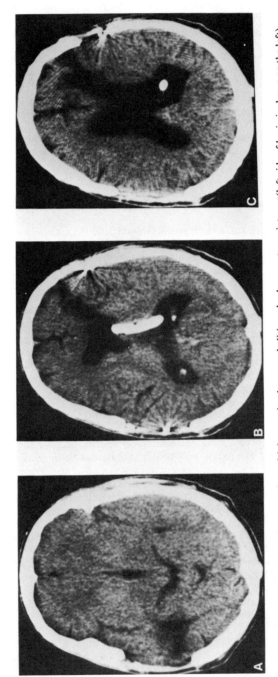

FIGURE 4. CT brain scan from a patient with herpes simplex encephalitis and subsequent craniotomy (left side of brain is shown on the left).

intractable epilepsy, who is well known in the literature as case H.M.[37] Although considerable seizure control was achieved in H.M., the procedure was soon rejected because neuropsychological studies of this patient revealed that bilateral medial temporal-lobe resection produced a pervasive and severe anterograde amnesia.[38] His amnesic condition persists unabated 31 years after the operation.[39] The surgical resection included the medial half of the tips of both temporal lobes and the tissue posterior to them, including the uncus, the amygdala, and the anterior 8 cm of the hippocampus and hippocampal gyrus. Evidence of bilateral tissue loss in this region was seen on a CT scan performed in 1984 (FIGURE 7, A and B). In addition, the cerebellar cistern was not well filled by the cerebellar vermis (FIGURE 7, C), indicating atrophy. The extent of cortical atrophy was consistent with his age, 58 (FIGURE 7, D).

Similarities and Differences among Etiologies

The etiologies of amnesia just described may be grouped according to the major area of brain insult: Cases of ACoA aneurysm are characterized by lesions of the

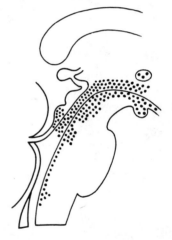

FIGURE 5. Diagram showing the topographical distribution of lesions in Wernicke's encephalopathy. (From Escourolle and Poirier.[8] With permission from the W.B. Saunders Company.)

posterior inferior medial frontal region and the basal forebrain; cases of closed head injury by diffuse involvement of white matter, particularly in the corpus callosum; cases of Korsakoff's syndrome by midline thalamic and hypothalamic lesions; and anoxia, herpes simplex encephalitis, stroke (in our patient), and bilateral medial temporal-lobe resection by lesions of the hippocampus and sometimes the amygdala. Accordingly, one set of analyses grouped patients by etiology and another set by locus of lesion.

Despite some commonality in locus of lesion among etiologically distinct groups, it is still necessary to consider etiology separately because each etiology of amnesia has its own characteristic brain insult; these biological differences may have important consequences for memory and other cognitive functions later on. Differences in the long-term outcome may be signaled by differences in the acute stage of the illnesses, including the presence and duration of cardiovascular and respiratory changes, loss of consciousness, complications such as increased intracranial pressure, and the presence of focal neurological deficits unrelated to the brain systems implicated in memory. In

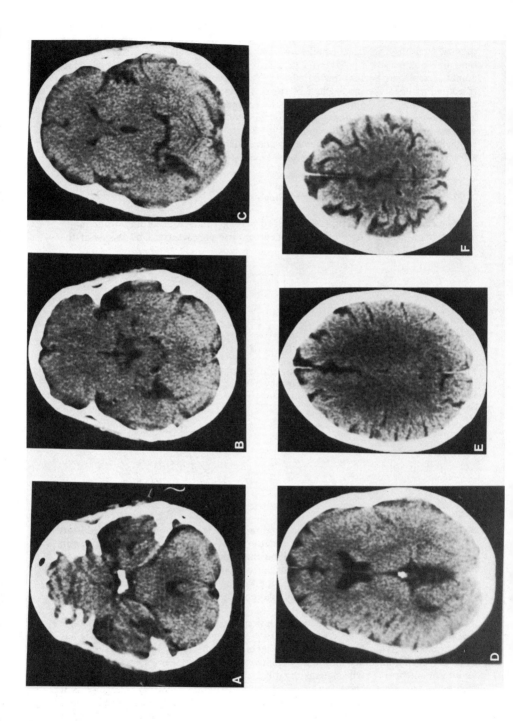

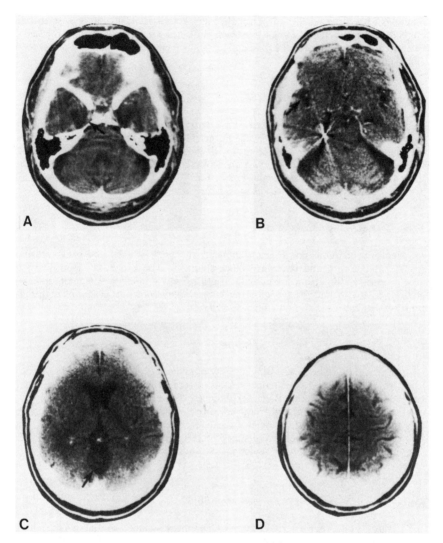

FIGURE 7. CT brain scan from a patient with bilateral medial temporal-lobe resection.

our series of cases, most of the patients with head injury and anoxia experienced days or weeks of unconsciousness, whereas the patients in the other etiologic groups did not. In addition, focal neurological abnormalities, such as hemiparesis, were observed in patients with ACoA aneurysm, head injury, stroke, and anoxia, but not in the others.

Neuropsychological Tests

In order to sample behavior as broadly as possible, our neuropsychological evaluation of the amnesic patients assessed mnemonic and nonmnemonic cognitive functions as well as mood and personality characteristics. This paper describes the methods and results for the cognitive tests. Within the memory system, it focused on fact learning, and excludes the dissociable memory phenomena that are preserved in global amnesia.[4,39]

Overall Intelligence and Global Memory

Overall intelligence was assessed in the early years of the study by means of the Wechsler-Bellevue Intelligence Scale, Forms I[40] and II,[41] and the Wechsler Adult Intelligence Scale,[42] and more recently with the Wechsler Adult Intelligence Scale–Revised.[43] A global rating of orientation, arousal, and memory function was obtained using the Wechsler Memory Scale, Forms I and II.[44] The Intelligence and Memory Scale scores were each expressed as numerically comparable quotients.

Immediate Memory

Measures of immediate memory capacity included forward and backward digit spans,[45] and foward and backward block spans.[46,47] The Brown-Peterson distractor task[48,49] assessed forgetting of consonant trigrams held in immediate memory at delays of 0, 3, 6, 9, 15, and 30 seconds; the longer delay intervals probably required a contribution from long-term memory as well.

Recall of Verbal and Nonverbal Material

The verbal recall tasks assessing long-term memory capacities required subjects to learn to criterion three word pairs,[50,51] and to recall the two prose passages and 10 paired associates from the Wechsler Memory Scale after a one-hour delay.[52] A composite score was calculated from the score for the prose passages divided by two plus the number of paired asssociates recalled correctly. The nonverbal recall tasks involved redrawing the Wechsler Memory Scale figures one hour after the initial recall test[52] and redrawing the Rey or Taylor complex figure one hour after making the initial copy.[53-55]

Recognition of Verbal and Nonverbal Material

The tests of long-term verbal recognition memory included continuous recognition of words, nonsense syllables, and numbers (Verbal Recurring Figures Test[56]), and forced-choice recognition of 30 words that had been processed at different levels of meaning,[51,57] and the content score from the Verbal Recency Test (see section on Cognitive functions of the frontal lobes). Recognition of nonverbal material was evaluated with 52 geometric figures and 52 nonsense shapes (Nonverbal Recurring Figures Test[58]). A nonverbal paired-associate learning task with three pairs of geometric shapes required learning to criterion with a three-choice recognition procedure.[51]

Cognitive Functions of the Frontal Lobes

The assessment of frontal-lobe capacities included four different kinds of tasks: problem-solving, using Milner's version of the Wisconsin Card-Sorting Test[59]; verbal fluency, using Thurstone's symbolic test[60,61]; route finding, using the Porteus Maze Test (Vineland Revision[62,63]), which yields both a test quotient and a qualitative error score; and the Verbal Recency Test, using a task that simultaneously tested memory for content and memory for order using four word lists of 16 items each.[64] In the latter test, only the order score was an index of frontal-lobe function; the content score was included with the recognition memory tests.

Language

The brief evaluation of language comprehension and production used the Token Test[65] and the Reporter's Test.[66] The Token Test was a quantitative measure of the ability to understand and respond to increasingly complex verbal commands. The Reporter's Test required the subject to translate the examiner's actions into verbal commands.

Spatial Abilities

The three spatial tasks each sampled a different spatial ability. A constructional test required copying the Rey or Taylor complex figure[54–55]; the drawing was scored quantitatively using strict criteria. The Body Scheme Test measured personal spatial orientation by requiring the subject to indicate the parts on his or her own body that corresponded to the parts indicated on a drawing of a person.[67] A route-finding task, the Visual Locomotor Mazes, assessed extrapersonal spatial orientation.[67]

Perception of Complex Visual Stimuli

The Hidden Figures Test measured the ability to detect a simple geometric figure embedded in a more complex one.[60,68,69] The Gollin Incomplete-Pictures Test evaluated the subject's perception of fragmented drawings of objects and animals in the initial test session, and evaluated perceptual learning one hour and 24 hours later.[70]

RESULTS

All statistical analyses were performed twice: In the first set, the patients were grouped by etiology, and in the second, they were grouped by lesion site. In order to compensate for the low statistical power consequent to the small samples, most analyses of individual tests used a .10 significance criterion and therefore should be considered exploratory. Other composite analyses that examined scores averaged within cognitive domains used the customary .05 significance criterion. Not all patients completed all neuropsychological tests; the tables in this section include the N for each group in order to facilitate interpretation of the results. Statistical analyses used raw test scores or ranks based upon these scores. In another type of comparison, prevalence of deficits on cognitive tests was reported for each etiologic group (TABLES 3 to 9) but was not analyzed statistically.

Definition of Deficit

On each test, the cut-off for a deficit was specified; these deficit criteria are noted in TABLES 3–9. Ideally, one would base such delineations on statistical manipulations of data from a separate normal control sample that matched each etiologic sample for age, sex, and premorbid intellectual level. Because the present study needs more subjects to complete such control groups, we derived definitions of deficits from three sources that were extrinsic to this study: normative data, performance of focal lesion groups that were significantly impaired, and experience gained from years of administering the tests. When normative data were used in the definition of deficits, the cut-off score was set at one standard deviation below the mean for achievement scores and above the mean for error scores. The exceptions were the Wechsler Intelligence and Memory Scales, where any score below the lowest value of the normal range (90 to 110) was considered to indicate a deficit. On tests for which the performance of focal lesion groups was used to define the deficit, the cut-off was the mean score of the impaired group, for example, the mean score achieved by patients with left temporal lobectomy on the Verbal Recurring Figures Test and by patients with right temporal lobectomy on the Nonverbal Recurring Figures Test.[56] Less systematic definitions of deficit grew out of discussions among investigators with extensive experience administering the tests described in this paper to control subjects and to patients with a variety of focal cerebral lesions; this was the sole criterion of deficit on only two tests, the Verbal Recency Test and the Visual Locomotor Mazes.

A Search for Differences among Etiologic Groups: Analyses of Raw Scores

Raw scores were analyzed by computing separate analyses of variance (ANOVAs) for each test individually; presentation of the results was organized according to the eight cognitive domains examined (Tables 3–9). Statistical comparisons of the different etiologic groups were confined to those with two or more subjects: the anterior communicating artery aneurysm, head injury, anoxia, and encephalitis groups. Oneway ANOVAs tested differences among the means for these four groups. When the significance level of the overall F-test was .10 or less, .05-level Tukey HSD (honestly significant difference) comparisons evaluated intergroup differences.[71] The Tukey tests are mentioned only when statistically significant. Scores for etiologic groups with one subject each were evaluated relative to the ranges of performance of the other amnesic groups and with respect to the deficit criteria described in the preceding section.

Overall Intelligence and Global Memory

Overall intelligence was highest for the patients with ACoA aneurysm, the woman with bilateral stroke, and H.M., the man with a bilateral medial temporal-lobe resection. The patient with Korsakoff's syndrome was lowest in overall intelligence. For all patients, Memory Quotients (MQ) were lower than Full Scale IQ ratings. Wechsler IQ-MQ differences of 25 or more points were observed for three of the eight aneurysm patients, one of the five head-injury patients, two of the three anoxia patients, one of the two postencephalitis patients, the woman with bilateral stroke, and H.M. Statistically significant differences among the four multi-patient groups were observed for Verbal IQ, $F(3, 14) = 3.16$, $p = .06$; Full Scale IQ, $F(3, 14) = 3.27$, $p = .05$; and MQ, $F(3, 14) = 3.07$, $p = .06$ (TABLE 3). The ACoA aneurysm patients scored highest on all three measures, and the head injury, anoxia, and encephalitis patients had lower and nearly identical means. The differences between the ACoA aneurysm and other groups in IQ and MQ resulted primarily from parallel differences on the Vocabulary ($p = .04$) and Digit Span ($p = .01$) subtests of the WAIS-R and on the Mental Control ($p = .01$) and Digit Span ($p = .01$) subtests of the Memory Scale.

Immediate Memory

Two of the four tests of memory span led to significant group differences. The ACoA aneurysm and encephalitis patients had mean forward and backward digit

TABLE 3. Comparison of Patients with Global Amnesia Due to Different Etiologies: Weschler Intelligence and Memory Scales

	Verbal I.Q.	Performance I.Q.	Full Scale I.Q.	Memory Quotient
Deficit Criterion Group	<90[a]	<90[a]	<90[a]	<90[a]
ACoA aneurysm				
Mean score	118.4	110.4	115.9	98.2
Prevalence of deficit	0/8	1/8	1/8	2/8
Closed head injury				
Mean score	101.8	92.8	98.0	75.8
Prevalence of deficit	0/5	2/5	0/5	5/5
Anoxia				
Mean score	99.7	96.7	98.0	75.7
Prevalence of deficit	1/3	0/3	1/3	2/3
Herpes simplex encephalitis				
Mean score	98.5	107.5	102.5	78.5
Prevalence of deficit	0/2	0/2	0/2	2/2
Korsakoff's syndrome				
Score	77	77	76	63
Presence of deficit	1	1	1	1
Stroke				
Score	116	103	111	77
Presence of deficit	0	0	0	1
Medial temporal-lobe resection				
Score	109	125	118	64
Presence of deficit	0	0	0	1

Source of deficit criterion: [a]normative data, [b]performance of impaired focal lesions groups, [c]clinical experience.

spans that were in the normal range and superior to those of the anoxia and head-injury patients: for forward span, $F(3, 14) = 4.01$, $p = .03$; for backward span, $F(3, 14) = 2.88$, $p = .07$ (TABLE 4). The ACoA aneurysm versus anoxia Tukey comparison was significant at the .05 level. The ACoA aneurysm and encephalitis groups were also the best on forward and backward block span: for forward span, $F(3, 11) = 5.16$, $p = .02$; for backward span, $F(3, 8) = 2.93$, $p = .10$. A split-plot factorial ANOVA of the Brown-Peterson distractor task data yielded the expected main effect for delay interval (recall was worse at longer intervals, $p < .001$), but neither the F ratios for between-etiology differences nor for the etiology × delay interaction approached significance.

TABLE 4. Comparison of Patients with Global Amnesia Due to Different Etiologies: Immediate Memory

Group	Digit Span		Block Span		Brown-Peterson Distractor Task (max. = 144)
	Forward	Backward	Forward	Backward	
Deficit Criterion	$<5^a$	$<4^a$	$<4^{a,c}$	$<3^{a,c}$	$<100^{a,c}$
ACoA aneurysm					
Mean score	7.6	5.9	6.4	5.5	102.4
Prevlance of deficit	0/8	1/8	0/7	0/6	3/7
Closed head injury					
Mean score	6.4	4.6	4.2	4.2	77.5
Prevalence of deficit	1/5	2/5	0/4	0/4	3/4
Anoxia					
Mean score	4.0	3.0	4.5	4.0	63.0
Prevalence of deficit	2/3	3/3	1/2	0/1	2/2
Herpes simplex encephalitis					
Mean score	6.5	3.5	6.5	5.0	77.5
Prevalence of deficit	0/2	1/2	0/2	0/1	2/2
Korsakoff's syndrome					
Score	5	3	5	4	55
Presence of deficit	0	1	0	0	1
Stroke					
Score	6	7	5	3	83
Presence of deficit	0	0	0	0	1
Medial temporal-lobe resection					
Score	5	5	5	4	76
Presence of deficit	0	0	0	0	1

Source of deficit criterion: [a] normative data, [b] performance of impaired focal lesions groups, [c] clinical experience.

Recall of Verbal and Nonverbal Material

None of these tests produced significant between-group differences (TABLE 5).

Recognition of Verbal and Nonverbal Material

The four etiologic groups differed on two tests of recognition: Verbal Recurring Figures, $F(3, 12) = 6.31, p = .01$; and Nonverbal Recurring Figures, $F(3, 12) = 2.97$,

TABLE 5. Comparison of Patients with Global Amnesia Due to Different Etiologies: Recall of Verbal and Nonverbal Material

	Rey Recall (max. = 36)	Verbal Paired Associates (trials to criterion) Initial	Delay	Delayed Recall Wechsler Memory Scale Items Verbal	Nonverbal
Deficit Criterion	$<18^{a,b}$	$>9^a$		$<12^a$	$<6^a$
Group					
ACoA aneurysm					
Mean score	9.4	16.8	11.0	5.2	2.2
Prevalence of deficit	7/8	5/7		8/8	7/8
Closed head injury					
Mean score	6.2	5.5	5.5	4.5	0.0
Prevalence of deficit	5/5	0/2		5/5	5/5
Anoxia					
Mean score	9.5	27.0	8.0	5.5	2.5
Prevalence of deficit	1/2	1/2		2/2	2/2
Herpes simplex encephalitis					
Mean score	6.0	49.0	22.0	5.5	0.0
Prevalence of deficit	1/1	2/2		2/2	2/2
Korsakoff's syndrome					
Score	1	19	31	2	0
Presence of deficit	1	1		1	1
Stroke					
Score	2	7	19	6	0
Presence of deficit	1	0		1	1
Medial temporal-lobe resection					
Score	0	49	68	1	0
Presence of deficit	1	1		1	1

Source of deficit criterion: [a]normative data, [b]performance of impaired focal lesions groups, [c]clinical experience.

$p = .07$ (TABLE 6). On both tests, the head-injury patients were particularly handicapped. For the Verbal Recurring Figures Test, Tukey comparisons between the mean scores of the encephalitis and head injury groups and between the mean scores of the ACoA aneurysm and head injury groups were significant. The one anoxia patient who took the Nonverbal Recurring Figures Test was extremely impaired on this test.

TABLE 6. Comparison of Patients with Global Amnesia Due to Different Etiologies: Recognition of Verbal and Nonverbal Material

| | Recurring Figures | | Nonverbal Paired Associates (trials to criterion) | | Verbal Depth of Processing (max. = 30) | Verbal Recency (errors; chance = 8) Content |
	Verbal (max. = 60)	Nonverbal (max. = 56)	Initial	Delay		
Deficit Criterion	<37[b]	<31[b]	>6[a]		<20[a]	>3[c]
Group						
ACoA aneurysm						
Mean score	28.6	24.5	8.0	13.3	18.6	4.5
Prevalence of deficit	7/8	6/8	3/7		4/7	5/8
Closed head injury						
Mean score	17.6	16.2	18.0	4.0	18.8	3.9
Prevalence of deficit	5/5	5/5	3/3		2/4	1/5
Anoxia						
Mean score	27.0	-4.0	17.5	5.0	16.0	5.3
Prevalence of deficit	1/1	1/1	2/2		2/2	3/3
Herpes simplex encephalitis						
Mean score	38.0	20.5	17.5	73.0	19.5	3.0
Prevalence of deficit	1/2	2/2	2/2		1/2	1/2
Korsakoff's syndrome						
Score	14	6	12	15	10	6
Presence of deficit	1	1	1		1	1
Stroke						
Score	26	4	33	16	19	5
Presence of deficit	1	1	1		1	1
Medial temporal-lobe resection						
Score	19	3	75	63	12	6
Presence of deficit	1	1	1		1	1

Source of deficit criterion: [a] normative data, [b] performance of impaired focal lesions groups, [c] clinical experience.

Cognitive Functions of the Frontal Lobes

None of these tests differed significantly by patient group (TABLE 7).

Language

The groups did not differ on the Token Test, but there was a significant effect on the Reporter's Test, $F(3, 11) = 4.10, p = .04$ (TABLE 8). The mean score for the anoxia group was substantially below the means for the other groups; the Tukey test comparing the ACoA aneurysm and anoxia groups was significant.

Spatial Abilities

The anoxia patients had the lowest Body Scheme scores (TABLE 8). As a consequence of this group's deficit, there was a .02-level main effect, $F(3, 10) = 5.49$, and a significant difference between the means of the ACoA and anoxia groups as shown by a Tukey test. There were no other between-group differences on spatial tests.

Perception of Complex Visual Stimuli

The means for the tests of visual perception showed no differences by etiology (TABLE 9).

A Search for Quantitative and Qualitative Differences among Etiologic Groups: Analysis of Ranks

The analyses of scores on individual tests revealed that the ACoA aneurysm group was the least impaired relative to the other amnesic groups. The next analysis explored whether the differences among groups were quantitative or qualitative. If the differences were quantitative, groups would differ in severity of deficit, irrespective of cognitive domain; statistically, a quantitative difference would be indicated by a significant group effect. If the differences were qualitative, patterns of spared and impaired performance from domain to domain would vary from group to group, and would be indicated by a group-by-domain interaction. In the present analysis, ranking procedures were used to form composite scores for each domain. All subjects were ranked on each of the test scores, and these ranks were transformed so as to approximate standard deviates ($M = 0, SD = 1$); positive scores indicated superior performance. The data from etiologic groups containing fewer than three patients were discarded, leaving 16 patients in the ACoA aneurysm, anoxia, and head injury groups. One of the 35 variables was omitted (the Wechsler Memory Quotient, because it confounded various memory functions). Only variables for which at least 13 of the 16 patients had scores and only cognitive domains containing at least 3 variables were retained; 18 variables qualified, and they were combined into five average ranks, one for each domain. A split-plot factorial ANOVA of the mean ranks tested for quantitative and qualitative group differences; groups formed the between-subjects factor, and domains formed the within-subjects factor.

TABLE 7. Comparison of Patients with Global Amnesia Due to Different Etiologies: Cognitive Functions of the Frontal Lobes

	Wisconsin Card Sorting		Fluency		Porteus Mazes		Verbal Recency (errors; chance = 8)
	No. of Cats.	No. of Cards	Verbal Total	Nonverbal Total	TQ	Qual.	Order
Deficit Criterion	$<4^b$		$<30^a$		$<90^a$	$>38^a$	$>5^c$
Group							
ACoA aneurysm							
Mean score	4.0	109.2	45.8	9.9	122.0	29.0	5.8
Prevalence of deficit	4/8		1/8		0/8	2/8	5/8
Closed head injury							
Mean score	6.0	93.3	40.8	7.8	122.0	31.5	7.4
Prevalence of deficit	0/3		1/5		0/2	1/2	4/5
Anoxia							
Mean score	3.3	118.0	21.0	7.0	105.0	26.0	7.3
Prevalence of deficit	1/3		2/3		1/2	0/2	3/3
Herpes simplex encephalitis							
Mean score	4.5	106.5	25.0	—	118.0	23.0	7.0
Prevalence of deficit	1/2		1/2		0/1	0/1	2/2
Korsakoff's syndrome							
Score	6	78	17	1	86	362	6
Presence of deficit	0		1		1	1	1
Stroke							
Score	6	74	79	15	129	22	7
Presence of deficit	0		0		0	0	1
Medial temporal-lobe resection							
Score	6	84	26	3	110	63	7.5
Presence of deficit	0		1		0	1	1

Source of deficit criterion: ^{a}normative data, ^{b}performance of impaired focal lesions groups, ^{c}clinical experience.

TABLE 8. Comparison of Patients with Global Amnesia Due to Different Etiologies: Language and Spatial Abilities

	Language		Spatial Abilities		
	Receptive Token Test (max. = 36)	Expressive Reporter's Test (max. = 26)	Rey Copy (max. = 36)	Body Scheme (max. = 35)	Visual Locomotor Mazes (max. = 44)
Deficit Criterion	<33[a]	<24[a]	<30[a,b]	<20[a]	<35[c]
Group					
ACoA aneurysm					
Mean score	34.5	24.5	27.6	27.0	30.7
Prevalence of deficit	1/7	2/7	6/8	1/7	5/6
Closed head injury					
Mean score	34.4	24.2	26.7	20.8	23.5
Prevalence of deficit	1/4	0/4	3/5	1/4	2/4
Anoxia					
Mean score	33.8	18.0	22.0	8.5	27.5
Prevalence of deficit	0/2	2/2	2/2	2/2	2/2
Herpes simplex encephalitis					
Mean score	34.5	24.2	23.0	25.0	30.5
Prevalence of deficit	0/2	1/2	1/1	0/1	2/2
Korsakoff's syndrome					
Score	30.5	10	16.5	9	11
Presence of deficit	1	1	1	1	1
Stroke					
Score	35	25.5	22	11	19
Presence of deficit	0	0	1	1	1
Medial temporal-lobe resection					
Score	31	17.5	27	12	23
Presence of deficit	1	1	1	1	1

Source of deficit criterion: [a] normative data, [b] performance of impaired focal lesions groups, [c] clinical experience.

Quantitative Differences

The three etiologic groups differed at the .01 significance level in mean rank across domains, $F(2,14) = 7.84$. The mean rank for the ACoA aneurysm group was .37, and the means for the anoxia and head injury groups were $-.51$ and $-.32$, respectively, indicating that the ACoA aneurysm patients generally performed better than the others across the five domains tested.

TABLE 9. Comparison of Patients with Global Amnesia Due to Different Etiologies: Perception of Complex Visual Stimuli

	Hidden Figures Test (max. = 61)	Gollin Incomplete-pictures Test (errors; max. = 100)		
		Initial	1-Hour Delay	24-Hour Delay
Deficit Criterion	$<17^a$	$>29^a$		
Group				
ACoA aneurysm				
Mean score	19.1	16.8	9.3	7.0
Prevalence of deficit	4/8	0/7		
Closed head injury				
Mean score	17.0	31.5	25.2	19.5
Prevalence of deficit	3/5	2/4		
Anoxia				
Mean score	17.0	26.0	21.0	19.0
Prevalence of deficit	1/3	0/1		
Herpes simplex encephalitis				
Mean score	19.0	26.0	17.0	14.0
Prevalence of deficit	0/1	0/1		
Korsakoff's syndrome				
Score	4	35	25	21
Presence of deficit	1	1		
Stroke				
Score	20	26	17	9
Presence of deficit	0	0		
Medial temporal-lobe resection				
Score	16	21	11	—
Presence of deficit	1	0		

Source of deficit criterion: ^{a}normative data, ^{b}performance of impaired focal lesions groups, ^{c}clinical experience.

Qualitative Differences

The group × domain interaction test searched for qualitative differences among etiologies. The interaction did not approach significance, $F(8, 48) = 1.30, p < .20$. It is important to note that the nonsignificant interaction test was more powerful than the previously reported significant test of the group main effect because the interaction test used a smaller, within-subjects error term. Together, the two ANOVA tests provide strong evidence that, subject to the limitations of our patient recruitment procedures, amnesic patients of different etiologies differed in overall level of cognitive functioning (the ACoA aneurysm patients performed best), and the pattern of performance across domains was similar for the eitologies studied.

One additional statistical technique was applied to the present data in another effort to determine whether etiologic groups differed in the pattern of deficits across domains. It, too, failed to find such differences. This analysis entered the normalized ranks for 24 variables into a disjoint (as opposed to hierarchical) cluster analysis algorithm. Only data from the ACoA aneurysm and head injury groups were included because of the relatively large sample sizes. Because the goal was to determine whether the etiologic groups could be distinguished on the basis of patterns of deficit, independent of the quantitative differences already described, all scores were adjusted by computing each subject's mean rank over all tests, and then subtracting that mean rank from each of the subject's scores. This procedure ensured that the data for each subject had an overall mean of zero, thereby eliminating differences in level of severity among etiologic groups. Corresponding to the inclusion of patients with either of two etiologies (aneurysm and head injury), the algorithm was forced to classify each of the 13 patients into either of two clusters. Because the algorithm did not use etiologic information, any correspondence between the cluster and etiologic classifications must have resulted from consistent pattern differences between etiologies. A 2 × 2 chi square test of association compared the two classifications; the p value was greater than .5, indicating no association whatsoever. A second cluster analysis, identical to the first except that it retained level information, led to a chi square value significant at the .06 level. Consistent with the ANOVA of ranks, the two cluster analyses jointly imply that the ACoA and head injury groups differed in degree rather than in kind of impairment.

Analyses Restricted to Memory Functions

The quantitative and qualitative analyses just reported encompassed combined data from measures of IQ, memory, frontal-lobe function, language, spatial capacities, and visual perception. Because the major questions concerned differences in mnemonic capacities, additional analyses were performed, procedurally similar to those above and using the same subjects, but incorporating only data from the memory tests and pooling the scores from tests of immediate memory, recall, and recognition tests. The results of the analysis restricted to memory functions were consonant with the results of the analysis for all cognitive functions: Groups differed significantly, $F(2, 14) = 4.66$, $p = .03$, indicating the presence of quantitative differences in mnemonic capacities; the group × test interaction was not significant, $F(4, 24) = 1.57$, $p < .20$, indicating the absence of qualitative differences. Similarly, a cluster analysis for qualitative differences based only upon memory tests failed to classify patients according to etiology, $p < .50$.

A Search for Differences among Lesion Groups: Analyses of Raw Scores

In the preceding sections, the analyses classified patients by etiology; in this and the next sections, the analyses classified patients by lesion site. In the latter analyses, the patients were grouped irrespective of etiology and on the basis of commonality of lesion. Thus, the patients with anoxia, herpes simplex encephalitis, stroke, or bilateral medial temporal-lobe resection were combined to form one group believed to have lesions of the medial temporal lobes; the patients with ruptured ACoA aneurysms were believed to have lesions of the posterior inferior medial frontal-basal forebrain regions; and the patients with closed head injury were believed to have diffuse involvement of white matter. As before, we began with analyses of raw scores of individual tests. The variables for which the previous analyses by etiology as well as the new analyses by lesion site yielded significance levels of .10 or less were Verbal IQ, Full Scale IQ, Memory Quotient, forward digit span, forward and backward block span, Body Scheme, and Verbal and Nonverbal Recurring Figures. In five instances the analyses by lesion were significant but the corresponding analyses by etiology were not: nonverbal paired-associate learning task (initial test, $p = .10$), Brown-Peterson distractor task ($p = .08$), and Gollin Incomplete-Pictures Test (one hour retest, $p = .05$; 24 hours, $p = .10$). The group with insult to the posterior inferior medial frontal-basal forebrain regions had the best performance of all measures.

A Search for Quantitative and Qualitative Differences among Lesion Groups: Analyses of Ranks

The ANOVA test for quantitative differences in ranks between lesion groups was significant at $p < .01$ when examining ranks in five cognitive domains, and was significant at $p = .03$ when examining ranks in the three memory domains. In the ANOVA test for qualitative differences, the lesion group by domain interaction did not approach significance for either the composite cognitive or memory domain analyses, $p < .50$ for each. The corresponding chi squre tests, which attempted to recapture lesion site classification from cluster analyses of the neuropsychological information, were significant neither for the cognitive variables ($p = .20$) nor for the memory variables ($p < .5$).

Comparisons among Individual Subjects

This section summarizes the test performance of the patients from the three etiologic groups with one subject: Korsakoff's syndrome, bilateral stroke, and bilateral medial temporal-lobe resection (H.M.). The patient with Korsakoff's syndrome had widespread cognitive impairment. Her scores were below the range of the scores for the aneurysm, head injury, anoxia, and encephalitis groups on most tests; in particular, her Wechsler Full Scale IQ was only 76 and her MQ 63. Thus, her amnesic syndrome resembled dementia insofar as she showed deficits on most nonmnemonic tasks as well as those focusing on memory. Nevertheless, she did perform the Wisconsin Card Sorting Test efficiently. In contrast, the stroke patient showed a moderately severe and relatively pure amnesia: her Wechsler IQ and Porteus Maze Test scores were above average (Full Scale IQ = 111, Porteus Test Quotient = 129), and her frontal-lobe and language functions were intact. Her greatest deficits relative to the other patients were on the delayed recall of the Rey figure and on the Nonverbal Recurring Figures Test. This finding is consistent with the decreased density noted in the right temporal lobe on CT scan. H.M. was more impaired than were patients in the other amnesic groups on tests of verbal and nonverbal recall and recognition, though not in immediate memory capacity. Despite above-average intelligence, he performed some language and spatial tests poorly. The latter deficits were selective and less marked than the memory impairment.

AN INTERPRETATION

The major question addressed in this paper was whether neurological diseases that differ in etiology or that differ in the brain regions affected produce fundamentally dissimilar global amnesias. Two kinds of statistical analyses were reported: those sensitive to quantitative differences in mnemonic and nonmnemonic capacities among etiologic or lesion groups (that is, differences in severity of impairment) and those sensitive to qualitative differences among etiologic or lesion groups (that is, to different patterns of sparing and loss of function). The results were straightforward: patients with global amnesia, whether grouped according to etiology (ACoA aneurysm, closed head injury, and anoxia) or according to locus of lesion (posterior inferior medial frontal—basal forebrain regions; diffuse involvement of white matter; and medial temporal lobe) differed in the severity of mnemonic and nonmnemonic deficits but not in the pattern of deficits. These findings of quantitative but not qualitative differences, therefore, are consistent with the view that there is one form of amnesia resulting from invasion of a single neural system for fact learning.

Group comparisons revealed that the aneurysm, or posterior inferior medial frontal—basal forebrain, group was superior on most tests across domains. This impairment of function among the other groups appears unrelated to differences among etiologic groups in the neural correlate of the acute symptoms. For example, neither patients with aneurysms nor patients with encephalitis, stroke, Korsakoff's syndrome, or bilateral medial temporal-lobe resection had any or notable loss of consciousness; yet, all the latter groups were more impaired than the aneurysm groups in the performance of memory and other cognitive tests.

Our conclusion seems to be at variance with the claims of other investigators that certain etiologically distinct amnesic groups manifest fundamentally different disorders of recent memory.[72,73] Specifically, dissociations have been reported between patients with diencephalic lesions and patients with dysfunction of medial temporal-lobe structures. In studies of forgetting rate, performance was normal in two instances of diencephalic lesions, Korsakoff's syndrome[74] and case N.A.,[75] whereas forgetting was said to be accelerated in two examples of medial temporal-lobe disorder, case H.M.[74] and patients who had recently undergone ECT.[75] Not only does the present finding of quantitative but not qualitative differences among several lesion groups pose problems for these claims, but in a separate study, we could not replicate Huppert and Piercy's finding in H.M.[76] Further, we did not observe abnormal forgetting rates in a group of patients believed to have severe bilateral degeneration of the hippocampus and amygdala, patients with Alzheimer's disease.[77] Nevertheless, we have by no means ruled out the possibility of qualitative differences among some amnesic patients; possibly our behavioral measures were insensitive to them. Evidence does exist of clear qualitative distinctions among etiologic groups in remote memory function.[78-80] Also, a study with monkeys found dissociations of memory capacities following lesions of different brain structures.[81]

One surprising finding in our own work was that some amnesic patients, particularly those with ACoA aneurysms, showed minimal or no memory deficits on some tests of new fact learning. Does this finding necessitate a modification of our definition of an amnesic syndrome? Probably not. These patients were considered amnesic because there was a loss of continuity and detail in their recollection of life's events. Although they sometimes had almost normal recall of very recent events, they showed an inability to reconstitute events that had occurred a few weeks or months ago. Consequently, they were unable to hold a job or live alone. Their handicap was not due to ancillary nonmnemonic cognitive deficits, although loss of motivation may have been a contributing factor in some cases. Despite being incapacitated in everyday life, their performance on formal testing was more efficient. Perhaps the delay intervals used in our laboratory memory tests were too short to elicit deficits consistently. This point is illustrated by the performance of one of our patients with amnesia due to anoxia (Corkin, unpublished data). He was trained on a tactual stylus maze for three consecutive days; each day's training consisted of three sessions two hours apart. His recall of the task at the beginning of sessions two and three on each of the three days was excellent. In contrast, on the second and third mornings before training began, he recalled neither the apparatus nor the task. At these times, attempts to prompt him (seating him at the apparatus, showing him the stylus and having him hold it, letting him feel the perimeter of the maze, and guiding his hand to the start and finish) did not benefit recall. Apparently, his fact-learning system was sufficiently intact to support recall after a two-hour delay interval, but too fragile to support recall after 21 hours. Although his deficit was mild compared to H.M.'s, it was clinically significant and presented a crippling problem for the patient.

Although the results of most analyses for etiologic groups were consonant with those for lesion groups, a few significant results were unique to analyses based upon etiology. Specifically, the patients with anoxia were impaired relative to the other groups on the Mental Control subtest of the Wechsler Memory Scale (counting backward from 20, saying the alphabet, counting by threes or fours), and on forward digit span; traditionally, these tasks have been considered to be gross estimates of attention.[82] In contrast, the anoxia patients were relatively efficient on the WAIS Vocabulary subtest, a test of semantic knowledge. These results suggest a general attentional disorder, which may have contributed to the severity of their mnemonic deficit. The possibility that an attentional deficit is germane to amnesic patients with anoxia needs to be explored more rigorously with specific tasks designed to test attention.

The present study of etiologically distinct amnesias also sheds light on the neurobiological substrate of fact learning in humans. The patients studied here included not only those with lesions of the medial temporal-lobe or midline diencephalic regions, the most frequently studied lesion groups, but also patients whose lesions implicated other regions. In particular, the patients with ruptured ACoA aneurysms had lesions invading the posterior inferior medial frontal areas and the basal forebrain; the patients with closed head injury had diffuse involvement of cerebral white matter. It may be that the functionally significant neural loss in the patients with aneurysms or head injuries was to medial temporal-lobe or medial thalamic regions, either directly or indirectly; alternatively, additional critical lesion sites may reside outside these regions, thereby extending the limits of the neural systems subserving memory formation. Mishkin and his collaborators, in their work with monkeys, have described a memory system consisting of two limbo-diencephalic pathways and the pathways' prefrontal targets,[83] which together may represent the neural substrate of the fact-learning system in humans. Of particular interest here is the prefrontal component of this system, which has received little attention in investigations of human amnesia, but which seems to be implicated in the present cases with ruptured ACoA aneurysms.

To date, researchers have not characterized the functional roles played by the different elements of the fact-learning system. It is difficult to imagine that such an extensive network with such clear anatomical differentiation lacks a parallel functional differentiation, and it is reasonable to expect that etiologically distinct amnesias with different neuropathological profiles would be distinguishable on behavioral grounds. Nonetheless, in our 21 patients with global amnesia, the only differences among etiologically defined groups across the range of memory tests were in severity of memory loss, a finding probably related in part to the extent of damage to this anatomical system, or to specific neurochemical divisions within it; of particular interest is the extent of interference with cholinergic pathways. In addition, in at least two etiologies of global amnesia, anoxia and Korsakoff's syndrome, the region of the fourth ventricle is involved, and it is tempting to speculate that loss of neurons in the locus coeruleus and the consequent deficiency of noradrenergic metabolism can contribute to the fact-learning disorder. This structure projects to the basal forebrain[84,85] and may cooperate with the limbo-diencephalic system in the learning and retention of new facts. The integrity of this source of noradrenergic input to the rest of the brain has been related to learning and memory performance in animals and humans,[86] although it has not been determined whether the locus coeruleus and noradrenergic neurotransmission are involved in memory processing itself or in nonmnemonic processes that influence performance on memory tests. In future research, it may be possible to characterize distinctive contributions to memory function of the locus coeruleus and limbo-diencephalic systems or elements of these systems, by administering noradrenergic and cholinergic agonists and antagonists to patients and animals with lesions in these areas, and measuring both mnemonic and nonmnemonic capacities involved in the performance of specific memory tests. In this way, it should be possible to detect any patterns of change within and across cognitive domains and relate them to the function of anatomical and chemical entities.

ACKNOWLEDGMENTS

We thank the following colleagues for permission to study patients under their care: H. Thomas Ballantine, Jr., M.D., Verne S. Caviness, Jr., M.D., John H. Growdon, M.D., Roberto Heros, M.D., F. Jacob Huff, M.D., Brenda Milner, Sc.D., Michael S. Perlman, M.D., Vincent Perlo, M.D., the late William B. Scoville, M.D., John F. Sullivan, M.D., Thomas E. Twitchell, M.D., Ken R. Winston, M.D., Bryan T. Woods, M.D., and Thomas Zeffiro, M.D. The research described here was undertaken at the MIT Clinical Research Center; we acknowledge with thanks the work of its staff.

REFERENCES

1. WHITTY, C. W. M. & O. L. LISHMAN. 1966. Amnesia in cerebral disease. *In* Amnesia. C. W. M. Whitty & O. L. Zangwill, Eds.: 36–76. Butterworth. London.
2. MILNER, B. 1962. Les troubles de la memoire accompagnant des lesions hippocampiques bilaterales. *In* Physiologie de l'Hippocampe. Pp. 257–272. Centre National de la Recherche Scientifique. Paris.
3. CORKIN, S. 1968. Acquisition of motor skill after bilateral medial temporal lobe excision. Neuropsychologia 6: 255–265.
4. COHEN, N. 1984. Preserved learning capacity in amnesia: evidence for multiple memory systems. *In* Neuropsychology of Memory. L. Squire & N. Butters, Eds.: 83–103. Guilford Press. London.
5. GRAF, P., L. R. SQUIRE & G. MANDLER. 1984. The information that amnesic patients do not forget. J. Exp. Psychol.: Learning, Memory & Cognition 10: 164–178.
6. SCHACTER, D. 1985. Ann. N.Y. Acad. Sci. (This volume.)
7. BRIERLY, J. B. 1961. Clinico-pathological correlations in amnesia. Geront. Clin. 3: 97.
8. ESCOUROLLE, R. & J. POIRIER. 1978. Manual of Basic Neuropathology. 2nd edit. W.B. Saunders Company. Philadelphia, PA.
9. GADE, A. 1982. Amnesia after operations on aneurysms of the anterior communicating artery. Surg. Neurol. 18: 46–49.
10. TALLAND, G. A., W. H. SWEET & H. T. BALLANTINE. 1967. Amnesic syndrome with anterior communicating artery aneurysm. J. Nervous Mental Disease 145: 179–192.
11. DUNKER, R. O. & A. B. HARRIS. 1976. Surgical anatomy of the proximal anterior cerebral artery. J. Neurosurg. 44: 359–367.

12. ALEXANDER, M. P. & M. FREEDMAN. 1984. Amnesia after anterior communicating artery aneurysm rupture. Neurology 34: 752–757.
13. DAMASIO, A. R., N. R. GRAFF-RADFORD, P. J. ESLINGER, H. DAMASIO & N. KASSELL. Amnesia following basal forebrain lesions. Unpublished manuscript.
14. STRICH, S. J. 1956. Diffuse degeneration of cerebral white matter in severe dementia following head injury. J. Neurol. Neurosurg. Psychiatry 19: 163–185.
15. STRICH, S. J. 1970. Lesions in the cerebral hemispheres after blunt head injury. In The Pathology of Trauma. S. Sevitt & H. B. Stoner, Eds.: 166–171. BMA House. London.
16. ADAMS, J. H., D. E. MITCHELL, D. I. GRAHAM & D. DOYLE. 1977. Diffuse brain damage of immediate impact type. Brain 100: 489–502.
17. LEVIN, H. S., A. L. BENTON & R. G. GROSSMAN. 1982. Neurobehavioral Consequences of Closed Head Injury. Oxford University Press. Oxford.
18. OPPENHEIMER, D. R. 1968. Microscopic lesions in the brain following head injury. J. Neurol. Neurosurg. Psychiatry 31: 299–306.
19. LANKSCH, W., T. GRUMME & E. KAZNER, Eds. 1979. Computed Tomography in Head Injuries. Springer-Verlag. New York.
20. LINDENBERG, R., R. S. FISHER, S. H. DURLACHER, W. V. LOVITT JR. & E. FREYTAG. 1955. Lesions of the corpus callosum following blunt mechanical trauma to the head. Am. J. Pathol. 31: 297–317.
21. RUSSELL, W. R. 1932. Cerebral involvement in head injury. Brain 35: 549–603.
22. BROOKS, D. N. 1972. Memory and head injury. J. Nerv. Mental Dis. 155: 350-355.
23. ILLIS, L. S. & J. V. T. GOSTLING. 1972. Herpes Simplex Encephalitis. Williams & Wilkins. Baltimore.
24. ADAMS, H. & D. MILLER. 1973. Herpes simplex encephalitis: A clinical and pathological analysis of 22 cases. Postgrad. Med. J. 49: 393–397.
25. DRACHMAN, D. A. & R. D. ADAMS. 1962. Herpes simplex and acute inclusion-body encephalitis. Arch. Neurol. 7: 61–79.
26. ADAMS, R. D. & M. VICTOR. 1981. Principles of Neurology. 2nd edit. McGraw-Hill. New York.
27. SYMONDS, C. P. 1966. Disorders of memory. Brain 89: 625.
28. VICTOR, M., R. D. ADAMS & G. H. COLLINS. 1971. The Wernicke-Korsakoff Syndrome. F.A. Davis Co. Philadelphia.
29. BUTTERS, N. 1984. Alcoholic Korsakoff's syndrome: An update. Sem. Neurol. 4: 226–244.
30. DELAY, J. & S. BRION. 1954. Syndrome de Korsakoff et corps mamillaires. L'Encephale 43: 193–200.
31. MAIR, W. G. P., E. K. WARRINGTON, & L. WEISKRANTZ. 1979. Memory disorder in Korsakoff's psychosis. A neuropathological and neuropsychological investigation of two cases. Brain 102: 749–783.
32. LISHMAN, W. A. 1981. Cerebral disorder in alcoholism: Syndromes of impairment. Brain 104: 1–20.
33. WINOCUR, G., S. OXBURY, R. ROBERTS, V. AGNETTI & C. DAVIS. 1984. Amnesia in a patient with bilateral lesions to the thalamus. Neuropsychologia 22: 123–143.
34. DIDE, M. & BOTCAZO. 1902. Amnesie continue, cecite cerbale pure, perte du sense topographique, ramollissement double du lobe lingual. Rev. Neurol. 10: 676–680.
35. VICTOR, M., J. B. ANGEVINE, E. L. MANCALL & C. M. FISHER. 1961. Memory loss with lesions of hippocampal formation. Arch. Neurol. 5: 244–263.
36. DEJONG, R. N., H. H. ITABASHI & J. R. OLSON. 1969. Memory loss due to hippocampal lesions. Arch. Neurol. 20: 339–348.
37. SCOVILLE, W. B., R. H. DUNSMORE, W. T. LIBERSON, C. E. HENRY & A. PEPE. 1953. Observations on medial temporal lobotomy and uncotomy in the treatment of psychotic states. In Psychiatric Treatment. 31: 347–369. Williams & Wilkins. Baltimore.
38. SCOVILLE, W. B. & B. MILNER. 1957. Loss of recent memory after bilateral hippocampal lesions. J. Neurol. Neurosurg. Psychiatry 20: 11–21.
39. CORKIN, S. 1984. Lasting consequences of bilateral medial temporal lobectomy: clinical course and experimental findings in H.M. Sem. Neurology 4: 252–262.
40. WECHSLER, D. 1941. The Measurement of Adult Intelligence. 2nd edit. Williams & Wilkins. Baltimore.

41. WECHSLER, D., Ed. 1946. The Wechsler-Bellevue Intelligence Scale, Form II. Manual for administering and scoring the test. The Psychological Corporation. New York.
42. WECHSLER, D., Ed. 1955. Manual for the Wechsler Adult Intelligence Scale. Psychological Corporation. New York.
43. WECHSLER, D., Ed. 1981. Manual for the Wechsler Adult Intelligence Scale—Revised. The Psychological Corporation. New York.
44. WECHSLER, D. & C. P. STONE. 1945. Wechsler Memory Scale. The Psychological Corporation. New York.
45. WECHSLER, D., Ed. 1944. The Measurement of Adult Intelligence. Williams & Wilkins. Baltimore, MD.
46. CORSI, P. 1972. Human memory and the medial temporal region of the brain. Unpublished doctoral dissertation. McGill University. Montreal.
47. MILNER, B. 1971. Interhemispheric differences in the localization of psychological processes in man. Brit. Med. Bull. **27**: 272–277.
48. BROWN, J. 1958. Some tests of the decay theory of immediate memory. Q. J. Exp. Psychol. **10**: 12–21.
49. PETERSON, L. R. & M. J. PETERSON. 1959. Short-term memory retention of individual verbal items. J. Exp. Psychol. **58**: 193–198.
50. INGLIS, J. 1959. A paired associate learning test for use with elderly psychiatric patients. J. Mental Sci. **105**: 440–443.
51. CORKIN, S., J. H. GROWDON, E. V. SULLIVAN, M. J. NISSEN & F. J. HUFF. 1985. Assessing treatment effects from a neuropsychological perspective. *In* Handbook for Clinical Assessment of Older Adults, L. Poon, Ed. American Psychological Association. Washington, DC.
52. MILNER, B. 1958. Psychological defects produced by temporal-lobe excision. Research Publications of the Association for Research in Nervous and Mental Disease **36**: 244–257.
53. REY, A. 1942. L'exam psychologique dans les cas d'encephalopathie traumatique. Arch. Psychol. **28**: 286–340.
54. OSTERREITH, P. & A. REY. 1944. Le test de copie d'une figure complexe. Arch. Psychol. **30**: 205–220.
55. TAYLOR, L. 1969. Localization of cerebral lesions by psychological testing. Clin. Neurosurg. **16**: 269–287.
56. MILNER, B. & D. KIMURA. 1964. Dissociable visual learning defects after unilateral temporal lobectomy in man. Presented at the Eastern Psychological Association Meeting. April, 1964. Philadelphia, PA.
57. CRAIK, F. I. M. & R. S. LOCKHART. 1972. Levels of processing: a framework for memory research. J. Verbal Learning Verbal Behavior **11**: 671–684.
58. KIMURA, D. 1963. Right temporal-lobe damage. Arch. Neurol. **8**: 264–271.
59. MILNER, B. 1963. Effects of different brain lesions on card sorting: the role of the frontal lobes. Arch. Neurol. **9**: 90–100.
60. THURSTONE, L. L. 1944. A Factorial Study of Perception. University of Chicago Press. Chicago, IL.
61. MILNER, B. 1964. Some effects of frontal lobectomy in man. *In* The Frontal Granular Cortex and Behavior. J. M. Warren & K. Akert, Eds. McGraw-Hill. New York.
62. PORTEUS, S. D, Ed. 1965. Porteus Mazes Test. Pacific Books. Palo Alto, CA.
63. LANDIS, C. & D. ERLICK. 1950. An analysis of the Porteus Maze-Test as affected by psychosurgery. Am. J. Psychol. **63**: 557–566.
64. CORKIN, S. 1980. A prospective study of the safety and efficacy of cingulotomy. *In* The Psychosurgery Debate. E. Valenstein, Ed.: 168–204. Freeman Press. San Francisco, CA.
65. DERENZI, E. & L. A. VIGNOLO. 1962. The token test: A sensitive test to detect receptive disturbances in aphasics. Brain **85**: 665–678.
66. DERENZI, E. & C. FERRARI. 1978. The reporter's test: A sensitive test to detect expressive disturbances in aphasics. Cortex **14**: 279–293.
67. SEMMES, J., S. WEINSTEIN, L. GHENT & H.-L. TEUBER. 1963. Correlates of impaired orientation in personal and extrapersonal space. Brain **86**: 747–772.

68. TEUBER, H.-L. & S. WEINSTEIN. 1956. Ability to discover hidden figures after cerebral lesions. Arch. Neurol. Psychiatry **76:** 369–379.
69. CORKIN, S. 1979. Hidden-figures test performance: lasting effects of unilateral penetrating head injury and transient effects of bilateral cingulotomy. Neuropsychologia **17:** 585–605.
70. CORKIN, S. 1982. Some relationships between global amnesia and the memory impairments in Alzheimer's disease. *In* Alzheimer's Disease: A Report of Progress in Research. S. Corkin, K. L. Davis, J. H. Growdon, E. Usdin, & R. J. Wurtman, Eds. **19:** 149–164. Raven Press. New York.
71. MILLER, R. G. JR. 1966. Simultaneous Statistical Inference. McGraw-Hill. New York.
72. LEHRMITTE, F. & J.-L. SIGNORET. 1972. Analyse neuropsychologique et differentiation des syndrome amnesiques. Rev. Neurol. **126:** 161–178.
73. SQUIRE, L. R. & N. J. COHEN. 1984. Human memory and amnesia. *In* Neurobiology of Learning and Memory. G. Lynch. J. L. McGaugh, & N. M. Weinberger, Eds.: 3–64. Guilford Press. New York.
74. HUPPERT, F. A. & M. PIERCY. 1979. Normal and abnormal forgetting in organic amnesia: effect of locus of lesion. Cortex **15:** 385–390.
75. SQUIRE, L. R. 1981. Two forms of amnesia: an analysis of forgetting. J. Neurosci. **1:** 635–640.
76. FREED, D. M., S. CORKIN & N. J. COHEN. 1984. Rate of forgetting in H.M.: A reanalysis. Society for Neuroscience Abstracts **10:** 383.
77. FREED, D. M. 1984. Rate of forgetting in Alzheimer's disease. Paper presented at the Annual Meeting of the Eastern Psychological Association. Baltimore, MD, April, 1984.
78. COHEN, N. J. & L. R. SQUIRE. 1981. Retrograde amnesia and remote memory impairment. Neuropsychologia **19:** 337–356.
79. CORKIN, S., N. J. COHEN & H. J. SAGAR. 1983. Memory for remote personal and public events after bilateral medial temporary lobectomy. Soc. Neurosci. Abstracts **9:** 28.
80. SAGAR, H. J., N. J. COHEN, S. CORKIN & J. H. GROWDON. 1985. Dissociations among processes in remote memory. Ann. N.Y. Acad. Sci. (This volume.)
81. ZOLA-MORGAN, S. & L. R. SQUIRE. 1982. Two forms of amnesia: rapid forgetting after medial temporal lesions but not after diencephalic lesions. Soc. Neurosci. Abstracts **8:** 24.
82. MATARAZZO, J. D. 1976. Wechsler's Measurement and Appraisal of Adult Intelligence. Williams & Wilkins. Baltimore.
83. MISHKIN, M. & J. BACHEVALIER. 1983. Object recognition impaired by ventromedial but not dorsolateral prefrontal cortical lesions in monkeys. Soc. Neurosci. Abstracts **9:** 29.
84. RAISMAN, G. 1966. Connexions of the septum. Brain **89:** 317–348.
85. MOORE, R. Y. 1978. Catecholamine innervation of the basal forebrain. I. The septal area. J. Comp. Neurol. **177:** 665–684.
86. QUARTERMAIN, D. 1983. The role of catecholamines in memory processing. *In* The Physiological Basis of Memory. J. A. Deutsch, Ed.: 387–423. Academic Press.

Priming of Old and New Knowledge in Amnesic Patients and Normal Subjects[a]

DANIEL L. SCHACTER

Unit for Memory Disorders
Department of Psychology
University of Toronto
Toronto, Canada M5S 1A1

Neuropsychological studies of memory pathology have demonstrated that amnesic patients who are characterized by diverse forms of neurological dysfunction are severely impaired on tasks that tap recall and recognition of recently studied information.[1-3] One feature of virtually all memory tasks on which amnesic patients are impaired is that they demand explicit recollection of the context and content of recent learning episodes. During the past decade, however, two kinds of evidence have established that amnesic patients can demonstrate relatively normal memory performance on implicit tests, which do not demand explicit recollection of a learning episode. One is that amnesic patients can acquire motor, perceptual, and cognitive skills in a normal or near-normal manner, even though they recall little or nothing of the learning episodes in which they acquired the skills.[4-7] A second kind of evidence that amnesic patients perform normally on implicit tests is provided by the phenomenon of repetition priming: A single exposure to an item on a list facilitates amnesics' processing of that item on a variety of retention tests that do not require explicit recollection of the study episode. Warrington and Weiskrantz,[8,9] for example, demonstrated that amnesics and controls showed a similar tendency to complete three-letter fragments of familiar words with items from a recently studied list. However, the amnesics' performance on a Yes/No recognition task was seriously impaired. Similar data have been reported by others.[10,11] Amnesics also exhibit intact repetition-priming effects, in the face of poor recall and recognition, on implicit tests such as lexical decision[7] and homophone spelling.[12]

The dissociation between priming and recollection in amnesia is paralleled by demonstrations in normal subjects that experimental variables that have large effects on recall and recognition have little or no effect on the magnitude of repetition priming in word completion,[13,14] word identification,[15,16] and lexical decision.[17,18] Moreover, the magnitude of priming effects on these tasks can be statistically independent of recognition memory performance.[12,14,18] The observed dissociations have led a number of investigators to propose that repetition-priming effects are mediated by a "memory system," "memory process," or "form of memory" that is relatively spared in amnesia and that can function independently of the damaged memory process or system that underlies conscious and explicit recollection.[3,4,10,11,14,19-22]

A fundamental question regarding the process or system that underlies repetition priming is whether it can support the acquisition of new knowledge or it is restricted to the activation of old, existing knowledge. One of the hallmarks of organic amnesia is the virtual absence of any capacity to retain new information. The possibility that the

[a]Supported by a Special Research Program grant from the Connaught Fund, University of Toronto, and by Research Grant No. U0361 from the Natural Sciences and Engineering Research Council of Canada.

implicit kind of memory that is involved in priming can support the creation of new knowledge is of considerable interest. However, intact repetition-priming effects in amnesics have been observed only with old information, such as familiar words. Thus, it can be argued that the normal performance of amnesics on implicit tests, such as word completion, represents a temporary increase in the activation level of old or existing knowledge.[10,19,22,23] Support for this idea derives from the work of Diamond and Rozin,[10] who found that amnesics exhibited no priming on a completion task when pseudowords were used as the experimental materials. They suggested that with the pseudowords there was no pre-established knowledge to activate, hence no priming was observed.

There is, however, evidence that amnesic patients may be able to acquire some new knowledge, even in the absence of conscious recollection. Schacter, Harbluk, and McLachlan[24] found that amnesics retained some new information about well-known and unknown people, even though they could not remember when or where they acquired it. In an experiment by Moscovitch,[25] amnesics and controls studied weakly related word pairs and later read over lists that contained either the same intact pairs, re-pairings of list items, or new pairs that had not appeared on the list. Moscovitch found that amnesics, as well as controls, read lists of old intact pairs faster than lists of new pairs. More importantly, he found that both groups of subjects read lists of old intact pairs faster than lists of old broken pairs, indicating that new relationships established at the time of study affected amnesics' performance. These data suggest that priming on implicit tests may reflect more than just the activation of existing knowledge and that it may reveal the presence of new knowledge. The purpose of the present article is to describe and discuss some recent research that attempts to determine the conditions under which priming can support new learning in amnesic patients.

PRIMING OF NEW INFORMATION IN WORD COMPLETION

Graf and Schacter[26] have explored whether normal retention of new associations by amnesics could be demonstrated with a word-completion task. We investigated this hypothesis by comparing probability of word completion in two conditions. In the same context condition, a preexperimentally unrelated cue and target were studied (e.g., *window*–REASON), and the study cue was present along with a three-letter fragment of the target on a word-completion test (e.g., *window*–REA___). In the different context condition, the target fragment appeared on the completion test with a word other than its list cue (e.g., *mold*–REA___). We reasoned that the presence of a new association between the unrelated cue and target would be demonstrated if probability of word completion in the same context condition exceeded probability of word completion in the different context condition. The major question of interest was whether completion performance of amnesics and controls is affected similarly by a new association between two words that is established for the first time on the study list.

Twelve amnesic patients of varied etiologies participated in the study. All had severe difficulties on standard memory tests such as paired-associate recall and Yes/No or forced-choice recognition. Twelve matched controls and twelve college students also participated. Subjects studied lists of words that were composed of either unrelated word pairs (e.g., *window*–REASON) or moderately related word pairs (e.g., *window*–GLASS). They were instructed to relate the two words by placing them in a sentence, because an earlier experiment with normal subjects indicated that priming of new information depends upon semantic processing.[26] The subsequent completion task contained some context pairings of items that had appeared together on the study list, and also contained different context pairs that represented re-pairings of A and B terms from the study list or included a new stimulus term that had not appeared on the study list along with a three-letter fragment of a list target. Other cue-fragment pairs had not appeared on the study list at all and were included to provide baseline data. Subjects were instructed to read over each pair and to complete each three-letter fragment with the first word that came to mind. Previous work has demonstrated that the instructions on a completion test influence performance markedly. When subjects are told to complete test fragments with the first word that comes to mind, amnesics and controls perform similarly; when subjects are told to complete the test fragments with words from the study list, normals' performance exceeds that of amnesics.[11] Following the completion test, a cued recall test was given in which the first members

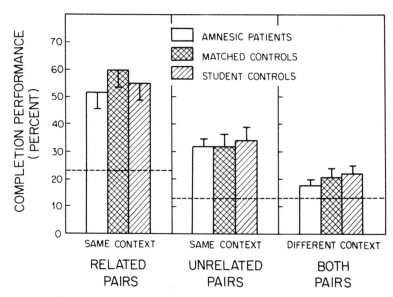

FIGURE 1. Mean word-completion performance for related and unrelated pairs in amnesic patients, matched controls, and student controls. The completion test presented the initial three letters of the response word from each study-list pair, either with the paired stimulus word from the study list (same context) or with another word (different context). A separate control group was used to obtain an estimate of baseline completion performance on the target response words, shown by the dashed lines. Vertical bars show the standard errors of the means.

of the word pairs were presented and subjects were asked to try to remember which word had been presented with each cue on the study list.

Consider first the outcome of the word-completion task. FIGURE 1 displays probability of word completion for unrelated and related pairs in the three groups of subjects. Probability of completing the targets in different context conditions significantly exceeded baseline levels, and there were no differences among groups. This finding is consistent with previous data indicating that presentation of a familiar word on a list enhances completion performance of amnesic patients in a normal manner. The critical new finding displayed in FIGURE 1 is that probability of completion was significantly higher in the same context conditions than in the different context conditions for amnesics, matched controls, and college students. Moreover, probability of completing the same context pairs did not differ among the three groups. These data demonstrate clearly that some sort of new association between previously unrelated pairs of words can be retained normally by amnesic patients. This new association is revealed when they are tested with a word-completion task.

The results of the cued-recall test, which was administered after the completion task, revealed a massive deficit on the part of the amnesic patients. The contrast between completion and cued recall is illustrated by FIGURE 2, which depicts cued-recall performance along with completion performance when pairs were tested in the same context. In contrast to the indistinguishable levels of the three groups on

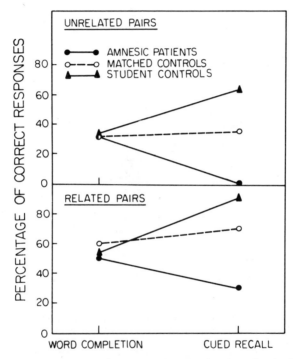

FIGURE 2. Mean word-completion performance for related and unrelated pairs in the same context condition, along with mean cued-recall performance, for the three subject groups.

completion, there were large differences on cued recall in both related and unrelated conditions.

The dissociation between completion and cued recall performance in amnesic patients suggests that qualitatively different forms of memory are tapped by the two tasks. It is possible, however, that amnesic patients simply form "weak" associations (cf. Milner[27]) that can be elicited on the completion task because there is more retrieval information on it than there is on the cued-recall test (e.g., window–REA___ versus window–_____). It would then follow that performance of matched controls and college students should also decline from completion to cued recall, although by a smaller amount, because both "weaker" and "stronger" associations can be contacted on the completion test, whereas only the "stronger" associations can be contacted on the recall test. Contrary to such a view, the data in FIGURE 2 indicate that both groups of controls produced more target items on the cued-recall test than on the completion test. Further information on this point is provided by a contingency analysis of the fate of individual items on the two tests. If the extra information on the completion test permitted amnesics and normals to gain access to weak associations, there should be few cases in which subjects fail to complete an item and then retrieve it on the cued-recall test. Subjects should not fail on a test that requires only weak associations for successful performance, and then succeed on a test that requires stronger associations. The contingency analysis was performed on those items that were tested in the same context on the completion test. It revealed that the conditional probability of failing to complete items that were recalled ($p(\overline{C}|R)$) was substantial in all conditions. For related word pairs, $p(\overline{C}|R)$ was 36% in amnesic patients, 32% in matched controls, and 44% in college students; for unrelated word pairs, $p(\overline{C}|R)$ was 62% in college students and 52% in matched controls (the analysis could not be performed on the amnesics' data, because cued recall of unrelated pairs was negligible). These data indicate that the "first thing that comes to mind" on the completion test represents a qualitatively different kind of mnemonic information than what is remembered on the cued-recall test.

The foregoing data indicate that the implicit form of memory that underlies repetition-priming effects goes beyond the mere activation of existing knowledge. The implicit form of memory makes possible the acquisition of a kind of new knowledge that can be retained and expressed normally by amnesic patients and that is specific to an individual encounter with a pair of pre-experimentally unrelated words. Old knowledge, however, may have played a critical role in the new learning observed in this experiment, because the target fragments were themselves part of pre-existing, integrated units—familiar words. It seems highly unlikely that amnesics would have revealed evidence of new learning had they been asked to give the first word that comes to mind to an unrelated cue without the benefit of the three-letter target fragments; after all, amnesics produced virtually no target items on the cued-recall test. A pilot study with four amnesic patients confirmed this expectation. When patients studied unrelated word pairs and were later asked to give the first word that came to mind in response to the cue word, without any target letters, no evidence of priming was observed. Considering the results of word-fragment completion studies more generally, it is apparent that amnesics demonstrate intact priming when part of a pre-existing unit, such as a familiar word, is present on the test and they respond by giving the rest of the unit. These observations lead to the suggestion that it is possible to demonstrate acquisition of new knowledge on a priming task only when part or all of a pre-existing unit is a target on the test. If this idea has general validity, amnesics should reveal evidence of priming with well-established units other than single words. Recent data that demonstrate normal priming of highly related paired associates in amnesia[28,29] are consistent with this notion, because primary associates such as *table*–CHAIR can be viewed as unitized representations (cf. Hayes-Roth[30]). The purpose of the next experiment is to test the generality of the idea that pre-existing units play a critical role in priming effects.

PRIMING OF PRE-EXISTING UNITS: EVIDENCE FROM LINGUISTIC IDIOMS

In this experiment, priming of unitized and non-unitized materials was compared by presenting subjects with idiomatic, unitized phrases such as *sour grapes* and *small* potatoes or with non-unitized phrases that were formed by recombining the components of the idioms (e.g., *sour potatoes, small grapes*). The first part of the phrases (e.g., *sour, small*) were included on a priming task in which subjects gave the first words that came to mind in response to these cues. The question of interest is whether amnesics and normals show priming for the unitized phrases and little or no priming for the non-unitized phrases. Idioms are of interest for two reasons. First, they constitute well-integrated bits of knowledge that behave in a unitized manner.[31] Second, the probability of giving the second word of the idiom to the first in a free-association task is virtually zero.[31] An idiom is thus unlike a highly related paired associate, such as *table*–CHAIR, in which subjects have a strong tendency to give the response to the stimulus in the absence of any experimental input. To the extent that priming is observed for idioms, then, it is the unitized nature of the representation that is crucial.

The experiment included three groups of subjects: six severely amnesic patients of diverse etiologies (closed-head injury, encephalitis, ruptured anterior communicating artery aneurysm, anoxia, and third ventricle tumor), six matched control subjects, and six college students. The 24 idioms that constituted the target materials were all two-word, adjective-noun phrases selected from the idioms of Horowitz & Manelis.[31] The idioms were randomly divided into three sets of eight. Within each set, pairs of idioms were rearranged to form non-unitized but meaningful phrases, yielding a total of three unitized sets and three non-unitized sets. For a given subject, one set of materials was studied in a unitized manner and one set was studied in a non-unitized manner. To obtain baseline data, the first word of the set that was not studied appeared on the priming test. Materials were completely counterbalanced across conditions.

Each of the two study sets was presented twice, in a blocked manner, at a rate of six seconds/phrase. Subjects were told to try to remember each two-word phrase and were given a brief sentence that specified the meaning of each unitized and non-unitized pair. Following presentation of the study phrases, subjects were told that they would fill out some forms before beginning the memory task. The first form contained a list of common first names (e.g., Frank, Mary). Subjects were told to write next to each one the first surname that came to mind. The second form represented the priming test, 74 common words that included the first words of the 24 critical phrases. Subjects were told that they should write next to each cue the first word that came to mind. Upon finishing the task, subjects were told to try to recall each of the two-word phrases that had been presented earlier. Two minutes were provided for free recall. Subjects were then given a sheet that contained the first words of the sixteen study phrases, and were instructed to try to remember the second word that had appeared with each cue at the time of study.

Consider first the results on the priming task. Consistent with expectations, baseline probability of giving the second word of the unitized idiom in response to the first was functionally zero; only one subject (an amnesic) provided a single target idiom in the baseline condition. There was, however, a substantial priming effect in the unitized condition that did not differ among subject groups (TABLE 1): Amnesics produced as many unitized responses from the study list as controls did. In sharp contrast, there was virtually no evidence of priming in the non-unitized condition for either amnesics or controls: Only one subject (a matched control) produced one target from a non-unitized phrase in response to the first member of the phrase.

An entirely different pattern of results was observed when subjects were asked to remember target items on the free- and cued-recall tests. On the free-recall test, amnesics remembered none of the unitized or non-unitized phrases, whereas matched controls and college students remembered many of them (TABLE 1). On the cued-recall test (TABLE 1), amnesics did not recollect a single non-unitized phrase and produced no more unitized phrases than they had on the priming test. By contrast, matched controls recalled 35% of the non-unitized phrases and came up with over twice as many unitized phrases as they had on the priming task. College students remembered 75% of both unitized and non-unitized phrases.

Consider how these data are related to those of Graf and Schacter concerning priming of new associations. The finding of no priming for non-unitized phrases supports the idea that the presence of the target letters was critical for the priming of unrelated paired-associates observed by Graf and Schacter. However, the finding of substantial priming with unitized phrases indicates that the target letters need not be present if the priming cue is part of a pre-existing unit. Taken together, these observations support the generality of the notion that intact priming in amnesics depends upon the presence of part of a pre-existing unit on the test. In addition, two features of the data are consistent with the idea that fundamentally different forms of memory are involved in recall and priming. First, amnesics exhibited virtually no explicit recollection, even though they showed normal priming of unitized phrases. Second, non-unitized phrases were recalled frequently by normal subjects—as frequently as unitized phrases by college students—but they were not susceptible to priming. If priming and recall were based upon the same form of memory, non-unitized

TABLE 1. Priming and Recall of Unitized and Non-unitized Phrases in Amnesic Patients, Matched Controls, and Student Controls

	Unitized phrases			Non-unitized phrases		
	PR	FR	CR	PR	FR	CR
Amnesic patients	.27	.00	.27	.00	.00	.00
Matched controls	.23	.31	.54	.02	.19	.35
Student controls	.29	.40	.75	.00	.44	.75
M	.26	.24	.52	.01	.21	.37

Note: PR = Priming; FR = Free Recall; CR = Cued Recall.

phrases should have been susceptible to priming, because they were available for recall.

METHOD OF VANISHING CUES: DISCONTINUITY BETWEEN PRIMING AND RECOLLECTION

The purpose of the next experiment was to examine in more detail the role played by the presence of the target letters on a test when amnesic patients attempt to learn a set of unrelated paired associates. The experiment was conducted in collaboration with Elizabeth Glisky and Endel Tulving. We used a procedure called the method of vanishing cues.[32] Patients are first shown the stimulus terms of unrelated paired associates on an Apple II+ microcomputer and are provided with the successive letters of the target until they guess it or the complete word is displayed on the screen (e.g., tobacco–B———; BO———; BOU——; BOUL——; BOULD—; BOULDE–; BOULDER). On the next trial, patients are given one less letter than they needed to identify the response on the first trial. This procedure continues over successive trials. Patients are always given one less letter on trial $n + 1$ than they needed to complete the target on trial n, and letters are added until they provide the correct response. The question of interest is whether the letter-by-letter withdrawal of target information enables patients to learn the new information in such a manner that they can provide the response to the stimulus in the absence of any target letters.

If pre-existing units play a crucial role in amnesic patients' performance, they should have relatively little difficulty when at least the initial letter of the target word, part of the pre-existing unit, is present. Thus, amnesics should show a relatively rapid reduction in number of letters required to complete the target in the presence of the stimulus term until the final target letter is withdrawn. The amnesics should then have a great deal of difficulty giving the target to the stimulus in the absence of any letters, because part of the pre-existing unit is no longer present in the response.

Four amnesic patients (two closed-head injury, one encephalitic, and one ruptured anterior communicating artery aneurysm) participated in an extended procedure that involved eight sessions, each consisting of eight trials. The materials were 12 unrelated paired associates consisting of six to seven letter common nouns. The general procedure was as described above.

The critical data with respect to the present concerns derive from an analysis of the number of trials required to make the initial reduction from n to $n - 1$ letters at each of the pairwise transition points in the task (i.e., the number of trials required to move for the first time from needing five letters to needing four, from four to three, three to two, two to one, and one to zero). These data indicated that amnesics took on average 1.7 trials to make each pairwise transition up until the final letter was withdrawn. At this point a large discontinuity was observed. Patients required a mean of 24.9 trials to produce the item for the first time in the absence of any target letters. Thus, the presence of the first letter of the target, part of the pre-existing unit, was of special importance for amnesics. Control studies suggest that college students have no more difficulty with the final reduction, from one letter to no letters ($\overline{X} = 1.1$ trials), than they have with any of the other reductions ($\overline{X} = 1.1$ trials). Matched control subjects have only slightly more difficulty with the final reduction ($\overline{X} = 2.6$ trials) than with the preceding ones ($\overline{X} = 1.5$ trials). It is not surprising that normals do not have severe difficulties upon withdrawal of the final letter, because subjects treat this task as one of deliberate recall (it is not possible to conceal the nature of the task when repeated trials are used). Normals are able to use conscious recall mechanisms to remember the response, whereas amnesics must rely heavily on priming and hence depend upon the presence of the target letters.

THEORETICAL ACCOUNTS OF INTACT PRIMING IN AMNESIA

The experiments discussed in this article contain three critical findings concerning repetition priming in amnesic patients. First, amnesic patients revealed intact priming of new information concerning the relation between two normatively unrelated words on a word-completion task that included the stimulus term and part of the response. Second, amnesics showed normal priming of unitized phrases and, like controls, showed no priming of non-unitized phrases, under conditions in which only the first word of the phrase was presented on a priming task. Third, amnesic patients had special difficulties upon withdrawal of the final target letter in the vanishing-cues procedure. The principal theoretical challenge presented by this pattern of findings is to account simultaneously for the fact that priming in amnesia includes new, contextually specific information, yet also depends heavily upon the presence of part of a pre-existing unit in the test response. Let us consider briefly the implications of these facts for several relevant theoretical positions.

One class of theories holds that repetition priming and conscious recollection do not tap fundamentally different forms of memory, but involve different retrieval processes that make contact with the same mnemonic representation of a prior episode.[16,33] By these views, amnesics exhibit intact priming because tasks such as word completion, word identification, and lexical decision bypass the intentional or reconstructive retrieval processing that is assumed to be defective in amnesics.[12,33,34] This general notion has no problem accounting for priming of new information, although it might have difficulty handling the outcome of the contingency analyses discussed earlier. If, however, a word-completion task simply represents one way of contacting a single representation of a prior episode, it is not obvious why there is significant priming for unitized pairs and no priming for non-unitized pairs or why the presence of an initial target letter in the vanishing-cues experiment affected amnesics' performance so dramatically.

Several theories have proposed that two fundamentally different types of memory (one impaired in amnesia, the other spared) are involved in priming and recollection. One version holds that priming reflects a process of activation of old information that is preserved in amnesia and relatively independent of the process of elaboration that is impaired in amnesia.[13,19] This view accounts nicely for the pre-existing unit data, because the activation process is assumed to operate by reaffirming relationships that are well established. But it may have difficulty accommodating the finding that amnesics demonstrate intact new learning on a completion task, because this goes beyond affirming an existing relationship. A somewhat different notion that encounters similar problems is that priming reflects the activation of a semantic-memory system that is spared in amnesia, whereas recall and recognition depend upon an episodic or cognitive system that is damaged (cf. References 22, 35, and 36). If a decontextualized semantic memory underlies priming, it is not clear how completion performance of amnesics and normals can reflect retention of a new, contextually specific relationship that was established during a single learning episode. Data reported by others concerning the modality specificity of priming effects raise further problems for this interpretation, as has been discussed elsewhere.[14,16] Another account holds that priming tasks such as word completion depend upon a procedural memory system (i.e. "knowing how") that is spared in amnesics, whereas recall and recognition depend upon a declarative memory system (i.e. "knowing that") that is impaired in amnesics.[3-5] It is not easy to see how this distinction would account for intact priming of entirely new associations in amnesics, nor is it clear how this distinction would explain the critical importance of the target letters on a priming test. For example, to account for the discontinuity observed in the vanishing-cue experiment, it would be necessary to argue that amnesics perform relatively well when given a cue such as *tobacco–B*——— because they can rely on procedural memory, and perform disastrously when given *tobacco*——— because they must then depend upon declarative memory. But why would the task be considered "procedural" when a single target letter is present and "declarative" when it is not? To accommodate these data, it may be necessary to transform the notions of "procedural" and "declarative" beyond recognition.

Most of the foregoing ideas are consistent with one of the critical findings noted earlier, but are inconsistent with the others. In the short space that remains, I will suggest the outlines of an approach that may help to make sense of both facts. These ideas are similar to, and represent extensions of, various other hypotheses that have been proposed to account for preserved priming in amnesia.[11,22,23,25,34] They are offered as preliminary and somewhat speculative hypotheses to be tested in future research.

Along with many other investigators, I view priming and recollection as manifestations of fundamentally different explicit and implicit forms of memory. In the present discussion, I want to focus upon the representations that may be involved in each kind of memory. Two types of representations are postulated, unitized structures and nested structures. Unitized structures, it is suggested, are involved in repetition priming. They represent well-integrated and established informational structures that are built by repeated activation and use of a common set of elements (cf. Shimamura and Squire[29]). Unitized structures can be activated in an all-or-none manner by a process of redintegration—the presence of part of the structure is sufficient to elicit the entire unit.[29,30] Examples of unitized structures would be words, idioms, and primary associates. A critical postulated feature of unitized structures is that they are modified by information in the local contexts in which they are activated and used. By "local context," I refer to the semantic information that is encoded when a unitized structure is activated, the modality in which the structure is activated, and the physical parameters of the activating stimulus. The newly encoded features of local context, though modifying the unitized structure and hence altering the conditions in which it can be contacted, do not yet serve as identifying features of the unit.[37] With sufficient repetition, the new information may eventually function as an identifying feature of the unit. Thus, unitized structures are not viewed as decontextualized or abstract pieces of semantic knowledge that are independent of contextual constraints. For example, there might be multiple unitized structures that correspond to a word such as "chair," each of which preserves specific information concerning particular local contexts in which they have been activated and used frequently.

Nested structures, in contrast, are formed as a function of a single experience, and are assumed to underlie conscious recall and recognition. Nested structures are similar to composite traces[38] or vertical associates.[23] They emerge from the combining of existing elements in such a manner that a new gestalt is formed with emergent properties that were not previously present. I use the word "nested" to highlight the suggestion that these structures are part of, and are only accessible through, the global contexts in which they were created. By "global context," I refer to a higher-order representation that contains information about the spatial and temporal features of the episode in which a nested structure is formed. When a subject studies a list of target words that are paired with unrelated cues, the global context (the time and place of occurrence) is similar for each target, whereas the local context, which is defined by the unrelated cues, is different for each item. Nested structures are recalled in a graded, rather than in an all-or-none manner, and are contacted through processes of resonance,[39] correlation,[38,40] or reconstruction,[41] but only when information concerning the global context is available. I refrain from using the term "episodic" memories here because, as noted earlier, unitized structures too can be changed by information encoded during a single episode.

It is suggested that in amnesia, unitized structures can be activated and modified normally. However, the creation of nested structures, of new gestalts or wholes,[23] is defective. Consider how the distinction between unitized structures and nested structures can be applied to amnesics' performance in the experiments described earlier. The intact priming of new associations can be viewed in terms of a normal modification of unitized structures by an encoded feature of local context (in this case, an unrelated word). Because modification of the unitized structure is seen as the source of new learning, it is not surprising that part of the pre-existing unit would have to be present on the test for priming to occur; as suggested earlier, the newly encoded features of local context do not serve as identifying features of the unit. Thus, in the vanishing cues experiment, the critical function of the initial letter may be to identify the recently modified unitized structure. In the absence of this information, performance depends upon contacting the nested structure, which is severely degraded or non-existent in amnesics, although it is available for normals to retrieve in appropriate test conditions. In the idioms experiment, amnesics show intact priming of unitized structures (e.g., *sour grapes*) and, like normals, show no priming of nested structures (e.g., *sour potatoes*). The lack of priming of nested structures is viewed as a consequence of their being tied to a global context that is not contacted in a priming task, because no attempt is made to reconstruct the study context. However, on a recall test, normals reconstruct the global context and gain access to the nested structures, whereas amnesics do not. By the present hypothesis, amnesics do not gain access to the nested structure because it was not retained or was retained in a degraded manner. It is also possible that amnesics cannot engage in reconstructive retrieval, and are thus unable to gain access to an existing nested structure. The issue requires further investigation.

This fragmentary outline reveals that the present approach takes a middle road between theories that view priming effects in amnesia as an activation of general, semantic knowledge and those that view priming as relying upon the same episodic knowledge as underlies conscious recall and recognition. Although the suggested notions are, of course, no more than preliminary hypotheses, they do suggest future experiments that otherwise might not be as readily perceived. For example, a basic issue concerns the building of new unitized structures, that is, the process by which the first part of an unrelated word pair comes to elicit the second on a priming test in the absence of any target letters. What conditions must be satisfied to build such a structure? Are new unitized structures built from, and hence dependent upon, nested structures? Or are they the result of repeated modification of existing unitized structures such that the modifying information eventually serves as an identifying feature of the unit? Is the building of new unitized structures similar in amnesics and normals, or is it fundamentally different? Detailed exploration of such questions could provide a more complete picture of the implicit form of memory that is preserved in amnesia and hence facilitate understanding of its relation to explicit recollection.

ACKNOWLEDGMENTS

I thank Elizabeth Glisky, Peter Graf, Morris Moscovitch, and Endel Tulving for helpful comments and discussion, and Carol A. Macdonald for valuable aid with preparation of the manuscript.

REFERENCES

1. HIRST, W. 1982. The amnesic syndrome: Descriptions and explanations. Psychol. Bull. **91:** 435–460.
2. SCHACTER, D. L. & H. F. CROVITZ. 1977. Memory function after closed head injury: A review of the quantitative research. Cortex **13:** 150–176.
3. SQUIRE, L. R. 1982. Comparisons between forms of amnesia: Some deficits are unique to Korsakoff's syndrome. J. Exp. Psychol.: Learn., Mem., Cog. **8:** 560–571.
4. COHEN, N. J. 1984. Amnesia and the distinction between procedural and declarative knowledge. *In* The Neuropsychology of Memory. L. R. Squire & N. Butters, Eds. Guilford Press. New York.
5. COHEN, N. J. & L. R. SQUIRE. 1980. Preserved learning and retention of pattern-analyzing skill in amnesia: Dissociation of "knowing how" and "knowing that." Science **210:** 207–209.
6. MILNER, B., S. CORKIN & H. L. TEUBER. 1968. Further analysis of the hippocampal amnesic syndrome: 14 year follow-up study of H. M. Neuropsychol. **6:** 215–234.
7. MOSCOVITCH, M. 1982. Multiple dissociations of functions in amnesia. *In* Human Memory and Amnesia. L. S. Cermak, Ed. Lawrence Erlbaum Associates. Hillsdale, NJ.
8. WARRINGTON, E. K. & L. WEISKRANTZ. 1970. Amnesic syndrome: Consolidation or retrieval? Nature **228:** 629–630.

9. WARRINGTON, E. K. & L. WEISKRANTZ. 1974. The effect of prior learning on subsequent retention in amnesic patients. Neuropsychol. **12:** 419–428.
10. DIAMOND, R., & P. ROZIN. 1984. Activation of existing memories in the amnesic syndrome. J. Abnorm. Psychol. **93:** 98–105.
11. GRAF, P., L. R. SQUIRE & G. MANDLER. 1984. The information that amnesic patients do not forget. J. Exp. Psychol.: Learn. Mem. Cog. **10:** 164–178.
12. JACOBY, L. L. & D. WITHERSPOON. 1982. Remembering without awareness. Can. J. Psychol. **36:** 300–324.
13. GRAF, P., G. MANDLER & P. HADEN. 1982. Simulating amnesic symptoms in normal subjects. Science **218:** 1243–1244.
14. TULVING, E., D. L. SCHACTER & H. STARK. 1982. Priming effects in word-fragment completion are independent of recognition memory. J. Exp. Psychol.: Learn. Mem. Cog. **8:** 336–342.
15. JACOBY, L. L. & M. DALLAS. 1981. On the relationship between autobiographical memory and perceptual learning. J. Exp. Psychol.: Gen. **110:** 306–340.
16. JACOBY, L. L. 1983. Remembering the data: Analyzing interactive processes in reading. J. Verb. Learn. Verb. Behav. **22:** 485–508.
17. FEUSTEL, T. C., R. M. SHIFFRIN & A. SALASOO. 1983. Episodic and lexical contributions to the repetition effect in word identification. J. Exp. Psychol.: Gen. **112:** 309–346.
18. SCARBOROUGH, D. L., L. GERARD & C. CORTESE. 1979. Accessing lexical memory: The transfer of word repetition effects across task and modality. Mem. & Cog. **7:** 3–12.
19. MANDLER, G. 1980. Recognizing: The judgment of previous occurrence. Psychol. Rev. **87:** 252–271.
20. SCHACTER, D. L. & M. MOSCOVITCH. 1984. Infants, amnesics, and dissociable memory systems. *In* Infant Memory. M. Moscovitch, Ed. Plenum. New York.
21. TULVING, E. 1983. Elements of Episodic Memory. Clarendon Press. Oxford, England.
22. WARRINGTON, E. K. & L. WEISKRANTZ. 1982. Amnesia: A disconnection syndrome? Neuropsychol. **20:** 233–248.
23. WICKELGREN, W. 1979. Chunking and consolidation: A theoretical synthesis of semantic networks, configuring in conditioning, S-R versus cognitive learning, normal forgetting, the amnesic syndrome, and the hippocampal arousal system. Psychol. Rev. **86:** 44–60.
24. SCHACTER, D. L., J. L. HARBLUK & D. R. MCLACHLAN. 1984. Retrieval without recollection: An experimental analysis of source amnesia. J. Verb. Learn. Verb. Behav. (In press.)
25. MOSCOVITCH, M. 1984. The sufficient conditions for demonstrating preserved memory in amnesia: A task analysis. *In* The Neuropsychology of Memory. L. R. Squire & N. Butters, Eds. Guilford Press. New York.
26. GRAF, P. & D. L. SCHACTER. 1984. Implicit and explicit memory for new associations in normal and amnesic subjects. J. Exp. Psychol.: Learn. Mem. Cog. (In press.)
27. MILNER, P. 1984. Amnesia: Some neurophysiological considerations. Presented to Canadian Psychological Association. Ottawa, 1984.
28. CERMAK, L. S. & M. O'CONNOR. 1983. The anterograde and retrograde retrieval ability of a patient with amnesia due to encephalitis. Neuropsychol. **21:** 213–274.
29. SHIMAMURA, A. P. & L. R. SQUIRE. 1984. Paired-associate learning and priming effects in amnesia: A neuropsychological study. J. Exp. Psych.: Gen. (In press.)
30. HAYES-ROTH, B. 1977. Evolution of cognitive structures and processes. Psychol. Rev. **84:** 260–278.
31. HOROWITZ, L. M. & L. MANELIS. 1972. Toward a theory of redintegrative memory: Adjective-noun phrases. *In* The Psychology of Learning and Motivation. G. H. Bower, Ed. Vol. 6. Academic Press. New York.
32. GLISKY, E., D. L. SCHACTER & E. TULVING. 1984. Vocabulary learning in amnesia: Method of vanishing cues. Presented to American Psychological Association. Toronto, 1984.
33. CRAIK, F. I. M. 1983. On the transfer of information from temporary to permanent memory. *In* Functional Aspects of Memory. D. E. Broadbent, Ed. Royal Society. London, England.
34. JACOBY, L. L. 1984. Incidental vs. intentional retrieval: Remembering and awareness as

separate issues. *In* The Neuropsychology of Memory. L. R. Squires & N. Butters, Eds. Guilford Press. New York.

35. KINSBOURNE, M. & F. WOOD. 1982. Theoretical considerations regarding the episodic-semantic memory distinction. *In* Human Memory and Amnesia. L. S. Cermak, Ed. Lawrence Erlbaum Associates. Hillsdale, NJ.

36. SCHACTER, D. L. & E. TULVING. 1982. Memory, amnesia, and the episodic/semantic distinction. *In* The Expression of Knowledge. R. L. Isaacson & N. E. Spear, Eds. Plenum Press. New York.

37. SPYROPOULOS, T. & J. CERASO. 1977. Categorized and uncategorized attributes as recall cues: The phenomenon of limited access. Cog. Psychol. **9:** 384–402.

38. EICH, J. M. 1982. A composite holographic associative recall model. Psychol. Rev. **89:** 627–661.

39. RATCLIFF, R. 1978. A theory of memory retrieval. Psychol. Rev. **85:** 59–108.

40. MURDOCK, B. B., JR. 1982. A theory for the storage and retrieval of item and associative information. Psychol. Rev. **89:** 609–626.

41. BADDELEY, A. D. 1982. Domains of recollection. Psychol. Rev. **89:** 708–729.

Different Memory Systems Underlying Acquisition of Procedural and Declarative Knowledge[a]

NEAL J. COHEN[b]

Department of Psychology
and
Clinical Research Center
Massachusetts Institute of Technology
Cambridge, Massachusetts 02139

HOWARD EICHENBAUM AND BEATRICE S. DEACEDO

Psychobiology Program
Wellesley College
Wellesley, Massachusetts 02181

AND

SUZANNE CORKIN

Department of Psychology
and
Clinical Research Center
Massachusetts Institute of Technology
Cambridge, Massachusetts 02139

Cognitive neuropsychological investigations of memory have begun to distinguish among different component processes and component systems of normal memory. In the present paper we show that amnesic patients with marked disorders of learning and memory demonstrate a striking dissociation between the memory processes or memory systems that support the acquisition of cognitive skills and the processes or systems that mediate the acquisition of new facts or other data-based knowledge. This dissociation is exhibited by normal control subjects as well. These data conform with a long tradition of introspectively based speculations on the difference between skill memory and memory for particular facts or events, and they suggest that this dissociation is honored by the nervous system. In-depth analyses of the knowledge acquired by amnesic patients and normal control subjects in learning the cognitive skills studied in this report permit some conclusions to be drawn about the characteristics of the dissociated memory phenomena, as they inform us about both the nature of preserved learning capacities in amnesia and the nature of the knowledge underlying skilled performance in all subjects, amnesic patients and control subjects alike.

[a]Supported by National Institute of Mental Health grants MH08280 and MH24433, and National Institutes of Health grants NS19698 and RR00088.
[b]Address all correspondence to: Neal J. Cohen, Ph.D., Department of Psychology, 330 G Ames Hall, The Johns Hopkins University, Charles & 34th Streets, Baltimore, MD 21218.

BACKGROUND

A number of investigations of amnesia have documented a domain of preserved learning capacities despite an otherwise severe and pervasive disorder of learning and memory. Perhaps the clearest example of preserved capacity is the ability of even the most severely amnesic patients to learn new skills. Thus, amnesic patients have demonstrated a normal capacity to acquire and retain a variety of motor, perceptual, and cognitive skills. Of importance for the present purposes is the dissociation between this impressive skill learning capacity and other aspects of memory performance: Normal acquisition and retention of skill can occur in amnesia despite (1) abnormally poor insight into the knowledge underlying the newly acquired skilled performance, (2) abnormally poor memory for the episodes during which the skills were learned, and (3) impaired memory-test performance for the information normally acquired in using the skills.

Evidence for the foregoing claim of dissociation is provided by a growing number of findings. The noted amnesic case H.M., who has had a profound and pervasive memory disorder since undergoing bilateral resection of medial temporal-lobe structures in 1953 for relief of chronic epilepsy,[1,2] learned a mirror-tracing task across three days of testing, without any indication in his verbal reports of his accumulating experience with the task.[3] Learning and retention of perceptual-motor skills have been exhibited in the continuous tracking task of rotary pursuit in a variety of examples of amnesia, including H.M.,[4] patients with Korsakoff's syndrome,[5-7] post-encephalitic patients,[5] patients receiving bilateral ECT,[7] and the diencephalic case N.A.[7] Learning and retention in these examples of amnesia equaled that of normal control subjects (except for H.M.; see Cohen[8]), though the patients typically could neither recognize the motor apparatus from session to session nor remember their previous experience with the task. Normal learning and retention of the perceptual skills required to read mirror-reversed text was reported for case N.A.,[9] patients receiving ECT,[9] patients with Korsakoff's syndrome,[9,10] and a mixed group of amnesic patients including some with mild Alzheimer's disease,[11] despite impaired recognition memory for the material that was read during training and little, if any, recollection of the training experiences themselves. The opposite pattern of results was reported on this task for patients with Huntington's disease, whose relatively poor performance on mirror reading contrasted with their excellent recognition of the stimuli and recall of the testing session.[10] Finally, patients with Korsakoff's syndrome learned to use a numerical rule (Fibonacci rule) across repeated exposures to examples of the rule, despite poor recollection of the training.[12]

Dissociations similar in form to the above examples can be observed in normal control subjects as well. In the work of Kolers on reading of geometrically inverted or otherwise transformed text, a dissociation was apparent between perceptual skill acquisition and memory for the material presented during training: The dramatic improvement exhibited by college students in the ability to read transformed text was uncorrelated with their ability to remember the content of the text.[13] Normal subjects also show a dissociation between the ability to acquire skills and the ability to introspect about the knowledge underlying the performance of skilled acts. Indeed, this dissociation is apparent in our everyday experience. Consider for a moment how to ride a bicycle. Our ability to articulate just how we coordinate steering and pedaling, how exactly we maintain balance at different speeds, exactly how and when we lean into a turn, and the other mechanics of actually riding is quite limited. The aspects of knowledge about bicycles to which we can gain access in explicit remembering seem restricted largely to knowledge of the make, color, appearance, and other physical characteristics of particular bicycles, to knowledge about the uses to which they can be put and the contexts in which they might be expected to appear, and to memory of specific experiences of riding or seeing them.

This dissociation between the ability to perform with skill and the inability to introspect about skilled performance is perhaps even more striking when considering expert performance. Posner pointed to this dissociation in skilled typists, who are much more proficient at typing the alphabet from "a" to "z" than at indicating on a schematic keyboard where each of the 26 letters is located spatially, even though they must "know" the location of each letter in order to type it.[14] To take a final example, despite John McEnroe's obvious expertise in tennis, it is doubtful whether he could provide a detailed account of the nature of his tennis skills or recount the precise circumstances in which different aspects of his game were acquired and refined. Consider, for example, how he serves the ball. How high and with how much force does he toss the ball? Where exactly in the tossed ball's trajectory does he start and finish his swing? How does the position of the racquet in his hand and the position of his hand with respect to his arm change during the course of a serve? And how do these relationships change according to the amount of spin imparted to the ball? But note that he would likely be able to recount in exquisite detail particular serves that he made or failed to make in numerous matches against various opponents. The point is that our everyday experience and that of experts conforms with empirical evidence in suggesting an important dissociation between the acquisition and performance of skills and the learning and retention of facts or other data-based knowledge.

THE PRESENT STUDIES

The present studies were conducted in order to further illuminate, in a single task, the dissociation between the acquisition and performance of skills and the learning and retention of new facts in both amnesic patients and normal control subjects. We focused on cognitive skills in the present studies. Acquisition was assessed with repeated testing on the Tower of Hanoi puzzle, a complex problem-solving task whose solution requires 31 steps (see below). Performance of amnesic patients and normal control subjects provided a set of striking demonstrations of the dissociation between skill acquisition and memory for facts, in conformance with previous work. In particular, the following dissociations in performance were observed: (1) Amnesic patients demonstrated normal learning of the puzzle despite otherwise severe memory impairment. (2) The ability of amnesic patients to solve the puzzle was reflected only poorly, if at all, in their verbal reports. (3) By the end of training, amnesic patients could solve the puzzle efficiently from any intermediate stage of completion; but their recognition performance failed to distinguish intermediate stages of completion that led to optimal solution and had been seen previously from configurations of the puzzle that did not lead to optimal solution and had not been previously encountered. Similarly, for control subjects: (4) Performance of control subjects on the puzzle was poorly correlated with their performance on standard recall or recognition tests of memory. (5) The acquisition by control subjects of increasingly sophisticated strategies for solving the puzzle was poorly reflected in their verbal reports. (6) The pattern of performance of control subjects in solving the puzzle from various optimal and nonoptimal configurations of the puzzle differed from the pattern of recognition memory performance on the same configurations.

Newly devised analyses of performance on the puzzle permitted new insights about the nature of the memory systems that give rise to these observed dissociations.

The Tower of Hanoi Puzzle

The Tower of Hanoi puzzle, shown schematically in FIGURE 1, consists of three pegs and five disks or blocks of various sizes. At the outset, the blocks are arranged on the leftmost "start" peg (peg A) in size order, with the largest on the bottom and the smallest on top. The task involves moving the blocks from the start peg and reassembling them in the original size order on the rightmost "goal" peg (peg C), obeying the following two rules: Only one block may be moved at a time and a larger block may never be placed on top of a smaller one. In the present studies, subjects were presented with either a wooden model of the puzzle and were asked to physically move the blocks from peg to peg, or with a video display of the puzzle controlled by an Apple IIe microcomputer and were asked to indicate to the examiner the block they wanted moved and the peg to which they wanted it moved. In the former case, the examiner recorded all moves made by the subjects; in the latter case, the examiner typed the appropriate command responses on the computer keyboard, causing the moves to be recorded and incorporated into each successive display.

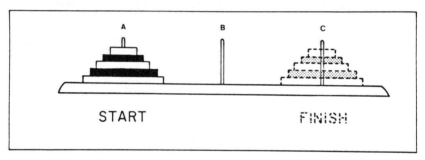

FIGURE 1. Schematic of the Tower of Hanoi puzzle. At the start of a trial, all five blocks are arranged in size order on peg A. Subjects are asked to move the blocks from the start peg and reassemble them in the original size order on peg C, moving only one block at a time and never placing a larger block on top of a smaller one.

The Tower of Hanoi puzzle has enjoyed wide use in the study of skill acquisition, for the following reasons. First, it can be solved with varying degrees of efficiency, subject to a variety of different solution strategies. With practice, subjects learn to solve the puzzle more efficiently, reducing the number of errors and superfluous moves as they adopt more sophisticated strategies. Previous work with the puzzle on normal control subjects has permitted the identification of a number of different strategies and has documented the evolution of these strategies across trials.[15–17] Accordingly, subjects can be presented with the puzzle on multiple occasions to promote the acquisition of the cognitive skills necessary to solve the puzzle optimally. Data from repeated trials can be analyzed with respect to the effects of practice on the degree of success of performance outcome and on the style of performance.

Second, the number of moves required for solution is too large, even when performing optimally (the minimum number of moves to solution is 31), to support a strategy in which the entire set of specific moves is remembered by rote. Rather, subjects must make use of the internal structure of the problem to organize the task into more manageable "chunks." That the puzzle has sufficient internal structure to support principled or organized (i.e., non-rote) solution methods follows from its membership in the class of transformational problems. In such problems, solution is reached through the execution of a logical series of steps.[17] Indeed, the outstanding feature of the Tower of Hanoi puzzle is its recursiveness; solution to the puzzle involves solving a series of sub-problems of the same kind. Thus, solution to the overall puzzle involves solving two four-block problems, each of which, in turn, incorporates solution of two three-block problems, each of which requires solving two two-block problems.

The recursive structure of the puzzle can be seen graphically by examining the "decision tree" or "state space" characterizing this problem (FIGURE 2). The nodes of the graph represent all possible puzzle configurations in the state space of the five-block problem. Lines connecting the nodes represent possible moves in solving the puzzle; through each move, one configuration of the puzzle is transformed into another. The upper corner of the triangular decision tree corresponds to the initial configuration of the puzzle, in which all five blocks are on peg A; the lower left corner represents all five blocks arranged on the middle peg (peg B); the lower right corner corresponds to arrangement of the five blocks on peg C. The 31-move optimal solution falls on the right-hand diagonal of the triangular decision tree, occupying the shortest path on the tree from peg A to peg C. There is only one sequence of moves that leads to optimal solution.

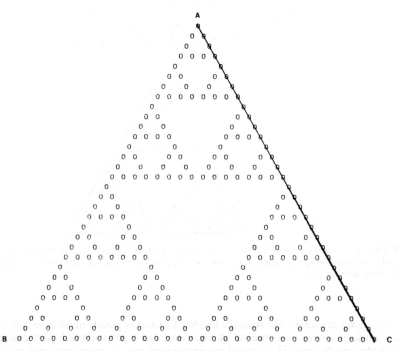

FIGURE 2. Graphic depiction of the problem space or decision tree for the Tower of Hanoi puzzle. The nodes of the graph represent all possible puzzle configurations; lines connecting the nodes represent moves through which one configuration of the puzzle is transformed into another. The optimal solution path, representing the solution accomplished in the fewest moves possible, falls on the right-hand diagonal of the decision tree.

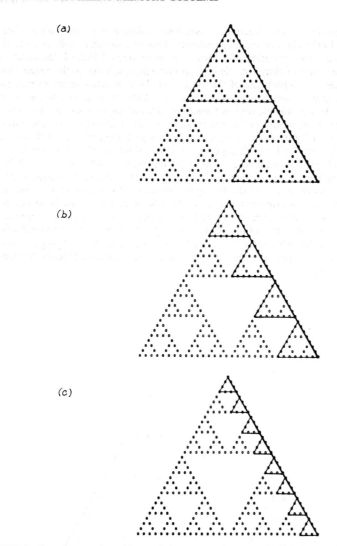

FIGURE 3. Component sub-problems of the Tower of Hanoi puzzle. Overall solution to the puzzle involves solving two four-block problems (a), four three-block problems (b), and eight two-block problems (c).

As shown in FIGURE 3, solving the five-block puzzle optimally involves solving two four-block problems, four three-block problems, and eight two-block problems, all arrayed along the right side of the triangular decision tree. A nonoptimal solution may involve moving down the left side of the decision tree, corresponding to placing various three-block, four-block, or even five-block configurations on an inappropriate peg. In solving the puzzle on a given trial, especially early in training, subjects may produce a sequence of moves involving optimal and nonoptimal configurations of the puzzle, and

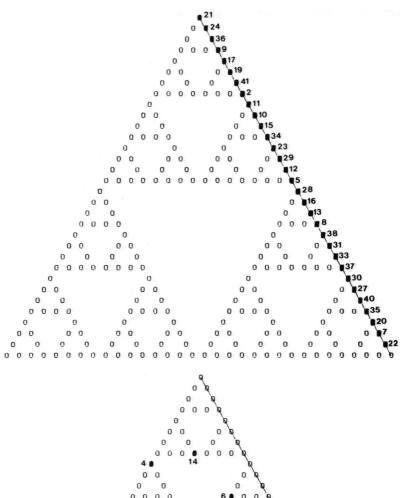
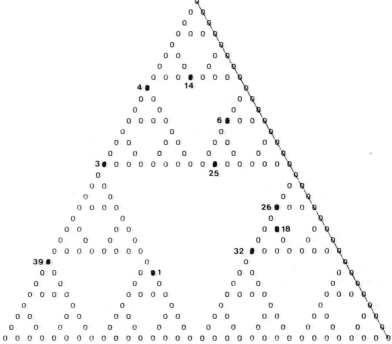

may solve a mixture of optimal and nonoptimal sub-problems. Note that the difference between optimal and nonoptimal sub-problems and among different optimal sub-problems is only their location in the decision space; the principles required for solution to each of the sub-problems are always the same, though the actual moves executed will vary.

Experimental Procedures and Analyses

Twelve amnesic patients and eight control subjects matched approximately to the patients for age, level of education, and IQ subtest scores, were challenged with finding the optimal solution to the Tower of Hanoi puzzle four times on each of four consecutive days. The patients comprised a number of etiologic types; bilateral medial temporal-lobe excision (case H.M.), posterior cerebral artery stroke, herpes simplex encephalitis, third ventricle tumor, closed-head injury, and ruptured aneurysm of the anterior communicating artery. Each subject was tested individually with the wooden model of the Tower of Hanoi puzzle.

Immediately following the last trial, each amnesic patient was a subject in two further experiments. In the first, patients were asked to solve the puzzle with the middle peg (peg B), and not the rightmost peg (peg C), serving as the goal. Successful performance on this task required a different sequence of moves than on the original task, though the problem had the same deep structure and could be solved using the same rules. In the second, patients were presented with the puzzle portraying each of nine different intermediate stages of completion, one at a time. Five of these puzzle configurations portrayed stages of completion in an optimal solution; subjects would have had previous exposure to these configurations and would have had experience in solving them. The other four configurations were not on the optimal solution path and were likely never to have been experienced previously. For each configuration, subjects were asked to perform two tasks: In a recognition task, subjects were asked to indicate whether a given configuration was a stage on the optimal path to solution; in the completion task, subjects were asked to identify the best next move to solve the puzzle from that particular configuration as the starting point.

Approximately one year after original training, six of the amnesic patients were retested on the puzzle. At this testing, subjects were presented individually with the puzzle displayed on a color video monitor rather than with the wooden version on which they received their original training. Given the change of presentation format, this one-year retention test provided a conservative estimate of long-term savings. All of the data from original testing and retesting come from a study reported by Cohen and Corkin.[18]

Sixteen Wellesley College undergraduates were also engaged in the present studies. They were presented individually with the puzzle displayed on a color video monitor. Subjects were asked to solve the puzzle four times in each of either two or three sessions spaced one week apart; half of the subjects were assigned randomly to each condition.

Immediately following the final trial, subjects were presented with 41 different intermediate stages of completion of the puzzle, one at a time. There were 31 configurations corresponding to all stages of an optimal solution (FIGURE 4, Top);

FIGURE 4. Intermediate configurations. All 31 stages of completion of the puzzle in an optimal solution (Top), together with 10 puzzle configurations corresponding to stages in some nonoptimal solution (Bottom), were presented to subjects in a randomized order. The numbers indicate the order in which the configurations were presented.

subjects would have had previous experience with these configurations. There were also 10 configurations corresponding to stages in a nonoptimal solution (FIGURE 4, Bottom) which were likely never to have been encountered previously. For each configuration, subjects were asked to perform a recognition task and a completion task, as described above. The data from training and intermediate configurations testing come from an undergraduate Honors Thesis by DeAcedo.[19]

The performance of all subjects was submitted to a number of analyses. Newly developed objectives analyses[20] permitted quantitation of performance on a large number of variables; for the present purposes, we shall focus on four primary variables. For each trial we calculated the number of moves to solution, for the overall puzzle as well as for each of the three-block and four-block sub-problems; the number of errors committed; the positions at which errors were committed; and the number of moves required to recover from each error. In addition, for the amnesic patients and matched control subjects, all experimental sessions were tape-recorded and the recordings transcribed. The resulting protocols were examined in an attempt to determine the solution strategies employed by the subjects, in the manner of previous investigators.[16,17] Finally, on the intermediate configurations testing, recognition performance was compared to completion performance for all subjects.

RESULTS

The major finding was a set of dissociations between skill acquisition and other types of memory performance. Each dissociation will be discussed in turn.

(1) Amnesic patients demonstrated normal learning of the puzzle despite otherwise severe memory impairment. Analysis of the number of moves to solution across trials indicated significant learning by both amnesic patients and control subjects, with no difference between groups (FIGURE 5). With practice, all subjects learned to commit fewer errors and to recover from their errors in fewer moves. H.M.'s performance on "critical choice points" provides a good example of this systematic improvement. Critical choice points refer to the four decision points during the course of each solution where most errors occur and where errors committed have the greatest negative consequences in terms of the number of moves required to recover. These decision points correspond to the opening move of each of the four three-block sub-problems of which the overall puzzle is composed. On the first day of testing, H.M. made errors at seven of the 16 critical choice points, each error requiring a mean of 8.2 moves and as many as 20 moves to correct; by contrast, on the last day of testing, H.M. made but one error from which he recovered in four moves. His improvement in performance can be seen most graphically in FIGURE 6, which shows his solution path for the first, a middle, and the last trials.

(2) The ability of amnesic patients to solve the puzzle was reflected only poorly, if at all, in their verbal reports. The impressive acquisition of the cognitive skills demonstrated by all of the amnesic patients contrasted markedly with their verbal reports before, during, and after each day's testing. Patients showed profoundly impaired recognition of their many encounters with the task and abnormally poor insight about the knowledge they were using to solve it. Thus, 8 of the 12 patients denied having ever seen the puzzle previously when queried at the start of the second testing day and none of the patients realized that they had completed four sessions when queried at the end of the fourth testing day. This finding was particularly striking in H.M. On each testing day, he denied having ever seen the puzzle previously when queried at the start of testing, he typically denied having solved the puzzle previously

when queried during the course of testing, and he always underestimated the number of daily encounters with the puzzle when requested to guess at the end of testing. In addition, H.M. claimed no knowledge of how to solve the puzzle even while solving it optimally. H.M.'s poor insight about the knowledge supporting his puzzle solution comes from remarks elicited by the examiner during and after each testing session. For example, during the final testing, H.M. asked the examiner on 13 different occasions whether he was permitted to move a block across two pegs, rather than only one; and on eight different occasions he claimed to be "stuck" and unable to think of any legal moves to continue working on the puzzle. These remarks and questions are very similar to ones made throughout all days of H.M.'s training; yet at this point he was reaching optimal solution consistently. The verbal reports of the entire amnesic group, like those of H.M., changed relatively little over the course of training compared to those of the control subjects, though the objective performance of both groups changed in parallel.

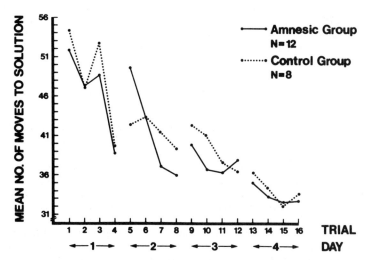

FIGURE 5. Performance on the Tower of Hanoi puzzle. Each of 12 amnesic patients and eight matched control subjects solved the puzzle four times on each of four consecutive days. Mean number of moves per solution is plotted for each trial for each group.

H.M.'s account of his performance elicited at the end of testing illustrates quite clearly the dissociation between performance of skill and verbalizable knowledge about skilled performance. H.M. claimed to have solved the puzzle in three moves, by placing the top four blocks on the middle peg in reverse order, then moving the largest block to the goal peg, and then placing the stack of four blocks right-side-up on the goal peg. This account of course violates the rules that prohibited moving more than one block at a time and placing larger blocks on top of smaller ones; yet his performance at this time clearly obeyed these rules. When this discrepancy was pointed out to H.M., the following dialogue ensued:[18]

    H.M.: Well, if you can only move one block at a time . . . No, I couldn't figure it
        out.
    N.C.: But, you did! See you just . . .
    H.M.: (interrupts) I did?

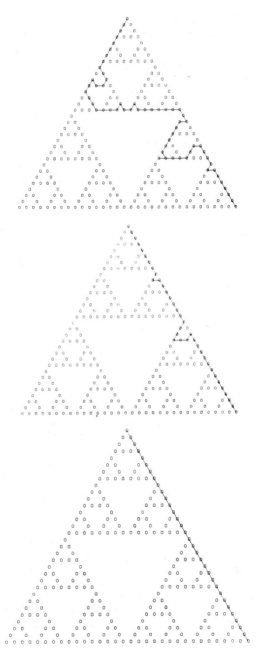

FIGURE 6. H.M.'s performance on the Tower of Hanoi puzzle. H.M.'s solution path is shown for the first (Top), twelfth (Middle), and last (Bottom) trials.

N.C.: And you did it very well, too.
H.M.: Funny, I was trying to figure it out, and I couldn't.

(3) By the end of training, amnesic patients could solve the puzzle efficiently from any intermediate stage of completion; but their recognition performance failed to distinguish intermediate stages of completion that led to optimal solution and had been solved previously from configurations of the puzzle that did not lead to optimal solution and had not been previously encountered. The amnesic patients performed near perfectly on completion of intermediate configurations, providing the best next move toward solution for 92% of the optimal and 92% of the nonoptimal configurations. However, their ability to distinguish optimal from nonoptimal configurations was near chance: Recognition of optimal configurations was 52% and recognition of nonoptimal configurations was 58%.

(4) Performance of control subjects on the puzzle was poorly correlated with their performance on standard recall or recognition tests of memory. Each of the subjects in the control group that was matched to the amnesic patients received nine recall tests of categorized word lists and three tests of verbal paired-associate learning. For each subject, mean performance on the recall tests and mean performance on the paired-associate learning tests was compared to the corresponding learning slope across trials for the Tower of Hanoi puzzle and correlations were determined. Rank order correlations were then calculated across subjects for each of the two test types. The mean rank-order correlation was only 0.12. The point is that whereas the recall and recognition memory performance of control subjects was far superior to that of the amnesic patients, it was no more related to the acquisition of cognitive skills than was the recall and recognition performance of the patients. Indeed, the mean rank-order correlation for the amnesic patients, each of whom received seven different types of memory test, was also near zero (0.09).

(5) The acquisition by control subjects of increasingly sophisticated strategies for solving the puzzle was poorly reflected in their verbal reports. For both the control group that was matched to the amnesic patients and the college-aged control group, the change over trials in performance success and in the method of puzzle solution was frequently at variance with their verbal reports. Whereas the subjects showed a systematic evolution toward more sophisticated goal-driven strategies and a relatively consistent pattern of improvement in objective performance across trials, verbal accounts were highly idiosyncratic, with large variance across individuals; and they changed relatively slowly across trials, often failing to reflect changes exhibited in the objective analyses of their performance. The systematic evolution of strategies and improvement on objective measures of performance can be seen most clearly in the analyses of the college-aged control subjects on the various sub-problems of the puzzle. Thus, inspection of FIGURE 7 reveals a difference in number of moves required to solve the two four-block sub-problems early, but not late, in training; after five or six trials, subjects apparently begin to treat the sub-problems equivalently. This transition is not reflected in the subjects' verbal reports, however, until later in training. A similar conclusion derives from the subjects' pattern of performance across trials on the three-block sub-problems (FIGURE 8). At first, performance on the opening move of each sub-problem (i.e., the critical choice points) differs markedly across sub-problems. For example, on the first trial (Top), success on critical choices across the four sub-problems was 37.5%, 50%, 0%, and 14.3%, respectively. By the eighth trial, performance on three of the four critical choices had begun to converge (Middle) and by the end of training (Bottom), performance on the four sub-problems was nearly equivalent. As with the four-block sub-problems, this orderly transition across trials

toward equivalent performance on formally equivalent sub-problems was not captured reliably in the subjects' verbal reports until later in training, if at all. It is important to note here that the students' verbal reports were often quite good; it is just that the timecourse of change in the reports did not accurately reflect the changes observed across trials in objective performance.

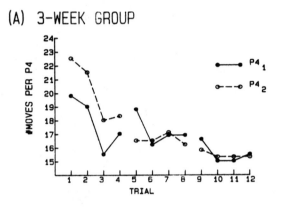

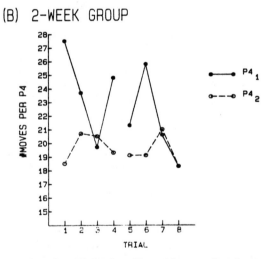

FIGURE 7. Performance on four-block sub-problems. Mean number of moves per solution for each of the two four-block sub-problems is shown for each trial for the college-aged control subjects receiving either 12 trials (A: three-week group) or eight trials (B: two-week group).

(6) The pattern of performance of control subjects in solving the puzzle from various optimal and nonoptimal configurations of the puzzle differed from the pattern of recognition memory performance on the same configurations. For the college-aged control subjects, completion performance was superior to recognition for configurations that were on the optimal solution path and would have been seen previously (94% correct versus 91% correct), whereas completion performance was inferior to recogni-

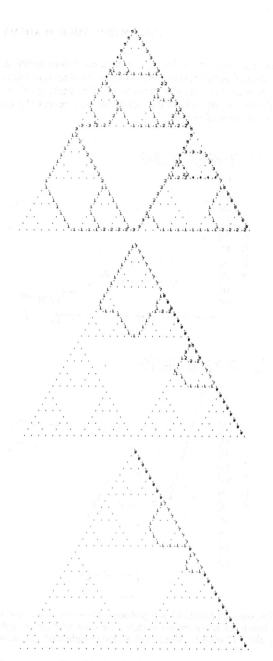

FIGURE 8. Performance on three-block sub-problems. Cumulative solution paths for eight college-aged control subjects (three-week group) on the first (Top), eighth (Middle), or last trial (Bottom). The numbers indicate how many of the eight subjects moved from any given configuration to any other on the trials shown. Changes in performance across trials occur particularly at the critical choice points, i.e., the opening move of each of the four three-block sub-problems.

tion for configurations that were not on the optimal solution path and may never have been previously encountered (64% correct versus 81% correct).

It is worth emphasizing that dissociation between completion and recognition performance was obtained despite the subjects' being relatively competent at both. Note, however, that this dissociation was exhibited by subjects with a particular amount of training on the Tower of Hanoi puzzle; they had had 8 or 12 learning trials. With more practice, both completion performance and recognition performance would likely approach ceiling too closely and the dissociation between them would disappear.

DISCUSSION

The present studies of the acquisition of cognitive skills required for amnesic patients and control subjects to learn the optimal solution to the Tower of Hanoi puzzle permit us to speculate about the nature of skill learning in this domain, and they speak more generally to the dissociation between the memory system mediating skill learning and the memory system mediating the learning of new facts or other data-based knowledge. Each of these issues will be discussed in turn.

Solving the Tower of Hanoi Puzzle: Acquisition of Cognitive Skills

The present studies of the Tower of Hanoi puzzle suggest that with practice amnesic patients and control subjects become better able to derive the solution to the puzzle without necessarily remembering explicitly the puzzle, the component steps of the puzzle, or a set of explicit rules for solving it. That is, we conclude that subjects are not looking at particular configurations and thinking: "Oh, I know this one. What I do here is to move block X to peg Y." Rather, they derive a solution from each configuration, more efficiently and more successfully each time. The evidence for this claim comes from the following findings: First, objective quantitative analyses of performance indicate that subjects learn to treat sub-problems of the puzzle equivalently although the specific moves required to solve each sub-problem actually differ. Second, practice produces not only a reduction in the number of errors committed, but also a reduction in the number of moves required to recover from each error. Thus, the actual paths taken by the subjects through the problem space, i.e., the actual sequence of moves made by the subjects, are different from trial to trial; yet their performance gradually approximates the optimal solution path. Third, in a control experiment in which subjects who had completed training on the puzzle were asked to solve the puzzle with the middle peg, and not the rightmost peg, serving as the goal, subjects solved the puzzle optimally within one session, although the actual sequence of moves required was different than in all of the training sessions. Fourth, and perhaps most directly relevant, subjects were able to reach optimal solution from a variety of intermediate configurations of the puzzle, whether or not the configurations were on the optimal solution path and whether or not they had been encountered previously; and the ability to complete the configurations was dissociated from the ability to recognize them. These findings, taken together, suggest that subjects acquire knowledge about the deep structure of the puzzle, permitting them to derive a solution that, with practice, approximates optimal solution.

The point is that after training, skilled performance on the Tower of Hanoi puzzle depends no more upon the explicit remembering of specific puzzle configurations or moves than skilled performance in tennis depends upon the explicit remembering of specific arm movements or arm trajectories. And in neither of these cases is it likely that performance is mediated by gaining access to a set of explicit rules and applying them. In the present case, successful performance is guided by the application of a recursive sub-goal strategy to match the recursive structure of the puzzle.

Dissociation between the Memory System Mediating the Acquisition of Cognitive Skills and the Memory System Mediating Learning of New Facts or Other Data-based Knowledge

The present findings emphasize the dissociation between acquisition of cognitive skills and memory for new facts or events in amnesic patients and normal control subjects. The findings are taken to be consistent with the proposal we have offered previously that accounts for the observed dissociation in performance by distinguishing between procedural and declarative memory systems.[7-9,21,22] Anderson, too, has relied on such a distinction in his more comprehensive attempts to model all of human memory,[23,24] though his views differ from ours in some important respects beyond the scope of this paper.[21] Our view has been presented in detail elsewhere. In brief, the procedural memory system permits the acquisition and expression of knowledge that guides performance without permitting or requiring this knowledge to be accessible to explicit remembering and to the processes mediating conscious introspection. Experience on a given task, such as the Tower of Hanoi puzzle, is taken to produce changes that are "dedicated" to the particular processing and action systems engaged by the task; they can only be expressed by again making use of the affected systems and need only make use of the affected systems to be expressed. In our example, memory would reside in changes in systems responsible for problem solving and the organization of action plans; it would be expressed only when these systems were again engaged in attempting to derive the solution to the puzzle. Note that a deficit in those systems responsible for problem solving and the organization of action plans would interfere selectively with learning the Tower of Hanoi puzzle, without other obvious memory problems. And indeed, there are some data to support this notion. Amnesic patients with Korsakoff's syndrome, who have damage to frontal-lobe regions implicated in problem-solving and planning processes, differ from other etiologies of amnesia by being unable to learn the puzzle (unpublished observations). Moreover, patients with damage restricted to these frontal-lobe regions are severely impaired on a somewhat simpler version of the present task, called the Tower of London.[25]

The way in which this procedural memory system preserves the effects of experience is taken to be akin to what Bruner called "memory without record" which, he argued, captures the way in which "encounters are converted into some process that changes the nature of an organism, changes his skills, or changes the rules by which he operates, but are virtually inaccessible in memory as specific encounters."[26] By contrast, the declarative memory system conforms to the traditional memory metaphor of experimental psychology by mediating the encoding of parsed events, storing and maintaining encoded information in some explicitly accessible form, and subsequently retrieving the stored information upon demand. In this system, new facts and other data-based knowledge, representing the specific results or outcomes of the operations engaged by the various processing and action systems, are accumulated. It is represented in a manner that Stitch[27] would call "promiscuous" to a variety of cognitive processes, including those mediating explicit remembering and conscious introspection. In our example of the Tower of Hanoi puzzle, this system would be responsible for the ability of normal subjects, but not amnesic patients, to remember specific puzzle configurations and moves, to recollect the episodes during which learning occurred, and to introspect about the nature of their solution to the puzzle. As these examples indicate, the declarative system permits past experience to exert an influence on present performance through the processes of explicit remembering, that is, by gaining access to explicitly stored information. William James took this type of memory processing to be prototypical of (long-term) memory; to him, the act of recollecting past events was the crucial feature of (long-term) memory. As he so aptly stated it: "An object which is recollected, in the proper sense of that term, is one which has been absent from consciousness altogether, and now revives anew. It is brought back, recalled, fished up, so to speak, from a reservoir in which, with countless other objects, it lay buried and lost from view."[28]

To summarize, the present account suggests that experience exerts its influence on subsequent performance in at least two ways. In one way, the basic systems engaged in processing information and expressing behavior are themselves modified in a dedicated manner, becoming better tuned to the relevant elements of the perceptual array and more effective in eliciting the appropriate performance routines. In the second way, the results our outcomes of engaging the various processing and action systems are stored in a promiscuous form, permitting the accumulation and explicit remembering of new facts and other data-based knowledge. In the course of normal experience, these two dissociable memory systems operate together, perhaps with other memory systems, to affect performance.

REFERENCES

1. SCOVILLE, W. B. & B. MILNER. 1957. Loss of recent memory after bilateral hippocampal lesions. J. Neurol. Neurosurg. Psychiatry 20: 11–21.
2. CORKIN, S. 1984. Lasting consequences of bilateral medial temporal lobectomy: Clinical course and experimental findings in H.M. Sem. Neurol. 4(2): 249–259.
3. MILNER, B. 1962. Les troubles de la memoire accompagnant des lesions hippocampiques bilaterales. In Physiologie de l'hippocampe. P. Passouant, Ed. Centre de la Recherche Scientifique. Paris.
4. CORKIN, S. 1968. Acquisition of motor skill after bilateral medial temporal lobe excision. Neuropsychologia 6: 255–265.
5. CERMAK, L. S., R. LEWIS, N. BUTTERS & H. GOODGLASS. 1973. Role of verbal mediation in performance of motor tasks by Korsakoff patients. Perceptual Motor Skills 37: 259–262.
6. BROOKS, D. N. & A. BADDELEY. 1976. What can amnesic patients learn? Neuropsychologia 14: 111–122.
7. COHEN, N. J. 1981. Neuropsychological evidence for a distinction between procedural and declarative knowledge in human memory and amnesia. Unpublished doctoral dissertation. University of California, San Diego.
8. COHEN, N. J. 1984. Preserved learning capacity in amnesia: Evidence for multiple memory systems. In Neuropsychology of Memory. L. R. Squire & N. Butters, Eds.:83–103. Guilford Press. New York.
9. COHEN, N. J. & L. R. SQUIRE. 1980. Preserved learning and retention of pattern analyzing skill in amnesia: Dissociation of knowing how and knowing that. Science 210: 207–210.
10. MARTONE, M., N. BUTTERS, M. PAYNE, J. BECKER & D. S. SAX. 1985. Dissociations between skill learning and verbal recognition in amnesia and dementia. Arch Neurol. (In press.)
11. MOSCOVITCH, M. 1982. A neuropsychological approach to perception and memory in normal and pathological aging. In Aging and Cognitive Processes. F. I. M. Craik & S. Trehub, Eds. Plenum Press. New York.
12. KINSBOURNE, M. & F. WOOD. 1975. Short-term memory processes and the amnesic syndrome. In Short-Term Memory. D. Deutsch & J. A. Deutsch, Eds. Academic Press. New York.
13. KOLERS, P. A. 1979. A pattern-analyzing basis of recognition. In Levels of Processing in

Human Memory. L. S. Cermak & F. I. M. Craik, Eds. Erlbaum Associates. Hillsdale, NJ.
14. POSNER, M. I. 1973. Cognition: An Introduction. Scott, Foresman and Company. Glenview, IL.
15. SIMON, H. A. 1975. The functional equivalence of problem solving skills. Cogn. Psychol. **7**: 268–288.
16. ANZAI, Y. & H. A. SIMON. 1979. The theory of learning by doing. Psychol. Rev. **86**: 124–140.
17. KARAT, J. A. 1982. A model of problem solving with incomplete constraint knowledge. Cogn. Psychol. **14**: 538–559.
18. COHEN, N. J. & S. CORKIN. 1985. Normal learning of the Tower of Hanoi puzzle despite amnesia. (In press.)
19. DEACEDO, B. S. 1984. Objective analyses of the knowledge underlying skilled performance on the Tower of Hanoi puzzle. Unpublished honors thesis. Wellesley College.
20. COHEN, N. J., H. EICHENBAUM, & B. S. DEACEDO. 1985. Analyses of cognitive skill acquisition. (In manuscript.)
21. COHEN, N. J. 1985. Neuropsychological analyses of memory: Identifying component memory processes. *In* Learning and Memory: A Biological View. J. L. Martinez & R. P. Kesner, Eds. Academic Press. New York. (In press.)
22. SQUIRE, L. R. & N. J. COHEN. 1984. Human memory and amnesia. *In* Neurobiology of Learning and Memory. J. McGaugh, N. Weinberger & G. Lynch, Eds.: 3–64. Guilford Press. New York.
23. ANDERSON, J. R. 1982. Acquisition of cognitive skill. Psychol. Rev. **89**: 369–406.
24. ANDERSON, J. R. 1983. The Architecture of Cognition. Harvard University Press. Cambridge, Massachusetts.
25. SHALLICE, T. 1982. Specific impairments of planning. Philosoph. Trans. R. Soc. London Ser. B **298**: 199–209.
26. BRUNER, J. S. 1969. Modalities of memory. *In* The Pathology of Memory. G. A. Talland & N. C. Waugh, Eds. Academic Press. New York.
27. STICH, S. P. 1978. Beliefs and subdoxastic states. Philos. Sci. **45**: 499–518.
28. JAMES, W. 1890. The Principles of Psychology. Henry Holt & Company. New York.

A Disconnection Analysis of Amnesia

ELIZABETH K. WARRINGTON

National Hospital
Queen Square
London W.C.1., England

INTRODUCTION

Lesions in all sectors of the cortex give rise to memory disorders[24] but none so devastating as can occur with relatively small sub-cortical lesions. Anterograde amnesia, one of the central components of the amnesic syndrome, can be so defective that patients are apparently completely unable to learn or retain ongoing events. Clinically there appears to be a global, virtually absolute deficit for all new learning and indeed it is not misleading to describe these patients as having a total loss of memories.[19]

However, over the last 15 years or so it has become increasingly clear that the amnesic deficit may not be so absolute nor so dense as either clinical impressions or conventional memory tests would suggest. The repertoire of tasks on which the amnesic patient demonstrates unexpectedly good evidence of retention grows annually. Indeed there appears to be a recent convergence of opinion that the analysis of the distinction between those tasks which the patient can and cannot do will yield the solution or at least the partial solution to the amnesic syndrome.

First, I shall give a very brief account of those retention skills that appear to be preserved or relatively preserved in the amnesic patients. Secondly, I will attempt to review in somewhat more detail experiments in which the amnesic patient was not merely quantitatively impaired but those in which a qualitative difference has been demonstrated. The critical experiments for my thesis are those in which the test stimuli were held constant and the method of testing retention manipulated and those in which the conditions of testing were held constant and the nature of the memoranda manipulated. Lastly, I shall attempt to summarize the arguments in favor of a disconnection hypothesis; specifically that there are cognitive mediational memory systems subserved by frontal lobe structures that are disconnected from semantic memory systems subserved by temporal lobe structures.

EVIDENCE OF PRESERVED RETENTION

Milner's[14] classic observation that one severely amnesic patient (HM) succeeded in learning a mirror drawing task, improving his performance both in terms of errors and time, over a three-day period, has been followed by numerous demonstrations of preserved retention. It was shown that amnesics can learn to recognize degraded perceptual stimuli and show retention over hours and even days.[29,33] Learning and retention of phonemically degraded stimuli appeared to be equally effective cues for recall.[34] Starr and Phillips[18] described an amnesic patient who was able to learn a new melody and recall it later when prompted. Eyelid conditioning has been demonstrated,[35] also the ability to reassemble jigsaw puzzles[2] and the retention of the principle in a problem-solving task.[11] These examples are not exhaustive.

We have previously suggested that the factor common to all those tasks on which learning and retention in the amnesic patient can be demonstrated is that they can be performed relatively automatically on the basis of differential strength of response. Thus we have suggested that there are two types of task on which the amnesic patient's performance is relatively unimpaired. First, simple incremental stimulus-response learning as exemplified by our eyelid conditioning experiment and the acquisition of motor skills, and secondly tasks in which the probability of response is primed or facilitated by repetition. It is now well documented that in normal subjects the mere exposure of or response to a verbal or visual stimulus can have priming/facilitatory effects lasting as long as weeks.[12,17] The relevance of 'priming' for amnesic retention has been particularly neatly demonstrated by Jacoby and Witherspoon.[7] Homophones presented in context, were first written to dictation. In a recognition memory task the amnesic group were unable to identify the words from the test list, yet when the words were represented (without the sentence context) the amnesics retained the original homphonic spelling of the word.

In our own studies we showed a significant repetition effect in verbal response times.[32] Presented with verbal stimuli subjects were required to respond with the superordinate category name, an exemplar from a category, and a semantic opposite. There was no significant difference between the amnesics and the controls in their speed of accessing this class of verbal information; but for the present argument I wish to emphasize that the size of the repetition effect was much the same for the two groups (in no instance was there a significant groups×conditions interaction term).

It is widely accepted that lesions of the post-rolandic cortices give rise to primary perceptual processing impairments and semantic memory deficits (i.e. memory for words, objects, concepts, etc.; a pool of facts shared by individuals). To take but a few examples from group studies: recognition of the degraded perceptual stimuli that provide an effective cue for the amnesic in a retention task has been shown to be impaired in patients with post-rolandic lesions of the right hemisphere.[26,27] More important, there is evidence that both verbal and visual semantics are subserved by structures within the post-rolandic regions of the left hemisphere. For example, verbal comprehension at a single word level (not attributable to perceptual impairments) was impaired in patients with left temporal lobe lesions.[3] Visual object matching by semantic categories was found to be impaired in patients with posterior left hemisphere lesions.[5,25,28] If we presuppose that the priming and repetition effects reflect the efficient functioning of these perceptual and semantic systems, then one would predict that these effects would be attenuated in patients with cortical damage. This prediction could, of course, easily be tested, however there is already some meager evidence to hand that suggests that patients with semantic memory deficits are quite unlike the classical amnesic patients.

I have described in some detail two patients (AB and EM) in whom it was argued that there was a selective impairment of semantic memory.[22] These patients had severe agnosic difficulties, the meanings of all but fairly common words and objects had been 'forgotten'. Yet they appeared to have reasonably good memory for ongoing events. Unlike the typical amnesic their conversation was not repetitive. Some quantitative data to support this impression was provided by their average or above average score on a forced-choice recognition memory test for colored reproductions of paintings. Colors were one of the few categories in either their verbal or visual semantics that appeared to be preserved and it seems likely that the ability to encode the color information from stimuli that were otherwise only crudely meaningful must have contributed to their very creditable performance on this task. By contrast, the amnesics scored at chance on this task. In spite of her very poor recall of word meanings EM's score on a conventional free recall task was at the lower limits of normal, a task on which the amnesics were markedly impaired.[4]

Such double dissociation of deficits strengthen the arguments that there are independent semantic memory systems that are impaired in patients with post-rolandic lesions but intact in patients with an amnesic syndrome due to subcortical lesions.

EVIDENCE FOR DIFFERENTIAL IMPAIRMENTS IN THE AMNESIC SYNDROME

Different Methods of Testing Retention

The first investigation of verbal learning in amnesic patients in which there was a differential effect of the method of testing retention, compared free recall, yes/no recognition, and cueing recall either by fragmented letters or by the initial letters.[30] The amnesic's performance was impaired when retention was tested using the two conventional techniques. However, using the two cueing techniques their performance was not significantly different from that of the control group. Furthermore the groups × conditions interaction term was significant. The main finding of this experiment, the differential impairment depending on the method of testing retention, was replicated in a later study.[31] In one of the agnosic patients (EM) described above, it was shown that the pattern of deficit was the opposite of that associated with the amnesic syndrome: namely a better performance on a verbal yes/no recognition memory task than on the cued recall task.[22]

In an early study, Baddeley and I[1] manipulated different encoding strategies in a verbal recall task. We compared the benefit of phonemic clustering (words that rhyme), semantic clustering (words from the same category), and visual imagery (subjects explicitly instructed to use visual imagery). The amnesic does in fact gain from phonemic and semantic clustering but not at all from the imagery instruction. This was an effective strategy for the control subjects, yet it did not appear to help the amnesic at all. This failure of visual imagery to aid recall was also noted in the patient, HM.[8]

The Effect of Stimulus Material

Normal subjects show very rapid forgetting when required to recall meaningless 'pointless' verbal stimuli. For example, if rehearsal is prevented a rapid decrement in performance, in a matter of seconds, occurs on the apparently simple task of say, the recall of three letters or three words. Using this, the Brown/Peterson paradigm, the recall of random word triplets (e.g. sweet-cross-coin, black-visit-tongue) was compared with recall of word triplets linked by semantic associations (e.g. feed-beggar-hungry, clock-slow-wind). It was found that the amnesic patients were as efficient as the controls in their ability to recall the meaningless word triplets (there were neither floor nor ceiling effects to mar this result). By contrast the meaningful stimuli resulted in a significantly greater gain for the control group than the amnesics.[23] Thus under constant conditions for recall, the amnesics show normal retention for one type of verbal stimuli, the random triplets, but are significantly impaired for the meaningful word triplets.

In two further experiments we used a paired-associate learning paradigm. First, we compared the recall of rhyme pairs, semantic category pairs, and noun-verb pairs. Although the rhymes condition was most difficult for the control group (their mean score was less than 40% correct) the amnesic group were not impaired on this difficult retention task. In contrast there was a highly significant deficit in the amnesic group for the semantic categories and noun-verb conditions.[32] Once again we have obtained the result that under identical conditions for recall, the amnesics show normal retention for one type of verbal stimulus, the rhyme pairs, but grossly impaired retention for the more meaningful verbal material, semantic category pairs and noun-verb pairs. Secondly, we manipulated the associative strength of the word pairs and we compared recall of close associates (e.g. paper-pencil, story-book) with more distant associates (e.g. letter-stamp, oven-heat). The amnesic groups' performance was impaired for both types of stimulus material. However, the groups×conditions interaction term was significant indicating that the amnesic group was relatively more impaired on the 'distant' pairs condition than the 'close' pairs.[32] It is worth noting that the association between the so-called 'distant' pairs was rather obvious and certainly sufficiently so to be beneficial to the normal subject.

A DISCONNECTION HYPOTHESIS

First, I began by discussing those tasks on which amnesics are relatively unimpaired and I argued that such evidence of learning and memory in many such tasks can be considered as priming or repetition effects that reflect the preservation of semantic memory and perceptual processing systems that are themselves impaired by post-rolandic lesions. Secondly, I have reviewed a number of studies in which a differential deficit, not a mere quantitative impairment, was demonstrated in the amnesic group. We have suggested that it is the greater potential for the operation of cognitive mediation processes that differentiate those conditions that fail to benefit the amnesic. Per force we are led to postulate the existence of a cognitive mediational memory system. We use the term to encompass memoranda organized by visual imagery, the formation of associative links, semantic schema, and many other similar cognitive mappings. Kapur[9] was able to demonstrate that it was imagery utilization that was defective in the amnesic patient not imagery formation per se. Similarly we would presuppose that the amnesic patient is impaired not in his ability to engage in cognitive mediation as such, but in those memory tasks in which the stored benefits of mediation are normally important. We have argued that recourse to such a memory system is at the core of an individual's long-term record of events and that this system is damaged or disconnected in the amnesic patient. On the whole we favor the disconnection hypothesis.[32]

We would argue that the integrity of both semantic memory systems and a cognitive mediational memory system are essential for the operation of efficient learning and recall. It is self-evident that both recall and recognition must be preceded by comprehension or identification, both facets of semantic memory. For example the failure to comprehend a word list, or identify objects would vitiate any attempt to recall the words or recognize the objects. Thus without prior comprehension cognitive memory would be contentless. It seems fairly likely that temporal lobe structures subserve semantic memory. Is it possible that these cortical structures have multiple functions, subserving not only semantic memory but also the postulated cognitive mediational memory systems? In view of the evidence of double dissociation of deficits between these two types of retention, such a dual function seems most improbable. Furthermore there is a better candidate! Memory deficits have been repeatedly demonstrated in patients with frontal lobe lesions. Hecaen[6] recorded a 20% incidence of selective memory impairment in a consecutive series of patients with frontal lobe lesions and he considered paired associate learning to be particularly vulnerable. In our own series we recorded an incidence of material-specific memory deficits in the region of 30% on recognition memory tasks.[24] Milner[15,16] has shown that patients with frontal lobe lesions are more impaired on memory tasks requiring the active manipulation and comparison of the memoranda (and it is perhaps such activity that imparts the quality of memories to recalled events). Kapur and Coughlan[10] have described in some detail a memory deficit with confabulation in a patient who had sustained frontal lobe damage. We have therefore suggested that structures in the frontal lobe subserve the cognitive mediational memory system, or some crucial component of it, and that this system is disconnected from temporal lobe semantic memory systems thus depriving the cognitive memory system of any meaningful input.

Perhaps the strength of the disconnection hypothesis derives not so much from behavioral/anatomical correlations as from the evidence of pathology. The sufficient lesion appears to lie in a very restricted locus. We have pathological data from two of our amnesic patients whom we had studied intensively over a number of years. These were both 'typical' severe amnesics and demonstrated all the phenomena I have described.[13]

In the brains of both patients there was marked gliosis, shrinkage in the medial nuclei of the mammillary bodies. In addition, there was a thin band of gliosis bilaterally between the wall of the third ventricle and the medial dorsal nucleus. There were two important negative findings: the dorsal medial nucleus and the hippocampi; both structures often implicated in the amnesic syndrome were considered to be normal in both cases.[21] We have argued that these "conspicuous and severe lesions in a relatively small zone of the diencephalon can be considered as the disconnecting structures in the mid-brain and in the temporal lobe (via connections from the entorhinal and parahippocampal regions to the hippocampus and subiculum and from the subiculum through the fornix to the mammillary bodies) from structures in the frontal lobes (via connections from the mammillary bodies) to the anterior and medial thalamus."[32] Thus the lesions can be considered on a 'route' between structures in the temporal lobe that subserve semantic memory and structures in the frontal lobe that are held to subserve a cognitive mediational memory system.

REFERENCES

1. BADDELEY, A. D. & E. K. WARRINGTON. 1973. Memory coding and amnesia. Neuropsychologia 11: 159–165.
2. BROOKS, D. N. & A. D. BADDELEY. 1976. What can amnesic patients learn? Neuropsychologia 14: 111–122.
3. COUGHLAN, A. K. & E. K. WARRINGTON. 1978. Word-comprehension and word-retrieval in patients with localised cerebral lesions. Brain 101: 163–185.
4. COUGHLAN, A. K. & E. K. WARRINGTON. 1981. The impairment of verbal semantic memory: a single case study. J. Neurol. Neurosurg. Psychiatry 44: 1079–1083.
5. DE RENZI, E., G. SCOTT & H. SPINNLER. 1969. Perceptual and associative disorders of visual recognition: relationship to the site of the cerebral lesion. Neurology 19: 634–642.
6. HECAEN, H. 1964. Mental symptoms associated with tumors of the frontal lobe. In The Frontal Granular Cortex and Behaviour. J. M. Warren & K. Akert, Eds.: 335–352. McGraw-Hill. New York.
7. JACOBY, L. L. & D. WITHERSPOON. 1982. Remembering without awareness. Can. J. Psychol. 32: 300–324.
8. JONES, M. K. 1974. Imagery as a mnemonic aid after left temporal lobectomy: Contrast between material specific and generalised memory disorders. Neuropsychologia 12: 21–30.
9. KAPUR, N. 1978. Visual imagery capacity of alcoholic Korsakoff patients. Neuropsychologia 16: 517–519.
10. KAPUR, N. & A. K. COUGHLAN. 1980. Confabulation and frontal lobe dysfunction. J. Neurol. Neurosurg. Psychiatry 43: 461–463.
11. KINSBOURNE, M. & F. WOOD. 1975. Short-term memory processes and the amnesic

syndrome. *In:* Short-Term Memory. D. Deutsch & J. A. Deutsch, Eds.: 257–291. Academic Press. New York.

12. LACHMAN, R. & J. L. LACHMAN. 1980. Picture naming: retrieval and activation of long-term memory. *In* New Directions in Memory and Aging. Proceedings of the George Talland Memorial Conference. L. W. Poon, J. L. Fozard, L. S. Cermak, D. Arenberg & L. W. Thompson, Eds.: 313–343. Lawrence Erlbaum. Hillsdale, NJ.

13. MAIR, W. G. P., E. K. WARRINGTON & L. WEISKRANTZ. 1979. Neuropathological and psychological examination of 2 patients with Korsakoff's psychosis. Brain **102:** 749–783.

14. MILNER, B. 1962. Les troubles de la Memoire accompagnant des lesions Hippocampiques Bilaterales. *In* Physiologie de l'hippocampe. (Colloques internationaux, no. 107: 257–272.) C.N.R.S. Paris.

15. MILNER, B. 1971. Interhemispheric difference in the localization of psychological processes in man. Brit. Med. Bull. **27:** 272–277.

16. MILNER, B. 1982. Some cognitive effects of frontal lobe lesions in man. Phil. Trans. R. Soc. London Ser. B **298:** 3–13.

17. SCARBOROUGH, D. L., C. CORTESE & H. S. SCARBOROUGH. 1977. Frequency and repetition effects in lexical memory. J. Exp. Psychol. Human Perception Performance **3:** 1–17.

18. STARR, A. & L. PHILLIPS. 1970. Verbal and motor memory in the amnestic syndrome. Neuropsychologia **8:** 75–88.

19. TALLAND, G. A. 1965. Deranged Memory: A psychonomic study of the amnesic syndrome. Academic Press. New York.

20. TAYLOR, A. M. & E. K. WARRINGTON. 1971. Visual agnosia: A single case report. Cortex **7:** 152–161.

21. VICTOR, M., R. D. ADAMS & G. H. COLLINS. 1971. The Wernicke Korsakoff syndrome. Blackwell. Oxford.

22. WARRINGTON, E. K. 1975. The selective impairment of semantic memory. Q. J. Exp. Psychol. **27:** 635–657.

23. WARRINGTON, E. K. 1981. The double dissociation of short and long-term memory deficits. *In* Human Memory and Amnesia. L. S. Cermak, Ed.: 61–76. Lawrence Erlbaum. Hillsdale, NJ.

24. WARRINGTON, E. K. 1984. Recognition memory test manual. NFER-Nelson Publishing Co. Ltd. Windsor, Berks.

25. WARRINGTON, E. K. 1985. Agnosia: the impairment of object recognition. *In* Handbook of Clinical Neurology. P. J. Vinken, G. W. Bruyn & H. L. Klawans, Eds. **45:** 333–349. Elsevier. Amsterdam.

26. WARRINGTON, E. K. & M. JAMES. 1967. Disorders of visual perception in patients with localised cerebral lesions. Neuropsychologia **5:** 253–266.

27. WARRINGTON, E. K. & A. M. TAYLOR. 1973. Contribution of the right parietal lobe to object recognition. Cortex **9:** 152–164.

28. WARRINGTON, E. K. & A. M. TAYLOR. 1978. Two categorical stages of object recognition. Perception **7:** 695–705.

29. WARRINGTON, E. K. & L. WEISKRANTZ. 1968. New method of testing long-term retention with special reference to amnesic patients. Nature **277:** 972–974.

30. WARRINGTON, E. K. & L. WEISKRANTZ. 1970. Amnesia: Consolidation or retrieval? Nature **228:** 628–630.

31. WARRINGTON, E. K. & L. WEISKRANTZ. 1974. The effect of prior learning on subsequent retention in amnesic patients. Neuropsychologia **12:** 419–428.

32. WARRINGTON, E. K. & L. WEISKRANTZ. 1982. Amnesia: A disconnection syndrome. Neuropsychologia **20:** 233–249.

33. WEISKRANTZ, L. & E. K. WARRINGTON. 1970. A study of forgetting in amnesic patients. Neuropsychologia **8:** 281–288.

34. WEISKRANTZ, L. & E. K. WARRINGTON. 1970. Verbal learning and retention in amnesic patients using partial information. Psychonom. Sci. **20:** 210–211.

35. WEISKRANTZ, L. & E. K. WARRINGTON. 1979. Conditioning in amnesic patients. Neuropsychologia **17:** 187–194.

Memory from Infancy to Old Age: Implications for Theories of Normal and Pathological Memory[a]

MORRIS MOSCOVITCH

Unit for Memory Disorders and
Centre for Research in Human Development
Department of Psychology
Erindale College
University of Toronto
Mississauga, Ontario L5L 1C6

Memory changes radically between infancy and extreme old age. Yet in reading the literature concerned with memory development one is struck by the apparent disconti-nuity between memory in infancy and memory during the rest of the life span. Admittedly, this may be simply a consequence of the radically different ways in which memory is tested in infants, who have no language and limited motor skills as compared to adults or even young children, in which these capacities are more fully developed. Yet, despite the attempts of many investigators to account for memory development in terms of a unitary system that grows or declines in capacity during the lifespan, it seems that infant memory has characteristics that made it fundamentally different from that of even very young children. As a student of neuropsychology, I was struck by the similarity between infant memory and organic amnesia. The memory tests on which infants succeeded were similar to those on which amnesic patients demonstrated preserved memory abilities, whereas those tests on which infants failed, amnesic patients also displayed a profound memory impairment.

In an extensive review comparing the memory of infants and organic amnesic patients, Dan Schacter and I[1] suggested that organic amnesia results from damage to a memory system that develops late in infancy. The preserved memory abilities of amnesic patients are dependent on the operation of a memory system that develops early in infancy and accounts for those functions that are characteristic of infant memory before 8–12 months.

In this paper I will review the arguments and evidence Schacter and I presented to support our hypothesis and compare our approach with that of other developmental psychologists, particularly Piaget and Inhelder. I will then consider the implications of our approach to theories of cognitive development, in particular to Piaget's theory on the relation between symbolic representation and memory. I will argue that the capacity for symbolic representation is not sufficient for the development of the late memory system. I will further suggest that the converse may be true: the full expression of symbolic representation in cognition and behavior is dependent on the emergence of the late memory system in infancy. I will then consider briefly the kind of changes that occur in memory between childhood and old age. Here I will suggest that the changes in memory performance do not depend on the development of new and different

[a]Supported by grants from Medical Research Council of Canada, the Ontario Mental Health Foundation, and the Connaught Foundation.

78

memory systems, but rather that the changes result from the maturation and deterioration of the memory system that is already in place by late infancy and from the acquisition and deployment of cognitive strategies that serve memory throughout life.

THEORIES OF INFANT MEMORY

It is said that children learn more between birth and two years than they do during any comparable period in their lives. Yet before reaching school-age and certainly before turning two, a child's memory for past events is notoriously poor or nonexistent. Although these two statements may seem paradoxical, they are not. Psychologists have reconciled them in two ways. One way is to assert that memory functions are similar throughout life, but that memory performance varies as a function of the tests that are administered. Given the appropriate tests, even infants can be shown to have a good memory.[2] The other way is to distinguish between different types of memory or forms of remembering, one of which develops early and the other later. According to the first approach, which I will call the single memory approach, memory only appears to be poor in very young children because they lack the means of demonstrating its existence. Appropriate techniques, such as habituation and conditioning, can reveal quite startling memory capacities in infants. These techniques rarely, if ever, require the infant or child to demonstrate that they can consciously recollect a particular episode by traditional recall or recognition procedures. Instead, they allow the investigator to infer that previous experience has a powerful and often long-lasting effect on the child's subsequent behavior. Despite the difference in testing procedures, some of these investigators assume that the principles governing memory performance are the same in infants and in adults. As a result, concepts from the adult memory literature, such as recognition,[3] recall, encoding, and retrieval[4] are invoked to explain or describe the infant's behavior without seriously considering the possibility that these concepts may take on a very different meaning when applied to such different populations in such different testing situations.

The alternative way of dealing with the paradox of preserved learning in the face of poor recollection, the way chosen by Piaget and Inhelder,[5] was to distinguish between different types of memory, what I will call the multiple memory approach. "Memory in the wide sense" is observed by noting the effects of any past experience on current or subsequent behavior. "Memory in the strict sense" is memory for a particular event at a particular time and place. According to Piaget and Inhelder, one can speak only of memory in the wide sense when referring to infants before the age of 1.5 to 2 years. Although their behavior can be modified by experience and "primitive recognition" of previously presented signals is possible, the infants cannot recognize or recall in the sense that they can bring to mind a previous event that they have experienced. The infant's failure to have memory in the strict sense was linked by Piaget and Inhelder to the absence of an appropriate representational system. For them, true recognition and recall, what I have called conscious recollection,[6,7] depends on symbolic representation which entails, in part, that objects can be brought to mind in their absence. These objects must have an existence independent of the actions that are performed on them. Before the development of symbolic representation, the infant relies on sensorimotor schemas. In such a representational schema, memory cannot be demonstrated by consciously recollecting an event, but simply by reactivating the procedures, operations, or actions performed initially on the object and during the event or by altering the schema that enables the infant to interact with the object. In short, the infant's behavior may be modified but without any recollection of a previous episode. Memory in the strict sense must therefore await the development of a symbolic representational system.

THEORIES OF AMNESIA AND AN EXPERIMENT

Research on traumatic amnesia in adult humans (and animals) has been concerned with similar theoretical issues. Human amnesia has a variety of etiologies, ranging from concussions, ECT, encephalitis, chronic alcoholism and vitamin deficiency, to neurosurgical excisions. The form that amnesia takes, therefore, may be different depending on the etiology, the structure of the brain that was damaged, and, perhaps, even the age and personality of the individual. All amnesias, however, have a variety of symptoms in common.[7] The hallmark symptom is that amnesic patients find it very difficult, if not impossible, to recollect post-traumatic events. That is, they have a profound anterograde memory deficit. Amnesic patients are nonetheless capable of acquiring new information, sometimes normally, despite having no conscious recollection of having acquired it. At first, it was thought that only perceptuomotor skills are acquired by amnesic patients whereas true cognitive skills were not.[8] Recently, however, it has been demonstrated by a number of investigators that amnesic patients can use letter fragments to recall words they had seen earlier,[9,10] they can solve anagrams faster the second time than the first,[11] they can solve the Tower of Hanoi as quickly as normal people,[12] and, given sufficient support, they can even show that they are capable of forming new associations between randomly paired words even after a single presentation.[13,14]

It is important to remember, however, that these demonstrations of relatively intact memory in the face of profound amnesia occur only when the following three conditions are satisfied[13]: the tasks are so highly structured that the goal of the task and the means to achieve it are apparent, the means to achieve the goal are available to the subject (i.e., the response and the strategies used to arrive at the goal are already in the subject's repertoire), success in achieving the goal can be had without reference to a particular postmorbid event or episode. With slight modification, these are the same conditions under which memory can be demonstrated in infants. Likewise, there are now two approaches to dealing with these paradoxical memory abilities of amnesic patients that are analogous to the approaches adopted by investigators of infant memory. The single-memory approach is based on the view that there is a single memory system whose operation and the memory it reveals varies with the tests used to probe it. Amnesic patients, like infants, may be incapable of revealing their memories except on tests such as habituation or dishabituation, conditioning, and priming that make no demands on conscious recollection. I will illustrate this point with a recent experiment conducted in collaboration with Mary Rees-Nishio.

A number of infant studies use psychophysiological measures, most typically heart rate, to gauge the infant's ability to process different types of information.[16] These measures are usually used in habituation-dishabituation paradigms in which the trials are often separated by a few seconds. As a result, studies employing these techniques necessarily involve a memory component and, in addition to cognitive or perceptual competence, these studies measure the infant's memory for previous events, however short-lived it may be. Rather than heart-rate, Rees-Nishio and I used the skin conductance response (SCR) as a psychophysiological index of memory and compared it with the more traditional measures of recognition and recall.

The study was concerned with a number of issues regarding the relation of emotion to memory, but I will present only those findings that are directly relevant to this discussion (for a detailed report see Rees-Nishio[15]). Subjects studied a set of emotional and non-emotional words. A week later they were shown the same words mixed with an equal number of emotional and non-emotional distractors. Their task was simply to say whether or not they recognized the word as one they had previously studied and indicate the confidence they had in their answer on a seven-point scale, with one as low confidence and seven as high confidence. Both of these can be considered traditional tests of conscious recollection. At the same time, the first skin conductance response (SCR) within eight seconds of word presentation was measured. The SCR is an electrophysiological index of habituation and arousal both of which may reflect "memory in the wide sense" for a previous event in that it tracks changes in neural

TABLE 1. Proportion Recognized (REC), Confidence Level (CONF), and Skin Conductance Response (SCR)

Group (N)			YES		NO	
			Old	New	Old	New
Young	Emotional	REC	.89	.31	.11	.69
(N = 20)	Words	CONF	6.47	5.40	4.55	5.31
		SCR	1.23	1.16	1.27	1.17
	Neutral	REC	.71	.28	.29	.72
	Words	CONF	6.03	5.01	3.85	4.83
		SCR	1.10	.96	1.02	1.00
Elderly	Emotional	REC	.82	.50	.18	.50
(N = 25)	Words	CONF	6.32	5.51	3.96	4.42
		SCR	.85	.73	.80	.76
	Neutral	REC	.63	.31	.37	.69
	Words	CONF	5.70	4.76	3.89	4.10
		SCR	.85	.70	.72	.75
Amnesic	Emotional	REC	.52	.40	.48	.60
(N = 6)	Words	SCR	.24	.19	.24	.13
	Neutral	REC	.50	.42	.50	.58
	Words	SCR	.22	.14	.22	.14

responsiveness to repeated stimulus exposure. If electrophysiological indices of memory are not dependent on the subjects making explicit reference to a previous event, as they seem not to be given the individual's lack of awareness of these responses, then it follows that the memory of amnesic patients, like that of infants, might be relatively intact when assessed with these techniques despite appearing grossly defective on traditional tests of recognition and recall. The dissociation between electrophysiological and recognition indices of memory would also be predicted on the basis of the conditions under which memory performance would be normal in amnesic patients.

As TABLE 1 shows, the predictions were generally confirmed. First, even in normal young and elderly control subjects, there was a dissociation between SCR and recognition. In general, the SCR was larger to "old" words seen the previous week than to "new" words, regardless of the subject's judgement or confidence rating. In amnesic patients this dissociation is even more striking because their recognition was virtually at chance, whereas their SCR clearly favored the "old" words.

This study is consistent with the task analysis view expressed earlier. Memory performance is determined by the demands of the task and the means used to assess it. Although useful, this task analysis approach is primarily descriptive. It does not explain why performance should appear normal on some tasks but not on others. Although the single memory point-of-view provides an adequate account of infant behavior—their limited motor and cognitive skills do not allow them to display what they remember except under special circumstances—it fares less well with amnesic patients who, aside from their memory deficit, have the cognitive and motor skills of the normal adult. Why then should amnesic patients display normal memory functioning under some circumstances and not others? The obvious answer that one measure is simply more sensitive than another has been discredited because performance on the more sensitive test has been shown to be independent of performance on the less sensitive one.[17-19] Were one test merely more sensitive than another, accurate performance on the less sensitive tests would predict similar performance on the same items of the more sensitive test leading to dependence between the two. Failure to answer the above question adequately is the major problem facing the single-memory theory of amnesia. For purposes of exposition, I now wish to turn to an alternative approach that at first glance deals with this problem more effectively.

This second approach has a simple solution to the above problem: it postulates the existence of multiple memory systems, only some of which are impaired in amnesia, the remainder being relatively spared. Some recent proposals[12,20] regarding the nature of the different systems have a great deal in common with Piaget and Inhelder's theories. Although I will note some serious problems with these views later in the paper, for the moment I will present them in a favorable light.

According to some advocates of the multiple memory system approach, what distinguishes one memory system from another is the nature of internal representations and the kind of mnemonic processes that these representations can support. The similarity between their argument and Piaget's goes even deeper in that the language used to describe the differences between the preserved and impaired memory systems in amnesic patients is one with which a Piagetian would be very comfortable.[7,12,17,20] The preserved memory system has been termed procedural, skill, or priming memory. Knowledge in this system is represented in terms of the procedures or operations that are necessary to perceive an object, read a word, learn a motor skill, or solve a problem, much like the sensorimotor representation that underlies an infant's cognition in the preoperational stage. Memory that is dependent on this system is manifested by improvement in performance that results from either reactivating or modifying the procedures and operations that are then run off more quickly and efficiently with practice. The memory that is observed in these circumstances is "memory in the wide sense" and is akin to Piaget's recognitory assimilation, in which recognition is dependent on the assimilation of the object or event to a previously existing sensorimotor schema.

The impaired memory system in amnesia, on the other hand, is often described as declarative and episodic. What is represented in this system are not procedures but their perceived outcomes, not sensorimotor operations, but symbols that can be accessed independently of the situation in which they were acquired. Although some investigators wish to restrict these symbolic representations to a propositional format, research on both normal and neurological patients suggests that a nonpropositional, analogue format is also available to conscious awareness. This too is consistent with Piaget's view that symbols first appear in the form of images. Without this symbolic representational system, conscious awareness as we experience it is not possible. It is these stored, symbolically represented outcomes of a previous experience that are consciously revived or retrieved during typical tests of recognition and recall. This is akin to Piaget's memory in the strict sense. By this view, amnesic patients fail either to store, retain, or gain access to the symbolically represented information of the content and context of an event. Consequently, the amnesic patient cannot consciously recollect a post-morbid experience, though that experience may affect his behavior via the preserved memory system.

From this multiple memory system point of view, the previous study on SCR and recognition would be interpreted in the following way. SCR reflects a kind of priming of previously activated sensory and perceptual operations and hence reflects memory processes in one system. Its operation may be independent of the other system that relies instead on consciously retrieving a previously experienced event and its appropriate context and consciously deciding whether a particular aspect of that event indeed occurred.

The study conducted with Rees-Nishio is similar to a class of recently published experiments that contrast memory as inferred by performance on priming tasks, which depend on reactivation of sensorimotor processes or procedures, with that on tasks of recognition and recall, which depend on consciously recollecting a previous episode. In these studies, subjects study or merely examine a list of words. The test phase usually consists of two parts. In the priming part, the subject is asked to identify a word that is perceptually degraded,[9] to decide whether a string of letters is an English word,[13] or to complete a word given some of its letters as cues.[14] In all these cases, no effort is made to have the subject recollect the previously studied word. As such, the tasks meet the three conditions set out earlier. In the conscious recollection part of the test phase, the subjects are required to recognize or recall the words that they had studied. In these experiments, as in Rees-Nishio's and mine, amnesic performance was normal when memory was tested by priming and severely impaired when it was tested by conscious recollection.

FIGURES 1 and 2 illustrate the results of one such study from our own laboratory. The paradigm we used was repetition priming in a lexical decision task that we borrowed from Scarborough et al.[21] By pressing a button subjects indicated whether a string of letters was a word or not. Their response latencies were recorded. Half the strings consisted of real English words and half did not. Half of all the items were repeated a second time at lags of 0, 7, or 29 items after the first presentation. Replicating the results of Scarborough et al., we found that subjects were 50 msec faster the second time than the first at deciding that an item was a word. This repetition priming effect did not decay over a lag of at least 29 items and, according to Scarborough et al., was even observed after a few days (FIGURE 1). Moreover, it did not transfer across mode of representation—there was no repetition priming effect between a picture and a word or between a spoken and a written word—suggesting that what underlay the effect was the reactivation of a very specific set of procedures or operations that was used to encode the material, not the reactivation of a symbolic or semantic representation of the item in question.[21] In addition, because the pattern of repetition priming effects were different and more short-lived for non-words, it suggested that the effect was dependent on reactivating a set of formerly laid down perceptual procedures that were typically used to identify known words (FIGURE 2).

The results of the experiment and their interpretation are again consistent with Piaget's notion that memory in this wide sense is dependent on recognitory assimilation. Of course, new sensorimotor schemas can get laid down, but these typically require more than one repetition. I will have more to say about this later. For now, I want to emphasize that the repetition priming effect is virtually identical in our

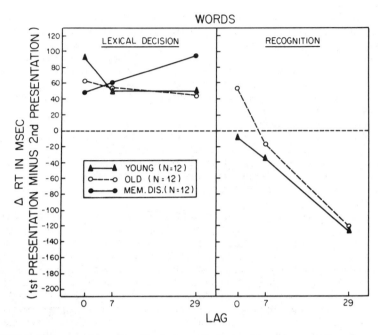

FIGURE 1. Differences in reaction time between the first and second presentation of a word in lexical decision task and recognition tasks. The second word was presented at lags of 0, 7, or 29 items after the first word. MEM. DIS. refers to patients with severe memory disorders.

amnesic patients as in our young and elderly control subjects, demonstrating that the amnesic patients' "memory" can appear normal under these testing conditions.

That their memory in the strict sense, namely conscious recollection of particular events, was severely compromised becomes evident as soon as the repetition priming paradigm was altered in the following way. Instead of deciding whether each letter string forms a word or not, the subject had to indicate whether this was the first or second time that the word appeared on the screen. Here we see that normal performance deteriorates with lag, although the rate was identical for young and old people. Many amnesic patients, however, performed at chance level even on the first presentation of an item. Their data, therefore, do not appear on the graph.

EARLY AND LATE DEVELOPING MEMORY SYSTEMS AND THEIR RELATION TO AMNESIA

Dan Schacter and I, in a review comparing the literature on memory in infants and in amnesic patients,[1] concluded that the memory system that develops early in infants, Piaget's "memory in the wide sense," is spared in amnesic patients whereas the system that develops late, "memory in the strict sense," is impaired. Because amnesia is often associated with bilateral damage to the hippocampus, frontal lobes, and related structures that typically develop late in mammals,[22,23] we felt that we were on safe ground in referring to the preserved and impaired systems as early and late, respectively. Also, the terms early and late carried very little theoretical baggage. It enabled us to capture the relevant distinctions between infant and child memory on the one hand, and amnesic and normal memory on the other, without committing ourselves to any particular theoretical view of the nature of the memory systems. We speculated that tests of habituation-dishabituation in infants had qualities similar to tests of priming in amnesic patients. Similarly, those paradigms that led to successful conditioning and learning in infants produced normal performance in amnesic patients and in animals with hippocampal lesions, whereas failure or anomalous performance in one group was likely to produce similar results in the other.

We may have erred in drawing analogies between the trouble that infants have on cross-modal matching tasks and the difficulty in obtaining cross-modality effects in some priming paradigms used with adults (see Schacter & Moscovitch,[1] pp. 189–191). First, it is not yet clear whether failures to find evidence for cross-modal matches early in infancy reflects methodological problems more than the infant's cognitive incompetence. Second, and perhaps more telling, is our own difficulty in demonstrating that all amnesic patients fail on tests of cross-modality matching. In our study, we had subjects inspect haptically or visually wire figures that were bent into nonsense shapes. The subject then had to choose the target item from two items presented in the same or in a different modality. The first four patients performed worse than control subjects in the cross-modal but not in the unimodal condition, whereas the next four subjects did not differ significantly from control subjects in either condition. What was most disconcerting was that performance did not vary in any obvious way with the severity of the amnesia. The most amnesic of our patients performed normally in this task!

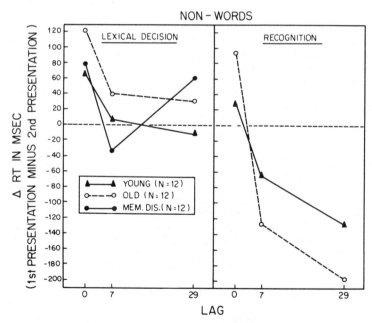

FIGURE 2. Differences in reaction time between the first and second presentation of a nonword in lexical decision and recognition tasks. The second nonword was presented at lags of 0, 7, or 29 items after the first word.

Research on primates indicates that successful cross-modal matching is dependent on the integrity of neural structures such as the frontal lobes and amygdala[24,25] that are often damaged in amnesic patients. Since we did not have good evidence of the site of the lesion in most of our patients, we could not determine whether performance on this task was correlated with damage to particular neural structures. Nonetheless, it is interesting and provocative that the areas that affect cross-modal matching in non-human primates, such as the amygdala and frontal lobes,[24,25] also develop relatively late in infancy. Although the parallel between infants and amnesic patients on cross-modal matching tasks may not apply to all amnesic patients, it may still apply to a subset of them and provide some insight into the nature of their particular memory deficit.

From a survey of the memory literature in infants we suggested that between 8–12 months of age, the late system has developed sufficiently to make its influence felt on the memory performance of most normal infants. This is significantly earlier than the time that Piaget and Inhelder set for the emergence of "memory in the strict sense" and serves as a signpost for marking a critical conceptual difference between our proposal and theirs. Having emphasized the similarities between our approach and Piaget and Inhelder's, I now wish to call attention to the differences.

THE RELATION BETWEEN THE DEVELOPMENT OF SYMBOLIC REPRESENTATION AND MEMORY IN INFANTS: IMPLICATIONS FROM STUDIES OF AMNESIA

To Piaget, or even to fellow travellers such as Mandler[26] or Nelson,[27] the development of symbolic representations is primary. The infant must first develop concepts that could be called to mind independently of the sensorimotor operations from which they emerged. Symbols are then acquired that stand for those concepts and through which the concepts could be accessed and manipulated in thought. Once the symbolic representational system is established, memory in the strict sense seems to be a natural extension of it. Evoking a concept to mind in the absence of the situation in which the concept was acquired has the same flavor in Piaget's and even Mandler's theorizing as recalling a previous event. The memory for a particular event is so inextricably tied to the representational schema necessary to encode and retrieve that event that it is difficult to separate the two conceptually. Piaget and Inhelder struggle to specify just what the differences are between evoking a concept or image to mind and evoking a particular event.

The research on amnesia forces one to consider symbolic representation and the voluntary evocation of a previous episode (not necessarily a concept), what I have called conscious recollection, as separable both conceptually and empirically. There is no doubt that an amnesic has developed the capacity for dealing with old symbolic representations. He can describe absent objects with which he is familiar, deal with abstract concepts, and, in some, but not all cases, recall remote pretraumatic events in great detail. Yet despite this capacity, the amnesic patient's ability to recollect post-traumatic (anterograde) episodic or semantic information remains severely impaired.

This research on adult amnesia has a number of implications for studies of cognitive development in infancy. First, and most obviously, it suggests that even after the capacity for symbolic representation is in place, recognition and recall of specific events or episodes must await the development of another process or system that allows for the conscious recollection of new memories. The second, and more subtle implication, is the converse of the first. At least one of the criteria for symbolic representation, the evocation of an object or concept in its absence, may be critically dependent, in many situations, on the development of the late memory system. From the vantage point of amnesia research, it is entirely possible for an infant to have developed the capacity for symbolic representation and nonetheless fail on specific tests of that capacity if successful performance depends on the recollection of particular past events. The capacity for symbolic representation may be present in the sense that the infant can have a conceptual system and form symbols that refer to those concepts.[26,28] The ability to express this capacity, however, may be confined only to early memory system tasks. For example, the infant may have developed the concept of object permanence and display it when tested in habituation-dishabituation paradigm, which depends on the early memory system, but not in a search task, which requires conscious recollection and depends on the late system. Before exploring these implications further, the results of experiments on object-permanence search tasks in amnesic patients should help bring this critical point into focus.[1,29]

$\overline{AB}$ OR STAGE IV ERROR IN INFANTS AND AMNESIC PATIENTS

As a test of our ideas we chose to look at the $\overline{AB}$ or stage IV error. Piaget[28] observed that 8–10-month-old infants can search successfully for an object hidden at location A. After repeatedly finding the object at A, most infants will continue to search for the object there even when, in full view, it is moved and hidden at a new location, B.

We decided to test for the presence of similar errors in amnesic patients for a number of reasons. First, this observation holds a central place in Piaget's account of the development of object permanence and, by extension, symbolic representation. According to Piaget, object permanence is achieved when the object can be called to mind independently of the perceptuomotor procedures performed on it. During Stage IV, the infant's concept of an object is still limited to the previous sensorimotor operations performed on it and these are elicited when the infant tries to find it. Since these operations were directed at a particular location in the past, they continue to be directed at the old location even though the object has been moved to a new one. Only later, when the capacity for symbolic representation has matured, can infants begin to search directly at the new location. In fact, it is on the basis of accurate performance on this task, that the development of symbolic representation is inferred. According to this interpretation, Stage IV errors should not be committed by individuals who have long ago developed object permanence.

A second reason for testing for Stage IV errors in amnesic patients, is that the phenomenon lends itself so readily to a memory interpretation. Such an interpretation had already been proposed by other infant researchers[29,30] but had been met with counterproposals that either defended Piaget's interpretation or advanced new inter- pretations. The area has a rich experimental and theoretical literature,[1,29,30] which is the third reason we decided to venture into these thoroughly tested waters to see if we can make our very own waves.

Six severely amnesic patients and six patients with mild cognitive deficits but less severe memory loss participated in the study. Except for the profound memory deficit of the amnesic patients that is reflected even in such gross measures as the MQ on the Wechsler Memory Scale, the two groups did not differ in age, education, or IQ (for the details of patient population see Schacter and Moscovitch[1]).

The tests were designed to resemble the infant tests as much as possible. The first test had two phases. In phase 1, the patient had to find an object immediately after the experimenter hid it behind a set of books located three meters behind the patient at location A. Following this immediate test, the experimenter engaged the patient in 2.5

minutes of conversation after which the patient was again asked to find the missing object. The cycle of hiding, immediate test, and delayed test was repeated until the patient found the object at location A on three successive delay trials. A different object was hidden each time. The same series of events occurred on the next trial, except the object was hidden at a new location, B, behind a plant or a book on top of a filing cabinet two meters to the left and a little behind the patient.

The resemblance between the performance of amnesic patients and infants extended to all phases of the experiment, as FIGURE 3 illustrates. All patients could locate the object at A even on the delay trials. On the delayed B trials, four of the six amnesic patients continued to search for the object at A instead of at B and expressed surprise when they found nothing there. When queried further, none could recall that an object had been hidden at the B location. In contrast, all the control patients remembered the location of the hidden object on all A and B trials.

Investigators who argue against a memory interpretation of the infant's failure on this task cite the observation that infants continue to search for the object at A even when it is not hidden at a new location but placed there out in the open and in full view of the infants. Phase 2 served as a further test of the memory interpretation. In phase 2 of the experiment, after two additional successful delayed searches at A, the object was placed on a desk in full view of the subject at location C, which was directly in front of location A. The subject could not avoid seeing the visible object at C when looking or searching at A. After an immediate test, the subject was engaged in conversation for two minutes before being asked to find the object that was placed in the room.

As FIGURE 3 illustrates, five of the six amnesic patients failed to locate the object on the C trial, despite its being directly visible to them. Four subjects looked directly past the visible object and searched again at A. When told immediately afterwards to examine the objects on the desk to see if the target object was located there, all the patients either denied it was there, still maintaining it was placed at A, or chose the wrong item. All but one of the control patients "found" the object at C, and the patient who failed corrected himself spontaneously.

The results of phase 2 indicate that failure to "find" visible objects can indeed be attributed to a poor memory and this, presumably, applies to infants as well. This interpretation was further supported by the amnesic patients' failure to recall correctly

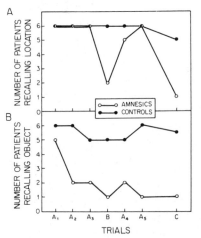

FIGURE 3. Delayed recall of location and object by amnesic and control patients on consecutive trials of an object search task conducted in different places in a testing room. Objects were hidden at an initial location (A) and a second location (B) and were visible at a third location (C). A different object was used on each trial.

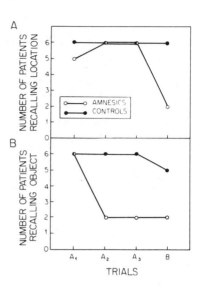

FIGURE 4. Delayed recall of location and object by amnesic and control patients on consecutive trials of an object search task conducted with a small container. Objects were hidden in one drawer of the container (A) for three trials and a second drawer (B) on the fourth trial. A different object was used on each trial.

the object for which they were searching. Except for the first A trial, amnesic patients' delayed object recall was very low in comparison (FIGURE 3) to the control group's. To test for the generalizability of our results, on a different occasion we hid the object in different drawers (locations A and B) of a small, plastic container. We found virtually identical results as in the large room condition (FIGURE 4).

The resemblance between the performance of amnesic patients and infants on the search task is striking. We called this analogue of the AB̄, or Stage IV, an error in amnesic patients the "mnemonic precedence effect." There is little doubt that the effect occurs in amnesic patients because of poor memory rather than a poorly developed object concept. At first glance, what is surprising is not their poor performance on the B and C trials, but their relatively normal performance on the A trials. If we consider the A trials as unique events that require little effortful processing to remember,[31] it becomes easier to understand how even amnesic patients do well on the A trials at relatively short delays. On the B and C trials, however, not only must the patients remember that event, but she must distinguish it from the previously repeated trials. Since it is established that amnesic patients are highly susceptible to proactive interference, their failure in the B and C trials and their intrusion of A trial responses is not only understandable but consistent with their performance on verbal analogues of this search task.[32]

To rule out a pure response perseveration interpretation of the mnemonic precedence effect, we administered the task to three patients with documented bilateral frontal lesions who exhibit the classical perseverative cognitive deficits associated with frontal lesions. All of these patients performed normally on the task.

The striking similarity between amnesic and infant performance on the search task suggests, but does not prove, that the underlying cause of the Stage IV error is the same for both groups—an impaired late memory system not a poorly developed symbolic representational system. This interpretation is supported by other research showing that memory is a significant factor in infant search tasks[30] and by other similarities in memory performance between the two groups.[1] Accepting this interpretation implies that the infant may have developed the concept of object permanence, that is a form of symbolic representation in a conceptual sense, but may not be able to evoke the object to mind voluntarily because this latter act requires the late memory system. This view predicts that so long as tests do not invoke the late memory system, object permanence can be shown to develop much earlier than Piaget claimed. A recent study by Baillargeon et al.[33] supports this prediction. By using a habituation-dishabituation paradigm, which by my criteria is associated with the early memory system, she found that 5-month-old infants who expect to see a solid object behind a screen increased their looking time when the screen tilted all the way backwards—an impossible feat if a solid object were already there. She interpreted her finding as evidence for the existence of a form of object permanence, and by inference symbolic representation, even in a 5-month-old infant.

The third major implication that follows from these considerations is that it is premature, if not altogether wrong, to link the early and late memory system exclusively with sensorimotor and symbolic representations, respectively. I have already argued that the capacity for symbolic representation is not sufficient either for the development or the continued operation of the late memory system. That symbolic representation is necessary for conscious recollection, however, seems likely, but is not proven.

With regard to the early memory system, there are strong indications from the amnesia literature that it can operate on symbolic or declarative representations, although typically its functions are associated with sensorimotor or procedural operations. Thus, in addition to learning mirror drawing and mirror-reading,[7,12,17] and solving jigsaw puzzles[11] and the Tower-of-Hanoi (somewhat stretching the concept of procedural or sensorimotor knowledge),[12] amnesic patients have also learned new facts about individuals,[34] formed associations between randomly paired words,[13,14] and even learned to redefine old words for use on a computer[35]—all this without any conscious recollection of having learned the material at all.[35]

Again, an experiment from my laboratory will illustrate this phenomenon. Amnesic patients and normal young and elderly subjects were presented with a list of 40 pairs of randomly associated words. After studying each of these pairs for three seconds, the subjects were required to read as quickly as possible a list of the original pairs, a list of recombined pairs in which a stimulus item from one pair was recombined with a response item from another pair, and a list of new pairs they had never seen

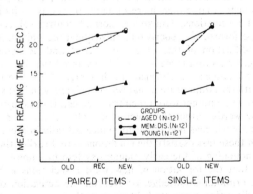

FIGURE 5. Reading time in seconds to old, recombined (REC), and new word pairs. The right panel shows the reading time when the old and new words are presented individually rather than as pairs. MEM. DIS. refers to patients with severe memory disorders.

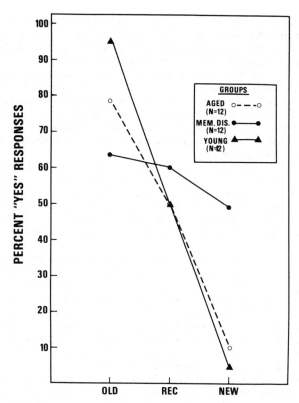

FIGURE 6. Proportion of positive "yes" responses to old, recombined (REC), and new items on a recognition test.

before. As FIGURE 5 indicates, amnesic patients like old and young control subjects, read the old pairs faster than either the recombined or new pairs indicating that they had formed novel associations. Unlike the normal control subjects, however, the amnesic patients performed very poorly on a subsequent recognition test (FIGURE 6).

In a later modification of this experiment, Graf and Schacter[14] had subjects complete a word given its first three letters. They showed that both amnesic patients and normal control subjects performed much better if the word fragment was presented along with the stimulus item that was associated with it at study rather than with a new word or with another word taken from the list. If the subjects were asked to recall the response words, rather than merely complete them, amnesic performance dropped dramatically whereas normal performance actually improved (see Schacter, this volume). Both these tasks satisfy the conditions stated earlier that are associated with preserved functioning of the early memory system in amnesia, yet it would be difficult to argue that the formation of new word associations is based simply on procedural or sensorimotor knowledge, or even on the activation of old memories, without seriously distorting currently held views of these concepts. A more parsimonious explanation is that the early memory system can operate on symbolic representations. It is important to note, however, that the domain over which this newly acquired information can act or be used, be it symbolic or sensorimotor, seems to be very much restricted to the context in which it was acquired. In the sense that it cannot be called to mind freely, the newly acquired information, though represented symbolically, still retains one of the characteristics associated with Piaget's sensorimotor stages. It is the capacity for calling voluntarily to mind newly acquired information or a newly experienced event (those may turn out to be the same) when it is removed from the supporting context of acquisition that may be one of the primary prerequisites for a normally functioning late-memory system. It does not, however, seem necessary to make it a defining characteristic of symbolic representations.

It is important to remember that these conjectures regarding the development of memory and symbolic representation are based on studies of amnesic patients. Although I believe that they are applicable to studies of infant memory, not enough research that is relevant to this point has been conducted on infants to know whether this belief is well-founded. Infant researchers typically accept Piaget's claim that representations are considered symbolic only when they can be evoked apart from the sensorimotor context in which they have been acquired. Yet this is the very question at issue in this paper. This criterion of "contextual freedom" is not simply conceptual, it is also methodological. By accepting Piaget's criterion one is forced to invoke the late memory system in testing for the presence of symbolic representations. Yet by shedding or relaxing the criteria, as Baillargeon did in her study, it becomes possible to show on tests that address the early memory system that the infant has the rudiments of symbolic representation. In such circumstances, we see that the infant indeed possesses the requisite knowledge for forming symbolic representations at much earlier stages than Piaget would have predicted.

This brings me to the last implication that studies of infant and amnesic memory have for each other. This implication is really more in the form of a proposal or conjecture that I think follows from the previous discussion. For symbolic representation to emerge fully and play the prominent role that it does in cognition, it needs the services of a well-developed late memory system.

The development of symbolic thought is as dependent on the late memory system as the latter is on the former. This statement may be stronger than is warranted given the evidence, yet I think it marks a clear distinction between the point of view expressed in this paper and that proposed by other developmental cognitive theorists. The development of the rudiments of symbolic representation may indeed be primary with respect to the development of the late memory system. Yet until the late memory system is functional, the infant's capacity for symbolic representation may remain largely hidden, much like the images and thoughts of a dream that cannot be sustained in the waking state. Once the late memory system is sufficiently developed, the rudiments of symbolically represented knowledge can be brought to mind more easily, manipulated in thought for extensive periods, and revived despite interference from other thoughts or activities. As a result, what was rudimentary and demonstrable through the early memory system could be elaborated into the full symbolic representations that characterize the concrete and formal operational stages of development. Once such a representation is formed and is stable, however, its elaboration and manipulation in thought may no longer require the operation of the late memory system but can occur independently of it. This certainly applies to well-learned concepts and may even apply to well-consolidated episodic memories.

This last conjecture is also derived from work with amnesic patients. There is much evidence that amnesic patients are capable of using their past conceptual knowledge well. Whether amnesic patients can also revive past episodic memories is a moot point, but the concensus is that at least some amnesic patients are normal in this regard.[7] Their deficit lies in consciously recollecting new semantic and episodic memories. The infant is like the amnesic patient in this way. Because he has virtually no past from which to draw his knowledge and is prevented from evoking any new symbolic representations until the late memory system is in place, the infant's cognitive development may appear more impoverished than it really is.

A BRIEF PROPOSAL ABOUT MEMORY DEVELOPMENT FROM EARLY CHILDHOOD TO OLD AGE

I do not wish to leave the impression that once the late memory system becomes functional in late infancy no other interesting changes occur. There is no doubt that memory improves dramatically from late infancy through childhood and adolescence and declines again in old age,[36–40] though what accounts for these changes is unresolved. What I wish to emphasize is that the emergence of the late memory system in infancy marks an important transition in memory development and to suggest that it might also underlie or make possible important changes in cognitive development,[39,40] particularly with regard to symbolic representation.

Are there, however, other significant transitions that can account for the changes that occur in memory during the rest of the life span? From a psychological and neuropsychological perspective, the safe answer would be "yes." It is commonplace to note that memory and cognition are linked. Whatever cognitive skill is acquired, be it language, number concept, or seriation, it is likely to influence some aspects of memory for information associated with that skill (see J. Moscovitch[41] for a thorough discussion and some very interesting experiments on this issue with special emphasis on the relation between memory and seriations[5]). If we accept the neuropsychological premise that cognitive skills are dependent on the development of neural structures that mediate that skill, then again, one would be forced to conclude that significant transitions in the development of memory coincide with the period during which these structures become functional. This is especially true for structures such as the frontal lobes that develop late and whose damage leads not only to cognitive deficits[42] but to specific memory deficits as well.[43,44]

Despite this evidence, I wish to propose that after the late memory system becomes functional, the major changes that occur in memory during the lifespan can be explained best, not by postulating many additional fundamental changes, but by the further maturation and later deterioration of the early and late system, and by the acquisition and loss of cognitive strategies that affect memory performance.[38–40,45] In short, in terms of memory function per se, the major changes that occur are changes in capacity and efficiency, not changes in fundamental memory processes. In addition, the child acquires knowledge both about the world and about how some aspects of memory and cognition work.[45] That knowledge can then be used either directly to help encode and retrieve information or indirectly to create strategies that can serve memory. By contrast, in normal aging there is a mild deterioration of the structures associated with the late memory system[46] as well as a reduction in working memory[47] or mental energy and attentional resources.[48] As a result, the normal elderly person's memory performance is impaired primarily on those tasks of conscious recollection that are effortful[31] and rely primarily on internal generation rather than external environmental support for successful performance.[49] Because the late memory system is not severely compromised, forcing the elderly person to adopt appropriate strategies and providing her with external support either in the form of a simple, easily organized task structure or cues, or both, can often raise her performance to the level of the young.[46,48] Once the late memory system is severely impaired, as in pathological forms of aging that may accompany institutionalization[50] or Alzheimer's disease,[46] these cognitive and environmental supports are of little use. Memory performance becomes more and more dependent on the early system and begins more and more, especially in Alzheimer patients, to resemble the memory processes of infants.

ACKNOWLEDGMENTS

I thank Meredyth Daneman, Howard Gardner, Jill Moscovitch, Dan Schacter, and Sandra Trehub for their very helpful comments. Don McLachlan kindly referred most of the patients to us and acted as a neurological consultant on the projects.

REFERENCES

1. SCHACTER, D. L. & M. MOSCOVITCH. 1984. Infants, amnesics, and dissociable memory systems. *In* Infant Memory. M. Moscovitch, Ed. New Plenum Press. New York.
2. FAGAN, J. F. 1984. Infant memory: history, current trends, relations to cognitive psychology. *In* Infant Memory. M. Moscovitch, Ed. Plenum Press. New York.
3. WERNER, J. S. & M. PERLMUTTER. 1979. Development of visual memory in infants. Adv. Child Behav. Dev. **14:** 1–56.
4. ROVEE-COLLIER, C. K. & J. W. FAGAN. 1981. The retrieval of memory in early infancy. *In* Advances in Infancy Research. L. P. Lipsitt, Ed. Vol. 1. Ablex. Norwood, NJ.
5. PIAGET, J. & B. INHELDER. 1973. Memory and Intelligence. Basic Books. New York.
6. BADDELEY, A. D. 1982. Amnesia: A minimal model and an interpretation. *In* Human Memory and Amnesia. L. S. Cermak, Ed. Lawrence Erlbaum. Hillsdale, NJ.
7. MOSCOVITCH, M. 1982. Multiple dissociations of function in amnesia. *In* Human Memory and Amnesia. L. S. Cermak, Ed. Lawrence Erlbaum Associates. Hillsdale, NJ.
8. CORKIN, S. 1968. Acquisition of motor skill after bilateral medial temporal-lobe excision. Neuropsych. **3:** 255–265.
9. WARRINGTON, E. K. & L. WEISKRANTZ. 1970. Amnesic syndrome: Consolidation or retrieval? Nature **228:** 628–630.
10. GRAF, P., L. R. SQUIRE & G. MANDLER. 1984. The information that amnesic patients do not forget. J. Exp. Psych.: Learn. Mem. Cog. **10:** 164–178.
11. BROOKS, D. N. & A. D. BADDELEY. 1976. What can amnesic patients learn? Neuropsychologia **14:** 111–122.
12. COHEN, N. J. 1984. Amnesia and the distinction between procedural and declarative knowledge. *In* The Neuropsychology of Memory. N. Butters & L. R. Squire, Eds. Guilford Press. New York.
13. MOSCOVITCH, M. 1984. The sufficient conditions for demonstrating preserved memory in amnesia: A task analysis. *In* The Neuropsychology of Memory. N. Butters & L. R. Squire, Eds. Guilford Press. New York.
14. GRAF, P. & D. L. SCHACTER. 1985. Implicit and explicit memory for new associations in normal and amnesic subject. J. Exp. Psych.: Learn. Mem. Log. (In press.)
15. REES-NISHIO, M. 1984. The relation between skin conductance response and memory for emotional and neutral words in normal young and elderly people and in amnesic patients. Doctoral dissertation. University of Toronto. Toronto, Ontario, Canada.
16. CHANG, H-W. & S. E. TREHUB. 1977. Infants' perception of temporal grouping in auditory patterns. Child Dev. **48:** 1666–1670.
17. SQUIRE, L. R., N. J. COHEN & L. NADEL. 1983. The medial temporal region and memory consolidation: A new hypothesis. *In* Memory Consolidation. H. Weingartner & E. Parker, Eds. Lawrence Erlbaum. Hillsdale, NJ.
18. JACOBY, L. L. & D. WITHERSPOON. 1982. Remembering without awareness. Can. J. Psych. **36:** 300–324.

19. TULVING, E., D. L. SCHACTER & H. A. STARK. 1982. Priming effects in word-fragment completion are independent of recognition memory. J. Exp. Psych: Learn. Mem. Cog. **8:** 336–342.
20. JOHNSON, M. 1983. A multiple entry modular memory system. *In* The Psychology of Learning and Motivation. G. H. Bower, Ed. Vol. 17. Academic Press. New York.
21. SCARBOROUGH, D. L., C. CORTESE & H. SCARBOROUGH. 1977. Frequency and repetition effects in lexical memory. J. Exp. Psych: Hum. Percep. Perf. **3:** 1–17.
22. CAMPBELL, B. A. & D. J. STEHOUWER. 1979. Ontogeny of habituation and sensitization in the rat. *In* Ontogeny of Learning and Memory. N. E. Spear & B. A. Campbell, Eds. Erlbaum. Hillsdale, NJ.
23. NADEL, L. & S. ZOLA-MORGAN. 1984. Infantile amnesia: A neurobiological perspective. *In* Infant Memory. M. Moscovitch, Ed. Plenum Press. New York.
24. PETRIDES, M. & S. D. IVERSON. 1976. Cross-modal matching and the primate frontal cortex. Science **192:** 1023–1024.
25. BACHEVALIER, J. & M. MISHKIN. 1982. The development of memories vs habits in infant monkeys. Paper presented to the International Organization of Psychophysiology.
26. MANDLER, J. M. 1984. Representation and recall in infancy. *In* Infant Memory. M. Moscovitch, Ed. Plenum Press. New York.
27. NELSON, K. 1984. The transition from infant to child memory. *In* Infant Memory. M. Moscovitch, Ed. Plenum Press. New York.
28. PIAGET, J. 1952. The Origins of Intelligence in Children. International Universities Press. New York.
29. SOPHIAN, C. 1980. Habituation is not enough: Novelty preferences, search, and memory in infancy. Merrill-Palmer Q. **26:** 239–257.
30. BJORK, E. L. & E. M. CUMMINGS. 1984. Infant search errors: Stage of concept development or stage of memory development. Mem. Cogn. **12:** 1–19.
31. HASHER, L. & R. T. ZACHS. 1979. Automatic and effortful processes in memory. J. Exp. Psych.: Gen. **108:** 356–388.
32. WINOCUR, G. & L. WEISKRANTZ. 1976. An investigation of paired-associate learning in amnesic patients. Neuropsych. **14:** 97–110.
33. BAILLARGEON, R., E. S. SPELKE & S. WASSERMAN. Object permanence in 5-month old infants. Cognition. (In press.)
34. SCHACTER, D. L., J. A. HARBLUK & D. R. MCLACHLAN. 1984. Retrieval without recollection: An experimental analysis of source amnesia. J. Verb. Learn. Verb. Behav. **23:** 593–611.
35. GLISKY, E. L., D. L. SCHACTER & E. TULVING. 1984. Vocabulary learning in amnesia: Method of vanishing cues. Paper presented at the Meeting of the American Psychological Association. Toronto, Canada.
36. CRAIK, F. I. M. & S. TREHUB. 1982. Aging and Cognitive Processes. Plenum Press. New York.
37. POON, L. W. 1980. New Directions in Memory and Aging. Erlbaum. Hillsdale, NJ.
38. BROWN, A. L. 1979. Theories of memory and the problems of development: Activity, growth, and knowledge. *In* Levels of Processing in Human Memory. L. S. Cermak & F. I. M. Craik, Eds. Erlbaum. Hillsdale, NJ.
39. PASCUAL-LEONE, J. 1978. Compounds, confounds, and models in developmental psychology: A reply to Trabasso and Foellinger. J. Exp. Child Psych. **26:** 18–40.
40. CASE, R., M. KURLAND & J. GOLDBERG. 1982. Operational efficiency and the growth of short-term memory span. J. Exp. Child Psych. **33:** 386–404.
41. MOSCOVITCH, J. 1975. How young children represent and reproduce organized visual material: Accounting for difficulty in drawing an array of seriated sticks. Doctoral thesis. University of Pennsylvania. Philadelphia.
42. MILNER, B. 1964. Some effects of frontal lobectomy in man. *In* The Frontal Granular Cortex and Behaviour. J. M. Warren & H. Akert, Eds.: 313–334. McGraw-Hill. New York.
43. MILNER, B. 1982. Some cognitive effects of frontal-lobe lesions in man. Phil. Trans. R. Soc. London **298:** 211–226.

44. PETRIDES, M. & B. MILNER. 1982. Deficits on subject-oriented tasks after frontal- and temporal-lobe lesions in man. Neuropsych. **20:** 249–262.
45. FLAVELL, J. H. 1978. Metacognitive development. *In* Structural-process Theories of Complex Human Behavior. J. M. Scandura & C. J. Brainerd, Eds. Sitjhoff. Leyden. The Netherlands.
46. MOSCOVITCH, M. 1982. A neuropsychological approach to perception and memory in normal and pathological aging. *In* Aging and Cognitive Processes. F. I. M. Craik & S. Trehub, Eds. Plenum Press. New York.
47. RABBITT, P. M. A. 1982. How do old people know what to do next? *In* Aging and Cognitive Processes. F. I. M. Craik & S. E. Trehub, Eds. Plenum Press. New York.
48. CRAIK, F. I. M. & M. BYRD. 1982. Aging and cognitive deficits: The role of attentional resources. *In* Aging and Cognitive Processes. F. I. M. Craik & S. E. Trehub, Eds. Plenum Press. New York.
49. CRAIK, F. I. M. 1983. On the transfer of information from temporary to permanent memory. Phil. Trans. R. Soc. London **302:** 341–359.
50. WINOCUR, G. 1982. Learning and memory deficits in institutionalized and non-institutionalized old people: an analysis of interference effects. *In* Aging and Cognitive Processes. F. I. M. Craik & S. Trehub, Eds. Plenum Press. New York.

Neural Systems of the Non-human Primate Forebrain Implicated in Memory[a]

GARY W. VAN HOESEN

Departments of Anatomy and Neurology
University of Iowa
Iowa City, Iowa 52242

INTRODUCTION

The word forebrain is a short-hand term used to designate those parts of the embryonic prosencephalon that later in development form the telencephalon and diencephalon. In the adult, it includes such structures as the cerebral cortex, limbic structures, basal ganglia, thalamus, and hypothalamus—the bulk of the neural contents of the cranium. Terms such as basal forebrain have gained popularity in recent years, but have a much more specific meaning. The basal forebrain refers to both cortical and subcortical structures located along the midline and base of the hemisphere ventral to the caudate nucleus, putamen, and globus pallidus. Such structures as the septum, nucleus accumbens, ventral pallidum, olfactory tubercle, olfactory cortex, substantia innominata, nucleus basalis of Meynert, diagonal band nuclei, and amygdala form the basal forebrain. The majority of these have a telencephalic origin, but they interdigitate with structures of diencephalic origin, and in some instances their lineage is yet to be ascertained.

Historically, much of the literature dealing with the neural correlates of memory has focused on a single or a small set of forebrain structures. In the absence of key neuroanatomical facts, a neural systems approach has not been possible. The list of anatomical structures that seem to play a role in memory has grown steadily in recent years and now includes many different parts of the forebrain. The hippocampus, parahippocampal gyrus, amygdala, anterior thalamic nucleus, dorsomedial thalamic nucleus, midline thalamic nuclei, mammillary body, and most recently, the nucleus basalis of Meynert would constitute the major items of the list. While individual structures undoubtedly play critical and unique roles with regard to certain aspects of memory, it is no longer tenable to view them as isolated entities. Indeed, much has been learned about the connections of all forebrain structures implicated in memory and a great deal is now known as well about their mutual anatomical interrelationships. The latter forms a basis for several neural systems related to memory.

A major feature of this newly acquired knowledge, which applies to all of the structures listed above, concerns their relationship with the association cortices. This previously unappreciated aspect of cortical anatomy is essential for understanding the neural basis of memory, since the association cortices play a dual role with regard to this aspect of behavior. On the one hand, they are instrumental in processes pertaining to the sensory analysis and integration of ongoing environmental events, while on the other hand they are repositories for the less labile and preserved abstractions of these same events. Thus, their output, whether it be to other forebrain structures that play a

[a]Supported by National Institutes of Health grants NS 14944 and NS POI 19632.

role in memory or to other areas, bears at least two marks: one that relates to current sensory events and another that reflects past reactions to the same or similar events. This report surveys some of the major neural systems of forebrain structures in higher mammals implicated in memory. These include the hippocampal formation, parahippocampal gyrus, amygdala, dorsomedial thalamus, and the nucleus basalis of Meynert. Particular attention is focused on interactions with the association and limbic cortices.

HIPPOCAMPAL FORMATION AND PARAHIPPOCAMPAL GYRUS

The hippocampal formation comprises three allocortical areas: the Ammonic pyramids that form the CA zones of the hippocampus (CA1, CA2, CA3); the dentate gyrus, including the so-called CA4 neurons that occupy its hilum; and the subicular cortices.[1] The latter includes the subiculum proper, a true allocortical zone, and two periallocortical zones, the presubiculum and parasubiculum. These latter two areas are associated closely with the hippocampal formation and have continuity with the subiculum proper in their deep layers. However, since they are multilayered periallocortical areas related also to the entorhinal cortex of the parahippocampal gyrus, it is most appropriate to include them with this part of the temporal cortex. Thus, they should be viewed as forming the medial boundary of the parahippocampal gyrus.

Cajal and his student, Lorente de Nó, published many pioneering observations on the cytoarchitecture, fiberarchitecture, and connections of the hippocampal formation. These studies represent some of their finer achievements.[2-4] This work led to a conceptualization of the hippocampal formation that persisted for many decades. It is only in recent years that their seminal findings have been embellished. Their major connectional contributions and a revised and more contemporary version are shown in FIGURE 1. The major input to the hippocampal formation was thought to arrive via two large white matter pathways, the fimbria-fornix system and what Cajal termed the temporo-ammonic or perforant pathway. These afferents were observed to terminate on the pyramidal cells of the hippocampus and the granule cells of the dentate gyrus. A two-part sequential series of intrinsic connections also was described. This entailed first, a massive projection from the dentate gyrus granule cells to the base of the apical dendrites of the CA3 pyramidal cells. This system, which sends no axons outside of the hippocampal formation, was termed the mossy fiber system. The second major intrinsic pathway, known as the Schaffer collateral system, was observed to arise from the CA3 pyramids and terminate on the dendrites of the adjacent CA1 pyramids.

The view that emerged from these studies of hippocampal anatomy held that input would arrive via the fimbria-fornix or perforant pathway and activate the pyramidal neurons directly, or indirectly, via the dentate gyrus and intrinsic pathways. Pyramidal axons entered the alveus and eventually the fimbria-fornix system and conveyed hippocampal output to other, largely subcortical, structures. There are no errors in this logic, and indeed, nearly all aspects of Cajal's careful research observations have been verified in more recent experimental neuroanatomical studies. He failed, however, to fully document an important extension of the intrinsic circuitry of the hippocampal formation, namely, CA1 projections to the adjacent subicular cortices.[5,6] The neurons that form this cortex, and not the hippocampal pyramids per se, are responsible for a large amount of hippocampal output[7,8] and nearly all of its diversity with regard to influencing other brain areas. For example, the CA3 pyramids project mainly to the septum in terms of extrinsic projections, although they also give rise to major intrinsic and commissural inter- and intrahippocampal projections.[9] With the exception of commissural projections, this is somewhat true for CA1 pyramidal neurons as well. However, the neurons that form the subicular cortices, and to a lesser extent those of the CA1 zone, have extensive extrinsic projections and divide hippocampal output into two major components; one to a variety of cortical areas and another to a variety of subcortical structures such as the basal forebrain, amygdala, thalamus, and hypothalamus.[7,10-12]

Another feature of hippocampal anatomy not described by early anatomists concerns the issue of afferent input, and in particular, the input to the entorhinal cortex. These investigators saw axons entering the entorhinal cortex, but heavy reliance on the Golgi method precluded ascertaining the exact origin. This meant that

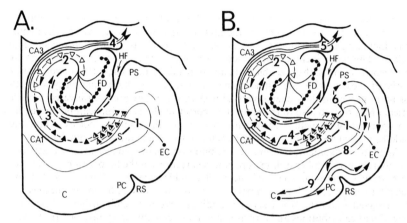

FIGURE 1. (A) depicts the major connectional anatomy of the hippocampal formation in cross-section as revealed by Cajal. Note that the entorhinal cortex (EC) projects via the perforant pathway (1) to the hippocampus (CA1-CA3) and fascia dentata (FD) or dentate gyrus. The latter's output, the mossy fibers (2), terminate on the CA3 pyramids. These give rise to the Schaffer collaterals (3), which terminate on the CA1 pyramids. Axons of CA1-CA3 exit the hippocampal formation via the fimbria-fornix (4). (B) depicts a partial update of Cajal's observations. Note that the CA1 pyramids project to the adjacent subiculum (4). This cortex and the CA pyramids project to the septum via the fornix (5), but it is largely subicular projections that course to the anterior thalamus and mammillary bodies. The subicular cortex also projects to several other cortical areas; the presubiculum (PS), the entorhinal cortex (EC), the perirhinal cortex (PC), and other parts of the cortex (C). These are shown schematically in pathways 6-9. The subicular cortices account largely for the diversity of hippocampal output (HF = hippocampal fissure and RS = rhinal sulcus).

the input to the major source of afferents to the hippocampal formation was left uncharacterized. It has been shown in recent studies that the entorhinal cortex receives powerful projection from many cortical areas in the temporal lobe[13-17] and from subcortical structures, such as the amygdala and midline thalamus.[18-20] It is important to note that amygdaloid input is derived from subdivisions of this structure that receive both limbic cortical input as well as input from association cortices located in both the frontal and temporal lobes.[21-25] Additionally, these same nuclei receive direct or indirect hypothalamic[25] and basal forebrain input.[26,27] Thus, input to the entorhinal cortex is extensive. It arises largely from the cortices that form the limbic lobe (the amygdala and the midline thalamus). In terms of cortex, proisocortical areas such as the posterior parahippocampal, cingulate, temporal polar, and posterior orbitofrontal cortices, and periallocortical areas such as the retrosplenial, presubicular, and parasubicular cortices are the major contributors. These transitional cortical areas, interposed between the allocortex and neocortex, receive major projections from both sensory specific and multimodal association cortices.[28-30] Altogether, it is clear that the entorhinal cortices receive potentially a significant portion of the sensory output generated by forebrain structures and that this includes both interoceptive and exteroceptive information. In structural terms, it could be argued that the entorhinal cortex would be privy to or receive a digest of nearly all neural reactions that the organism responds to both internally as well as externally and many of the combinations and permutations that could result.

Comment

The hippocampal formation is the focal point for a major forebrain neural system that is interconnected with the sensory specific association cortices and the multimodal association cortices. Unquestionably, this is a widespread system that involves much of the cortical mantle. As mentioned, the cortices that form the limbic lobe in general, and the amygdala and posterior parahippocampal area in particular, are the major mediators of critical links within this system. They receive input from the various association cortices and either project directly to the hippocampal formation or first to the entorhinal cortex which then projects to the hippocampal formation. The most compact part of this latter system is the perforant pathway, the major output system of the entorhinal cortex. It mediates a powerful excitatory input to the hippocampal formation that culminates in extrinsic output to the septum via the fimbria-fornix or intrinsic output to the subicular cortices. These latter areas then project to several basal forebrain areas, including the amygdala, various diencephalic nuclei, and many parts of the limbic lobe. The cortices that form the limbic lobe complete the circuitry of this neural system by projecting powerfully to the association cortices.[31] Some of these relationships are summarized schematically in FIGURE 2.

AMYGDALA

As cited in the previous section, the amygdala receives a powerful input from the cerebral cortex and from a host of subcortical structures of both diencephalic and mesencephalic origin. The latter includes such structures as the hypothalamus, periaqueductal gray, peripeduncular nucleus, ventral tegmental area, supramammillary nucleus, and various midline thalamic nuclei.[25,26,32]

Unlike the hippocampal formation, whose input is derived largely from periallocortical and proisocortical limbic lobe areas that receive input from the association cortices, many of the latter project directly to the amygdala without relays in the limbic lobe. For example, the visual association cortices of the lateral temporal neocortex, the so-called inferotemporal cortices, send direct projections to the lateral amygdaloid nucleus and to some extent the laterobasal amygdaloid nucleus.[21-23,29,33] Some of these investigators have also shown that the auditory association cortex of the superior temporal gyrus also projects directly to the lateral amygdaloid nucleus. Input related to somatic sensation also converges on this nucleus from the insular cortex.[34]

Although neocortical input from various association cortices constitutes a major source of input to the lateral amygdaloid nucleus, it would be erroneous to characterize corticoamygdaloid input as derived largely from the neocortex. Indeed, the proisocortices, periallocortices, and allocortices make a major contribution in this respect.[24] For example, much of the lateral nucleus receives input from the insular, temporal polar, and orbitofrontal cortices. This terminates largely in the medial part of the lateral nucleus. The basal complex of the amygdala, consisting of the laterobasal, accessory basal, and mediobasal nuclei, receives cortical projections that are derived almost exclusively from the proisocortices and the periallocortices. These nuclei compose the largest area of the amygdala, and thus, limbic lobe input must be regarded as the major source of cortical input to this structure. The accessory basal nucleus, for example, receives strong projections from the temporal polar cortex, the insular cortex, the

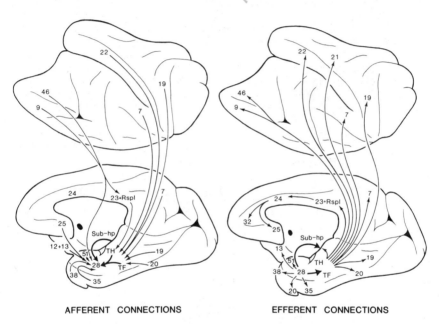

AFFERENT CONNECTIONS   EFFERENT CONNECTIONS

FIGURE 2. This depicts the major afferent and efferent connections of the parahippocampal cortices on lateral and medial views of the monkey hemisphere. The periallocortical and proisocortical parahippocampal cortices (areas 28, TF and TH) are major staging areas for hippocampal input from the association and other limbic cortices, and a major mediator of hippocampal output to the cortex. Cortical areas are after Brodmann and Bonin and Bailey (Rspl = retrosplenial cortex and Sub-hp = subicular and hippocampal cortices).

medial frontal cortex, and to some extent, the orbitofrontal cortex. The mediobasal nucleus is not well characterized in terms of input, but receives strong projections from the perirhinal and subicular cortices.[10] The laterobasal nucleus receives input from many of the cortical areas listed above, but additionally, is characterized by having a major input from the anterior cingulate cortex. The subiculum and entorhinal cortices also project to part of the basal amygdaloid complex.

The central amygdaloid nucleus is unusual in the sense that it receives input derived from all types of cortex. For example, it receives input from the lateral temporal isocortex, the temporal polar, orbitofrontal and insular proisocortex, the entorhinal periallocortex, and the periamygdaloid and primary olfactory allocortex.

The superficial nuclei of the amygdala, such as the medial nucleus and the various cortical nuclei receive input largely from allocortical origin such as the subicular and periamygdaloid cortices.[24] Some of the major cortical relationships of the amygdala in terms of input are summarized in FIGURES 3 and 4.

For many years it was believed that the major input and output relationships of the amygdala were with the hypothalamus. Such connections of course, do exist,[25] but the diversity of amygdaloid output is far more extensive than appreciated previously. For example, the lateral nucleus and some components of the basal complex project strongly to the entorhinal cortex,[35] the major source of cortical input to the hippocampal formation. Additionally, the basal amygdaloid complex has strong reciprocal interconnections with the subiculum, the major source of hippocampal output.[10,35] From these studies it is clear that the amygdala is very much interrelated with the hippocampal formation in structural terms and that these two temporal bedfellows undoubtedly influence each other.

Non-hypothalamic subcortical projections arise from several amygdaloid nuclei and link this structure with many parts of the neuraxis. Of special interest here are powerful projections to parts of the basal forebrain, including the nucleus basalis of Meynert.[36] Additional non-hypothalamic subcortical projections course to the dorsomedial thalamic nucleus[37-39] and to several autonomic centers in the brainstem.[36,40]

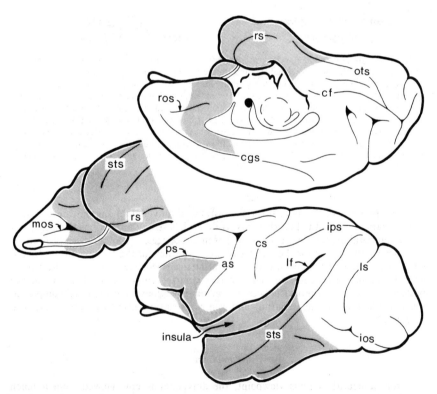

FIGURE 3. This depicts the topography of frontal, temporal, and insular cortical areas that give rise to direct corticoamygdaloid projections in the monkey.

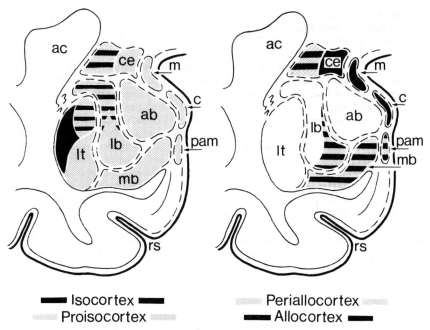

■■ Isocortex ■■   ▦ Periallocortex ▦
▦ Proisocortex ▦   ■■ Allocortex ■■

FIGURE 4. The left side of the illustration shows the topography of iso- or neocortical (black) and proisocortical limbic lobe (shaded) input to the amygdala derived from anterograde tracing studies in the monkey. Note the overlap laterally and that the amygdala as a whole is dominated by limbic lobe input. In fact, only the lateral part of the lateral nucleus receives iso- or neocortical input exclusively. The right side of the illustration shows the topography of periallocortical and allocortical input to the amygdala. Note that its distribution overlaps substantially and is shifted to medial parts of the amygdala (ab = accessory basal nucleus, ac = anterior commissure, c = corticoamygdaloid area, ce = central nucleus, lb = laterobasal nucleus, lt = lateral nucleus, m = medial nucleus, mb = mediobasal nucleus, pam = periamygdaloid cortex, and rs = rhinal sulcus).

Perhaps, some of the more surprising aspects of amygdaloid anatomy described in recent years concerns the fact that this structure has strong projections to many parts of the temporal association, insular, and frontal cortices.[34,37,38,41-43] These projections have been well-studied for the latter two areas, but not for the former. In the frontal lobe, these projections end on certain parts of the isocortices that form the frontal granular cortex, the frontal agranular cortex, and the cingulate, medial frontal, and posterior orbitofrontal proisocortices. Powerful projections from the basal complex of the amygdala to the neostriatum and ventral striatum also have been described recently.[44]

Comment

From a neural systems viewpoint, the amygdala is now viewed from a much broader perspective than in previous years. The more classic interrelationships with the hypothalamus and olfactory system, although largely valid, are only two of many unique features that characterize its anatomy. For example, the amygdala has powerful direct interconnections with much of the anterior cortex of the limbic lobe and with neocortical areas of both the frontal and temporal lobes. Additional smaller projections have been reported to terminate in the premotor cortices and limbic lobe area 24, both of which project directly to the supplementary motor cortex. Additional projections connect the amygdala with the neostriatum and ventral striatum. Certain amygdaloid nuclei also project strongly to basal forebrain areas like the nucleus basalis of Meynert whose axons provide a powerful cholinergic input to the cortex in general, but especially to the premotor, motor, and somatosensory cortices. Descending amygdaloid projections from the central amygdaloid nucleus also provide input to autonomic centers in the brainstem. While much of the input to the amygdala, particularly from subcortical areas, cannot be characterized well in functional terms, this is not the case for amygdaloid output. Overall, it can be concluded that amygdaloid output is very much directed toward the origin of effector systems that influence motor, endocrine, and autonomic areas along the full extent of the cerebral neuraxis. In this regard, it is very much unlike the hippocampal formation whose output to such areas is either less strong or more indirect, and instead shifted more toward the association cortices. The amygdala, however, is by no means isolated from these neural systems, since it has reciprocal connections with selective parts of the association and limbic cortices and with both the major source of input to the hippocampal formation, the entorhinal cortex, and its major output area, the subiculum. Additionally, the basal amygdaloid complex has direct projections to a major thalamic association nucleus, the dorsomedial complex, and the former receives a strong subicular projection.

NUCLEUS BASALIS OF MEYNERT

The neurons that form the nucleus basalis of Meynert have attracted substantial attention since retrograde tracing studies have shown consistently that they project to the cerebral cortex.[45-49] Such projections had been suggested in earlier ablation experiments, but the magnitude of this projection was not appreciated. It was not demonstrated clearly that probably all of the nucleus basalis of Meynert projects to the cortex and all parts of it. While these findings were of interest in relation to previous physiologic observations, they took on added significance with the demonstration (FIGURE 5) that the majority of these neurons contain cholinergic enzymes and in fact provide the major source of cholinergic input to the cortex.[48,50] Thus, they mirror the projections of their counterparts in the diagonal band nuclei and medial septum that project to the allocortices of the hippocampal formation. Of substantial additional interest in the recent literature is the observation that these neurons are depleted in Alzheimer's disease and the suggestion that this may form the etiological basis for the dementia and memory impairment that forms the clinical hallmark of this disorder.[51] It seems well established that cortical levels of acetylcholine drop precipitously in Alzheimer's disease,[52] and this may be due to alterations in the nucleus basalis of Meynert.

The neurons that form the nucleus basalis are large, hyperchromatic, multipolar, and fusiform-shaped cells that lie among the many ascending and descending limbic, hypothalamic, and brainstem pathways that course through the basal forebrain. Part of the nucleus is found within the substantia innominata, although in reality, cholinergic neurons span the anterior-posterior expanse of the ventral surface of the hemisphere all the way from the septum to the midbrain. They have a lateral extension as well that follows the course of the anterior commissure into the temporal lobe.[47,50] Scattered acetylcholinesterase and choline acetyltransferase positive neurons are also found within the internal and external medullary fibers of the globus pallidus, in the lateral hypothalamus, and in the dorsal parts of various amygdaloid nuclei. It seems likely that a disease process selectively affecting such widespread and scattered neurons must in all likelihood affect membrane or cytologic characteristics that are unusually unique to these neurons.

The output of the nucleus basalis to the cortex has been well-characterized in the rat and monkey. These studies reveal that a rather rigid topography exists with regard

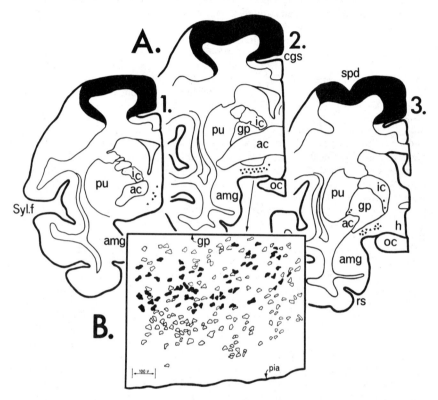

FIGURE 5. (A) Three coronal sections through a horseradish peroxidase injection (blackened area) in areas 4 and 6 of the rhesus monkey. Triangles show the distribution of retrogradely labeled cells in the nucleus basalis of Meynert. (B) Camera lucida drawing from section 2 showing cellular profiles of labeled cells. Blackened profiles denote nucleus basalis neurons positive for both retrogradely transported horseradish peroxidase and acetylcholinesterase. (ac = anterior commissure, amg = amygdala, cgs = cingulate sulcus, gp = globus pallidus, h = hypothalamus, ic = internal capsule, oc = optic chiasm, pu = putamen, rs = rhinal sulcus, spd = superior precentral dimple, Syl. f. = Sylvian fissure.) (From Mesulam, M. M. & G. W. Van Hoesen. 1976. *Brain Research* **109:** 152–157. With permission from Elsevier Biomedical Division.)

to where in the cortical mantle they terminate.[49,50,53,54] Additionally, it has been demonstrated recently that the nucleus basalis projects to the basal complex of the amygdala.[26,27] However, beyond these observations, little else is known about the efferent connections of the nucleus basalis of Meynert, and there remains a fundamental need for further study of this in experimental neuroanatomy. Suggestive evidence has been provided that nucleus basalis axons project at least as far caudally as the midbrain.[46]

The input to the nucleus basalis of Meynert is better understood. In terms of cortex, it has been shown that it receives projections from only a small percentage of the cortical areas to which it sends axons.[55] These include such areas as the olfactory, orbitofrontal, anterior insular, temporal polar, entorhinal, and medial temporal cortices—all components of the limbic lobe. Subcortical projections to the nucleus basalis arise from the septum, nucleus accumbens, hypothalamus, amygdala, preoptic nucleus, and from the peripeduncular nucleus of the midbrain.[47,56-58]

Comment

From a neural systems viewpoint, many statements can be made about the unusual connectivity of the nucleus basalis of Meynert. For example, the widespread projections to the cortex and the fact that acetylcholine serves as the transmitter for these projections are of fundamental importance. These facts put these neurons in a pharmacologically specific class much like serotonergic neurons in the raphe complex, noradrenergic neurons in the locus coeruleus, and dopaminergic neurons in the ventral tegmental area.[48] Like these neurons, many of their projections are not reciprocated by projections from the cortex they innervate. The input to nucleus basalis neurons seems topographically organized and rather specific. At least two investigations have reported afferent input that seemingly "picks out" the clusters of nucleus basalis neurons. Some of these originate in the amygdala and may provide a highly specific, albeit indirect, manner for this structure to exert its influence on widespread parts of the cortical mantle. These projections arise from amygdaloid nuclei that receive intrinsic amygdaloid projections, suggesting that, at least in so far as the amygdala is concerned, its output to the nucleus basalis reflects output related to much of the structure. In this context, it should not be overlooked that the subiculum of the hippocampal formation projects both to the basal complex of the amygdala and to other basal forebrain areas that project to the nucleus basalis. Thus, a highly synthesized output from the hippocampal formation seems to be a likelihood. On these grounds and on those that demonstrate limbic cortical input, it would seem indisputable that the major input to the nucleus basalis is from nearly the entirety of what one thinks of as limbic system. The nucleus basalis of Meynert seems uninfluenced directly by the major part of the cortex to which it projects, and only indirectly influenced after the whole sequence of cortico-limbic connections is retraced.

Finally, it is important to highlight the fact that the nucleus basalis of Meynert receives direct projections from the hypothalamus. These are incompletely understood, but suggest at least a structural basis for the theoretical belief that the internal state of the organism can indirectly influence both the motor and the sensory manner by which the organism interacts with its external environment. Such well-documented behavioral observations have not had strong anatomical backing in the past. In this regard, however, it should be noted that several limbic structures receive hypothalamic projections and project back to the cortex. Thus, the nucleus basalis of Meynert might not be unique in this regard.

DORSOMEDIAL THALAMIC NUCLEUS

The dorsomedial thalamic nucleus has been implicated in a host of behavioral changes in humans including visuo-spatial processing, attention, dementia, aphasia, temporal disorientation, and memory. Some authors attribute damage to this nucleus as the etiological basis for the debilitating cognitive changes that occur in the alcoholic-Korsakoff syndrome.[59] Evidence from penetrating wounds[60] and thalamic infarcts[61] to some extent support this contention despite the radically different nature of the process that creates the lesion. The literature regarding prefrontal lobotomy would also seem of relevance here, since one would think that this surgical treatment would cause extensive retrograde cellular changes in the dorsomedial thalamic nucleus. However, only a subset of the behavioral changes listed above was observed in individuals having this procedure, and proportedly, these were confined largely to the realm of personality changes.

The dorsomedial thalamic nucleus is a large midline association nucleus that has powerful interconnections with the prefrontal granular association cortex.[62] From a cytoarchitectural viewpoint it is a complex nucleus composed of at least three cytoarchitecturally different regions. These form partially concentric and adjacent subdivisions, with the third ventricle at their core and along their dorsal surface. From the midline, and extending laterally, the subdivisions are named the pars magnocellularis, pars parvocellularis, and pars multiformis.[63] In general terms, they have topographically organized reciprocal connections with the prefrontal cortex in the non-human primate.[62,64,65] For example, the pars magnocellularis, the most medial subdivision of the dorsomedial nucleus, projects to and receives projections from the posterior orbital, anterior cingulate, and medial frontal cortex. The pars parvocellularis projects to and receives projections from the prefrontal association cortex dorsal and ventral to the principal sulcus and the anteriormost parts of the orbitofrontal cortex. The pars multiformis is the lateralmost subdivision of the dorsomedial nucleus and sends projections to and receives projections from the periarcuate cortex in the anterior bank of the arcuate sulcus.

At the outset, it must be stated that the connections of the dorsomedial nucleus are understood poorly, with, of course, the exception of those to the prefrontal cortex. In fact, known input and output relationships with other structures are decidedly sparse in comparison to the motor and sensory nuclei of the thalamus and even other association nuclei, such as the pulvinar.

Some evidence, however, is accumulating that enables at least a partial characterization of this structure. For example, early ablation-degeneration experiments identified another cortical projection to this large nucleus from the lateral temporal cortex.[21] Additional evidence suggests that certain cortical areas of the limbic lobe, such as the anterior cingulate cortex, have connections with the dorsomedial nucleus.[66] This is of some interest since this part of the cingulate cortex (Brodmann's area 24) sends axons into descending motor pathways and directly to the supplementary motor cortex.

A direct input from the amygdala to the dorsomedial nucleus has been known for over twenty years. Recent autoradiographic experiments buttress and extend these findings.[18,38,39] These projections arise from the basal complex of the amygdala and terminate in the more medial parts of the dorsomedial nucleus. The mediobasal nucleus seems to be the primary focus for this projection, although other basal nuclei (laterobasal and accessory basal) appear to contribute as well. These axons course largely via the ventroamygdalofugal pathway and the inferior thalamic peduncle. Curiously, the temporal cortical projections to the dorsomedial nucleus and those that arise from the amygdala are not reciprocated by thalamocortical or thalamoamygdaloid projections. Additional input from the ventral pallidum, substantia nigra, septum, superior colliculus, and hypothalamus have been reported.

Comment

Anatomically, the neural systems of the dorsomedial thalamic nucleus are the least well-known of forebrain structures implicated in memory. The position of this nucleus ventral to two large fiber systems, the fimbria-fornix and corpus callosum, its encasement within the internal medullary lamina of the thalamus, and the fact that the mammillothalamic tract traverses its ventral parts, undoubtedly has discouraged experimental study. Therefore, attention is focused squarely on the amygdalothalamic and temporothalamic projections since they clearly link the dorsomedial nucleus with temporal structures known to play a role in some aspects of memory. For example, the lateral temporal cortex, the so-called inferotemporal cortices, has been characterized as playing a mnemonic role in certain perceptual learning tasks. Also, the mediobasal amygdaloid nucleus, which contributes strongly to the amygdalothalamic projection, is a direct recipient of subicular output from the hippocampal formation.[10] Finally, recent anatomical findings reveal that the frontal association cortices that receive powerful input from the dorsomedial nucleus themselves receive projections from the hippocampal formation and project to the cortex around the rhinal sulcus, which, in turn, projects directly to the subiculum.

The findings themselves may be sufficient to implicate the dorsomedial thalamic nucleus in at least some aspects of memory. However, a cautionary note is worth sounding. Several midline nuclei of the thalamus project directly to the hippocampal formation, entorhinal cortices, and amygdala. These include the nucleus reuniens, the paracentral nucleus, and the thalamic paraventricular nucleus. These are likely involved in hemorrhagic and non-hemorrhagic infarcts to the midline thalamus and even in penetrating wounds. Their involvement in the alcoholic-Korsakoff patient seems likely as well since these nuclei lie immediately anterior to the dorsomedial nucleus. Until more is known about the neural associations of the latter, it might be worthwhile to stress midline thalamic damage in conjunction with memory impairments rather than implicating a single nucleus for the behavioral changes.

CONCLUSIONS

It is obvious that a substantial amount is known regarding the neural connections of forebrain structures implicated in memory. For example, with regard to all such structures, there is now a reasonable understanding of how they are connected with those parts of the cerebral cortex activated by events in the sensory world. This varies considerably in its directness, with some structures such as the amygdala receiving direct projections from modality-specific sensory association cortices, and others like the nucleus basalis of Meynert, receiving cortical input from only limbic lobe areas. Many of the latter, however, receive either sensory specific association or multimodal association projections. The issue of multimodal input itself is an interesting one, and nearly all structures implicated in the structural basis of memory receive projections from cortical areas that receive more than one sensory input. This is particularly evident in the case of the dorsomedial thalamic nucleus, which receives projections from multimodal areas in the frontal lobe, and the hippocampal formation, which receives input from multimodal areas of the superior temporal sulcus and posterior parahippocampal cortices.

Likewise, there is now a reasonable understanding of the efferent connections of forebrain structures implicated in memory including those directed back to the cerebral cortex. As with the afferent connections of these structures, substantial variations in directness exist. For example, the nucleus basalis of Meynert has extensive projections to nearly all parts of the cerebral cortex, while the dorsomedial thalamic nucleus projects exclusively to the frontal granular cortex and the anterior parts of the limbic lobe. The latter is true for the amygdala as well, but frontal projections from this structure appear not to reach the dorsal prefrontal cortex. Additionally, amygdaloid projections also course to the insular cortex and to the association cortices in the anterior parts of the temporal lobe. The output of the hippocampal formation is mediated largely via the subiculum and to some extent the CA1 sector of the hippocampal formation. These projections terminate largely in the cortex of the limbic lobe, before widespread projections from the latter back to the association cortices.

Finally, a more complete understanding of interconnectivity between structures implicated in memory now exists. Much of this has been known, and has formed a significant portion of classic limbic system teaching, but new facts gathered in recent years greatly embellish the picture. For example, the demonstration of interconnectivity between the amygdala and hippocampal formation has provided at last a structural underpinning for many previous physiological findings that suggested such a relationship. These are strong connections that involve principally the basal complex and both the entorhinal cortex and subiculum. Other connections of possible major importance entail amygdaloid projections to the basal forebrain and, particularly, to the nucleus basalis of Meynert. They arise from various parts of the basal amygdaloid complex as well as from the central amygdaloid nucleus, a part of the amygdala that receives major intrinsic amygdaloid projections. Finally, although amygdaloid projections directly to the dorsomedial thalamic nucleus have been known for several years, recent investigations have pinpointed the exact cells of origin within the amygdala. Interestingly, these arise from those parts of the basal amygdaloid complex that receive a strong direct projection from the hippocampal formation and an indirect hippocampal projection via the entorhinal cortex.

ACKNOWLEDGMENTS

The author thanks Dr. A. R. Damasio for many thoughtful discussions of this topic and L. J. Kromer and P. Reimann for editorial and photographic assistance.

REFERENCES

1. BLACKSTAD, T. W. 1956. Commissural connections of the hippocampal region of the rat, with specific reference to their mode of termination. J. Comp. Neurol. 105: 417–538.
2. CAJAL, S. RAMÓN Y. 1901. Trabajos del laboratorio de investigaciones biologicas de la universidad de Madrid. Tomo I: 1,141,159,189. In Studies on the Cerebral Cortex. L. Kraft, Ed. and Transl. 1955. Yearbook Publ., Inc. Chicago.
3. LORENTE DE NÓ, R. 1933. Studies on the structure of the cerebral cortex. I. The area entorhinalis. J. Psychol. Neurol. 45: 381–438.
4. LORENTE DE NÓ, R. 1934. Studies on the structure of the cerebral cortex. II. Continuation of the study of the ammonic system. J. Psychol. Neurol. 46: 113–177.
5. HJORTH-SIMONSEN, A. 1973. Some intrinsic connections of the hippocampus in the rat: An experimental analysis. J. Comp. Neurol. 147: 145–162.
6. ANDERSEN, P., B. H. BLAND & J. D. DUDAR. 1973. Organization of the hippocampal output. Exp. Brain Res. 17: 152–168.
7. SWANSON, L. W. & W. M. COWAN. 1975. Hippocampo-hypothalamic connections: Origin in subicular cortex, not Ammon's horn. Science 189: 303–304.
8. MEIBACH, R. C. & A. SIEGEL. 1975. The origin of fornix fibers which project to the mammillary bodies of the rat: A horseradish peroxidase study. Brain Res. 88: 518–522.
9. SWANSON, L. W. & W. M. COWAN. 1977. An autoradiographic study of the organization of the efferent connections of the hippocampal formation in the rat. J. Comp. Neurol. 172(1): 49–84.

10. ROSENE, D. L. & G. W. VAN HOESEN. 1977. Hippocampal efferents reach widespread
     areas of the cerebral cortex and amygdala in the rhesus monkey. Science 198: 315–317.
11. SWANSON, L. W., J. M. WYSS & W. M. COWAN. 1978. An autoradiographic study of the
     organization of intrahippocampal association pathways in the rat. J. Comp. Neurol.
     181(4): 681–716.
12. SORENSON, K. E. & M. T. SHIPLEY. 1979. Projections from the subiculum to the deep layers
     of the ipsilateral presubicular and entorhinal cortices in the guinea pig. J. Comp. Neurol.
     188: 313–334.
13. VAN HOESEN, G. W., D. N. PANDYA & N. BUTTERS. 1972. Cortical afferents to the
     entorhinal cortex of the rhesus monkey. Science 175: 1471–1473.
14. VAN HOESEN, G. W. & D. N. PANDYA. 1975. Some connections of the entorhinal (area 28)
     and perirhinal (area 35) cortices of the rhesus monkey. II. Efferent connections. Brain
     Res. 95: 39–59.
15. SHIPLEY, M. T. 1975. The topographic and laminar organization of the presubiculum's
     projection to the ipsi- and contralateral entorhinal cortex in the guinea pig. J. Comp.
     Neurol. 160: 127–146.
16. VAN HOESEN, G. W., D. L. ROSENE & M.-M. MESULAM. 1979. Subicular input from
     temporal cortex in the rhesus monkey. Science 205: 608–610.
17. AMARAL, D. G., R. INSAUSTI & W. M. COWAN. 1983. Evidence for a direct projection from
     the superior temporal gyrus to the entorhinal cortex in the monkey. Brain Res.
     275: 263–277.
18. KRETTEK, J. E. & J. L. PRICE. 1974. Projections from the amygdala to the perirhinal and
     entorhinal cortices and the subiculum. Brain Res. 71: 150–154.
19. HERKENHAM, M. 1978. The connections of the nucleus reuniens thalami: Evidence for a
     direct thalamo-hippocampal pathway in the rat. J. Comp. Neurol. 177: 589–610.
20. AMARAL, D. G. & W. M. COWAN. 1980. Subcortical afferents to the hippocampal
     formation in the monkey. J. Comp. Neurol 189: 573–591.
21. WHITLOCK, D. G. & W. J. H. NAUTA. 1956. Subcortical projections from the temporal
     neocortex in Macaca mulatta. J. Comp. Neurol. 106: 183–212.
22. HERZOG, A. G. & G. W. VAN HOESEN. 1976. Temporal neocortical afferent connections to
     the amygdala in the rhesus monkey. Brain Res. 115: 57–69.
23. TURNER, B. H., M. MISHKIN & M. KNAPP. 1980. Organization of the amygdalopetal
     projections from modality-specific cortical association areas in the monkey. J. Comp.
     Neurol. 191: 515–543.
24. VAN HOESEN, G. W. 1981. The different distribution, diversity and sprouting of cortical
     projections to the amygdala in the rhesus monkey. In The Amygdaloid Complex. Y. Ben
     Ari, Ed.: 77–90. Elsevier/North Holland. New York.
25. AMARAL, D. G., R. B. VEAZEY & W. M. COWAN. 1982. Some observations on hypothala-
     mo-amygdaloid connections in the monkey. Brain Res. 252: 13–27.
26. AGGLETON, J. P., M. J. BURTON & R. E. PASSINGHAM. 1980. Cortical and subcortical
     afferents to the amygdala of the rhesus monkey (Macaca mulatta). Brain Res. 190: 347–
     368.
27. WOOLF, N. J. & L. L. BUTCHER. 1982. Cholinergic projections to the basolateral amygdala:
     A combined Evans blue and acetylcholinesterase analysis. Brain Res. Bull. 8: 751–763.
28. PANDYA, D. N. & H. G. J. M. KUYPERS. 1969. Cortico-cortical connections in the rhesus
     monkey. Brain Res. 13: 13–36.
29. JONES, E. G. & T. P. S. POWELL. 1970. An anatomical study of converging sensory
     pathways within the cerebral cortex of the monkey. Brain 93: 793–820.
30. SELTZER, B. & D. N. PANDYA. 1976. Some cortical projections to the parahippocampal area
     in the rhesus monkey. Exp. Neurol. 50: 146–160.
31. VAN HOESEN, G. W. 1982. The primate parahippocampal gyrus: New insights regarding its
     cortical connections. Trends Neurosci. 5: 345–350.
32. MEHLER, W. R. 1980. Subcortical afferent connections of the amygdala in the monkey. J.
     Comp. Neurol. 190: 733–762.
33. KLINGER, J. & P. GLOOR. 1960. The connections of the amygdala and of the anterior
     temporal cortex in the human brain. J. Comp. Neurol. 115: 333–369.

34. MUFSON, E. J., M.-M. MESULUM & D. N. PANDYA. 1981. Insular interconnections with the amygdala in the rhesus monkey. Neurosci. 6(7): 1231–1248.
35. KRETTEK, J. E. & J. L. PRICE. 1977. Projections from the amygdaloid complex and adjacent olfactory structures to the entorhinal cortex and to the subiculum in the rat and cat. J. Comp. Neurol. 172(4): 723–752.
36. PRICE, J. L. & D. G. AMARAL. 1982. An autoradiographic study of the projections of the central nucleus of the monkey amygdala. J. Neurosci. 1(11): 1242–1259.
37. NAUTA, W. J. H. 1961. Fibre degeneration following lesions of the amygdaloid complex in the monkey. J. Anat. 95: 515–531.
38. PORRINO, L. J., A. M. CRANE & P. S. GOLDMAN-RAKIC. 1981. Direct and indirect pathways from the amygdala to the frontal lobe in rhesus monkeys. J. Comp. Neurol. 198: 121–136.
39. AGGLETON, J. P. & M. MISHKIN. 1984. Projections of the amygdala to the thalamus in the cynomolgus monkey. J. Comp. Neurol. 222: 56–68.
40. HOPKINS, D. A. & G. HOLSTEGE. 1978. Amygdaloid projections to the mesencephalon, pons and medulla oblongata in the cat. Exp. Brain Res. 32: 529–547.
41. JACOBSON, S. & J. Q. TROJANOWSKI. 1975. Amygdaloid projections to prefrontal granular cortex in rhesus monkey demonstrated with horseradish peroxidase. Brain Res. 100: 132–139.
42. KRETTEK, J. E. & J. L. PRICE. 1977. Projections from the amygdaloid complex to the cerebral cortex and thalamus in the rat and cat. J. Comp. Neurol. 172(4): 687–722.
43. AVENDANO, C., J. L. PRICE & D. G. AMARAL. 1983. Evidence for an amygdaloid projection to premotor cortex but not to motor cortex in the monkey. Brain Res. 264: 111–117.
44. KELLEY, A. E., V. B. DOMESICK & W. J. H. NAUTA. 1982. The amygdalostriatal projection in the rat—an anatomical study by anterograde and retrograde tracing methods. Neurosci. 7(3): 615–630.
45. KIEVIT, J. & H. G. J. M. KUYPERS. 1975. Basal forebrain and hypothalamic connections to the frontal and parietal cortex in the rhesus monkey. Science 187: 660–662.
46. DIVAC, I. 1975. Magnocellular nuclei of the basal forebrain project to neocortex, brain stem, and olfactory bulb: Review of some functional correlates. Brain Res. 93: 385–398.
47. JONES, E. G., H. BURTON, C. B. SAPER & L. W. SWANSON. 1976. Midbrain, diencephalic and cortical relationships of the basal nucleus of Meynert and associated structures in primates. J. Comp. Neurol. 167(4): 385–420.
48. MESULAM, M.-M. & G. W. VAN HOESEN. 1976. Acetylcholinesterase containing basal forebrain neurons in the rhesus monkey project to neocortex. Brain Res. 109: 152–157.
49. PEARSON, R. C. A., K. C. GATTER, P. BRODAL & T. P. S. POWELL. 1983. The projection of the basal nucleus of Meynert upon the neocortex in the monkey. Brain Res. 259: 132–136.
50. MESULAM, M.-M., E. J. MUFSON, A. I. LEVEY & B. H. WAINER. 1983. Cholinergic innervation of cortex by the basal forebrain: Cytochemistry and cortical connections of the septal area, diagonal band nuclei, nucleus basalis (substantia innominata), and hypothalamus in the rhesus monkey. J. Comp. Neurol. 214: 170–197.
51. WHITEHOUSE, P. J., D. L. PRICE, A. W. CLARK, J. T. COYLE & M. R. DE LONG. 1981. Alzheimer disease: Evidence for selective loss of cholinergic neurons in the nucleus basalis. Ann. Neurol. 10: 122–126.
52. DAVIES, P. & A. J. F. MALONEY. 1976. Selective loss of central cholinergic neurons in Alzheimer's disease. The Lancet: 1403.
53. WENK, H., V. BIGL & V. MEYER. 1980. Cholinergic projections from magnocellular nuclei of the basal forebrain to cortical areas in rats. Brain Res. Rev. 2: 295–316.
54. FIBIGER, H. C. 1982. The organization and some projections of cholinergic neurons of the mammalian forebrain. Brain Res. Rev. 4: 327–388.
55. MESULAM, M.-M. & E. J. MUFSON. 1984. Neural inputs into the nucleus basalis of the substantia innominata (Ch. 4) in the rhesus monkey. Brain Res. 107: 253–274.
56. NAUTA, W. J. H. & W. HAYMAKER. 1969. Hypothalamic nuclear and fiber connections. In The Hypothalamus. W. Haymaker, E. Anderson & W. J. H. Nauta, Eds. C. C. Thomas. Springfield, IL.

57. SAPER, C. B., L. W. SWANSON & W. M. COWAN. 1979. Some efferent connections of the rostral hypothalamus in the squirrel monkey (Saimiri sciureus) and cat. J. Comp. Neurol. **184:** 205–242.
58. PRICE, J. L. & D. G. AMARAL. 1981. An autoradiographic study of the projections of the central nucleus of the monkey amygdala. J. Neurosci. **1**(11): 1242–1259.
59. VICTOR, M., R. D. ADAMS & G. H. COLLINS. 1971. *In* The Wernicke-Korsakoff Syndrome. F. A. Davis. Philadelphia.
60. SQUIRE, L. R. & R. Y. MOORE. 1979. Dorsal thalamic lesion in a noted case of chronic memory dysfunction. Ann. Neurol. **6:** 505–506.
61. GRAFF-RADFORD, N. R., P. J. ESLINGER, A. R. DAMASIO & T. YAMADA. 1984. Nonhemorrhagic infarction of the thalamus: Behavioral, anatomical and physiological correlates. Neurology **34:** 14–23.
62. AKERT, K. 1964. Comparative anatomy of the frontal cortex and thalamocortical connections. *In* The Frontal Granular Cortex and Behavior. J. M. Warren & K. Akert, Eds.: 372–396. McGraw-Hill. New York.
63. OLSZEWSKI, J. 1952. The Thalamus of the Macaca mulatta. An atlas for use with the stereotaxic instrument. S. Karger. Basel.
64. TOBIAS, T. J. 1975. Afferents to prefrontal cortex from the thalamic mediodorsal nucleus in the rhesus monkey. Brain Res. **83:** 191–212.
65. TANAKA, D. 1976. Thalamic projections of the dorso-medial prefrontal cortex in the rhesus monkey (Macaca mulatta). Brain Res. **110:** 21–38.
66. ARIKUNI, T., M. SAKAI & K. KUBOTA. 1983. Columnar aggregation of prefrontal and anterior cingulate cortical cells projecting to the thalamic mediodorsal nucleus in the monkey. J. Comp. Neurol. **220:** 116–125.

Strategies for the Development of Anii
Models of Human Memory Impairments"

DAVID S. OLTON

Department of Psychology
The Johns Hopkins University
Baltimore, Maryland 21218

INTRODUCTION

The validity of any model is ultimately tested by its ability to predict effects in the system that is being modeled. In the context of this volume, predictions in three areas are of interest: (1) The brain mechanisms involved in normal memory; (2) the pathological changes that produce memory impairments; (3) the therapeutic interventions that alleviate memory impairments. Any model that can make correct predictions in these three areas will be judged successful.

The discussion here assumes that behavioral testing of non-human mammals is a critical step in the development of a successful model. This approach has a set of features that allows it to make unique contributions complementing those of other approaches. For example, neuropsychological experiments with people are providing a catalog of the types of memory that are most likely to be spared or impaired in amnesic syndromes, and some information about the types of brain damage most likely to produce these syndromes (see articles by Cohen, Corkin, Moscovitch, Schacter, and Weingartner in this volume). However, the therapeutic benefit to the individual being tested must always take precedence over the gathering of knowledge to help others. Hence, severe limitations are placed on the techniques and procedures that can be used in experiments with people. Experiments with animals are necessary to obtain the necessary precision of manipulation and accuracy of measurement.

Experiments with invertebrates have provided a great deal of information about the general neural mechanisms involved in habituation, conditioning, and other behaviors, all of which involve memory of some kind.[1-4] However, memory impairments in people typically affect only some types of memory processes, and these syndromes are produced by damage in only some areas of the brain (see articles by Cohen, Corkin, Milner, Moscovitch, Schacter, and Weingartner in this volume). Hence, the animals being tested must be similar to people psychologically (to assess the same types of memory) and neurologically (to examine the same areas of the brain).

The incredible growth of neuroscience has described the neural components of the normal central nervous system and the types of pathological changes that can assault it. However, the questions addressed in this article have to do with the functional implications of this knowledge for memory. The most elegant description of the central nervous system itself is of no help until it can be linked to aspects of memory. Hence, behavioral testing is necessary to interrelate the information from neuroscience with that from psychology.

If the logic of this reasoning is sound, then the type of behavioral testing that is carried out in the experiments will have a significant influence on the rapidity with

[a]Supported in part by Research Grant MH 24213.

113

which we can develop animal models to make accurate predictions in the three areas mentioned above (see articles by Bartus and Kesner in this volume).[5-8] The issues do not concern just the brain mechanisms, pathology, or their treatments, but the specific application of these to memory. This last element requires behavioral tests with non-human mammals.

The desirability of non-human mammalian animal models does not imply that the welfare of the animal being tested can be ignored. Indeed, the similarity of the non-human mammalian brain to that of humans implies a shared set of cognitive and emotional processes. However, people have chosen not to give animals all the same rights that we give ourselves, and as long as that value judgment persists, animals offer the opportunity to gather information that is not obtainable in any other way.

STEPS IN DEVELOPING AN EFFECTIVE ANIMAL MODEL

The ultimate test of the validity of any model is its ability to predict effects in the system that is being modeled, and any strategy that develops a valid model will be judged successful. Still, some routes to this goal are more likely to be successful than others, and some time spent evaluating the relative merits of the alternatives prior to choosing one may help reach the goal more productively.[9]

Dissociations

At the core of any model must be the ability to demonstrate behavioral dissociations, differences in the magnitude of the effect of an independent variable on performance in different behavioral tasks. These dissociations are necessary to interpret the empirically observed effects on an independent variable, to determine the extent to which it alters memory and other psychological processes, and to relate the results to the types of memory impairments seen in people. In essence, information about the effects of a variable on a single behavior is uninterpretable by itself; only a pattern of behavioral effects can lead to useful conclusions about the psychological processes affected by this variable.[7]

This reasoning is a vital part of the definition of an amnesic syndrome, which is a disproportionate failure of performance on tasks that require memory relative to general intellectual function. The single observation that performance is impaired in a test of memory is of little value; correct performance on that test involves not only memory, but a whole group of psychological functions. Poor performance could be due to an impairment of any of these functions: perception, motivation, motor coordination, etc. Independent manipulation of the importance of memory and other psychological functions in other tasks is necessary to determine the extent to which a failure of memory is responsible for the empirically observed changes in choice accuracy.

Sensitivity and Selectivity

A test should be sensitive to and selective for certain types of memory. Sensitivity is desirable so that changes in memory will be reflected by changes in behavior. A sensitive test acts as an amplifier so that even small changes in memory produce large and readily observable changes in behavior. Selectivity is desirable so that alterations in psychological processes other than the type of memory being studied will have little effect on behavior. A selective task acts as a filter, minimizing the effects of other areas on behavior.

Empirically observed changes in behavior can be used to make inferences about memory processes only to the extent that memory is a powerful and singular influence on this behavior. A highly selective and sensitive task helps to make correct inferences.

Performance of Normal Animals

Normal animals should be tested in the task to be certain that they use memory to perform correctly. Relevant, redundant strategies are often available to reach the same goal, and specialized testing procedures are necessary to be certain that animals actually use the type of memory that the experimenter wishes to study. "Clever Hans" was an excellent example of the way in which animals can fool experimenters. Hans was a horse that appeared to understand and remember numbers spoken to him by people. When given a number, he pawed the ground with his foot that number of times. In reality, of course, Hans looked at his trainer for a cue, which was a change in facial expression when Hans had pawed the ground the appropriate number of times. This strategy was detected by changing the experimental situation so that Hans' trainer did not know the number actually given to Hans; Hans then failed to paw the ground correctly.

The recent emphasis on cognitive representations in animal memory[10,11] and ethological analyses of memory[12-14] have both shown that animals can be quite clever if given the appropriate kind of test. Knowing the natural predispositions of an animal can help us design effective and productive experimental procedures. However, special tests must be included to be certain that the animal is being clever in relevant ways. The results of these tests must indicate that the animals are using the desired memory processes to perform correctly.

Performance of Animals with Altered Brain Function

Animals with experimentally induced pathological changes similar to those producing amnesia in humans are tested in the task. If the task is selective for and sensitive to the types of memory that are impaired in amnesic syndromes, and animals actually use this type of memory in the task, then the choice accuracy of these brain damaged animals should be affected by these manipulations. Likewise, the types of pharmacological alterations known to improve or impair memory in normal people should also improve and impair, respectively, choice accuracy in the task.

Interpretation of Observed Behavioral Changes

The empirically observed changes in choice accuracy must be shown to be due to changes in memory rather than to alterations in other psychological processes. Even though the task may meet all of the other criteria described above, the changes in choice accuracy may still reflect the influence of variables other than memory. This step requires careful attention to experimental design and the logic of strong inference.[15] In essence, the critical role of memory is never directly proven. Rather, the argument for memory is made by excluding other possible explanations.

For this step, two different approaches have been taken. For between-task dissociations, a battery of tasks is used, each of which is relatively sensitive to and selective for psychological processes other than memory. If performance in these tasks is normal, then the empirically observed changes in choice accuracy in the task that is sensitive to and selective for memory are most likely due to changes in memory itself. If performance in these tasks is also affected, then the changes in choice accuracy in the original task may be produced by factors other than alterations in memory.[5,16]

For within-task dissociations, a single task is used and the importance of the memory component of the task is altered. The number of items to be remembered, the length of time for which they have to be remembered, the extent to which other information interferes with memory—these and other variables can all affect the extent to which memory is required for accurate choices. If a manipulation does indeed affect memory, then as the experimental variables are changed to increase the importance of memory for performance of the task, choice accuracy in the group with the impaired memory should change differentially as compared to that in the control group, producing an interaction. If a manipulation does not affect memory, then no interaction should be seen, leaving either no effect or a main effect.[17,18]

DELAYED CONDITIONAL DISCRIMINATIONS, HIPPOCAMPAL FUNCTION, AND MEMORY

I will illustrate these points with a set of tasks testing rats in mazes. Rats were chosen because they have brains and memories sufficiently similar to those of humans so that cross-species comparisons can be reasonably made,[19] and they are readily available. Mazes were chosen as the testing apparatus because memory processes have been productively investigated here, providing a substantial empirical and theoretical framework in which to interpret the results.[20,21] A delayed conditional discrimination (DCD, described below) was used as the principle test. It assesses the type of memory often impaired by brain damage in humans, is easily incorporated into experimental designs using dissociations to identify the psychological mechanisms responsible for observed behavioral changes, and has been the object of extensive theoretical analyses.[22]

At the beginning of each trial in a DCD, one or more stimuli are presented. During the subsequent delay interval, these stimuli are removed. At the end of the delay, the animal is given a choice between two or more responses. The one that is correct depends upon the stimuli that were present at the beginning of that particular trial. Because the stimuli at the beginning of each trial change from trial to trial, the correct response at the end of the trial also changes. The only way the animal can identify which response is correct at the end of the trial is to determine which stimulus was present at the beginning of that particular trial.

Many of the tasks on the Weschler Memory Scale require this type of memory, and severe impairments on this scale (as compared to performance on the general intelligence scale) are a critical element in defining an amnesic syndrome. Many other types of tests and everyday experiences require this type of memory.[23]

In a DCD in a maze, rats remember the stimulus presented at the beginning of the trial to choose the correct response at the end of the trial.[20,24] Special care must be taken to eliminate the influence of non-mnemonic variables (such as response patterns) on choice behavior; if choice behavior is affected by variables other than memory, then inferences about memory are severely compromised because the experimenter cannot determine the extent to which any given choice is affected by the variables influencing memory or by those influencing other psychological processes. The control of response patterns in mazes has received a great deal of attention and is obviously important. However, these same issues arise in any testing procedure.

Damage to temporal lobe structures and anti-cholinergic drugs produce impairments in choice accuracy in a DCD.[25-28] These same manipulations in humans can produce amnesia, suggesting that the choice accuracy of animals in this type of task can reflect changes in the function of brain systems that are involved in memory in humans.

Dissociations show that the impairments in choice accuracy in a DCD as a result of temporal lobe damage or anti-cholinergic drugs are due primarily to impairments of memory rather than to impairments of other types of cognitive processes. Both between-task and within-task dissociations as outlined above have supported this conclusion.[17,27,29]

Between-Task Dissociations

One experiment incorporated two types of memory discriminations in the same apparatus, a modified T-maze.[30] The usual DCD took place in the arms of the maze. At the beginning of each trial, one pellet of food was placed at the end of each arm. Each trial had two runs. For the forced run, a block of wood was placed at the entrance of one arm forcing the rat to enter the other arm where he ate the pellet of food. For the choice run, the block of wood was removed from the maze allowing the rat to choose either arm. However, food was located only in the arm not entered during the forced run. Thus, the correct response (going to the left or right arm) at the end of the trial was conditional upon the arm entered at the beginning of that particular trial.[20]

Intramaze cues or response chains were not used to choose correctly. Rather, each arm was identified by its spatial location and the correct arm during the choice run at the end of the trial was determined by remembering the location of the arm that was entered during the forced run at the beginning of that trial.

The second memory task took place on the stem of the maze. A barrier divided the stem along its length (perpendicular to the arms). An opaque curtain hung at the end of each side of the stem by arms. A clear Plexiglas barrier was located behind one of the curtains so the rat could not reach the arms by going through that curtain. No barrier was placed behind the other curtain so the rat could reach the arms by going through that curtain.

Two mazes were in distinctive spatial locations. The side of the stem with the barrier was different in each location. The maze in one location had the open side of the stem on the right, the maze in the other location had the open side of the stem on the left. Thus, in order to choose correctly in the stem, the rat had to remember a conditional discrimination: When in the maze in the first location, go down the right side of the stem; when in the maze in the second location, go down the left side of the stem. This conditional discrimination did not have a temporal (delay) component to it, however. Because the side of the stem that was open did not vary from trial to trial, the rat did not have to remember which side was entered on any specific trial (although the rat did have to remember that in general one side of the stem had been blocked while the other had been open).

Bilateral lesions of the fimbria-fornix, a major extrinsic fiber pathway of the hippocampus, produced a severe and permanent impairment of choice accuracy in the DCD in the arms. These lesions had no effect on choice accuracy in the discrimination in the stem. Consequently, the poor choice accuracy in the discrimination in the arms is not likely to be caused by an impairment of any psychological process required for accurate choice behavior in the stem. Using this type of subtractive logic, explanations based on changes in perception, sensory-motor coordination, or motivation can be eliminated. Thus, the most likely reason for the impairment in the DCD in the arms is a failure of the type of memory required for that task. As with human amnesic syndromes, the animal model shows that even while some types of memory may be severely impaired, other types may proceed normally.[27]

Within-Task Dissociations

The difficulty of the memory component of the DCD can be manipulated in many ways. The amount of information to be remembered can be manipulated by having many arms radiating from the choice points and varying the number that are visited before a choice is made. The length of time for which this information is to be remembered can be manipulated by allowing the rat to visit some arms and removing him from the maze for varying periods of time before being allowed to complete the trial. The amount of interference can be manipulated by altering temporal parameters (the delay interval and the intertrial interval) and the familiarity of the stimuli.

For normal rats, the probability of a correct response was greater when only a few arms were to be remembered for a short period of time. It decreased with a positively accelerated function with increases in the number of arms to be remembered and the length of the delay interval during which they were to be remembered.[24]

Following damage to temporal lobe structures or injections of anti-cholinergic drugs, choice accuracy was minimally impaired with only one arm to be remembered for an interval of a few seconds. With increasing numbers of arms and longer delays, however, choice accuracy declined precipitously, much faster than that seen with normal rats. Thus, an interaction occurred between brain function and choice accuracy as the difficulty of the task increased.

BASAL FOREBRAIN AND MEMORY

Severe memory impairments accompany the onset of Alzheimer's disease in humans (see articles by Corkin and Weingartner in this volume). These impairments may be associated with pathology of the basal forebrain cholinergic system (see article by Price in this volume), which includes the nucleus basalis magnocellularis (NBM) and the medial septal area (MSA). Specific conclusions about the role of the NBM and MSA in memory cannot be obtained from this clinical material; at autopsy, pathological changes are widespread and the psychological changes involve more than just memory. An animal model in which specific damage is localized to the NBM and MSA is necessary to determine if pathological changes limited to these areas are sufficient to cause memory impairments.

Lesions in the NBM and MSA were made in rats by injecting ibotenic acid into these areas. Histological examination indicated that most of the magnocellular neurons at the site of the injection were destroyed. Neurochemical assays of choline acetyl transferase (ChAT), an enzymatic marker for cholinergic cells in the NBM and MSA, showed that ChAT was reduced to approximately 50% of its normal value in the appropriate projection areas (frontal cortex for NBM, hippocampus for MSA). Thus, the lesions were successful in producing localized damage.[31]

The behavioral changes following these lesions resulted from a selective impairment of memory. Rats were first trained preoperatively on the split stem T-maze as described previously. They were given the appropriate surgery and tested postoperatively. Control operations caused little change in choice accuracy in either the stem or arm discrimination. Lesions of the NBM or MSA alone, or both together, impaired choice accuracy in the arm discrimination, but not in the stem discrimination. When the delay interval between the forced run and the choice run on the arm discrimination was increased from its usual five seconds to 10 minutes, the rats with lesions had a relatively greater decrease in choice accuracy than the control rats. Thus, between-task and within-task dissociations both suggest that the behavioral changes following these basal forebrain lesions were due to an impairment of memory rather than to disruption of some other psychological function.[30]

These experiments were not intended to provide a model of the pathological changes involved in Alzheimer's disease. Putting acute, specific lesions in the brain of young animals in no way mimics the chronic widespread degeneration seen in elderly people. However, the experiments were designed to examine the behavioral changes following substantial but selective damage to the basal forebrain; as long as the lesions are appropriately located, the mechanisms producing them are of little consequence for this analysis. The focus is on the functional consequences of the damage, not on the process that actually produces the damage. The results show that these lesions were sufficient to produce an impairment of memory. They provide information about the ways in which the brain normally processes memory and the pathological changes that can produce memory impairments. They are consistent with the suggestion that the memory impairments in patients with Alzheimer's disease are due to the pathological changes in the NBM and MSA. If this conclusion is supported by further testing, the magnitude of the memory impairments exhibited by these patients may be a way of assessing the pathological state of the NBM and MSA during the course of the disease.

Current experiments are examining the effects of pharmacological interventions on choice accuracy in the DCD in the arm discrimination. Drug treatments that improve selectively the choice accuracy of rats in the arm discrimination most likely do so by having a specific effect on memory.

DISCUSSION

Because animal models are so important in the understanding of the pathological bases of memory impairments and the therapeutic interventions to alleviate them, explicit criteria to evaluate the relative validity of different models can help to decide which models are likely to be the most productive. The steps outlined here have been valuable in developing this particular approach. However, they are not the only ones that might be considered, and other models have been used effectively. Consequently, the comments here are not to be taken as a fixed set of requirements that should be adhered to rigorously. Rather, they are a beginning point for further discussion about the ways in which we can produce productive animal models that will help us improve human memory.

ACKNOWLEDGMENTS

I thank D. Hepler, M. Shapiro, G. Wenk, and C. Wible for helpful comments on the manuscript, and E. Picken for typing.

REFERENCES

1. CAREW, T. J., R. D. HAWKINS & E. R. KANDEL. 1983. Differential classical conditioning of a defensive withdrawal reflex in *Aplysia californica*. Science **219**: 397–400.

2. HAWKINS, R. D., T. W. ABRAMS, T. J. CAREW & E. R. KANDEL. 1983. A cellular mechanism of classical conditioning in Aplysia: Activity-dependent amplification of presynaptic facilitation. Science **219**: 400–404.
3. KANDEL, E. R. & J. H. SCHWARTZ. 1982. Molecular biology of learning: Modulation of transmitter release. Science **218**: 433–443.
4. WALTERS, E. T. & J. H. BYRNE. 1983. Associative conditioning of single sensory neurons suggests a cellular mechanism for learning. Science **219**: 405–407.
5. BARTUS, R. T., C. FLICKER & R. L. DEAN. 1983. Logical principles for development of animal models of age-related memory impairments. *In* Assessment in Geriatric Psychopharmacology. T. Crook *et al.,* Eds.: 263–293. Mark Powley Associates, Inc. New Canaan, CT.
6. MISHKIN, M., B. J. SPIEGLER, R. C. SAUNDERS & B. L. MALAMUT. 1982. An animal model of global amnesia. *In* Alzheimer's Disease: A Report of Progress. S. Corkin *et al.,* Eds.: Raven Press, New York. Aging **19**: 235–248.
7. OLTON, D. S. 1983. The use of animal models to evaluate the effects of neurotoxins on cognitive processes. Neuro. Tox. Tera. **98**(6): 635–640.
8. WENK, G. & D. S. OLTON. 1984. Lesion analyses as a tool in neurobehavioral toxicology. *In* Behavior Toxicology. Z. Annau, Ed. (In press.)
9. WEISKRANTZ, L. 1968. Some traps and pontifications. *In* Analysis of Behavioral Change. L. Weiskrantz, Ed.: 415–429. Harper & Row, Publishers. New York.
10. ROITBLAT, H. L. 1982. The meaning of representation in animal memory. Behav. Brain Sci. **5**: 353–372.
11. ROITBLAT, H. L., T. G. BEVER & H. S. TERRACE. 1983. Animal Cognition. Lawrence Erlbaum Associates. Hillsdale, NJ.
12. KAMIL, A. C. 1977. Systematic foraging by a nectar-feeding bird, the Amakihi (*Loxops virens*). J. Comp. Physio. Psych. **92**: 388–396.
13. KAMIL, A. C. & T. D. SARGENT. 1981. Foraging Behavior: Ecological, Ethological, and Psychological Approaches. Garland STPM Press. New York.
14. SHETTELWORTH, S. J. & J. R. KREBS. 1982. How marsh tits find their hoards: The roles of site preference and spatial memory. J. Exp. Psychol.: Anim. Behav. Proc. **8**(4): 354–375.
15. PLATT, J.R. 1964. Strong inference. Science **146**(3642): 347–353.
16. ZORNETZER, S. F. & J. ROGERS. 1983. Animal models for assessment of geriatric mnemonic and motor deficits. *In* Assessment in Geriatric Psychopharmacology. T. Crook *et al.,* Eds.: 301–317. Mark Powley Associates. New Canaan, CT.
17. JARRARD, L. E. 1975. Role of interference in retention by rats with hippocampal lesions. J. Comp. Physiol. Psych. **89**: 400–408.
18. MISHKIN, M. 1982. A memory system in the monkey. Phil. Trans. R. Soc. Lond. Ser. B **298**: 85–95.
19. OLTON, D. S. 1978. Characteristics of spatial memory. *In* Cognitive Aspects of Animal Behavior. S. H. Hulse *et al.,* Eds.: 341–373. Lawrence Erlbaum Associates. Hillsdale, NJ.
20. OLTON, D. S. 1979. Mazes, maps, and memory. Am. Psych. **34**: 583–596.
21. OLTON, D. S. 1982. Spatial abilities of animals: Behavioral and neuroanatomical analyses. *In* Spatial Abilities' Developmental and Physiological Foundations. M. Potegal, Ed.: 353–360. Academic Press. New York.
22. HONIG, W. K. 1978. Studies of working memory in the pigeon. *In* Cognitive Processes in Animal Behavior. S. H. Hulse *et al.,* Eds.: 211–248. Lawrence Erlbaum Associates. Hillsdale, NJ.
23. SCHACTER, D. L. 1983. Amnesia observed: Remembering and forgetting in a natural environment. J. Abn. Psych. **92**(2): 236–242.
24. OLTON, D. S. 1984. The temporal context of spatial memory. Proc. R. Acad. Sci. (In press.)
25. BURESOVA, O. & J. BURES. 1982. Radial maze as a tool for assessing the effect of drugs on the working memory of rats. Psychopharm. **77**: 268–271.
26. HIRAGA, Y. & T. IWASAKI. 1984. Effects of cholinergic and monoaminergic antagonists and tranquilizers upon spatial memory in rats. Pharm. Biochem. Beh. **20**: 205–207.
27. OLTON, D. S. 1984. Animal models of human amnesia. *In* The Neuropsychology of Memory. L. R. Squire & N. Butters, Eds.: 367–373. Guilford Press. New York.

28. WATTS, J., R. STEVENS & C. ROBINSON. 1981. Effects of scopolamine on radial maze performance in rats. Pharm. Biochem. Beh. **26:** 845–851.
29. WIRSCHING, B. A., R. J. BENINGER, K. JHAMANDAS, R. J. BOEGMAN & S. R. EL-DEFRAWY. 1984. Differential effects of scopolamine on working and reference memory of rats in the radial maze. Pharm. Biochem. Beh. **20:** 659–662.
30. WENK, G. L., D. HEPLER & D. OLTON. 1984. Lesions in nucleus basalis magnocellularis and medial septal area of rats produce qualitatively similar memory impairments. J. Neurosci. (In press.)
31. WENK, G. L., B. CRIBBS & L. MCCALL. 1984. Nucleus basalis magnocellularis: Optimal coordinates for selective reduction of choline acetyltransferase in frontal neocortex by ibotenic acid injections. Exp. Brain Res. **82:** 1–6.

Correspondence between Humans and Animals in Coding of Temporal Attributes: Role of Hippocampus and Prefrontal Cortex

RAYMOND P. KESNER

Department of Psychology
University of Utah
Salt Lake City, Utah 84112

Investigators interested in understanding the neurobiological basis of memory have had a long term interest in studying patients with a variety of memory disturbances. On the basis of a large number of descriptive and formal tests with these patients, researchers have identified a number of critical neural regions (e.g., hippocampus, cerebral cortex) that subserve the encoding, storage, and retrieval of mnemonic information and have developed a set of specific theories of brain-memory function. In addition, these patients have provided a great impetus for animal researchers to search for correspondence in brain function and memory. This latter emphasis is based on the assumption of evolutionary continuity of brain-mediated mnemonic functions.

In the past the search for animal models of human memory pathology has not been entirely successful. However, a modicum of success has emerged in the last five years. What factors might have contributed to this success? First, there has been the development of new information-processing theoretical frameworks with an emphasis not only on the process of information storage and retrieval, but also on the structural organization of memory. As a result, these new theoretical frameworks have led to the development of new tests providing a richer description of human amnesic syndromes. Second, great progress has been made in the development of scanning techniques to assess potential brain damage in living organisms as well as in the development of new techniques (e.g., histochemical and neurochemical) to evaluate the consequences of brain damage. Third, there has been the development of new tasks and theories to study mental processes in animals as an alternative to the behaviorist tradition. Fourth, there is a recognition that brain damage in humans is rarely complete within a region and that more often than not it involves more than one neural region.

There are of course still many problems, but the outlook is more optimistic. Some of the major problems in developing good animal models of human memory pathology lie in the importance of language processing in humans, the difficulty in determining the exact underlying neural pathology, the interconnectedness of the central nervous system, and the great variety of theoretical interpretations of the extant data.

The purpose of this paper is to present a few experiments demonstrating that rats with hippocampus lesions have a comparable pattern of mnemonic deficits to humans with presumed hippocampus damage. Furthermore, I will attempt to show that rats with medial prefrontal cortex lesions display memory dysfunctions that are similar to those observed in frontal cortex damaged patients. Finally, I will present data showing that rats with either medial septum or nucleus basalis magnocellularis lesions have memory deficits similar to those that have been described in Alzheimer's patients.

122

HIPPOCAMPUS

Humans

One of the cardinal features of the amnesic syndrome seen in humans with presumed hippocampus damage is the inability to maintain new temporal-spatial information over time. As a consequence, patients forget rather quickly specific events or experiences that occur in their daily lives. In contrast, they are able to communicate normally at least about events that have occurred prior to their brain damage or that are occurring at present.

More formally, there are at least two ways of demonstrating that these patients can process and maintain information for short but not long time periods. The first is to

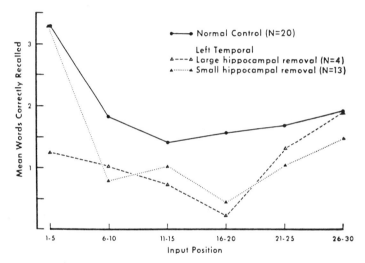

FIGURE 1. Serial position curves for immediate recall of a list of 30 unrelated concrete words. Results for normal control subjects and for patients tested after left temporal lobectomy and subdivided according to the extent of hippocampal removal. The mean number of words recalled is plotted as a function of presentation position summed over five words. (From Milner.[8] By permission of Elsevier Press.)

present a single item of information to a subject and ask for retention of that item at short and long temporal delays. The finding is that hippocampus-damaged patients can remember information at short but not long delays. Often this phenomenon has been interpreted as a reflection of accelerated forgetting.[1,2] The second is to present a list of items of information to the subject and ask for recall or recognition of the items. In normal subjects one observes a serial position curve with better performance for the first items (primacy effect) and the last items (recency effect) compared to items located in the middle of the list. It has been proposed by some theorists that the primacy effect reflects information storage in long-term memory, while the recency effect reflects information processing in short-term memory.[3] However, it should be noted that there are other interpretations for the serial position effect. For example, it has been suggested that the recency effect reflects automatic availability of information requiring little attention, whereas the primacy effect reflects the utilization of controlled or effortful attention-directing activity.[4-6] Others have suggested that the ends (primacy and recency) of a list are more distinctive and therefore are remembered better than the interior positions.[7]

Milner[8] presented a list of 30 words to patients with small or large left hippocampus lesions and asked for immediate free recall. The results are shown in FIGURE 1 and indicate that patients with large hippocampus lesions were impaired compared to controls in remembering the first items of the list (primacy), but could remember as well as controls the last items of the list (recency). Using the same task similar results were found for H.M.[8] One interpretation of these findings is that hippocampus-damaged patients can maintain information for only short time periods, resulting in good retention for the last items of a list, but can not maintain information for long time periods, resulting in a deficit in retention of the early items of a list. It is of course also possible that maintaining information for longer time periods can increase the probability of activation of controlled processes rendering the first items more available and more distinctive during the retention test.

It should be noted that the deficit is primarily in the processing of new temporal-spatial information. Thus, one would expect sparing in the processing of new stimulus-response or affect-laden information. This observation has led to the suggestion that the hippocampus codes declarative, but not procedural information.[9] One would also expect sparing in the processing of spatio-temporal information learned prior to brain damage. This latter observation has led to the idea that the hippocampus codes data-based information (working memory), but not expectancy-based information (reference memory).[10,11]

Animals

For many years attempts to develop an animal model of the human amnesic syndrome (with presumed hippocampus damage) have been unsuccessful. A number of suggestions have been made to resolve this discrepancy. The first and simplest idea is that the function of the hippocampus is different in animals and humans. A second possibility is that the amnesic syndrome produced by medial temporal lobe lesions in humans is not due to hippocampus damage, but to damage of other structures. For example, Horel[12] suggested that damage to the temporal stem containing input and output pathways of temporal cortex and amygdala was necessary for memory impairment. This idea is based on an extensive review of the literature and on the experimental observation that cuts of the temporal stem in monkeys abolished a preoperatively learned visual pattern discrimination. Mishkin,[13] on the other hand, suggested that the amnesic syndrome is due not only to hippocampus damage, but due to a combination of hippocampus plus amygdala damage. He demonstrated in monkeys that in a delayed object matching-to-sample task neither amygdala nor hippocampus lesions alone produced a deficit, but a severe performance deficit was observed with combined lesions.

A third possibility is that the hippocampus is critically involved in some aspect of long-term memory, but that the tasks used to test memory in animals are not equivalent to those used to test human memory. For example, Iversen[14] has argued that the major effect of hippocampus lesions leading to long-term memory deficits is excessive interference. Since most animal tests tend to be simple and very repetitive, there often is little interference and deficits might not be expected.

Based on the assumption that in the past inadequate tests of memory function have been employed, I would like to demonstrate that more complex tests of mnemonic function might indeed reveal that the same pattern of deficits described above for amnesic patients apply to hippocampus-damaged rats. Previously, it was demonstrated that subseizure levels of electrical stimulation of the dorsal hippocampus during or after a training trial can result in a disruption of retention at a long-term retention test (minutes to hours) without altering performance on a short-term retention test (seconds to minutes) in a one-trial passive avoidance, one-trial appetitive learning, and eight-choice spatial-matching-to-sample tasks.[15-17] It is assumed that electrical stimulation serves as a temporary disruptive agent of normal dorsal hippocampus function. One could argue, however, that electrical stimulation of the hippocampus does not represent a comparable condition to that seen with brain damage in amnesic patients. In order to rectify this situation, animals were prepared with lesions of the hippocampus and tested in tasks aimed at demonstrating that hippocampus-damaged rats have dysfunctions that are similar to what has been observed in amnesic patients with presumed hippocampus damage.

In the first study, rats were trained to perform in an Olton eight-arm radial maze.[18] Following acquisition, animals received during the study phase of the trial (one per day) a piece of Froot Loop cereal reinforcement in one of the eight arms of the maze. The arm containing the food was varied randomly from day to day. Ten seconds after finding the food, the animal was returned to its home cage for either a 1 min or 2 hr delay period. Following the delay period the animal was returned to the maze and given a retention test (test phase). Correct performance during the test phase required the animal to return to the previously reinforced arm (i.e., the animal had to use a "win-stay" rule) in order to receive an additional piece of Froot Loop cereal. After extensive training rats could remember (made few errors) the correct arm after a 1 min or 2 hr delay period.

Animals then received dorsal hippocampus lesions and were retested for 16 trials at each delay period. Results indicated that the lesioned animals made no errors at 1 min delay, but made many more errors at 2 hr delay. These results are consistent with previous findings using electrical brain stimulation of the hippocampus in the same task.[16] They also support the idea that hippocampus-lesioned animals can apply the "win-stay" rule for relatively short delay periods resulting in normal performance, but cannot apply the rule at long delay periods (perhaps because of inability to use active control processes) resulting in a deficient long-term memory performance. Note also that one can interpret these data as representing an example of accelerated forgetting and thus are consistent with the Huppert and Piercy data.[1]

In a second study[19] rats were trained on an eight-arm radial maze for Froot Loop reinforcement. After extensive training each animal was allowed on each trial (one per day) to visit all eight arms in an order that was randomly selected for that trial. The sequencing of the eight arms was accomplished by sequentially opening of Plexiglas doors (one at a time) located at the entrance of each arm. This constituted the study phase. Immediately (within 20 sec) after the animal had received reinforcement from the last of the eight arms (i.e., completed the study phase), the test phase began. Only one test was given for each trial and consisted of opening two doors simultaneously. On a random basis either the first and second, fourth and fifth, or seventh and eighth doors that occurred in the sequence were selected for the test. The rule to be learned leading to an additional reinforcement was to choose the arm that occurred earlier in the sequence. All rats displayed a serial position curve, e.g., prominent retention (better than chance [50%] performance) for the recency and primacy components of the list, but no retention (chance performance) for the middle portion of the list (FIGURE 2). It is important to note that this is the first demonstration of a prominent serial position curve in rats (for more detail on methods see Kesner & Novak).[19] Some animals then received a dorsal hippocampus lesion, while other animals served as sham-operated

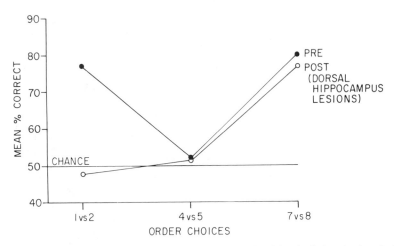

FIGURE 2. Mean percent correct responses as a function of serial order before (pre) and after (post) small dorsal hippocampus lesions.

controls. Since the sham operation had no deleterious effect on the serial position curve, the sham animals were subsequently subjected to dorsal hippocampus lesions. Results are shown in FIGURE 2 and indicate that the lesioned animals had excellent retention only for the recency component of the list, but no retention (chance performance) for the primacy component. All animals were then given additional tests at 10-min delay between study and test phases. Under those conditions hippocampus-lesioned animals performed at chance level for all items of the list indicating that they had no memory for order information.

In a third study rats were trained on an eight-arm radial maze with Froot Loop reinforcement. After extensive training each animal was allowed on each trial (one per day) to visit a sequence of five arms, which was selected on a pseudo-random basis. This constituted the study phase. Immediately after the animal had received reinforcement from the last of the five arms, the test phase began. Only one test was given for each trial and consisted of opening two doors simultaneously, with one door representing an arm previously visited for that trial and the other door representing a novel arm for that trial. The rule to be learned leading to an additional reinforcement was to choose the arm that had been previously visited during the study phase of the trial (win-stay). Each animal received 40 tests with eight tests for each of the serial positions.

Rats display a serial position curve for memory of items given that a win-stay rule is required.[14] After training animals received dorsal hippocampus lesions followed by an additional 40 trials with eight tests for each serial position. Results are shown in FIGURE 3 and indicate that hippocampus-lesioned animals show good memory only for the last item of the list (recency component), but poor memory for the early items of the list (primacy component).

The results of the last two experiments are remarkably similar to the performance of amnesic patients, including H.M., on memory for a list of items,[8] in that hippocampus damage disrupted the primacy but not the recency component of the serial position curve. Furthermore, with an additional delay between presentation and retention test the hippocampus-lesioned animals demonstrated no retention, a finding that is similar to what has been described clinically with amnesic patients.

Thus, there is a correspondence in mnemonic function in the hippocampus of rats and humans. From a theoretical viewpoint, I have proposed that the hippocampus codes and is activated by both temporal and spatial attributes of memories associated with specific events or episodes.[21] Since it is assumed that activation of the hippocampus is triggered primarily by events in the external environment, the hippocampus might represent a data-based operational system capable of maintaining critical temporal-spatial information over time. The duration of this activation might be a direct function of the extent of damage. Thus, the ability of animals with partial hippocampus lesions and of patients with presumed partial hippocampus damage to remember spatio-temporal information for only short time periods might be a function of the remaining intact hippocampus.

PREFRONTAL CORTEX

Humans

Damage to the prefrontal cortex in humans results in a number of intellectual and behavioral deficits. Among these are personality disorders, lack of initiative or spontaneity, disorders of cognitive function and spatial orientation, poor movement programming, and reduced corollary discharge. With respect to mnemonic information processing, it has been proposed that humans with prefrontal cortex damage have deficits for information concerning short-term temporal aspects of their environment, i.e., they cannot remember the order in which information was experienced, plan and create a complex ordered set of motor movements, or program a temporally ordered set of activities. Experimental evidence in support of this hypothesis comes from the

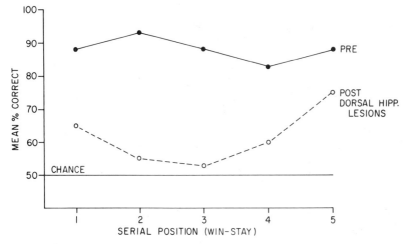

FIGURE 3. Mean percent correct responses as a function of serial position (win-stay) before (pre) and after (post) small dorsal hippocampus lesions.

observation that frontal cortex–damaged patients can remember that certain words or pictures have been presented, but cannot discriminate the more from the less recent. Thus, memory for item information is intact, but memory for order information is impaired.[22] In addition, frontal cortex–damaged patients have been shown to be impaired in a short-term memory task in which two stimuli had to be remembered for a 60 sec time interval (paired-comparison task).[23] This task requires short-term temporal memory for two events, implying that frontal cortex–damaged patients can not remember the order of stimulus presentation. In another experiment, frontal cortex–damaged patients were impaired in their ability to self-order a sequence of stimuli presented one at a time.[24]

The above-mentioned cognitive disorders are most likely to occur from damage to the dorsolateral region of the prefrontal cortex, while changes in social behavior, affect, and behavioral spontaneity are most likely due to damage to the orbital-frontal region.

Animals

In monkeys, dorsolateral prefrontal cortex lesions result in deficits in the temporal ordering of events, a finding that is comparable to what has been described in humans. This temporal ordering deficit is evidenced by impairments in delayed response, delayed alternation, and delayed matching-to-sample tasks as well as self-ordering of a sequence of responses.[24,25] Based upon the above-mentioned findings, it has been suggested that the prefrontal cortex is primarily involved in temporal structuring of information in short-term memory.[26]

In rats, lesions of the medial prefrontal cortex produce in most studies a deficit in DRL performance as well as deficits in a temporal go/no-go alternation task and a delayed alternation task.[27,28] Deficits have also been observed in tasks in which rats emit a specific sequence of behavioral responses requiring temporal organization.[29] However, there are no studies describing comparable behavioral deficits to what have been described in humans, including a dissociation for item-order information.[22]

In order to test whether there is a correspondence in function of prefrontal cortex in rats and humans, rats were tested for item and order memory for a list of items (places on a maze).

Rats were trained on an eight-arm radial maze for Froot Loop reinforcement. After extensive training, each animal was allowed on each trial (one per day) to visit four arms in an order that was randomly selected for that trial (study phase). The sequencing of the four arms was accomplished by sequentially opening of Plexiglas doors (one at a time) located at the entrance of each arm. Immediately after the animal had received reinforcement from the last of the four arms, the test phase began. During the test phase the animal was given two tests—one to test order memory and one to test item memory. The test for order memory consisted of opening of either the first and second, second and third, or third and fourth door that occurred in the sequence. The rule to be learned leading to an additional reinforcement was to choose the arm that occurred earlier in the sequence. The test for item memory consisted of opening of a door that was previously visited for that trial and a door that was not. The rule to be learned resulting in an additional reinforcement was to choose the arm previously visited during the study phase of the trial (win-stay rule). The order of presentation of the two tests was varied randomly.

Following extensive training, animals performed better than chance for each item or order position on both tests (FIGURE 4). The animals then received medial prefrontal cortex aspiration lesions. After recovery from surgery animals were given an additional thirty-two tests. Results are shown in FIGURE 4 and indicate that prefrontal cortex–lesioned animals had an order memory deficit for all items, but had excellent item memory for the first item of the list with impaired item memory for the remaining items of the list. The possibility exists that poor performance for item information was due to the variable temporal-spatial sequences presented during the study phase. To test this possibility the lesioned animals were trained with a constant sequence (e.g., the same four arms were always selected) followed by tests of item and order memory. The results are shown in FIGURE 5 and indicate that prefrontal cortex–lesioned animals had excellent item memory for all items of the list, but had no memory for the order of presentation of the items. In additional tests it was shown that this order deficit

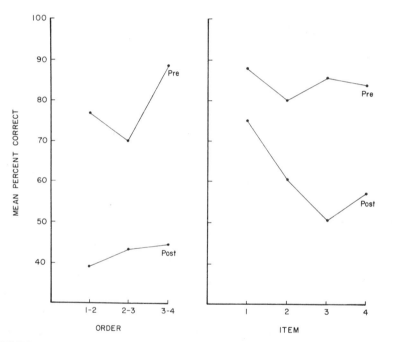

FIGURE 4. Mean percent correct responses as a function of serial order and serial position (item) before (pre) and after (post) medial prefrontal cortex lesions.

appeared even when the animals were allowed to self-order the items during the study phase or when the list length was only two items.

Thus, rats can remember the occurrence, but not the temporal ordering of spatial events, suggesting that there is a correspondence between rats and humans with respect to the mnemonic functions of prefrontal cortex.

From a theoretical viewpoint I would like to propose that the prefrontal cortex codes temporal attributes of repeatedly occurring events to be stored in the form of a temporal map (temporal reference memory). Since it is assumed that the prefrontal cortex can be activated independent of events in the external environment, the

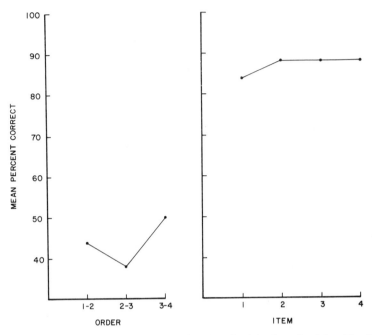

FIGURE 5. Mean percent correct responses as a function of serial order and serial position (item) using an invariant order for the study phase in medial prefrontal cortex lesioned animals.

prefrontal cortex might represent an expectancy-based operational system providing access to temporal rules and temporal ordering of information. Thus, the prefrontal cortex and hippocampus differentially process temporal attributes of mnemonic information. The hippocampus codes "real" time or the processing of information based on data input ("bottom-up" processing), while the prefrontal cortex codes "abstract" time or the processing of information based on expectancies ("top-down" processing).

ALZHEIMER'S DISEASE

Hippocampus

There is one neurological disorder known as Alzheimer's disease that might involve both the hippocampus and prefrontal cortex as well as other cortical regions. The behavioral hallmark of this disease is deterioration of memory, but changes in feeling, conduct, sleep, sexual activity, motor coordination, awareness, social habits, and communication are often present. In early stages of Alzheimer's disease, the pattern of memory deficits is very similar to that of hippocampus-damaged patients. As an illustration, Miller[30] presented twelve unrelated words to demented and control patients followed by an immediate test of free recall. Results are shown in FIGURE 6. Compared to controls, demented patients had an impaired primacy effect and a slightly impaired recency effect.

The parallel between the pattern of memory deficits in Alzheimer's and hippocampus-damaged patients suggests that the function of the hippocampal formation is impaired in Alzheimer's patients. Indeed, hippocampal neurons of these patients exhibit dendritic atrophy as well as abnormal dendritic growth patterns,[31] and there are large increases in neurofibrillary tangles, neuritic (senile) plaques, and granulo-vacuolar degeneration of pyramidal cells.[32]

In addition to these anatomical changes, there are specific changes in the cholinergic system as indicated by profound decreases in choline acetyltransferase (ChAT) and acetylcholinesterase (AChE) activity in the hippocampal formation.[33]

In order to test whether there is a correspondence between animals and humans in terms of the importance of cholinergic innervation to the hippocampus, rats were tested on the order memory task described above.[19,20] After extensive pretraining rats received electrolytic lesions of the medial septum. Following recovery from surgery, the animals were given 24 tests with eight tests for each choice position. The animals were divided into two groups based on subsequent histochemical analysis of AChE. The first group consisted of animals with unilateral or incomplete depletion of cholinergic input to the hippocampus. The results are shown in FIGURE 7 and indicate that there was an order memory deficit only for the primacy, but not the recency component of the serial position curve. These data are consistent with the pattern of results found in rats with

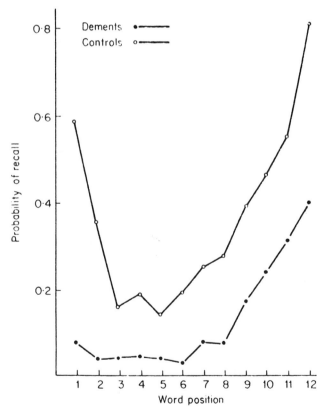

FIGURE 6. Recall of words as function of their position in the list. (From Miller.[30] By permission of Pergamon Press.)

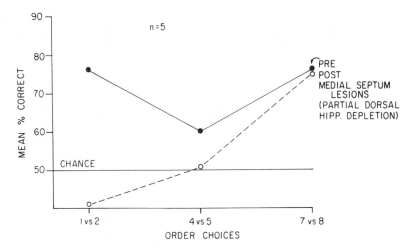

FIGURE 7. Mean percent correct responses as a function of serial order position before (pre) and after (post) medial septum lesions with partial dorsal hippocampus depletion of cholinergic input.

dorsal hippocampus lesions, patients with partial hippocampus damage, and patients in early stages of Alzheimer's disease.[8,19,30]

The second group consisted of animals with complete bilateral dorsal hippocampus depletion of cholinergic input. The results are shown in FIGURE 8 and indicate an order memory deficit for all items of the list. These data are consistent with the performance

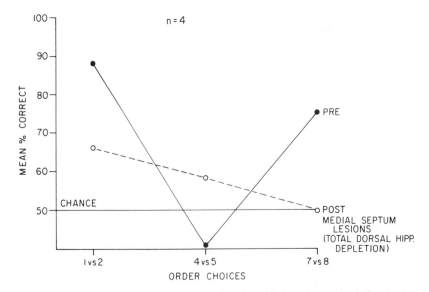

FIGURE 8. Mean percent correct responses as a function of serial order position before (pre) and after (post) medial septum lesions with total dorsal hippocampus depletion of cholinergic input.

expectation of patients with advanced Alzheimer's disease, who presumably have greater loss of cholinergic function.

Since the greater the cholinergic depletion of the hippocampus the greater the deficit in maintaining information over time, the hypothesis suggesting that the hippocampus maintains temporal-spatial information over time is supported. In addition there is a strong possibility that the cholinergic input represents the critical neurotransmitter involved in maintaining information concerning the occurrence of events or episodes.

Prefrontal Cortex

Even though in the early stages of Alzheimer's disease there are primarily deficits in the primacy with slight impairment of the recency components of the serial position

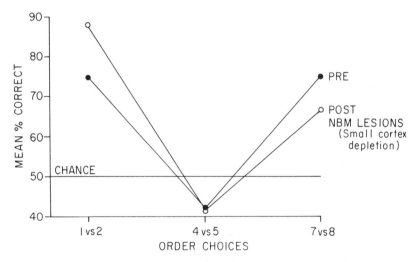

FIGURE 9. Mean percent correct responses as a function of serial order position before (pre) and after (post) nucleus basalis magnocellularis lesions with small cortex depletion of cholinergic input.

curve,[30] in later stages of Alzheimer's disease there is, in addition to the primacy deficit, also a marked recency deficit.[34] These impairments in memory for the most recent items are similar to what have been described in patients with parietal or frontal cortex damage.[35,36]

The above parallel between the memory deficits in later Alzheimer's disease and cerebral cortex–damaged patients suggests that the anatomy and function of the cerebral cortex might also be altered in Alzheimer's patients. Indeed in Alzheimer's patients one finds in the neocortex dendritic atrophy as well as abnormal dendritic growth patterns,[37] and large increases in neurofibrillary tangles and neuritic senile plaques.[32] There are also specific changes in the central cholinergic system as indicated by large decreases in levels of ChAT and AChE in the neocortex without measurable changes in norepinephrine, dopamine, 5-hydroxytryptamine, or γ-amino-butyric acid.[38,39]

It has recently been shown that there is a loss of neurons in the basal forebrain of Alzheimer's patients[40] and that the cholinergic fibers in the neocortex may be involved in plaque formation.[41]

In order to test whether there is a correspondence between animals and humans in terms of the importance of cholinergic innervation to the cerebral cortex (especially prefrontal), rats were tested on the order memory task described above. After extensive pretraining rats received ibotenic acid lesions of the nucleus basalis magnocellularis (NBM). Following recovery from surgery animals were given 24 tests with eight tests for each choice position. The animals were then divided into two groups based on subsequent histochemical analysis of AChE. The first group consisted of animals with unilateral or incomplete depletion of cholinergic input to the medial prefrontal cortex. The results are shown in FIGURE 9 and indicate that there was a slight deficit only for the recency component of the serial position curve, but no deficit for the primacy

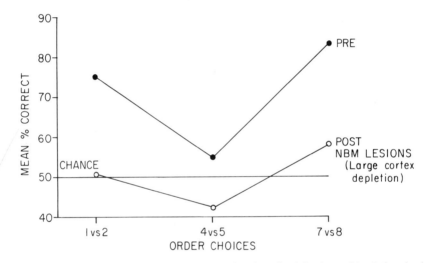

FIGURE 10. Mean percent correct responses as a function of serial order position before (pre) and after (post) nucleus basalis magnocellularis lesions with large cortex depletion of cholinergic input.

component. These data are consistent with the slight deficit seen in the recency part of the serial position curve in early stage Alzheimer's patients.[30] The second group consisted of animals with complete bilateral medial prefrontal cortex depletion of cholinergic input. The results are shown in FIGURE 10 and indicate an order memory deficit for all items of the list. These data are consistent with the performance expectation of patients with advanced Alzheimer's disease.

It appears that the cholinergic input to the medial prefrontal cortex is critical for the operation of a temporal map. Thus, one critical deficit of Alzheimer's patients with presumed alteration of the medial septum-hippocampus and the basal forebrain-dorsolateral prefrontal cortex cholinergic systems is the inability to code both the data- and expectancy-based components of temporal attributes of mnemonic information.

In conclusion, I have attempted to demonstrate that for the medial septum-hippocampus system and the basal forebrain-prefrontal cortex system there is a correspondence between rats and humans in terms of the structural organization of memory.

REFERENCES

1. HUPPERT, F. A. & M. PIERCY. 1979. Normal and abnormal forgetting in organic amnesia: Effect of locus of lesion. Cortex **15**: 385–390.
2. SQUIRE, L. R. 1981. Two forms of human amnesia: An analysis of forgetting. J. Neurosci. **1**: 635–640.
3. ATKINSON, R. C. & R. M. SHIFFRIN. 1968. Human memory: A proposed system and its control processes. *In* Advances in the Psychology of Learning and Motivation, Research and Theory. K. W. Spence & J. T. Spence, Eds. Vol. 2. Academic Press. New York.
4. DIMATTIA, B. V. & R. P. KESNER. 1984. Serial position curves in rats: Automatic vs. controlled information processing. J. Exp. Psych.: Animal Behav. Proc. **10**: 557–563.
5. HASHER, L. & R. T. ZACKS. 1979. Automatic and effortful processes in memory. J. Exp. Psych.: Gen. **108**: 356–388.
6. SHIFFRIN, R. M. & W. SCHNEIDER. 1977. Controlled and automatic human information processing. II. Perceptual learning, automatic attending, and a general theory. Psych. Rev. **3**: 1–17.
7. EBENHOLTZ, S. M. 1972. Serial learning and dimensional organization. *In* The Psychology of Learning and Motivation. G. H. Bower, Ed. Vol. 5. Academic Press. New York.
8. MILNER, B. 1978. Clues to the cerebral organization of memory. *In* Cerebral Correlates of Conscious Experience. P. A. Buser & A. Rougeul-Buser, Eds. Elsevier. Amsterdam.
9. COHEN, N. J. & L. R. SQUIRE. 1980. Preserved learning and retention of pattern analyzing skill in amnesia: Dissociation of knowing how and knowing that. Science **210**: 207–210.
10. OLTON, D. S., J. T. BECKER & G. E. HANDELMANN. 1979. Hippocampus, space and memory. Beh. Brain Sci. **2**: 352–359.
11. LAYLANDER, J. A., D. R. BEERS & R. P. KESNER. 1984. Dissociation of expectancy-based and data-based information processing of a list learning task following partial hippocampus lesions. Neurosci. Abstr. **10**: 135.
12. HOREL, J. 1978. The neuroanatomy of amnesia. A critique of the hippocampal memory hypothesis. Brain **101**: 403–445.
13. MISHKIN, M. 1978. Memory in monkeys severely impaired by combined but not by separate removal of amygdala and hippocampus. Nature **273**: 297–298.
14. IVERSEN, S. D. 1976. Do hippocampal lesions produce amnesia in animals? Int. Rev. Neurobiol. **19**: 1–49.
15. BERMAN, R. F. & R. P. KESNER. 1976. Posttrial hippocampal, amygdaloid and lateral hypothalamic electrical stimulation: Effects upon memory of an appetitive experience. J. Comp. Physiol. Psych. **90**: 260–267.
16. BIERLEY, R. A., R. P. KESNER & J. M. NOVAK. 1983. Episodic long-term memory in the rat: Effects of hippocampal stimulation. Behav. Neurosci. **97**: 42–48.
17. KESNER, R. P. & H. S. CONNER. 1974. Effects of electrical stimulation of limbic system and midbrain reticular formation upon short- and long-term memory. Phys. Behav. **12**: 5–12.
18. OLTON, D. S. & R. J. SAMUELSON. 1976. Remembrance of places passed: Spatial memory in rats. J. Exp. Psych.: Animal Beh. Proc. **2**: 97–116.
19. KESNER, R. P. & J. M. NOVAK. 1982. Serial position curve in rats: Role of the dorsal hippocampus. Science **218**: 173–174.
20. KESNER, R. P., M. O. MEASOM, S. L. FORSMAN, & T. H. HOLBROOK. 1985. Serial position curves in rats: Order memory for episodic spatial events. Anim. Learning Beh. (In press.)
21. KESNER, R. P. 1984. The neurobiology of memory: Implicit and explicit assumptions. *In* Neurobiology of Learning and Memory. J. L. McGaugh, G. Lynch & N. M. Weinberger, Eds.: 111–118. Guilford Press. New York.
22. MILNER, B. 1971. Interhemispheric differences in the localization of psychological processes in man. Brit. Med. Bull. **27**: 272–277.

23. MILNER, B. 1964. Some effects of frontal lobectomy in man. *In* The Frontal Granular Cortex and Behavior. J. M. Warren & K. Akert, Eds. McGraw-Hill. New York.
24. PETRIDES, M. & B. MILNER. 1982. Deficits on subject-ordered tasks after frontal- and temporal-lobe lesions in man. Neuropsych. **20:** 249–262.
25. ROSENKILDE, C. E. 1979. Functional heterogeneity of the prefrontal cortex in the monkey: A review. Beh. Neural Biol. **25:** 301–345.
26. FUSTER, J. M., Ed. 1980. The Prefrontal Cortex: Anatomy, Physiology, and Neuropsychology of the Frontal Lobe. Raven Press. New York.
27. JOHNSTON, V. S., M. HART & W. HOWELL. 1974. The nature of the medial wall deficit in the rat. Neuropsych. **12:** 497–503.
28. ROSENKILDE, C. E. & I. DIVAC. 1975. DRL performance following anteromedial cortical ablations in rats. Brain Res. **95:** 142–146.
29. BARKER, D. J. 1967. Alterations in sequential behavior of rats following ablation of midline limbic cortex. J. Comp. Phys. Psych. **3:** 453–604.
30. MILLER, E. 1971. On the nature of the memory disorder in presenile dementia. Neuropsych. **9:** 75–81.
31. SCHEIBEL, M. E., R. D. LINDSAY, U. TOMIYASU & A. B. SCHEIBEL. 1976. Progressive dendritic changes in aging human limbic system. Exp. Neurobiol. **53:** 420–430.
32. TOMLINSON, B. E. 1977. Morphological changes and dementia in old age. *In* Aging and Dementia. W. L. Smith & M. Kinsbourne, Eds. Spectrum Publications, Inc. New York.
33. PERRY, E. K., G. BLESSED & B. E. TOMLINSON. 1978. Changes in brain cholinesterases in senile dementia of Alzheimer type. Neuropath. App. Neurobiol. **4:** 273–277.
34. MILLER, E. 1981. The nature of the cognitive deficit in senile dementia. *In* Aging: Clinical aspects of Alzheimer's disease and senile dementia. N. E. Miller & G. D. Cohen, Eds. Vol. 15. Raven Press. New York.
35. SHALLICE, T. & E. K. WARRINGTON. 1970. Independent functioning of verbal memory stores: A neuropsychological study. Q. J. Exp. Psych. **22:** 261–273.
36. MILNER, B. 1982. Some cognitive effects of frontal-lobe lesions in man. Phil. Trans. R. Soc. Lond. Ser. B **298:** 211–226.
37. SCHEIBEL, M. E., R. D. LINDSAY, U. TOMIYASU & A. B. SCHEIBEL. 1975. Progressive dendritic changes in aging human cortex. Exp. Neurol. **47:** 392–403.
38. BOWEN, D. M., C. B. SMITH, P. WHITE & A. N. DAVISON. 1976. Neurotransmitter-related enzymes and indices of hypoxia in senile dementia and other abiotrophies. Brain **99:** 459–469.
39. PERRY, E. K., B. E. TOMLINSON, G. BLESSED, K. BERGMANN, P. H. GIBSON & R. H. PERRY. 1978. Correlation of cholinergic abnormalities with senile plaques and mental test scores in senile dementia. Brit. Med. J. **2:** 1457–1459.
40. WHITEHOUSE, P. J., D. L. PRICE, R. G. STRUBLE, A. W. CLARK, J. T. COYLE & M. R. DELONG. 1982. Alzheimer's disease and semile dementia: Loss of neurons in the basal forebrain. Science **215:** 1237–1239.
41. STRUBLE, R. G., L. C. CORK, P. J. WHITEHOUSE & D. L. PRICE. 1982. Cholinergic innervation in neuritic plaques. Science **216:** 413–414.

The Neuropsychology of Memory: New Links between Humans and Experimental Animals

L. R. SQUIRE[a] AND S. ZOLA-MORGAN

Veterans Administration Medical Center, San Diego
and Department of Psychiatry
School of Medicine
University of California
La Jolla, California 92093

Study of how memory is organized in the brain has taken a major forward step in the last few years. As several articles in this volume describe, animal models of human amnesic syndromes have now been achieved. This new and tighter link between work on humans and animals is going to make potentially solvable certain problems that previously could not be addressed systematically. The description of what particular function, what aspect of memory, is damaged in amnesia is continually improving[1-4] and animal models should permit these ideas about function to be linked to anatomy and structure. In addition, some questions about function can be explored more thoroughly in behavioral studies of animals who are amnesic[5-7] than in humans.

This chapter illustrates the utility of this new link between human and animal studies by considering three topics that have figured prominently in recent discussions of the neuropsychology of memory: the concept of memory consolidation; the idea that there are two different kinds of memory, only one of which is affected in amnesia; and the question of which structures in the medial temporal region must be damaged to produce the strikingly selective deficit that is termed amnesia.

Amnesia is characterized by an impaired ability to acquire new information and by difficulty remembering at least some information that was acquired prior to the onset of amnesia. Patients who develop an amnesic syndrome can be disabled in their daily lives to the point of requiring supervisory care. Their deficiency in new learning isolates them from most kinds of social activity, and makes them unable to engage effectively in many of the normal activities of daily living. Cooking a simple meal, for example, places enough burden on memory that the amnesic patient cannot accomplish the required steps without losing his way and forgetting what has already been done, what needs to be done next, what the ringing of the timer was supposed to mean, and so on. Yet despite this severe disability, amnesia is often under-appreciated in the clinic because the impairment can be so pure. For example, case N.A.,[8,9] became amnesic following an accident with a miniature fencing foil that resulted in damage to his left dorsal thalamus. He has a full-scale Wechsler Adult Intelligence Scale (WAIS) IQ of 124, a Wechsler Memory Scale (WMS) of 97 and has no noticeable defect of higher mental function other than a severe verbal memory problem. Indeed, now at the age of 46, 24 years after his injury in 1960, he is an agreeable and well-mannered gentleman with a pleasant sense of humor who would probably be accepted into any circle of conversation without special recognition. Eventually, however, observers would notice

---

[a]Address correspondence to: L. Squire, VA Medical Center, 3350 La Jolla Village Drive, San Diego, California 92161.

that he cannot learn the names of his companions, keep up with a prolonged conversation that keeps to a single topic, or enter into discussions about recent events. It has been known for a long time that amnesia can be caused by damage to one of two parts of the brain, the medial temporal region or the midline of the diencephalon.[10-12] Many questions remain about the exact identity of the important structures within these regions. The animal models that are now available should be able to answer these questions within the next few years.

MEMORY CONSOLIDATION

The historic concept of consolidation[13] was brought firmly to neurobiological studies by McGaugh.[14] Consolidation refers to the idea that memory storage is not instantaneous but develops gradually after initial learning. Based on studies of electroconvulsive therapy (ECT) and retrograde amnesia, we have elaborated this concept and suggest that memory can continue to change in long-term memory for as long as a few years after initial learning.[15] Resistance to disruption develops as forgetting occurs. The medial temporal region plays an obligatory role in maintaining the organization of memory during this time period, but eventually this region is not needed for storage or retrieval of memory. These ideas are based in part on the findings that ECT can affect memories formed one or two years ago without affecting memories formed prior to that time. In addition, case H.M. has consistently been described as having a temporally limited retrograde amnesia and good memory of his early life.[16]

Until recently, these data and the ideas that go with them did not make a clear connection to the data from experimental animals. The data from human amnesia suggested that consolidation can continue for a long time after learning.[17] In contrast, the data from animals, based on paradigms that seemed to reproduce the conditions that cause human amnesia, suggested that consolidation is relatively rapid and is completed within seconds or minutes after learning.[14,18]

A recent study found evidence for continuity between the data from humans and from experimental animals.[19] Mice were given a single training trial in a passive avoidance task, a much-used paradigm for studying memory in rodents.[20] Half the animals later received four treatments of electro convulsive shock (ECS), spaced one hour apart, at one of seven different times after training (1 day to 12 weeks). The other half of the animals received sham ECS. Retention was tested on a single trial two weeks after the treatment in order to allow dissipation of possible proactive effects of ECS on the subsequent retention measure. Four separate ECS were used to mimic the circumstances of human ECT, where one treatment is known to exert less retrograde amnesia than several treatments.[21]

The results were that memory for the avoidance task in the sham-treated mice persisted for more than 12 weeks, although the mice exhibited gradual forgetting of the passive-avoidance habit during this interval. ECS caused a loss of memory when it was given within three weeks after training. The susceptibility of memory to disruption by ECS gradually diminished during the three weeks after training. Thus, retrogarde amnesia covered a considerable portion of the lifetime of the habit. FIGURE 1 compares these results obtained for mice given ECS and tested on the passive avoidance task to previous results obtained for patients given ECT and tested on memory for past one-season television programs.[22] The forms of the curves are similar. The passive avoidance task in mice is forgotten during a period of many weeks and retrograde amnesia covered one to three weeks. Memory for television programs is lost gradually over the years and retrograde amnesia covered a period of a few years.

These findings suggest that consolidation is not a fixed, automatic process. Its rate and duration can vary, depending on the course of normal forgetting. As time passes after learning, details are lost through forgetting, and the original representation is resculpted by subsequent events, by rehearsal, and by the learning of related information. In the end, what survives has been reorganized and has become more resistant to disruption. These findings in mice and humans, based on formal experimental methods, agree with earlier reports of case H.M.[23] and post-encephalitic patients[24] who were said to have temporally limited retrograde amnesia based on interview methods. A recent formal study of H.M.[25] also found evidence for temporally limited retrograde amnesia. Accordingly, it seems reasonable to think that the medial temporal region is ordinarily involved in memory storage processes for as long as a few years after initial learning and that after that time it is either less involved or not at all involved in memory storage.

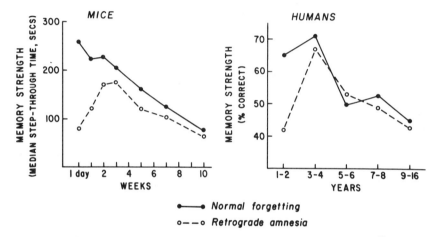

FIGURE 1. Temporally graded retrograde amnesia in mice and humans.[19]

TWO KINDS OF MEMORY

A major new concept for our understanding of memory and the brain is that there are two kinds of memory. Only one of these requires the integrity of the medial temporal region and is affected in amnesia. We have referred to the memory that is affected in amnesia as declarative memory and have described it as a memory system that acquires information about facts or episodes. Memory for skills or procedures, what we have termed procedural knowledge, is preserved in amnesia.[3,26,27] It is now known that it survives retrograde amnesia as well.[28] That is, a skill can be taught prior to a course of ECT and survive the ECT, although patients are afterwards unable to remember that they had learned a skill or to supply the information that they had acquired while using the skill.

Several different names have been applied to the two kinds of memory considered here (TABLE 1). Many, but not all, of these distinctions were derived specifically to address the data concerning what human amnesic patients can and cannot do, or what animals who have lesions of the structures presumed to be damaged in human amnesia can and cannot do. Some of the distinctions come from the literature of cognitive

TABLE 1. Two Kinds of Memory

A	B	Reference
Fact	Skill	The media
Declarative	Procedural	Cohen & Squire[26]
Memory	Habit	Mishkin[29]
Knowing that	Knowing how	Ryle[30]
Locale	Taxon	O'Keefe & Nadel[31]
Cognitive mediation	Semantic	Warrington & Weiskrantz[32]
Conscious recollection	Skills	Moscovitch[33] and Baddeley[34]
Elaboration	Integration	Mandler[35]
Memory with record	Memory without record	Bruner[36]
Autobiographical	Perceptual	Jacoby and Dallas[37]
Representational	Dispositional	Thomas[38]

Note: Numbers in reference column indicate reference numbers at end of chapter.

psychology. One of them comes from developmental psychology; another comes from philosophy. The declarative-procedural distinction that we have used in the context of human amnesia was used originally in the literature of artificial intelligence.[39] Not all the distinctions are identical. The terms in a column seem sometimes broader and sometimes narrower than other terms in the same column.

But these differences seem small compared to the significance of the general idea that two fundamentally different forms of memory should be distinguished. In our view, the terms in column A describe a memory system or process that is accessible to conscious awareness, adapted for one-trial learning, and dependent on the brain system that is damaged in amnesia. The terms in column B describe a system or process that is more automatic, not accessible to conscious awareness, adapted for incremental learning, and independent of the brain system damaged in amnesia. What makes this distinction important is the idea that it is biologically meaningful, a distinction that is honored by the nervous system.

The term declarative, which we have used, captures the notion that one kind of memory can be "declared"; it can be brought to mind explicitly, as a proposition or an image. The capacity for declarative memory may be a relatively recent feat of evolution, appearing early in the vertebrates with the development of the hippocampus, and the capacity for declarative memory may be ontogenetically delayed.[40-42] Procedural knowledge, by contrast, can be expressed only through performance, and the contents of this knowledge are not accessible to awareness. Procedural knowledge is considered to be phylogenetically primitive and ontogenetically early.

Two distinctions have been omitted from TABLE 1, because they make a different point about memory (FIGURE 2). We agree with Tulving and his colleagues[43,44] that the episodic-semantic distinction, which has something interesting to say about the structure of normal memory, is a subset of declarative (or propositional) memory. As discussed elsewhere, both episodic and semantic memory are impaired in amnesia.[27] That conclusion holds both for anterograde and retrograde memory impairment. If one surveys from the remote past of amnesic patients, rather than from the recent past, then both episodic and semantic memory are preserved to an equivalent extent.[45] We take a similar view of the working-reference memory distinction, which was developed from work with hippocampus-damaged rats trained in a particular apparatus.[46] That is, the working-reference memory distinction is a subset of declarative memory as Tulving[43] also suggested. At the least this classification should have heuristic value. All the distinctions shown in FIGURE 2 cannot be correct, when considering how to characterize the amnesia that follows a particular brain lesion.

WHICH STRUCTURES IN THE MEDIAL TEMPORAL REGION MUST BE DAMAGED TO PRODUCE AMNESIA?

The insight that only one kind of memory is affected in amnesia indicates that the amnesic syndrome is a much narrower syndrome than previously thought. This insight more than any other has made it possible to define the tasks appropriate for studying amnesia in experimental animals and to understand the patterns of successful and impaired performance in animals with brain lesions. To date, the development of animal models of amnesia have been most successful in the monkey.

In trying to identify which structures in the medial temporal region must be damaged to produce amnesia, interest has focused on the hippocampal formation and the amygdala. Much of the initial work has been done with the delayed non-matching to sample task, a task sensitive to human amnesia.[47] The task itself was developed for use with monkeys several years ago.[48,49] On the first trial the monkey displaces a junk object to obtain a raisin reward. In the test phase, which can be presented many minutes or even hours later, the monkey sees the original object together with a novel object, and must displace the novel object to find a raisin reward. Subsequent trials use different pairs of junk objects taken from a large set of several hundred objects.

FIGURE 3 shows the results from three different laboratories, where the effects of separate hippocampal (H) lesions and combined hippocampal-amygdala (H-A) lesions have been evaluated with the delayed non-matching to sample task. The results show clearly that the combined H-A lesions produced a larger deficit than the hippocampal lesions alone. We had originally proposed[12] that H-A lesions may produce more amnesia than H lesions, because the hippocampus is incompletely destroyed in the latter case, but completely destroyed in the former. Indeed, our review of the literature had indicated that the anterior portion of the hippocampus was often spared in studies attempting to damage the hippocampus selectively. However, it now appears that this explanation is incorrect and cannot account for the greater effect on memory of H-A lesions as compared to H lesions. In our study ($N = 7$, FIGURE 3), the H lesions in four of the seven monkeys have now been examined histologically and were found to be complete in each case. Selective H lesions were also demonstrated to be complete in another recent study[53] in which monkeys with H-A lesions were concurrently tested and found to have a greater impairment. Thus, it appears that insofar as performance on the delayed non-matching task is concerned, removal of the hippocampus alone does

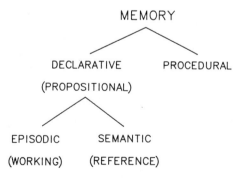

FIGURE 2. A preliminary taxonomy of memory systems. Episodic and semantic memory, and working and reference memory, are considered to be subsets of declarative or propositional memory.

DELAYED
NON-MATCHING TO SAMPLE

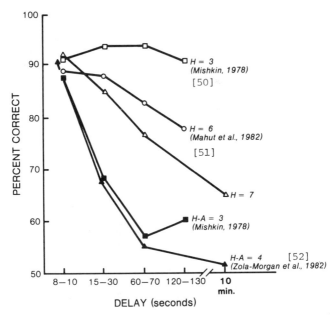

FIGURE 3. Data from three laboratories comparing the effects of hippocampal (H) versus conjoint hippocampal-amygdala (H-A) lesions on the delayed non-matching to sample task. (H = 7: monkeys with lesions of the hippocampus tested in our laboratory; numbers in brackets indicate reference numbers.)

not result in as severe an impairment as is found following conjoint removal of the hippocampus and the amygdala.

The next question that should be asked is how impaired are the monkeys with selective H lesions. Are they normal? Or are they impaired; and if so, are they impaired to a meaningful degree? FIGURE 4 shows data from the same three laboratories represented in FIGURE 3. Here the performance of monkeys with hippocampal lesions is compared to the perfomance of normal monkeys. Although the degree of deficit varies, the data from all three laboratories agree that H monkeys are significantly impaired. The right panel of FIGURE 4 shows the averaged data from the three groups of monkeys with H lesions and the three normal groups, combining data for two-minute and 10-minute delays. The impairment of the monkeys with H lesions is clear. The overall group difference is highly significant. At the longest delay, 12 normal monkeys scored 90% correct, and 16 monkeys with hippocampal lesions scored 78% correct.

While these comparisons are illuminating, what one really wants to know is whether this impairment following lesions restricted to the hippocampal formation is clinically meaningful. If a patient had this lesion, would he or she be substantially disabled in memory performance? One way to think about this problem is to recall the extent to which distraction can exacerbate the impairment of amnesic patients. Distraction occurs normally between the time an event is learned and the time it is needed in recall. It is well known that distraction-filled delays increase the deficit in amnesic patients; and sometimes, when overt rehearsal is possible, distraction is needed to produce any deficit at all.[54]

These considerations suggested to us that it would be worthwhile to evaluate the effects of distraction on memory in monkeys. Accordingly, we tested the effects of introducing irrelevant extra sample trials during the retention interval of the delayed non-matching to sample task.[55] On half of the delay trials at 15 and 30 seconds, an irrelevant object was introduced during the delay, and monkeys displaced it to obtain a raisin. FIGURE 5 shows the results of such a manipulation in the case of H-A monkeys performing delayed non-matching to sample at delays up to 30 seconds. The distraction brought the performance of the operated monkeys to chance. For example, H-A monkeys tested at a delay of 30 seconds between sample and choice trials scored 61% correct when there was no distraction and 48% correct when distraction was introduced. This result shows that distraction can have a large effect on the performance of operated monkeys just as it can exacerbate the impaired performance of human amnesic patients. It will be important to test monkeys with selective hippocampal lesions on the distraction procedure.

Turning back to the finding that the deficit following conjoint H-A lesions was larger than the deficit following H lesions, one must also try to understand the reason for the additional deficit in monkeys with the conjoint lesion. Accordingly, we have begun to evaluate the contribution of the structural damage beyond hippocampus that occurs in monkeys with conjoint H-A lesions, i.e. in lesions where it is intended to add an amygdala lesion to a hippocampal lesion. When an amygdala lesion is done in the

DELAYED NON-MATCHING TO SAMPLE

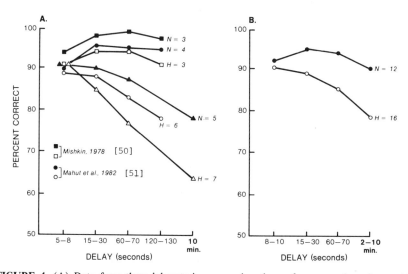

FIGURE 4. (A) Data from three laboratories comparing the performance of monkeys with hippocampal (H) lesions to that of normal (N) monkeys on the delayed non-matching to sample task. (N = 5, H = 7: normal monkeys and monkeys with lesions of the hippocampus tested in our laboratory; numbers in brackets indicate reference numbers.) (B) Combined data for all the normal (N) monkeys and monkeys with hippocampal (H) lesions in (A). Scores for the 2-minute and 10-minute delays have been combined.

DELAYED NON-MATCHING TO SAMPLE

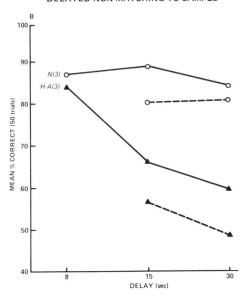

FIGURE 5. Delayed non-matching to sample performance by three normal monkeys (N) and three monkeys with conjoint lesions of the hippocampus and amygdala (H-A). For half the 15-second and 30-second delay trials (dashed lines), a distraction task was introduced during the delay.[55]

ordinary way by a fronto-temporal surgical approach, the extra damage includes most prominently the entorhinal cortex and perirhinal cortex. In an effort to avoid damage to these areas, Dr. David Amaral of the Salk Institute in La Jolla, California has assisted us in preparing a group of monkeys with amygdala lesions using a specially designed stereotaxic procedure. These lesions were made using four separate electrode placements on each side, and the brains from two animals prepared in this way have been examined histologically. The lesions of the amygdala were circumscribed and complete and the surrounding tissue, including entorhinal and perirhinal cortex, was spared. Three additional monkeys prepared in the same way have been trained and tested in delayed non-matching to sample, but have not yet come to histology. These monkeys showed signs of reduced fear, a behavioral effect that has been reported to appear only when amygdala damage is complete or nearly complete.[56]

Thus far, only two laboratories have tested monkeys on the delayed non-matching to sample task following amygdala lesions (FIGURE 6). The conventional lesion that involves amygdala, together with portions of entorhinal and perirhinal cortex, produced a small, but significant deficit.[50] The newly devised lesion that spares the extra-amygdala areas produced no deficit at all, even at a delay of 10 minutes.[57] These two findings raise the possibility that damage to the surrounding cortical areas rather than damage to the amygdala itself may be responsible for adding to the deficit found following hippocampal lesions alone (FIGURE 3). However, these data can only raise the possibility, and direct studies will be needed to decide the issue. A direct study of this question would evaluate monkeys with a hippocampal lesion plus a circumscribed amygdala lesion against monkeys with a hippocampal lesion plus a lesion limited to those portions of entorhinal cortex and perirhinal cortex that are typically damaged during conventional amygdala surgery.

There is one final point that will require attention before the identity of the medial temporal structures important in amnesia can be established with certainty. The deficit produced by the candidate lesion(s) must be demonstrated on a variety of tasks, in the same way that the deficit in human amnesia can be shown to hold across a variety of learning and memory tasks. FIGURE 7 summarizes data from four different tasks that are sensitive to the effects of H-A lesions.[55] These tasks are each sensitive to human amnesia, although the particular requirements of the tasks vary. Together with tests of skill learning, which can be accomplished normally by monkeys with these lesions,[58] these problems may be considered to constitute a battery for testing monkeys for the presence of an amnesic syndrome. It will therefore be important to test monkeys with hippocampal lesions on each of these tasks. Eventually, this same analysis could be extended to diencephalic amnesia by testing monkeys with lesions of medial dorsal thalamic nucleus,[59,60] mammillary bodies,[61] and combined lesions of these structures.

CONCLUSION

The availability of animal models for the clinical syndrome of amnesia is a cause for optimism and excitement. The way is clear now for identifying the structures, both in the medial temporal region and in the diencephalic midline, that cause amnesia.

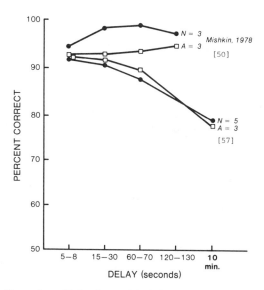

**DELAYED
NON-MATCHING TO SAMPLE**

FIGURE 6. The effects of two kinds of amygdala lesions on delayed non-matching to sample performance: surgical lesions of the amygdala with additional damage to entorhinal and perirhinal cortex[50]; stereotaxic lesions of the amygdala and no additional cortical damage.[57] Numbers in brackets indicate reference numbers.

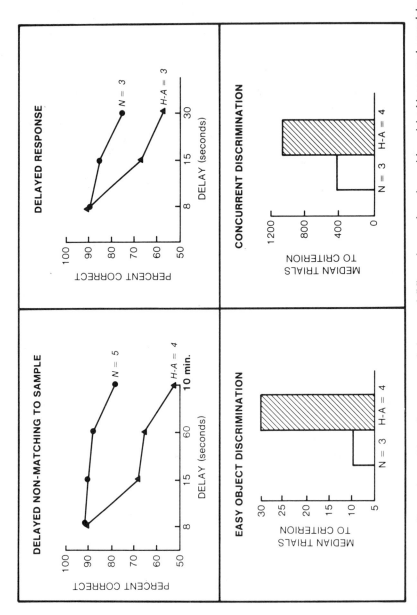

FIGURE 7. Performance on four tasks sensitive to human amnesia by normal (N) monkeys and monkeys with conjoint hippocampal-amygdala (H-A) lesions.[55]

This work, together with anatomical and physiological data, should lead to the identification of a particular brain system that has an identified function in normal cognition. This in turn can lead to more detailed neurobiological studies. In this sequence, even studies carried out at a cellular level promise to maintain a clear link to functional questions about memory and the human brain.

REFERENCES

1. SQUIRE, L. R. 1982. The neuropsychology of human memory. Annu. Rev. Neurosci. **5**: 241–273.
2. SQUIRE, L. R. & N. BUTTERS, Eds. 1984. The Neuropsychology of Memory. Guilford Press. New York.
3. COHEN, N. J. 1985. Different memory systems underlying acquisition of procedural and declarative knowledge. Ann. N.Y. Acad. Sci. (This volume.)
4. WARRINGTON, E. 1985. A disconnection analysis of amnesia. Ann. N.Y. Acad. Sci. (This volume.)
5. KESNER, R. P. 1984. Correspondence between humans and animals in coding of temporal attributes: role of hippocampus and prefrontal cortex. Ann. N.Y. Acad. Sci. (This volume.)
6. MISHKIN, M. 1984. Global amnesia in the monkey. Ann. N.Y. Acad. Sci. (This volume.)
7. OLTON, D. S. 1985. Criteria for establishing and evaluating animal models. Ann. N.Y. Acad. Sci. (This volume.)
8. TEUBER, H. L., B. MILNER & H. G. VAUGHAN. 1968. Persistent anterograde amnesia after stab wound of the basal brain. Neuropsychologia **6**: 267–282.
9. KAUSHALL, P. I., M. ZETIN & L. R. SQUIRE. 1981. A psychosocial study of chronic, circumscribed amnesia. J. Nervous Mental Dis. **169**: 383–389.
10. MAIR, W. G. P., E. K. WARRINGTON & L. WEISKRANTZ. 1979. Memory disorder in Korsakoff's psychosis: A neuropathological and neuropsychological investigation of two cases. Brain **102**: 749–783.
11. MISHKIN, M. 1982. A memory system in the monkey. Phil. Trans. R. Soc. London Ser. B **298**: 85–95.
12. SQUIRE, L. R. & S. ZOLA-MORGAN. 1983. The neurology of memory: The case for correspondence between the findings for man and non-human primate. *In* The Physiological Basis of Memory. 2nd edit. J.A. Deutsch, Ed.: 200–268. Academic Press. New York.
13. MULLER, G. E. & A. PLZECKER. 1900. Experimentelle Beitrage zur Lehre vom Gedachtniss [Experimental contributions to the theory of memory]. Zeitschr. Psychol. **1**: 1–288.
14. MCGAUGH, J. L. & M. L. HERZ. 1972. Memory Consolidation. Albion. San Francisco.
15. SQUIRE, L. R., N. J. COHEN & L. NADEL. 1984. The medial temporal region and memory consolidation: A new hypothesis. *In* Memory Consolidation. H. Weingartner & E. Parker, Eds. Lawrence Erlbaum Associates. Hillsdale, NJ.
16. CORKIN, S. 1984. Lasting consequences of bilateral medial temporal lobectomy: Clinical course and experimental findings in H.M. Seminars Neurol. **4**: 249–259.
17. RUSSELL, W. R. & P. W. NATHAN. 1946. Traumatic amnesia. Brain **69**: 280–300.
18. CHOROVER, S. L. 1974. An experimental critique of "Consolidation Studies" and an alternative "model-systems" approach to the biophysiology of memory. *In* Neural Mechanisms of Learning and Memory. M.R. Rosenzweig & E.L. Bennett, Eds.: 561–582. MIT Press. Cambridge.
19. SQUIRE, L. R. & C. W. SPANIS. 1984. Long gradient of retrograde amnesia in mice: continuity with the findings in humans. Behav. Neurosci. **98**(2): 345–348.
20. JARVIK, M. R. & R. KOPP. 1967. An improved one-trial passive avoidance learning situation. Psychol. Reports. **21**: 221–224.
21. SQUIRE, L. R. 1984. Opinion and facts about ECT. Can Science help? Commentary for Behavioral and Brain Sciences **7**: 34–37.
22. SQUIRE, L. R., P. C. SLATER & P. M. CHACE. 1975. Retrograde amnesia: temporal gradient in very long-term memory following electroconvulsive therapy. Science **187**: 77–79.

23. MILNER, B., S. CORKIN & H. L. TEUBER. 1968. Further analysis of the hippocampal amnesic syndrome: 14-year follow-up study of H.M. Neuropsychologia **6:** 215–234.
24. ROSE, F. C. & C. P. SYMONDS. 1960. Persistent memory defect following encephalitis. Brain **83:** 195–212.
25. SAGAR, D. M., N. J. COHEN & S. CORKIN. 1985. Dissociations among processes in remote memory. Ann. N.Y. Acad. Sci. (This volume.)
26. COHEN, N. & L. R. SQUIRE. 1980. Preserved learning and retention of pattern analyzing skill in amnesia: Dissociation of knowing how and knowing that. Science **210:** 207–209.
27. SQUIRE, L. R. & N. J. COHEN. 1984. Human memory and amnesia. *In* Neurobiology of Learning and Memory. G. Lynch, J.L. McGaugh & N.M. Weinberger, Eds. Guilford Press. New York.
28. SQUIRE, L. R., N. J. COHEN & J. A. ZOUZOUNIS. 1984. Preserved memory in retrograde amnesia: sparing of a recently acquired skill. Neuropsychologia **22:** 145–152.
29. MISHKIN, M., B. MALAMUT & J. BACHEVALIER. 1984. Memories and habits: two neural systems. *In* Neurobiology of Learning and Memory. G. Lynch, J.L. McGaugh & N.M. Weinberger, Eds. Guilford Press. New York.
30. RYLE, G. 1949. The Concept of Mind. Hutchinson. San Francisco.
31. O'KEEFE, J. & L. NADEL. 1978. The Hippocampus as a Cognitive Map. Oxford University Press. London.
32. WARRINGTON, E. K. & L. WEISKRANTZ. 1982. Amnesia: A disconnection syndrome. Neuropsychologia **20:** 233–248.
33. MOSCOVITCH, M. 1982. Multiple dissociations of function in amnesia. *In* Human Memory and Amnesia. L. Cermak, Ed.: 337–370. Lawrence Erlbaum Associates. Hillsdale, NJ.
34. BADDELEY, A. 1982. Implications of neuropsychological evidence for theories of normal memory. Phil. Trans. R. Soc. London Ser. B **298:** 59–72.
35. MANDLER, G. 1980. Recognizing: The judgment of previous occurrence. Psychological Rev. **87:** 252–271.
36. BRUNER, J. S. 1969. Modalities of memory. *In* The Pathology of Memory. G.A. Talland & N.C. Waugh, Eds.: 253–259. Academic Press. New York.
37. JACOBY, L. L. & M. DALLAS. 1981. On the relationship between autobiographical memory and perceptual learning. J. Exp. Psychol. Gen. **3:** 306–340.
38. THOMAS, G. J. 1984. Memory: Time Binding in Organisms. *In* Neuropsychology of Memory. L.R. Squire & N. Butters, Eds.: 374–384. Guilford Press. New York.
39. WINOGRAD, R. 1975. Frame representations and the declarative-procedural controversy. *In* Representation and Understanding. D. Bobrow & A. Collins, Eds. Academic Press. New York.
40. SQUIRE, L.R. 1985. Memory and the Brain. *In* Brain, Cognition, and Education. S.L. Friedman, K.A. Klivington & R.W. Peterson, Eds. Academic Press. New York. (In press.)
41. SCHACTER, D. L. & M. MOSCOVITCH. 1984. Infants, amnesics, and dissociable memory systems. *In* Infant Memory. M. Moscovitch, Ed. Plenum Press. New York.
42. NADEL, L., & S. ZOLA-MORGAN. 1984. Toward the understanding of infant memory: Contributions from animal neuropsychology. *In* Infant Memory. M. Moscovitch, Ed. Plenum Press. New York.
43. TULVING, E. 1985. Multiple learning and memory systems. *In* Psychology in the 1990's. K. Lagerspetz & P. Niemi, Eds. North-Holland. Amsterdam. (In press.)
44. SCHACTER, D. L. & E. TULVING. 1982. Memory, amnesia, and the semantic/episodic distinction. *In* Expression of Knowledge. R.L. Isaacson & N.E. Spear, Eds.: 33–65. Plenum Press. New York.
45. ZOLA-MORGAN, S., N. J. COHEN & L. R. SQUIRE. 1983. Recall of remote episodic memory in amnesia. Neuropsychologia **21:** 487–500.
46. OLTON, D. S., J. T. BECKER & G. E. HANDELMANN. 1979. Hippocampus, space, and memory. Behav. Brain Sci. **2:** 313–365.
47. SQUIRE, L. R. & S. ZOLA-MORGAN. Unpublished observations.
48. GAFFAN, D. 1974. Recognition impaired and association intact in the memory of monkeys after transection of the fornix. J. Comp. Physiol. Psychol. **86:** 1100–1109.

49. MISHKIN, M. & J. DELACOUR. 1975. An analysis of short-term visual memory in the monkey. J. Exp. Psychol.: Anim. Behav. Processes 1: 326–334.

50. MISHKIN, M. 1978. Memory in monkeys severely impaired by combined but not by separate removal of amygdala and hippocampus. Nature 273: 297–298.

51. MAHUT, H., S. ZOLA-MORGAN & M. MOSS. 1982. Hippocampal resections impair associative learning and recognition memory in the monkey. J. Neurosci. 2: 1214–1229.

52. ZOLA-MORGAN, S., L. R. SQUIRE & M. MISHKIN. 1982. The neuroanatomy of amnesia: amygdala-hippocampus versus temporal stem. Science 218: 1337–1339.

53. MURRAY, E. A. & M. MISHKIN. 1984. Combined removal of the amygdala and hippocampus in monkeys produces severe tactual as well as visual memory deficits. J. Neurosci. (In press.)

54. MILNER, B. 1972. Disorders of learning and memory after temporal lobe lesions in man. Clin. Neurosurg. 19: 421–446.

55. ZOLA-MORGAN, S. & L. R. SQUIRE. 1985. Medial temporal lesions in monkeys impair memory in a variety of tasks sensitive to amnesia. Behav. Neurosci. (In press.)

56. AGGLETON, J. P. & M. MISHKIN. 1982. A comparison of amygdaloid and hippocampal projections to the thalamus in monkeys. Soc. Neurosci. Abstr. 8: 836.

57. ZOLA-MORGAN, S. & L. R. SQUIRE. 1984. Performance of monkeys with separate and combined lesions of hippocampus and amygdala on delayed nonmatching to sample. Soc. Neurosci. Abstracts 9: 27.

58. ZOLA-MORGAN, S. & L. R. SQUIRE. 1984. Preserved learning in monkeys with medial temporal lesions: sparing of motor and cognitive skills. J. Neurosci. 4(4): 1072–1085.

59. AGGLETON, J. P. & M. MISHKIN. 1983. Memory impairments following restricted medial thalamic lesions in monkeys. Exp. Brain Res. 52: 199–209.

60. ZOLA-MORGAN, S. & L. R. SQUIRE. 1985. Lesions of the dorsal medial thalamic nucleus in monkeys cause amnesia. Ann. Neurol. (In press.)

61. SAUNDERS, R. C. 1983. Impairment in recognition memory after mammillary body lesions in monkeys. Soc. Neurosci. Abstracts 9: 28.

Peripheral and Central Adrenergic Influences on Brain Systems Involved in the Modulation of Memory Storage[a]

JAMES L. McGAUGH

Center for the Neurobiology of Learning and Memory
and Department of Psychobiology
University of California
Irvine, California 92717

There are two major and equally important reasons for studying memory in animals. First, as the articles in this volume amply attest, the phenomena of learning and memory in animals are of great interest. On the assumption that most behavior is learned, questions concerning the nature of learning and memory have dominated psychological theory and research for decades. Laboratory animals, usually rats, cats, dogs, or rabbits have been used as sources of facts and principles of learning and memory as well as arbiters of theoretical controversy.[1] Ethological studies of less domesticated animals have attempted to reveal the nature and role of learning and memory in animal adaptation.[2] Throughout the relatively brief history of research on animal learning and memory there has been a parallel interest in the physiological mechanisms underlying learning and memory. Pavlov's purpose in investigating conditioned reflexes was to gain insights in brain physiology.[3] Since the turn of the century each successive decade has provided new techniques for investigating brain mechanisms as well as new hypotheses and theories concerning the anatomical, physiological, cellular, and biochemical bases of learning and memory. Here too, studies of animal learning have been central in arbitration of theoretical controversy.

A second major reason for studying animal learning and memory is based on the assumption that studies using animals provide useful models of human learning and memory. The current acceleration of interest in animal studies of learning and memory seems to be motivated primarily by interests in understanding human memory and in developing therapy for memory disorders. This interest is, of course, the major concern of the present volume. It is worth noting that interest in principles of human learning and memory was implicit in earlier research on animal learning. Hull's highly influential book, *Principles of Behavior*,[4] was based primarily on findings of studies of animal learning. Hull was, however, not constrained by the sources of his principles. In the preface to his book he wrote:

> ... this book attempts to present in an objective, systematic manner the primary, or fundamental, molar principles of behavior. It has been written on the assumption that all behavior, individual and social, moral and immoral, normal and psychopathic, is generated from the same primary laws; ... Consequently, the present work may be regarded as a general introduction to the theory of all the behavioral (social) sciences.[4] (pg v)

Skinner's book, *The Behavior of Organisms*,[5] was based exclusively on studies of learned behavior in rats. However, Skinner, like Hull showed little constraint in applying his principles to human behavior.[6]

[a]Supported by U.S. Public Health Service Research Grants AG 0058 and MH 12526 and the Office of Naval Research, Contract N00014-84-K-0391.

VALIDITY OF ANIMAL MODELS

Thus, the use of animal models of human learning and memory is a well-established tradition. At one level, this use of animal research seems quite reasonable. At the very least, animal models of learning and memory have face value. Animals, like humans, learn, show retention of the learned behavior, and with time and interference, forget. Many of the detailed findings of animal learning and memory are like those obtained in human studies.[7] Thus, there is reasonably good correspondence between many aspects of animal and human memory. This correspondence stands in contrast to animal models of other human behavior. It is not clear that there are valid animal models of human depression, schizophrenia, or attentional disorders. It is of interest to note that the absence of models with face-validity has not precluded the use of animal behavior in screening drugs for potential use in the treatment of these human behavioral disorders. It might be that more effective treatments could be developed if there were face-valid animal models of these disorders.

However, face-validity of an animal model of human behavior might also be misleading. The fundamental problem is that there is no ready means of determining whether the similarities in behavior are homologous or merely analogous. Bees, birds, and bats all learn. They also fly, and it is clear that their ability to fly is not based on homologous mechanisms. Do the same principles of learning apply to animal and human learning and memory or are there fundamental differences arising from special adaptive requirements? For example, does our use of language cause us to learn and remember in ways unavailable to lower species? Do the spatial abilities of rats[8] enable them to learn about their environments in a way that are unavailable to us? If there are fundamental differences in learning and memory, are there also common features in animal and human memory? Are we and lower animals alike in the way we learn about the events of the day, in learning things to be afraid of and things to like? There are of course, many species of animals and, consequently, there may well be basic differences among species in forms of learning. There may also be aspects of learning common among lower species as well as humans. The evidence of conservation in evolution would argue strongly for continuity. Is our learning and memory in some fundamental ways like that of the marine molluscs *Aplysia* and *Hermissenda,* which are used extensively in cellular studies of learning and memory?[9,10] Assessment of the adequacy of animal models of memory require, ultimately, that we find answers to these questions. The usefulness of animal models of human learning and memory will depend upon whether the features and mechanisms of animal and human memory are in some basic sense homologous.

IMPAIRMENT AND ENHANCEMENT OF MEMORY IN ANIMALS

Animal studies have proved highly useful in investigation of retrograde amnesia and enhancement of memory. This area of research is particularly relevant to the question of the appropriateness of animal models of memory since the basic experimental and theoretical issues it addresses grew out of experimental as well as clinical observations of human memory. The Perseveration-Consolidation hypothesis, which was originally proposed as an explanation for retroactive interference in human forgetting[11] was also considered to provide an explanation for retrograde amnesia produced by head injury.[12] Early findings that electroconvulsive therapy (ECT) treatments impaired memory in human patients[13] led to studies of the effects of electroconvulsive shock (ECS) on retention in laboratory animals.[14] Recent studies of the effects of ECT on memory in human patients have confirmed and greatly extended these findings.[15] Studies of learning and memory in animals have also greatly extended the findings of the early studies of the effects of ECS on retention. There is now extensive evidence that the retention of newly learned information can be impaired or enhanced by administration of a variety of treatments shortly after training.[16] These findings have generally been interpreted as suggesting the treatments alter memory by modulating time-dependent processes underlying memory storage.[17,18] The effects of posttraining treatments on memory appear not to be restricted to any one task or restricted set of tasks: Both retrograde amnesia and enhancement of memory are found with a wide variety of tasks including active avoidance, inhibitory avoidance, discrimination learning, maze learning (with appetitive motivation), latent learning, spatial alternation, and sensory pre-conditioning.[19] Enhancement of memory has been found with a variety of posttraining treatments including electrical stimulation of the brain, several CNS stimulants, and adrenergic hormones as well as neuropeptides.[18,20,21] The fact that the effects are obtained with such a wide range of experimental tasks and treatments suggests that the treatments have a common influence on some general process or processes involved in the storage of recent experiences. It is perhaps worth emphasizing that modulating influences are not restricted to drugs influencing only a few transmitters. These findings may be instructive for research seeking memory enhancers for use in treatment of human memory dysfunction. Focus on specific brain transmitter systems might well prove to be too restrictive and, at the same time, unnecessary. While there is some evidence that memory in human subjects can be influenced by several classes of drugs and hormones,[22,23] the findings, to date, are clearly not as robust as those obtained in experiments with laboratory animals. The reasons for this are not yet clear. It might be that only certain forms of learning are susceptible to modulating influences. Or, it might be that the optimal conditions for demonstrating the effects of drugs on human memory have not yet been determined. One of the major problems facing studies of the effects of drugs on memory is that enhancing effects are typically found within a fairly narrow range of doses. The dose-response curve is usually an inverted-U. Further, the effect of a given dose varies with the specific task and training conditions used. From an experimental perspective, such findings suggest that determining effective drug doses in human studies may be difficult. From a practical perspective the findings also suggest that drugs known to have a narrow range of effective doses in animal studies are likely to be of limited use in the treatment of human memory disorders.

HORMONAL MODULATION OF MEMORY

Adrenergic catecholamines and peptide hormones, including ACTH and vasopressin are among the treatments that have been shown to affect retention when administered to animals after training.[24] As with drugs, the hormones tend to affect retention in a narrow range of doses. It is well-known that these hormones (as well as others) are released from the adrenal medulla and pituitary when animals are given stimulation of the kind typically used in training.[21] Several years ago Gold and I suggested that hormones released at the time of a learning experience may serve as endogenous modulators of memory storage.[25] According to this view, posttraining susceptibility to memory-modulating influences serves an important adaptive function: The period of susceptibility allows hormones released by experiences to influence memories of the experiences by modulating time-dependent memory storage processes.

An unfortunate consequence of the susceptibility is that it also provides opportunity for accidents that produce retrograde amnesia. Fortunately, conditions that impair memory, such as head injury, occur infrequently.

The findings of many recent studies using animals provide support for the view that hormones released during learning play an important role in the normal physiology of memory storage. Studies in my laboratory have focused on adrenergic hormones. In previous work, Gold[26] found that, in low doses, epinephrine enhanced rats' retention of an inhibitory avoidance task. Recently, we found that the enhancing effect of epinephrine on memory is not restricted to aversively motivated tasks. Epinephrine also enhances retention of an appetitively motivated discrimination task.[27] Such generality is required, of course, if it is assumed that epinephrine has a general role as in the modulation of memory storage. A different interpretation would be required were epinephrine effects restricted to learning based on aversive motivation.

The findings of other recent studies indicate that the memory-influencing effects of ECS and other treatments may involve adrenergic systems. Gold and Sternberg[28] found, for example, that adrenergic antagonists block the amnestic effects of several drugs, including pentylenetetrazol, cycloheximide, and diethyldithiocarbamate, as well as the effects of electrical stimulation of the frontal cortex and amygdala. Adrenergic antagonists also block the enhancing effects of electrical stimulation of the brain. As FIGURE 1 shows, posttraining electrical stimulation of the frontal cortex enhances retention in animals trained on an active avoidance task with low footshock and impairs retention in animals trained with high footshock. Both the enhancing and impairing effects of the brain stimulation were blocked in animals given the beta-antagonist, propranolol, prior to training.[29]

The hypothesis that endogenous adrenergic hormones are involved in the modulation of memory storage is also supported by evidence that the effects of posttraining electrical stimulation of the amygdala are altered by adrenal demedullation or denervation.[30] In these studies, rats were implanted bilaterally with amygdala electrodes and then given sham adrenal surgery or were demedullated or denervated. They were then trained on inhibitory and active avoidance tasks. Amygdala stimulation was administered immediately after training and retention was tested 24 hours following training. FIGURE 2 shows the effects found with demedullated rats trained in the inhibitory avoidance tasks. With these training conditions, retention performance was not significantly affected by either the electrode implanatation or the adrenal demedullation. However, retention was significantly impaired in the demedullated implanted controls. Demedullation altered the effect of amygdala stimulation: Amygdala stimulation impaired retention in animals with intact adrenal medullae but enhanced retention in demedullated rats (in comparison with controls that were implanted and demedullated). Highly similar results were obtained with denervated rats and with an active avoidance task.

Other recent evidence supports the interpretation that these effects of adrenal demedullation are due specifically to depletion of adrenal epinephrine.[31] First, as the findings summarized in FIGURE 3 indicate, the retention deficit seen in demedullated rats with implanted amygdala electrodes is attenuated by posttraining administration of epinephrine. Second, posttraining amygdala stimulation impairs retention in demedullated rats if epinephrine is administered after training but immediately prior to the stimulation. If epinephrine is administered after the stimulation, retention is enhanced, as it is in demedullated rats that are not given posttraining epinephrine. These findings indicate that the effect of amygdala stimulation on retention depends upon epinephrine levels present at the time of the stimulation. If peripheral epinephrine is present at the time of the stimulation (either because epinephrine is released by

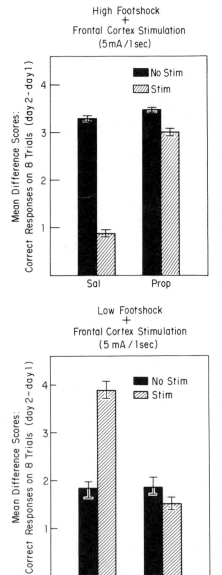

FIGURE 1. Effects of posttraining frontal cortex stimulation (5 mA/1 sec) on retention of an active avoidance response. Saline or propranolol was administered prior to training. (A) High footshock (750 μA). (B) Low footshock (500 μA).

the training stimulation or because it was administered prior to the stimulation) retention is impaired. If epinephrine is depleted, the amygdala stimulation enhances retention.

AMYGDALA INVOLVEMENT IN MEMORY MODULATION

Our findings are consistent with the view that epinephrine affects memory by influencing brain systems involved in memory storage. Further, the findings of our

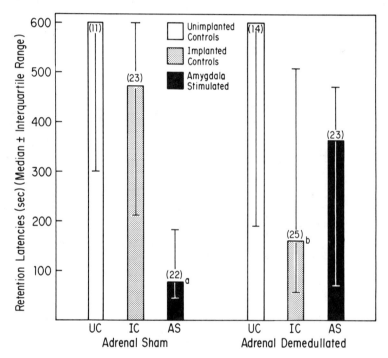

FIGURE 2. Effects of posttraining amygdala stimulation on retention of inhibitory avoidance in adrenal-demedullated and sham-operated rats: a = $p < 0.01$ compared with UC and IC sham controls, and $p < 0.05$ compared to adrenal AS group; b = $p < 0.02$, compared with IC sham controls.

studies of the effects of amygdala stimulation add to the growing evidence suggesting that the amygdala may be part of a brain system involved in memory consolidation. The recent studies of Mishkin[32] and Squire and his colleagues[33] indicate that, in monkeys, lesions of the amygdala and hippocampus produce a severe memory deficit that appears to model that seen in the patient, H.M. While comparable studies of the effects of combined amygdala and hippocampal lesions have not as yet been conducted in studies using rats, amygdala lesions seriously impair retention. In recent experiments, for example, we found that, in rats, retention is impaired by lesions made prior to training as well as posttraining lesions of the amygdala if the lesions are made within

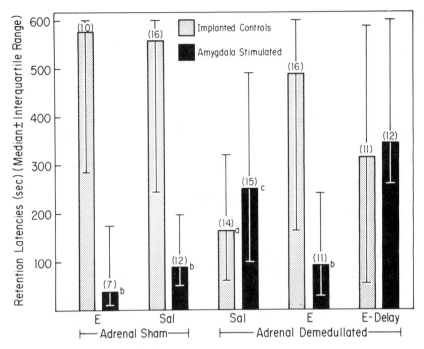

FIGURE 3. Effect of posttraining epinephrine and amygdala stimulation on retention of inhibitory avoidance in adrenal-demedullated and sham-control rats: a = $p < 0.05$, compared with IC sham controls and demedullated IC immediate and delayed epinephrine groups; b = $p < 0.05$ compared with IC sham controls and demedullated IC epinephrine groups; c = $p < 0.02$ compared with adrenal-sham amygdala-stimulated group (Mann-Whitney U-tests).

several days following the training. It seems unlikely that the amygdala is a site of storage since lesions made 10 days after training do not significantly impair retention.[34] We have also found that the effects of amygdala stimulation on memory are blocked by lesions of the stria terminalis[35] as well as by administration of naloxone into the bed nucleus of the stria terminalis prior to the amygdala stimulation.[36] These findings indicate that the effects of amygdala stimulation on memory are due to influences mediated by the stria terminalis.

The findings of several other recent studies from my laboratory have provided additional evidence that the enhancing effects of peripheral epinephrine involve the amygdala. For example, as is shown in FIGURE 4, the effects of posttraining epinephrine on memory are blocked in rats with stria terminalis lesions.[37] Posttraining epinephrine effects on memory are also blocked in rats given intra-amygdala injections of propranolol immediately prior to the administration of epinephrine.[38] These findings suggest that epinephrine affects memory either through influences on the amygdala or through influences elsewhere that require cooperative outputs from the amygdala.

In a series of studies Gallagher and her colleagues[39] have shown that, in rats, retention can be altered by administration of adrenergic antagonists (as well as opiate agonists and antagonists) directly into the amygdala. Further, intra-amygdala administration of high doses of norepinephrine impairs retention.[40] Recently, we found (FIGURE 5) that retention is enhanced by posttraining intra-amygdala administration of low doses of norepinephrine and that the enhancement is blocked if propranolol is administered with the epinephrine.[41] These findings are consistent with the view that peripheral epinephrine may influence the amygdala through activation of adrenergic receptors in the amygdala. At present, however, little is known about the detailed mechanisms by which peripheral adrenergic hormones affect brain systems. While it is generally held that adrenergic hormones do not pass the blood-brain barrier it may well be that they do under some conditions.

FIGURE 6 presents a simple model of the involvement of peripheral hormones and central systems in the modulation of memory storage. The model assumes that the strength of storage in a memory system is influenced by a memory modulation system. The modulation system is activated by sensory stimulation and, also, by influences from peripheral hormones. As I indicated above, several lines of evidence suggest that the amygdala may be part of the proposed memory modulation system. For example, if the amygdala is part of a modulating system, then disruption of the stria terminalis, a major amygdala pathway, should be expected to interfere with the modulating effects of the amygdala. Further, disruption of the stria terminalis should, according to the model, also block the enhancing effect of peripheral epinephrine on memory. And, if the modulating effects of the amygdala are influenced through influences of adrenergic hormones on the amygdala the effects of the stimulation should vary with peripheral levels of epinephrine. The findings of the recent studies summarized above generally fit well with this simple model.

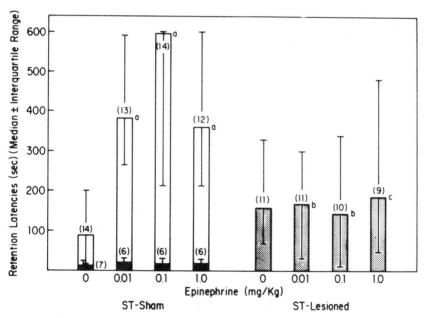

FIGURE 4. Effects of posttraining epinephrine on inhibitory avoidance retention in sham controls and ST-lesioned rats. Black bars represent the non-footshock controls. a = different from the ST sham/saline controls, $p < 0.01$; b and c = different from the corresponding ST sham/epinephrine groups, $p < 0.05$ and $0.05 < p < 0.10$, respectively; Mann-Whitney two-tailed U-tests.

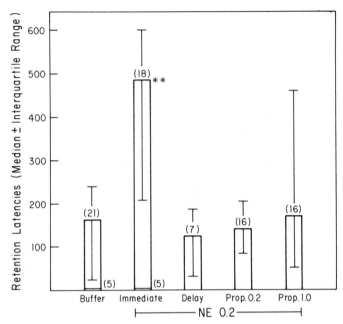

FIGURE 5. Effects of posttraining intra-amygdala administration of norepinephrine and propranolol (doses in μg) on retention. NE was ineffective when administered two hours posttraining. Propranolol blocked the effect of immediate posttraining NE. ** = $p < 0.05$, compared with buffer controls.

ADRENERGIC INVOLVEMENT IN MEMORY DYSFUNCTION

The model shown in FIGURE 6 suggests that memory disorders can result from interference with sites of memory storage, brain systems involved in the modulation of memory storage, or with hormonal systems that activate the modulating systems. There is ample evidence that brain lesions produce memory disorders. However, there is, as yet, only modest evidence that different brain systems have the roles proposed in the model. There is considerable evidence that memory is altered by conditions affecting the functioning of the peripheral adrenergic system. Further, there is some evidence suggesting that age-related deficits in memory may be related to a decline in

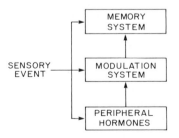

FIGURE 6. Interaction of peripheral hormones with central modulating and memory systems.

the functioning of the adrenergic system. A number of studies have reported that, in rats and mice, retention of newly learned information declines with age.[42] There is also evidence suggesting that, in comparison with young animals, plasma levels of epinephrine are lower following a stressful stimulus.[43] If the impaired retention seen in older animals is due at least in part to decreased release of adrenal epinephrine, then it should be possible to attenuate the retention deficit by administering epinephrine. FIGURE 7 shows the effects of posttraining administration of epinephrine on retention in young and old mice. As can be seen, the epinephrine markedly enhanced retention in old as well as young animals.[44] These results are consistent with the view that the age-related decline in retention may be related to a decline in adrenergic function. The findings also clearly indicate that older animals remain sensitive to the enhancing effects of epinephrine on retention.

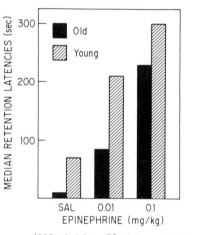

FIGURE 7. An age comparison of epinephrine modulation of memory in mice. Epinephrine facilitates retention performance in both young and old mice in aversive training. One-trial inhibitory avoidance. Retention is expressed as latency to reenter the shock compartment 24 hours after aversive training (600 μA footshock for 2 sec).

CONCLUDING COMMENTS

It seems clear that, at least in rats and mice, memory storage processes are subject to experimental as well as endogenous modulating influences. Some of the findings appear to fit reasonably well with the findings of studies of memory modulation and memory dysfunction in humans. Whether these animal models are adequate models of human memory remains to be seen. If they are not, then it will be of great interest to know why the findings of studies of animal memory differ from those of human memory. If the models have at least some degree of validity they should prove useful in the development of effective treatments for human memory dysfunction.

ACKNOWLEDGMENTS

I thank Cathy Bennett, Debra Sternberg, and K.C. Liang for their contributions to research reported in this paper.

REFERENCES

1. HILGARD, E. R. & G. H. BOWER. 1966. Theories of Learning. 3rd edit. Appleton-Century-Crofts. New York.
2. MANNING, A. 1976. Animal learning: ethological approaches. *In* Neural Mechanisms of Learning and Memory. M. R. Rosenzweig & E. L. Bennett, Eds. The MIT Press. Cambridge, MA.
3. PAVLOV, I. P. 1927. Conditioned Reflexes. Oxford University Press. London.
4. HULL, C. L. 1943. Principles of Behavior. Appleton-Century-Crofts. New York.
5. SKINNER, B. F. 1938. The Behavior of Organisms: an Experimental Analysis. Appleton-Century-Crofts. New York.
6. SKINNER, B. F. 1953. Science and Human Behavior. Macmillan. New York.
7. WINOGRAD, E. 1971. Some issues relating animal memory to human memory. *In* Animal Memory. W. K. Honig & P. H. R. James, Eds. Academic Press. New York.
8. O'KEEFE, J. & L. NADEL. 1978. The Hippocampus as a Cognitive Map. Oxford University Press. Oxford.
9. KANDEL, E. 1979. Cellular aspects of learning. *In* Brain Mechanisms in Memory and Learning from the Single Neuron to Man. M. A. B. Brazier, Ed. Raven Press. New York.
10. ALKON, D. L. 1982. A biochemical basis for molluscan associative learning. *In* Conditioning: Representation of Involved Neural Functions. C. D. Woody, Ed. Plenum Press. New York.
11. MUELLER, G. E. & A. PILZECKER. 1900. Experimentelle Beitrage zur Lehre vom Gedachtniss. Z. Psychol. **1:** 1–288.
12. MCDOUGALL, W. 1901. Experimentelle Beitrage zur Lehre vom Gedachtniss by G. E. Mueller and A. Pilzecker. Mind **10:** 388–394.
13. FLESCHER, G. 1941. I. L'amnesia retrograda dopo l'electroschok: contributo allo studio della patogenesi della amnesie in genere. Schweiz. Arch. Neurol.Psychiat. **48:** 1–28.
14. DUNCAN, C. P. 1949. The retroactive effect of electroshock on learning. J. Comp. Physiol. Psychol. **42:** 32–44.
15. SQUIRE, L. R. & N. J. COHEN. 1982. Remote memory, retrograde amnesia, and the neuropsychology of memory. *In* Human Memory and Amnesia. L. S. Cermak, Ed. Lawrence Erlbaum Associates. Hillsdale, NJ.
16. MCGAUGH, J. L. & M. J. HERZ. 1972. Memory Consolidation. Albion Publishing Co. San Francisco.
17. MCGAUGH, J. L. 1976. Cognition and consolidation. *In* Knowing, Thinking, and Believing (Festschrift for Professor David Krech). L. Petrinovich & J. L. McGaugh, Eds. Plenum Press. New York.
18. GOLD, P. E. & S. F. ZORNETZER. 1983. The mnemon and its juices; neuromodulation of memory processes. Behav. Neural Biol. **38:** 151–189.
19. MCGAUGH, J. L. 1968. Drug facilitation of memory and learning. *In* Psychopharmacology: A Review of Progress. D. H. Efron, Ed. U.S. Government Printing Office. Washington, D.C. PHS Publ. No. 1836.
20. MCGAUGH, J. L. & P. E. GOLD. 1976. Modulation of memory by electrical stimulation of the brain. *In* Neural Mechanisms of Learning and Memory. M. R. Rosenzweig & E. L. Bennett, Eds. The MIT Press, Cambridge, MA.
21. MCGAUGH J. L. 1983 Hormonal influences on memory. Annu. Rev. Psychol. **34:** 297–323.
22. DAVIES, P. 1985. Ann. N.Y. Acad. Sci. (This volume.)
23. WEINGARTNER, H. 1985. Ann. N.Y. Acad. Sci. (This volume.)
24. DEWIED, D. 1980. Pituitary neuropeptides and behavior. *In* Central Regulation of the Endocrine System. K. Fuxe, T. Hokfelt & R. Luft, Eds. Plenum Press, New York.
25. GOLD, P. E. & J. L. MCGAUGH. 1975. A single-trace two-process view of memory storage processes. *In* Short-Term Memory. D. Deutsch & J. A. Deutsch, Eds. Academic Press, New York.
26. GOLD, P. E. & R. VAN BUSKIRK. 1976. Effects of posttrial hormone injections on memory processes. Horm. Behav. **7:** 509–517.
27. STERNBERG D. B., P. E. GOLD & J. L. MCGAUGH. Unpublished findings.

28. GOLD, P. E. & D. B. STERNBERG. 1978. Retrograde amnesia produced by several treatments. Evidence for a common neurobiological mechanism. Science 209: 836–837.
29. STERNBERG, D. B., P. E. GOLD & J. L. McGAUGH. 1983. Memory facilitation and impairment with supraseizure electrical brain stimulation: Attenuation with pretrial propranolol injections. Behav. Neural Biol. 38: 261–268.
30. BENNETT, C., K. C. LIANG & J. L. McGAUGH. 1985. Depletion of adrenal catecholamines alters the amnestic effect of amygdala stimulation. Behav. Brain Res. 15.
31. LIANG, K. C., C. BENNETT & J. L. McGAUGH. Peripheral epinephrine modulates the effects of posttraining amygdala stimulation on memory. Behav. Brain Res. (In press.)
32. MISHKIN, M. 1985. Ann. N.Y. Acad. Sci. (This volume.)
33. SQUIRE, L. & S. ZOLA-MORGAN. 1983. The neurology of memory: The case for correspondence between the findings for human and nonhuman primate. In The Physiological Basis of Memory. J. A. Deutsch, Ed. Academic Press. New York.
34. LIANG, K. C., J. L. McGAUGH, J. L. MARTINEZ, JR., R. A. JENSEN, B. J. VASQUEZ & R. B. MESSING. 1982. Posttraining amygdaloid lesions impair retention of an inhibitory avoidance response. Behav. Brain Res. 4: 237–249.
35. LIANG, K. C. & J. L. McGAUGH. 1983. Lesions of the stria terminalis attenuate the amnestic effect of amygdaloid stimulation on avoidance responses. Brain Res. 274: 309–318.
36. LIANG, K. C., R. B. MESSING & J. L. McGAUGH. 1983. Naloxone attenuates amnesia caused by amygdaloid stimulation: The involvement of a central opioid system. Brain Res. 271: 41–49.
37. LIANG, K. C. & J. L. McGAUGH. 1983. Lesions of the stria terminalis attenuate the enhancing effect of post-training epinephrine on retention of an inhibitory avoidance response. Behav. Brain Res. 9: 49–58.
38. LIANG, K. C. & J. L. McGAUGH. Unpublished findings.
39. GALLAGHER, M., B. S. KAPP, J. P. PASCOE & P. R. RAPP. 1981. A neuropharmacology of amygdaloid systems which contribute to learning and memory. In The Amygdaloid Complex. Y. Ben-Ari, Ed. Elsevier. North Holland.
40. ELLIS, M. E. & R. P. KESNER. 1983. The noradrenergic system of the amygdala in aversive information processing. Behav. Neurosci. 97: 399–415.
41. LIANG, K. C. & J. L. McGAUGH. Unpublished findings.
42. KUBANIS, P. & S. F. ZORNETZER. 1981. Age-related behavioral and neurobiological changes: A review with an emphasis on memory. Behav. Neural Biol. 31: 115.
43. McCARTY, R. 1981. Aged rats: Diminished sympathetic-adrenal medullary responses to acute stress. Behav. Neural Biol. 33: 204.
44. STERNBERG, D. B., J. L. MARTINEZ, JR., P. E. GOLD & J. L. McGAUGH. 1985. Epinephrine attenuates age-related deficits in retention of inhibitory avoidance learning. (Submitted for publication.)

Role of β-Endorphin
in Behavioral Regulation[a]

IVAN IZQUIERDO[b] AND CARLOS A. NETTO

Laboratório de Neuroquímica
Departamento de Bioquímica
Instituto de Biociencias
Universidade Federal do Rio Grande do Sul (U.F.R.G.S.–centro)
90.000 Porto Alegre, RS, Brazil

Experiences may modify behavior. Acquisition of such changes is called learning. Retention and retrieval of learned information is called memory. Memory can only be evaluated by measuring retrieval in a test session, so the processes that lead from learning to retrieval (consolidation, storage, availability for retrieval, recall) can only be inferred.

The concept of the chain of events, experiences → learning → retention → retrieval, applies to all forms of memory, regardless of whether they may be classified according to the duration of the training-test interval (eg., early vs. late) or to the promptness of retrieval, or to their resistance to external variables, or even to the neural systems involved. Therefore, the present article will ignore those classifications, since it will examine data descriptively in terms of the simple chain of events mentioned above. The findings commented on here, or others obtained using similar animal models,[1-3] may be relevant only to the simpler or more general aspects of human memory. Functions of great importance for mental illness,[4] such as the role of memory in the sense of personal identity ("I am who I am because I remember"), of time ("I had breakfast after I got up"), of space ("I came from south of the Equator"), or of history ("Mongolians arrived here before Columbus"), are left largely untouched by the present findings or others of their kind or their interpretation.

Pharmacologic or other treatments applied before training may affect retrieval through influences on any of the components of the chain (learning, retention, retrieval). Posttraining treatments may in principle affect retention or retrieval. Pretest treatments may affect recall, retrieval, or variables that may complicate retrieval at the time of testing, such as new learnings or performance variables.

At least some types of learning (those more "biologically significant" or arousing or stressful) are accompanied by a number of neurohumoral and hormonal changes during and after training or testing.[1-7] Most of these changes are unspecific as to learning, but reflect instead the degree of arousal or stress associated with the experience.[1,3,5,6] Many of these changes may affect memory during the posttraining period or at the time of testing. Agents that modify the endogenous systems involved, or injection of the neurotransmitters or hormones themselves, may affect retrieval measured in minutes, hours, or days after the experience.[3] Therefore, posttraining or pre-test treatments in general are invariably applied in the context of a highly dynamic neurochemical state that may vary with the type of learning, the time of the day, previous experiences, or the species under study; and, in addition, posttraining or

[a]Work supported by FINEP and CNPq, Brazil.
[b]Correspondence to: Dr. Ivan Izquierdo, Departamento de Bioquímica, Instituto de Biociencias, UFRGS (centro), 90.000 Porto Alegre, RS, Brazil.

pre-test treatments may modify the neurohumoral or hormonal changes that occur simultaneously.[1-3,8] Thus, the effect of these treatments may be subject to great variation. Some generalizations are, however, possible; and some of the interactions between posttraining or pre-test system and endogenous systems involved in memory modulation have been identified.[3,6-9]

The present article studies the influence on memory of one major brain system, the medial basal hypothalamic β-endorphin system that projects mostly to periventricular regions of the brain.[10] This influence has been studied in a variety of neurohumoral and hormonal contexts, and it is possible to draw a number of conclusions as to its physiological role. As will be seen, some of these conclusions may bear on aspects of the pathology of memory.

NALOXONE FACILITATION AND β-ENDORPHIN INHIBITION OF LATE RETRIEVAL

The first evidence that endogenous opioids may be involved in memory processes was provided by experiments showing that the posttraining injection of the opiate receptor antagonist, naloxone, facilitates retrieval of a wide variety of aversive and nonaversive behaviors in rats, measured one or more days after training.[11-17] The effect can also be obtained with pre-training injections of naloxone,[15,18,19] and with posttraining injections of other opiate antagonists.[12] The decreasing order of potency of opiate antagonists for producing late retrieval facilitation roughly follows their decreasing order of affinity for opiate μ receptors: diprenorphine $\geq$ naltrexone $\geq$ naloxone > levallorphan $\gg$ dextrallorphan = 0.[12]

Opiate agonists given shortly before[18,19] or after training[5,16,20-24] disrupt retrieval of many aversive and nonaversive tasks measured one or more days after training in rats. This effect is competitively antagonized by naloxone[25] and is shared by a number of opiate agonists, including endogenous peptides, morphine,[15,16] and levorphanol.[11] The decreasing order of potency of endogenous opioid peptides for this effect also follows their decreasing order of affinity for μ receptors: β-endorphin > Met- or Leu-enkephalin $\gg$ dynorphin[1-13] = 0.[25-28] The posttraining inhibitory effect of β-endorphin or Met-enkephalin on late retrieval may be obtained with as little as 5 or 25 ng of these substances given intracerebroventricularly,[24] which suggests that the effect is centrally mediated. The systemic ED_{50} of β-endorphin is 1 μg/kg $\simeq$ 140 ng/rat.[5,25,27] Approximately 20% of a systemically injected dose of β-endorphin reaches the cerebrospinal fluid within 2 hr from injection[30] and is apparently metabolized shortly after penetration into the brain matter.[30,31] Therefore, the receptors involved in the posttraining effects of naloxone or β-endorphin on memory appear to be opiate μ receptors located very near the walls of the brain ventricles.[28,31,32] The brain β-endorphin system indeed projects mostly to periventricular regions.[10]

ACTIVATION OF THE BRAIN β-ENDORPHIN SYSTEM BY BEHAVIORAL EXPERIENCES

The effects of opiate antagonists and of endogenous opioids on memory discussed in the previous section obviously suggest the participation of endogenous opioids in memory regulation at the posttraining period.

There are three groups of endogenous opioid systems in the brain: the enkephalin system, whose active compounds are Met- and Leu-enkephalin, derived from a precursor protein called pro-enkephalin;[33] and is scattered over 20-or-so short-axon neuron systems all over the brain;[10] the β-endorphin system, whose active substance is β-endorphin, derived from a precursor protein called pro-opiocortin, and whose cell bodies are in the medial basal hypothalamus and project to the periventricular region;[10] and the dynorphin system, which produces various forms of dynorphin, derived from a precursor protein called pro-dynorphin or neo-endorphin, which is also scattered over many regions of the brain.[34]

Posttraining intraperitoneal or intracerebroventricular administration of dynorphin over a very wide dose range (0.008 to 25 μg/kg i.p., or 1 to 25 ng/rat, i.c.v.) has no effect on the late retrieval of two different tasks in rats,[28] so it may be ruled out from participation in posttraining memory regulation processes. In addition, it is a very poor agonist at μ receptors,[34] which is a further argument against a physiological role of dynorphin in memory.

The pre-training administration of the enkephalins markedly disrupts acquisition of aversive and nonaversive tasks at doses lower than those that influence late retrieval.[27] No such effect is observed with β-endorphin over a wide dose range.[18,19,27] This rules the enkephalins out as possible physiological participants in learning and memory processes; if they were, they would make learning impossible. A further, and strong, argument against any such role for the enkephalins is that tasks whose retrieval is strongly influenced by opiate agonists and antagonists, such as habituation and shuttle avoidance,[16,17,20] are not accompanied by a release of brain Met-enkephalin.[35]

On the contrary, a very wide variety of behavioral procedures are accompanied by a decrease of brain β-endorphin–like immunoreactivity, which is interpreted as due to release and subsequent degradation of β-endorphin.[5,6,9,29,36,37] It cannot be interpreted

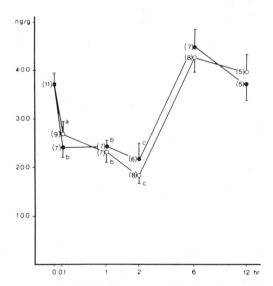

FIGURE 1. Ordinates: β-endorphin–like immunoreactivity of rat diencephalon, expressed as ng β-endorphin/g wet tissue. Abscissae: time of sacrifice (in hr) after one step-down inhibitory avoidance trial (0.8 mA footshock) (filled circles) or after simple exposure to the training apparatus with no footshock. Data shown as means ± S.E. Number of animals per group shown in parentheses. Significant differences from intact controls (i.e., from time 0) in Duncan multiple range test: [a] at $p < 0.05$ level; [b] at $p < 0.01$ level; [c] at $p < 0.005$ level.

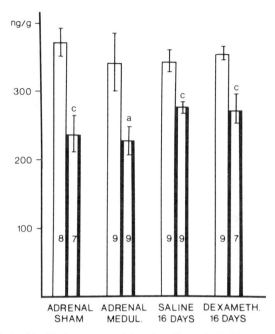

FIGURE 2. β-Endorphin–like immunoreactivity of rat diencephalon, expressed as mean ± S.E. ng β-endorphin/g wet tissue, in control rats and in animals sacrificed 6 min after a step-down inhibitory avoidance trial (0.8 mA footshock) (columns with light and with heavy vertical bars respectively), 20 or more days after an adrenal sham operation or a bilateral adrenal medullecto-my, or 1 day after a 16-day course of daily i.p. saline (1 ml/kg) or 0.2 mg/kg dexamethasone. *N* is shown in the histograms. Differences between trained and control animals was significant in all cases in a Duncan multiple range test: [a] at *p* < 0.005 level; [c] at *p* < 0.01 level.

by synthesis inhibition because the synthesis of β-endorphin immunoreactive material takes hours[38] and the decrease caused by training develops in minutes[9] (FIGURES 1, 2, and 4). Furthermore, as far as is know, the synthesis of that material can only be inhibited by blocking general protein synthesis. The behavioral procedures that are followed by a decrease of brain β-endorphin–like immunoreactivity are accompanied by an increase, rather than by an inhibition of brain protein synthesis.[39]

The decrease of brain β-endorphin–like immunoreactivity caused by behavioral experiences may be observed in the whole brain[5,6,37] or in a fraction of the brain that includes the whole hypothalamus, ventral thalamus, and/or preoptic region;[9,36] i.e., the region that contains all the cell bodies and most of the projections of the brain β-endorphin system.[10] Pituitary and plasma β-endorphin levels are not affected by most of the behavioral procedures;[29,36,37] only intense footshock stimulation repeated over 25 min may be followed by a simultaneous pituitary decrease and plasma increase of β-endorphin–like immunoreactivity;[29,36] in that case, possibly this substance is cosecreted with ACTH by the hypophysis.[40] Pro-opiocortin is a common precursor to ACTH and β-endorphin.[34,38]

The decrease of brain β-endorphin caused by training corresponds to the apparent release of 20 to 40 ng of β-endorphin per brain (FIGURES 1, 3, and 4).[5,6,9,29,36,37] This amount corresponds to doses of β-endorphin that affect late retrieval when given intracerebroventricularly.[24,32] Thus, in view of the evidence discussed so far, it seems reasonable to postulate a role for the brain β-endorphin system in memory regulation. The behavioral procedures that are accompanied by a brain β-endorphin release comprise a variety of aversive and non-aversive situations: simple exposure to a 50 × 25 × 25 cm training box for a few seconds with no footshocks; step-down inhibitory avoidance training in the same box using either low (0.3 mA) or high (0.8 mA) intensity footshocks; testing of inhibitory avoidance learning in the same box with no footshocks; exposure to one 1.0 mA, 30-sec inescapable footshock; exposure to fifty 1.0 mA escapable foot-shocks over 25 min; habituation to the presentation of 50 low-level 1 kHz tones over 25 min; 50 tone-footshock shuttle avoidance trials; extinction of the shuttle avoidance learning using 50 tones and no footshocks.[5,6,9,29,36,37] When any of these tasks is repeated for a second time there is no release of brain β-endorphin on the second time; however, when animals are trained in one task and tested in another (for example, trained with tones alone and tested on shuttle avoidance or vice versa), there is again a release of brain β-endorphin on the test session.[5,9] Thus, the change cannot be correlated with any specific type of learning, with duration of the behavioral experiences, with the sensory or motor requirements, the degree of arousal or stress associated with each task, or with the presence or absence of pain; but it can be, instead, correlated with the novelty inherent to each task.[9]

Footshock-motivated training is accompanied, as is known, by a transient hypersecretion of pituitary ACTH[3,7,40] and of adrenal medullar epinephrine.[7] The injection of these hormones may be followed by a decrease of diencephalic β-endorphin–like immunoreactivity similar to that caused by training.[41] The brain β-endorphin response to training, however, is not mediated by pituitary ACTH or by adrenal epinephrine; it persists unaltered in rats with bilateral adrenal medullectomy, or in animals that receive 0.2 mg/kg of dexamethasone daily over 16 days (FIGURE 2), a treatment that suppresses the pituitary ACTH response to stress.[42]

NEURAL PATHWAY INVOLVED IN THE ACTIVATION OF THE BRAIN β-ENDORPHIN SYSTEM BY BEHAVIORAL EXPERIENCES

The medial basal hypothalamus receives neural afferents from the septo-hippocampo-subiculum system through the fornix;[43] from the lateral septum, tuberculum olfactorium, and other frontal regions through anterior fibers entering at the suprachiasmatic region;[44-46] and from the mesencephalic reticular formation and the locus ceruleus through posterior fibers.[43,44] If the response of the medial basal hypothalamic β-endorphin system to novelty is mediated by any of those three groups of fibers, it should be suppressed by a surgical section of the pathway involved. Rats were submitted to surgical section of each of these three main groups of fibers stereotaxically under ether anesthesia. Placement of the lesions is shown in FIGURE 3. Twenty-two to thirty-two days after surgery, intact animals, rats submitted to sham brain surgery (holes drilled in the skull with no penetration of the knife assembly), and animals in each lesion group, were either taken from their home cages and sacrificed right away (controls), or submitted to one trial of step-down inhibitory avoidance learning using a 0.8 mA footshock and sacrificed 6 min after training. This procedure had been previously found to release diencephalic β-endorphin (FIGURES 1 and 2).[9,36] Diencephalic (i.e., hypothalamic plus ventral thalamic) β-endorphin like immunoreactivity was measured in all animals by a conventional radioimmunoassay.[5,6,9,29,36,37,40,42] The β-endorphin response to training was abolished by the dorsal fornix lesion but not by the other hypothalamic deafferentations (FIGURE 4). Therefore, integrity of the

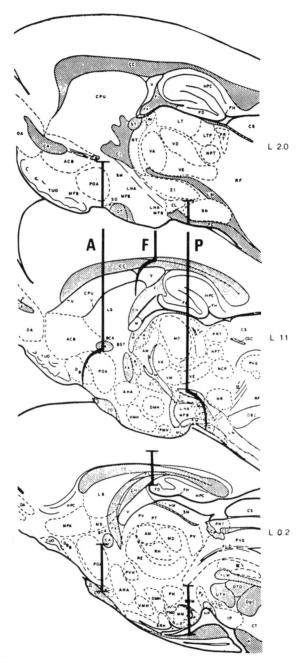

FIGURE 3. Placement and extension of the knife cuts, A (anterior hypothalamic deafferentation), F (dorsal fornix transsection), and P (posterior hypothalamic deafferentation) shown in lateral planes 0.2, 1.1, and 2.0 of the atlas by De Groot.[47] Shape and size of the knife is shown in plane L = 1.1, which is 0.1 mm lateral to actual plane of penetration. Horizontal bars shown in planes L = 0.2 and 2.0 show the approximate spread of the cuts.

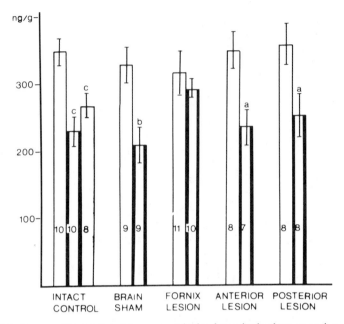

FIGURE 4. Same as FIGURE 2, but in groups submitted to a brain sham operation or to the lesions shown in FIGURE 3, 20 or more days after surgery. The fornix cut abolished the diencephalic β-endorphin response to training; in all other groups, the difference between trained and control animals was significant in a Duncan multiple range test: [a] at $p < 0.001$ level; [b] at $p < 0.01$ level; [c] at $p < 0.005$ level. In an intact control group, it is shown that both avoidance training (heavy vertical bars) and simple exposure to the apparatus (see caption to FIGURE 1) caused a depletion of diencephalic β-endorphin immunoreactivity to about the same extent.

pathway that sends signals from the septo-hippocampo-subiculum system to the medial basal hypothalamic β-endorphin system appears to be essential for the response of the latter to training.

Gray[43] proposed that the hippocampus and subiculum play a key role in the detection of novelty. Others[48,49] have suggested that the hippocampus is important for the correct recognition of contextual and discriminative stimuli, a role that is not at odds with the one suggested by Gray.[43] Thus, it seems reasonable to postulate that recognition of novelty by the hippocampo-subiculum system may be an important first step, or the actual trigger, of the brain β-endorphin response to training, which may be considered as a response to novelty.[9]

The rather protracted time course of this response (hours, see FIGURE 1) precludes its repetition too soon after the system is activated by some significant experience. This raises precisely the point of "significance" of the experiences; it is possible that the brain β-endorphin system does not respond just to any novel situation, but only to those that are somehow particularly striking to the animal. While we do not know what may be particularly striking for a rat, we can guess that being grabbed by a human, taken out of their home cage, placed in a strange environment, and then submitted to behavioral manipulations may signify something new and striking for a rat, particularly the first time. We also know from our own experience that even though many new things may happen to us every day, only a few strike us as being particularly novel and significant.

EFFECTS OF β-ENDORPHIN ON EARLY RETRIEVAL

As was mentioned in the previous sections, β-endorphin is released in the brain by many behavioral experiences and disrupts the retrieval of these experiences when it is measured one or more days later; an effect opposite to, and antagonized by, naloxone.

Immediate retrieval is not affected by β-endorphin. An injection of this peptide prior to training in multi-trial aversive or non-aversive tasks does not affect acquisition curves of those tasks;[18,19] such curves are presumed to be a function of trial-to-trial retrieval.[6] As shown in FIGURE 5, the pre-training injection of 1.0 μg/kg of β-endorphin i.p. does not affect retrieval of a step-down inhibitory avoidance task measured at 0, 1, or 2 hr after training; at 6 hr, however, retrieval is inhibited. A new injection of the same amount of the peptide prior to testing prevents this inhibition. This last finding is consonant with many previous observations on the facilitatory effect of pre-test β-endorphin on retrieval;[32,50,51] this effect may be observed both when retrieval measured 24 hr after training is disrupted by posttraining β-endorphin administration[50,51] or in normal animals;[8,32] and it may be obtained both with systemic or with intracerebroventricular injections of the peptide.[32]

Thus, β-endorphin does not affect retrieval immediately. In fact, its pre-test injection may even restore retrieval when it had been disrupted by previous treatments,

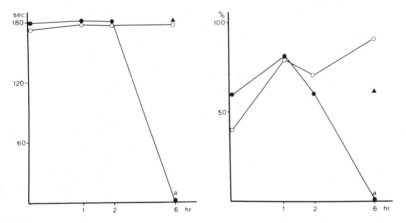

FIGURE 5. Influence of a pre-training injection of saline (1 ml/kg, i.p.) (open circles) or of β-endorphin (1.0 μg/kg, i.p.) (filled circles) on retrieval of step-down inhibitory avoidance measured 0, 1, 2, or 6 hr after training (injections given 6 min before training). In both graphs, training-test interval is shown in the abscissae and there are 10 animals per group. In the left-hand graph, ordinates represent training-test step-down latency difference in sec (median). In the right-hand graph, the ordinates represent the percentage of animals at maximum latency (180 sec). β-Endorphin had no effect on any of the two measures of retrieval at 0, 1, or 2 hr training-test intervals, but it reduced both at 6 hr ([a] significant difference at $p < 0.001$ level in Mann-Whitney U test vs. saline at same interval). Another injection of the same dose of β-endorphin given 6 min prior to testing abolished this effect (black triangles, also different from [a] at $p < 0.001$ level).

or actually enhance retrieval; its deleterious effect becomes manifested only several hours after the peptide is released or injected, and then it can be overcome by another injection of β-endorphin. It may be noted, by the way, that these results rule out the previously advanced interpretation that β-endorphin affects consolidation.[5,6,18–20,23] It does not; animals that receive β-endorphin after training may retrieve very well when tested again under the influence of the drug. It is not known whether the resistance of early retrieval to injected β-endorphin is due to a persistent action of this substance at receptors during hours after training. The parallelism between this resistance of retrieval to the disruptive effect of β-endorphin (FIGURE 5) and the time course of the recovery of the depletion of brain β-endorphin induced by training (FIGURE 1) is indeed striking. A role of β-endorphin metabolites at other-than-opiate receptors at that time may be possible.

Since, as was said, brain β-endorphin is not released in test sessions unless these involve a change of task,[9] these findings suggest a form of state dependency. Beginning several hours after training (FIGURE 5), memories acquired under the influence of injected β-endorphin (i.e., of β-endorphin in excess of the amount that is endogenously released) become dependent on the renewed presence of this peptide for retrieval. A further comment on the problem of state dependency will be found below.

INTERACTION OF THE BRAIN β-ENDORPHIN SYSTEM WITH HORMONES INVOLVED IN MEMORY MODULATION

Posttraining administration of ACTH, epinephrine, vasopressin, or of the peripheral norepinephrine releaser, tyramine, affects retrieval of aversive tasks measured one or more days after training.[3,7,8,23,51,52] When training is accompanied by a presumably low endogenous release of these substances, as is the case of inhibitory avoidance acquired using low intensity footshock, they induce late retrieval facilitation; when training is accompanied by a high endogenous release, their posttraining administration inhibits late retrieval.[1,3,7,8,23,51,52] The effect of the hormones is probably mediated peripherally at least in the case of ACTH and epinephrine, since it may be obtained with systemic but not with intracerebroventricular injections.[52] Posttraining facilitation of late retrieval by ACTH, epinephrine, norepinephrine, or vasopressin may be secondary to a reflex activation[3] of central catecholaminergic mechanisms.[7,53] The effect is potentiated by naloxone and blocked by β-endorphin.[23] It has been proposed that these substances also influence central catecholaminergic mechanisms, naloxone by antagonizing and β-endorphin by inducing a presumably presynaptic inhibition of those mechanisms.[17,29] The depression of late retrieval caused by high doses of ACTH, epinephrine, tyramine, or vasopressin[3,7,23,52,54] may be due to a release of brain β-endorphin;[23] such a release has been demonstrated at least for ACTH and epinephrine.[41] Late retrieval inhibition by the hormones is counteracted by posttraining naloxone and potentiated by posttraining β-endorphin administration.[23]

Thus, the brain β-endorphin system may interact with the hormones that modulate memory at the posttraining period at two levels, in both cases tending to "push" their combined effect to the inhibitory side.

When given prior to testing, β-endorphin, ACTH, epinephrine, and tyramine facilitate the retrieval of aversive behaviors learned 24 hr before.[8,23,32,51] The effect is observed in normal animals[8,32] and also in animals whose late retrieval had been inhibited by a posttraining administration of these substances.[8,23,50,51] Retrieval facilitation by pre-test administration of these drugs is also peripherally mediated,[32] is not observed in animals treated with posttraining naloxone,[8] and is antagonized by a simultaneous pre-test injection of naloxone.[8] Thus, it is possible that it depends on the release of β-endorphin after training and at the time of testing and that it represents state-dependency on endogenous β-endorphin.[8,9] It is possible, however, that the hormones may participate by themselves in the induction of state-dependency,[55,56] particularly in the case of learning acquired using strong aversive stimulation and therefore presumably accompanied by a large endogenous release of the hormones.[7,9] In such cases, reversal of the amnesia induced by posttraining ACTH or epinephrine by their pre-test administration is better when the same drug is used twice, than when one is used after training and the other on the test session.[50,51,57] These results may clearly be interpreted in terms of state dependency induced by injection of these substances,[50,51,57] but do not necessarily indicate that such a dependency develops in untreated animals merely as a consequence of their endogenous release.

ON THE ROLE OF β-ENDORPHIN IN BEHAVIORAL REGULATION

Evidence presented so far shows that a variety of behavioral experiences activate the β-endorphin system, apparently as a result of novelty; that this activation is mediated by the septo-hippocamposubicular system; and that this seems to play a role in regulation of the retrieval of learned behavior, as suggested by the experiments using naloxone, whose effects cannot be explained by an interference with other endogenous opioid systems since these are either inactive or ineffective in relation to behavior.

Activation of the brain β-endorphin system by novel experiences would permit adequate retrieval for some time, so animals may react to the experience; would simultaneously facilitate the retrieval of older memories that may help the animal to examine the present experience in a proper context so as to develop coping strategies; and then would set information on the new experience aside until it may be needed once again, possibly when another new experience strikes the animal enough as to stimulate its brain β-endorphin system once more.[9]

The series of events described in the preceding paragraph is merely inferred from what is now known about the effects of β-endorphin on early and late retrieval β-endorphin may obviously play a very important role in adaptive behavior. No doubt, the rather long recovery time of the brain β-endorphin system once it has been activated (FIGURE 1) may preclude its reutilization too soon after activation; it cannot be used just every time that animals are confronted with something new, and its function must be reserved for events that are particularly striking to the animals (see above).

Two major problems are, why does memory acquired under the influence of β-endorphin become dependent on it for retrieval, and why does this dependency take hours to develop (FIGURE 5); as many hours, in fact, as it takes for diencephalic β-endorphin levels to recover from training-induced depletion (FIGURE 1).

With regard to the dependency of retrieval on β-endorphin, it is important to note that all the tasks studied so far in which this happens are indeed accompanied by a release of brain β-endorphin.[9] This release is of similar magnitude across tasks, regardless of their nature, duration, degree of arousal, presence of pain, response requirements, etc.[5,6,9,29,36,37] It is possible that there may be behavioral experiences that are not accompanied by a release of brain β-endorphin when animals are exposed to them for a first time, but we have not found any such situation. Obviously, such tasks, if they exist, would not depend on β-endorphin for early or late retrieval. It could well be that tasks acquired while brain β-endorphin stores are low (FIGURE 1) may belong to that category (see below). The fact that the release of brain β-endorphin is of similar magnitude in all the tasks we studied suggests that the amount released is just sufficient to permit a reasonably good retrieval of those tasks even in the absence of a new release or of an injection of this peptide. The posttraining effect of naloxone suggests that late retrieval could in fact be somewhat better if endogenous β-endorphin were not acting at the time of training.[5,6] Certainly if the peptide or other opiate receptor agonists are present after training in excess, as occurs when they are injected, retrieval becomes too dependent on it. In fact, in animals treated with 1.0 μg/kg of β-endorphin before (FIGURE 5) or after[50,51] training, retrieval cannot be measured at all unless they receive another similar dose of the peptide prior to testing.

With regard to the long time it takes for the dependency of retrieval on β-endorphin to develop (more than 2 hr, FIGURE 5), there are at least three possible explanations. One is that during that time memory depends on other systems for retrieval. Another is that β-endorphin activity persists for many hours after its release, perhaps at other-than-opiate receptors, and perhaps through actions of non-immunoreactive metabolic products of the peptide. The third possibility is that the β-endorphin released by training triggers some long-lasting process that makes memory independent of the peptide for retrieval.

A NOTE ON ELECTROCONVULSIVE SHOCK

Electroconvulsive shock (ECS) is still widely used in the treatment of severe depression. One of its major side effects is severe retrograde amnesia; i.e., a pronounced impairment of the late retrieval of events that happened prior to the ECS. ECS is followed by a multitude of neurohumoral and hormonal changes, among which a depletion of brain catecholamines,[58] β-endorphin,[59] and Met-enkephalin,[35] and a hypersecretion of pituitary ACTH,[60] vasopressin,[61] and gonadotrophins.[62] Pituitary and plasma β-endorphin immunoreactivity is unaffected by ECS.[59]

The amnesic effect of ECS is antagonized by naloxone.[63] This, together with the effect of ECS on brain opioids,[35,59] suggests that its amnestic effect is mediated by a massive release of these substances.

Rats were submitted to the various hypothalamic deafferentation procedures shown in FIGURE 3. Twenty to thirty days after surgery they were submitted to step-down inhibitory avoidance training using a 0.5 mA footshock and then to transcorneal ECS (15.0 mA, 2 sec) and to a retention test 24 hr later. The amnesic effect of ECS was abolished by the posterior hypothalamic deafferentation but not by the anterior lesion or the fornix transection (TABLE 1). Thus, if the amnestic effect of ECS is due to a hyperactivation of brain opioid systems,[35,59,63] this is mediated by posterior and not by other neural afferents to the hypothalamus. The ventral noradenergic bundle is a likely candidate for this mediation, since ECS is known to deplete brain norepinephrine.[58] Parenthetically, the endocrine effects of ECS[60-62] may be ruled out from an involvement in ECS amnesia, since hormone hypersecretions are mediated by fornical[64] and anterior hypothalamic afferents.[45,46]

A CAUTIONARY NOTE ON NEUROCHEMICAL MEMORY MODULATION

Whatever the importance of neurohumoral and hormonal mechanisms in memory, it must not be overlooked that, as has been known for decades, the strength of motivation is a major factor in determining the strength of retention and retrieval. A

TABLE 1. Influence of Posttraining Transcorneal ECS (15 mA, 2 sec) on Retrieval of Step-down Inhibitory Avoidance (0.5 mA, 60 Hz Training Footshock) Measured 24 Hours after Training in Intact Rats and in Rats Submitted to Various Brain Operations

| | Median (interquartile range) Training Test Step-down Latency Difference (sec) | |
Group	no ECS	ECS
Intact control	180 (180/180)	−1 (−1/4)^a
	(10)	(10)
Sham-operated	180 (176/180)	0 (−1/3)^a
	(10)	(10)
Fornix lesion	44 (7/99)^b	−1 (−2/4)^a
	(10)	(10)
Anterior lesion	180 (72/180)	0 (−2/5)^a
	(9)	(10)
Posterior lesion	180 (175/180)	180 (180/180)
	(9)	(10)

N shown in parentheses. ^{a}Significant difference from same group, no ECS ($p < 0.001$); ^{b}significant difference from intact control or sham-operated with no ECS, $p < 0.01$ (Mann-Whitney test, one-tailed).

sufficiently strong motivation may overrule the influence of inhibitory modulatory factors, as shown in TABLE 2. The fornix lesion that abolishes the brain β-endorphin response to training (FIGURE 3) makes retrieval poor in animals trained for step-down inhibitory avoidance using a 0.5 mA footshock, but not in animals trained with a 0.8 mA footshock. Similarly, animals trained with the 0.5 mA footshock are more sensitive to the disruptive influence of ECS than those trained with the 0.8 mA footshock. We do not know to what extent this influence of the strength of motivation on retrieval is due to neural factors, or to the motivation-dependent hormonal changes[1,7] examined in a previous section.

TABLE 2. Effects of a Previous Bilateral Transection of the Fornix and of Immediate Posttraining ECS (15 mA, 60 Hz), on Retrieval of Step-down Inhibitory Avoidance Acquired Using Either a 0.5 or a 0.8 mA Footshock, Measured 24 hr after Training

| | Median (interquartile range) Training Test Step-down Latency Difference (sec) | |
Group	0.5 mA	0.8 mA
Intact control	180 (180/180)	180 (180/180)
	(10)	(10)
Fornix lesion	44 (7/99)^a	160 (111/180)^c
	(10)	(8)
ECS	−1 (−1/4)^b	172 (35/180)^c
	(10)	(10)

N shown in parentheses. The three 0.5 mA groups are the same as in TABLE 1. ^{a}Significant difference from intact control groups at $p < 0.01$ level; ^{b}same, at $p < 0.001$ level; ^{c}same, at $p < 0.05$ level and in addition significantly different from same group trained with 0.5 mA footshock at $p < 0.025$ level (Mann-Whitney U tests, one-tailed).

A NOTE ON MEMORY DYSFUNCTIONS, PARTICULARLY IN THE OLD

The brain of old rats has a reduced number of opiate binding sites,[65] a reduced amount of β-endorphin–like immunoreactivity in the hypothalamus, and an excess in the frontal lobes.[66] Thus, depending on the region, or on the predominance of one or other deficit, there may be a hyper- or a hypofunction of brain opioid mechanisms in old rats. It is clear from the preceding sections that both a hyper- and a hypofunction of the brain β-endorphin system may result in memory impairment; the former, through an inhibition of late retrieval that results, in practice, in retrograde amnesia; the latter, through an insufficient "marking" of significant new memories for later retrieval.

Naloxone has been recently reported to ameliorate the amnesia that accompanies Alzheimer's disease.[67] Thus, it is possible that this disease includes a hyperfunction of brain opioid mechanisms, possibly those mediated by β-endorphin. More research into this question is desirable.

REFERENCES

1. GOLD, P. E. & J. L. MCGAUGH. 1975. A single-trace, two-process view of memory storage processes. In Short-Term Memory. D. & J. A. Deutsch, Eds.: 355–378. Academic Press. New York.
2. GOLD, P. E. & S. F. ZORNETZER. 1983. The mnemon and its juices: neuromodulation of memory processes. Behav. Neural Biol. 38: 151–189.
3. MCGAUGH, J. L. 1983. Hormonal influences on memory storage. J. Am. Psychol. Assoc. 38: 161–174.
4. BRAIN, Sir R. 1955. Diseases of the Nervous System. Oxford University Press. Oxford.
5. IZQUIERDO, I., D. O. SOUZA, M. A. CARRASCO, R. D. DIAS, M. L. PERRY, S. EISINGER, E. ELISABETSKY & D. A. VENDITE. 1980. Beta-endorphin causes retrograde amnesia and is released from the rat brain by various forms of training and stimulation. Psychopharmacology 70: 173–177.
6. IZQUIERDO, I., R. D. DIAS, M. L. PERRY, D. O. SOUZA, E. ELISABETSKY & M. A. CARRASCO. 1982. A physiological amnesic mechanism mediated by endogenous opioid peptides, and its possible role in learning. In Neuronal Plasticity and Memory Formation. C. Ajmone-Marsan & H. Matthies, Eds.: 89–111. Raven Press. New York.
7. GOLD, P. E. & R. L. DELANOY. 1981. ACTH modulation of memory storage processing. In Endogenous Peptides and Learning and Memory Processes. J.L. Martinez, Jr., R.A. Jensen, R.B. Messing, H. Rigter & J.L. McGaugh, Eds.: 79–98. Academic Press. New York.
8. IZQUIERDO, I. & R. D. DIAS. 1984. Influence on memory of the posttraining and pre-test injection of ACTH, vasopressin, epinephrine or β-endorphin, and their interaction with naloxone. Psychoneuroendocrinology 9: in press.
9. IZQUIERDO, I., D. O. SOUZA, R. D. DIAS, M. A. CARRASCO, N. VOLKMER, M. L. S. PERRY & C. A. NETTO. 1984. Effect of various behavioral training and testing procedures on brain β-endorphin-like immunoreactivity and the possible role of β-endorphin in behavioral regulation. Psychoneuroendocrinology 9: 381–389.
10. BLOOM, F. E. & J. F. MCGINTY. 1981. Cellular distribution and function of the endorphins. In Endogenous Peptides and Learning and Memory Processes. J. L. Martinez, Jr., R. A. Jensen, R. B. Messing, H. Rigter & J. L. McGaugh, Eds.: 199–230. Academic Press. New York.
11. GALLAGHER, M. & B. S. KAPP. 1978. Opiate administration into the amygdala. Effects on memory processes. Life Sci. 23: 1972–1978.
12. GALLAGHER, M. 1982. Naloxone enhancement of memory processes: effects of other opiate antagonists. Behav. Neural Biol. 35: 375–382.
13. GALLAGHER, M., R. A. KING & N. B. YOUNG. 1983. Opiate antagonists improve spatial memory. Science 221: 975–976.

14. JENSEN, R. A., J. L. MARTINEZ, JR., R. B. MESSING, V. SPIEHLER, B. J. VASQUEZ, B. SOUMIREU-MOURAT, K. C. LIANG & J. L. MCGAUGH. 1978. Morphine and naloxone alter memory in the rat. Soc. Neurosci. Absts. **4:** 260.

15. MESSING, R. B., R. A. JENSEN, J. L. MARTINEZ, JR., V. R. SPIEHLER, B. J. VASQUEZ, B. SOUMIREU-MOURAT, K. C. LIANG & J. L. MCGAUGH. 1979. Naloxone enhancement of memory. Behav. Neural Biol. **27:** 266–275.

16. IZQUIERDO, I. 1979. Effect of naloxone and morphine on various forms of memory in the rat: possible role of endogenous opiate mechanisms in memory consolidation. Psychopharmacology **66:**199–203.

17. IZQUIERDO, I. & M. GRAUDENZ. 1980. Memory facilitation by naloxone is due to release of dopaminergic and beta-adrenergic systems from tonic inhibition. Psychopharmacology **67:** 265–268.

18. IZQUIERDO, I. 1980. Effect of beta-endorphin and naloxone on acquisition, memory and retrieval of shuttle avoidance and habituation learning in rats. Psychopharmacology **69:** 111–115.

19. IZQUIERDO, I. 1980. Effect of a low and a high dose of β-endorphin on acquisition and retention in the rat. Behav. Neural Biol. **30:** 460–464.

20. IZQUIERDO, I., A. C. M. PAIVA & E. ELISABETSKY. 1980. Posttraining intraperitoneal administration of Leu-enkephalin and beta-endorphin causes retrograde amnesia for two different tasks in rats. Behav. Neural Biol. **28:** 246–250.

21. MARTINEZ, J. L., JR. & H. RIGTER. 1980. Endorphins alter acquisition and consolidation of an inhibitory avoidance response in rats. Neurosci. Lett. **19:** 197–201.

22. IZQUIERDO, I. & R. D. DIAS. 1981. Retrograde amnesia caused by Met-, Leu-, and des-Tyr-Met-enkephalin in the rat and its reversal by naloxone. Neurosci. Lett. **22:** 189–193.

23. IZQUIERDO, I. & R. D. DIAS. 1983. Effect of ACTH, epinephrine, β-endorphin, naloxone, and of the combination of naloxone or β-endorphin with ACTH or epinephrine on memory consolidation. Psychoneuroendocrinology **8:** 81–87.

24. LUCION, A. B., G. ROSITO, D. SAPPER, A. L. PALMINI & I. IZQUIERDO. 1982. Intracerebroventricular administration of nanogram amounts of β-endorphin and Met-enkephalin causes retrograde amnesia in rats. Behav. Brain Res. **4:** 111–115.

25. IZQUIERDO, I. 1982. β-Endorphin and forgetting. Trends Pharmacol. Sci. **3:** 455–457.

26. IZQUIERDO, I. 1982. The role of an endogenous amnesic mechanism mediated by brain β-endorphin in memory modulation. Braz. J. Med. Biol. Res. **15:** 119–134.

27. DIAS, R. D., M. A. CARRASCO & I. IZQUIERDO. 1982. Effect of the pre-training administration of β-endorphin, Met-, Leu-, and des-Tyr-Met-enkephalin on acquisition and retention of a shuttle avoidance response in rats. Braz. J. Med. Biol. Res. **15:** 55–60.

28. IZQUIERDO, I., M. A. M. R. DE ALMEIDA & V. R. EMILIANO. 1984. Posttraining β-endorphin, but not dynorphin$_{1-13}$, causes retrograde amnesia for two different tasks in rats. Psychopharmacology (In press).

29. IZQUIERDO, I., M. L. PERRY, R. D. DIAS, D. O. SOUZA, E. ELISABETSKY, M. A. CARRASCO, O. A. ORINGHER & C. A. NETTO. 1981. Endogenous opioids, memory modulation and state dependency. In Endogenous Peptides and Learning and Memory Processes. J. L. Martinez, Jr., R. A. Jensen, R. B. Messing, H. Rigter & J. L. McGaugh, Eds.: 269–290. Academic Press. New York.

30. HOUGHTEN, R. A., R. W. SWANN & C. H. LI. 1980. β-Endorphin: stability, clearance behavior, and entry into the central nervous system after intravenous injection of the tritiated peptide in rats and rabbits. Proc. Natl. Acad. Sci. USA **77:** 4588–4591.

31. IZQUIERDO, I. 1983. Some persisting myths about β-endorphin and related substances. Trends Pharmacol. Sci. **4:** 108–109.

32. ALMEIDA, M. A. M. R. DE & I. IZQUIERDO. 1984. Effect of the intraperitoneal and intracerebroventricular administration of ACTH, epinephrine or β-endorphin on retrieval of an inhibitory avoidance task in rats. Behav. Neural Biol. **40:** 119–122.

33. ROSSIER, J. 1982. Pro-enkephalin sequencing and the advent of cDNA technologies. Trends Neurosci. **5:** 179–180.

34. WEBER, E., C. J. EVANS & J. D. BARCHAS. 1983. Multiple endogenous ligands for opioid receptors. Trends Neurosci. **6:** 333–336.

35. CARRASCO, M. A., M. L. PERRY, R. D. DIAS, S. WOFCHUK & I. IZQUIERDO. 1982. Effect of tones, footshocks, shuttle avoidance, and electroconvulsive shock on Met-enkephalin immunoreactivity of rat brain. Behav. Neural Biol. **34:** 1–4.
36. PERRY, M. L. S., R. D. DIAS, M. A. CARRASCO & I. IZQUIERDO. 1983. Effect of step-down inhibitory avoidance training on β-endorphin-like immunoreactivity of rat hypothalamus and plasma. Braz. J. Med. Biol. Res. **16:** 339–343.
37. PERRY, M. L. S., M. A. CARRASCO, R. D. DIAS & I. IZQUIERDO. 1984. β-Endorphin like immunoreactivity of brain, pituitary gland and plasma of rats submitted to postnatal protein malnutrition. Peptides **5:** 15–20.
38. CRINE, P., S. BENJANNET, N. G. SEIDAH, M. LIS & M. CHRÉTIEN. 1977. In vitro biosynthesis of β-endorphin, γ-lipotropin and β-lipotropin by the pars intermedia of beef pituitary glands. Proc. Natl. Acad. Sci. USA **74:** 4276–4280.
39. IZQUIERDO, I., D. A. VENDITE, D.-O. SOUZA, R. D. DIAS, M. A. CARRASCO & M. L. S. PERRY. 1983. Some neurochemical effects of behavioral training and their relevance to learning and memory modulation. *In* Neural Transmission, Learning and Memory. R. Caputto & C. Ajmone-Marsan, Eds.: 221–235. Raven Press. New York.
40. ROSSIER, J., E. D. FRENCH, C. RIVIER, N. LING, R. GUILLEMIN & F. BLOOM. 1977. Foot shock induced stress increases β-endorphin levels in blood but not brain. Nature **270:** 618–620.
41. CARRASCO, M. A., R. D. DIAS, M. L. PERRY, S. WOFCHUK, D. O. SOUZA & I. IZQUIERDO. 1982. Effect of morphine, ACTH, epinephrine, Met-, Leu- and des-Tyr-Met-enkephalin on β-endorphin immunoreactivity of rat brain. Psychoneuroendocrinology **7:** 229–234.
42. ROSSIER, J., E. FRENCH, C. GROS, S. MINICK, R. GUILLEMIN & F. E. BLOOM. 1980. Adrenalectomy, dexamethasone or stress alters opioid peptides levels in rat anterior pituitary but not intermediate lobe or brain. Life Sci. **25:** 2105–2112.
43. GRAY, J. A. 1982. The Neuropsychology of Anxiety: an Enquiry into the Function of the Septo-hippocampal System. Clarendon Press. Oxford.
44. IZQUIERDO, I. & A. B. MERLO. 1966. Potentials evoked by stimulation of the medial forebrain bundle in rats. Exp. Neurol. **14:** 144–159.
45. HALÁSZ, B. & R. A. GORSKI. 1967. Gonadotrophic hormone secretion in female rats after partial or total interruption of neural afferents to the medial basal hypothalamus. Endocrinology **80:** 608–622.
46. HALÁSZ, B., J. VERNIKOS-DANIELLIS & R. A. GORSKI. 1967. Pituitary ACTH contents in rats after partial or total interruption of neural afferents to the medial basal hypothalamus. Endocrinology **81:** 921–924.
47. DE GROOT, J. 1959. The Rat Forebrain in Stereotaxic Coordinates. N. V. Noord-Hollandsche Uitgevers Maatschapij. Amsterdam.
48. HIRSH, R. 1974. The hippocampus and contextual retrieval of information from memory: A theory. Behav. Biol. **12:** 421–444.
49. WINOCUR, G. & M. GILBERT. 1984. The hippocampus, context, and information processing. Behav. Neural Biol. **40:** 27–43.
50. DIAS, R. D. & I. IZQUIERDO. 1983. Memory modulation by the administration of ACTH, adrenaline or β-endorphin after training or prior to testing in an inhibitory avoidance task in rats. Braz. J. Med. Biol. Res. **16:** 333–337.
51. IZQUIERDO, I. & R.D. DIAS. 1983. The influence of adrenergic receptor antagonists on the amnestic and antiamnestic actions of adrenaline and tyramine. Psychopharmacology **80:** 181–183.
52. ALMEIDA, M. A. M. R. DE, F. P. KAPCZINSKI & I. IZQUIERDO. 1983. Memory modulation by post-training intraperitoneal, but not intracerebroventricular, administration of ACTH or epinephrine. Behav. Neural Biol. **39:** 277–283.
53. BOHUS, B., L. CONTI, G. L. KOVÁCS & D. H. G. VERSTEEG. 1982. Modulation of memory processes by neuropeptides: interaction with neurotransmitter systems. *In* Neuronal Plasticity and Memory Formation. C. Ajmone-Marsan & H. Matthies, Eds.: 75–88. Raven Press. New York.
54. HAGAN, J. J., B. BOHUS & D. de WIED. 1982. Post-training vasopressin injections may facilitate or delay shuttle-box avoidance extinction. Behav. Neural Biol. **36:** 211–228.

55. SPEAR, N. E. The Processing of Memories, Forgetting and Retention. Lawrence Erlbaum Associates. Hillsdale, NJ.
56. RICCIO, D. C. & J. T. CONCANNON. 1981. ACTH and the reminder phenomena. *In* Endogenous Peptides and Learning and Memory Processes. J. L. Martinez, Jr., R. A. Jensen, R. B. Messing, H. Rigter & J. L. McGaugh, Eds.: 117–142. Academic Press. New York.
57. IZQUIERDO, I. & R. D. DIAS. 1983. Memory as a state-dependent phenomenon: role of ACTH and epinephrine. Behav. Neural Biol. **38:** 144–151.
58. PETERS, D. A. V., H. ANISMAN & B. A. PAPPAS. 1978. Monoamines and aversively motivated behaviors. *In* Psychopharmacology of Aversively Motivated Behavior. H. Anisman & G. Bignami, Eds.: 257–343. Plenum Press. New York.
59. DIAS, R. D., M. L. PERRY, M. A. CARRASCO & I. IZQUIERDO. 1981. Effect of electroconvulsive shock on β-endorphin immunoreactivity of rat brain, pituitary gland, and plasma. Behav. Neural Biol. **32:** 265–268.
60. ALLEN, J. P., D. DENNEY, J. W. KENDALL & P. H. BLACHLY. 1974. Corticotropin release during ECT in man. Am. J. Psychiat. **131:** 1225–1228.
61. SOELBERG SØRENSEN, P., M. HAMMER & T. G. BOLWIG. 1982. Vasopressin release during electroconvulsive therapy. Psychoneuroendocrinology **7:** 303–308.
62. RYAN, R. J., D. W. SWANSON, G. FAIRMAN, W. E. MAYBERRY & A. J. SPADONI. 1970. Effects of convulsive electroshock on serum concentrations of follicle stimulating hormone, luteinizing hormone, thyroid stimulating hormone and growth hormone in man. J. Clin. Endocr. Metab. **30:** 51–58.
63. CARRASCO, M. A., R. D. DIAS & I. IZQUIERDO. 1982. Naloxone reverses retrograde amnesia induced by electroconvulsive shock. Behav. Neural Biol. **34:** 352–357.
64. ROBERTS, E. & S. MATTHYSSE. 1970. Neurochemistry: at the crossroads of neurobiology. Ann. Rev. Biochem. **39:** 777–820.
65. JENSEN, R. A., R. B. MESSING, V. R. SPIEHLER, J. L. MARTINEZ, JR., B. J. VASQUEZ & J. L. McGAUGH. 1980. Memory, opiate receptors and aging. Peptides **1:** (Suppl. 1.) 197–201.
66. GAMBERT, S., T. L. GARTHWAITE, C. H. PONTZER & T. C. HAGEN. 1980. Age-related changes in central nervous system beta-endorphin and ACTH. Neuroendocrinology **31:** 252–255.
67. REISBERG, B., S. H. FERRIS, R. ANAND, P. MIR, V. GEIBEL, M. J. DE LEON & E. ROBERTS. 1983. Effects of naloxone in senile dementia: a double-blind trial. N. Eng. J. Med. **308:** 721–722.

Noradrenergic Modulation of Selective Attention: Its Role in Memory Retrieval

SUSAN J. SARA

Laboratoire de Physiologie Nerveuse
Department de Psychophysiologie
Centre National de la Recherche Scientifique
Gif/Yvette, France

INTRODUCTION

The biological significance of memory lies in its utilization in organizing an adaptive response to an environmental demand.[1] Despite this intuitively appealing functional view, there has been relatively little research effort devoted to the psychobiology of memory retrieval processes, even though memory lends itself to study through retrieval. However it is evaluated, be it through observation of the behavior of a rat in a maze, a human subject engaged in verbal reporting, or even an electrophysiological event, the memory trace is implied through its retrieval. Hence, our research efforts have been focused on the psychological factors and underlying physiological processes which might modulate memory retrieval.

"Remembering," Tulving suggests, "is the joint product of information stored in the past and information present in the immediate cognitive environment of the remember" (p. 352).[2] Such a view of memory retrieval places emphasis on attentional mechanisms, since the efficacy of retrieval will depend not only on the strength of the putative trace, but also on the appropriate selection of relevant stimuli present in the remembering environment.

These stimuli comprise the discriminative CS associated with response-reinforcement contingencies and the context. The context includes endogenous homeostatic information (hunger, thirst, hormonal status) as well as all stimuli in the external environment other than the nominal CS. We will argue that the context plays an essential role in memory retrieval processes and that memory dysfunction might involve deficits in contextual control of responding.

CONTEXT IN CONDITIONING AND REMEMBERING

Konorski suggested that "one need not think only of building on or looking beyond conditioning to deal with higher cognitive processes, for higher cognitive processes may be found in the conditioning situation itself."[3] Even the most basic learning involves not merely an association between the unconditioned stimulus (UCS) and the conditioned stimulus (CS), but a complex integration of information from the whole internal and external environment of the organism. This implies the involvement of attention, perception, and memory in the ongoing conditioning process. A similar view was put forth independently by Underwood,[4] who emphasized that memory is multidimensional. Attributes that are processed during learning, but do not include the nominal stimulus, are the context or background stimuli.

178

Lending support to Konorski's idea of the importance of the whole environment in learning and memory is the fact that presentation of contextual cues before the retention test is a very effective way of alleviating experimental amnesia.[5] Contextual cues may also alleviate memory deficits in rats with hippocampal lesions.[6] Furthermore, some clinicians have proposed that human amnesic syndromes, especially Korsakoff's, might be due, at least in part, to a failure to treat contextual information.[7,8]

Data from our laboratory indicate that spontaneous forgetting is likewise alleviated by pretest exposure to contextual cues.[9,10] Rats trained to run a maze (FIGURE 1) consisting of successive left-right choices for food reinforcement forget after four weeks. If the animal is exposed to the experimental room near the start box immediately prior to the retention test, the performance is improved to the level of the last training trial. (FIGURE 2)

Control experiments show that there is a specificity in the treatment. Placing the animal in another room or even in a different place in the experimental room has no effect.[11] If the reminder treatment occurs 24 hr or 1 hr before the test, there is only marginal facilitation.[12] It is important to note that this cue procedure does not contain

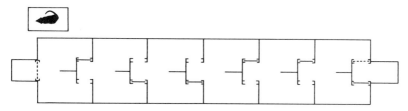

FIGURE 1. Schematic diagram of the six-unit spatial discrimination maze. The barriers can be placed at either side. The usual choice sequence is LRRLLR or RLLRRL. The square at the left of the maze represents the wire mesh "reminder" box.

any information concerning response-reinforcement contingencies. Yet, animals exposed to the context make fewer errors in less time than control animals. This leads to the conclusion that this contextual cue procedure alleviates forgetting by facilitating memory retrieval.

Contemporary learning theory has emphasized the role of background stimuli in elaborating the conditioned response by showing contextual specificity in conditioned responding, latent inhibition, and extinction. This phenomenon has been integrated into a theory of conditioning that holds that associations are formed between the UCS and the context as well as between the UCS and the nominal CS. In this view the context is on a par with the nominal stimulus in the acquisition of the conditioned response, supposedly either as a part of a compound stimulus or as a CS1, in a higher order conditioning relationship.[13-15]

On the other hand, the context can facilitate responding in the presence of the CS even though the context itself does not appear to have strong association with the UCS, i.e. it does not, by itself, elicit the CR.[16] These authors suggest that contextual cues somehow "potentiate retrieval of associations to the CS" (p. 383)[16] by some undefined mechanism. These data fit well within the theoretical framework provided by Spear,[17] who holds that the context is an attribute that acts as a retrieval cue. In the next section we propose a mechanism by which the context might facilitate responding independent

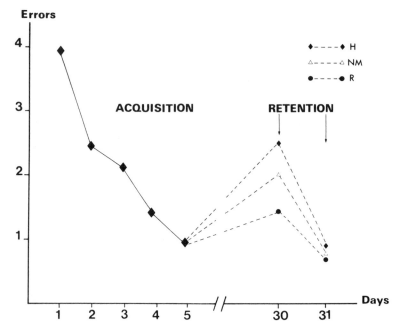

FIGURE 2. Mean time to run the maze (a) and mean number of errors (b) for the five training trials and the two retention tests. The training to Test 1 interval was 25 days; the Test 1 to Test 2 interval was 24 hr. Note the retention deficit in the two control groups (Group NM, nonmanipulated animals; Group H, animals habituated to the reminder) at Test 1, and the recovery of performance at Test 2. The reminded animals (Group R) did not show this deficit. These data are based on a 4 unit maze. (From Deweer et al.[9] With permission from *Animal Learning and Behavior.*)

of its ability to elicit the CR itself, but dependent, nevertheless, upon an association with the UCS.

CONTEXTUAL CUE REMINDER AND THE TRUNCATED CONDITIONED REFLEX

An initial conceptual framework for a proposed mechanism of action of the contextual cue facilitation of responding is provided by the work of Kupalov, a student of Pavlov. Many years ago, Kupalov[18] postulated a mechanism of conditioned regulation of arousal or "cortical tonus." He named this particular type of CR the truncated conditioned reflex (TCR); the CS eliciting this tonic response is the experimental context in which the reinforcement was delivered. Contextual stimuli elicit a TCR that involves an increase in arousal, attention, and expectancy. It puts the nervous system into a functional mode that facilitates cognitive integrative activity such as perception, stimulus selection, and response organization, which are necessary for an adaptive response to the environmental demands. Konorski later reiterated the importance of distinguishing between the consummatory CR and what he called the preparatory CR, the establishment of which is necessary before the specific, adaptive CR can be elaborated.[3]

The preparatory response or TCR may be physiologically equivalent to the orienting reponse (OR), which is an unconditioned increase in attention or arousal in the presence of novelty. The important difference between the two is that the OR occurs spontaneously. The context, on the other hand, elicits a tonic preparatory response through association with the reinforcement (US).

There are distinguishing features of this context—US association, according to Konorski—it is established very rapidly and it is highly resistant to extinction. If this association be highly resistant to forgetting as well, this could account for the fact that the context acts as an effective reminder in the spontaneous forgetting paradigms discussed in the previous section. The retention deficits seen in human and non human subjects when the environmental context is changed between acquisition and testing,[2,17] could also be explained if the preparatory tonic response elicited by the context is a necessary condition for efficient retrieval. In its absence, performance diminishes. Moreover, investigations of conditioned tonic responding to the context and its influence on subsequent CRs have been carried out in humans showing beneficial effects of tonic response to the context on discrimination performance.[19]

Kupalov believed that the discovery of the reticular activating system, by Magoun in 1949, some years after his proposal of the TCR, provided a brain mechanism for this putative response, lending strong support to the concept of conditioned regulation of cortical excitation, and thus attention and expectancy.[18] Studies in our laboratory have shown that electrical stimulation of the mesencephalic reticular formation (MRF), immediately before the retention test can, indeed, facilitate retrieval in the same forgetting paradigm described above, perhaps by enhancing the TCR elicited by the pretest handling and brief exposure to the context before being placed into the maze.[20]

Given the existence of the TCR, the question arises as to how the increased level of arousal provided by the conditioned response to context facilitates memory retrieval as manifested by more accurate discrimination in the maze. The question can be addressed at two levels: first, what are the cognitive processes particularly implicated in accurate discrimination, and second, what are the underlying brain systems involved in these processes.

SELECTIVE ATTENTION AND LOCUS COERULEUS-FOREBRAIN PROJECTION

Memory retrieval processes, viewed within the conceptual framework outlined above, must be intimately related to perception, attention, and stimulus selection, so the study of memory retrieval might begin with a consideration of those factors involved in cognitive functions.

Evidence from several different lines of research have implicated catecholamines, particularly noradrenaline (NE), in the modulation of attention. Both electrophysiological studies and behavioral analysis after neurotoxic lesions have suggested that the locus coeruleus projection to the cortex and hippocampus, via the dorsal bundle, might be involved in modulation of attention.

Electrophysiological Studies

Electrical stimulation of the locus coeruleus at intensities too low to produce inhibition of spontaneous cell firing in the forebrain can potentiate responses in the somatosensory cortex to peripheral input.[21] Cortical neurons are capable of a large range of responses to the same stimulus and NE seems to bias subthreshold sensory input to a detectable level. Neuronal responses in the hippocampus to biologically significant stimuli (e.g. stimuli previously associated with the reinforcement) are enhanced in the presence of NE.[22] The result is an improvement in the signal-to-noise ratio. Both of these series of experiments have been taken by their authors to provide evidence that the locus coeruleus-forebrain projections constituting the telencephalic NE system are intimately involved in the regulation of selective attention.

This functional interpretation of electrophysiological results raises two important questions. First, what are the behavioral or environmental conditions under which the LC is activated to perform its sensory gating function? This question has been addressed by Aston-Jones and Bloom[23] who have found that LC neurons were inhibited during grooming and consummatory behavior and that they responded robustly to environmental stimuli of many modalities. These data further support the role of LC in enhancement of signal-to-noise ratios and attention, in this case, to changes in environmental input or novelty. A demonstration of habituation of the response when the stimuli become familiar and enhancement of responses when the stimuli have been paired with reinforcement would add some genuine support to this view.

Neurotoxic Lesions and Selective Attention

A second question raised by the hypothesis that forebrain NE regulates selective attention is whether changes in this system have any impact on behavior that might reflect attention. This question can be addressed in a number of ways. The preferred technique is to decrease NE function selectively through neurotoxic injections to the dorsal bundle (DB). This procedure leaves the dopaminergic system intact as well as the brainstem noradrenergic system, but produces almost total depletion of NE in cortex and hippocampus. The literature concerning the cognitive effects of such lesions is large and discordant.

One of the problems in interpreting the literature concerning NE and attention in the rat is that of the validity of the measure of attention, and this could account for the lack of reliable results. Most investigators have used such paradigms as latent inhibition or blocking to evaluate attention and these studies have produced mixed results. On the other hand, the literature has been carefully reviewed recently by Robbins et al.,[24] who contend that, in spite of the abundance of negative results, there is sufficient evidence to justify the conclusion that DB-lesioned rats have difficulty in stimulus selection and/or maintaining attention to the "relevant dimension" once selected. Their own results showing clear-cut acquisition deficits in complex discrimination tasks lend weight to this conclusion. However, they fail to find a lack of latent inhibition in DB-lesioned rats, in a simpler task where there is no acquisition deficit.

In addition to the problem of a valid behavioral measure, another reason for the discrepancies in the literature concerning neurotoxic lesions and attention might have to do with recovery or functional reorganization after these lesions. Receptors become hypersensitive after lesion, so that any spared presynaptic function will become increasingly efficacious over time. Furthermore, the NE system is particularly susceptible to neuronal sprouting after damage. Functional recovery might well vary according to strain of rats, handling, diet, housing, and of course, amount of sparing after the lesion, leading to difficulty in replicating results.

Improvement of Selective Attention through Stimulation of LC

Early studies of Fuster showed that stimulation of the MRF facilitates fine discrimination thresholds in the monkey.[25] Such an approach, using LC stimulation, might be useful in evaluating the functional significance of NE-induced change in signal-to-noise ratio. It is surprising that there are, to our knowledge, no such studies designed to address the question as to whether the increase in electrophysiological response to biologically significant stimuli in the presence of NE really represents an increase in selective attention at a cognitive level.

Two series of experiments provide some indirect evidence. Prolonged stimulation of LC in young rats can facilitate learning several weeks later.[26] In aging mice there is improved long term memory retention after prolonged LC stimulation.[27] The mechanism of action of this prolonged stimulation whose effects are so long-lasting is not known, although in the former series of studies, there was a long-lasting increase in alpha adrenoreceptors. Whether the improved learning and retention performance is due to increased attention remains an open question. Indeed, as pointed out above, a major problem in validating at a behavioral level the conclusions drawn from electrophysiological studies is the measure of selective attention in the rat. The complex discrimination procedure of Robbins,[24] which reliably reveals DB lesion deficits, might be useful in this respect.

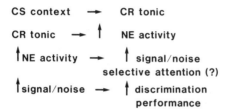

FIGURE 3. Schematic representation of a model based on the multidimensional view of memory.

NORADRENALINE AND MEMORY RETRIEVAL

Based on the multidimensional view of memory outlined above, which emphasizes attention processes in the retrieval of memory, we propose a working model by which contextual cue reminders enhance those cognitive processes intimately involved in memory retrieval. The context, through its association with the reinforcement, comes to elicit a tonic response, a component of which is increased firing of LC neurons. This increased activity in the LC releases NE in the forebrain. In the presence of NE, hippocampal and cortical neurons are inhibited in their spontaneous firing and neuronal response to "significant" stimuli are enhanced. In this case, "significant" stimuli are the discriminative stimuli, not necessarily those specified by the experimenter, that predict response contingencies for the animal. Schematically the model can be summarized in FIGURE 3.

This model makes two simple predictions. (1) Pharmacological or physiological interventions that enhance NE activity to a certain optimal level should facilitate memory retrieval. Treatments that block NE activity should block the contextual cue reminder effect. (2) Exposure to contextual cue reminders that enhance discrimination performance after a long retention interval should increase NE utilization in cortex and/or hippocampus. We have tested these predictions in the spontaneous forgetting paradigm mentioned in a previous section.

Spontaneous Forgetting Paradigm

Most of the studies reported here have used the experimental design and, with a few exceptions, behavioral procedures, as were used in the studies concerned with reminder effects and MRF stimulation, described above. The maze task used in these experiments is depicted in FIGURE 1.

Forgetting is defined operationally as a significant increase in errors between the last training trial and the retention test. Forgetting is considered to be alleviated when there is no difference between the last training trial and the test trial after a treatment, and there is a significant difference between the treated group and control group. The error measure is considered to be the most valid measure of retention; some treatments significantly improve performance as measured by errors without having significant effect on run time. The contrary—a significant decrease in run time with no effect on errors—has never been seen in our experiments. All pharmacological interventions take place just before retention test, three or four weeks after training, when forgetting can be expected in control animals. Preliminary studies are always carried out to determine the effects of a substance on locomotor activity and food motivation.

Pharmacological Studies

Amphetamine stimulates release and blocks reuptake of both NE and DA in the central nervous system as well as having a stimulating effect on the sympathetic nervous system. There are advantages to this lack of specificity on initial investigation of the role of catecholamines in memory retrieval, since its broad range of physiological effects increases the chance of finding behavioral effects and thus determining the experimental paradigms that best lend themselves to more specific pharmacological

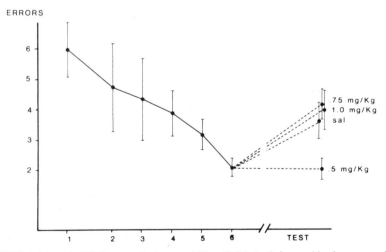

FIGURE 4. Mean (±SEM) errors during acquisition (Trials 1–6) for combined groups and at retention test three weeks later, for the four treatment groups. Injections of amphetamine or saline were made 20 min before the retention test. Note the forgetting in the saline, 1.0 and 0.75 mg/kg amphetamine groups, and the alleviation of forgetting by 0.50 mg/kg amphetamine. (From Sara & Deweer.[29] With permission from *Behavioral Neural Biology*.)

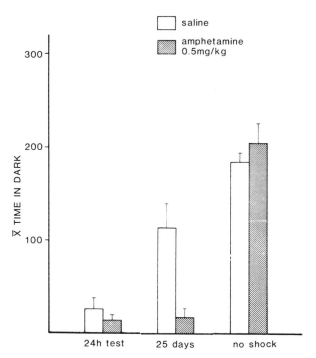

FIGURE 5. Mean time in the dark during the 5 min retention test. White bars, saline; striped bars, .5 mg/kg amphetamine, 20 min before retention test. Note robust avoidance learning in rats tested 24 hr after training and significant retention deficit in rats tested 25 days after training. This deficit is alleviated by pretest amphetamine. Amphetamine has no effect on avoidance in trained rats (group 24 hr) and no effect on dark preference in untrained rats (group 25 days). A replication showed no effect of amphetamine on rats submitted to non contingent FS and tested 25 days later. (Fom Sara.[30] With permission from *Physiological Psychology*.)

investigation. Amphetamine has been employed extensively in learning and memory studies and, for the most part, small doses have been found to facilitate learning and attenuate experimentally induced amnesia when given after training or before retention test.[28] Using the spontaneous forgetting paradigm described above, we have found that doses up to .5 mg/mg, which have little effect on locomotor activity, alleviate forgetting when injected before the retention test. As can be seen in FIGURE 4, higher doses have no effect. Subsequent studies showed that when the rats are retested 24 hr later, without the drug, they maintain their good performance. There is no effect of the drug at any stage of acquisition.[29]

In another series of experiments,[30] it was found that the same low doses of amphetamine can facilitate retrieval in an inhibitory avoidance task after a long retention interval (FIGURE 5). Since the behavioral requirements and motivation are so different in the two tasks. these results lend weight to the interpretation of the maze results in terms of facilitation of memory retrieval and not merely task performance.

While the effect of systemically administered amphetamine is quite reliable, the action could be either on the peripheral or central nervous system or both. This question has received much attention in the literature and has been addressed by several strategies, including use of amphetamine analogs that are devoid of central action, or central injections of amphetamine, with inconclusive results.[28] Intracerebroventricular (icv) injections of amphetamine in the maze forgetting paradigm produced results that were not as robust and reliable as with systemic injections. Since the results of experiments using systemic treatments showed that a facilitative effect was highly dose dependent, the marginal effects found with central injections might be improved upon using a wide range of doses (Sara, unpublished results).

The facilitative effect of amphetamine may be acting through the noradrenergic system or the dopaminergic system. In an early attempt to test our hypothesis concerning the role of NE modulation of cortical and hippocampal activity in memory retrieval, NE injected directly into the hippocampus by means of permanently indwelling cannula produced a nonsignificant tendency for animals treated with .25 μg to make more errors at test than controls. The tendency to impair performance might

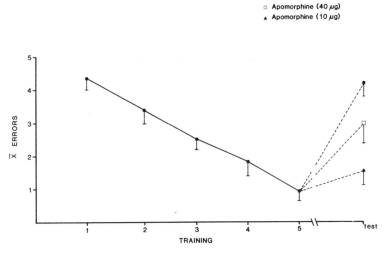

FIGURE 6. Mean (±SEM) number of errors for the combined groups during each day of training and mean number of errors for each treatment group at retention test, 25 days after the last training trial. Note forgetting in saline group and alleviation of forgetting in group treated with 10 μg Apo before retention test (From Sara et al.[33] With permission from Behavioural Brain Research.)

be an indication that NE applied locally at that concentration blocks NE release by presynaptic action at α-2 receptors.[31]

Attempts to block the reminder effect with systemic injections of the noradrenergic beta receptor antagonist, propranolol, were also unsuccessful. In the light of these results and in spite of the attractiveness of the model outlined above, we turned our attention to the DA system to see if the amphetamine facilitation (and possibly the reminder effect) could be due to DA release. Another reason for interest in DA came from some new evidence that DA agonists could reverse experimentally induced amnesia when injected before the retention test.[32]

Systemic injections of apomorphine (apo), a DA receptor agonist, had no effect at

TABLE 1. Dopamine and Metabolites in Striatum after Intraventricular Injection of Apo (ng/mg protein)

	DA	DOPAC	DA/DOPAC	HVA
Control	242.1	16.75	11.35	12
10 μg Apo	255.3	17.5	19	8.5
40 μg Apo	183	15.93	10.37	8.41

There were no significant differences.

.1 mg/kg. This is a dose that is considered to have postsynaptic effects, but is not large enough to produce hyperactivity. Smaller doses, which allegedly have presynaptic inhibitory effects on the DA system, increased run time, but had no effect on errors. Doses larger than .1 mg/kg produced hyperactivity, which precluded collection of meaningful data in the maze. On the other hand, preliminary studies showed that icv injections of apo never produced hyperactivity or stereotypy. Injections of 10 μg alleviated forgetting, while the larger dose had no effect (FIGURE 6).

Since there was very little literature concerning the behavioral and neurochemical effects of icv injections of apo, and since the behavioral effects we observed were notably different than those after systemic injections, we examined the effects of these icv injections on striatal, hippocampal, and cortical amines, using HPLC analysis. The unexpected results can be seen in TABLES 1 and 2. The dose that facilitated memory retrieval had no effect on striatal DA, but produced increases in cortical and hippocampal NE. The larger, behaviorally ineffective dose did not produce this effect.[33] Why icv and systemic injections of apo should produce such different results, both behavioral and neurochemical, might have to do with different target structures reached when the drug arrives in brain through the cerebral spinal fluid or through the blood stream. We have discussed this in depth elsewhere.[33]

We next examined the ability of the DA antagonist, haloperidol, to block the reminder effect. The experiment had originally been designed to test the interaction between reminder effect and drug treatment, with the hypothesis that the reminder would be ineffective when DA receptors were inactivated. The surprising results were that haloperidol at .5 mg/kg facilitated maze performance in both reminded and nonreminded rats. The results of a replication, in which smaller doses were used along with the previously effective dose, can be seen in FIGURE 7. It should be noted that the hypomotility and slight catalepsy that occurs at this dose in open field observations is not seen in hungry rats during the 30 sec test trial.

It has been reported very recently that systemically administered haloperidol increased firing of LC neurons.[34] This could occur either through blockade of

TABLE 2. Noradrenaline and Metabolites in Various Brain Regions after Intraventricular Injection of Apomorphine (ng/mg protein)

	Hypothalamus			Hippocampus	Cortex		
	NE	MHPG	NE/MHPG	NE	NE	MHPG	NE/MHPG
Control	46.62	1.92	22.77	2.98	6	1.87	3.44
10 μg Apo	35.39	.87	11.14	8.5[a]	14.82[b]	2.04	9.245
40 μg Apo	29.02	1.36	20.15	5.64	4.79	1.44	4.65

Values are group medians. N = 5 control, N = 4, 10 μg Apo, 40 μg Apo. 1 MHPG value in each group was lost in hippocampus samples so the data are not presented. [a].10 > p > .05 two tailed, [b]p < .05 two tailed.

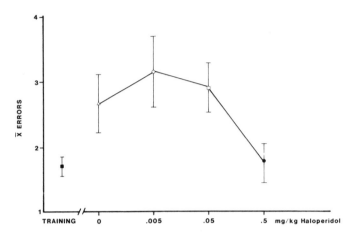

FIGURE 7. Mean (±SEM) number of errors at the last training trial for combined groups and at retention test, 25 days after last training trial. Note forgetting in saline and .005 and .05 mg/kg treated rats and alleviation of forgetting in the group receiving .5 mg/kg haloperidol before retention test.

inhibitory DA receptors recently described in the LC[35] or through direct action of haloperidol on somatodendritic LC adrenoreceptors. (α2 receptors). Further evidence for noradrenergic effects of haloperidol is found in that it enhances release of NE from rat cerebral cortex, and these authors suggest that it is probably due to its blockading effects on presynaptic α-2 receptors.[36]

Yohimbine is a relatively selective alpha-2 antagonist at low doses and increases NE turnover in selective brain regions.[37] Our next experiments examined the effect on

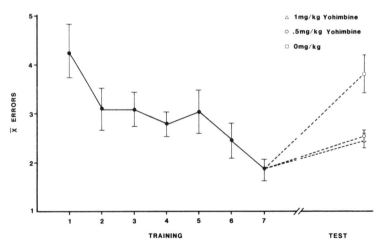

FIGURE 8. Mean (±SEM) number of errors during training for the combined groups. Note forgetting in saline-treated rats and significant reduction in errors in both groups of rats treated with yohimbine before retention test.

memory retrieval of blocking these receptors. The results are shown in FIGURE 8; rats treated with either dose of yohimbine make fewer errors than rats treated with saline. The treatment had no effect on time to run the maze, nor on spontaneous locomotion or exploration as measured in the holeboard.

The results of these pharmacological experiments, though incomplete, strongly implicate the noradrenergic system in memory retrieval in the maze task. The studies should be completed by a demonstration of prevention of the reminder effect by a NE postsynaptic receptor blockade. Propranolol was inactive at the dose used, but it is more likely that alpha receptors are involved and studies are planned in which post-synaptic alpha receptor blockade will be effected in conjunction with the reminder procedure.

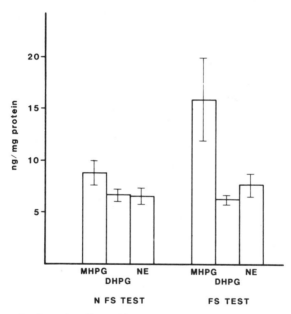

FIGURE 9. Amount of noradrenaline and its metabolites, MHPG and DHPG in hippocampus of rats exposed to the context in which they had been mildly shocked 24 hr earlier. FS = footshock and NFS = non shocked controls. The increase in MHPG in shocked controls is significant.

Neurochemical Studies

The aim of this series of experiments, done in collaboration with V. Leviel and B. Guibert, has been to test the hypothesis that memory retrieval is facilitated by contextual cue reminders because these cues elicit a conditioned increase in NE activity. In the first experiment, the rats were trained in the maze and then divided into four matched groups. After the usual retention interval, the rats were exposed to the training context and either run in the maze or decapitated immediately after exposure to the context. Control animals in the nonreminded condition were placed in a similar wire mesh cage in a context that had never been associated with the reinforcement and then run in the maze or sacrificed. Brains were dissected into hypothalamus, hippocampus, cortex, and striatum. Subsequent HPLC analysis measured NE, DA, serotonin, and metabolites. There were no differences between reminded and nonreminded rats for any of the neurotransmitters or metabolites measured. In this experiment we were only able to measure free 3-methoxy-4-hydroxyphenyl-ethylene glycol (MHPG), which amounts to only about 10% of the total MHPG in the rat brain. Since our samples from discrete brain regions were small, there was relatively little free MHPG detectable and certainly not in sufficient quantity to show any treatment effects. Yet it is this metabolite of NE that would provide the most valid indication of a conditioned response of the system, since MHPG is the end product of the utilization of NE. However, increase in turnover of NE without changes in amine levels has been reported by several investigators.[38] A method for measuring MHPG sulfate has since been developed in our laboratory and we intend to repeat this experiment, measuring total MHPG in various brain regions.

Using this recently available analysis of MHPG sulfate in preliminary experiments, we have been able to show an increase in total MHPG in the hippocampus after exposure to the environment in which the rat had received mild footshock 24 hours previously (FIGURE 9). This increase is not seen in the entorhinal cortex, the only other region examined in this study. It should be noted that there are no differences in NE, itself, nor in dihydroxyphenylglycol (DPHG), a metabolite of NE that appears earlier in the metabolic process. This lack of difference in neurotransmitter or early metabolites agrees with our earlier results in the maze study.

Conditioned increases in whole brain MPHG have been reported before,[39] but an important difference in that earlier study and our own lies in the amount of stress involved in the conditioning situation. In the Cassens et al. study, rats were submitted to intense footshocks intermittently for 90 minutes. The exposure to the context 24 hours later also lasted 90 minutes. In our experiment, the rats received five mild shocks over a period of 30 seconds; the retention test likewise lasted 30 seconds. We are presently trying to demonstrate an increase in MHPG upon exposure to a context in which the rat has received a distinctive positive UCS (sweetened condensed milk). This would lend support to the argument that it is the significance of the context in predicting reinforcement that elicits the NE response and not the stress itself.

CLINICAL CONSIDERATIONS

After an extensive review of the literature concerning the role of LC in human neurological and psychiatric disorders, van Dongen[40] concludes that there are certain underlying symptoms involved in a number of disorders that might be attributed to disturbances in NE transmission. He suggests from the available evidence that impairments of perceptual organization and memory found in some Parkinson's patients and in those suffering from Alzheimer's disease are actually caused by dysfunction of the LC. Support for this interpretation comes from recent evidence of loss of NE cells in LC and concomitant decrease in cortical NE in Alzheimer's patients compared to control brains of the same age at death.[41] Moreover, several new psychogeriatric drugs, reputed to improve cognitive functioning in the elderly, increase firing in the LC of the anesthetized rat.[42] This opens up a promising area of research into therapeutics involving direct manipulation of the NE system (see Olpe, this volume).

McEntee and Mair[43] have found that Korsakoff patients have decreased MHPG in spinal fluid and that this loss is correlated with performance on memory tasks. Clonidine, an alpha receptor agonist, improves cognitive performance in these patients without having its usual sedative effect. The sedative effect of clonidine in normal subjects is thought to be due to stimulation of alpha-2 presynaptic receptors, which overrides its postsynaptic effect. The absence of sedative effect in Korsakoff patients suggests degeneration of presynaptic elements. Support for this has been provided by the marked decrease in cortical NE after thiamine deprivation in a rat Korsakoff model.

Orienting Response, Truncated Conditioned Reflex and Amnesia

Korsakoff patients also have deficits in the orienting response to novelty. NE involvement is suggested by the fact that the specific OR deficit can be reversed by clonidine.[43] The amnesia is likely to be due in part to impairment in information processing at the time of acquisition due to this attention deficit.

As suggested above, the OR and the TCR are very likely to involve the same physiological systems and may even be the same response, the former being unconditioned and the latter conditioned. Thus with a deficit in the OR, it would be reasonable to expect a deficit in the TCR as well. Retrieval failure resulting from the diminished TCR or preparatory response to context might then also contribute to the memory deficit, along with the loss of the OR and its resultant encoding deficit.

CONCLUSION

Context-dependent increases in LC activity prepare the system for effective retrieval by enhancing selective attention to relevant stimuli. Direct and indirect support for this proposition has been presented here. The most convincing support comes from the alleviation of forgetting seen with drugs that enhance LC firing. Further evidence is found in the conditioned increase in NE turnover upon exposure to the context. Finally, deficits in noradrenergic function in diseases involving memory dysfunction[40–43] and the efficacy of drugs that improve noradrenergic function in improving memory in these patients[42,32] provide clinical support for this conclusion.

ACKNOWLEDGMENTS

The experiments reported here were carried out in collaboration with Bernard Deweer, Bernard Hars, Gisela Grecksch, Vincent Leviel, Bernard Guibert, Mark Hongenaert, and Abdelwahab Mahjoub. Technical assistance was provided by Michele Dumas and Gerard Le Floch. David Olton and Steven Zornetzer gave helpful suggestions for improving the manuscript.

REFERENCES

1. FESSARD, A. 1970. Approche neurophysiologique des problèmes de la mémoire. *In* La Mémoire. D. Bovet, A. Fessard, C. Flores, N. Frijda, B. Inhelder, B. Milner & J. Piaget, Eds. Presses Universitaires de France. Paris.
2. TULVING, E. & D. THOMPSON, 1973. Encoding specificity and retrieval processes in episodic memory. Psychol. Rev. **80:** 352–373.
3. KONORSKI, J. 1967. Integrative Activity of the Brain. Chicago University Press.

4. UNDERWOOD, B. 1969. Attributives of memory. Psychol. Rev. **76:** 559–573.
5. SARA, S. J. 1974. Recovery from hypoxia and ECS-induced amnesia after a single exposure to the training environment. Physiol. Behav. **10:** 85–89.
6. WINOCUR, G. & J. OLDS. 1978. Effects of context manipulation on memory and reversal learning en rats in hippocampal lesions. J. Comp. Physiol. Psychol. **92:** 312–321.
7. WINOCUR, G. & M. KINSBOURNE. 1978. Contextual cueing as an aid to Korsakoff amnesics. Neuropsychologia **16:** 671–682.
8. HUPPERT, F. & M. PIERCY. 1982. In search of the functional locus of amnesic syndromes. *In* Human Memory and Amnesia. L. S. Cermak, Ed. Lawrence Erlbaum. Hillsdale, NJ.
9. DEWEER, B., S. SARA & B. HARS. 1980. Contextual cues and memory retrieval in rats: alleviation of forgetting by a pretest exposure to background stimuli. Anim. Learn. Behav. **8**(2): 265–272.
10. DEWEER, B. & S. J. SARA. 1981. Alleviation of forgetting by a pretest exposure to background stimuli: Role of delay and duration of cueing. Behav. Brain Res. **2:** 254–255.
11. DEWEER, B. Memory retrieval in rats: critical role of contextual similarity between training and testing. Behav. Brain Res. **5:** 97–98.
12. DEWEER, B. & S. SARA. 1984. Background stimuli as a reminder after spontaneous forgetting: role of duration of cueing and cueing-test interval. Anim. Learn. Behav. (In press.)
13. WAGNER, A. 1976. Priming in STM: an information-processing mechanism for self-generated depression in performance. *In* Habituation: perspectives from child development, animal behavior and neurophysiology. T. J. Tighe & R. N. Leaton, Eds. Lawrence Erlbaum. Hillsdale, NJ.
14. LUBOW, R. B., R. B. RIFKIN & M. ALEK. 1976. The context effect: the relationship between stimulus preexposure and environmental preexposure determines subsequent learning. J. Exp. Psychol.: Anim. Behav. Proc. **2:** 38–47.
15. RESCORLA, R. & A. WAGNER. 1973. A theory of Pavlovian conditioning: variations in the effectiveness of reinforcement and nonreinforcement. *In* Classical Conditioning II: Current Research and Theory. A. H. Black & W. Prokasy, Eds. Appleton-Century-Crofts. New York.
16. BALAZ, M. A., S. CAPRA, P. HARTL & R. R. MILLER. 1981 Contextual potentiation of acquired behavior after devaluing direct context-US association. Learn. Motiv. **12:** 383–397.
17. SPEAR, N. 1978. The processing of memories: forgetting and retention. Lawrence Erlbaum. Hillsdale, NJ.
18. KUPALOV, P. S. 1961. Some normal and pathological processes in the brain. Ann. N.Y. Acad. Sci. **92:** 813–1198.
19. KIMMEL, M. D., N. BIRBAUMER, T. ELBERT, W. LUTZENBERGER & B. ROCKSTROH. 1983. Conditioned tonic stimulus control of nonspecific arousal. Pavlov. J. Biol. Sci. **18:** 136–143.
20. SARA, S. J., B. DEWEER & B. HARS. 1980. Reticular stimulation facilitates retrieval of a "forgotten" maze habit. Neurosci. Lett. **18:** 211—217.
21. WATERHOUSE, B. D., H. MOISES & D. WOODWARD. 1980. Locus coeruleus stimulation potentiates somatosensory cortical neuronal responses to afferent synaptic inputs. Soc. Neurosci. Abst. **6:** 446.
22. SEGAL, M. & F. BLOOM. 1976. Norepinephrine in the rat hippocampus. III—stimulation of nucleus locus coeruleus in the awake rat. Brain Res. **107:** 499–511.
23. ASTON-JONES, G. & F. BLOOM. 1981. Norepinephrine-containing locus coeruleus neurons in behaving rats exhibit pronounced responses to non noxious environmental stimuli. J. Neurosci. **1:** 887–900.
24. ROBBINS, T. W., B. EVERETT, P. FRAY, M. GASKIN, M. CARLI & C. DE LA RIVA. The roles of central catecholamines in attention and learning. *In* Behavioral Models and the Analysis of Drug Action. M. Spregelstein & A. Levy, Eds. Elsevier. Amsterdam.
25. FUSTER, J. & A. UYEDA. 1962. Facilitation of tachistoscoptic performance by stimulation at midbrain tegmental points in the monkey. Exp. Neurol. **6:** 384–406.

26. ZORNETZER, S. 1985. Catecholamine system involvement in age related memory dysfunction. Ann. N.Y. Acad. Sci. (This volume.)

27. VELLEY, L., B. CARDO & J. BOCKAERT. 1981. Modulation of rat brain and adrenoreceptor population four weeks after stimulation of nucleus locus coeruleus. Psychopharmacology **74:** 226–231.

28. QUARTERMAIN, D. 1983. The role of catecholamines in memory processing. *In* The Physiological Basis of Memory. J. A. Deutsch, Ed. 2nd edit. John Wiley. New York.

29. SARA, S. J. & B. DEWEER. 1982. Memory retrieval enhanced by amphetamine after a long retention interval. Behav. Neural Biol. **36:** 146–160.

30. SARA, S. J. 1984. Forgetting of a conditioned emotional response and its alleviation by pretest amphetamine. Physiol. Psychol. **12:** 17–22.

31. AGHAJANIAN, G. 1982. Central noradrenergic neurons: a locus for the functional interplay between alpha-2 adrenoceptors and opiate receptors. J. Clin. Psychiatry **43**(6): 20–24.

32. QUARTERMAIN, D., M. JUDGE & E. FRIEDMAN. 1983. Role of lisuride and other dopamine agonists in memory retrieval processes. *In* Lisuride and other Dopamine Agonists. D. Calne, Ed. Raven Press. New York.

33. SARA, S. J., G. GRECKSCH & V. LEVIEL. 1984. Intra cerebral ventricular apomorphine alleviates spontaneous forgetting and increases cortical noradrenaline. Behav. Brain Res. **13:** 43–52.

34. DINAN, T., R. SHAVER & G. ASTON-JONES. 1983. Haloperidol alters activity of locus coeruleus neurons. Soc. Neurosci. Abst. **2:** 1000.

35. MCRAE-DEGEURCE, A. & H. MILON. 1983. Serotonin and dopamine afferents to the rat locus coeruleus: a biochemical study after lesioning of the ventral mesencephalic tegmental-A10 region and the raphe dorsalis. Brain Res. **263:** 344–347.

36. AKENHEIL, M. Neuroleptics. *In* Psychopharmacology Part 2: Clinical Psychopharmacology. H. Hippius & G. Winokur, Eds. Expecta Medical. Amsterdam.

37. GOLDBERG, M. & D. ROBERTSON. 1983. Yohimbine: a pharmacological probe for study of the alpha-2-adrenoreceptor. Pharmacol. Rev. **35:** 143–180.

38. THIERRY, A-M. 1973. Effect of stress on various characteristics of norepinephrine metabolism in central noradrenergic neurons. *In* Neurohumoral and Metabolic Aspects of Injury. A Kovack & H. Stone, Eds. Spitzer. New York.

39. CASSENS, G., M. ROFFMAN, A. KURUG, R. ORSULAK & J. SCHILDKRANT. 1980. Alterations in brain norepinephrine metabolisms induced by environmental stimuli previously paired with inescapable shock. Science **209:** 1138–1139.

40. VAN DONGEN, P. 1981. The human locus coeruleus in neurology and psychiatry. Progr. Neurobiol. **17:** 97–139.

41. IVERSEN, L. I., M. N. ROSSOR, G. P. HILLS, M. ROTH, C. Q. MOUNTJOY, S. L. FOOTE, J. H. MORRISON & F. E. BLOOM. 1983. Loss of pigmented dopamine beta hydroxylase positive cells from locus coeruleus in senile dementia of Alzheimer's type. Neurosci. Lett. **39:** 95–100.

42. OLPE, H., M. STEINMANN & R. JONES. 1985. Locus coeruleus as a target for psychogeriatric agents. Ann. N.Y. Acad. Sci. (This volume.)

43. MCENTEE, W. & R. MAIR. 1978. Memory impairment in Korsakoff's patients: a correlation with brain noradrenergic activity. Science **102:** 905–906.

Arginine Vasopressin, Stress, and Memory[a]

GEORGE F. KOOB, CHRISTINE LEBRUN,
JOE L. MARTINEZ, JR.,[b] ROBERT DANTZER,[c]
MICHEL LE MOAL,[c] AND FLOYD E. BLOOM

Division of Preclinical Neuroscience and Endocrinology
Department of Basic and Clinical Research
Scripps Clinic and Research Foundation
La Jolla, California 92037
[b]Department of Psychology
University of California
Berkeley, California 94720
[c]Unite 259 Institut National de la Santé et
de la Recherche Medicale
Psychobiologie des Comportments Adaptatifs
Domaine de Carreire, Rue Camille-Saint Saens
33077 Bordeaux, France

INTRODUCTION

Physiological Actions of Vasopressin

Arginine vasopressin (AVP), synthesized in the hypothalamo-hypophysial system and released from the posterior pituitary, has the physiological responsibility for conserving water. This action, for which AVP is called antidiuretic hormone (ADH), is effected by making the distal renal tubules more permeable to water [for review see Sawyer[1]]. The usual physiological stimulus for the release of the hormone is dehydration, or plasma hyperosmolarity, and it is generally accepted that osmoreceptors in the region of the brain with highest concentrations of vasopressin immunoreactivity mediate this response. Inhibition in the release of vasopressin results in a diuresis of dilute urine, a condition known as diabetes insipidus. Lesions placed anywhere along the hypothalamic neurohypophysial system are associated with permanent diabetes insipidus.

Another important non-renal action of antidiuretic hormone is its pressor effect,[1] justifying the hormone's alternate name, AVP. This vasopressor effect is mediated directly as vasoconstriction on the smooth muscles of the vascular system,[2] and may be physiologically significant during hypovolemic or hypotensive crises.[3] This effect seems to require doses of vasopressin considerably higher than needed for maximal antidiuresis.[4] Also, AVP may function as a releaser of corticotropin and may modulate the action of corticotropin releasing factor.[5,6]

[a]Supported in part by National Institute of Neurological and Communicative Diseases and Stroke grant NS 20912-01 and National Science Foundation grant NT 8215308 to G.F.K, and by Office of Naval Research grant N 00014-82-K-0408 to J.L.M. Jr.

Behavioral Actions of Vasopressin—The "Memory" Hypothesis

AVP also produces important behavioral changes in addition to these classical endocrine actions. In the pioneering classical work by De Wied,[7] removal of the posterior lobe of the pituitary gland in the rat interfered with the maintenance of shuttle-box active avoidance response. This deficit was restored by treatment with pitressin or lysine-vasopressin. Interestingly, centrally administered AVP did not reverse these deficits observed in hypophysectomized rats.[8]

Later studies showed that AVP, itself, administered to normal rats subcutaneously, intraventricularly, or intracerebrally could prolong extinction of active avoidance

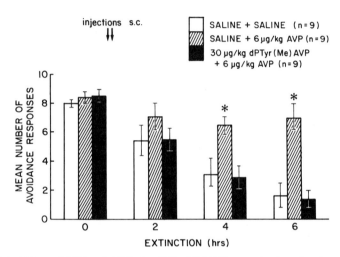

FIGURE 1. Effects of AVP and AVP plus dPTyr(Me)AVP on extinction of active avoidance behavior. After three days of training, rats meeting the criteria of at least seven successful avoidances during the first 10 trials of extinction were injected subcutaneously (s.c.) with saline (twice at 2.0-min intervals), AVP plus saline, or AVP plus dPTyr(Me)AVP immediately after the first set of 10 extinction trials on day 4. Rats receiving AVP show persistent avoidance throughout the 6-hr of observation, when tested on 10 trials at each of the three next 2-hr intervals, whereas rats receiving either saline with no peptide or both peptides extinguished this active avoidance behavior at similar rates. Open squares, saline + saline (N = 9); Hatched squares, saline + AVP, 6 μg per kg (N = 9); Solid squares, dPTyr(Me)AVP, 30 μg per kg + AVP, 6 μg per kg. *Significantly different from both the saline with no peptide and both peptides groups; $p < 0.05$ Newman-Keuls test following analysis of variance (From Le Moal et al.[27] With permission from the AAAS.)

behavior[9–11] and could enhance retention in inhibitory (passive) avoidance.[12–14] Indeed, numerous studies have led De Wied and colleagues to suggest that AVP has a physiological role in "memory," particularly memory consolidation, and that this action is mediated directly in the central nervous system through an action on catecholamine substrates.[8,15–20] However, with few exceptions, the data regarding a role for vasopressin, itself, in "memory" come from studies employing aversively motivated tasks. This observation and failures to replicate some of the previously reported observations, particularly with regard to inhibitory avoidance effects[21,22] and the "memory" deficits associated with the Brattleboro genetic defect (rats genetically deficient in AVP),[23] have led to some controversy as to the role of AVP in memory.[16,17,24,25]

Vasopressin Antagonists—A Role for Visceral Signals?

Work with the recently developed vasopressin antagonists has reopened some of the questions raised by this earlier work of De Wied and associates. A pressor antagonist analog of arginine vasopressin, [1-deaminopenicillamine, 2-(O-methyl) tyrosine] AVP [dPTyr(Me)AVP][26] given in doses that prevented the pressor response, also blocked the effects of subcutaneously injected AVP on prolongation of active avoidance (FIGURE 1).[27] Similar results were observed with combinations of peripheral injections of the antagonist and central injections of AVP.[28] This antagonist also blocked the effects of AVP on inhibitory avoidance behavior and on an appetitive water finding task, but at somewhat higher doses (FIGURE 2).[29,30] These effects suggested to us that signals from peripheral sources may play an important role in the subsequent behavioral changes of vasopressin.

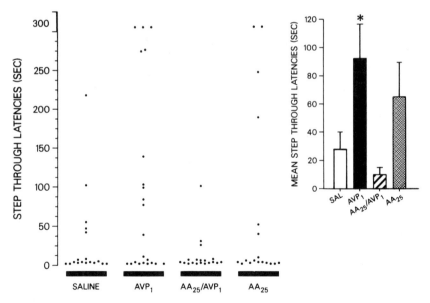

FIGURE 2. Effects of AVP, dPTyr(Me)AVP plus dPTyr(Me)AVP on retention of inhibitory avoidance task. The drugs were injected subcutaneously immediately after the acquisition trial. Data represent the individual scatter diagram of latency scores during the retention test, 24 hours after the acquisition trial. Saline ($N = 18$); AVP, 1 μg/rat ($N = 22$); dPTyr(Me)AVP, 25 μg/rat + AVP, 1 μg/rat ($N = 19$); dPTyr(Me)AVP, 25 μg/rat ($N = 18$). Insert shows the mean latency score (± S.E.M.) produced by each group during the retention test. *Significantly different from saline group ($p < 0.05$ t-test) (From Lebrun et al.[29] With permission from Life Sciences.)

TABLE 1. Antagonism of AVP-Induced Prolongation of Extinction

Active avoidance	AVP-Antagonist (S.C.)	AVP-Antagonist (I.C.V.)
AVP (S.C.)	Yes	Yes[a]
AVP (I.C.V.)	Yes	?
Inhibitory (passive) avoidance	AVP-Antagonist (S.C.)	AVP-Antagonist (I.C.V.)
AVP (S.C.)	Yes	Yes
AVP (I.C.V.)	Yes	Yes

[a]But only at doses high enough to reverse peripheral pressor effects. S.C. = subcutaneously and I.C.V. = intracerebroventricularly.

Separate but Parallel Central and Peripheral AVP Systems

These observations have prompted significant effort to distinguish between these two hypotheses: a central memory action or a peripheral physiologic activation of the CNS. Some controversy still exists as to the final resolution. For example, in two recent studies De Wied and associates have shown that a new analog of vasopressin [pGlu^4, Cyt^6] AVP 4–8 (AVP$^{4-8}$) is much more active than AVP itself in facilitating passive avoidance when injected peripherally post training.[31] This analog has no pressor activity and these effects can be reversed by an even more potent AVP pressor antagonist,[32] even when the antagonist is injected in nanogram amounts[32] intracerebroventricularly. Similar results were obtained using AVP itself,[32] leading De Wied and associates to conclude that both peripherally and centrally derived AVP act via an action on CNS receptors.

Work in our laboratory using the pressor antagonist [dPTyr(Me)AVP] and extinction of active avoidance has provided evidence for precisely the opposite conclusion. The pressor antagonist reverses the effects of AVP administered subcutaneously only doses sufficient to reverse the peripheral pressor effects, i.e., 6000 nanograms I.C.V. (TABLE 1).[14] Similar effects have been observed for the facilitation of performance in the water finding task.[33] Peripheral administration of this antagonist also readily reverses the central effects of non pressor enhancing doses of AVP in active avoidance, suggesting that the antagonist readily crosses the blood-brain barrier (TABLE 1). Thus, although we do confirm the original effects of AVP on aversive and appetitive behavioral performance, our recent data differ importantly. Specifically, our current work leads to a conclusion that is dramatically different than the views of De Wied and associates. We hypothesize that there are two AVP systems operating on behavior, one central and the other peripheral; although these systems may ultimately act on a similar behavioral substrate, they do so by different and independent mechanisms.

Behavioral Mechanism of Action for Vasopressin

The hypothesis for a behavioral mechanism of action for these behavioral effects of AVP varies to some extent with the aforementioned position regarding a peripheral versus central site. For example, the "peripheralists" can list a whole series of unconditioned effects of AVP that ultimately could contribute to a behavioral state sufficient to prolong or augment aversive or stress-motivated behavior. AVP produces pressor effects, aversive effects (AVP acts as an unconditioned stimulus for conditioned taste and place aversion), and motor effects,[34] and even can be found in the autonomic nervous system.[35]

Indeed, Sahgal and colleagues have argued that the reputed "memory" enhancing action of AVP observed in the inhibitory avoidance task may be due to an arousal effect.[22] Here, in a series of tests these investigators found little evidence of a consistent and reliable improvement in passive avoidance in all rats treated with AVP, but instead significant bimodal scores, i.e., scores clustered at the low end of the distribution where the rats re-enter quickly (less than 205 sec) or the scores clustered at the high end (scores in excess of 300 sec) (FIGURE 2).[23,29,36] These authors suggest that AVP acts on the inverted U-shaped relationship where poor performance is observed if the subject is a low arousal state, but at very high levels of arousal, performance is impaired.[37] According to this hypothesis, AVP administration immediately following the shock trial will increase arousal and this in turn will improve consolidation in under-aroused rats but disrupt consolidation in over-aroused animals, thus producing the bimodal distribution described above.[22] This motivational hypothesis of Sahgal and associates may point to a possible explanation for many of the previously reported effects of AVP including those reported for appetitive tasks. However, a motivational explanation also leads to a consideration of the behavioral function of AVP in terms of the well-documented role of endogenous AVP in meeting homeostatic challenge.

Vasopressin and Stress

It is well accepted that emotional stimuli or stress[38] induce changes in the release of hormones from the anterior as well as the posterior lobe of the pituitary, including the release of AVP and oxytocin.[39-41] Although some treatments appear not to release AVP in the rat,[42] clear evidence for release of both plasma and central AVP has been observed following various osmotic or hypovolemic challenges.[43-46] The demonstrated efficacy of this pressor antagonist [dPTyr(Me)AVP[26]] to reverse the behavioral effects of exogenously administered AVP (see above) provided a powerful tool by which to examine the possible functional significance of AVP in mediating the behavioral responses produced by physiological challenges known to release vasopressin. In a recent study in our laboratory, a potent peripheral osmotic stimulus, the intraperitoneal injection of hypertonic saline at doses known to release AVP both centrally and peripherally,[44,45] produced similar behavioral effects on extinction of active avoidance to those produced by exogenously administered AVP.[47] The prolongation of active avoidance induced by this osmotic stimulus was reversed by pretreatment with peripheral injections of the pressor antagonist, again suggesting a peripheral role for endogenously released AVP in these behavioral effects (FIGURE 3).

These results demonstrate that an interoceptive osmotic challenge (hypertonic saline), known to release AVP, can mimic the effects of AVP on learned behavior, and the reversal of this behavioral effect by the AVP receptor antagonist suggests a causal relationship between the endogenously released AVP and the behavioral change. Similar doses of the AVP antagonists have been used to reverse the behavioral effects of exogenously administered AVP in a variety of learning tasks.[23] However, it is unlikely that the antagonist effect in the present experiment is due to an action of the antagonist on its own, independent of released AVP, since we have never observed any behavioral effects with this antagonist in reversing shock-induced prolongation of active avoidance except at doses of 10 μg–100 μg/rat.[11]

Finally, these data with hypertonic saline reopen the question of the nature of brain pituitary interactions. One question that remains unanswered is what anatomic or molecular substrate, peripheral or central mediates this behavioral response. For example, little evidence exists to show that AVP itself crosses the blood-brain barrier, particularly at doses that would be liberated from the pituitary under conditions of the present experiment.[23] In addition, central AVP pathways exist independently of the classical hypothalamo-posterior pituitary projection,[48] and both central and peripheral AVP are released by the osmotic challenge used here.[44,45] Also as described above, the AVP antagonist can reverse the effects of centrally administered AVP, but the AVP antagonist when injected centrally will only reverse the behavioral effects of peripherally injected AVP in doses sufficient to reverse the peripheral pressor effects of these same doses.[14] Thus, in the present experiment the basis for the behavioral change

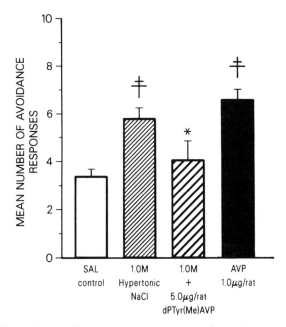

FIGURE 3. Effects of the AVP antagonist on the prolongation of extinction produced by hypertonic saline. Data shown represent only those from the III extinction session, but results from extinction IV were identical. ‡Significantly different from saline. $p < 0.05$; *Significantly different from hypertonic saline alone. ‡$p < 0.05$ Student's t test following a significant overall analysis of variance for each logical grouping. Number of subjects were 83, 52, 21, and 42 for the saline, 1.0 M NaCl, 1.0 M NaCl + 5.0 μg dPTyr(Me)AVP, and AVP groups, respectively.

resulting from osmotic challenge could be a release of AVP from both central and peripheral sources acting independently but in a homologous fashion.[49] This possibility of independent but homologous function for pituitary peptides in the central nervous system remains a hypothesis worthy of further exploration.

These results also have important implications for our conceptualization of the role of AVP in behavior and in a sense, for our conceptualization of brain-body interactions in memory. Clearly, an AVP reserve sufficient to change, or even mobilize, behavior is available both in the periphery and the central nervous system in situations of extreme challenge. It will be critical to determine that other interoceptive or exteroceptive cues can activate this system, and how this mechanism works, if at all, in normal behavior.

SUMMARY

Arginine vasopressin (AVP) has been shown to have several non-renal actions including the potentiation of learned avoidance behavior in rats and improvement in cognitive functioning in humans. Research in our laboratory has confirmed these behavioral effects in rats using both peripheral and central injection of AVP. We have begun to examine the physiological basis for these effects. Peripheral administration of a vasopressor AVP antagonist reversed the prolongation of extinction produced by peripherally administered AVP in both active and passive avoidance, but also reversed the aversive unconditioned effects of AVP. However, central administration of the vasopressor AVP antagonist reversed peripheral effcts of AVP only at doses shown to act peripherally to reverse vasopressor effects of AVP. An osmotic stress in doses known to liberate endogenous AVP mimicked the behavioral effects of exogenously administered AVP, and this stress effect was reversed by the AVP antagonist. These results support our hypothesis of separate but parallel AVP systems in the pituitary and brain with a role in behavioral adaptation to certain types of stress.

REFERENCES

1. SAWYER, W. H. 1964. Vertebrate neurohypophysial principles. Endocrinol. **75:** 981–990.
2. ALTURA, B. M. 1967. Evaluation of neurohumoral substances in local regulation of blood flow. Am. J. Physiol. **212:** 1447–1454.
3. ROCHA E. SILVA, JR., M. & M. ROSENBERG. 1969. The release of vasopressin in response to haemorrhage and its role in the mechanism of blood pressure regulations. J. Physiol. **202:** 535–557.
4. STRAUS, M. B. 1957. Body Water in Man. pp. 82–104. Little Brown and Co. Boston.
5. PEARLMUTTER, A. F., E. RAPINO & M. SAFFRAN. 1974. A semi-automated in vitro assay for CRF activities of peptides related to oxytocin and vasopressin. Neuroendocrinol. **15:** 106–119.
6. GILLIES, G. E. & S. J. LOWRY, 1979. Corticotropin releasing factor may be modulated by vasopressin. Nature **278:** 463–464.
7. DEWIED, D. 1965. The influence of the posterior and intermediate lobe of the pituitary and pituitary peptides on the maintenance of a conditioned avoidance response in rats. Eur. J. Neuropharmacol. **4:** 157–167.
8. DE WIED, D. & J. JOLLES. 1982. Neuropeptides derived from pro-opiocortin: behavioral, physiological and neurochemical effects. Physiol. Rev. **62:** 976–1059.
9. DE WIED, D. 1971. Long term effect of vasopressin on the maintenance of a conditioned avoidance response in rats. Nature **232:** 58–60.
10. DE WIED, D. 1976. Behavioral effects of intraventricularly administered vasopressin and vasopressin fragments. Life Sci. **19:** 685–690.
11. KOOB, G. F., M. LE MOAL, O. GAFFORI, M. MANNIN, W. H. SAWYER, J. RIVIER & F. E. BLOOM. 1981. Arginine vasopressin and a vasopressin antagonist peptide: opposite effects on extinction of active avoidance in rats. Regul. Peptides 2:153–163.
12. BOHUS, B., R. ADER & D. DE WIED. 1972. Effects of vasopressin on active and passive avoidance behavior. Horm. Behav. 3: 191–197.
13. BOHUS, B., G. L. KOVACS & D. DE WIED. 1978. Oxytocin, vasopressin and memory: opposite effects on consolidation and retrieval processes. Brain Res. **157:** 414–417.
14. LEBRUN, C., M. LE MOAL, G. F. KOOB & F. E. BLOOM. 1984. Vasopressin pressor antagonist injected centrally, reverses peripheral behavioral effects of vasopressin but only at doses that reverse increases in blood pressure. Regul. Peptides. (In press.)
15. DE WIED, D. & D. H. G. VERSTEEG. 1979. Neurohypophyseal principles and memory. Fed. Proc. **38:** 2348–2354.
16. DE WIED, D. 1984. The importance of vasopressin in memory. Trends Neurosci. **7:** 62–64.
17. DE WIED, D. 1984. The importance of vasopressin in memory. Trends Neurosci. **7:** 109.
18. DE WIED, D. & B. BOHUS. 1979. Modulation of memory processes by neuropeptides of

hypothalamic-neurohypophyseal origin. *In* Brain Mechanisms in Memory and Learning. From the Single Neuron to Man. M. A. B. Brazier, Ed. Raven Press. New York.

19. KOOB, G. F. & F. E. BLOOM. 1982. Behavioral effects of neuropeptides: endorphins and vasopressin. Ann. Rev. Physiol. **44:** 571–582.

20. VAN WIMERSMA GREIDANUS, T. B., J. M. VAN REE & D. DE WIED. 1983. Vasopressin and memory. Am. J. Psych. **20:** 437–458.

21. HOSTETTER, G., S. L. JUBB & G. P. KOZLOWSKI. 1980. An inability of subcutaneous vasopressin to affect passive avoidance behavior. Neuroendocrin. **30:** 174–177.

22. SAHGAL, A. & C. WRIGHT. 1983. A comparison of the effects of vasopressin and oxytocin with amphetamine and chlordiazepoxide on passive avoidance behavior in rats. Psychopharmacol. **80:** 88–92.

23. LE MOAL, M., R. DANTZER, P. MORMEDE, A. BADUEL, C. LEBRUN, A. ETTENBERG, D. VAN DER KOOY, J. WENGER, S. DEYO, G. F. KOOB & F. E. BLOOM, 1984. Behavioral effects of peripheral administration of arginine vasopressin: A review of our search for a mode of action and a hypothesis. Psychoneuroenodocrinol. **9:** 319–341.

24. GASH, D. M. & G. J. THOMAS. 1983. What is the importance of vasopressin in memory processes? Trends Neurosci. **6:** 197–198.

25. GASH, D. M. & G. J. THOMAS. 1984. Reply from Don M. Gash and Garth J. Thomas. Trends Neurosci. **7:** 64–65.

26. BANKOSKI, K., M. MANNING, J. HALDER & W. H. SAWYER. 1978. Design of potent antagonists of the vasopressor response to arginine vasopressin. J. Med. Chem. **21:** 850–853.

27. LE MOAL, M., G. F. KOOB, L. Y. KODA, F. E. BLOOM M. MANNING, W. H. SAWYER & J. RIVIER. 1981. Vasopressor receptor antagonist prevents behavioral effects of vasopressin. Nature **291:** 491–493.

28. LE MOAL, M., G. F. KOOB, P. MORMEDE, R. DANTZER & F. E. BLOOM. 1982. Vasopressin pressor antagonist reverses central behavioral effects of vasopressin. Neurosci. Abstr. **8:** 368.

29. LEBRUN, C. J., H. RIGTER, J. L. MARTINEZ, JR., G. F. KOOB, M. LE MOAL & F. E. BLOOM. 1984. Antagonism of effects of vasopressin (AVP) on inhibitory avoidance by a vasopressor antagonist peptide [dPtyr(Me)AVP]. Life Sci. **35:** 1505–1512.

30. ETTENBERG, A., M. LE MOAL, G. F. KOOB & F. E. BLOOM. 1983. Vasopressin potentiation in the performance of a learned appetitive task: Reversal by a pressor antagonist analog of vasopressin. Pharmacol. Biochem. Behav. **18:** 645–647.

31. BURBACH, J. P. H., F. L. KOVACS, D. DE WIED, J. W. VAN NISPEN & H. M. GREVEN. 1983. A major metabolite of agenine vasopressin in the brain is a highly potent neuropeptide. Science **221:** 1310–1312.

32. DE WIED, D., O. GAFFORI, J. M. VAN REE & W. DE JONG. 1984. Central target for the behavioral effects of vasopressin neuropeptides. Nature **305:**276–278.

33. ETTENBERG, A. 1985. Intracerebroventricular application of a pressor antagonist of vasopressin prevents both the "memory" and "aversive" actions of vasopressin. Behav. Brain Res. (In press.)

34. ETTENBERG, A., D. VAN DER KOOY, M. LE MOAL, G. F. KOOB & F. E. BLOOM. 1983. Can aversive properties of peripherally-injected vasopressin account for its putative role in memory? Behav. Brain Res. **7:** 331–350.

35. HANLEY, M. R., H. P. BENTON, S. L. LIGHTMAN, K. TODD, E. A. BONE, P. FRETTEN, S. PALMER, C. J. KIRK & R. H. MICHELL. 1984. A vasopressin-like peptide in the mammalian sympathetic nervous system. Nature **309:**258–261.

36. SAHGAL, A., A. B. KEITH, C. WRIGHT & J. A. EDWARDSON. 1982. Failure of vasopressin to enhance memory in a passive avoidance task in rats. Neurosci. Lett. **28:** 87–92.

37. BERLYNE, D. E. 1960. Conflict, Arousal, and Curiosity. McGraw-Hill Publishing Co. New York.

38. SELYE, H. 1980. Selye's Guide to Stress Research. pp. v-xiii. van Nostrand Reinhold Co. New York.

39. O'CONNOR, W. J. & E. B. VERNEY. 1942. The effect of removal of the posterior lobe of the pituitary on inhibition of water diuresis by emotional stress. Q. J. Exp. Physiol. **31:** 393–408.

40. PICKFORD, M. 1969. Neurohypophysis-antidiuretic (vasopressor) and oxytocic hormones. *In* The Hypothalamus. W. Haymaker, E. Anderson, W. J. H. NAUTA & W. J. H. NAUTA, Eds.: 463–505. Thomas. Springfield, IL.
41. KENDLER, K. S., R. E. WEITZMAN & D. A. FISHER. 1978. The effect of pain on plasma arginine vasopressin concentrations in man. Clin. Endocrinol. 8:89–94.
42. KEIL, L. C. & W. B. SEVERS. 1977. Reduction in plasma vasopressin levels of dehydrated rats following acute stress. Endocrinol. 100: 30–38.
43. KNEPEL, W., D. NUTTO, H. ANHUT & G. HERTTING. 1982. Vasopressin and B-endorphin release after osmotic and non-osmotic stimuli: effect of naloxone and dexamethasone. Eur. J. Pharmacol. 77: 299–306.
44. DUNN, I. L., T. J. BRENNAN, A. E. NELSON & G. L. ROBERTSON. 1973. The role of blood osmolality and volume in regulating vasopressin secretion in the rat. J. Clin. Invest. 52: 3212–3219.
45. RODRIGUEZ, F., J. DEMOTES–MAINARD, J. CHAUVEAU, D. POULAIN & J. D. VINCENT. 1983. Vasopressin release in the rat septum in response to systemic stimuli. Neurosci. Abstr. 9: 445.
46. DEYO, S. N., W. J. SHOEMAKER, A. ETTENBERG, F. E. BLOOM & G. F. KOOB. 1984. Subcutaneous administration of behaviorally effective doses of arginine vasopressin results in brain uptake in only the median eminence. (Submitted for publication.)
47. KOOB, G. F., R. DANTZER, F. RODRIGUEZ, F. E. BLOOM & M. LE MOAL. 1984. Osmotic stress mimics effects of vasopressin on learned behavior. Neurosci. Abstr. 10: 169.
48. BUIJS, R. M. 1978. Intra- and extrahypothalamic vasopressin and oxytocin pathways in the rat: pathways to the limbic system, medulla oblongata and spinal cord. Cell. Tiss. Res. 192: 423–435.
49. IVERSEN, S. D. 1981. Neuropeptides: do they integrate body and brain? Nature 291:454.

Phosphoprotein Regulation of Memory Formation: Enhancement and Control of Synaptic Plasticity by Protein Kinase C and Protein F1

ARYEH ROUTTENBERG[a]

Cresap Neuroscience Laboratory
Northwestern University
Evanston, Illinois 60201

INTRODUCTION: PROTEIN F1 AND NEUROBEHAVIORAL PLASTICITY

The reactivity of synaptic relationships has been proposed to be regulated by post-translational modification of brain proteins.[34] This hypothesis was advanced on the basis of the discovery that behavioral activation of the brain of the intact organism altered *in vitro* phosphorylation of particular brain proteins.[38]

Protein phosphorylation, a control mechanism for the regulation of cellular protein function,[10,32] has been suggested to play a role in the regulation of synaptic and behavioral plasticity of vertebrates[33] and invertebrates.[3,13]

Shortly after the studies on protein phosphorylation of Weller and Rodnight[47] and Ueda, Maeno and Greengard,[46] we reported on a new cyclic AMP independent phosphoprotein substrate.[9] Initially referred to as band F, it has a molecular weight similar to Protein F1 (47 kD). Of the phosphoproteins studied, it was the most rapidly phosphorylated in the absence of cyclic AMP and the most heavily phosphorylated 30 min after reaction initiation.[37] Studies of *in vivo* phosphorylation also suggested that Protein F1 was rapidly phosphorylated.[23] In our initial studies in 1974 we confirmed the presence of an 80 kD protein band described by Ueda *et al.*[46] whose phosphorylation was stimulated by cyclic AMP.

The selective participation of this cyclic AMP independent 47 kD phosphoprotein in plasticity was first suggested by a behavioral experiment.[38] In this study we introduced the "back-phosphorylation" or "ad hoc" method to the study of brain phosphoproteins.[35] It was reasoned that if an environmental event regulated brain protein phosphorylation, then such regulation should be detectable *in vitro* if one preserved the alteration until the time of the *in vitro* reaction. We found, in a series of studies reviewed elsewhere,[33,34] that such regulation could indeed be preserved. Behavioral treatment did, in fact, alter the *in vitro* phosphorylation state of a 47 kD phosphoprotein.[7,38,39] Another phosphoprotein, designated Protein F2 (mol wt = 41,000; pI = 6.5) and later identified as the alpha subunit of pyruvate dehydrogenase,[24] was also increased in its phosphorylation following training.[24] We have focused on Protein F1 because, as will be discussed, it is membrane bound, localized to the synapse, brain specific, and directly related to synaptic plasticity monitored electrophysiologically.

[a]With the assistance of R. Nelson, D. Lovinger, and R. Akers. Supported by MH25281 and AFOSR 83-0335.

Since our past behavioral work on protein phosphorylation has been reviewed,[33–35] I shall mention briefly a recent report from our laboratory given at the Neuroscience Society.[1] In this experiment we determined the effects of training in an environment involving storage of spatial information[31] on *in vitro* protein phosphorylation of hippocampal tissue specimens. An alteration in Protein F1 phosphorylation selective to the dorsal hippocampus was observed immediately after performance in a well-learned spatial environment (the eight-arm radial maze). This occurred in two different behavioral paradigms (win-shift or win-stay).[8]

We interpret these results as follows: certain select behavioral events can stimulate synaptic plasticity in particular brain locations. Indeed, one can observe behaviorally induced alterations in hippocampal plasticity monitored electrophysiologically.[45] Such plasticity, in turn, could be directly related to alterations of Protein F1 phosphorylation. Our recent electrophysiological studies directly test this interpretation.

Shortly after our initial reports on the existence of a 47 kD brain phosphoprotein now termed Protein F1, Zwiers *et al.*[50] described an ACTH-sensitive, cyclic nucleotide–independent phosphoprotein (termed band 6 then and B-50 in later work) with a similar (48,000) molecular weight. As was later suggested both by the Utrecht group[49] and our laboratory,[23] Protein F1 and Protein B-50 appeared to be identical. Recent evidence[27,28] has confirmed this view. Using two-dimensional gel electrophoresis or "protein fingerprinting," a powerful tool for identification of protein substrates based both on molecular weight and on charge, Protein F1 and Protein B-50 appear to be identical.

Protein F1, on this basis, is brain-specific,[17] enriched in synaptic membranes,[30,43] and its phosphorylation is stimulated by calcium and inhibited by neuropeptides such as ACTH and dynorphin.[48–50] These data provide important clues to the function of Protein F1. Particularly intriguing is the brain specificity of Protein F1. In addition, its kinase, while not brain specific, is distributed uniquely in brain[15] at the subcellular level. Thus, the brain-specific membrane-localized Protein F1 may have functions that are unique to brain tissue. In our view, this is related to plasticity of synapses and consequent information storage processes.

SYNAPTIC PHYSIOLOGY AND PHOSPHOPROTEIN METABOLISM

Our behavioral studies pointed to an important role of post-translational regulation of synaptic reactivity by phosphorylation of select brain proteins. We now wished to determine whether a direct link could be established between the phosphorylation state of these identified proteins and synaptic reactivity measured electrophysiologically.

To achieve this we have studied the enhancement of synaptic reactivity in the intact hippocampus.[41,42] High frequency stimulation of the perforant path produces long-term enhancement (LTE) or potentiation (LTP) of the evoked synaptic potential in the dentate gyrus. In this presentation we shall refer to short-term alterations in reactivity lasting minutes as LTP[5] and long-term alterations lasting hours or days as LTE.[21] Although the mechanisms may be quite different in the two cases this enhanced synaptic response can be observed immediately after the first potentiating train and can persist for several hours, or several days in chronic preparations.

The particular pathway studied is pathological in Alzheimer's disease. In particular, the layer II cells of the entorhinal cortex, the cells of origin of the perforant path to the dentate gyrus, are severely necrotic (see van Hoesen, this volume). Thus, knowledge of the type of plasticity present in this pathway and the definition of the molecular basis for this plasticity may be of some relevance to the presumed loss of synaptic plasticity and consequent memory dysfunction observed in this dementing illness.

Methods

Using both anesthetized and chronically prepared male adult rat subjects, stimulating electrodes were placed in the perforant path to evoke synaptic responses recorded with a micropipette placed in the dentate gyrus. The region of granule cell excitation was defined by the presence of a negative-going population spike superimposed on a positive-going population EPSP and the reversal of these field potentials during laminar profile analysis (see Lomo[19] for an example). We have therefore

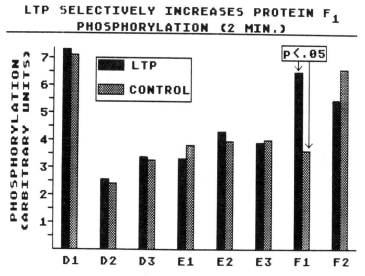

FIGURE 1. Selective activation of Protein F1 phosphorylation 5 min after completion of long-term potentiation procedures. After a 2 min *in vitro* reaction, electrophoresis, autoradiography, and microdensitometry of individual protein bands (D1 through F2), analysis of LTP effect revealed a significant increase only on Protein F1 phosphorylation.

defined the tissue specimen for subsequent dissection of the dorsal hippocampal tissue used for *in vitro* phosphorylation analysis by electrophysiological criteria.

After baseline was established, eight trains of eight 0.4 msec cathodal pulses were delivered (one train every 30 sec) to produce an enhancement of the synaptic response.

After enhancement procedures, the change from baseline was monitored for selected durations, at which time, the brain was rapidly frozen (<5 sec to elimination of brain activity) *in situ*.

Procedures for preparation of the tissue, *in vitro* phosphorylation, and densitometric analysis of phosphate content of electrophoretically separated phosphoproteins have been described in detail elsewhere.[24]

PROTEIN F1 PHOSPHORYLATION SELECTIVELY INCREASED FOLLOWING SYNAPTIC ENHANCEMENT

Synaptic enhancement significantly increased the phosphate content of a 47 kD protein.[41,42] In addition, we observed that this increase was selective for Protein F1 (FIGURE 1). That is, long-term enhancement produced no detectable alterations in phosphate content among the other phosphoprotein bands studied. The specific change in F1 phosphorylation was further restricted to the LTP condition, and was not observed when stimulation of the pathway at low frequency was used.

ENHANCEMENT MAY ACTIVATE F1 KINASE

One major advantage of using the *in vitro* technique to study events occurring *in vivo* is that it is possible to perform several different *in vitro* assays on a tissue sample taken from an individual subject that has received only one *in vivo* treatment. One may therefore characterize the specific biochemical mechanisms altered by synaptic plasticity using assays that assess endogenous phosphorylation, kinase activity, and subcellular distribution after osmotic shock. Moreover, given the time-dependent nature of synaptic plasticity one may determine whether these biochemical properties change as a function of the duration after LTP.

We have recently demonstrated, for example, that the increase in Protein F1 phosphorylation *in vitro* following enhancement can be observed with extremely short reaction durations and micromolar concentrations of ATP. Such reaction conditions almost wholly depend on the level of kinase activity, since less than 1% of Protein F1 substrate available would be phosphorylated. Moreover, the selectivity of the alteration in Protein F1 is also observed under these conditions. This suggests that the enhancement procedure is likely to activate Protein F1 kinase. A direct test of this suggestion has recently been carried out.[2]

SYNAPTIC ENHANCEMENT PREDICTED BY PROTEIN F1 PHOSPHORYLATION STATE

If the change in synaptic strength does actually depend on the state of phosphorylation of Protein F1, then one would predict that the extent of synaptic enhancement would be directly related to Protein F1 phosphate content. In support of this prediction, we found that a direct relation ($r = +0.906$, $p < .01$) exists between F1 phosphate content and change in spike amplitude. Interestingly, the direct relation between F1 phosphorylation and synaptic reactivity was observed to be greatest with the 10 sec reaction suggesting an important role for Protein F1 kinase in synaptic plasticity. The direct relation was selective as no other phosphoprotein studied demonstrated a significant relationship with changes in synaptic reactivity.

PLASTICITY AND GROWTH: LONG-LASTING CHANGES IN PROTEIN F1 PHOSPHORYLATION FOLLOWING ENHANCEMENT

We have sought to determine how long the change in F1 phosphorylation might last and, if present, how might such long-term alterations in plasticity be brought about. We have recently observed that Protein F1 phosphorylation *in vitro* is elevated three days after the induction of LTP in awake, freely moving animals with chronically implanted electrodes.[20] As in our short term studies lasting 5 min, the increase in phosphorylation is selective for Protein F1. These studies also demonstrated a significant relation of Protein F1 phosphorylation with the persistence of the poten-tiated response. As we observed little relation of Protein F1 phosphorylation with the magnitude of change in the synaptic response, this suggests the possibility that Protein F1 may be less important in determining the magnitude of the synaptic response, and more concerned with the persistence of that response. Thus, the biochemical processes necessary for the synaptic response itself would be regulated by a mechanism separate from that concerned with the persistence of change in the response. In our view, Protein F1 plays a role in this latter process. We have considered two quite different mechanisms that may contribute to the long-lasting alterations in Protein F1 phospho-rylation.

Protein Kinase C is Protein F1 Kinase

The surprising three-day persistence of change in the phosphorylation state of the Protein F1 substrate may, in fact, be understood in terms of already available evidence on the regulation of Protein F1 kinase. The evidence for this is based on our recent identification of this kinase[2] as the same as protein kinase C, the novel Ca^{2+}- and phospholipid-dependent kinase of Takai et al.[44] We have demonstrated that Protein F1 is stimulated both by a calcium- and a phospholipid-dependent mechanism and that exogenous kinase C stimulates the phosphorylation of Protein F1. This finding places the regulation of synaptic reactivity within the framework of a newly discovered but critical multifunctional enzyme that is both linked to receptor processes and to cellular growth mechanisms.

Because Protein F1 is regulated by kinase C, it is attractive to think that long-term persistent changes in Protein F1 may be related to the permanent alterations in kinase C brought about by protease regulation of protein kinase C activity.[16] It has been shown that the catalytic subunit becomes permanently active following the calcium-dependent activation of a protease that frees the catalytic subunit from the regulatory subunit. Following this liberation of the catalytic subunit, calcium is no longer required for the phosphotransferase reaction, since the catalytic domain is fully exposed by the proteolytic step. If this mechanism were operative during LTP one would predict an increase in the amount of the protein kinase C catalytic subunit (kinase M) in hippocampal tissue from subjects demonstrating LTP that lasts for days.

One will need to know whether the mechanism for increase in F1 phosphorylation observed after 5 min (LTP) may be different from that observed after three days (LTE). Specifically, long-term regulation of Protein F1 phosphorylation may occur via an irreversible action of the protease. Short-term regulation may occur following elevation of intracellular calcium. It may be the case, then, that LTE increases Protein F1 phosphorylation by activation of this protease. This hypothesis can be evaluated by studying the amount of calcium-independent phosphorylation of Protein F1 that occurs before and after enhancement procedures. We would expect an increase in "kinase M"—the catalytic subunit of protein kinase C—following enhancement and thus, an increase in calcium-independent phosphorylation of F1 substrate following enhancement.

Calcium-activated Translocation of Protein Kinase C

It has been demonstrated that calcium increases the affinity (possibly by charge screening) of the negatively charged kinase C for the normally negatively charged inner membrane.[44] We have recently modeled this process *in vitro* by incubating non-shocked synaptosomes in control, EGTA, or 2 mM calcium conditions, then applying osmotic shock, and finally running the *in vitro* phosphorylation reaction using calcium buffered at 50 μM in all three reaction conditions.[2] The prediction was that F1 phosphorylation in osmotically shocked synaptosomes would be highest in those preparations previously treated with calcium. This was based on the presumption that calcium would increase the amount of kinase bound to the membrane.

We have recently confirmed this prediction and have found that 10 μM calcium is sufficient to hold the kinase to the membrane. Moreover, the addition of calcium during the initial osmotic shock appears to have a persistent effect, since a subsequent osmotic shock does not remove the kinase from the substrate.

These results model a scenario for LTP: following high frequency stimulation, an elevation of intracellular calcium provokes an increased association of cytosolic or loosely bound F1 kinase to Protein F1 in the membrane. This translocation may be quite persistent, but the duration of such persistence is not yet known. To test the predictive value of this model we have recently determined whether Protein F1 phosphorylation is increased in osmotically shocked membranes following long-term enhancement. In a recently completed study,[2] this prediction was confirmed by a high positive correlation between the level of synaptic enhancement and the extent of F1 phosphorylation present in osmotically shocked membranes pelleted at 150,000×g. These results are compatible with the view that translocation of F1 kinase is a crucial step in the regulation of synaptic reactivity. [Note added in proof: Recent evidence demonstrated the existence of kinase C translocation following LTP.[2a]]

Our laboratory has provided the first direct evidence for a specific role of protein kinase C in brain. It has not escaped our attention that the multifunctional protein kinase C is associated with both secretory events[12,29] and with growth.[4,6] Such functions already documented in peripheral non-neural systems may be related to the synaptic plasticity function we have proposed for protein kinase C in brain. Based on the view that plasticity in the adult may be a form of controlled growth regulated by calcium,[18] it is attractive to think that such control is mediated, on a brain regional basis, through the protein kinase C system. Thus, both the regulation and expression of growth may occur through calcium regulation of the protein kinase C system.

Though we have not tested this view with tissue from animals subjected to a behavioral experience, our earliest behavioral studies reviewed above did use an osmotically shocked synaptosome preparation. This recommends the view that alterations in the mechanisms regulating Protein F1 following LTP may also occur during information storage. Specifically, it is reasonable to think that information storage is a consequence of an elevation in protein F1 phosphorylation, possibly brought about by translocation of its kinase or calcium-activated protease.

PLASTIC BRAIN REGIONS AND PROTEIN KINASE C REGULATION OF PROTEIN F1

It has often been suggested that only certain brain regions serve a plastic function. However, what differentiates such regions from non-plastic regions remains unknown. I propose the hypothesis that the capacity for plasticity in a brain locus is regulated by Protein F1 function. This function could be regulated by translocation or by protease mechanisms that would adjust the level of synaptic plasticity in that region.

These considerations lead to the prediction that Protein F1 phosphorylation would distinguish between plastic and non-plastic brain locations. In confirmation of this view we have found such a distinction in monkey cerebral cortex. It is known that temporal lobe mechanisms of information processing play a distinctive role in the storage of visual experience.[22] We have found in an analysis of old world monkey (*M. nemistrima*) neocortex that those cortical regions with higher-order information processing, in contrast to the visual cortex, for example, have the highest levels of Protein F1 phosphorylation.[27,28] It will be fruitful to determine whether these brain regional differences in Protein F1 phosphorylation might be related to a specific change in the protease that regulates the kinase, the amount of F1 substrate, or an alteration in translocational mechanisms.

MOLECULAR MECHANISM FOR NORMAL AND PATHOLOGICAL MEMORY IMPAIRMENT

This review suggests the hypothesis that memory may be formed by the regulated activation of particular brain phosphoproteins. If memory loss were related to a breakdown in function of such an endogenous phosphorylation system, then one would expect to find alterations in Protein F1 phosphorylation in such cases. In an earlier series of studies on brain protein phosphorylation and aging[40] we did not observe selective alterations in a particular phosphoprotein. We now know that this result occurred because we did not adequately preserve the *in vivo* state of certain brain phosphoproteins. In a recent study[20] performed in collaboration with Drs. Barnes and McNaughton, University of Colorado, Boulder, we have taken these factors of preservation into account. We have now obtained evidence that Protein F1 phosphorylation is significantly lower in aged animals relative to younger adult subjects. With such evidence it may be fruitful to determine the mechanism for the decrease in F1 phosphorylation in senescence. These results may also be relevant to the study of protein phosphorylation in post-mortem human tissue, both in aging[40] and in Alzheimer's disease. Our studies on the cerebral cortex of non-human primate[27] may provide a useful foundation for understanding alterations in phosphoprotein metabolism in human cortex following diseases of mentation.

REFERENCES

1. AKERS, R. F., S. T. CAIN, G. GONZALES-MARISCAL, D. M. LOVINGER, R. B. NELSON & A. ROUTTENBERG. 1983. Hypothesis: A 47kD phosphoprotein (F1) serves as molecular trigger for synaptic plasticity. Soc. Neurosci. Abstr. **9:** 1030.
2. AKERS, R. & A. ROUTTENBERG. 1985. Protein kinase C phosphorylates a protein directly related to synaptic plasticity. Brain Res. (In press.)
2a. AKERS, R. F., P. COLLEY, D. LINDEN, D. M. LOVINGER, K. MURAKAMI & A. ROUTTENBERG. 1985. Protein kinase C activity is translocated to the membrane following hippocampal synaptic plasticity. Fed. Proc. **44:** 1421.
3. ALKON, D. L. 1982. Biochemical analysis of associative learning. *In* Behavioral Models and the Analysis of Drug Action. Proc. of the 27th OHOLO Conf. M. Y. Spiegelstein & A. Levy, Eds.: 71-87. Elsevier Biomedical Press. Amsterdam.
4. ASHENDEL, C. L., J. M. STALLER & R. K. BOUTWELL. 1983. Protein kinase activity associated with a phorbol ester receptor purified from mouse brain. Cancer Res. **43:** 4333–4337.
5. BLISS, T. V. P. & T. LOMO. 1973. Long-lasting potentiation of synaptic transmission in the dentate area of the anesthetized rabbit following stimulation of the perforant path. J. Physiol. **232:** 334–356.
6. BOYNTON, A. L., J. F. WHITFIELD & L. P. KLEINE. 1983. Ca + +/phospholipid dependent

protein kinase correlates to the ability of transformed liver cells to proliferate in Ca+ + deficient medium. Biochem. Biophys. Res. Commun. 115: 383–390.

7. CAIN, S. & A. ROUTTENBERG. 1983. Neonatal handling selectively alters the phosphorylation of a 47,000 MW protein in male rat hippocampus. Brain Res. 267: 192–195.

8. COLLIER, T. J., J. S. MILLER, J. TRAVIS & A. ROUTTENBERG. 1982. Dentate gyrus granule cells and memory: Electrical stimulation disrupts memory for places rewarded. Behav. Neural Biol. 34: 227–239.

9. EHRLICH, Y. H. & A. ROUTTENBERG. 1974. Cyclic AMP regulates phosphorylation of three protein components of rat cerebral cortex membranes for thirty minutes. FEBS Lett. 45: 237–243.

10. GISPEN, W. H. & A. ROUTTENBERG. 1982. Prog. Brain Res. 56: 1–454.

11. GREENGARD, P. 1979. Cyclic nucleotides, phosphorylated proteins, and the nervous system. Fed. Proc. 38: 2208–2217.

12. IMAI, A., S. NAKASHIMA & Y. NOZAWA. 1983. The rapid polyphosphoinositide metabolism may be a triggering event for thrombin-mediated stimulation of human platelets. Biochem. Biophys. Res. Commun. 110: 108–115.

13. KANDEL, E. R. & J. H. SCHWARTZ. 1982. Molecular biology of learning: Modulation of transmitter release. Science 218: 4571.

14. KAWAHARA, Y., Y. TAKAI, R. MINAKUCHI, K. SANO & Y. NISHIZUKA. 1980. Possible involvement of Ca^{2+}-activated, phospholipid-dependent protein kinase in platelet activation. Biochem. J. 88: 913–916.

15. KIKKAWA, U., Y. TAKAI, R. MINAKUCHI, S. INOHARA & Y. NISHIZUKA. 1982. Calcium-activated, phospholipid-dependent protein kinase from rat brain. J. Biol. Chem. 257: 13341–13348.

16. KISHIMOTO, A., N. KAJIKAWA, M. SHIOTA & Y. NISHIZUKA. 1983. Proteolytic activation of calcium-activated, phospholipid-dependent protein kinase by calcium-dependent neutral protease. J. Biol. Chem. 258: 1156–1164.

17. KRISTJANSSON, G. I., H. ZWIERS, A. B. OESTREICHER & W. H. GISPEN. 1982. Evidence that the synaptic phosphoprotein B-50 is localized exclusively in nerve tissue. J. Neurochem. 39: 371–378.

18. LLINAS, R. & M. SUGIMORI. 1982. Calcium conductances in purkinje cell dendrites: Their role in development and integration. Prog. Brain Res. 51: 323–334.

19. LOMO, T. 1971. Patterns of activation in a monosynaptic cortical pathway: The perforant path input to the dentate area of the hippocampal formation. Exp. Brain Res. 12: 18–45.

20. LOVINGER, D., R. AKERS, R. NELSON, C. BARNES, B. MCNAUGHTON & A. ROUTTENBERG. 1985. A selective increase in hippocampal protein F1 phosphorylation directly related to three day growth of long term synaptic enhancement. Brain Res. (In press.)

21. MCNAUGHTON, B. L. 1982. Long-term synaptic enhancement and short-term potentiation in rat fascia dentata act through different mechanisms. J. Physiol. 324: 249–262.

22. MISHKIN, M. 1982. A memory system in monkeys. Phil. Trans. R. Soc. Lond. Ser. B 298: 85–95.

23. MITRIUS, J. C., D. G. MORGAN & A. ROUTTENBERG. 1981. In vivo phosphorylation following ^{32}P-orthophosphate injection into neostriatum or hippocampus: Selective and rapid labeling of electrophoretically-separated brain proteins. Brain Res. 212: 67–81.

24. MORGAN, D. G. & A. ROUTTENBERG. 1981. Brain pyruvate dehydrogenase: phosphorylation and enzyme activity altered by a training experience. Science 214: 470–471.

25. MORGAN, D. G. & A. ROUTTENBERG. 1980. Evidence that a 41K dalton phosphoprotein is pyruvate dehydrogenase. Biochem. Biophys. Res. Commun. 95: 509–512.

26. MORRIS, M. E., K. KRNJEVIC & N. ROPERT. 1983. Changes in free Ca+ + recorded inside hippocampal neurons in response to fimbrial stimulation. Soc. Neurosci. Abstr. 9: 395.

27. NELSON, R., D. FRIEDMAN, J. B. O'NIELL, M. LEWIS & A. ROUTTENBERG. 1983. Protein phosphorylation and opioid receptor gradients in monkey cerebral cortex: phosphorylation state of a 47kD phosphoprotein. Soc. Neurosci. Abs. 9: 585.

28. NELSON, R., R. F. AKERS & A. ROUTTENBERG. 1984. Does protein kinase C activity regulate neural plasticity and its time-dependent processes? Soc. Neurosci. 10: 1180.

29. NISHIZUKA, Y. 1983. Phospholipid degradation and signal translation for protein phosphorylation. TIBS 8: 13–16.

30. OESTREICHER, A. B., H. ZWIERS, P. SCHOTMAN & W. H. GISPEN. 1981. Immunohisto-
     chemical localization of a phosphoprotein (B-50) isolated from rat brain synaptosomal
     plasma membranes. Brain Res. Bull. 6: 145–153.
31. OLTON, D. S. 1983. Memory functions and the hippocampus. In Neurobiology of the
     Hippocampus. W. Seifert, Ed.: 335–373. Academic Press. New York.
32. ROSEN, O. M. & E. G. KREBS. Eds. 1981. Protein Phosphorylation. Cold Spring Harbor
     Laboratory. Cold Spring Harbor, NY.
33. ROUTTENBERG, A. 1979. Anatomical localization of phosphoprotein and glycoprotein
     substrates of memory. Progr. Neurobiol. 12: 85–113.
34. ROUTTENBERG, A. 1982. Memory formation as a post-translational modification of brain
     proteins. In Mechanisms and Models of Neural Plasticity. Proc. VIth Intl. Neurobiol.
     IBRO Symp. Learning and Memory. C.A. Marsden & H. Matthies, Eds.: 17–24. Raven
     Press. New York.
35. ROUTTENBERG, A. 1982. Identification and back-titration of brain pyruvate dehydrogenase.
     Progr. Brain Res. 56: 349–374.
36. ROUTTENBERG, A. 1983. Phosphoproteins: Protagonists of plasticity in particular pathways.
     In Memory Neurobiology. G. Lynch, J. McGaugh & N. Weinberger, Eds.: 479–490. The
     Guilford Press. New York.
37. ROUTTENBERG, A. & Y. H. EHRLICH. 1975. Endogenous phosphorylation of four cerebral
     cortical membrane proteins: role of cyclic nucleotides, ATP, and divalent cations. Brain
     Res. 92: 415–430.
38. ROUTTENBERG, A., Y. H. EHRLICH & R. RABJOHNS. 1975. Effect of a training experience
     on phosphorylation of a specific protein in neocortical and subcortical membrane
     preparations. Fed. Proc. 34: 293.
39. ROUTTENBERG, A. & G. E. BENSON. 1980. In vitro phosphorylation of a 41,000-MW
     protein band is selectively increased 24 hr after footshock or learning. Behav. Neural Biol.
     29: 168.
40. ROUTTENBERG, A., D. G. MORGAN, R. G. CONWAY, M. J. SCHMIDT & B. GHETTI. 1981.
     Human brain protein phosphorylation in vitro: Cyclic AMP stimulation of electrophoreti-
     cally-separated substrates. Brain Res. 222: 323–333.
41. ROUTTENBERG, A., D. LOVINGER, S. CAIN, R. AKERS & O. STEWARD. 1983. Effects of
     long-term potentiation of perforant path synapses in the intact hippocampus on in vitro
     phosphorylation of a 47kD protein (F1). Fed. Proc. 42: 755.
42. ROUTTENBERG, A., D. LOVINGER & O. STEWARD. 1985. Selective increase in the phospho-
     rylation of a 47kD protein (F1) directly related to long-term potentiation. Behav. Neural
     Biol. 43: 3–11.
43. SORENSON, R. G., L. P. KLEINE & H. R. MAHLER. 1981. Pre-synaptic localization of
     phosphoprotein B-50. Brain Res. Bull. 7: 56–61.
44. TAKAI, Y., A. KISHIMOTO, Y. IWASA, Y. KAWAHARA, T. MORI & Y. NISHIZUKA. 1977.
     Calcium-dependent activation of a multifunctional protein kinase by membrane phos-
     pholipids. J. Biol. Chem. 254: 3692–3695.
45. THOMPSON, R. F. 1981. Increases in the monosynaptic population spike responses of the
     dentate gyrus during classical conditioning. Neurosci. Res. Prog. Bull. 20: 693–695.
46. UEDA, T., H. MAENO & P. GREENGARD. 1973. Regulation of endogenous phosphorylation
     of specific proteins in synaptic membrane fractions from rat brain by adenosine
     3':5'-monophosphate. J. Biol. Chem. 248: 8295–8305.
47. WELLER, M. & R. RODNIGHT. 1971. Turnover of protein bound phosphorylserine in
     membrane preparations of ox brain catalyzed by intrinsic kinase and phosphatase
     activity. Biochem. J. 124: 183–250.
48. ZWIERS, H., V. J. ALOYO & W. H. GISPEN. 1981. Behavioral and neurochemical effects of
     the new opioid peptide dynorphin-(1-13): Comparison with other neuropeptides. Life Sci.
     28: 2545–2551.
49. ZWIERS, H., J. JOLLES, V. J. ALOYO, A. B. OESTREICHER & W. H. GISPEN. 1982. ACTH
     and synaptic membrane phosphorylation in rat brain. Progr. Brain Res. 56: 405–417.
50. ZWIERS, H., H. D. VELDHUIS, P. SCHOTMAN & W. H. GISPEN. 1976. ACTH, cyclic
     nucleotides, and brain protein phosphorylation in vitro. Neurochem Res. 1: 669–677.

A Critical Review of the Role of the Cholinergic System in Human Memory and Cognition[a]

PETER DAVIES

Departments of Pathology and Neuroscience
Albert Einstein College of Medicine
Bronx, New York 10461

INTRODUCTION

The aim of this paper is to briefly and critically review the evidence suggesting a major role for the cholinergic system in human memory and cognition. There are three essentially distinct areas of research that have led to the development of the "cholinergic hypothesis." These are (1) studies using anticholinergics in normal human volunteers; (2) direct examination of the status of the cholinergic system in subjects with disorders of memory and cognition; and (3) Attempts to improve memory and cognitive function with cholinomimetics in both normal subjects and patients with appropriate dysfunctions. We will examine each of these three lines of evidence, attempting to critically evaluate the strengths and weaknesses of the results obtained.

EFFECTS OF ANTICHOLINERGICS

That anticholinergics produce deficits in short-term memory function has been known for decades. The by-now classical studies of Drachman[1,2] are an excellent example of this type of investigation. Using low doses of scopolamine in young volunteers, Drachman and his colleages have demonstrated robust deficits in memory function, with smaller deficits in other aspects of cognitive function. The changes produced are not reversed by stimulants such as amphetamines, but can be ameliorated by the cholinesterase inhibitor physostigmine. Thus the evidence is consistent with a role for the cholinergic system in memory and perhaps in other cognitive functions. Scopolamine is the drug most frequently used in studies of this type, precisely because its effects are so reproducible. Why shouldn't all anticholinergics behave the same? Shouldn't it be possible to accurately model disorders of memory and cognition with anticholinergics? There are several complicating factors to be considered when evaluating experiments such as those of Drachman et al. First and foremost is the complexity of the cholinergic system itself. For the purposes of this article, the central nervous system (CNS) can be considered to have three distinct groups of cholinergic neurons.[3–5] The first is the "motor system," comprising the motor neurons as well as many of the neurons of the cranial nerve nuclei. These neurons are essentially exclusively an output system and probably have little or no role in memory or cognition.

[a]The author is supported by grants from National Institutes of Health (AG02478 and MH38623), the McKnight Foundation, and the Joyce Mertz-Gilmore Foundation. He is the Commonwealth Fund Fellow at Albert Einstein College of Medicine.

The second group is the striatal cholinergic neurons of the caudate and putamen (in the human, there are very few cholinergic neurons in the globus pallidus).[6,7] One function of these cells is in extrapyramidal motor control: whether or not striatal cholinergic neurons have any role in memory and/or cognition is not clear. There is a body of data to indicate a role for the striatum in cognition, but a review of these data is outside the scope of this paper.[8] The third and probably key system for memory and cognition is made up by the basal forebrain neurons, which innervate the cerebral cortex and hippocampus. These neurons of the nucleus basalis of Meynert and the diagonal band supply about 80% of the cholinergic innervation to the cortex and hippocampus,[9,10] both structures clearly being important for memory and cognition. The administration of anticholinergics clearly has the potential to interfere with the activities of all three cholinergic systems equally or to selectively attack one or more. Various factors may be important, such as regional distribution of the drug in brain, regional variations in receptor concentrations and/or affinity for the drug, and even regional variations in the baseline activity of the system. (It is not often appreciated that an antagonist must compete with the natural transmitter to block the receptor: this will be easier at a relatively inactive synapse, where there is little competing transmitter.) It is also important to appreciate that there are two cholinergic receptors in the CNS, nicotinic and muscarinic. Most cholinergic antagonists show selectivity for one or the other receptor type, whilst a disorder of cholinergic neurons would denervate both types. Whether or not both receptor types are important for cognition is not entirely clear; although there are many more muscarinic than nicotinic receptors in brain,[11,12] and many more usable muscarinic antagonists, there is a body of literature to suggest a role for nicotinic receptors in aspects of cognition[13,14] As the above discussion should make clear, the use of drugs in an attempt to dissect the role of the cholinergic system in memory and cognition is extremely complex. Several potential confounding factors should be considered. Some or perhaps all of the above may account for the differences between the effects of individual drugs, even when test tube studies indicate strong similarities. For example, atropine and scopolamine behave in a very similar fashion in test tube studies of receptor binding, while scopolamine produces much more dramatic effects on short term memory than does atropine.[15] The best one can conclude is that with certain specific anticholinergics, a robust deficit in memory function can be demonstrated. Certain anticholinergics can also produce deficits in other aspects of cognition: together these data are consistent with some role for the cholinergic system in human memory and cognition.

STATUS OF THE CHOLINERGIC SYSTEM IN DISORDERS WITH MEMORY DYSFUNCTION

Evidence of cholinergic dysfunction in human disorders involving memory loss and cognitive deficits is largely limited to studies of Alzheimer's disease. In this case, it is clear from numerous studies that a marked cholinergic deficiency is very consistently found.[16,17] In reference to the previous section, it is interesting to note that this deficiency is limited to only one of the three cholinergic systems of the CNS: the nucleus basalis of Meynert/diagonal band neurons are affected while the striatal and motor systems are not.[18] Interpretation of the relationship between the cholinergic deficit and the major symptoms of the disease is very difficult. On the one hand, correlations between the degree of the cholinergic deficiency and the extent of the cognitive deficit[19] could simply result from both being indicative of the severity of the disease and do not imply any causal relationship. How can we establish the role of the cholinergic system in cognitive function from studies of brain tissue? Our group has been approaching this problem in a correlative fashion, examining brain tissue from patients who were given a variety of psychometric tests prior to death.[20] Obviously, linear regression analysis can be used to search for relationships between test scores and chemical assays of the status of the cholinergic system (usually and most of the time, reliably assessed by measurement of choline acetyltransferase activity, abbreviated ChAT). Data from 64 completely unselected cases (unselected means selected simply because the data were available), analyzed by linear regression, indicate a relationship between cortical ChAT activity and the Blessed Functional Inventory score,[21] the latter being a rather gross index of level of cognitive function. The correlation coefficient is -0.329, which with 64 pairs of data gives a statistical significance of $p < 0.01$. This is evidence of a rather loose relationship, but since these patients are completely unselected for pathology or disease, any relationship at all is surprising. In analyzing these data further, we formulated the hypothesis that a low level of ChAT in cortex was not compatible with reasonable levels of cognitive function. To test this hypothesis, we defined normal levels of ChAT activity as the mean value from a group of individuals whose psychometric test scores indicated normal cognition. Taking this mean value and subtracting two standard deviations of the mean, we analyzed the test scores of patients whose ChAT levels were below the mean minus two standard deviations. Only six of our 64 patients had ChAT activities below this level: all six were profoundly demented, the best making 20 out of a possible 33 errors on the Blessed. In this group of cases, a low ChAT activity in cortex was highly predictive of dementia. In fact of all the post mortem markers, a low ChAT activity in more than one cortical region was the best predictor of dementia. It is noteworthy that a few cases had low ChAT activity in only a single cortical region, usually as the result of focal vascular disease. The effects of the lesions on cognitive function were, as is predictable, highly dependent on the location of the lesion. Although analyses of the results from this group of patients support the basic hypothesis that without cholinergic function normal cognition is impossible, the results show that there is more than one cause of dementia. We have several patients who have very respectable cortical ChAT activity but are profoundly demented. Precisely what is wrong with these patients is not yet clear. Thus we believe that defective cholinergic transmission always results in dementia, but dementia is not always due to defective cholinergic transmission. When we exclude the odd cases and include only those with either no pathology or with varying degree of pathology of the Alzheimer type, we find very strong correlations between degree of cognitive deficit and extent of reduction in ChAT activity. Correlations are strongest between scores on memory tests and hippocampal ChAT activity, where correlation coefficients are in the range of -0.6. Even in the remaining patients, hippocampal ChAT activity is the best post mortem predictor of scores on test of recent memory, correlation coefficients being in the range of -0.5. This brief overview of the results of our own studies, along with those of others, suggests a role for deficits in the cholinergic system contributing to the generation of dementia. However, it is perhaps the third line of research that will contribute most to our understanding of the role of the cholinergic system in cognition.

IMPROVEMENT IN COGNITIVE FUNCTION THROUGH ENHANCEMENT OF CHOLINERGIC FUNCTION

Before considering how cholinergic transmission might be enhanced, a step away from cognition and memory is instructive. In Parkinson's disease, there is a deficiency of dopamine, which, when treated with L-Dopa, alleviates the symptoms of the disorder. There are also deficiencies of noradrenaline, serotonin, gamma-aminobutyric acid, met-enkephalin, and cholecystokinin octapeptide.[22,23] However, clinicians do not have to worry about these other deficits in most patients, because most of the time all that needs to be done is to carefully regulate the dosage of L-dopa. Thus although multiple transmitter deficits are measurable, only one is significant to the patients ability to function. Is the cholinergic deficit the functionally significant one in patients with Alzheimer's disease? We won't really know until we can reliably enhance cholinergic transmission in people and measure the effects on memory and cognitive function. This is the key to unlocking the mystery of the cause of symptoms in Alzheimer patients. The plain fact is that we do not yet know how to reliably and safely enhance cholinergic transmission in the CNS of people. There is at this time only one drug that can reliably reverse the effects of drugs like scopamine and atropine in people, and that drug is physostigmine. Perhaps significantly, physostigmine is the only agent (to the best of my current knowledge) that has produced statistically significant improvements in carefully characterized Alzheimer patients in double-blind studies at more than one center.[24-26] Why isn't it easier to manipulate central cholinergic transmission in humans? It is very unfortunate that there are several barriers to doing this. First and foremost is the widespread nature of the peripheral cholinergic system. Virtually every neuromuscular junction in the body is a cholinergic synapse, so we have to be extremely careful about what we give to people. Too much acetylcholine at a neuromuscular junction is as bad as too little. Witness the extreme toxicity of the nerve gases and weapons of chemical warfare: virtually all of the most potent agents turn out to block the degradation of acetylcholine by inhibition of one or more cholinesterases. The importance of the peripheral cholinergic system is also evident in evolutionary terms. Many of the more potent snake and spider venoms turn out to act through blocking peripheral nicotinic acetylcholine receptors.

A further problem may turn out to be the existence of inhibitory presynaptic muscarinic receptors on central cholinergic nerve terminals.[27,28] These receptors act to suppress transmitter release when activated, thus attempts to enhance transmitter release or to use muscarinic agonists might result in a decrease in transmitter release from the terminal. Their existence may also present an unusual avenue for therapy: if an antagonist selective for presynaptic receptors could be found, it would actually enhance acetylcholine output.

What is needed is an agent or agents that selectively enhance central cholinergic transmission. None appear to be available at this time, so it is impossible to accurately test the hypothesis that the memory loss and decline in cognitive function experienced by patients with Alzheimer's disease are the direct result of a deficiency of cholinergic transmission. However, given the weight of the studies cited in this article, it would seem that if there is a key transmitter for memory, and perhaps for other aspects of cognitive function, the best bet for that transmitter would be acetylcholine.

ACKNOWLEDGMENTS

Much of our work cited in this paper was done in collaboration with Drs. Robert Terry, Robert Katzman, Paula Fuld, and Ted Brown.

REFERENCES

1. DRACHMAN, D. A. & J. LEAVITT. 1974. Human memory and the cholinergic system. Arch. Neurol. 30: 113–121.

2. DRACHMAN, D. A. & B. J. SAHAKIAN. 1980. Memory and cognitive function in the elderly. A preliminary trial of physostigmine. Arch. Neurol. **37:** 674–675.
3. ARMSTRONG, D. A., C. B. SAPER, A. I. LEVEY, B. H. WAINER & R. D. TERRY 1983. Distribution of cholinergic neurons in rat brain: demonstration by immunocytochemical localization of choline acetyltransferase. J. Comp. Neurol., **216:** 1184–1190.
4. MESULAM, M. M., E. J. MUFSON, A. I. LEVEY & B. H. WAINER. 1983. Cholinergic innervation of cortex by basal forebrain: cytochemistry and cortical connections of the septal area, diagonal band nuclei, nucleus basalis (substantia innominata) and hypothalamus in the Rhesus monkey. J. Comp. Neurol. **214:** 170–197.
5. COYLE, J. T., D. L. PRICE & M. R. DELONG. 1983. Alzheimer's Disease: A disorder of cortical cholinergic innervation. Science **219:** 1184–1190.
6. DAVIES, P. & S. FEISULLIN. 1982. A search for discrete cholinergic nuclei in the human ventral forebrain. J. Neurochem. **39:** 1743–1747.
7. GASPER, P., F. JAVOY-AGID, A. PLOSKA & Y. AGID. 1980. Regional distribution of neurotransmitter synthesizing enzymes in the basal ganglia of the human brain. J. Neurochem. **34:** 278–283.
8. TEUBER, H-L. 1976. Complex functions of basal ganglia. *In* The Basal Ganglia. M. D. Yahr, Ed.: 151–168. Raven Press. New York.
9. JOHNSON, M. V., M. MCKINNEY & J. T. COYLE 1979. Evidence for a cholinergic projection to neocortex from neurons in the basal forebrain. Proc. Natl. Acad. Sci. USA **76:** 5392–5396.
10. LEHMANN, J., J. I. NAGY, S. ATMANJA & H. C. FIBIGER. 1980. The nucleus basalis magnocellularis: the origin of a cholinergic projection to the neocortex of the rat. Neuroscience **5:** 1161–1174.
11. DAVIES, P. & S. FEISULLIN. 1981. Post mortem stability of alpha bungarotoxin binding sites in mouse and human brain. Brain Res **216:** 449–453.
12. DAVIES, P. & A. H. VERTH. 1977. Regional distribution of muscarinic acetyl choline receptors in normal and Alzheimer-type dementia brains. Brain Res. **138:** 385–392.
13. ROSECRANS, J. A. & W. T. CHANCE. 1977. Cholinergic and non-cholinergic aspects of the discriminative stimulus properties of nicotine. Adv. Behav. Biol. **22:** 155–185.
14. HUNTER, B., S. F. ZORNETZER, M. E. JARVIK & J. L. MCGAUGH. 1977. Modulations of learning and memory: effects of drugs influencing neurotransmitters. *In* Handbook of Psychopharmacology. L. L. Iversen, S. Iversen & S. Snyder, Ed. **8:** 531–578. Plenum Press. New York.
15. HULME, E. C., N. J. M. BIRDSALL & A. S. V. BURGEN. 1978. The binding of antagonists to brain muscarinic receptors. J. Molec. Pharmacol. **14:** 737–750.
16. DAVIES, P. 1983. An update on the neurochemistry of Alzheimer's Disease. Adv. Neurol. **38:** 75–86.
17. BARTUS, R. T., R. L. DEAN, B. BEER & A. S. LIPPA. 1982. The cholinergic hypothesis of geriatric memory dysfunction. Science **217:** 408–417.
18. ROSSER, M. N., N. J. GARRETT, A. L. JOHNSON, C. Q. MOUNTJOY, M. ROTH & L. L. IVERSEN. 1982. A post-mortem study of the cholinergic and GABA systems in senile dementia. Brain **105:** 313–330.
19. PERRY, E. K., B. E. TOMLINSON, G. BLESSED, K. BERGMANN, P. H. GIBSON & R. H. PERRY. 1978. Correlation of cholinergic abnormalities with senile plaques and mental test scores in senile dementia. Brit. Med. J. **2:** 1457–1459.
20. FULD, P. A., R. KATZMAN, P. DAVIES & R. D. TERRY. 1982. Intrusions as a sign of Alzheimer's Disease: Chemical and pathological verification. Ann. Neurol. **11** 155–159.
21. BLESSED, G., B. E. TOMLINSON & M. ROTH. 1968. The association between quantitative measures of dementia and of senile changes in the grey matter of elderly subjects. Brit. J. Psychiat. **114:** 797–811.
22. HORNYKIEWICZ, O. 1973. Dopamine in basal ganglia. Brit. Med. Bull. **29:** 172–178.
23. JAVOY-AGID, F., M. RUBERG, H. TAQUET, J. M. STUDLER, M. GARBARG, C. LLORENS, J. C. SCHWARTZ, D. GROUSELLE, K. G. LLOYD, R. RAISMAN & Y. AGID. 1982. Biochemical neuroanatomy of the human substantia nigra (pars compacta) in normal and Parkinsonian subjects. Adv. Neurol. **35:** 151–163.

24. PETERS, B. & H. S. LEVIN. 1979. Effects of physostigmine and lecithin on memory in Alzheimer's Disease. Ann. Neurol. **6:** 219–221.
25. THAL, L. J., P. A. FULD, D. M. MASUR & N. D. SHARPLESS. 1983. Oral physostigmine and lecithin improve memory in Alzheimer's Disease. Ann. Neurol. **13:** 491–494.
26. DAVIS, K. L., R. C. MOHS, W. G. ROSEN, B. S. GREENWALD, M. I. LEVY & T. B. HORVATH. 1983. Memory enhancement with oral physostigmine in Alzheimer's Disease. New Eng. J. Med. **308:** 721.
27. MCKINNEY, M. & J. T. COYLE. 1982. Regulation of neocortical muscarinic receptors: effects of drug treatment and lesions. J. Neurosci. **2:** 97–105.
28. KRNJEVIC, K. 1977. Acetyl choline receptors in vertabrate CNS. *In* Handbook of Psychopharmacology. L. L. Iversen, S. D. Iversen & S. Snyder, Eds. **6:** 97–125. Plenum Press. New York.

Catecholamines and Cognitive Decline in Aged Nonhuman Primates

AMY F.T. ARNSTEN AND
PATRICIA S. GOLDMAN-RAKIC

Section of Neuroanatomy
Yale University
New Haven, Connecticut 06510

The neural machinery required for cognitive processing in primates is not well understood. More than likely, however, higher order cognitive abilities involve the synaptic interaction of a number of neural pathways and neurotransmitters. Indeed, in a nervous system as complex as that of humans, it is difficult to conceive of a lesion in one system that does not engender changes in other synaptically related systems. The same complexity undoubtedly pertains to the processes of deterioration that occur in the aging brain. Much recent research has emphasized the relationship between cholinergic dysfunction and cognitive decline in the aged, particularly in patients with Alzheimer's disease, where dementia is accompanied by loss of cholinergic cells. However, it is also apparent that many other neurotransmitter systems degenerate with increasing age, and some of these deteriorate further in Alzheimer's disease. Amongst these various neurochemical changes, there is evidence that levels of the catecholamines, dopamine and norepinephrine, decrease with advancing age and that noradrenergic levels may be depleted even more in some brain regions of Alzheimer's patients. This chapter examines the role of catecholamine loss in the cognitive decline exhibited by aged nonhuman primates whose cognitive deficits resemble those associated with normal aging in humans.

ANATOMICAL DISTRIBUTION OF CATECHOLAMINES IN PRIMATE NEOCORTEX

The distribution of catecholamines (CA) in the cortex of the rodent brain has been known for many years. Dopamine cells project selectively to the prefrontal and anterior cingulate regions[1] while noradrenergic cells project uniformly to all cortical areas.[2] The diffuse nature of the noradrenergic projection has influenced hypotheses of the possible functions of these neurotransmitters toward the view of a general or diffuse neurochemical action. Although early reports suggested that this pattern of CA innervation might also be found in the primate, recent results from biochemical,[3] fluorescence histochemical,[4] and immunocytochemical[5] analyses agree that norepinephrine (NE), as well as dopamine (DA), shows marked regional variation in the primate neocortex.

Dopamine levels in the monkey cortex are highest in the prefrontal cortex and decrease along the fronto-occipital axis such that only trace amounts are found in visual cortex (FIGURE 1).[3] Intermediate levels are found in the premotor and motor cortex and in the temporal lobe. Even within the frontal lobe, examination of histofluorescence material reveals selectivity in the DA distribution.[4] DA fibers are

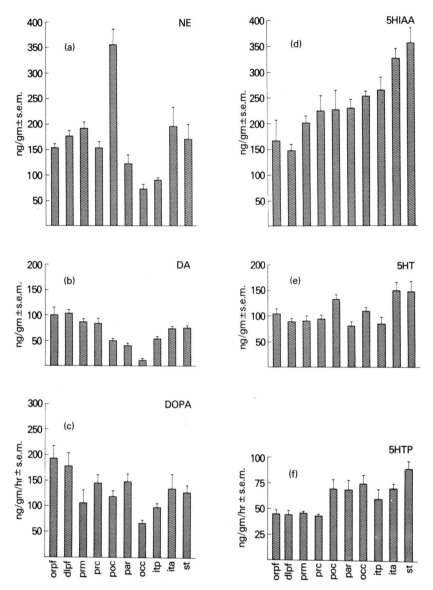

FIGURE 1. The ng/g tissue concentration of (a) norepinephrine, (b) dopamine, (d) S-hydroxyindoleacetic acid, and (e) serotonin as well as the hourly ng/g accumulation of (c) DOPA and (f) 5-HTP in 10 areas of neocortex in young adult rhesus monkeys. Abbreviations: orpf = orbital prefrontal cortex, dlpf = dorsolateral prefrontal cortex, prm = premotor cortex, prc = precentral gyrus (motor cortex), poc = postcentral gyrus (somatosensory cortex), par = posterior parietal cortex, occ = occipital cortex (includes area 17), itp = inferior temporal gyrus, posterior, ita = inferior temporal gyrus, anterior, st = superior temporal gyrus. (From Brown *et al.*[3] With permission from *Brain Research*.)

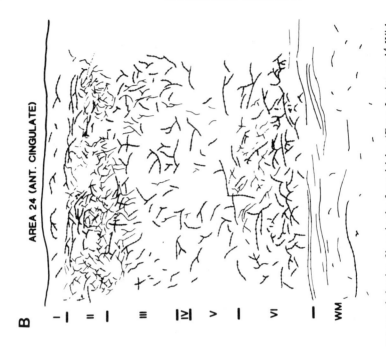

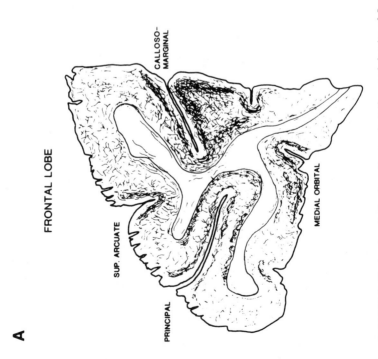

FIGURE 2. Regional variation in pattern, orientation, and density of fluorescent catecholamine fibers in the frontal lobe. (From Levitt *et al.*[4] With permission from *Journal of Comparative Neurology.*)

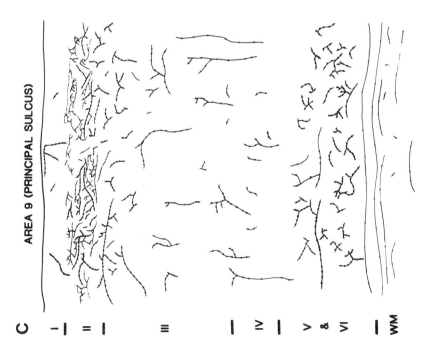

particularly dense in anterior cingulate, dorsolateral (around the principal sulcus), and orbital cortex, but are less concentrated in areas in between (FIGURE 2).

Norepinephrine, like DA, exhibits an anterior-posterior gradient (FIGURE 1). However, the NE gradient is more irregular and exhibits a marked deviation from linearity; notably, NE reaches its peak concentration in the somatosensory cortex.[3] Intermediate levels are found in the frontal and anterior temporal lobes, while the lowest amount of NE, like DA, is found in occipital cortex. In contrast, most areas of the frontal lobe are innervated in a dense manner.[4]

The laminar distribution of CA-containing fibers also appears to differ in rat and monkey. In contrast to the rat neocortex, layer I of monkey neocortex receives little CA innervation. Instead, most areas of rhesus monkey cortex contain two CA-rich laminae, one superficial and one deep layer. This bilaminar pattern is particularly pronounced in granular cortex, where the CA terminal input is often concentrated in layers II and V, and the CA fibers run parallel to the pial surface. Most agranular regions contain more evenly distributed CA axons throughout all cortical layers, although two, more densely innervated laminae can be discerned in some areas. Careful examination of both the fluorescence and immunocytochemical material reveals unique patterns of axonal organization between and even within defined cortical areas. For example, within the prefrontal cortex, the density, pattern, and orientation of CA fibers vary greatly between adjacent cortical areas (FIGURE 2). These intricate regional patterns raise the possibility that CA may have selective targets and hence specialized functions within each individual cortical field.

THE RELATIONSHIP OF CATECHOLAMINES TO COGNITIVE FUNCTION

The prefrontal cortex in monkeys is extensively interconnected with the hippocampus,[6] amygdala,[7] dorsomedial thalamus,[8] locus coeruleus,[9] and nucleus basalis[10] (FIGURE 3). With connections to so many structures implicated in memory function, it is not surprising that several areas of prefrontal cortex are critical foci for normal performance of two spatial memory tasks, the spatial delayed response and delayed

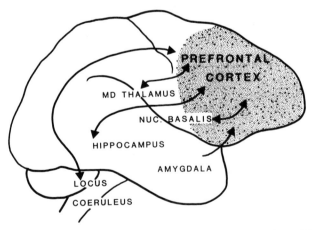

FIGURE 3. Diagrammatic representation of prefrontal cortical connections with subcortical structures implicated with memory function.

INJECTED   ABLATED

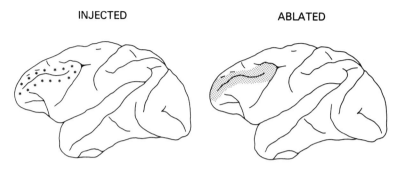

left lateral view

FIGURE 4. The region of prefrontal cortex surrounding the principal sulcus that was injected with 6-OHDA or vehicle (left) or ablated (right) in young adult rhesus monkeys.

alternation tasks.[11] In delayed response, one of two wells is baited in sight of the animal, the wells are covered with identical cardboard plaques, and a screen is lowered to remove them from the animal's view. After a prescribed delay the screen is raised and the animal allowed to choose a well. In delayed alternation the monkey does not see the well being baited and instead must remember which side he chose correctly on the last trial and alternate his response. Monkeys with bilateral ablations of the prefrontal cortex, particularly in the region surrounding the principal sulcus, are profoundly impaired at both of these tasks. These animals are not amnesic, per se; they are able to perform a go/no-go alternation task[12] and are not impaired on a recognition memory task; delayed nonmatch-to-sample.[13] However, they seem to have particular trouble with spatial working memory and are especially vulnerable to interference. Frontally lesioned monkeys are more easily distracted[14,15] and the presentation of irrelevant stimuli disrupts their performance of delayed response testing even at very short delays.[16] Humans with prefrontal cortical lesions similarly are more distractable[17] and unable to overcome interference.[18] Thus one of the functions of the dorsolateral prefrontal cortex appears to involve the ability to correctly guide behavioral response, possibly by suppression of competing responses to interfering events.

The presence of catecholamines, particularly dopamine, appears to be essential for the cortex surrounding the principal sulcus to function properly. 6-OHDA-induced catecholamine depletions restricted to the dorsolateral PFC, like ablations of this same area (FIGURE 4), resulted in marked deficits on the delayed alternation task.[19] The neurotoxic lesions did not impair performance on a nonfrontal task, a visual pattern discrimination. Thus, a CA depletion in a circumscribed region of the PFC produced a cognitive deficit selective to the function of that cortical area.

The deficits on the delayed alternation task were most pronounced in the monkeys with large DA depletions (FIGURE 5; DA decreased by 87%, NE by 76%). These animals had received the NE reuptake inhibitor DMI in conjunction with the 6-OHDA. The animals who were injected with 6-OHDA without DMI were only slightly impaired on the task (FIGURE 5); these monkeys had a smaller DA loss (56%) and a large NE depletion (85%). The vehicle-injected control animals had slight CA depletions in the dorsolateral PFC (DA decreased by 27%, NE by 34%), and were not impaired on the task (FIGURE 5). Thus performance of the delayed alternation task seemed to be related directly to the extent of DA loss in the principal sulcus region.

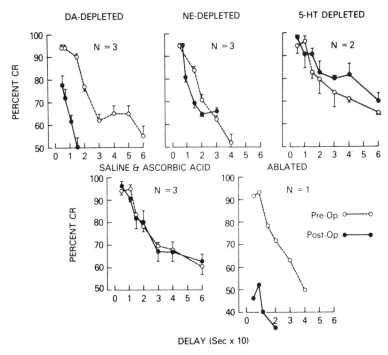

FIGURE 5. Delay function for cortical treatment leading to maximal depletion of dopamine (DA), norepinephrine (NE), or sertotonin (5-HT) in the principal sulcus and for ablation. Each point is based on a minimum of 40 test trials at each delay value. (From Brozoski et al.[19] With permission from the AAAS.)

Similar findings have been observed in rats following 6-OHDA lesions of an analogous area of cortex.[20]

PHARMACOTHERAPY FOR COGNITIVE DEFICITS IN NONHUMAN PRIMATES

As is well known, endogenous loss of dopamine in the neostriatum of Parkinson's patients can be successfully treated by the dopamine precursor L-dopa. Monkeys with selective depletions of CAs in the specific regions of cortex offered further support for the importance of catecholamines in PFC function, but also the first evidence that the cognitive deficits expressed by 6-OHDA–lesioned monkeys were improved by pharmacological treatment. Furthermore, the effective drugs were those that facilitate CA transmission. The poor performance of the DA-depleted monkeys was improved by the administration of the CA precursor L-dopa (50 mg/kg) and the DA receptor agonist apomorphine (0.02–0.08 mg/kg; FIGURE 6).[19] These drugs had no effect preoperatively or on the behavior of the animals in the other treatment groups, including animals with frontal ablations.

The noradrenergic alpha-2 receptor agonist clonidine also improved the performance of the DA-depleted animals.[19] However, this drug additionally improved the performance of the animals with large NE depletions (FIGURE 7) and the vehicle-treated controls, but had no effect pre-operatively and little effect on animals with PFC ablations (Brozoski, unpublished results). In contrast to the dopamine agonists, clonidine's effects appear related to the degree of NE depletion, as the animals with the largest NE depletions were improved by the smallest doses, and those without NE loss were unaffected by the drug. These clonidine results, like those with apomorphine and L-dopa, are consistent with drug actions at super-sensitive post-synaptic receptors in the cortex and encourage the possibility of effective drug "replacement therapy" for cognitive impairments related to neurotransmitter deficiencies.

CATECHOLAMINES AND AGE-RELATED COGNITIVE DECLINE

The pattern of cognitive impairment that develops in aged monkeys bears a marked resemblance to that produced by lesions to the dorsolateral PFC.[21] Both aged and frontally lesioned monkeys perform poorly on the delayed response task, particularly at long delays.[22] In general there is a direct relation between the age of the monkey and the delays at which it is able to perform, such that the oldest monkeys perform well at only the shortest delays (e.g. FIGURE 11). The delayed response deficit displayed by aged and frontally lesioned monkeys results, at least partially, from an increased

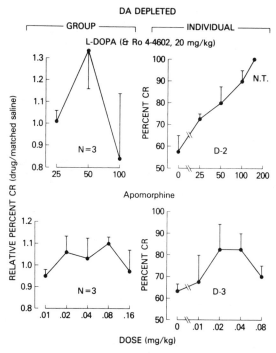

FIGURE 6. Dose-response functions for the DA-depleted group (left) and for representative individual animals. Data for each drug session were compared to mean performance on matched saline test sessions. N.T. = animal would not perform at this dose.

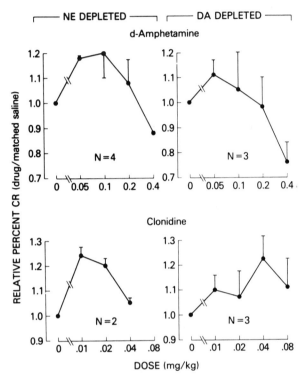

FIGURE 7. Dose-response functions for D-amphetamine (top) and clonidine (bottom) for the group with large NE depletions (left) and with large DA depletions (right). Data for each drug session were compared to mean performance on matched saline test sessions (Brozoski, unpublished results).

susceptibility to interference from distracting stimuli and poor inhibition of prepotent response tendencies.[23] Both aged and frontally lesioned monkeys usually are capable of learning visual discriminations but have difficulty when they must reverse their responses.[21]

The similarity of the response profiles between aged and frontally lesioned monkeys suggests that the prefrontal cortex may be particularly vulnerable to deterioration with advancing age. It is interesting in this regard that the prefrontal cortex has amongst the highest levels of neuritic plaques in the aged monkey brain and that plaque formation may begin in this cortical region.[24] These plaques have been stained with antisera to markers for several types of neurotransmitters, including CAT, tyrosine hydroxylase, and dopamine beta hydroxylase,[25] suggesting that plaques may be associated with the degeneration of ascending aminergic pathways to the cortex.

Indeed, our biochemical analysis of monoamine levels in the brains of aged rhesus monkeys revealed substantial depletions in cortical catecholamine levels compared to those of young animals.[26] In this study, measurements were made throughout the cortical mantle and in many subcortical structures from brains of rhesus monkeys ranging in age from 2–3 years (adolescent) to 10–18 years ("young" aged). Of the many regions studied, only the prefrontal and temporal cortices displayed large (50%) depletions in dopamine with increased age (FIGURE 8). The CA precursor L-dopa was reduced by approximately 60% in all sensory and association cortical areas including the PFC (FIGURE 9). It is quite likely that even greater depletions, particularly in NE, would be found in older monkeys (18–30+ years). These findings of reduced DA and

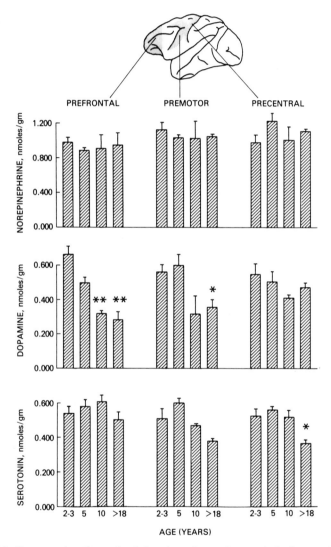

FIGURE 8. Concentration of norepinephrine, dopamine, and serotonin in three major cortical subdivisions of the frontal lobe. Concentration is in nmoles/g with S.E.M. indicated on the bars. Asterisks indicate significance of comparisons between the 2–3 yr age group and each of the other age groups: *p = 0.05, **p = 0.01. (From Goldman-Rakic & Brown.[26] With permission from *Neurosciences.*)

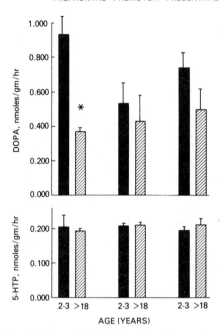

FIGURE 9. Accumulation of L-dopa and 5-HTP in prefrontal, premotor, and precentral cortex of 2–3 (solid bars) and 18 (thatched bars) year-old monkeys. Value are in nmoles/g/hr with S.E.M. indicated. * = 0.05 compared to 2–3 years old. (From Goldman-Rakic & Brown.[2] With permission from *Neurosciences*.)

L-dopa levels in cortex are constant with reports of decreased fluorescence intensity in the CA cell bodies of the substantia nigra and locus coeruleus in aged monkeys.[27] Similar studies of monoamine levels in aged rodents[28] and aged humans[29] also report deterioration of CA systems, including decreased levels of CA receptors.[30,31] Although previous research has accentuated the role of cholinergic loss in age-related cognitive decline, the results from these studies indicate that deterioration of CA systems also may contribute to the cognitive deficits of the aged.

PHARMACOLOGICAL TREATMENT OF AGED MONKEYS

As CA agonists improved the cognitive performance of young, 6-OHDA–lesioned monkeys, we were encouraged to examine whether these drugs similarly might prove effective "replacement therapy" for aged monkeys with endogenous CA depletions. This investigation examined the behavior of five aged rhesus monkeys, ranging in age from 18 to 30+ years. In agreement with Bartus' findings, these animals were all impaired on the frontal tasks, spatial delayed alternation and delayed response (FIGURE 10). Only one animal (#121) additionally was unable to perform a task sensitive to inferotemporal cortical damage, a visual pattern discrimination. We thus wished to determine whether CA agonists would improve the aged monkeys' performance of the two-well spatial delayed response task, which is so sensitive to prefrontal damage. In order to see the effects of each dose of drug on performance at a variety of delays, the animals were trained on a variable delayed response task. In this task five delays occurred quasi-randomly and varied between 0 seconds and the delay which resulted in chance performance for each animal. Drug testing began after the monkeys had achieved a stable baseline of performance on this task. Each animal was tested twice a week, with at least two days separating each test session. On one day the animal received a single dose of drug, and on the other a placebo treatment according to random assignment. The experimenter testing the animal was unaware of the drug treatment conditions. A variety of drugs that had improved the young, experimentally lesioned animals were tried with the aged animals. Examination of a drug continued until a dose-response curve with selected replications was completed.

To date, neither L-dopa nor apomorphine have had beneficial effects in the aged monkeys. However, the alpha-2 agonist, clonidine, produced robust improvements in delayed response performance in a dose-related manner (FIGURE 11). At the highest doses tested, performance was impaired by the sedative effects of the drug. The one monkey who was impaired on the visual discrimination task was the only animal who was not consistently improved by clonidine. Marked clonidine improvements were found with the 30+-year-old monkey. At the most effective dose, four of the five aged monkeys were able to achieve near perfect performance. This improvement was most apparent at the longer delays (FIGURE 12). Clonidine's beneficial effects on delayed response performance do not seem to be secondary to the hypotensive or sedative effects of the drug, as neither the hypotensive agent, propranolol, nor the sedative diazepam improved performance. We presently are examining the possible neurochemical mechanisms underlying clonidine's ability to ameliorate cognitive deficits.

TRIALS TO CRITERION

	Delayed Response (5 sec)	Delayed Alternation (5 sec)
Young:	463 ± 58	387 ± 92
Old:	failed*	failed
	890	failed
	failed	failed**
	648	failed
	failed	failed

FIGURE 10. Comparison of the performance of young adult and aged (18–30+ years) rhesus monkeys on two tasks sensitive to prefrontal cortical damage. Aged monkeys frequently failed to reach criterion of 90% correct within 1000 trials. *Within 1,000 trials, **also failed visual pattern discrimination.

Dose/response profiles are consonant with clonidine having actions at post-synaptic receptors.

One question of interest is whether clonidine's beneficial effects result in any way from a facilitation of dopaminergic activity, particularly as our biochemical data indicate that this catecholamine is the more vulnerable to deterioration with increasing age. In rodents, there is evidence that noradrenergic innervation of the ventral tegmental area has excitatory actions only on those dopaminergic cells projecting the PFC.[32] Thus clonidine might increase the firing of meso-cortical DA cells. Alternatively, the higher clonidine doses could have direct actions on dopamine receptors,

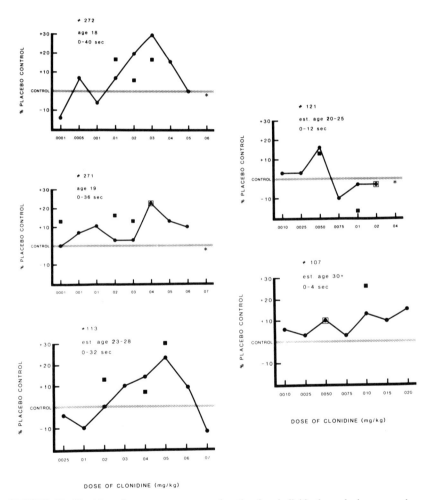

FIGURE 11. Clonidine dose-response curves for the five individual aged rhesus monkeys performing a variable delayed response task. Data are collapsed across delays and compared to matched saline control performance. Squares represent replications of a particular dose; asterisk indicates that the animal was too sedated to test.

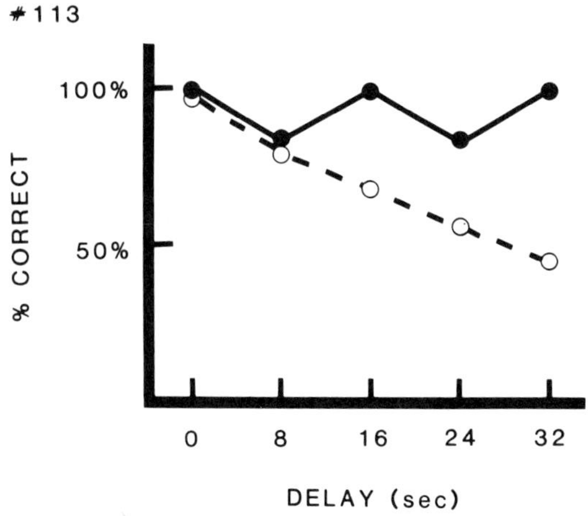

#113

FIGURE 12. Delay-response function for a representative aged monkey following administration of saline (open circles) or clonidine (0.05 mg/kg, the most effective dose for this animal; closed circles).

particularly as NE and DA appear to develop special interactions when either system is damaged.[33]

The investigation of adrenergic interactions with other neurotransmitters may be especially relevant in aging studies where behavioral deficits undoubtedly reflect the disintegration of various, interdependent neurochemical systems. The interaction of noradrenergic and cholinergic effects in cortex may be of particular interest as both of these neurotransmitter systems deteriorate in Alzheimer's disease. In rodent cortex, cholinergic excitatory effects are facilitated by stimulation of alpha receptors,[34] suggesting that the beneficial effects of cholinergic and alpha agonists in primates could be synergistic if given in combination. These issues are currently being studied in our laboratory, and may lead to superior, potential treatments for age-related cognitive disorders in humans.

RELEVANCE TO HUMAN DISORDERS

As with aged monkeys, aged humans often develop memory problems whereby they have difficulties recalling information following a delay with a distraction.[35] These impairments are even more evident in patients with Alzheimer's disease[35] where heightened susceptibility to interference[36] and poor selective attention[37,38] may accompany and contribute to profound mnemonic deficits.

Although much research has emphasized the loss of acetylcholine in Alzheimer's disease (AD), it is now evident that other neurotransmitter systems are depleted as well.[39-41] For this reason, the aged monkey is at present the most appropriate model for disorders associated with human aging. Experimental depletions of cholinergic or adrenergic structures in young monkeys may be useful in demonstrating the influence of one or another neurotransmitter on behavior, but cannot approximate the condition of multiple system involvement that seems to exist in AD. As in aged monkeys,[26] examination of CA content in tissues from Alzheimer's brains has shown that catecholamines are depressed compared to age-matched controls; NE particularly is depleted in the prefrontal and temporal cortex.[42-44] Consonant with decreased NE in cortex, several investigators have found extensive cell loss in the locus coeruleus of

Alzheimer's brains, particularly in the presenile form of the disease.[45–47] Although Perry et al.[44] found that decreases in cortical (Brodmann's areas 10 and 21) DBH levels did not significantly correlate with either locus coeruleus cell loss or dementia scores, Adolfsson et al.[42] found a significant negative correlation between intellectual deterioration and NE levels in the cingulate gyrus and hypothalamus.

In contrast to NE levels, adrenergic receptors do not appear to be lost further in AD,[48] raising the possibility that agonists that act directly on NE receptors may help to restore lost noradrenergic function. As the alpha-2 receptor agonist, clonidine, improved the cognitive performance of aged monkeys, it is conceivable that this drug might have similar beneficial effects in patients suffering from AD. There are reports that clonidine is capable of improving another patient population with both memory deficits and indices of NE loss, patients with Korsakoff's syndrome.[49] These clinical results encourage the possibility that clonidine may be efficacious in the treatment of other cognitive disorders that are associated with a loss of brain catecholamines.

REFERENCES

1. THEIRRY, A. M., G. BLANE, A. SOBEL, L. STINUS & L. GLOWINSKI. 1973. Dopamingeric terminals in the rat cortex. Science 182: 499–501.

2. MOORE, R. Y. & F. E. BLOOM. 1979. Central catecholamine neuron systems: Anatomy and physiology of the norepinephrine and epinephrine systems. Ann. Rev. Neurosci. 2: 113–168.

3. BROWN, R. M., A. M. CRANE & P. S. GOLDMAN. 1979. Regional distribution of monoamines in the cerebral cortex and subcortical structures on the rhesus monkey: Concentrations in vivo synthesis rates. Brain Res. 168: 133–150.

4. LEVITT, P., P. RAKIC & P. S. GOLDMAN-RAKIC. 1984. Region-specific distribution of catecholamine afferents in primate cerebral cortex: A fluorescence histochemical analysis. J. Comp. Neurol. 227: 23–36.

5. MORRISON, J. H., S. L. FOOTE, D. O'CONNOR & F. E. BLOOM. 1982. Laminar, tangential and regional organization of the nordrenergic innervation of monkey cortex: dopamine-β-hydroxylase immunohistochemistry. Brain Res. Bull. 9: 309–319.

6. GOLDMAN-RAKIC, P. S., L. D. SELEMON & M. L. SCHWARTZ. 1984. Dual pathways connecting the dorsolateral prefrontal cortex with the hippocampal formation and parihippocampal cortex in the rhesus monkey. Neuroscience. 12: 719–743.

7. PORRINO, L. J., A. M. CRANE & P. S. GOLDMAN-RAKIC. 1981. Direct and indirect pathways from the amygdala to the frontal lobe in monkeys. J. Comp. Neurol. 198: 121–136.

8. GOLDMAN, P. S. 1979. Contralateral projections to the dorsal thalmas from the frontal association cortex in the rhesus monkey. Brain Res. 166: 166–171.

9. ARNSTEN, A. F. T. & P. S. GOLDMAN-RAKIC. 1984. Selective prefrontal cortical projections to the region of the locus coeruleus and raphe nuclei in the rhesus monkey. Brain Res. 306: 9–18.

10. MESULAM, M. M. & E. J. MUFSON. 1984. Neural inputs into the nucleus basalis of the substantia innomineta (ch 4) in the rhesus monkey. Brain 107: 253–272.

11. GOLDMAN, P. S. & H. E. ROSVOLD. 1979. Localization of function within the dorsolateral PFC of the rhesus monkey. Exp. Neurol. 27: 291–304.

12. GOLDMAN, P. S., H. E. ROSVOLD, B. VEST & T. W. GALKIN. 1971. Analysis of the delayed-alternation deficit produced by dorsolateral prefrontal lesions in the rhesus monkey. J. Comp. Physiol. Psychol. 77: 212–220.

13. MISHKIN, M. & J. BACHEVALIER. 1983. Object recognition impaired by ventromedial but not dorsolateral PFC lesion in monkeys. Soc. Neurosci. Abstr. 9: 29.

14. MALMO, R. B. 1942. Interference factors in delayed response in monkeys after removal of frontal lobes. J. Neurophysiol 5: 295–308.

15. GRUENINGER, W. E. & K. H. PRIBAM. 1969. Effects of spatial and nonspatial distractors on

performance latency of monkeys with frontal lesions. J. Comp. Physiol. Psychol. **68:** 203–209.
16. BARTUS, R. T. & T. E. LEVERE. 1977. Frontal decortication in rhesus monkeys: a test of the interference hypothesis. Brain Res. **119:** 233–248.
17. KNIGHT, R. T., S. A. HILLARD, D. L. WOODS & H. J. NEVILLE. 1981. The effects of frontal cortex lesions on event-related potentials. Electroenceph. Clin. Neurophysiol. **52:** 571–582.
18. STUSS, D. T., E. F. KAPLAN, D. F. BENSON, W. S. WEIR, S. CHIVILLI & F. F. SARAZIN. 1982. Evidence for the involvement of orbitofrontal cortex in memory functions: an interference effect. J. Comp. Psychol. **7:** 913–925.
19. BROZOSKI, T. J., R. M. BROWN, H. E. ROSVOLD & P. S. GOLDMAN. 1970. Science **215:** 929–932.
20. SIMON, H. B., SCATTON & M. LEMOAL. 1980. Dopaminergic A10 neurons are involved in cognitive functions. Nature **286:** 150–151.
21. BARTUS, R. 1979. Effects of aging on visual memory, sensory processing and discrimination learning in a nonhuman primate. In Sensory Systems and Communication in the Elderly. J. M. Ordy & K. Brizzee, Eds. Raven Press. New York.
22. BARTUS, R. T., D. FLEMING & H. R. JOHNSON. 1978. Aging in the rhesus monkey: debilitating effects on short-term memory. J. Gerontology **33:** 858–7871.
23. BARTUS, R. T. & R. L. DEAN. 1979. Recent memory in aged non-human primates: hypersensitivity to visual interference during retention. Exp. Aging Res. **5:** 385–400.
24. STRUBLE, R. G., L. C. CORK, D. L. PRICE, JR., D. L. PRICE & R. T. DAVIS. 1983. Distribution of neuritic plaques in the cortex of aged rhesus monkeys. Soc. Neurosci. **9:** 927.
25. PRICE, D. L., P. J. WHITEHOUSE, R. G. STRUBLE, D. L. PRICE, JR., L. C. CORK, J. C. HEDREEN & C. A. KITT. 1983. Basal forebrain cholinergic neurons and neuritic plaques in primate brain. Biological Aspects of Alzheimer's Disease. Banbury Rep. **15:** 65–77.
26. GOLDMAN-RAKIC, P. S. & R. M. BROWN. 1981. Regional changes of monoamines in cerebral cortex and subcortical structures of aging rhesus monkeys. Neurosci. **6:** 177–187.
27. SLADEK, J. R. & B. C. BLANCHARD. 1981. Age-related declines in perikaryl monoamine histofluorescence in the Fisher 344 Rat. Aging. **17:** 13–21.
28. FINCH, C. E. 1978. Age-related changes in brain catecholamines; A synopsis of findings in C57BL (6) Mice and other rodent models. Adv. Exp. Med. Biol. **113:** 15–39.
29. CARLSSON, A. 1981. Aging and brain neurotransmitters. In Strategies for the Development of an Effective Treatment for Senile Dementia. T. Crook & S. Gershon, Eds.: 83–104.
30. MISRA, C. H., H. S. SHELAT & R. C. SMITH. 1980. Effect of age on adrenergic and dopaminergic receptor binding in rat brain. Life Sci. **27:** 521–526.
31. WINBLAD, B., R. ADOLFSSON, A. CARLSSON & C-G. GOTTFRIES. 1982. Biogenic amines in brains of patients with Alzheimer's disease. Aging **19:** 26.
32. HERVE, D., G. BLANC, J. GLOWINSKI & J. P. TASSIN. Reduction of dopamine utilization in the prefrontal cortex but not in the nucleus accumbens after selective destruction of noradrenergic fibers innervating the ventral tegmental area in the rat. Brain Res. **237:** 510–516.
33. TASSIN, J. P., H. SIMON, D. HERVE, G. BLANC, M. LE MOAL, M. GLOWINSKI, JR. & J. BOCKAERT. 1982. Non-dopaminergic fibers may regulate dopamine-sensitive adenylate cyclase in the prefrontal cortex and nucleus accumbens. Nature **295:** 696–698.
34. WATERHOUSE, B. D., H. C. MOISES, & D. J. WOODWARD. 1981. Alpha-receptor mediated facilitation of somatosensory cortical neuronal responses to excitatory synaptic inputs and iontophoretically applied acetylcholine. Neuropharm. **20:** 907–920.
35. OSBORNE, D. P., JR. E. R. BROWN & C. T. RANDT. 1982. Qualitative changes in memory function: Aging and dementia. Aging **19.**
36. WILLIAMS, M. 1956. Studies of perception in senile dementia—Cue selection as a function of intelligence. Br. J. Med. Psych. **29:** 177–302.
37. NISSEN, M. J., S. CORKIN & J. H. CROWDON. 1984. Attentional focusing in amnesia and Alzheimer's Disease. (Submitted for publication.)
38. REISBERG, B., S. H. FERRIS, M. J. DE LEON & T. CROOK. 1982. The global deterioration

scale for assessment of primary degenerative dementia. Am. J. Psychiatry **139**: 1136–1139.

39. DAVIES, P., R. KATZMAN & R. D. TERRY. 1980. Reduced somatostatin-like immunoreactivity in cerebral cortex from cases of Alzheimer's Disease and Alzheimer's senile dementia. Nature **288**: 279–280.
40. ROSSOR, M. N., P. C. EMSON, C. Q. MOUNTJOY, M. ROTH & L. L. IVERSEN. 1980. Reduced amounts of immunoreactive somatostatin in the temporal cortex in senile dementia of Alzheimer type. Neurosci. Lett. **20**: 373–377.
41. BOWEN, D. M., S. J. ALLEN, J. S. BENTON, M. J. GOODHARDT, E. A. HAAN, A. M. PALMER, N. R. SIMS, C. C. T. SMITH, J. A. SPILLANE, M. M. ESERI, D. NEARY, J. S. SNOWDON, G. K. WILCOCK & A. N. DAVISON. 1983. Biochemical assessment of serotonergic and cholinergic dysfunction and cerebral atrophy in Alzheimer's Disease. J. Neurochem. **41**: 266–272.
42. ADOLFSSON, R., C. G. GOTTFRIES, B. E. ROOS & B. WINBLAD. 1979. Changes in the brain catecholamines in patients with dementia of Alzheimer Type. Brit. J. Psychiat. **135**: 216–223.
43. BENTON, J. S., D. M. BOWEN, S. J. ALLEN, E. A. HAAN, A. N. DAVISON, D. NEARY, R. P. MURPHY & J. S. SNOWDEN. 1982. Alzheimer's Disease as a disorder of isodendritic core. Lancet **20**: 456.
44. PERRY, E. K., B. E. TOMLINSON, G. BLESSED, R. H. PERRY, A. J. CROSS & T. J. CROW. 1981. Neuropathological and biochemical observations on the noradrenergic system in Alzheimer's Disease. J. Neurol. Sci. **51**: 279–237.
45. FORNO, L. S. 1978. The locus coeruleus in Alzheimer's Disease. Neuropath. Exp. Neurol. **37**: 614.
46. TOMLINSON, B. E., D. IRVING & G. BLESSED. 1981. Cell loss in the locus coeruleus in senile dementia of Alzheimer type. J. Neurol. Sci. **49**: 419–428.
47. IVERSEN, L. L., M. N. ROSSOR, G. P. REYNOLDS, R. HILLS, M. ROTH, C. Q. MOUNTJOY, S. L. FOOTE, J. H. MORRISON & F. E. BLOOM. 1983. Loss of pigmented dopamine-β-hydroxylase positive cells from locus coeruleus in senile dementia of Alzheimer's type. Neurosci. Lett. **39**:95–100.
48. BLOXHAM, C. A., E. K. PERRY, R. H. PERRY & J. M. CANDY. 1984. Neuropathological and neurochemical correlates of Alzheimer type and Parkinsonian dementia. (Submitted for publication.)
49. MCENTEE, W. J. & R. G. MAIR. 1980. Memory enhancement in Korsakoff's psychosis by clonidine: further evidence for a noradrenergic deficit. Ann. Neurol. **7**: 466–470.

Changes in Cerebrospinal Fluid Associated with Dementia

LEON J. THAL

Department of Neurology
Albert Einstein College of Medicine
Bronx, New York 10461

Cerebrospinal fluid (CSF) represents a unique material in that it is the only substance of central nervous system origin that is readily available to the clinician for analysis. Its rate of formation, approximately 0.35 ml/min or 500 ml per day, is remarkably constant. CSF is secreted from the choroid plexus and ultimately absorbed by the arachnoid villi. Since CSF bathes the brain and spinal cord, it is likely that biochemical alterations, changes in activity, or the development of pathological states may be reflected by changes in the CSF.

CSF analysis has been used for a wide variety of functions including determining the presence of infection, tumors, and the presence of abnormal antibodies. The chemical composition of CSF may aid in the diagnosis of diseases in which an alteration in neurotransmitter function occurs. Neurotransmitter metabolites are readily measurable in CSF and provide an index of neurotransmitter function in adjacent brain tissue. The best known alteration in CSF neurotransmitter metabolite level is the decrease in homovanillic acid (HVA), a metabolite of dopamine, in the CSF of patients with Parkinson's disease.[1] A second clinically important abnormality is the elevation of CSF IgG in certain chronic infections, such as syphilis or viral encephalitis, and in multiple sclerosis.

In Alzheimer's disease and most other dementias there is presently no biochemical marker available for the clinician or researcher to confirm the clinical diagnosis. Since a number of transmitter and protein abnormalities have been defined in the brains of Alzheimer disease patients, many investigators have attempted to find a suitable biological marker in CSF for Alzheimer disease and other dementias.

ROUTINE ANALYSIS AND PROTEINS

Routine analysis of CSF glucose, protein, and cell count does not distinguish Alzheimer's disease patients from age-matched controls, although some investigators have reported a decrease in total protein[2,3] as shown in TABLE 1. More recently, several reports of abnormal proteins in CSF of dementia patients have appeared. Using CSF enriched in CSF-specific proteins coupled with isoelectric focusing, abnormal protein patterns were found in all CSF samples from Alzheimer patients, but in no patients with multi-infarct dementia or controls.[4] Agarose gel electrophoresis of CSF has also been reported to show abnormal bands in the gamma-globulin region in five out of eight Alzheimer patients.[5] The possibility that abnormal proteins are present in CSF seems quite plausible in view of the presence of paired helical filaments, an abnormal brain protein found in the brains of patients with Alzheimer's disease. However, the marked insolubility of the paired helical filament may result in the release of little or no abnormal protein into CSF, making clinical detection quite difficult.

TABLE 1. Protein Content of Cerebrospinal Fluid

Source	Controls	Alzheimer's	Percent Decrease
Lumbar CSF[2]	58 ± 3.6(9)	48 ± 2.9(21)[a]	17
Ventricular CSF[3]	107 ± 19(14)	40 ± 3.9(21)[b]	63

Values are in mg/100 ml ± S.E. Number of samples in parentheses. [a]$p < 0.05$, [b]$p < 0.025$.

CONVENTIONAL NEUROTRANSMITTERS

Glutamic acid decarboxylase (GAD), the synthetic enzyme for γ-aminobutyric acid (GABA), is decreased in Alzheimer's disease[6] as is GABA itself.[7] However, GAD is profoundly affected by agonal states and the interpretation of the available data is open to question. Several groups have reported an approximately 50% decrease in CSF GABA in several neurological disorders including Alzheimer's disease and Huntington's chorea[8,9] as shown in TABLE 2. However, more recent work has noted lower overall levels, a decline in CSF GABA with aging, and no change in CSF GABA in Alzheimer's disease when using age matched controls.[10] While the definitive study of CSF GABA in dementia remains to be done, based on the data currently available, it seems unlikely that changes in GABA levels will be either large enough or specific enough to be useful as a marker for Alzheimer's disease.

CATECHOLAMINES AND SEROTONIN

During normal aging, there is a decline in regional dopamine, norepinephrine, and serotonin content.[11-15] The enzymes, tyrosine hydroxylase and aromatic amino acid decarboxylase, decrease while monoamine oxidase B increases.[16] In Alzheimer's disease, decreases in cortical norepinephrine and serotonin as well as decreases in striatal and hypothalamic dopamine have been reported.[17] Loss of locus coeruleus cells further bolsters the concept of a noradrenergic loss in Alzheimer's disease.[18] Whether these changes are specific for Alzheimer's disease and whether neurotransmitter changes that are generally less than 50% are clinically meaningful remains an open question.

Catecholamine and serotonin metabolites are readily detectable in lumbar CSF. Since the majority of dopamine is in the basal ganglia, homovanillic acid (HVA) is an excellent index of central dopaminergic metabolism.[18] The major norepinephrine metabolite, 3-methoxy-4-hydroxyphenylglycol (MHPG), arises largely from central norepinephrine metabolism,[20] while the major serotonin metabolite, 5-hydroxyindoleacetic acid (5-HIAA), is derived largely from spinal cord.[21]

Major changes in the metabolism of these transmitters should be reflected by

TABLE 2. Cerebrospinal Fluid GABA Content

Controls	Alzheimer's	Percent Decrease
230 ± 24(26)[9]	120 (3)	48
239 ± 13(42)[8]	144 ± 36(5)[a]	40
28.3 ± 7.5(8)[10]	26.3 ± 4.4(14)	7

All values are in pmoles/ml ± S.E. Number of samples are in parentheses. [a]$p < 0.001$.

TABLE 3. Cerebrospinal Fluid HVA

Controls	Alzheimer's	Percent Decrease
60 ± 7.1(20)[22]	23 ± 4.3(15)[a]	62
67.5 ± 3.7(8)[10]	27.5 ± 4.2(16)[b]	59
23.3 ± 3.2(8)[23]	20.2 ± 3.2(14)	13
52.0 ± 4.7(32)[25]	46.4 ± 7.6(11)	11
33 ± 16(12)[24]	29 ± 12(5)	10

All values are in ng/ml ± S.E. Number of subjects in parentheses. [a] $p < 0.01$, [b] $p < 0.001$.

changes in CSF. Some investigators have reported about a 50% decrease in lumbar HVA in Alzheimer's disease[10,22] while others have reported no change[23-25] (TABLE 3). Two reports note normal MHPG levels in lumbar CSF[23,25] while most authors agree that 5-HIAA remains unchanged.[10,22,23] Overall, decreases in HVA seem to be fairly consistent in a subgroup of patients with dementia and the decrease appears to be more pronounced as the dementia advances. HVA levels, however, do not decline in only Alzheimer's disease and, therefore, they do not represent a specific finding for this disease.

CHOLINERGIC SYSTEMS

Of all the neurotransmitter changes in Alzheimer's disease, the decrease in presynaptic cholinergic markers is the most profound. Choline acetyltransferase (CAT) is decreased by 85–90% in cortex;[6,26] acetylcholinesterase (ACHE) is similarly decreased.[6] Direct measurements of acetylcholine (ACH) are difficult because this compound is rapidly hydrolyzed. While no large scale studies of ACH in Alzheimer's disease have been carried out, one investigator reported a significant correlation between CSF ACH levels and test scores on a memory-information test in patients with Alzheimer's disease.[27] ACHE has been reported to be decreased in lumbar CSF[2] and ventricular CSF[3] from Alzheimer patients. Others have reported no difference as indicated in TABLE 4. The available data, suggesting a decrease in ACHE, must be cautiously interpreted, since if the ACHE values are corrected for CSF protein content, significant differences disappear. This observation suggests that the apparent decline in ACHE may be a dilutional effect secondary to ventricular enlargement during the dementing process. Nevertheless, because of the importance of the cholinergic system in Alzheimer's disease, attempts to establish a valid CSF cholinergic marker are justified.

TABLE 4. Cerebrospinal Fluid Acetylcholinesterase

Controls	Alzheimer's	Percent Decrease
37.5 ± 3.3(9)[2]	25.1 ± 1.6(21)[a]	−33
15.2 ± 3.5(14)[3]	5.7 ± 1.7(9)[a]	−63
13.3(46)[6]	13.6(28)	+2
26 ± 1.3(32)[25]	27 ± 2(11)	+4

All values are in nmoles/min/ml ± SE. All are lumbar fluids except Appleyard,[2] which is ventricular fluid. Number of samples in parentheses. [a] $p < 0.005$ and [b] $p < 0.025$.

NEUROPEPTIDES

A large number of neuropeptides have been measured in brain tissue from patients with Alzheimer's disease including somatostatin, cholecystokinin, vasoactive intestinal peptide, enkephalin, thyrotropin releasing hormone, neurotensin, vasopressin, oxytocin, and Substance P. The only peptides showing definite abnormalities in Alzheimer's disease include the well established decrease in somatostatin[28-30] and a single report of a smaller decrease in Substance P.[31]

There are three reports of a decrease in CSF somatostatin in Alzheimer's disease averaging approximately 50%[25,32,33] and one report of no change in patients with early dementia[34] as indicated in TABLE 5. Although changes in somatostatin are likely to be confirmed in future series of patients studied, decreases have also been found in Huntington's chorea,[35] Parkinson's disease,[36] and multiple sclerosis.[37] The decrease in CSF somatostatin may well parallel the decrease in brain concentrations. However, considerable overlap exists between patients with dementia and controls.

A number of other peptides have also been examined in the CSF of patients with Alzheimer's disease. These include the finding of normal VIP levels,[38] both elevated[39] and depressed[40] vasopressin concentrations, and decreased TRH levels.[32] These CSF neuropeptide data are too scanty for interpretation, since most studies involve small numbers of patients and a wide variation of the values.

TABLE 5. Cerebrospinal Fluid Somatostatin

Controls	Alzheimer's	Percent Decrease
$48 \pm 6.9(17)^{32}$	$12.9 \pm 2(16)^a$	73
$52 (19)^{25}$	$22 (11)^b$	58
$46.6 \pm 4.1(15)^{33}$	$31.3 \pm 3.1(21)^b$	33
$34.9 \pm 3.9(8)^{34}$	$34 \pm 4.8(5)$	3

All values are in pg/ml $\pm$ SE. Number of samples in parentheses. $^a p < 0.001$ and $^b p < 0.05$.

USE OF CSF TO MONITOR DRUG THERAPIES

A number of therapeutic trials have been conducted using compounds that may augment cholinergic transmission. A key issue that must be raised during such trials is whether or not the administered compound reaches the central nervous system. To answer this question, the compound in question, or a metabolite, may be measured in CSF to estimate entry of the compound into brain. Thus, after L-DOPA treatment in Parkinson's disease, CSF HVA levels increase markedly[41] while after L-5-hydroxytryptophan treatment, CSF 5-HIAA levels increase.[42] Following choline treatment for memory loss in Alzheimer's disease, CSF choline levels increase,[43] suggesting that the lack of clinical improvement following choline administration is not due to a failure of choline to reach the brain.

Treatment of Alzheimer patients with oral physostigmine has resulted in extremely variable degrees of improvement. One investigator noted improvements in retrieval from long-term storage that vary from 3 to 79 in different patients with a decrease in intrusions, or incorrect responses, ranging from 10 to 71%.[34] When CSF cholinesterase inhibition was measured as an index of entry of physostigmine into the central nervous system, it became apparent that patient response to physostigmine correlated with CSF cholinesterase inhibition. Multiple factors including gastrointestinal absorption, peripheral metabolism, transport across the blood-brain barrier, and central metabolism may ultimately influence brain and CSF levels of administered compounds. As technology improves, we should be able to measure an increasingly large number of administered compounds in CSF, such as tetrahydroaminoacridine, a cholinesterase inhibitor, and 4-amino-pyridine, a compound that stimulates the release of acetylcholine.

FUTURE DIRECTIONS

Although it seems unlikely that detection of a single neurotransmitter abnormality in Alzheimer's disease will ever be powerful enough to biochemically identify individuals with the disease, a pattern of neurotransmitter abnormalities might emerge that is unique to this disorder. For example, the disease may be characterized by selective decreases in acetylcholine and somatostatin, while in other dementing illnesses, other patterns of neurotransmitter deficits may appear.

A second approach may be an even more powerful tool for identifying afflicted individuals. It seems likely that abnormal antigens are present in the brains of Alzheimer patients. For example, paired helical filaments represent an unusual protein not found in normal brain tissue. Other antigens may also be present in Alzheimer's disease. The use of monoclonal antibody techniques may allow for the identification of minute quantities of specific antigens released into CSF from brain tissue. Identification of these antigens may result in the development of a highly sensitive and specific method of identifying individuals with this disease.

REFERENCES

1. BERNHEIMER, H. W., W. BIRKMAYER & P. HORNYKIEWICZ. 1966. Cerebrospinal fluid proteins in multi-infarct and senile dementia. J. Neurol. Sci. **49:** 293–303.
2. SOININEN, H. T., T. HALONEN, & P. J. RIEKKINEN. 1981. Acetyl-cholinesterase activities in cerebrospinal fluid of patients with senile dementia of the Alzheimer type. Acta Neurol. Scand. **64:** 217–224.
3. APPLEYARD, M. E., A. D. SMITH, G. K. WILCOCK & M. M. ESIRI. 1983. Decreased CSF acetylcholinesterase activity in Alzheimer's disease. Lancet **ii:** 452.
4. WIKKELS, C., C. BLOMSTRAND & L. RÖNNBÄCK. 1981. Cerebrospinal fluid proteins in multi-infarct and senile dementia. J. Neurol. Sci. **49:** 293–303.
5. WILLIAMS, A., N. PAPODOPOULOS & T. N. CHASE. 1980. Demonstration of CSF gamma-globulin banding in presenile dementia. Neurology **30:** 882–884.
6. DAVIES, P. 1979. Neurotransmitter-related enzymes in senile dementia of the Alzheimer type. Brain Res. **171:** 319–327.
7. ROSSOR, M. N., P. C. EMSON, L. L. IVERSEN, C. O. MOUNTJOY, M. ROTH, J. FAHRENKRUG & J. F. REHFELD. 1982. Neuropeptides and neurotransmitters in cerebral cortex. Aging **19:** 15–24.
8. BALA MANYAM, N. V., L. KATZ, T. HARE, J. GERBER & M. GROSSMAN. 1980. Levels of γ-aminobutyric acid in cerebrospinal fluid in various neurologic disorders. Arch. Neurol. **37:** 352–355.
9. ENNA, S. J., L. STERN, G. WASTEK & H. YAMAMURA. 1977. Cerebrospinal fluid γ-aminobutyric acid variations in neurological disorders. Arch. Neurol. **34:** 683–685.
10. BAREGGI, S. R., M. FRANCESCHI, L. BONINI, L. ZECCA & S. SMIRNE. 1982. Decreased CSF concentrations of homovanillic acid and γ-aminobutyric acid in Alzheimer's disease, age, or disease-related modifications? Arch. Neurol. **39:** 709–712.
11. BERTLER, A. 1961. Occurrence and localization of catechol amines in the human brain. Acta Physiol. Scand. **51:** 97–107.

12. CARLSSON, A. & B. WINDBLAD. 1976. Influence of age and time interval between death and autopsy on dopamine and 3-methoxytyramine levels in human basal ganglia. J. Neurol. Trans. **38:** 271–276.

13. NIES, A., D. S. ROBINSON, J. M. DAVIS & L. RAVARIS. 1973. Changes in monoamine oxidase with aging. *In* Psychopharmacology and Aging. C. Eisdorfer & W. E. Fann, Eds.: 41–54. Plenum Press. New York.

14. ROBINSON, D. S. 1975. Changes in monoamine oxidase and monoamines with human development and aging. Fed. Proc. **34:** 103–107.

15. ROBINSON, D. S., J. M. DAVIS, A. NEIS, R. W. COLBURN, J. N. DAVIS, H. R. BOURNE, W. E. BUNNEY, D. M. SHAW & A. J. COPPER. 1972. Aging, monoamines and monoamine-oxidase levels. Lancet **1:** 290–291.

16. MCGEER, E. G. 1978. Aging and neurotransmitter metabolism in the human brain. *In* Alzheimer's Disease: Senile Dementia and Related Disorders. R. Katzman, R. D. Terry & K. L. Bick, Eds.: 427–440. Raven Press. New York.

17. WINDBLAD, B., R. ADOLFSSON, A. CARLSSON & C.-G. GOTTFRIES. 1982. Biogenic amines in brains of patients with Alzheimer's disease. Neurol. **39:** 25–33.

18. BONDAREFF, W., C. O. MOUNTJOY & M. ROTH. 1981. Selective loss of neurones of origin or adrenergic projection to the central cortex (nucleus locus coeruleus) in senile dementia. Lancet **1:** 783–784.

19. WOOD, J. H. 1980. Site of origin and concentration gradients of neurotransmitters, their metabolites and cyclic nucleotides in cerebrospinal fluid. *In* Neurobiology of Spinal Fluid. I. J. H. Wood, Ed. Plenum Publishing Corp. New York.

20. CHASE, T. N., E. K. GORDON & L. K. Y. NG. 1973. Norepinephrine metabolism in the central nervous system of man: Studies using 3-methoxy-4-hydroxyphenylethylene glycol levels in cerebrospinal fluid. J. Neurochem. **21:** 581–587.

21. BULAT, M. 1977. On the cerebral origin of 5-hydroxyindole-acetic acid in the lumbar cerebrospinal fluid. Brain Res. **122:** 388–391.

22. GOTTFRIES, C.-G. & B. E. ROOS. 1973. Acid monoamine metabolites in cerebrospinal fluid from patients with presenile dementia. Acta Psychiat. Scand. **49:** 257–263.

23. MANN, J. J., M. STANLEY, A. NEOPHYTIDES, M. J. DE LEON, S. H. FERRIS & S. GERSHON. 1981. Central amine metabolism in Alzheimer's disease: in vivo relationship to cognitive deficit. Neurobiol. Aging **2:** 57–60.

24. BOWEN, D. M., N. R. SIMS, J. S. BENTON, G. CURZON, A. N. DAVISON, D. NEARY & D. J. THOMAS. 1981. Treatment of Alzheimer's disease—a cautionary note. Lancet **II:** 1016.

25. WOOD, P. L., P. ETIENNE, S. LAL, S. GAUTHIER, S. CAJAL & N. P. V. NAIR. 1982. Reduced lumbar CSF somatostatin levels in Alzheimer's disease. Life Sci. **31:** 2073–2079.

26. BOWEN, D. M., C. B. SMITH, D. WHITE & A. N. DAVISON. 1976. Neurotransmitter-related enzymes and indices of hypoxia in senile dementia and other abiotrophies. Brain **99:** 459–496.

27. DAVIS, K. L., J. HSIEK, M. I. LEVY, T. B. HORVATH, B. M. DAVIS & R. C. MOHS. 1982. Cerebrospinal fluid acetylcholine, choline and senile dementia of the Alzheimer's type. Psychopharm. Bull. **18:** 193–195.

28. DAVIES, P. & R. D. TERRY. 1981. Cortical somatostatin-like immunoreactivity in cases of Alzheimer's disease and senile dementia of the Alzheimer's type. Neurobiol. Aging **2:** 9–14.

29. ROSSOR, M. M., P. C. EMSON, C. O. MOUNTJOY, M. ROTH & L. L. IVERSEN. 1980. Reduced amounts of immunoreactive somatostatin in the temporal cortex in senile dementia of the Alzheimer type. Neurosci. Lett. **20:** 373–377.

30. PERRY, R. H., G. J. DOCKRAY, R. DIMALINE, E. G. PERRY, G. BLESSED & B. E. TOMLINSON. 1981. Neuropeptides in Alzheimer's disease, depression, and schizophrenia. A post mortem analysis of vasoactive intestinal peptide and cholecystokinin in cerebral cortex. J. Neurol. Sci. **51:** 465–472.

31. CRYSTAL, H. A. & P. DAVIES. 1982. Cortical Substance P-like immunoreactivity in cases of Alzheimer's disease and senile dementia of the Alzheimer type. J. Neurochem. **38:** 1781–1784.

32. ORAM, J. J., J. EDWARDSEN & P. H. MILLARD. 1981. Investigation of cerebrospinal fluid neuropeptides in idiopathic senile dementia. Gerontology **27:** 216–223.

33. BEAL, M. F., J. H. GROWDON & M. F. MAZAREK. 1984. CSF somatostatin in dementia. Neurology **34** (supplement): 120.
34. THAL, L. J., D. M. MASUR, P. A. FULD, N. S. SHARPLESS & P. DAVIES. 1983. Memory improvement with oral physostigmine and lecithin in Alzheimer's disease. *In* Biological Aspects of Alzheimer's Disease. R. Katzman, Ed. Banbury Report. Vol. 15. Cold Spring Harbor Laboratory. New York.
35. CRAMER, H., J. KOHLER, G. OEPEN, G. SCHOMBURG & E. SCHROTER. 1981. Huntington's chorea-measurements of somatostatin, Substance P and cyclic nucleotides in the cerebrospinal fluid. J. Neurol. **225**: 183–187.
36. DUPONT, E., S. E. CHRISTENSEN, A. P. HANSEN, B. F. OLIVARIUS & H. ORSKOV. 1982. Low cerebospinal fluid somatostatin in Parkinson disease: An irreversible abnormality. Neurology **32**: 213–314.
37. SØRENSEN, K. V., S. E. CHRISTENSEN, E. DUPONT, A. P. HANSEN, E. PEDERSEN & H. ORSKOV. 1980. Low somatostatin content in cerebrospinal fluid in multiple sclerosis. Acta Neurol. Scand. **61**: 186–191.
38. SHARPLESS, N. S., L. J. THAL, M. J. PERLOW, K. TABADDOR, J. M. WALTZ, K. N. SHAPIRO, I. M. AMIN, J. ENGEL, JR. & P. H. CRANDEL. 1984. Vasoactive intestinal peptide in cerebrospinal fluid peptides. (In press.)
39. TSUJI, M., S. TAKUHUSHI & S. AKAZAWA. 1981. CSF vasopressin and cyclic nucleotide concentrations in senile dementia. Psychoneuroendocrinology **6**: 171–176.
40. SØRENSEN, P. S., M. HAMMER, S. VORSTRUP & F. GJENIS. 1983. CSF and plasma vasopressin concentrations in dementia. J. Neurol. Neurosurg. Psych. **46**: 911–916.
41. DAVIDSON, D. L. W., C. M. YATES, C. MAWDSLEY, I. A. PULLAR & H. WILSON. 1977. CSF studies on the relationship between dopamine and 5-hydroxytryptamine in Parkinsonism and other movement disorders. J. Neurol. Neurosurg. Psych. **40**: 1136–1141.
42. THAL, L. J., N. S. SHARPLESS, L. WOLFSON & R. KATZMAN. 1980. Treatment of myoclonus with L-5-hydroxytryptophan and carbidopa: Clinical, electrophysiological and biochemical observations. Ann. Neurol. **7**: 570–576.
43. CHRISTIE, J. E., I. M. BLACKBURN, A. I. M. GLEN, S. ZEISEL, A. SHERING & C. M. YATES. 1979. Effects of choline and lecithin in CSF choline levels and in cognitive function in patients with presenile dementia of the Alzheimer type. Brain **5**: 377–387.

Catecholamine System Involvement in Age-related Memory Dysfunction

STEVEN F. ZORNETZER[a]

Office of Naval Research
Arlington, Virginia 22217

INTRODUCTION

There is a large and growing literature describing the many age-related psychobiological changes associated with memory decline in aging.[11,22,42,44] The reader interested in delving further into these topics should additionally consider these excellent reviews.

Pioneering studies by Ruch[65] and Gilbert[35] demonstrated clearly that, relative to young adults, the aged exhibit a decline in performance on tests of learning and memory capabilities. Once age-related performance deficits were established, experimental attention focused on identifying the particular aspects of cognitive functioning that are impaired with aging. There has been, and continues to be, a decided lack of agreement on this matter. In particular, changes in both nonspecific processes and in memory-specific processes have been invoked to account for the same behavioral performance deficits.[36] The complicated task of localizing the source of cognitive impairment associated with aging is our goal as students of brain and behavior.

NEUROBIOLOGICAL STUDIES

The Search for a Neurobiological Substrate

There is an important caveat that needs to be mentioned from the outset. The study of neurobiological and associated behavioral changes occurring with normal aging is often blurred by the study of these same phenomena in age-related "pathological" conditions. This is best illustrated by the recent proliferation of interest in, and new data pertaining to, senile dementia of the Alzheimer's type (SDAT). If, as some have suggested (see below), SDAT is nothing more than an acceleration of normal aging processes, then data obtained from normal aging animals (which do not develop SDAT) may indeed be a valid model for studying some aspects of human SDAT. Conversely, clinical-pathological correlates of human SDAT may provide important insights into normal aging. Of course, we should keep in mind that this need not be the case at all, and that the basic assumption may be faulty, i.e., data obtained from normal aged organisms might have little or no relationship to SDAT and vice versa.

[a]Mailing Address: Dr. Steven F. Zornetzer, Associate Director for Life Sciences, Office of Naval Research, 800 North Quincy Street, Arlington, Virginia 22217.

SDAT as a Research Focal Point

A common deficit in both normal aging and SDAT is a decline in memory. The dramatic loss of cholinergic neurons observed in senile dementia of the Alzheimer's type (SDAT) has led to the hypothesis that degeneration of cholinergic systems may be responsible for the loss of higher order function in these individuals. Recent data suggest that there is a relation between the severity of the clinical expression of SDAT and transmitter-specific changes in cholinergic neurons located in the basal forebrain.[13,21,59] These cholinergic neuron changes are believed to occur specifically in magnocellular cholinergic basal forebrain systems located in the medial septum, diagonal band of Broca, and nucleus basalis of Meynert. These data, coupled with the recent hypothesis[61] that degenerating cholinergic neurons and terminals originating in basal forebrain give rise to neuritic plaques, support the growing conventional wisdom that pathogenetic processes primary to the basal forebrain cholinergic system are closely associated with SDAT.

Since SDAT is thought to represent an acceleration of normal aging processes, it has been proposed that cholinergic dysfunction may underlie normal age-related memory deficits.[24,25] The finding that, in young subjects, blockage of cholinergic systems results in interruption of normal memory processes[23] has strengthened this hypothesis. Disturbingly, however, interventive strategies designed to stimulate cholinergic systems have not resulted in significant generalized improvement in age-related memory loss.[30,54,55,70]

Multiple Neurotransmitter Involvement

Although basal forebrain cholinergic activity has taken "center stage" with respect to its pathogenetic importance in age-related memory loss, it is very unlikely, given our current knowledge of brain complexity, that any single neurotransmitter would selectively and exclusively be involved in disorders of cognitive function and memory.[37,71] Other neurotransmitter systems have been implicated in normal memory processes, particularly catecholamines and opioids.[34,53,68,73] A growing literature has also described multiple neurochemical,[33,62,67] neuroanatomical,[47,64] and behavioral[7,8,10,36,45,74] changes in aged animals. It is therefore possible that aged-related memory deficits may result from concurrent changes in several neurotransmitter systems. This point can be made even more strongly in the case of SDAT, in which widespread degeneration and cell loss is seen in postmortem tissue.[15,16] Rather than review the entire morphologic and neurotransmitter literature on age-related brain changes, let us focus upon available data for noncholinergic neuronal systems believed to employ primarily a single neurotransmitter. For purposes of both example and personal interest, the paragraphs below will focus on the noradrenergic nucleus locus coeruleus (LC).

Vijayashankar and Brody[69] were the first to report significant cell loss of LC neurons in senescent human brain. These data were extended by Bondereff et al.,[12] who recently reported that in patients with SDAT, cell loss in LC was significantly greater than occurred with normal aging. Further, two subclasses of Alzheimer's patients could be identified; a group having severe cognitive impairment and 80% cell loss in LC, and a less impaired group with correspondingly less LC cell loss. Most recently, Mann et al.[50] compared directly, cell loss and nucleus volume changes in both nucleus basalis and the LC from brains of Alzheimer's patients. Their findings indicated that in individuals under 80 years of age, the extent of cellular loss and damage in the LC exceeded that in nucleus basalis. Collectively, these data are particularly exciting for a number of reasons. First, the LC system, like the basal forebrain cholinergic system, constitutes a neurotransmitter-specific (norepinephrine) brain region that shows significant cell loss with both normal aging and SDAT. Second, and importantly, the extent of cell loss in LC appears directly correlated with the degree of impaired cognitive function. This second point is interesting in that it parallels the observations and speculations that the four major pathomnemonic findings in Alzheimer's disease (neurofibrillary tangles, senile plaques, granulo-vacuolar degeneration, and Hirano bodies) are similarly related in prevalence to the severity of impaired cognitive function. Accordingly, all of these changes are also found in normal aged brains, but they are quantitatively more frequent in brains from SDAT patients.[4] These data from the noradrenergic LC suggest that age-related cognitive decline may be quantitatively related to transmitter-specific dysfunction(s).

Other, more functional data, support these morphological findings regarding catecholamine-specific cell loss in normal aging and SDAT. Several investigations have reported reduced activity of catecholamine systems in aged rat brain.[3,31,32] Further, a reduced activity with age of tyrosine hydroxylase, the rate limiting enzyme in the synthesis of catecholamines, has been reported for man[20,52] and rodents.[3] Postmortem studies in man have reported reduced levels of dopamine (DA) and norepinephrine (NE) related to age.[2,18]

Clearly, from this brief discussion of the data describing age-related changes in catecholamine systems, there is good reason for us to consider the possibility that these systems, particularly the noradrenergic nucleus locus coeruleus, may be as important as the age-related changes occurring in basal forebrain cholinergic systems, which have received greater attention. Further, there is considerable additional support for the idea that the LC system plays an essential modulatory role in metabolic,[1] sensorimotor,[5] attentional,[51] and higher order (memory) functions,[73] in normal-aged subjects. These data, coupled with both published and new data (see below) from my own laboratory, strongly reinforce the hypothesis that functional decline of the noradrenergic LC system may be directly implicated in normal age-related cognitive decline and the more precipitous functional decline observed in SDAT.

Recent anatomical studies have suggested that there are several brain loci where functional interactions could occur between the locus coeruleus, nucleus basalis, and other neurotransmitter-defined systems of interest (e.g., the dopamine cells of the substantia nigra-ventral tegmental area and the widespread opiate-containing systems). Of particular interest here are the interactions between noradrenergic (NE) neurons of the locus coeruleus and cholinergic neurons (ACh) of the nucleus basalis. Although it is known that LC axons traverse the basal forebrain regions that contain nucleus basalis neurons,[28,29] there has not been convincing evidence that LC innervates these neurons. Based on the density of the LC fibers in these regions, such a projection would be sparse at best. Likewise, a projection from nucleus basalis neurons to the locus coeruleus has not been demonstrated. The presence of moderately dense AChE-positive neuropil in, and around, the LC could be the dendrites of AChE-positive cells (choliceptive but not cholinergic) or another cholinergic input. A more likely site of noradrenergic-cholinergic interaction is in the cerebral cortex, where dense noradrenergic[57] and cholinergic[41] innervation overlaps, especially in layers I and II. A more isolated, but nonetheless dense, catecholamine innervation of layer II of supragenual cortex arises in the central tegmental area.[48,56] Connections between the two major catecholamine cell groups could provide a second level of interaction. These include the innervation of the LC by the ventral tegmental area and a possible reciprocal innervation of the ventral tegmental area by the LC.[43]

Another important consideration to keep in mind is the role of opiate interactions with the catecholamine and cholinergic systems. In this regard, there is some evidence for anatomical projections of opiate-containing neurons to cholinergic neurons of the basal forebrain (Fallon, personal communication) and locus coeruleus.[38] Reciprocal projections of the cell groups to opiate-containing cells are unknown, but based on the widespread localization of opiate cell bodies and terminals, such connections may exist and could be significant in the etiology of SDAT.

As an interim summary, it can be concluded that a number of projections could account for interactions between cholinergic, catecholaminergic, and opiate systems as they relate to SDAT. The regions of greatest potential for interaction of cholinergic and catecholaminergic systems are the superficial layers of the cerebral cortex.

In 1976, studies were begun in young adult rodents implicating an important role of the nucleus locus coeruleus in memory processes.[72,73] These studies were amplified and further supported by others.[37,71] One particularly interesting study[68] reported that pharmacological inhibition of brain NE synthesis resulted in impaired memory. Administration of NE directly into forebrain ventricular systems, thereby bypassing synthesis inhibition, restored normal memory function.

As discussed above, aged organisms, ranging from man to mice, develop memory dysfunction. Recently, my laboratory has begun studying these age-related memory impairments in aged rats and mice.[44,45,74] One conclusion from the data obtained to date is that, generally, aged rodents do not have severe acquisition or learning deficits. Rather, they have an accelerated loss of recently acquired information, i.e., they forget faster then do young rodents. This accelerated loss of recently acquired information appears quite general to a variety of learning-memory situations (i.e., short-term, intermediate-term, and long-term memory[74]).

Considerable interest and effort has been (and is being) devoted to developing effective interventive, usually pharmacologic, strategies to ameliorate these age-related memorial and cognitive deficits.[26,39,40,49,66] In general, two main thrusts are being used. The first involves administration of agents that increase the efficacy of the cholinergic system in the brain. Such treatments include precursor loading with lecithin and/or choline[14,55] or administration of cholinesterase inhibitors.[25] The second thrust has led to the development of a new class of pharmacologic agents, the nootropics, believed to improve cognitive function in the aged. Accordingly, agents such as piracetam, hydergine, vincamine, centrophenoxine, etc., which have varied actions on brain blood flow and/or metabolism,[6] are being tested. To date, their efficacy in improving cognitive function in the elderly is not convincing.

A careful evaluation of each of these research thrusts leads to two observations: there has been an excessively narrow and exclusive focus upon the cholinergic system and memory impairment and the data reported thus far are collectively neither convincing nor impressive (with occasional notable exception[9]). Perhaps the latter observation is derived from the former observation?

Manipulation of central catecholamines in aging brain represents an additional strategy to supplement the two research strategies described briefly above. The NE-containing locus coeruleus (LC) is certainly another candidate transmitter-specific system likely to be involved in cognitive function. The fact that LC neurons and their terminal field receptors show widespread age-related changes, makes it an ideal system to study. Accordingly, the question asked in the study reported below was, "Can experimental manipulation of the LC alter normally expected age-related memory decline?" The results provide exciting new data suggesting that age-related memory failure in senescent rodents can be significantly retarded as a result of direct LC modulation. A brief description of these experiments follows.

The initial phase of the experiment simply documented, using the male C57BL/6J mouse, that aged (24 months) animals remember more poorly than young (5 months) controls. To demonstrate this, we used a single-trial step-down inhibitory avoidance apparatus.[45] The results are shown in FIGURE 1.

The second phase of the experiment was designed to test directly the hypothesis stated above. Groups of mice, either five months or 18 months at the start of the experiment, were surgically prepared, using stereotaxic procedures, with chronic indwelling electrodes targeted bilaterally for the LC. This is a well-established procedure in my laboratory.[60]

Following a 10-day postsurgical recovery period, the mice began an electrical stimulation regimen consisting of regular stimulation of the LC at 48-hour intervals for a period of six months. Thus, at the termination of this prolonged intermittent electric stimulation period, mice were either 11 months or 24 months of age. Stimulation parameters were either 100 μA or 50 μA current at 60 HZ using 0.1 msec biphasic pulses. Each stimulation session lasted 10 minutes, with stimulation actually administered intermittently during this period.

The third phase of the experiment began one week after the last electrical stimulation was administered. All mice were trained in the step-down inhibitory avoidance task. Mice were then tested 24 hours later for retention of the shock avoidance response. Following the behavioral experiments, all mice were sacrificed and electrode tip location was histologically verified. As the results shown in FIGURE 2 indicate, 24-month-old sham-stimulated mice typically forget (i.e., have a shorter step-down latency) the inhibitory avoidance response when tested 24 hours after learning. The data from the 24-month-old mice having had received chronic and repeated LC electrical stimulation are shown in FIGURE 2.

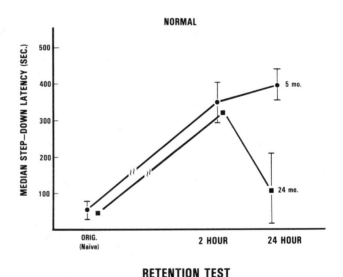

FIGURE 1. Median step-down latency (sec.) of aged and young C57BL/67 male mice. The figure indicates that original step-down latencies in naive mice did not differ between young and aged groups. When tested two hours after training, both young and aged mice had a long step-down latency suggesting good memory of the inhibitory avoidance response. Independent groups of mice tested 24 hours after training indicated that aged, but not young, mice now had a significant ($p < .02$) performance deficit suggesting memory loss.

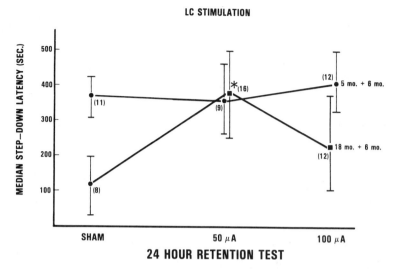

FIGURE 2. The effects of prior six month intermittent electrical stimulation of the LC upon memory of the inhibitory avoidance response. All stimulation was ended one week prior to training. The data indicate that stimulation at 50 μA current resulted in significant facilitation in performance in aged mice. Young mice, curiously, were not affected by the treatment. The higher current level (150 μA) did not result in significant facilitation of performance.

As these data indicate, regular repeated prior electrical stimulation of the LC resulted in an improved performance compared to aged controls, when tested 24 hours after learning. In fact, performance of the LC-stimulated (50 μA) aged mice were indistinguishable from that of young controls.

Surgical intervention and electrode implantation in the brain represent a rather extreme procedure for ameliorating age-related memory decline. In an attempt to circumvent this problem a pharmacological approach seemed more desirable. Accordingly, our first pharmacological approach to LC activation involved the use of piperoxane, an α_2-noradrenergic receptor blocking agent shown to have an excitatory action upon LC neurons[19] when administered systemically. Piperoxane is believed to activate LC neurons by directly blocking auto- and collateral inhibition in the LC. These intranuclear inhibitory projections utilize the α_2-receptor. Thus, α_2 blockade results in release from inhibition and greater LC cell firing.[19] Presumably, elevated LC cell firing would result in correspondingly greater synaptic release of NE at the many terminal fields of the LC in forebrain and other brain regions.

The experimental protocol was designed to parallel the electrical stimulation experiment just described. Mice, five months and 18 months of age, at the start of the experiment were divided into independent groups. Animals received either 0.5 or 1.5 mg/kg piperoxane or saline i.p. Injections were given once every 48 hours for six months. Injection sites were systematically varied to avoid producing peritoneal irritation or infection.

At the end of the six-month drug administration period, all mice had a one-week drug-free period prior to behavioral training and memory testing. At the end of this week, mice were trained and tested on the step-down inhibitory avoidance task, as described previously.

The results of this experiment are shown in FIGURE 3. Twenty-four-month old mice who had received repeated administration of piperoxane showed no performance deficit compared to young controls. Aged saline control mice performed as expected, i.e., these mice had a significant age-related performance deficit when tested 24 hours after training. It should be noted that prior long-term piperoxane treatment did not appear to alter initial step-down latencies in the mice. This observation would argue against the possibility that the piperoxane effect was due merely to altered activity or anxiety levels. These data are interpreted to suggest that piperoxane, a pharmacological agent capable of increasing LC cell activity, is also capable of significantly reducing age-related memory impairment.

A final experiment in this series evaluated forgetting in a normal young control population compared to normal aged and experimentally treated aged mice from the above described experiments. The rationale for this experiment was to evaluate the dynamics of forgetting in young and aged groups in order to determine whether the experimentally treated aged mice who demonstrated "youthful" 24-hour retention also demonstrated "youthful" memory decay over longer periods. Such forgetting would suggest that the memory storage processes in the LC-stimulated and/or piperoxane-injected aged animals were similar to those processes normally occurring in young animals. Dissimilar forgetting curves between treated aged mice and young controls might suggest that the "youthful" 24-hour retention in aged mice was not an accurate predictor of memory trace strength in the aged mice. In this experiment, mice were tested for retention of step-down inhibitory avoidance seven days and again at 14 days after original 24-hour testing. In this design all mice were tested on three separate ocassions. Ideally, independent groups of animals would be used in such a paradigm to avoid potential confounding problems associated with different rates of extinction etc., which might occur among different groups of subjects. Due to limited numbers of aged mice this was not possible in the present experiment.

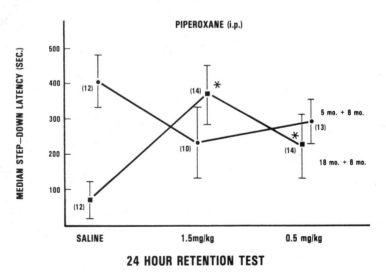

FIGURE 3. The effects of prior six month injection, at 48 hour intervals, of piperoxane upon memory of the inhibitory avoidance response. Drug administration was ended one week prior to training. The data indicate that both doses of piperoxane (0.5 and 1.5 mg/kg, i.p.) resulted in significant improvement in performance of aged, but not young, mice.

FORGETTING

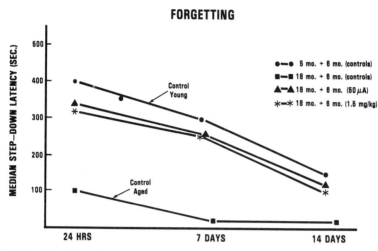

FIGURE 4. The effects of prior experimental treatment in aged mice upon forgetting of the inhibitory avoidance step-down response over a 14-day period. The data indicate that both direct electrical stimulation of the LC (50 μA) and i.p. piperoxane administration (1.5 mg/kg) resulted in forgetting in aged mice indistinguishable from that of young mice.

The results of this experiment are shown in FIGURE 4. Normal aged control mice show rapid forgetting of the inhibitory avoidance response, with significant loss of performance at 24-hours and essentially naive behavior by seven days. Normal young controls evidence significant retention performance at 24-hours, seven days, and 14 days. As FIGURE 4 indicates, there is a decline in retention performance throughout this fourteen day post-training period. Both groups of previously treated (either 50 μA electrical stimulation delivered to the LC or i.p. injections of 1.5 mg/kg piperoxane) aged mice evidenced forgetting that was not statistically different from normal aged mice. These data support the suggestion that LC-directed interventive strategies administered during a period of life preceding senescence, can serve to protect memory processes from normally occurring age-related decline.

If the LC plays an important role in sustaining youthful memory, then aged animals with poor memory, when compared to aged animals with good memory, might be expected to show differences in the LC. Experiments were performed in collaboration with Drs. Frances Leslie and Sandra Laughlin at University of California at Irvine to investigate this. For this study, aged CFW mice (24–26 months) were used. Mice were first trained and tested for 24-hour retention in a step-through inhibitory avoidance apparatus. Following testing, mice were coded and sacrificed. A complete series of serial sections through the LC was obtained for each animal. Sections were Thionen stained. Two independent raters counted each section using as an identification criterion, the presence of a nucleolus within the soma of LC neurons. Counts were compared and averaged between the two observers. Inter-observer variability was not statistically significant (<5%). After all tissue was analyzed, the code was broken and the data analyzed according to behavioral performance. The results are shown in FIGURE 5. As the data show, a significant correlation between good retention performance 24 hours after training and the total LC cell count was found. Those mice with poor retention performance generally had fewer cells in LC than those mice with good retention performance. Studies are in progress to enlarge this data base and further explore these exciting results.

As a summary statement for this experiment, the data do support the hypothesis that loss of noradrenergic function emanating from the LC contributes to age-related memory impairment.

The implications taken from these new findings are very important. First, the data suggest that age-related memory loss need not be inevitable. Appropriate interventive strategies can at least delay their onset. The extent to which this delay can be maintained relative to life-span is not understood at present. Many more careful experiments need to be conducted. Second, activation of LC electrical activity appears to be an important condition leading to the persistence of youthful memory function

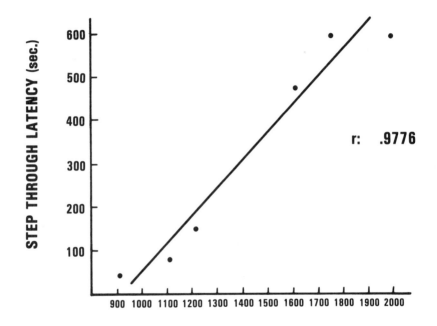

LC CELL COUNT

FIGURE 5. The relationship between LC cell number and 24-hour retention performance in aged CFW mice. The data indicate a significant relationship between LC cell number and retention performance.

into senescence. The result of both the electrical stimulation and the piperoxane treatments would suggest the locus coeruleus is a common target for the site of action of the two treatments. The question of what is necessary versus sufficient LC activation, *vis a vis* memory function, is not presently understood. The six-month protocol used in the two experiments described above was chosen based upon the assumption that if LC cell function was normally diminished during aging, the point of onset for such diminished function would likely be during middle age, which for the

C57BL/67 mouse is about 18 months.[33] Accordingly, long-term artificial activation of the LC was provided in an attempt to sustain and/or mimic greater LC functional output. At this juncture, it is important to determine the mechanism through which LC activation serves to sustain youthful memory function in aged rodents and the optimal parameters for obtaining improved memory function. Presumably the effect is in some way related to cellular changes occurring, or perhaps not occurring, at distant terminal projection fields receiving LC synaptic endings. One very interesting possibility is that NE-containing LC terminals and/or postsynaptic receptors modulate basal forebrain cholinergic activity directly. Alternatively, LC terminals may interact at common cortical postsynaptic target sites with cholinergic terminals. In either case, loss of normal LC function with aging might result in diminished cholinergic efficacy. This testable hypothesis awaits further study.

REFERENCES

1. ABRAHAM, W. C., R. L. DELANOY, A. J. DUNN & S. F. ZORNETZER. 1979. Locus coeruleus stimulation decreases deoxyglucose uptake in mouse cerebral cortex. Brain Res. **172:** 387–392.
2. ADOLFSSON, R., C. G. GOTTFRIES, B. E. ROOSE & B. WINDBLAD. 1979. Postmortem distribution of dopamine and homovanillic acid in human brain, variations related to age and a review of the literature. J. Neurol. Transmission **45:** 81–105.
3. ALGERI, S. 1978. Biochemical changes in central catecholaminergic neurons of the senescent rat. In Neuro-psychopharmacology. Proc. 10th Congr. Collegium International Neuropsychopharmacologicum. (Quebec, July 1976) Vol. 2. Pergamon Press. Oxford.
4. APPEL, S. H. 1981. Alzheimer's Disease. In Brain Neurotransmitters and Receptors in Aging and Age-Related Disorders. S. J. Enna *et al.*, Eds. Vol. 17. Raven Press. New York.
5. ASTON-JONES, G. & F. E. BLOOM. 1981. Norepinephrine-containing locus coeruleus neurons in behaving rats exhibit pronounced responses to non-noxious environmental stimuli. J. Neurosci. **1:** 887–900.
6. BAN, T. A. 1978. Vasodilators, stimulants and anobolic agents in the treatment of geropsychiatric patients. In Psychopharmacology: A Generation of Progress. M. A. Lipton, A. Dimascio & K. F. Killiam, Eds. Raven Press. New York.
7. BARNES, C. A. 1979. Memory deficits associated with senescence: A neurophysiological and behavioral study in the rat. J. Comp. Physiol. Psychol. **93:** 74–101.
8. BARTUS, R. T. 1979. Physostigmine and recent memory: Effects in young and aged non-human primates. Science **206:** 1087–1089.
9. BARTUS, R. T. & R. L. DEAN. 1980. Facilitation of aged primate memory via pharmacological manipulation of central cholinergic activity. Neurobiol. Aging **1:**145–152.
10. BARTUS, R. T., R. L. DEAN III & D. L. FLEMMING. 1979. Aging in the rhesus monkey: Effects on visual discrimination learning and reversal learning. J. Gerontol. **34:** 209–219.
11. BARTUS, R. T., R. L. DEAN, B. BEER & A. S. LIPPA. 1982. The cholinergic hypothesis of geriatric memory dysfunction. Science **217:** 408–417.
12. BONDAREFF, W., C. Q. MOUNTJOY & M. ROTH. 1982. Loss of neurons of origin of the adrenergic projection to cerebral cortex (nucleus locus coeruleus) in senile dementia. Neurology **32:** 164–168.
13. BOWEN, D. M., C. B. SMITH, P. WHITE, M. J. GOODHART, J. A. SPILLANE, R. H. A. FLACK & A. N. DAVISON. 1977. Chemical pathology of the organic dementias. Brain **100:** 397–426.
14. BOYD, W. D., J. GRAHAN-WHITE, G. BLOCKWOOD, I. GLEN & J. McQUEEN. 1977. Clinical effects of choline in Alzheimer senile dementia. Lancet **2:** 711.
15. BRODY, H. 1970. Structural changes in the aging nervous system. In Interdisciplinary Topics in Gerontology. H. T. Blumenthal, Ed. **7:** 9–21. Karger. New York.

16. BRODY, H. 1976. An examination of cerebral cortex and brain stem aging. *In* Aging: Neurobiology of Aging. R. D. Terry & S. Gershon, Eds. Raven Press. New York.
17. CANESTRARI, R. E. 1968. Age changes in acquisition. *In* Human Aging and Behavior. G. A. Talland, Ed.: 169–187. Academic Press. New York.
18. CARLSSON, A. & B. WINBLAD. 1976. The influence of age and time interval between death and autopsy on dopamine and 3-methoxytyramine levels in human basal ganglia. J. Neural Transmission **83:** 271–276.
19. CEDARBAUM, J. M. & G. K. AGHAJANIAN. 1976. Noradrenergic neurons of the locus coeruleus: Inhibition by epinephrine and activation by the α_2-antagonist piperoxane. Brain Res. **112:** 413–419.
20. COTE, L. J. & L. T. KREMZNER. 1976. Changes in neurotransmitter systems with increasing age in human brain. Trans. Am. Soc. Neurochem. p. 83.
21. DAVIES, P. & A. MALONEY. 1976. Selective loss of central cholinergic neurons in Alzheimer's disease. Lancet **ii:** 1403.
22. DEAN, R. L., J. SCOZZAFAVA, J. A. GOAS, B. REGAN, B. BEER & R. T. BARTUS. 1981. Age-related differences in behavior across the life-span of the C57BL/6J mouse. Exp. Aging Res. **7:** 427–451.
23. DRACHMAN, D. A. 1977. Memory and cognitive function in man: Does the cholinergic system have a specific role? Neurology **27:** 783–790.
24. DRACHMAN, D. A. & J. LEAVITT. 1974. Human memory and the cholinergic system: A relationship to aging? Arch. Neurol. **30:** 113–121.
25. DRACHMAN, D. A. & B. J. SHAKIAN. 1980. Memory and cognitive function in the elderly. Arch. Neurol. **37:** 674–675.
26. ETIENNE, P., S. GAUTHIER, G. JOHNSON, B. COLLIER, T. MENDIS, D. DASTOOR, M. COLE & H. F. MULLER. 1978. Clinical effects of choline in Alzheimer's disease. Lancet **1:** 500–509.
27. FALLON, J. H. 1984. The islands of Calleja complex II; connections of medium and large-sized cells. Brain Res. Bull. (In press.)
28. FALLON, J. H. & R. Y. MOORE. 1978. Catecholamine innervation of the basal forebrain III, olfactory tubercle, and piriform cortex. J. Comp. Neurol. **180:** 533–544.
29. FALLON, J. H., D. A. KOZRELL & R. Y. MOORE 1978. Catecholamine innervation of the basal forebrain II, Amygdala, suprarhinal cortex and entorhinal cortex. J. Comp. Neurol. **180:** 509–532.
30. FERRIS, S. H., G. SATHANANTHAN, B. REISBERG & S. GERSHON. 1979. Long-term choline treatment of memory-impaired elderly patients. Science **205:** 1039–1040.
31. FINCH, C. E. 1973. Catecholamine metabolism in the brains of aging male mice. Brain Res. **52:** 267–276.
32. FINCH, C. E. 1976. The regulation of physiological changes during mammalian aging. Q. Rev. Biol. **51:** 49–83.
33. FINCH, C. E. 1978. Age-related changes in brain catecholamines: A synopsis of findings in C57BL/6J mice and other rodent models. *In* Advances in Experimental Medicine and Biology. C. E. Finch, D. E. Potter & A. D. Kenny, Eds. **113.** Parkinson's Disease II. Plenum Press. New York.
34. GALLAGHER, M. & B. S. KAPP. 1978. Manipulation of opiate activity in the amygdala alters memory processes. Life Sci. **23:** 1973–1978.
35. GILBERT, J. G. 1941. Memory loss in senescence. J. Abn. Social Psychol. **36:** 73–86.
36. GOLD, P. E. & J. L. MCGAUGH. 1975. Changes in learning and memory during aging. *In* Neurobiology of Aging. I. M. Ordy & K. R. Brizzee, Eds. Plenum Press. New York.
37. GOLD, P. E. & S. F. ZORNETZER. 1983. The mnemon and its juices: Neuromodulation of memory processes. Behav. Neural Biol.
38. HERKENHAM, M. & C. G. PERT. 1982. Light microscopic localization of brain opiate receptors: A general autoradiographic method which preserves tissue quality. J. Neurosci. **2:** 1129–1149.
39. HIER, D. B. & L. R. CAPLAN. 1980. Drugs for senile demantia. Drugs **20:** 74–80.
40. HUGHES, J. R., J. G. WILLIAMS & R. D. CURRIER. 1976. An ergot alkaloid preparation (hydergine) in the treatment of dementia: Critical review of the clinical literature. J. Am. Geriatric Soc. **24:** 490–497.

41. JACOBOWITZ, D. M. & M. PALKOVITZ. 1974. Topagraphic atlas of catecholamine and acetyl-cholinesterase-containing neurons in the rat brain I. Forebrain (telencephalon, diencephalon). J. Comp. Neurol. 157: 13–28.

42. JENSEN, R. A., R. B. MESSING, J. L. MARTINEZ, B. J. VASQUEZ, V. R. SPIEHLER & J. L. MCGAUGH. 1981. Changes in brain peptide systems and altered learning and memory processes in aged animals. In Endogenous Peptides and Learning and Memory Processes. J. L. Martinez et al., Eds. Academic Press. New York.

43. JONES, B. E. & R. Y. MOORE. 1977. Ascending projections of the locus coeruleus in the rat II: autoradiographic study. Brain Res. 127: 23–53.

44. KUBANIS, P. & S. F. ZORNETZER. 1981. Age-related behavioral and neurobiological changes: A review with an emphasis on memory. Behav. Neural Biol. 31: 115–172.

45. KUBANIS, P., G. GOBBEL & S. F. ZORNETZER 1981. Age-related memory deficits in Swiss mice. Behav. Neural Biol. 32: 241–247.

46. KUBANIS, P., S. F. ZORNETZER & G. FREUND. 1982. Memory and postsynaptic cholinergic receptors in aging mice. Pharmacol. Biochem. Behav. 17: 313–322.

47. LANDFIELD, P. W., G. ROSE, L. SANDLES, T. WOHLSTADTER & G. LYNCH. 1977. Patterns of astroglial hypertrophy and neuronal degeneration in the hippocampus of aged, memory-deficient rats. J. Gerontol. 32: 3–12.

48. LINDVALL, O., A. BJORKLAND, R. Y. MOORE & J. STENEVI. 1974. Mesencephalic dopamine neurons projecting to neocortex. Brain Res. 81: 325–331.

49. LOEW, D. M. 1980. Pharmacological approaches to the treatment of senile dementia. In Aging of the Brain and Dementia. L. Amaducci, A. N. Davidson & P. Antuono, Eds. Vol. 13. Raven Press. New York.

50. MANN, D., P. YATES & B. MARCYNINK. 1984. A comparison of changes in the nucleus basalis and locus caeruleus in Alzheimer's disease. J. Neurol. Neurosurg. Psychiatry 47: 201–203.

51. MASON, S. T. 1981. Noradrenaline in the brain: Progress in theories of behavioral function. Prog. Neurobiol. 16: 263–303.

52. MCGEER, E. G. & P. L. MCGEER. 1973. Some characteristics of brain tyrosine hydroxylase. In New Concepts in Neurotransmitter Regulation. A. J. Mandell, Ed. Plenum Press. New York.

53. MESSING, R. B., R. A. JENSEN, J. L. MARTINEZ V. R. SPIEHLER, B. J. VASQUEZ, B. SOUMIREU-MOURAT, K. C. LIANG & J. L. MCGAUGH. 1979. Naloxone enhancement of memory. Behav. Neural Biol. 27: 266–275.

54. MOHS, R. C., K. L. DAVIS, J. R. TINKLENBER, L. HOLLISTER, J. A. YESAVAGE & B. S. KOPELL. 1979. Choline chloride treatment of memory deficits in the elderly. Am. J. Psychiatry 136: 1275–1277.

55. MOHS, R. C., K. L. DAVIS & J. R. TINKLENBERG. 1980. Choline chloride effects on memory in the elderly. Neurobiol. Aging 1: 21–25.

56. MOORE, R. Y. & F. E. BLOOM. 1978. Central catecholamine neurone systems: Anatomy and physiology of the dopamine systems. Annu. Rev. Neurosci. 1: 129–169.

57. MORRISON, J., R. GRZANNA, M. MOLLIVER & J. COYLE. 1978. The distribution and orientation of noradrenergic fibers in neocortex of the rat: An immunofluorescence study. J. Comp. Neurol. 181: 17–40.

58. OLIVERIO, A. & D. BOVET. 1966. Effects of age on maze learning and avoidance conditioning of mice. Life Sci. 5: 1317–1324.

59. PERRY, E., R. PERRY, G. BLESSED & B. TOMLINSON. 1977. Necropsy evidence of central cholinergic deficits in senile dementia. Lancet 1: 189.

60. PRADO DE CARVALHO, L. & S. F. ZORNETZER. 1981. The involvement of the locus coeruleus in memory. Behav. Neural Biol. 31: 173–186.

61. PRICE, D. L., P. J. WHITEHOUSE, R. G. STRUBLE, A. W. CLARK, J. T. COYLE, M. R. DELONG & J. C. HEDRENN. 1982. Basal forebrain cholinergic systems in Alzheimer's disease and related dementias. Neurosci. Comment 1: 84–92.

62. PONZIO, F., N. BRUNELLO N. & S. ALGERI. 1978. Catecholamine synthesis in brain of aging rats. J. Neurochem. 30: 1617–1620.

63. RANKIN, J. L. & D. H. KAULSER, 1979. Adult age differences in false recognitions. J. Gerontol. **34:** 58–65.
64. ROGERS, J., M. A. SILVER W. J. SHOEMAKER & F. E. BLOOM 1980. Senescent changes in a neurobiological model system: Cerebellar Purkinje cell electrophysiology and correlative anatomy. Neurobiol. Aging **1:** 3–11.
65. RUCH, F. L. 1934. The differentiative effects of age upon human learning. J. Genet. Psychiatry **11:** 261–286.
66. SCOTT, F. L. 1979. A review of some current drugs used in the pharmacotherapy of organic brain syndrome. In Aging, Physiology and Cell Biology of Aging. A. Cherkin, C. E. Finch, N. Kharasch, T. Makinodon, F. L. Scott & B. S. Strehler, Eds. Vol. 8. Raven Press. New York.
67. SIMPKINS, J. W., G. P. MUELLER, H. H. HUANG & J. MEITES. 1977. Evidence for depressed catecholamine and enhanced serotonin metabolism in aging male rats: Possible relation to gonadotrophin secretion. Endocrinology **100:** 1672–1678.
68. STEIN, L., J. D. BELLUZZI & C. D. WISE. 1975. Memory enhancement by central administrations of norepinephine. Brain Res. **84:** 329–335.
69. VIJAYASHANKAR, N. & H. BRODY. 1979. A quantitative study of the pigmental neurons in the nuclei locus coeruleus and subcoeruleus in man as related to aging. J. Neuropathol. Exp. Neurol. **38:** 490–497.
70. VROULIS, G. A. & R. C. SMITH 1981. Cholinergic drugs and memory disorders in Alzheimer's type dementia. In Brain Neurotransmitter and Receptors in Aging and Age-Related Disorders. S. J. Enna, T. Samorajski & B. Beer, Eds. Raven Press. New York.
71. ZORNETZER, S. F. 1978. Neurotransmitter modulation and memory: A new pharmacological phrenology? In Psychopharmacology: A generation of progress. M. A. Lipton, A. DiMascio & K. F. Killam, Eds. Raven Press. New York.
72. ZORNETZER, S. F. & M. GOLD. 1976. The locus coeruleus: Its possible role in memory consolidation. Physiol. Behav. **16:** 331–336.
73. ZORNETZER, S. F., W. C. ABRAHAM & R. APPLETON. 1978. Locus coeruleus and labile memory. Pharmacol. Biochem. Behav. **9:** 227–234.
74. ZORNETZER, S. F., R. THOMPSON & J. ROGERS. 1982. Rapid forgetting of aged rats. Behav. Neural Biol. **36:** 49–60.

Memory Function and Brain Biochemistry in Normal Aging and in Senile Dementia

BENGT WINBLAD AND JOHN HARDY

Departments of Geriatric Medicine and Pathology

LARS BÄCKMAN AND LARS-GÖRAN NILSSON

Department of Psychology
University of Umeå
S-901 87 Umeå, Sweden

PSYCHOLOGICAL ASPECTS OF AGING AND MEMORY

The distinctive feature of the literature on normal aging and memory is that of interactions between age and type of task. Typically, the interactions are characterized of pronounced age differences in favor of young adults in "non-guided" free recall or paired associate learning tasks and reduced or eliminated differences in tasks wherein different kinds of contextual support are provided.[55,94] Such results have been obtained by contrasting memory performance of young and old adults in a non-guided task to their performance in tasks where organizational strategies,[50,51] instructions to use verbal mediators,[48,49] or imagery instructions[25,100,101] are provided by the experimenter at encoding. Other demonstrations of this pattern of data are given in studies showing smaller or reduced age differences when the experimenter supplies copy cues as in recognition[30,46] or category cues as in cued recall[52,57] as compared to free recall tasks. Also, the studies by Smith[98] and Ceci and Tabor[28] as well as several studies on levels of processing and aging represent cases in point. Smith[98] and Ceci and Tabor[28] observed eliminated age differences in memory when category cues were provided at encoding and retrieval, respectively, whereas a number of studies employing orienting tasks prior to recognition tests[31,39,65] have reported invariance across the adult age span. Taken together these studies suggest that there is an age difference with respect to the need of environmental support for achieving maximal memory performance: The elderly need more than the younger adults.[32] This state of affairs also actualizes the concept of compensation, i.e. older adults are apparently capable of compensating for deficits in episodic remembering by utilizing various types of contextual aids. The concept of compensation was faintly outlined by Luria[59] in his work on brain damage and recovery from neurological impairments. More recently, the concept has also been used by O'Connor and Hermelin[77] and Rönnberg and Nilson[92] in the area of sensory handicaps and modality effects.

The concept of compensation is closely related to an interactionistic view of remembering.[13,33,53,71–73] Interactionistic accounts of memory emphasize the interplay between the cognitive capabilities of the individual and the actual task demands as the principal determinants for the understanding of memory. In the present context, this implies that the use of the concept of compensation incessantly forces the investigator to determine which properties of the tasks promote age effects and which do not and then to relate this task analysis to a conceptualization of age differences in mental operations.

In the studies cited on normal aging and memory the compensatory memory behavior in the aged was accomplished by means of experimenter-provided support through hints or instructions at encoding and/or additional retrieval information. In a series of experiments from our own laboratory we have investigated the possibility that compensatory capabilities in the elderly could be demonstrated as a function of properties inherent in the to-be-remembered (TBR) materials as well. This was done by employing a new memory task introduced by Cohen,[29] memory for so-called subject-performed tasks (SPTs). In SPTs, the subjects are instructed to perform consecutive acts either with real-life objects (e.g., bounce the ball, smell the perfume, lift the spoon) or without any objects (e.g., nod in agreement, stand up, clap your hands) for a later recall test.

SPTs differ from standard verbal memory tasks in the sense that they allow a multimodal encoding and each modality possesses a variety of aspects on which encoding may be based. Each SPT is read aloud by the experimenter whereby the auditory modality is activated. The visual system is stimulated throughout the presentation of SPTs. The tactual mode is involved, since the subjects are instructed to act physically. Also, some SPTs (e.g., eat the raisin, smell the perfume) bring about activity in the gustatory and olfactory modes. With respect to the variety of aspects, encoding the SPTs can be accomplished on the basis of color, shape, sound, motor aspects, texture, taste, and smell, besides the verbal aspects. The task properties of multimodality and richness of aspects distinguish SPTs from standard verbal memory

TABLE 1. Mean Proportion Correct Immediate Free Recall (IFR) and Delayed Free Recall (DFR) of SPTs, Words, and Sentences

	IFR			DFR		
Age Group (years)	SPTs	Words	Sentences	SPTs	Words	Sentences
Young (17–31)	.69	.76	.59	.56	.60	.42
Middle-aged (39–52)	.66	.70	.48	.51	.48	.30
Old (58–85)	.60	.46	.32	.45	.30	.15

tasks in which the presentation is typically unimodal and the number of aspects is (by definition) limited to the verbal features of the TBR items.

The initial hypothesis put forward was that the unique task properties of SPTs might constitute contextual support that the elderly could utilize with the result that age differences in memory could be reduced or eliminated. In the first study[23] we tested young, middle-aged, and old adults on immediate free recall (IFR) and delayed free recall (DFR) of words, sentences, and SPTs. Exactly the same verbal information was presented in sentences and SPTs (e.g., bounce the ball, nod in agreement). In words, the noun of each sentence or SPT comprised the TBR information. IFR and DFR data told the same story. As can be seen in TABLE 1 there were no age differences on free recall of SPTs, whereas typical age differences in favor of the young adults were found in the two verbal tasks. Informal interviews with the participants in the Bäckman and Nilsson[22] study revealed that many of the subjects (regardless of age) reported that they retrieved the SPTs by "imagining that they performed them once again." Since it is known from several paired-associate learning studies that old adults benefit more than young adults from imagery instructions[25,100,101] it seemed warranted to investigate whether the SPTs were so "imagery provoking" that no instructions would be needed. That is, to study the role of imagery for the lack of age differences on free recall of SPTs. To achieve this objective Bäckman and Nilsson[23] tested young and old adults on IFR and DFR of sentences, sentences with imagery instructions and SPTs. The results

TABLE 2. Mean Proportion Correct Immediate Free Recall (IFR) and Delayed Free Recall (DFR) of SPTs, Sentences with Imagery Instructions, and Sentences

	IFR			DFR		
Age Group (years)	SPTs	Sentences with Imagery	Sentences	SPTs	Sentences with Imagery	Sentences
Young (18–25)	.65	.64	.58	.53	.51	.40
Old (56–89)	.62	.46	.42	.47	.27	.22

of this study are portrayed in TABLE 2. Pronounced age differences were observed in the two former tasks, whereas the lack of age differences on free recall of SPTs was replicated. Accordingly, the hypothesis about imagery as a critical factor for the SPT data gained no support.

The reason why SPTs are multimodal and contextually rich is twofold. First, this is due to the fact the real-life objects are used in the experimental setting. Secondly, it depends upon the request that subjects act physically throughout the experiment. The sole purpose in the Bäckman[20] study was to investigate the relative importance of the use of real-life objects and the active physical manipulation for the elderly's success on free recall of SPTs.

This was accomplished by keeping the presence of real-life objects constant while varying the subjects' motor activity during encoding. Young and old adults were tested in IFR and DFR of SPTs and sentences and objects. The same verbal expressions and real-life objects were used as TBR items in both tasks. The only difference between the tasks was that the participants in SPTs were requested to perform the acts implied by the imperatives (e.g., draw a circle, smell the flower) physically, whereas subjects assigned to sentences and objects were instructed not to act physically. For the third time, no age differences were observed on IFR and DFR of SPTs, while the young adults outperformed the older adults when the subjects were not allowed to interact physically with the objects (TABLE 3).

The main conclusion to be drawn from this series of experiments is that old, healthy adults have the ability to demonstrate compensatory memory behavior by utilizing a multimodal and contextually rich encoding environment whereby age differences in free recall can be avoided. Here, the importance of an active motor manipulation during encoding as a "compensatory trigger" in the aged should be especially emphasized.

The SPT paradigm is used in an ongoing study[24] testing free and cued recall of SPTs and sentences in four groups: 73 year olds, 82 year olds, mildly and moderately impaired subjects with Alzheimer's disease/senile dementia of Alzheimer type (AD/SDAT). Preliminary data for the two groups of intact aged subjects replicate the findings of Bäckman[20] and Bäckman and Nilsson[23] by showing a pronounced improvement in SPT recall compared to sentence recall. Furthermore, even the two AD/

TABLE 3. Mean Proportion Correct Immediate Free Recall (IFR) and Delayed Free Recall (DFR) of SPTs and Sentences and Objects

	IFR		DFR	
Age Group (years)	SPTs	Sentences and Objects	SPTs	Sentences and Objects
Young (18–30)	.61	.62	.51	.49
Old (60–75)	.57	.46	.50	.30

SDAT groups improve memory performance remarkably on free and cued recall of SPTs compared to free and cued recall of sentences (TABLE 4). Although these results are encouraging, it should be pointed out that the samples of AD/SDAT subjects are relatively small. Further research is needed before any definite conclusions can be drawn regarding the ability in AD/SDAT subjects to improve recall performance by means of a multisensory and contextually rich encoding environment involving motor action.

The initially presented guided verbal memory tasks (GVTs) where the experimenter provides the subjects with hints, instructions, or cues share basic properties with the SPTs beside the fact that both types of tasks reduce or eliminate age differences in memory. One striking similarity arises when comparing SPTs and GVTs in terms of the attentional guidance provided by the tasks. In SPTs, the experimenter presents sentences in an imperative form (e.g., lift the spoon, break the match) and the subjects are instructed to perform these acts accordingly. Thus, the nature of the task is goal-directed: The subjects are forced to focus their attention on the performance of the acts with the purpose of subsequently encoding them. Similarly, in GVTs the experimenter causes the subjects to pay attention to different aspects of the TBR information (e.g., superordinate categories, verbal mediators, imagery aspects, cues)

TABLE 4. Mean Proportion Correct Immediate Free Recall and Cued Recall of SPTs and Sentences

	Free Recall		Cued Recall	
Group	SPTs	Sentences	SPTs	Sentences
73 year olds	.56	.29	.70	.37
82 year olds	.46	.28	.65	.36
Mildly demented (75–82)[a]	.29	.05	.49	.06
Moderately demented (79–86)[a]	.12	.02	.19	.02

[a]AD/SDAT

by informing the subjects that these aspects actually exist and can be used as mnemonic aids. Hence, in SPTs as well as in GVTs the present task demands and the instructions provided cause an attentional increase due to contextual guidance in both cases. This increase in the focusing of attention on the part of the subjects should be contrasted to standard free recall of paired-associate learning tasks in which no such external aids are provided; the subjects are free to perceive, attend to, and memorize the TBR information in any way they prefer. Obviously these non-guided tasks are relatively free from explicit attentional guidance. If a certain group of subjects has a deficit in the ability to selectively focus the attention on those stimulus features that promote optimal memory performance, it seems reasonable to suggest that these subjects should be especially penalized in such non-guided tasks. Actually, several investigators within the area of aging and attention have suggested that the aging process is accompanied by a decrement in the selective aspect of attention.[58,87,96] There are also data on card sorting[40,88] and problem solving[47] suggesting an age impairment in the ability to focus the attention on the important stimulus features while simultaneously closing out irrelevant information. A very interesting aspect of this literature is that there appears to be no age-related decline when relevant and irrelevant stimuli are partitioned by color or spatial position,[60,107] i.e. when the subjects' attention is strongly guided by the task demands. In addition to these psychological data, neuropsychological theory and data[3,56] suggest that the neural mechanisms assumed to mediate attentional functioning decline most rapidly with increased age.

The point to be made is that the reduction or elimination of age differences in memory in GVTs and SPTs fits well into the notion of a deficit in the elderly to selectively focus the attention on the relevant stimulus features: When the task and the instructions provided provoke an increase in the focusing of attention age differences in memory decrease. This does not imply that we should abandon other explanations of the presence/absence of age differences in memory. On the contrary, we argue that a multifactorial approach that embraces interactions between the individual level (neurochemical, neuroanatomical, neuropsychological, psychological) and the contextual level (task dimensions, environmental support) constitute the most fruitful point of departure for our everlasting search for what happens with memory as one gets older.[21,34] One way of achieving such an objective is to try to relate the present psychological data, the task analyses, and the interactions between cognitive capabilities and the environmental support to basic neurochemical data. In this paper we will emphasize the necessity of focusing of attention and motor action during encoding for the elderly's success in episodic remembering as the main points of this gap-bridging.

Now we turn to a presentation of biochemical data on normal and pathological aging and finally the psychological data and the lines of reasoning presented here will be linked together with some neuroanatomical and neurochemical findings.

BIOCHEMICAL CHANGES IN NORMAL AGING

The process of normal aging of the human brain has been described as a weight loss, atrophy, and increased ventricular volume.[9] Morphological studies have shown neuron loss in some brain regions,[14,38,45,68,102] but there are other regions without neuron loss.[70] A decrease in neuronal connectivity may also take place in the aging process.[9,19,38] The effects of increasing age on acetylcholine, catecholamine, and serotonin metabolism in brain have been studied extensively.[6,26,86]

The activities of the catecholamine synthesizing enzyme tyrosine hydroxylase appear to decrease with age in humans[68] predominantly during the first three decades of life and more slowly thereafter. Similarly, another catecholamine-forming enzyme DOPA decarboxylase declines with age. Post mortem investigations of the human brain have given support for age-related changes in the rate of monoamine turnover. Carlsson and Winblad[27] thus found a negative correlation between levels of DA and age in the basal ganglia in individuals over 20 years. In an ongoing study (Carlsson, Nyberg, and Winblad, unpublished data) we have analyzed 76 patients (18–95 yrs) who had mainly died of acute heart failure or due to an accident. None of these "normal" patients had any recorded history of psychiatric or neurological disease that might have influenced the metabolism. Eight different brain regions were analyzed for their content of catecholaminergic and serotonergic markers. The results are schematically summarized in TABLE 5. Significant changes with age were noted only in a few instances. In nucleus caudatus, dopamine levels decreased significantly with age and the same findings were seen in the putamen. In cortex gyrus cinguli noradrenaline concentrations were reduced. In hippocampus, the only significant change was a decrease in noradrenaline. When the material was grouped into age groups it was noted that in nucleus caudatus and putamen, dopamine was significantly down in the three highest age groups (about 79 years) compared to two or more of the younger groups (data not shown). In contrast, hippocampal noradrenaline was significantly down only

TABLE 5. Age Dependence of Neurotransmitters

Neurotransmitter	Gyrus cinguli	Hippocampus	Caudate	Putamen	Hypothalamus	Mesencephalon
5-HT	—	—	—	—	—	↑
5-HIAA	—	—	—	—	—	—
DA	—	—	▼	▼	—	—
HVA	↑	—	—	—	—	—
NA	▼	▼	—	—	▼	—
HMPG	—	—	—	—	—	
MAO-B	▲	▲	▲		▲	
CAT	—	—	—	—		

N = 23 to 76 control case.
↓ $p < 0.05$, ▼ $p < 0.01$.
Data from Carlsson, Nyberg, and Winblad (to be published).

in the oldest group (i.e. above 89 years). In cortex gyrus cinguli and hypothalamus, significantly lower noradrenaline concentrations were seen only in the noradrenaline group 65–69 years old, whereas the downward trend in the older age groups was not altogether clear-cut. The pattern of age-related reduction of noradrenaline differs from that of dopamine with significant reduction in cortex gyrus cinguli, hippocampus, and hypothalamus, but not in the striatal nuclei. The role of noradrenaline as a modulator of attention is well documented in the literature[4,66] and extensively discussed by Susan Sara (see this volume).

In normal aging and senile dementia the cortical motor areas are relatively spared from neurodegenerative changes.[17] In addition, dopamine is of importance for motor functions, the most obvious example being Parkinson's disease. The amounts of dopamine went down in all but two brain regions (cortex gyrus cinguli and hippocampus) in this study and significantly so in nucleus caudatus and putamen; these findings are in line with earlier reports.[1,2] The role of dopamine in motor function and its stability with age in hippocampus may provide a neurochemical basis for an explanation of preservation of memory when the subjects are allowed to act physically during encoding.

As for the serotonin system in aging, this study, like earlier ones[18,43] found few signs of an age dependence in this system. The exception was a positive correlation with age for serotonin in mesencephalon.

The age-related rise in MAO activity is now well established. It seems to be confined to the B form of the enzyme. This may be due to an increase of the extraneuronal tissue.

The decline of memory function with normal aging of the brain has been attributed to changes in the cholinergic system.[6] The cholinergic enzyme choline acetyltransferase, which can be considered as a marker for presynaptic cholinergic activity, has been found to be reduced in activity in different brain areas with normal aging.[67,79] Our present material for choline acetyl transferase measurements consisted of only few cases and no certain conclusions could be drawn from our own data. Changes in postsynaptic activity with a decreased number of receptors and/or changes in receptor affinity of function with increasing age could be another explanation for decreased memory function. The effect of age on muscarinic receptor binding sites in the brain in normal aging is unclear and both unchanged[37] and decreased numbers of binding sites[16,81,103] have been reported in cortical areas in the brain. In hippocampus[74] a decrease in muscarinic binding sites with age was reported.

In summary, the catecholaminergic transmitter systems (noradrenaline and dopamine) seem to be mainly affected in normal aging. The process of aging results in a dopamine depletion in striatal nuclei but not in hippocampus, whereas the content of noradrenaline is reduced primarily in the limbic regions cortex gyrus cinguli, hippocampus, and hypothalamus. The serotonergic and cholinergic systems are not affected to the same extent. It is well known that aged people acquire changes in memory function, altered sleeping habits, an increased frequency of depression, an increased frequency of Parkinson's disease and of course an increased frequency of senile dementia. Our findings invite the speculation that neuronal damage in early life together with the age-induced reduction in neuronal function may have pathogenetic importance for the changes observed in memory functions.

BIOCHEMICAL FINDINGS IN SENILE DEMENTIA

Although the histopathological features of AD/SDAT have been known for a long time, neurochemical research has mainly been undertaken in the last 15 years. In view of the clinical picture and the widespread degeneration in the brain, it is unlikely that a single neurotransmitter is selectively affected. It has long been clear that transmitters other than acetylcholine, such as noradrenaline and serotonin,[1,2,54] are also affected. This must be considered when looking into the etiology, pathogenesis, and memory disorders associated with AD/SDAT.

In a recent study[44] different neurotransmitters were examined in brain specimens from 14 patients with AD/SDAT and 16 controls. The data are summarized in TABLE 6.

In the four AD/SDAT-brain regions investigated, the concentration of serotonin and noradrenaline were significantly reduced while 3-methoxy-4-hydroxyphenylglycol was increased. In the caudate nucleus of the AD/SDAT brains the concentrations of dopamine and homovanillic acid were significantly reduced although this has not been reported by all groups. The activity of choline acetyl transferase was reduced in the four brain regions investigated, showing a general reduction in the acetylcholine system in AD/SDAT brains. Thus, at least three neurotransmitter pathways are affected in AD/SDAT with moderate or severe loss of cell bodies of origin and depletion of the neurotransmitter and its related enzymes in nerve terminal regions. These affected pathways are the noradrenergic cells in locus coeruleus with widespread projections throughout the brains,[8,61] the serotonergic raphe nuclei with widespread

TABLE 6. Alzheimer Dependence of Neurotransmitters as Compared to Age-matched Controls

Neurotransmitter	Gyrus cinguli	Hippocampus	Caudate	Hypothalamus
HT	↓	↓	↓	—
5-HIAA	—	—	—	—
DA			↓	—
HVA	↑	—	↓	—
NA	—	↓	↓	↓
HMPG	↑	↑	↑	—
MAO-B	↑	↑	—	↑
CAT	↓	↓	↓	—

↑ $p < 0.05$, ↓ $p < 0.01$.

TABLE 7. Acetylcholine in Alzheimer's Disease

	Reference	Comments
Histological Evidence for Neuronal Deficits		
Cell loss in nucleus basalis complex	Pilleri[84] Whitehouse et al.[104] and many others	That cells are lost is established; the extent of the loss varies considerably between reports
Tangles in the nucleus basalis complex	Ishii[54]	This study has not been repeated yet
Biochemical Evidence for Neuronal Deficits		
Loss of acetylcholine esterase	Pope[85] Atack et al.[5] and many others	Not a specific marker
Loss of choline acetyl transferase	Davies and Maloney[36] Bowen et al.[10] Perry et al.[79] and many others	Extent of reported deficits varies considerably and has been correlated to the severity of disease[80]
Reduction in biopsy material acetylcholine synthesis	Sims et al.[97]	

projections throughout the brain,[62] and the cholinergic systems of the basal forebrain complex, which project to the cortex and hippocampus.[104] When reviewing the literature most work has concentrated on acetylcholine in Alzheimer's disease; this will therefore be reviewed first.

Acetylcholine

The main finding (made in post mortem brain) is a considerable loss of choline acetyl transferase, a presynaptic marker for cholinergic neurons, particularly in the hippocampus and temporal cortex (TABLE 7).[10,35,36,44,75,79,91] The extent of the reported loss varies considerably between groups but reaches significant levels in all reports. Choline acetyl transferase in other brain regions may also be affected although this finding is less consistent.[90] Losses in other presynaptic markers for cholinergic neurons appear to be similar in general terms to the loss in choline acetyl transferase indicating that the decrement is not enzyme specific. Thus, synaptosomal choline uptake is reduced in Alzheimer's disease,[93] acetylcholine esterase, although not purely a presynaptic marker for cholinergic neurons[41] is reduced[5,35,85] as is pyruvate dehydrogenase (which may be specifically enriched acetylcholinergic neurons).[82] These findings have been confirmed and considerably extended in biopsy work,[97] which have shown that acetylcholine synthesis and release from tissue prisms are also reduced in Alzheimer's disease. The histological correlate of the biochemical loss is reduced cell numbers in a nucleus basalis complex[84,104] and the presence of tangles in this nucleus.[54]

Of particular importance has been the correlative studies showing relationships between intellectual impairment, the amount of pathological abnormalities (i.e. numbers of plaques and tangles), and the loss of choline acetyl transferase in the temporal cortex.[80] These findings have been largely repeated.[12,105] The losses in presynaptic markers do not appear to be mirrored by losses in post synaptic muscarinic receptors. Reports have shown these to have either normal levels[37,89,103,106] or reduced only in a subpopulation of Alzheimer's sufferers.[106] The possibility of receptor compensation has been raised.[76]

Noradrenaline

A noradrenergic deficit in Alzheimer's disease has been found by all groups who have investigated this possibility (TABLE 8). Thus noradrenaline concentrations and dopamine beta-hydroxylase levels have been reported to be reduced in Alzheimer's disease[1,2,42,108] and cell losses in the locus coeruleus have been frequently documented.[8,63,64] In addition, large number of tangles have been reported in the locus coeruleus neurons.[54] Experiments on human biopsy material have shown that noradrenaline uptake is reduced compared with other surgical material,[7] indicating that the noradrenaline deficit is not an artifact of the end stage of the disease. The distribution of the loss of adrenergic innervation is not well established although the hypothalamus appears to be severely affected and the hippocampus less so.[44] The noradrenergic deficit may therefore not occur in the same brain regions as the acetylcholine deficit. Comparisons of the relative sizes of the losses of noradrenaline and acetylcholine systems are thus fraught with difficulty, especially since the decrements do not necessarily occur in the same brain regions. The only direct comparisons of cell numbers and relative losses in the substantia innominate and the locus coeruleus in Alzheimer's disease revealed a larger although more variable loss in the latter.[64] The failure to obtain significant correlations between either the numbers of plaques and tangles or the clinical symptoms and the loss of dopamine beta hydroxylase in the temporal cortex is not surprising therefore,[83] since this area was presumably selected for comparison because of its particularly severe cholinergic deficit.[79] Indeed significant correlations have been obtained between the severity of the clinical symptoms and the noradrenergic deficits in the hypothalamus.[1,2]

Serotonin

Losses of serotonin (TABLE 9) innervation in Alzheimer's disease have been documented by measurement of serotonin and hydroxyindole acetic acid concentra-

TABLE 8. Noradrenaline in Alzheimer's Disease

	Reference	Comments
Histological Evidence for Neuronal Deficits		
Cell loss in the locus coeruleus	Mann *et al.*[63] and others	Cell loss has been confirmed in all reports.
Tangles in the locus coeruleus	Ishii[54]	This study has not been repeated yet.
Biochemical Evidence for Neuronal Deficits		
Loss of noradrenaline	Adolfsson *et al.*[1,2] Yates *et al.*[108] and others	A reduction in NA content has been reported by all investigators addressing this issue. The hypothalamus and striatal regions appear to be most affected but reports vary in this respect.
Loss of dopamine β-hydroxylase	Perry *et al.*[83]	Only measured in temporal cortex; not correlated with disease severity in this area.
Reduction in biopsy material noradrenaline uptake	Benton *et al.*[7]	

TABLE 9. Serotonin in Alzheimer's Disease

	Reference	Comments
Histological Evidence for Neuronal Deficits		
Cell loss in the raphé nuclei	Menn and Tates[62]	Not yet repeated
Tangles in the raphé	Ishii[54]	Not yet repeated
Biochemical Evidence for Neuronal Deficit		
Loss of serotonin	Adolfsson et al.[1,2]	Not yet investigated by other
	Gottfries et al.[44]	groups
Loss of imipramine binding	Bowen et al.[11]	Not yet repeated. Probably not a completely specific marker
Reduction in biopsy material serotonin uptake	Benton et al.[7]	

tions[1,2,44] and imipramine binding[11] to post mortem human brain tissue. In addition, a reduction of serotonin uptake into biopsy specimens of Alzheimer's disease when compared with other surgical material has been reported[7,11] again suggesting that the results obtained with post mortem material are not artifacts of the final stages of the disease. These biochemical observations correlate with reports of reduced cell counts and the presence of tangles in the raphe nuclei.[54,62] There have been, as yet, no attempts to correlate the serotonergic deficit with the pathological symptoms but again the impression seems to be that the loss of serotonin innervation does not mirror either the loss in cholinergic innervation or adrenergic innervation.[1,2,35]

Dopamine

Reduced dopamine concentration (TABLE 10) in striatal and extrastriatal regions have been reported in some patients.[1,2,44] Reductions in dopamine metabolite concentrations have also been reported in both brain and spinal fluid studies.[1,2,42,44,78,99] There have been no reports of cell counts in the substantia nigra in Alzheimer's disease. It could be that a dopamine deficit is found in a subgroup of patients with Alzheimer's disease; certainly a rather large proportion of Alzheimers patients develop Parkinson-like symptoms. Whether it is these patients who have reduced dopamine and homovanillic acid levels is not known.

TABLE 10. Dopamine in Alzheimers Disease

	Reference	Comments
Histological Evidence for Neuronal Deficits		
Cell counts in substantia nigra		No reports
Tangles in the substantia nigra		Ishii[54] reported no tangles in the substantia nigra
Biochemical Evidence for Neuronal Deficit		
Loss of dopamine	Gottfries et al.[44]	Not confirmed by other groups, see for example Yates et al.
Loss of homovanillic acid	Adolfsson et al.[1,2] Gottfries et al.[42]	A reduction in CSF MVA has been confirmed Palmer et al.

GENERAL SUMMARY

One might argue that the decrease in the number of brain cells as a function of age could be the source of the functional age deficits in memory performance. However, this possibility seems less likely since the actual loss of neurons up to advanced age is relatively small. There are no good estimates of the loss of synapses. Golgi staining of cortical neurons would indicate that there is a loss with higher age. So far, however, the most convincing data of marked loss with age appear at the biochemical level.

Most human data fail to demonstrate a decrease in cholinergic and serotonergic activity as a function of normal aging, although there is a loss of corresponding receptors. In AD/SDAT, however, there is a marked damage to these systems. Conceivably, acetylcholine may be providing informational rather than tone setting or balancing influence on memory function. This may explain the failure of cholinomimetic drugs to improve memory in AD/SDAT due to their inability to supply the informational properties of normal neuronal transmission.

The catecholamines, noradrenaline and dopamine are both lost in normal aging and to a much higher degree in AD/SDAT. Animal data show that noradrenaline deficiency results in scattered attention. Such a pattern might also exist in the intact aged and through guidance by means of instructions, contextual cues, and a richer TBR information, the elderly are being forced to attend. This may promote and supersede the normal functions of the noradrenaline system by directions from external rather than internal influences, conceivably by potentiating the remaining noradrenaline neurons. The cortical motor areas are relatively spared from neuro-degenerative changes in normal aging and in AD/SDAT and this might provide a neuroanatomical basis for the elderly's and mildly to moderately demented patients' success in memory performance when motor action is involved. The role of dopamine in motor function and its stability with age in hippocampus may also provide a neurochemical basis for the preservation of memory when the subjects are allowed to act physically during encoding.

ACKNOWLEDGMENT

We are grateful to David Morgan Ph.D for constructive comments on this paper.

REFERENCES

1. ADOLFSSON R., C. G. GOTTFRIES, B. E. ROOS & B. WINBLAD. 1979. Brit. J. Psychiat. **135:** 216-223.
2. ADOLFSSON, R., C. G. GOTTFRIES, B. E. ROOS & B. WINBLAD. 1979. J. Neural. Transm. **45:** 81–105.
3. ALBERT, M. S. & E. KAPLAN. 1980. Organic implications of neuropsychological deficits in the elderly. *In* New Directions in Memory and Aging. L. W. Poon, J. L. Fozard, L. S. Cermak, D. Arenberg & L. W. Thompson, Eds. L. Erlbaum. Hillsdale, NJ.
4. ARCHER, T. 1981. Scand. J. Psych. **23:** 61–71.
5. ATACK, J. R., E. K. PERRY, J. R. BONHAM, R. H. PERRY, B. E. TOMLINSON, G. BLESSED & A. FAIRBAIRN. 1983. Neurosci. Lett. **40:** 199–204.
6. BARTUS, R. T., R. L. DEAN, B. BEER & A. S. LIPPA. 1982. Science **217:** 408–417.
7. BENTON, J. S., D. M. BOWEN, S. J. ALLEN, E. A. HANN, A. N. DAVISON, D. NEARY, R. P. MURPHY & J. S. SNOWDON. 1982. Lancet **I: 456.**
8. BONDEREFF, W., C. Q. MOUNTJOY & M. ROTH. 1981. Lancet **I:** 783–784.

9. BOWEN, D. M., C. B. SMITH, P. WHITE, R. H. A. FLACK, L. H. CARRASCO, J. L. GEDYE & A. N. DAVISON. 1977. Brain 100: 427–453.
10. BOWEN, D. M., C. B. SMITH, P. WHITE & A. N. DAVISON. 1976. Brain 99: 459–496.
11. BOWEN, D. M., S. J. ALLEN, J. S. BENTON, M. J. GOODHARDT, E. A. HAHN, A. M. PALMER, N. R. SIMS, C. C. T. SMITH & J. A. SPILANE. 1983. J. Neurochem. 40: 266–272.
12. BOWEN, D. M. 1984. Paper read at the Third Zurich meeting on senile dementia.
13. BRANSFORD, J. D. 1979. Human Cognition. Learning, understanding and remembering. Belmont. Wadsworth.
14. BRODY, H. 1955. J. Comp. Neurol. 102: 511–556.
15. BRODY, H. 1973. Development and Aging in the Nervous System. pp. 121–133. Academic Press. New York.
16. BROOKSBANK, B. W. L., M. MARTINEX, D. J. ATKINSON & R. BALAZS. 1978. Dev. Neurosci. 1: 267–284.
17. BRUN, A. & L. GUSTAFSSON. 1976. Arch. Psychiat. Nervenkr. 223: 15–33.
18. BUCHT, G., R. ADOLFSSON, C. G. GOTTFRIES, B. E. ROOS & B. WINBLAD. 1981. J. Neural. Transm. 51: 185–203.
19. BUELL, S. J. & P. D. COLEMAN. 1979. Science 206: 854–856.
20. BÄCKMAN, L. 1984. Human Learning. (In press.)
21. BÄCKMAN, L. 1984. Doctoral dissertation. Department of Psychology. University of Umeä. Sweden.
22. BÄCKMAN, L. & L. G. NILSSON. 1984. Human Learning 3: 53–69.
23. BÄCKMAN, L. & L. G. NILSSON. 1984. Exp. Aging Res. (In press.)
24. BÄCKMAN, L., T. KARLSSON, A., HERLITZ, L. G. NILSSON & B. WINBLAD. 1984. How to improve recall performance in patients suffering from Alzheimer's disease. (Manuscript in preparation.)
25. CANESTRARI, R. E. 1968. In Human Aging and Behavior. G. A. Talland, Ed. Academic Press. New York.
26. CARLSSON, A., R. ADOLFSSON, S. M. AQUILONIUS, C. G. GOTTFRIES, L. ORELAND, L. SVENNERHOLM & B. WINBLAD. 1980. In Neuroendocrine and Neuropsychiatric Aspects. M. Goldstein et al., Eds.: 295–304. Plenum Press. New York.
27. CARLSSON, A. & B. WINBLAD. 1976. J. Neural. Transm. 38: 271–276.
28. CECI, S. J. & L. TABOR. 1981. Exp. Aging Res. 7: 147–158.
29. COHEN, R. L. 1981. Scand. J. Psych. 22: 267–282.
30. CRAIK, F. I. M. 1971. Q. J. Exp. Psych. 23: 316–319.
31. CRAIK, F. I. M. Age differences in human memory. 1977. In Handbook of the Psychology of Aging. J. E. Birren & K. W. SCHAIE, Eds. Van Nostrand. New York.
32. CRAIK, F. I. M. 1983. Phil. Trans. R. Soc. London 302: 341–359.
33. CRAIK, F. I. M. 1985. Paradigms in human memory research. In Perspectives on Learning and Memory. L. G. Nilsson & T. Archer, Eds. Lawrence Erlbaum. Hillsdale, NJ.
34. CRAIK, F. I. M. & J. C. RABINOWITZ. 1984. Age differences in the acquisition and use of verbal information. In Attention and Performance. H. Bouma & D. G. Bouwhuis, Eds. Vol. 10. Lawrence Erlbaum. Hillsdale, NJ.
35. DAVIES. P. 1979. Brain Res. 171: 319–327.
36. DAVIES, P. & A. J. MALONEY. 1976. Lancet II: 1403.
37. DAVIES, P. & A. H. VERTH. 1977. Brain Res. 138: 385–392.
38. DEKOSKY, S. T. & N. H. BASS. 1982. Neurology 32: 1227–1233.
39. ERBER, J. T., T. G. HERMAN, & J. BOTWINICK. 1980. Exp. Aging Res. 6: 341–348.
40. FARKAS, M. S. & W. J. HOYER. 1980. J. Gerontol. 35: 207–216.
41. FIBIGER, H. C. 1982. Brain Res. Rev. 4: 327–328.
42. GOTTFRIES, C. G. & B. E. ROOS. 1973. Acta Psychiat. Scand. 49: 257–263.
43. GOTTFRIES, C. G., L. ORELAND, Å. WIBERG & B. WINBLAD. 1974. Lancet II: 360–361.
44. GOTTFRIES, C. G., R. ADOLFSSON, S. M. AQUILONIUS, A. CARLSSON, S. Å. ECKERNÄS, A. NORDBERG, L. ORELAND, L. SVENNERHOLM, Å. WIBERG & B. WINBLAD. 1983. Neurobiol. Aging 4: 261–271.
45. HENDERSON, G., B. E. TOMLINSON & P. H. GIBSON. 1980. J. Neurol. Sci. 46: 113–136.
46. HOWELL, S. C. 1972. J. Gerontol. 27: 346–371.

47. HOYER, M. S., G. W. REBOK & S. M. SVED. 1979. J. Gerontol. **34:** 553–560.
48. HULICKA, I. M. & J. L. GROSSMAN. 1967. J. Gerontol. **22:** 46–51.
49. HULICKA, I. M., H. STERNS & J. L. GROSSMAN. 1967. J. Gerontol. **22:** 274–280.
50. HULTSCH, D. F. 1969. Dev. Psychol. **1:** 673–678.
51. HULTSCH, D. F. 1971. Dev. Psychol. **4:** 338–342.
52. HULTSCH, D. F. 1975. Dev. Psychol. **11:** 197–201.
53. HULTSCH, D. F. & C. A. PENTZ. 1980. Encoding, storage and retrieval in adult memory: The role of model assumptions. *In* New Directions in Memory and Aging. L. W. Poon, J. L. Fozard, L. S. Cermak, D. Arenberg & L. W. Thompson, Eds. Lawrence Erlbaum. Hillsdale, NJ.
54. ISHII, T. 1966. Acta Neuropath. **6:** 181–187.
55. KAUSLER, D. H. 1982. Experimental Psychology and Human Aging. John Wiley. New York.
56. KINSBOURNE, M. 1980. Attentional dysfunctions and the elderly: Theoretical models and research perspectives. *In* New Directions in Memory and Aging. L. W. Poon, J. L. Fozard, L. S. Cermak, D. Arenberg & L. W. Thompson, Eds. Lawrence Erlbaum. Hillsdale, NJ.
57. LAURENCE, M. W. 1967. Psychon. Sci. **9:** 209–210.
58. LAYTON, B. 1975. Psychol. Bull. **82:** 875–883.
59. LURIA, A. R. 1973. The Working Brain: An Introduction to Neuropsychology. Penguin Books Ltd. London.
60. MADDEN, D. J. 1983. Dev. Psychol. **19:** 499–507.
61. MANN, D. M. A. 1983. Mechanisms of Ageing and Development. **23:** 73–94.
62. MANN, D. M. A. & P. O. YATES. 1983. J. Neurol. Neurosurg. Psychiat. **46:** 96.
63. MANN, D. M. A. & J. LINCOLN, P. O. YATES, J. E. STAMP & S. TOPER. 1979. Brit. J. Psychiat. **136:** 533–541.
64. MANN, D. M. A. & P. O. YATES & B. MARCYNIUK. 1984. J. Neurol. Neurosurg. Psychiat. **47:** 201–203.
65. MASON, S. E. 1979. Dev. Psychol. **15:** 467–469.
66. MASON, S. T. & S. D. IVERSEN. 1979. Brain Res. Rev. **1:** 107–137.
67. MCGEER, E. G. & P. L. MCGEER. 1976. Neurobiol. Ageing. pp. 389–403. New York.
68. MCGEER, P. L., E. G. MCGEER & J. S. SUZUKI. 1977. Arch. Neurol. **34:** 33–35.
69. MCGEER, H. C. FIBIGER, P. L. MCGEER & V. WICKSON. 1971. Exp. Gerontol. **6:** 391.
70. MONAGLE, R. D. & H. BRODY. 1974. J. Comp. Neurol. **155:** 61–66.
71. NILSSON, L. G. 1979. Functions of memory. *In* Perspectives on Memory Research. L. G. Nilsson, Ed. Lawrence Erlbaum. Hillsdale, NJ.
72. NILSSON, L. G. 1980. Acta. Neurol. Scand. **62:** 62–74.
73. NILSSON, L. G. 1984. New functionalism in memory research. *In* Psychology in the 1990s. K. Lagerspetz & P. Niemi, Eds. North Holland Publishing Company. Amsterdam.
74. NORDBERG, A. & B. WINBLAD. 1981. Life Sci. **29:** 1937–1944.
75. NORDBERG, A., R. ADOLFSSON, S. M. AQUILONIUS, S. MARKLUND, L. ORELAND & B. WINBLAD. 1980. Aging **13:** 169–171.
76. NORDBERG, A., C. LARSSON, R. ADOLFSSON, I. ALAFUZOFF & B. WINBLAD. 1983. J. Neural Transm. **56:** 13–19.
77. O'CONNOR, N. & B. HERMELIN. 1978. Seeing and hearing and space and time. Academic Press. San Francisco.
78. PALMER, A. M., N. R. SIMS, D. M. BOWEN, D. NEARY, J. PALO, J. WIKSTRÖM & N. A. DAVISON. 1984. J. Neurol. Neurosurg. Psychiat. **47:** 481–484.
79. PERRY, E. K., P. H. GIBSON, G. BLESSED, R. H. PERRY & B. E. TOMLINSON. 1977. J. Neurol. Sci. **34:** 257–265.
80. PERRY, E. K., B. TOMLINSON, G. BLESSED, K. BERGMANN, P. H. GIBSON & R. H. PERRY. 1978. Br. Med. J. **2:** 1427–1429.
81. PERRY, E. K. 1980. Age Aging **9:** 1–8.
82. PERRY, E. K., R. H. PERRY, B. E. TOMLINSON, G. BLESSED & P. H. GIBSON. 1980. Neurosci. Lett. **18:** 105–110.
83. PERRY, E. K., G. BLESSED, B. TOMLINSON, R. H. PERRY, T. J. CROW, A. J. CROSS, G. J. DOCKRAY, R. DIMALINE & A. ARREGUI. 1981. Neurobiol. Aging **2:** 251–256.

84. PILLERI, G. 1966. Psychiat. Neurol. **152:** 65–103.
85. POPE, A., H. H. HESS & E. LEWIN. 1965. Trans. Amer. Neurol. Assoc. **89:** 15–16.
86. PRADHAN, S. M. 1980. Central neurotransmitters and ageing. Life Sci. **26:** 1643–1656.
87. RABBITT, P. 1965. Age and discrimination between complex stimuli. *In* Behaviour, Aging, and the Nervous System. A. T. Welford & J. E. Birren, Eds. C. C. Thomas. Springfield, IL.
88. RABBITT, P. 1965. J. Gerontol. **20:** 233–238.
89. REISINE, T. D., H. I. YAMAMURA, E. D. BIRD, E. SPOKES & S. T. ENNA. 1978. Brain Res. **159:** 477–481.
90. ROSSOR, M. N. 1982. Lancet **II:** 1200–1204.
91. ROSSOR, M. N., P. C. EMSON, C. Q. MOUNTJOY, M. ROTH & L. L. IVERSEN. 1980. Neurosci. Lett. **20:** 373–377.
92. RÖNNBERG, J. & L. G. NILSSON. 1982. Representation of auditory information based on a functionalistic perspective. *In* The Representation of Speech in the Peripheral Auditory System. R. Carlson & B. Granström, Eds. Elsevier Biomedical Press. Amsterdam.
93. RYLETT, R. J., M. J. BALL & E. H. COLHOUN. 1983. Brain Res. **289:** 169–176.
94. SALTHOUSE, T. A. 1982. Adult Cognition. Springer Verlag. New York.
95. SAMORAJSKI, T. 1977. J. Am. Geriat. Soc. **25:** 337–348.
96. SCHONFIELD, D. 1974. Am. Psychologist **29:** 796–801.
97. SIMS, N. R., D. M. BOWEN, S. J. ALLEN, C. C. T. SMITH, D. NEARY, D. J. THOMAS & A. N. DAVISON. 1983. Neurochem. **40:** 503–509.
98. SMITH, A. D. 1977. Dev. Psychol. **13:** 326–331.
99. SOININEN, H., E. MACDONALD, M. REKONEN & P. J. RIEKKINEN. 1981. Acta Neurol. Scand. **64:** 101–107.
100. THOMAS, J. C. & H. RUBEN. 1973. Age and mnemonic techniques in paired-associate learning. Paper presented at the Gerontological Society Conference. Miami, 1973.
101. TREAT, N. J., L. W. POON & J. L. FOZARD. 1978. Exp. Aging Res. **4:** 235–253.
102. VIJAYASHANKAR, N. & H. BRODY. 1979. J. Neuropathol. Exp. Neurol. **38:** 490–497.
103. WHITE, P., M. J. GOODHART, J. P. KEET, C. R. HILEY, L. H. CARASO, J. E. K. WILLIAMS & D. M. BOWEN. 1977. Lancet **1:** 668–671.
104. WHITEHOUSE, P. J., D. L. PRICE, R. G. STRUBLE, A. W. CLARS, J. T. COYLE & M. R. DELONG. 1982. Science **215:** 1237–1239. 1982.
105. WILCOCK, J. K., M. M. ESIRI, D. M. BOWEN & C. C. T. SMITH. 1982. J. Neurol. Sci. **57:** 407–417.
106. WOOD, P. L., P. ETIENNE, S. LAL, N. P. V. NAIR, M. H. FINLAYSON, S. GAUTHER, J. PALO, M. HALTIO, A. PAETAU & E. D. BIRD. 1983. J. Neurol. Sci. **62:** 211–217.
107. WRIGHT, L. L. & J. W. ELIAS. 1979. J. Gerontol. **34:** 704–708.
108. YATES, C. M., J. SIMSON, A. GORDON, A. J. F. MALONEY, Y. ALLISON, I. M. RITCHIE & A. URQUHART. 1983. Brain Res. **280:** 119–126.

Human Cerebral Metabolism: Studies in Normal Subjects and Patients with Dementia and Amnesia[a]

JOHN C. MAZZIOTTA[b]

Department of Neurology
Division of Biophysics and Nuclear Medicine
Department of Radiological Sciences
UCLA School of Medicine and
Laboratory of Nuclear Medicine
Los Angeles, California 90024

The investigation of human cerebral cognitive and memory functions has been one of the most difficult and challenging endeavors of the last century. Investigators have used a wide range of physiological, pharmacological, and neuropsychological techniques to examine these issues and many of those approaches are described in these proceedings. While the results of these studies have been impressive and have improved our understanding of normal and abnormal cerebral function, relatively little is known about the local biochemistry and physiology of these processes in humans. Positron computed tomography (PET) has provided previously unavailable insights into the local physiological relationships of the human brain and has the capability to provide specific information about human cognitive and mnestic processes.

Positron computed tomography can no longer be considered a new discipline. It has been applied to the study of normal subjects as well as patients with all of the major neuropsychiatric disorders.[29,31,37] These studies have demonstrated, for the first time, local cerebral responses to physiological stimuli in normals. In patients, PET has demonstrated cerebral pathophysiology expressed through a wide range of biochemical and physiological variables that are able to be measured with this technique. The purpose of this chapter is to describe the principles of PET and its application to normal subjects and patients, with particular reference to the results and strategies of studies aimed at understanding normal and abnormal memory function.

POSITRON COMPUTED TOMOGRAPHY

PET is an analytic, noninvasive measurement tool for determining local cerebral function in humans. PET is already able to provide information about local cerebral blood flow (LCBF), oxygen (LCMRO$_2$), and glucose (LCMRGLc) metabolic rates and extraction fractions as well as cerebral blood volume.[31] These physiological

[a]Partially supported by Department of Energy contract AM 03-76-SF00012, National Institutes of Health Grants R01-6M-248388 and P01-NS-15-654, National Institute of Mental Health Grant R01-MH-37916-02 and donations from the Jennifer Jones Simon Foundation. J.C.M. is the recipient of Teacher Investigator Award 1K07-00588-03-NSPA from the National Institute of Neurologic, Communicative Disease and Stroke.
[b]Address correspondence to: John C. Mazziotta, Department of Neurology, Reed Neurologic Institute, UCLA School of Medicine, Los Angeles, CA 90024.

269

measurements are made possible by using biologically active compounds labeled with positron emitting isotopes of carbon, nitrogen, oxygen, fluorine, and others. With these compounds it is possible to label substrates, substrate analogs, and drugs and use them . *in vivo* without disturbing their biochemical properties or behavior. The basic components that constitute the major methodological elements of PET include: analytic PET instrumentation, positron-labeled compounds, and tracer kinetic mathematical models (FIGURE 1).

PET imaging devices make use of the unique physical properties of positron decay that allow for the acquisition of high resolution quantifiable cross-sectional images of the human brain.[29,31] These compounds are administered either by intravenous injection or inhalation. After a period of time, predicted by the tracer kinetic model, images are obtained that can be mathematically converted to the physiological process of interest. Final image resolution is presently in the range of 8–18 mm. The NeuroECAT PET device (FIGURE 2)[13] has a spatial resolution of 10 mm. The theoretical limit of resolution is on the order of a few millimeters. Details about these systems and the resulting accuracy of the quantitative capabilities of PET have been previously described in detail.[13,26,29,31,46]

The short physical half-lives of positron-emitting radioisotopes require that a cyclotron for their production be available at or close to the site of PET imaging. Many labeled compounds are available for measuring biochemical and physiological processes.[31] However, the problem of actually achieving these measurements is far more complex. The measurement of physiological processes requires careful selection of the labeled compound, the process to study, and the use of tracer kinetic models within the limitations imposed by PET for human studies.[31] Most of the studies performed thus far have used oxygen-15–labeled compounds to examine cerebral blood flow, oxygen metabolism, and extraction and fluorine-18–labeled fluorodeoxyglucose (FDG) to examine cerebral glucose utilization. These variables are of greatest interest because they normally provide the supply-demand basis of local function in the brain. That is to say, under normal conditions, glucose and oxygen metabolism are held in a constant relationship, and flow is determined by metabolic demand (i.e., metabolic regulation of flow or flow-metabolism coupling).[31,38,41] The combined use of these measurements allows for the characterization of cerebral stoichiometry (i.e., the numerical relationship between chemical processes) of the normal and diseased human brain. Whereas CBF and metabolism are reasonably coupled in normal states, this is not the case in abnormal states, where CBF, $CMRO_2$, and CMRGLc can be uncoupled in unpredictable ways.[31] For a detailed discussion of tracer kinetic methods and positron-labeled compounds the reader is referred to recent reviews.[29,31,32,37]

STUDIES OF NORMAL SUBJECTS WITH PET

The measurement of functional brain responses with PET has been clearly demonstrated by the use of sensory, motor, and neurobehavioral stimulation paradigms in normal subjects.[20] The effects of visual,[11,19,25,30,36,42] auditory,[11,22–24] somatosensory,[2,11] and motor tasks[21,40] have already been reported in normal individuals. In these investigations PET was used typically with FDG to determine glucose utilization rates. Since gross structural brain abnormalities are typically not found in patients with dementia and amnestic syndromes, the functional aspects of PET imaging are particularly interesting and important in the study of such patients.

Stimulation studies involving the visual system have demonstrated the expected topographic representation of retinal areas in the primary visual cortex.[11,25,30,36,42]

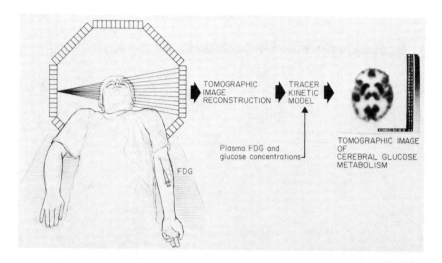

FIGURE 1. (Top) The sequence of events involved in the PET measurement of local cerebral metabolic rate of glucose (LCMRGLc) with F-18 2-fluoro-2-deoxy-D-glucose (FDG). At 40 min after intravenous injection of FDG, tomographic data are collected and cross-sectional images are reconstructed of the F-18 tissue activity distribution. Plasma FDG and glucose concentrations are entered into the computer of the tomograph that also contains the operational equation of the FDG tracer kinetic model. Images are then converted to local cerebral metabolic rate for glucose in units of mg or micromoles·min⁻¹·100 g⁻¹ of tissue. Tomographic images are displayed on television monitors with a gray scale in proportion to local cerebral metabolic rate for glucose with black being the highest value. Numerical values are shown beside the scale. (Bottom) The NeuroECAT (CTI, Inc., Oak Ridge, TN) positron computed tomographic system. (From Phelps *et al.*[32] With permission from *Annals of Internal Medicine.*)

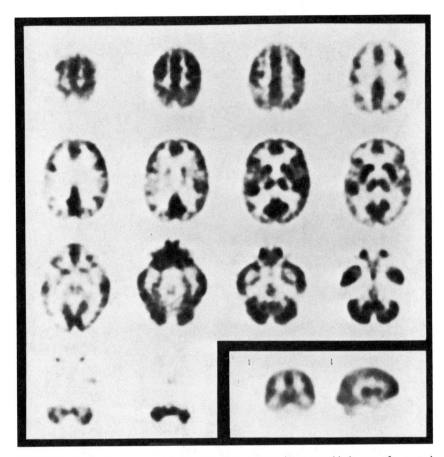

FIGURE 2. Cerebral glucose metabolism. Positron computed tomographic images of a normal subject studied with FDG to measure glucose metabolism using the NeuroECAT positron computed tomograph. Both tomographic and two-dimensional rectilinear images (lower right corner) are obtainable with this device. Note the details of the cerebral anatomy: Top row, cerebral cortical gyri, and sulci; second row, basal ganglia, thalamus, and visual cortex shown in the two right-most images; third row, temporal lobe, brain stem, and cerebellum, including cerebellar cortex, vermis, and dentate nuclei (two right-most images). Gray scale of the images is proportional to the glucose metabolic rate with black being highest. The left hemisphere is shown at the left of these and all subsequent images. (From Phelps et al.[31] With permission from *Journal of Cerebral Blood Flow and Metabolism*.)

Binocular stimuli have produced symmetrical metabolic responses of the primary and secondary visual cortical areas confirming in man the 50% functional input from each eye to both visual cortices.[36] Phelps et al.[30] demonstrated that the magnitude of the cortical response in both primary and secondary visual areas increased with stimulus complexity. In patients with lesions of the visual pathway that were outside of the occipital cortex, PET methods have revealed the appropriate functional deficits that correlated with the behavioral symptoms even in cases where X-ray computed tomography (XCT) imaging of the visual cortical areas was normal.[36,39]

Other PET studies in normal right-handed subjects who received auditory stimuli have demonstrated that cerebral metabolic responses correlated with the content of the stimulus and in some cases with the strategy employed by the subject to solve a particular auditory task.[24] Nonverbal stimuli consisting of chords activated right hemisphere regions in the posterior temporal, inferior parietal, and temporo-occipital zones. Verbal stimuli produced mirror image asymmetries and activations in metabolism in the left hemisphere.

In subjects given auditory recognition tasks with a specific memory requirement, additional cerebral structures were activated.[24] High resolution PET imaging was obtained from subjects listening to verbal, monaural auditory stimuli (Sherlock Holmes story) who were required to remember specific aspects of its content. Images from these subjects demonstrated increases in glucose utilization that were similar to subjects asked only to listen to the story without the memory component. However, in addition to the large areas of left > right cortical activations in glucose metabolism, bilateral activations of mesial temporal structures (FIGURE 3) were seen only in the stimulated state and never in control conditions.[24] This was a complex task involving

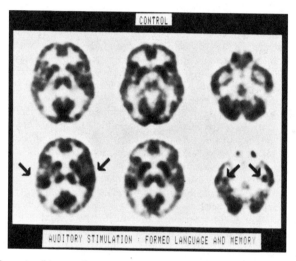

FIGURE 3. Two sets of images from normal subjects studied with FDG to determine glucose utilization in a control (top row) and stimulated state (bottom row). Images were obtained with the NeuroECAT PET device. The top row of images was obtained from a subject with no auditory stimulation (ears plugged but eyes open). The bottom row of images was obtained from a subject listening to a factual story monoaurally and told to remember as many details of the story as possible. He was additionally told that he would be paid in proportion to how much information he could recall on a subsequent examination. Note the activation of the primary auditory cortex situated bilaterally in the posterior transverse, temporal cortical zone. The left-right metabolic asymmetries in this area closely parallel known anatomical asymmetries for these zones in the human brain (i.e., the region on the left is larger, wedge shaped and more posterior than its counterpart on the right). Note also on the lowest plane (bottom right image), activation of the mesial temporal lobe during the stimulation task. The two black dots located adjacent to the mesial temporal cortex are in the anatomical position of the hippocampus and parahippocampal gyri. It is not clear whether these mesial temporal responses are the result of the auditory task itself, attentional factors, the memory requirements of the task, some combination of these factors, or some other components of the paradigm (see text). (From Mazziotta et al.[24] With permission from *Neurology*.)

auditory perception, decoding, and encoding of material that the subject was asked to remember, therefore, it was not possible to specifically identify which cerebral structures were responding to which aspects of this complex task. However, in other auditory stimulation paradigms, in which no memory requirement was demanded of the subject, mesial temporal responses (hippocampus, parahippocampus) were not seen. At present, it is unclear whether this mesial temporal response is a result of certain aspects of the auditory task itself, attentional factors, the memory requirement of the task, some combination of these factors, or some other component of the paradigm.

The ability to activate cerebral structures consistently in a functional way using neurobehavioral paradigms and PET allows for the selective stimulation of these areas in patients with minimal abnormalities on "resting" or baseline PET studies. Thus, the investigator may use stimulation paradigms involving either behavioral tasks or drugs to stress local regions of the brain and demonstrate minimal, latent cerebral dysfunction, much in the way a cardiologist uses treadmill testing to document latent abnormalities in coronary artery blood supply. Just as Penfield and his colleagues[28] investigated human cortical phenomena through intraoperative stimulations, PET studies in normals will provide similar information in a more physiological and noninvasive fashion.

The understanding of how specific sensory, motor, cognitive, and mnestic tasks activate brain structures will be helpful in classifying patients with dementia and amnestic syndromes. It is interesting to consider how such a strategy might be used with PET.[20] In patients with complex partial epilepsy and clinical and EEG evidence of a temporal lobe focus, PET studies have revealed focal hypometabolism for glucose of the affected temporal lobe in resting FDG studies.[6,7,16] Selective activation of mesial temporal structures through a specific auditory-mnestic stimulation paradigm (FIGURE 3)[24] could exaggerate the metabolic abnormality in the affected temporal lobe when compared to the contralateral side or to a normal control population. That is, the response of the abnormal temporal region may be attenuated and the stimulus-induced metabolic response diminished unilaterally. The use of such provocative behavioral stimuli, and potentially the use of pharmacological stimuli,[35] can enhance the interpretability of such studies and provide previously unavailable information about the structure-function relationships of memory processes. Functional activation studies performed with PET, therefore, serve not only to map the normal cerebral responses of the human subjects to stimuli but can also be developed as probes to stress minimally dysfunctioning brain tissue in patients with suspected or known abnormalities.[20]

STUDIES IN PATIENTS

The study of pathophysiology in patients with cerebral disorders using PET has a number of distinctive advantages over evaluating such patients with imaging techniques that only demonstrate brain structure. Since the brain consists of vastly interconnected networks of functional units, structural damage at a focal site will cause functional disruptions at many distant areas. The correlation of behavioral and clinical abnormalities with structural information, therefore, is limited to conclusions based on the small zone of anatomical injury and assumptions about projections into and out of this site. Functional imaging techniques allow for direct visualization of physiological altered sites at a distance from the zone of structural damage (FIGURE 4).

Patients followed serially after an acute cerebral injury (e.g., infarction) have demonstrated that their functional lesions (PET) are larger in volume and distribution

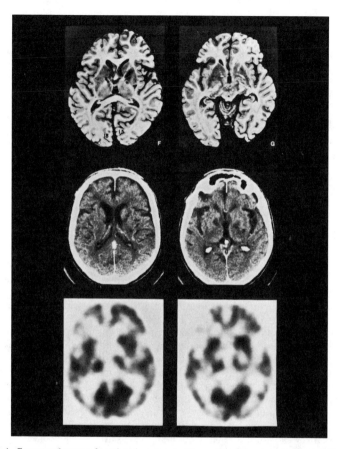

FIGURE 4. Structural versus functional anatomy. Three sets of images obtained with different methods from a patient with multiple infarct dementia. This patient had X-ray computed tomographic images (center row) and PET images of glucose utilization (bottom row) on the same day. Seven days later the patient died of non-neurological causes and had gross and microscopic evaluation of the brain (top row). Both forms of structural imaging (X-ray CT and post-mortem) demonstrate multiple small lacunar infarctions of the caudate, putamen, thalamus, and internal capsule. Neither of the structural imaging techniques demonstrated abnormalities of the cortex. Histologic examination did not reveal significant differences in neuronal cell counts between the left and right frontal cortices. Functional brain imaging of glucose metabolism with PET, however, demonstrates widespread abnormalities of the frontal cortex particularly on left. These distant functional effects probably represent disconnection of afferent and efferent fiber systems between the frontal cortical areas and subcortical zones. These disconnections most likely resulted from the lacunar infarcts seen structurally. Behavioral correlations, therefore, are more complete and comprehensive when evaluated by pathophysiology measures determined with PET than with structural or anatomical imaging techniques such as X-ray CT or post-mortem examination.

than structural abnormalities (XCT).[31] These functional lesions change and frequently improve dynamically over days, weeks, and months after the time of initial damage. Functional imaging, therefore, provides a much more comprehensive correlation with clinical signs, symptoms, and patient behavior than structural imaging techniques. Discrete structure-function relationships can be observed by using a combination of structural (XCT, NMR) and functional (PET) methods in the same individual.

As noted above, cerebral stoichiometry can be evaluated in patients by the use of multiple tracers and PET in the same scanning session.[31] This information allows one to describe the complex biochemical interactions that occur in a given patient in the course of an injury which produces a behavioral syndrome such as amnesia or dementia. These data may provide important insights into the pathophysiology that underlies specific disease states. Direct observation of pharmacology can also be evaluated with PET either by measuring the influence of pharmacological doses of drugs on nonspecific processes, such as blood flow and metabolism, or by using a positron-labeled ligand directly to measure cerebral pharmacokinetics *in vivo*.[1,53]

As an example of the capabilities of PET to study patients with cognitive and memory dysfunction, descriptions of PET results in patients with dementia and amnestic syndromes follow.

Patients with Dementia

Studies in demented patients were among the initial clinical projects using PET and results are now available from investigations that measured LCBF, LCMRGLc, and LCMRO$_2$ in patients with dementias resulting from various neurodegenerative processes.[3–5,8–10,17,18] While most studies have concentrated on Alzheimer's disease, data are also available for multiple infarct dementia and Huntington's disease.

A problem in interpreting PET studies in patients with cerebral atrophy is the issue of partial volume effects.[12,26] That is, since the PET instrument has a spatial resolution inadequate to resolve cortical structures with 100% accuracy, metabolic rates obtained for cortical structures in patients with atrophy will be the product of tissue mixtures that include cortex, white matter, and cerebrospinal fluid (CSF) spaces.[26] This nonuniform averaging of tissue zones (e.g., cortex with CSF spaces, particularly with enlarged cerebral sulci) may artifactually reduce cortical metabolic rates. In Alzheimer's disease it is well known that large numbers of cells are lost (46% of large neurons in the temporal cortex and 40% of neurons in the frontal cortex[47]). However, it is unclear whether reduced metabolism in the cortex reflects neuronal cell death or abnormal function of preserved neurons. To answer such questions corrections of the PET measured metabolic rates will have to be made to account for both partial volume effects and reduced numbers of total neurons. In addition, as noted by Foster *et al.*[8] the correlation of abnormal neuropsychological factors and focal areas of hypometabolism from PET data must be interpreted cautiously due to the difficulties of applying correlational statistics for multiple comparisons between partially interdependent variables.

Despite these problems, the data thus far available from PET demonstrate a positive correlation between the severity of dementia and the reductions in glucose or oxygen metabolism of the brain as a whole.[4,9,17] This is in contrast with XCT data of brain structure in which consistency is lacking between behavioral disability and XCT measurements of cerebral atrophy. Cerebral measurements of brain atrophy from XCT in demented patients overlap substantially with atrophy seen in elderly, but otherwise normal, individuals. In patients with Alzheimer's disease, focal abnormalities in metabolism have been most severe in the frontal, parietal, and temporal cortex and least severe in the primary visual, motor, and sensory cortical areas (FIGURE 5). The glucose metabolic rates in demented patients have been consistently lower than those found in age-matched normal populations.

Foster et al.[8] and Chase et al.[4] examined patients with Alzheimer's disease who had specific predominant symptoms and measured glucose metabolism in these subgroups. Patients included those with specific constructional abnormalities, language abnormalities, and pure memory disorders. In the group with abnormal spatial and constructional test scores, a 31% LCMRGLc decrease in the right parietal cortex

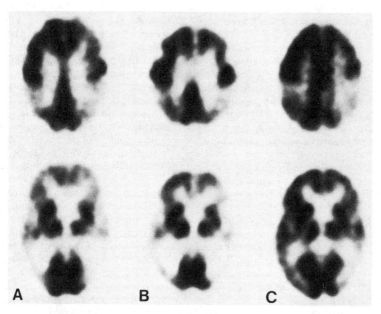

FIGURE 5. FDG-PET scans of glucose metabolism in three patients with Alzheimer's disease. Metabolic rates are depressed globally, particularly in the parietal cortex. Metabolic rates for the caudate and thalamus are depressed only slightly. This is the reverse of patients with Huntington's disease where striatal metabolism is maximally depressed and cortical values are normal (FIGURE 7). (From Kuhl et al.[17] With permission from *Journal of Cerebral Blood Flow Metabolism.*)

(relative to the left) was found whereas those with specific language abnormalities had metabolic decrements of 18% in the left fronto-parieto-temporal region relative to the right side. Patients with predominantly memory abnormalities had no left-right metabolic asymmetries. In these patients, who had little evidence of cerebrovascular disease and who were on no medication, it was concluded that focal abnormalities could be identified in the metabolic images that correlated with the predominant clinical symptoms.

DeLeon et al.[5] found that the maximal suppression of glucose metabolism occurred in the parietal cortex (24%) and that an overall cortical and subcortical metabolic depression of 17–24% could be found in Alzheimer's patients as compared with age-matched controls. Freidland et al.[10] in similar group of patients (N = 10) found maximal decreases in FDG activity in the parieto-temporal regions as compared with age-matched controls. This decrement was proportional to the severity of the patient's dementia and compared well with the distribution of metabolic depression found by Chase et al.[4] and Kuhl et al.[17] In this latter study[17] high resolution FDG-PET imaging was performed in patients with severe Alzheimer's disease and severe atrophy on XCT but little evidence of cerebrovascular disease. These patients (N = 6, mean age = 64) had a global decrease in LCMRGLc of 33%. Maximal cortical LCMRGLc depressions occurred in parietal cortex where the reduction was 47% relative to age-matched normals. Fronto-temporal cortical reductions in metabolism were 28% while subcortical regions had glucose reductions of only 12% (FIGURE 5).

Overall, FDG-PET studies of Alzheimer's disease patients have demonstrated global reductions in metabolic activity with maximal focal abnormalities in the parieto-temporal regions followed by frontal cortical abnormalities. The least affected areas in these patients have included the primary sensory-motor cortex and subcortical structures. The severity of the dementia appears to be inversely related to the metabolic rate and specific cognitive abnormalities revealed on clinical examination have been reflected by focal cortical metabolic rate reductions. No specific information has thus far been provided about mesial temporal structures in patients with Alzheimer's disease and symptoms of memory dysfunction.

Frackowiak et al.[9] examined Alzheimer's disease patients at various stages in the dementing process and compared them with patients suffering from multiple-infarct dementia. Twenty-two patients with a mean age of 66 ± 9 years were studied with mild to moderate dementia. Of this group, 13 patients had presumed Alzheimer's disease. In all patients, coupled reductions in blood flow and oxygen utilization were found. These reductions were 50% for gray matter and 23% for white matter. Oxygen extraction fractions were normal in all cases. As with the studies of glucose metabolism, a significant negative correlation was seen between the severity of the dementia and the magnitude of the blood flow and oxygen utilization variables. When compared to control populations, 20% reductions in CBF and CMRO$_2$ were found in subjects with moderate dementia as opposed to 35% reductions in patients with severe dementia. No significant left-right asymmetries for flow or oxygen utilization were reported for this group. No evidence of increased oxygen extraction fraction was found in Alzheimer's patients or patients with multiple-infarct dementia. The authors concluded that chronic ischemia was not the cause of either of these two types of dementing processes.

Focal decreases in oxygen utilization have been seen in patients with multiple infarct dementia in studies measuring both oxygen utilization and glucose metabolism.[9,17] Kuhl et al.[17] examined multiple-infarct dementia patients using PET and FDG to measure glucose metabolism (FIGURE 6). In this study a total of 39 cerebral abnormalities were found through the combined use of PET and XCT. In lesions with abnormalities identified by both imaging modalities, metabolic rate reductions averaged 48%. In lesions identified with PET but missed by XCT (N = 24), average metabolic rate reductions were only 17%. Five lesions were detected by XCT but not identified in images of glucose metabolism. All of these lesions occurred in white matter and it is uncertain whether they could have been detected with PET using image display parameters more suitable for examining white matter zones.

The discrepancy between the number of lesions seen with XCT versus PET may reflect the functional imaging capacity of the latter modality. It may be that focal small infarcts detected by XCT produce metabolic suppression at distant sites (FIGURE 4). The distant functional lesions would have no structural counterpart and, therefore, would only be demonstrated by functional imaging techniques such as PET. In this manner, a single structural abnormality seen on XCT could have multiple areas of metabolic suppression demonstrated with PET as a result of the multiple efferent projections emanating from the structural abnormality. This hypothesis awaits further documentation with combined XCT and PET studies of patients with focal lesions.

Bustany *et al.*[3] examined carbon-11–labeled methionine incorporation in patients with mild and severe dementia. As was found with metabolic rate determinations for glucose and oxygen, protein synthesis was inversely related to the severity of the

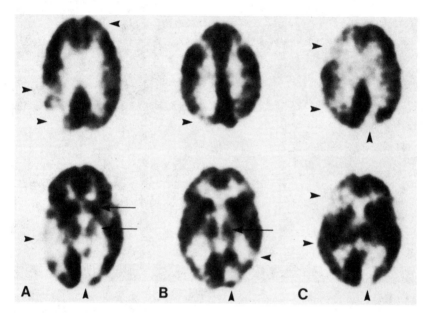

FIGURE 6. FDG-PET scans of glucose utilization in three patients with multiple infarct dementia. Global metabolic rates are depressed and there are multiple focal metabolic defects scattered throughout the brain (arrows). Notice the difference in these studies when compared with studies of patients with Alzheimer's disease (FIGURE 5) or Huntington's disease (FIGURE 7). (From Kuhl *et al.*[17] With permission from *Journal of Cerebral Blood Flow Metabolism.*)

dementia. The patients with mild dementia demonstrated a 19 ± 4% reduction in frontal cortical methionine incorporation whereas patients with severe dementia had reductions of 67% when compared to age-matched controls.

Patients with Huntington's disease have been examined with PET to determine glucose utilization rates.[18] While these patients consistently demonstrated profound striatal hypometabolism, they typically had preserved cortical metabolic rates (FIGURE 7). No correlation was found between the duration of the disease process or the severity of the dementia and either global or focal metabolic rates for glucose utilization. Again, no specific information has thus far been reported in Huntington's patients for metabolic activity of focal regions of the temporal lobe particularly the medial surface.

Overall, PET studies of patients with dementing processes have demonstrated abnormalities previously inaccessible with conventional imaging techniques. Studies are under way at the present time to correlate functional abnormalities of metabolism, blood flow, and protein synthesis in patients with early dementia and predominant

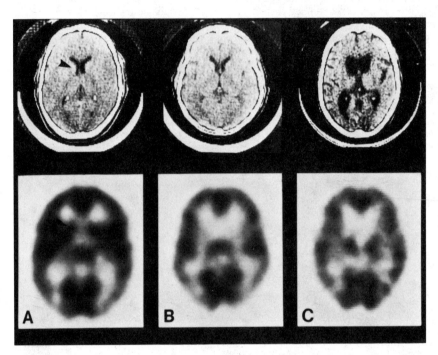

FIGURE 7. Local cerebral glucose metabolism in Huntington's disease demonstrated by X-ray CT and PET. All PET images were obtained using FDG to measure glucose metabolism. (A) Normal subject demonstrating the normal structural and metabolic appearance of the caudate nucleus (arrow) and putamen. (B) Patient with early clinical Huntington's disease, demonstrating a normal structural appearance of the caudate nucleus on X-ray CT but profound hypometabolism of the caudate and putamen in the PET image. (C) Patient with late Huntington's disease, demonstrating both structural (cortical and subcortical atrophy) and functional abnormalities of the caudate and putamen, bilaterally. Such studies demonstrate that functional (as measured by glucose metabolism) abnormalities of the basal ganglia in patients with early Huntington's disease precede structural cell loss sufficient to produce changes in X-ray CT images. (From Kuhl et al.[18] With permission from the Annals of Neurology.)

symptoms of memory dysfunction. The correlation of behavioral parameters in these patients with the physiological information from PET about the focal brain regions should prove to be extremely important in attempting to understand the pathophysiological basis for memory dysfunction in patients with dementing processes. The patterns that emerge may be disease specific or may show common abnormalities irrespective of the etiological entity involved but common to the behavioral syndrome of the memory disorder. As noted in the section on normal stimulation studies, behavioral and pharmacological interventions in such patients may enhance the ability to detect subtle "resting" PET abnormalities in these patients with dementia and memory dysfunction.[20]

Patients with Pure Amnestic Syndromes

Relatively few PET studies have been performed in patients with isolated memory defects that were not part of a more generalized dementing process.[27,49-51] Volpe *et al.* studied blood flow and oxygen utilization in patients with amnesia following global hypoxic-ischemia brain injury,[49,51] rupture and repair of anterior communicating artery aneurysms,[50] and in a single patient with transient global amnesia.[49]

The patients with global hypoxic-ischemic brain injury had stable amnesias lasting a number of years. The neuropsychological characteristics of this syndrome include intact short term memory, severely depressed free recall, and less depressed recognition of visual and verbal material.[52] These patients had normal cortical and thalamic blood flow and oxygen utilization when compared with controls but demonstrated bilateral decreases in oxygen utilization in mesial temporal regions despite having normal blood flow values for the same location. This flow-metabolism mismatch resulted in decreased oxygen extraction fractions for the mesial temporal zones. A similar result was reported by this group for the patients with rupture and repair of anterior communicating artery aneurysms.[50]

In the single patient evaluated with transient global amnesia, two PET studies were performed, one in the amnestic state and one following resolution of the amnesia.[49] X-ray CT images of this patient were normal. As in the patients described above, the patient with transient global amnesia had decreases in oxygen extraction fractions for the mesial temporal lobe that resolved one day after her clinical recovery.

Thus, in patients with amnesia from a variety of mechanisms, a common feature reported in preliminary studies by Volpe and coworkers was decreased oxygen extraction in the mesial temporal lobe. The relationship between global flow and metabolism and focal mesial temporal abnormalities in oxygen extraction remain to be fully defined. However, these preliminary observations by Volpe *et al.*[49-51] demonstrate the ability of PET to identify common physiological abnormalities in patients with amnestic syndromes caused by a variety of different mechanisms. This work represents the first example of physiological imaging in patients with pure amnestic syndromes.

Metter *et al.*[27] used FDG and PET to measure glucose utilization in eight patients who had either aphasia or amnesia following language-dominant hemisphere lesions. All but two patients had lesions secondary to ischemic infarction and all had either aphasia or amnesia. One exception was the well-studied patient N.A.,[14,45,48] who 19 years earlier had an injury with a fencing foil that resulted in damage to the medial thalamus (as reported from X-ray CT images). His major residual deficit has been a severe verbal memory amnesia with no language abnormality. The second patient without cerebral infarction had dominant hemispheric cortical damage resulting from posttraumatic surgical debridement of the left temporal lobe.

Marked metabolic depression was found in the thalamus and caudate in all patients reported by Metter *et al.*[27] Patients with subcortical infarcts had only mild left-sided cortical metabolic depressions, while the patients with cortical lesions showed marked cortical metabolic reductions. Aphasic symptoms were mild in the patients with subcortical lesions but were moderate to severe in the cortically damaged patients. All subjects showed severe verbal memory dysfunctions. The only common abnormality in the two groups was metabolic reductions in the thalamus and severe verbal memory dysfunction. The authors felt that these findings suggested a relationship between verbal memory and thalamic function.

CONCLUSION

Structural imaging techniques such as X-ray and proton nuclear magnetic resonance computed tomography have limited potential for providing insights into the pathophysiological basis of dementia and amnestic syndromes. Functional imaging with PET has already provided new information about the normal response of the human brain to physiological stimuli and to the patterns of pathophysiological derangement that can occur in disease processes associated with dementia and amnesia.[31] A number of refinements in techniques and methodology will improve the potential to study these issues in greater detail.

Spatial and temporal resolution of PET methods should improve in the near future. Devices are already planned[34] that should have spatial resolution capacities for neurological studies in the range of 4–5 mm. With spatial resolution in this range, detailed anatomy of the hippocampus, thalamus, and other nuclear substructures of the brain will be identifiable. Such images will also provide more accurate quantitative information about physiological processes occurring in small cerebral structures.

Techniques that use oxygen-15–labeled compounds to measure cerebral blood flow and oxygen metabolism provide the means to reduce the measurement period (i.e., the stimulation time for behavioral paradigms) from the 30 to 40 minutes now required with FDG, to 1–5 minutes. These stimulus duration reductions will minimize concerns about habituation and acclimatization to the testing environment.[15,20] In addition, the better dosimetry characteristics of short-lived positron-emitting isotopes like oxygen-15 will allow for multiple administrations in the same subject in the same setting. With such a strategy, a memory paradigm could be varied in such a way as to dissect apart components of a complex task into perception, decoding, encoding, and recall.[20] Such paradigms will require sophisticated attention to neuropsychological controls and will need sophisticated models for appropriate analysis of the resultant data. However, these techniques hold great promise for providing insights into the complex and perhaps heterogeneous functional systems that take part in different memory processes.

Once developed, behavioral paradigms that are aimed at memory function analysis in normals can be transferred to patient populations. As described above, these paradigms would be used as probes to stimulate areas of minimal brain dysfunction, evaluate functional reserve of damaged tissue, and examine the recovery process of patients with brain injuries.[20] In patients with amnestic syndromes secondary to acute events (e.g., transient global amnesia, hypoxic-ischemic injury) behavioral paradigms administered serially over the recovery period may allow for objective evaluation of this process. In patients with degenerative disorders such as Alzheimer's and Huntington's disease, serial studies should demonstrate functional systems that are responsible for preserving function in the face of ongoing structural damage.

The ability to measure cerebral protein synthesis rates *in vivo* in humans[33] with PET may allow for strategies of understanding the possible role of this process in memory formation. While paradigms and strategies that would employ protein synthesis measurements are difficult to design, the potential to make such measurements should stimulate interest and activity in this area. This is especially pertinent since an abundant literature exists from animal experimentation on the relationship between cerebral protein synthesis and memory.

The ability to examine drug effects using PET will be another area of future interest with relevance to memory function and its abnormalities. The effects of pharmacological doses of drugs on blood flow and metabolism as well as protein synthesis can be evaluated locally and *in vivo* with PET. Additionally, positron-labeled drugs can be studied directly in brain to examine sites of binding and pharmacokinetic behavior in normal and abnormal human subjects.[1,53]

Lastly, a great deal of research has focused on animal models of memory in recent decades. The tracer kinetic method provides a straightforward and objective means of evaluating the relevance of animal models to human conditions. Physiological measurements of blood flow, metabolism, protein synthesis, and ligand binding can be made in animals with autoradiography[43,44] and in humans with PET.[31] Since both studies can now be performed with a common technique (i.e., the tracer kinetic method) the results obtained from both PET and autoradiography can be scrutinized for similarities and differences. The PET methods can be used to evaluate or refute animal models of specific human amnestic disorders and normal memory function. The selected models can then be used to explore these processes in experimental paradigms that are either too invasive or logistically too complex to perform in patients.

The study of normal memory function, dementia, and amnestic disorders with PET is at an early stage. Many problems remain to be investigated and will require methodological improvements or experimental design strategy refinements for their success. However, the available techniques provide previously unobtainable information in humans and the potential to evaluate the relevancy and limits of accuracy of animal models in the study of memory systems. These issues represent unique and challenging new endeavors for the neurosciences.

ACKNOWLEDGMENTS

Special thanks to Bruce Volpe, M.D. and his colleagues for contributing data and valuable comments; to UCLA PET investigators: David Kuhl, Michael Phelps, Jerome Engel Jr., Jeffrey Metter, and Walter Riege for their generous contributions. In addition, gratitude is expressed to Patrick Welton for editorial assistance and to Anita Powers for preparing the manuscript. Artwork and illustrations were prepared by Lee Griswold.

REFERENCES

1. BARON, J. C., D. ROEDA, C. MUNARI, C. CROUZEL, J. P. CHODKIEWICZ & D. COMAR. 1983. Brain regional pharmacokinetics of ^{11}C-labeled diphenylhydantoin: Positron emission tomography in humans. Neurology 33: 580–585.
2. BUCHSBAUM, M. S., H. H. HOLCOMB, J. JOHNSON, A. C. KING & R. KESSLER. 1983. Cerebral metabolic consequences of electrical cutaneous stimulation in normal individuals. Human Neurobiol. 2: 35–38.
3. BUSTANY, P., J. F. HENRY & J. DEROTROU, et al. 1983. Local cerebral metabolic rate of ^{11}C-L-methionine in early stages of dementia, schizophrenia, and Parkinson's disease. J. Cereb. Bld. Flow. Met. 3(Suppl. 1): S492–S493.
4. CHASE, T. N., N. L. FOSTER, P. FEDIO, et al. 1983. Alzheimer's disease: Local cerebral metabolism studies using ^{18}F-fluorodeoxyglucose positron emission tomography techniques. In Aging of the Brain. D. Samuel et al., Eds.: 143–154. Raven Press. New York.
5. DELEON, M. J., S. H. FERRIS, A. E. GEORGE, et al. 1983. Positron emission tomographic studies of aging and Alzheimer's disease. Am. J. Neurol. 4: 568–571.
6. ENGEL, J. JR., D. E. KUHL, M. E. PHELPS & J. MAZZIOTTA. 1982. Interictal cerebral

glucose metabolism in partial epilepsy and its relation to EEG changes. Ann. Neurol. **12:** 510–517.
7. ENGEL, J. JR., W. J. BROWN, D. E. KUHL, M. E. PHELPS, J. C. MAZZIOTTA & P. H. CRANDALL. 1982. Pathological findings underlying focal temporal lobe hypometabolism in partial epilepsy. Ann. Neurol. **12:** 518–528.
8. FOSTER, N. L., T. N. CHASE, P. FEDIO et al. 1983. Alzheimer's disease. Focal cortical changes shown by positron emission tomography. Neurology **33:** 961–965.
9. FRACKOWIAK, R. S., C. POZZILLI, N. J. LEGG, et al. 1981. Regional cerebral oxygen supply and utilization in dementia. Brain **104:** 753–778.
10. FRIEDLAND, R. P., T. F. BUDINGER, E. GANZ et al. 1983. Regional cerebral metabolic alterations in dementia of the Alzheimer type: Positron emission tomography with [18F] fluorodeoxyglucose. J. Comput. Assist. Tomogr. **7:** 590–598.
11. GREENBERG, J., M. REIVICH, A. ALAVI et al. 1981. Metabolic mapping of functional activity in human subjects with the [18F] fluorodeoxyglucose technique. Science **212:** 678–680.
12. HOFFMAN, E. J., S. C. HUANG & M. E. PHELPS. 1979. Quantitation in positron emission computed tomography: 1. Effect of object size. J. Comp. Assist. Tomogr. **3:** 299–308.
13. HOFFMAN, E. J., M. E. PHELPS & S. C. HUANG. 1983. Performance evaluation of a positron tomograph designed for brain imaging. J. Nucl. Med. **24:** 245–257.
14. KAUSHALL, P. I., M. ZETIN & L. R. SQUIRE. 1981. A psychological study of chronic circumscribed amnesia. J. Nervous Mental Disorders **169:** 383–389.
15. KEARFOTT, K., D. A. ROTTENBERG & B. T. VOLPE. 1983. Design of steady-state positron emission tomography protocols for neurobehavioral studies: CO15O and 19Ne. J. Comput. Assist. Tomogr. **7:** 51–58.
16. KUHL, D. E., J. ENGEL JR., M. E. PHELPS & C. SELIN. 1980. Epileptic patterns of local cerebral metabolism and perfusion in humans determined by emission computed tomography of 18FDG and 13NH3. Ann. Neurol. **8:** 348–360.
17. KUHL, D. E., E. J. METTER. W. H. RIEGE et al. 1983. Local cerebral glucose utilization in elderly patients with depression, multiple infarct dementia and Alzheimer's disease. J. Cereb. Bld. Flow Met. 3 (Suppl 1): S494–S495.
18. KUHL, D. E., M. E. PHELPS, C. H. MARKHAM et al. 1982. Cerebral metabolism and atrophy in Huntington's disease determined by 18FDG and computed tomographic scan. Ann. Neurol. **12:** 425–434.
19. KUSHNER, M., A. ROSENQUIST, A. ALAVI et al. 1982. Macular and peripheral visual field representation in the striate cortex demonstrated by positron emission tomography. Ann. Neurol. **12:** 89.
20. MAZZIOTTA, J. C. & M. E. PHELPS. 1984. Human sensory stimulation and deprivation. PET results and strategies. Ann. Neurol. **15**(Suppl): S50–S60.
21. MAZZIOTTA, J. C. & M. E. PHELPS. 1984. Positron computed tomography studies of cerebral metabolic responses to complex motor tasks. Neurology **34**(Suppl. 1): 116.
22. MAZZIOTTA, J. C., M. E. PHELPS & R. E. CARSON. 1984. Tomographic mapping of human cerebral metabolism. Subcortical responses to auditory and visual stimulation. Neurology **34:** 825–828.
23. MAZZIOTTA, J. C., M. E. PHELPS & E. HALGREN. 1983. Local cerebral glucose metabolic responses to audio-visual stimulation and deprivation: Studies in humans subjects with positron CT. Human Neurobiol. **2:** 11–23.
24. MAZZIOTTA, J. C., M. E. PHELPS & R. E. CARSON et al. 1982. Tomographic mapping of human cerebral metabolism: Auditory stimulation. Neurology **32:** 921–937.
25. MAZZIOTTA, J. C., M. E. PHELPS, E. HALGREN, R. E. CARSON, S. C. HUANG & J. BAYER. 1983. Hemispheric lateralization and local cerebral metabolic blood flow responses to physiologic stimuli. J. Cereb. Bld. Flow Met. **3**(Suppl 1): S246–S247.
26. MAZZIOTTA, J. C., M. E. PHELPS, D. PLUMMER et al. 1981. Quantitation in positron computed tomography: 5. Physical-anatomical factors. J. Comput. Assist. Tomogr. **5:** 734–743.
27. METTER, E. J., W. H. RIEGE, W. R. HANSON et al. 1983. Comparison of metabolic rates, language and memory in subcortical aphasia. Brain Lang. **19:** 33–47.

28. PENFIELD, W. & T. RASMUSSEN. 1950. The Cerebral Cortex of Man. Macmillan. New York.
29. PHELPS, M. E. 1981. Positron computed tomography studies of cerebral glucose metabolism: Theory and application in nuclear medicine. Sem. Nucl. Med. 11: 32–49.
30. PHELPS, M. E., D. E. KUHL & J. C. MAZZIOTTA. 1981. Metabolic mapping of the brain's response to visual stimulation: Studies in man. Science 211: 1445–1448.
31. PHELPS, M. E., J. C. MAZZIOTTA & S. C. HUANG. 1982. Study of cerebral function with positron computed tomography. J. Cereb. Bld. Flow Met. 2: 113–162.
32. PHELPS, M. E., H. R. SCHELBERT & J. C. MAZZIOTTA. 1983. Positron computed tomography for studies of myocardial and cerebral function. Ann. Int. Med. 98: 339–359.
33. PHELPS, M. E., J. R. BARRIO, S. C. HUANG, R. KEEN, H. CHUGANI & J. C. MAZZIOTTA. 1984. Criteria for the tracer kinetic measurement of protein synthesis in man with positron CT. Ann. Neurol. 15(Suppl): S192–S202.
34. PHELPS, M. E., S. C. HUANG, E. J. HOFFMAN, D. PLUMMER & R. CARSON. 1981. An analysis of signal amplification using small detectors in positron emission tomography. J. Comput. Assist. Tomogr. 6: 551–565.
35. PHELPS, M. E., J. C. MAZZIOTTA, R. GERNER et al. 1983. Human cerebral glucose metabolism in affective disorders: Drug-free states and pharmacologic effects. J. Cereb. Bld. Flow Met. 3(Suppl 1): S7–S8.
36. PHELPS, M. E., J. C. MAZZIOTTA, D. E. KUHL et al. 1981. Tomographic mapping of human cerebral metabolism: Visual stimulation and deprivation. Neurology 31: 517–529.
37. RAICHLE, M. E. 1983. Positron emission tomography. Ann. Rev. Neurosci. 6: 249–267.
38. REIVICH, M. 1964. Arterial pCO_2 and cerebral hemodynamics. Am. J. Physiol. 206: 25–35.
39. REIVICH, M., W. COBBS, A. ROSENQUIST et al. 1981. Abnormalities in local cerebral glucose metabolism in patients with visual field defects. J. Cereb. Bld. Flow Met. 1(Suppl 1): S471–S472.
40. ROLAND, P., E. MEYER, Y. YAMAMOTO et al. 1981. Dynamic positron emission tomography as a tool in neuroscience: Functional brain-mapping in normal human volunteers. J. Cereb. Bld. Flow Met. 1(Suppl 1): S463–S464.
41. ROY, C. S. & C. S. SHERRINGTON. 1890. On the regulation of the blood supply of the brain. J. Physiol. (Lond.) 11: 85–108.
42. SCHWARTZ, E. L., D. R. CHRISTMAN & A. WOLF. 1984. Human primary visual cortex topography imaged via positron tomography. Brain Res. 294: 225–230.
43. SOKOLOFF, L. 1981. Localization of functional activity in the central nervous system by measurement of glucose utilization with radioactive deoxyglucose. J. Cereb. Bld. Flow Met. 1: 7–36.
44. SOKOLOFF, L., M. REIVICH, C. KENNEDY, M. H. DESROSIERS, C. S. PATLAK, K. D. PETTIGREW, O. SAKURADA & M. SHINOHARA. 1977. The [^{14}C]deoxyglucose method for the measurement of local cerebral glucose utilization: Theory, procedure and normal values in the conscious and anesthetized albino rat. J. Neurochem. 28: 897–916.
45. SQUIRE, L. R. & R. Y. MOORE. 1979. Dorsal thalamic lesion in a noted case of human memory dysfunction. Ann. Neurol. 6: 503–506.
46. TER-POGOSSIAN, M. M. 1981. Physical aspects of emission CT. In Radiology of the Skull and Brain: Technical Aspects of Computed Tomography. T. H. Newton & D. G. Potts, Eds.: 4372–4388. CV Mosby Co. St. Louis.
47. TERRY, R. D., A. PECK, R. DETERESA, R. SCHECTER & D. S. HOROUPIAN. 1981. Some morphometric aspects of the brain in senile dementia of the Alzheimer type. Ann. Neurol. 10: 184–192.
48. TEUBER, H. L., B. MILNER & H. G. VAUGHN. 1968. Persistent anterograde amnesia after stab wound of the basal brain. Neuropsychologia 6: 267–282.
49. VOPLE, B. T., P. HERSCOVITCH, M. E. RAICHLE, W. HIRST & M. S. GAZZANIGA. 1983. Cerebral blood flow and metabolism in human amnesia. 1983. J. Cereb. Bld. Flow Met. 3(Suppl 1): S5–S6.
50. VOLPE, B. T., P. HERSCOVITCH & M. E. RAICHLE. 1984. Positron emission tomography

defines metabolic abnormality in mesial temporal lobes of two patients with amnesia after rupture and repair of anterior communicating artery aneurysm. Neurology 34(Suppl): 188.

51. VOLPE, B. T., P. HERSCOVITCH & M. E. RAICHLE. 1984. PET evaluation of patients with amnesia after cardiac arrest. Stroke 15: 16.

52. VOLPE, B. T. & W. HEARST. 1983. Characterization of an amnesic syndrome following hypoxic ischemic injury. Arch. Neurol. 40: 436–440.

53. WAGNER, H. N., H. D. BURNS, R. F. DUNNALS, D. F. WONG, B. LANGSTROM, T. DUEFFLER, J. J. FROST, H. T. RAVERT, J. M. LINKS, S. B. ROSENBLOOM, S. E. LUKAS, A. V. KRAMER & M. J. KUHAR. 1983. Imaging dopamine receptors in the human brain by positron tomography. Science 22: 1264–1266.

The Functional Organization of the Basal Forebrain Cholinergic System in Primates and the Role of this System in Alzheimer's Disease[a]

DONALD L. PRICE[b]

Departments of Pathology, Neurology, and Neuroscience

LINDA C. CORK

Division of Comparative Medicine and Department of Pathology

ROBERT G. STRUBLE

Department of Pathology

PETER J. WHITEHOUSE

Departments of Neurology and Neuroscience

CHERYL A. KITT

Department of Pathology

AND

LARY C. WALKER

Department of Pathology
Neuropathology Laboratory
The Johns Hopkins University School of Medicine
Baltimore, Maryland 21205

INTRODUCTION

Recent investigations in the basal forebrain cholinergic system, which includes neurons in the medial septum, diagonal band of Broca (dbB), and nucleus basalis of Meynert (nbM), suggest that these neurons contribute to memory processing (for review, see Bartus *et al.*[7] and Coyle *et al.*[17]). This hypothesis is supported by the observation that this neuronal system shows pathological changes in Alzheimer's

[a]Supported by U.S. Public Health Service (NIH NS 15721, NS 17074, NS 10580, NS 07179, AG 03359, MH 00868, NS 15417, NS 20471), The McKnight Foundation, The Commonwealth Fund, the NIH Biomedical Research Support (RR5378), the Alfred P. Sloan Foundation, and funds from Point-of-View, Inc. L.C.C. is supported by a Research Career Development Award (NIH NS 00488).

[b]Correspondence to: Donald L. Price, M.D., Neuropathology Laboratory, 509 Pathology Building, The Johns Hopkins University School of Medicine, 600 North Wolfe Street, Baltimore, MD 21205.

disease (AD) and several other types of dementia[4,50,55,61,74,77,78,81–83] associated with reduced cholinergic markers in cortex.[9,11,12,18,53,65–67]

The present review focuses on the anatomy and physiology of this system in primates, the effects of aging on this system, the consequences of experimental lesions of the primate basal forebrain, and the changes occurring in this neuronal population in AD, in aged individuals with Down's syndrome and in certain demented patients with Parkinson's disease (PD).

ANATOMY AND PHYSIOLOGY OF THE PRIMATE BASAL FOREBRAIN CHOLINERGIC SYSTEM

The medial septum, nucleus of the dbB, and nbM of primates show high levels of choline acetyltransferase (ChAT) activity.[43] Many acetylcholinesterase (AChE)-rich neurons in these regions show ChAT immunoreactivity,[32,45,48,70] a marker specific for cholinergic neurons.[40] Recent anterograde tracing studies indicate that septal-dbB cholinergic neurons project through the fimbria-fornix to the hippocampus, while nbM neurons project via a ventral pathway to the amygdala and through medial and lateral pathways to the medial and lateral parts of neocortex.[38] These neurons give rise to topographical projections to amygdala, hippocampus, and neocortex.[23,35,36,38,44,45,51] Within nonhuman primate neocortex, there is some regional variability in ChAT activity: the temporal lobe and motor cortex have the highest levels of enzyme activity, prefrontal cortex has an intermediate level, and occipital neocortex has the lowest activity.[41] Selective lesions in the nbM, achieved by local injections of ibotenic acid, reduce cortical ChAT activity (up to 70%), indicating that these neurons provide the major cholinergic innervation of primate neocortex and that the density of cortical innervation by this system may not be uniform.[73]

At present, the physiology of the basal forebrain cholinergic system is not well understood. Neurons of the nbM show firing patterns distinct from adjacent cell groups in basal ganglia.[21] NbM neurons are tonically active but, in behavioral paradigms, can increase or decrease their rates of discharge in response to a variety of manipulations, including delivery of a reward.[63,64]

EFFECTS OF AGING ON THE BASAL FOREBRAIN CHOLINERGIC SYSTEM

Aged nonhuman primates show cognitive and mnemonic abnormalities that have certain parallels in aged humans.[19,57] To determine whether these age-associated impairments extend to recognition memory, rhesus monkeys of varying ages (3–6, 14–17, and 27–30 years of age) were trained on a delayed nonmatch-to-sample task using trial-unique stimuli. To date, our older animals have shown a moderate impairment in performance.[57] On the basis of pharmacological studies,[5,6,24] it has been suggested that some of these deficits, including those involving short-term memory,[8] may result, in part, from abnormalities in the cholinergic innervation of forebrain targets.

Recently, we have begun to examine substrates of age-associated deficits in aged nonhuman primates.[62,63,68,69] Our initial studies have focused on senile plaques—the most striking microscopic brain abnormality occurring in aged monkeys.[69,70,85] Plaques also occur in amygdala, hippocampus, and neocortex of aged humans[75] and (in greater numbers) in individuals with AD.[76] Enlarged, frequently argentophilic, axons and synaptic terminals occur in senile plaques in proximity to extracellular deposits of amyloid.[85] Since some senile plaques contain AChE,[25,54,69] an enzyme enriched in cholinergic axons of the nbM,[31,33,71] we hypothesized that some of the AChE-containing neurites in plaques may be derived from nbM neurons.[60,61,69] AChE activity is also present in some noncholinergic neurons projecting to cortex: noradrenergic nerve cells in the locus coeruleus, dopaminergic neurons in the substantia nigra and ventral tegmental area, serotonergic neurons in the raphe nucleus,[3,13] and somatostatinergic and gamma-aminobutyric acid (GABA)ergic neurons intrinsic to cortex.[20,46] Therefore, some AChE-containing abnormal axons and neurites in cortices of aged primates could be derived from these (and possibly other) populations of nerve cells. To further examine this hypothesis, ChAT immunoreactivity was visualized in the brains of aged (17–32 years of age) rhesus monkeys.[39] Many normal ChAT-positive fibers were seen. In addition, several patterns of axonal abnormalities were observed in aged primate neocortex and amygdala. Individual intracortical axons showed multiple nodular varicosities along their course, and clusters of these immunoreactive multivaricose neurites were sometimes associated with variable amounts of amyloid. These observations were interpreted to indicate that some neurites present in some plaques were abnormal cholinergic axons derived from the nbM.[39] Recent work in aged monkeys and humans has shown that monoaminergic[37] and several peptidergic systems, particularly somatostatinergic neurons, are involved in the formation of neurites in senile plaques.[72]

These findings indicate that neurons in the basal forebrain cholinergic system and in other neuronal systems innervating cortex show structural abnormalities suggestive of distal axonopathy. This axonal pathology could represent ongoing degeneration, abortive regeneration, or an admixture of these processes. If we are to understand the mechanisms underlying these changes, it will be important to devise new strategies to investigate cytoskeletal alterations in affected neurons and their distal axons. For example, in motor neurons, dramatic pathological changes in the axonal cytoskeleton have been attributed to abnormalities in axonal transport.[16,27–30,59] Transport studies of this type are difficult to perform in the nbM-cortical system. With information about the behavior of motor neurons as a background, probes of the axonal cytoskeleton (e.g., antibodies against epitopes of neurofilaments, microtubule-associated proteins, etc.) may be used to clarify these issues.[30]

CONSEQUENCES OF EXPERIMENTAL LESIONS OF THE BASAL FOREBRAIN CHOLINERGIC SYSTEM

Monkeys with bilateral partial lesions of the nbM show modest reductions in the activities of AChE and ChAT in cortex;[73] however, monkeys do not show behavioral deficits unless challenged with scopolamine,[1] a drug that blocks muscarinic receptors. The scopolamine sensitivity of lesioned animals suggests that asymptomatic moderate reductions in cortical cholinergic activity may be made clinically manifest by treatment with anticholinergics. As described below, approximately 50% of individuals with PD eventually develop dementia,[10,42] and some of these individuals have lesions in the basal forebrain cholinergic system.[4,14,50,81] Thus, it is not surprising that, when some PD patients are treated with anticholinergics to relieve motor symptoms, they develop confusion and dementia.[22] In our experimental animals, as in this clinical setting, the administration of anticholinergics reduces cholinergic function sufficiently to produce cognitive impairments.

However, animals with more extensive lesions involving the medial septum, dbB, and nbM show overt abnormalities on behavioral tests.[2] These results suggest that combined damage to the medial septum/dbB (which projects to hippocampus) in conjunction with damage to the nbM (which projects to amygdala and neocortex) may be necessary to produce impairments in recognition memory. Denervation of these targets, whose integrity is a prerequisite for adequate performance of the nonmatch-to-sample task,[47] is then sufficient to impair recognition memory.

BASAL FOREBRAIN CHOLINERGIC SYSTEM IN ALZHEIMER'S DISEASE, DOWN'S SYNDROME, AND PARKINSON'S DISEASE

Changes have also been noted in basal forebrain cholinergic neurons in older patients with Down's syndrome and in some patients with PD.[4,15,49,50,55,61,74,81,83] In AD, these nerve cells frequently contain neurofibrillary tangles[84] and the number of large neurons in the substantia innominata is reduced. However, in one case, nbM neurons were not greatly decreased in number but were reduced in size;[51] in some cases, reductions in cortical ChAT activity are greater than the decrease in nbM cell number.[56] Nevertheless, changes in nbM neurons are thought to be responsible for reductions in cholinergic markers in AD.[9,11,12,18,53,65,67] The activity of ChAT is also reduced in the forebrains of elderly individuals with Down's syndrome,[86] many of whom have the histopathological stigmata of AD.[61] Recent studies indicate that the number of neurons in the nbM is reduced in these patients.[15] Similarly, some demented patients with PD show decreased cortical cholinergic markers[66] and reductions in numbers of nbM neurons.[4,14,50,79] In concert with evidence for cytoskeletal pathology involving these cells, e.g., neurofibrillary tangles and senile plaques, our findings support the idea that basal forebrain neurons undergo chronic structural and functional changes which may long antedate cell death. Thus, dysfunction and death of basal forebrain cholinergic neurons appear to be major factors in the production of cortical cholinergic deficits in several human disorders associated with dementia.

The relationship of basal forebrain cholinergic neurons to the formation of plaques in AD is uncertain. In AD, there is a correlation between reductions in ChAT activity, the presence of plaques, and the presence of dementia;[54] some plaques show AChE-containing neurites.[25,54] Some neurites in plaques certainly are derived from AChE-containing systems, including the basal forebrain cholinergic system. However, in some types of human dementia, dysfunction (and death) of basal forebrain cholinergic neurons may not be associated with plaque formation. Examples of cortical cholinergic deficits without plaques can be found in cases of PD,[50,81] dementia pugilistica,[78] and Pick's disease.[77]

The evidence outlined above indicates that, in some diseases, nbM neurons dysfunction and die with no discernible abnormality demonstrated in distal axonal fields, while, in aging and AD, dysfunction of these neurons results in a distal axonal pathology manifested as neurites in plaques. The strategies adopted for the study of transmitter-specific markers in plaques in aged nonhuman primates should prove useful for clarifying these issues in aged humans and in individuals with AD and related disorders. Moreover, using antibodies directed against cytoskeletal and other neuronal constituents,[34] it should be possible to explore some of the mechanisms underlying the axonal (neurite) and perikaryal (neurofibrillary tangle) pathologies in these disorders. For example, in preliminary studies (Price et al., personal observation), we have observed similarities in the patterns of distribution of specific neurofilament epitopes in neurites in plaques of aged monkeys and humans with AD. Studies using antibodies against such constituents, particularly those important in determining cellular and axonal volume and those participating in intracellular motility, may provide clues to the mechanisms contributing to the formation of neurofibrillary tangles and abnormal neurites in senile plaques.

CONCLUSION

The basal forebrain cholinergic system, which includes neurons in the medial septum, dbB, and nbM, provides the major cholinergic innervation of amygdala, hippocampus, and neocortex. In aged nonhuman primates, these neurons (and several other neuronal populations) show structural changes, particularly in their distal axons. Some of these axons participate in the formation of senile plaques. In nonhuman primates, partial experimental destruction of these cholinergic neurons is associated with a sensitivity of certain memory tasks to the effects of anticholinergics. Similar observations have been made in parkinsonian patients treated with anticholinergics. Animals with larger lesions show overt deficits on visual recognition memory tasks. Finally, evidence from several laboratories indicates that dysfunction and death of cholinergic neurons are important pathological processes in several human disorders associated with memory impairments, including AD, some cases of PD, and elderly individuals with Down's syndrome.

ACKNOWLEDGMENTS

The authors gratefully acknowledge helpful discussions with our colleagues Drs. John C. Hedreen, Mahlon R. DeLong, Susan J. Mitchell, Jocelyn Bachevalier, Russell T. Richardson, John Lehmann, Arthur W. Clark, Thomas Aigner, George R. Uhl, Joseph T. Coyle, Manuel F. Casanova, Krystyna Wisniewski, Nancy Sternberger, Ludwig Sternberger, and Mortimer Mishkin and Ms. Sharon Presty. Mrs. Carla Jordon provided excellent secretarial assistance. Mr. Mark Becher and Mr. Richard Altschuler assisted with the immunocytochemical studies. Drs. Bruce H. Wainer, Allan I. Levey, Paul M. Salvaterra, and Garrett R. Crawford generously provided antiChAT monoclonal antibodies used in some of our original studies. We gratefully acknowledge the support of Dr. Kenneth R. Brizzee and the Caribbean Primate Center at the University of Puerto Rico.

REFERENCES

1. AIGNER, T., J. AGGLETON, S. J. MITCHELL, D. PRICE, M. DELONG & M. MISHKIN. 1983. Effects of scopolamine on recognition memory in monkeys after ibotenic acid injections into the nucleus basalis of Meynert. Neurosci. Abstr. **9:** 826.

2. AIGNER, T., S. MITCHELL, J. AGGLETON, M. DELONG, R. STRUBLE, D. PRICE & M. MISHKIN. 1984. Effects of scopolamine and physostigmine on recognition memory in monkeys after ibotenic acid injections into the area of the nucleus basalis of Meynert. *In* Alzheimer's Disease: Advances in Basic Research and Therapies. Proceedings of the Third Meeting of the International Study Group on the Treatment of Memory Disorders Associated with Aging. R. J. Wurtman, S. H. Corkin & J. H. Growdon, Eds.: 429. Zurich.

3. ALBANESE, A. & L. L. BUTCHER. 1979. Locus coeruleus somata contain both acetylcholinesterase and norepinephrine: direct histochemical demonstration on the same tissue section. Neurosci. Lett. **14:** 101–104.

4. ARENDT, T., V. BIGL, A. ARENDT & A. TENNSTEDT. 1983. Loss of neurons in the nucleus
    basalis of Meynert in Alzheimer's disease, paralysis agitans, and Korsakoff's disease.
    Acta Neuropathol. (Berl.) **61:** 101–108.
5. BARTUS, R. T. 1979. Aging in the rhesus monkey: specific behavioral impairments and
    effects of pharmacological intervention. *In* Recent Advances in Gerontology, Proc. XI
    Int. Congr. Gerontol. H. Orimo, K. Shimado, M. Iriki & D. Maeda, Eds.: 225–227.
    Excerpta Medica. Amsterdam.
6. BARTUS, R. T. & H. R. JOHNSON. 1976. Short-term memory in the rhesus monkey:
    disruption from the anti-cholinergic scopolamine. Pharmacol. Biochem. Behav. **5:** 39–
    46.
7. BARTUS, R. T., R. L. DEAN, III, B. BEER & A. S. LIPPA. 1982. The cholinergic hypothesis of
    geriatric memory dysfunction. Science **217:** 408–417.
8. BARTUS, R. T., D. FLEMING & H. R. JOHNSON. 1978. Aging in the rhesus monkey:
    debilitating effects on short-term memory. J. Gerontol. **33:** 858–871.
9. BIRD, T. D., S. STRANAHAN, S. M. SUMI & M. RASKIND. 1983. Alzheimer's disease: choline
    acetyltransferase activity in brain tissue from clinical and pathological subgroups. Ann.
    Neurol. **14:** 284–293.
10. BOLLER, F., T. MIZUTANI, U. ROESSMANN & P. GAMBETTI. 1980. Parkinson disease,
    dementia, and Alzheimer disease: clinicopathological correlations. Ann. Neurol. **7:** 329–
    335.
11. BOWEN, D. M. 1983. Biochemical assessment of neurotransmitter and metabolic dysfunc-
    tion and cerebral atrophy in Alzheimer's disease. Biological aspects of Alzheimer's
    disease. Banbury Rep. **15:** 219–231.
12. BOWEN, D. M., C. B. SMITH, P. WHITE & A. N. DAVISON. 1976. Neurotransmitter-related
    enzymes and indices of hypoxia in senile dementia and other abiotrophies. Brain
    99: 459–496.
13. BUTCHER, L. L., K. TALBOT & L. BILEZIKJIAN. 1975. Acetylcholinesterase neurons in
    dopamine-containing regions of the brain. J. Neural Transmis. **37:** 127–153.
14. CANDY, J. M., R. H. PERRY, E. K. PERRY, D. IRVING, G. BLESSED, A. F. FAIRBAIRN & B. E.
    TOMLINSON. 1983. Pathological changes in the nucleus of Meynert in Alzheimer's and
    Parkinson's diseases. J. Neurol. Sci. **59:** 277–289.
15. CASANOVA, M. F., L. C. WALKER, P. J. WHITEHOUSE & D. L. PRICE. 1985. Abnormalities
    of the nucleus basalis in Down's syndrome. Ann. Neurol. (In press.)
16. CORK, L. C., J. W. GRIFFIN, C. CHOY, C. A. PADULA & D. L. PRICE. 1982. Pathology of
    motor neurons in accelerated hereditary canine spinal muscular atrophy. Lab. Invest.
    46: 89–99.
17. COYLE, J. T., D. L. PRICE & M. R. DELONG. 1983. Alzheimer's disease: a disorder of
    cortical cholinergic innervation. Science **219:** 1184–1190.
18. DAVIES, P. & A. J. F. MALONEY. 1976. Selective loss of central cholinergic neurons in
    Alzheimer's disease. Lancet **2:** 1403.
19. DAVIS, R. T. 1978. Old monkey behavior. Exp. Gerontol. **13:** 237–250.
20. DELFS, J. R., C-H. ZHU & M. A. DICHTER. 1983. Coexistence of acetylcholinesterase and
    somatostatin-immunoreactivity in neurons cultured from rat cerebrum. Science **223:** 61–
    63.
21. DELONG, M. R. 1971. Activity of pallidal neurons during movement. J. Neurophysiol.
    34: 414–427.
22. DESMET, Y., M. RUBERG, M. SERDARU, B. DUBOIS, F. LHERMITTE & Y. AGID. 1982.
    Confusion, dementia and anticholinergics in Parkinson's disease. J. Neurol. Neurosurg.
    Psychiatry **45:** 1161–1164.
23. DIVAC, I. 1975. Magnocellular nuclei of the basal forebrain project to neocortex, brain stem,
    and olfactory bulb. Review of some functional correlates. Brain Res. **93:** 385–398.
24. DRACHMAN, D. A. & J. L. LEAVITT. 1974. Human memory and the cholinergic system. A
    relationship to aging? Arch. Neurol. **30:** 113–121.
25. FRIEDE, R. L. 1965. Enzyme histochemical studies of senile plaques. J. Neuropathol. Exp.
    Neurol. **24:** 477–491.
26. GOLDMAN-RAKIC, P. S. & R. M. BROWN. 1981. Regional changes of monoamines in

cerebral cortex and subcortical structures of aging rhesus monkeys. Neuroscience **6:** 177–187.

27. GRIFFIN, J. W., L. C. CORK, P. N. HOFFMAN & D. L. PRICE. 1984. Experimental models of motor neuron degeneration. *In* Peripheral Neuropathy, Vol. I. P. J. Dyck, P. K. Thomas, E. H. Lambert & R. Bunge, Eds.: 621–635. W.B. Saunders. Philadelphia.
28. GRIFFIN, J. W., K. E. FAHNESTOCK, D. L. PRICE & P. N. HOFFMAN. 1983. Microtubule-neurofilament segregation produced by β,β′-iminodipropionitrile: evidence for the association of fast axonal transport with microtubules. J. Neurosci. **3:** 557–566.
29. GRIFFIN, J. W., P. N. HOFFMAN, A. W. CLARK, P. T. CARROLL & D. L. PRICE. 1978. Slow axonal transport of neurofilament proteins: impairment by β,β′-iminodipropionitrile administration. Science **202:** 633–635.
30. GRIFFIN, J. W., D. L. PRICE & P. N. HOFFMAN. 1983. Neurotoxic probes of the axonal cytoskeleton. Trends Neurosci. **6:** 490–495.
31. HEDREEN, J. C., S. J. BACON & D. L. PRICE. 1985. An improved histochemical technique for acetylcholinesterase-containing axons. J. Histochem. Cytochem.
32. HEDREEN, J. C., S. J. BACON, L. C. CORK, C. A. KITT, G. D. CRAWFORD, P. M. SALVATERRA & D. L. PRICE. 1983. Immunocytochemical identification of cholinergic neurons in the monkey central nervous system using monoclonal antibodies against choline acetyltransferase. Neurosci. Lett. **43:** 173–177.
33. HEDREEN, J. C., G. R. UHL, S. J. BACON, D. M. FAMBROUGH & D. L. PRICE. 1984. Acetylcholinesterase-immunoreactive axonal network in monkey visual cortex. J. Comp. Neurol. **226:** 246–254.
34. IHARA, Y., C. ABRAHAM & D. J. SELKOE. 1983. Antibodies to paired helical filaments in Alzheimer's disease do not recognize normal brain proteins. Nature **304:** 727–730.
35. JONES, E. G., H. BURTON, C. B. SAPER & L. W. SWANSON. 1976. Midbrain, diencephalic and cortical relationships of the basal nucleus of Meynert and associated structures in primates. J. Comp. Neurol. **167:** 385–420.
36. KIEVIT, J. & H. G. J. M. KUYPERS. 1975. Basal forebrain and hypothalamic connections to frontal and parietal cortex in the rhesus monkey. Science **187:** 660–662.
37. KITT, C. A., W. C. MOBLEY, R. G. STRUBLE, L. C. CORK, L. C. WALKER, M. W. BECHER, T. JOH & D. L. PRICE. 1984. Contribution of catecholaminergic systems to neurites in plaques of aged primates. Ann. Neurol. **16:** 118.
38. KITT, C. A., D. L. PRICE, M. R. DELONG, R. G. STRUBLE, S. J. MITCHELL & J. C. HEDREEN. 1982. The nucleus basalis of Meynert: projections to the cortex, amygdala, and hippocampus. Soc. Neurosci. Abstr. **8:** 212.
39. KITT, C. A., D. L. PRICE, R. G. STRUBLE, L. C. CORK, B. H. WAINER, M. W. BECHER & W. C. MOBLEY. 1984. Evidence for cholinergic neurites in senile plaques. Science **226:** 1443–1445.
40. KUHAR, M. J. 1976. The anatomy of cholinergic neurons. *In* Biology of Cholinergic Function. A. M. Goldberg & I. Hanin, Eds.: 3–27. Raven Press. New York.
41. LEHMANN, J., R. G. STRUBLE, P. G. ANTUONO, J. T. COYLE, L. C. CORK & D. L. PRICE. 1984. Regional heterogeneity of choline acetyltransferase activity in primate neocortex. Brain Res. **322:** 361–364.
42. LIEBERMAN, A., M. DZIATOLOWSKY, M. KUPERSMITH, M. SERBY, A. GOODGOLD, J. KOREIN & M. GOLDSTEIN. 1979. Dementia in Parkinson disease. Ann. Neurol. **6:** 355–359.
43. MCKINNEY, M., R. G. STRUBLE, D. L. PRICE & J. T. COYLE. 1982. Monkey nucleus basalis is enriched with choline acetyltransferase. J. Neurosci. **7:** 2363–2368.
44. MESULAM, M.-M. & G. W. VAN HOESEN. 1976. Acetylcholinesterase-rich projections from the basal forebrain of the rhesus monkey to neocortex. Brain Res. **109:** 152–157.
45. MESULAM, M.-M., E. J. MUFSON, A. I. LEVEY & B. H. WAINER. 1983. Cholinergic innervation of cortex by the basal forebrain: cytochemistry and cortical connections of the septal area, diagonal band nuclei, nucleus basalis (substantia innominata), and hypothalamus in the rhesus monkey. J. Comp. Neurol. **214:** 170–197.
46. MESULAM, M.-M. & M. DICHTER. 1981. Concurrent acetylcholinesterase staining and gamma-aminobutyric acid uptake of cortical neurons in culture. J. Histochem. Cytochem. **29:** 306–308.
47. MISHKIN, M. 1978. Memory in monkeys severely impaired by combined but not by separate removal of amygdala and hippocampus. Nature **273:** 297–298.

48. NAGAI, T., P. L. MCGEER, J. H. PENG, E. G. MCGEER & C. E. DOLMAN. 1983. Choline acetyltransferase immunohistochemistry in brains of Alzheimer's disease patients and controls. Neurosci. Lett. 36: 195–199.

49. NAGAI, T., T. PEARSON, F. PENG, E. G. MCGEER & P. L. MCGEER. 1983. Immunohistochemical staining of the human forebrain with monoclonal antibody to human choline acetyltransferase. Brain Res. 265: 300–306.

50. NAKANO, I. & A. HIRANO. 1984. Parkinson's disease: neuron loss in the nucleus basalis without concomitant Alzheimer's disease. Ann. Neurol. 15: 415–418.

51. PEARSON, R. C. A., K. C. GATTER & T. P. S. POWELL. 1983. The cortical relationships of certain basal ganglia and the cholinergic basal forebrain nuclei. Brain Res. 261: 327–330.

52. PEARSON, R. C. A., M. V. SOFRONIEW, A. C. CUELLO, T. P. S. POWELL, F. ECKENSTEIN, M. M. ESIRI & G. K. WILCOCK. 1983. Persistence of cholinergic neurons in the basal nucleus in a brain with senile dementia of the Alzheimer's type demonstrated by immunohistochemical staining for choline acetyltransferase. Brain Res. 289: 375–379.

53. PERRY, E. K., R. H. PERRY, G. BLESSED & B. E. TOMLINSON. 1977. Necropsy evidence of central cholinergic deficits in senile dementia. Lancet 1: 189.

54. PERRY, E. K., B. E. TOMLINSON, G. BLESSED, K. BERGMANN, P. H. GIBSON & R. H. PERRY. 1978. Correlation of cholinergic abnormalities with senile plaques and mental test scores in senile dementia. Br. Med. J. 2: 1457–1459.

55. PERRY, R. H., J. M. CANDY & E. K. PERRY. 1983. Some observations and speculations concerning the cholinergic system and neuropeptides in Alzheimer's disease. Biological aspects of Alzheimer's Disease. Banbury Rep. 15: 351–361.

56. PERRY, R. H., J. M. CANDY, E. K. PERRY, D. IRVING, G. BLESSED, A. F. FAIRBAIRN & B. E. TOMLINSON. 1982. Extensive loss of choline acetyltransferase activity is not reflected by neuronal loss in the nucleus of Meynert in Alzheimer's disease. Neurosci. Lett. 33: 311–315.

57. PRESTY, S. K., L. C. CORK, D. L. PRICE, R. G. STRUBLE, L. C. WALKER, J. BACHEVALIER & M. MISHKIN. 1984. Aged rhesus monkeys (Macaca mulatta) are moderately impaired in visual recognition. Soc. Neurosci. Abstr. 10: 74.

58. PRICE, D. L., L. C. CORK, R. G. STRUBLE, C. A. KITT, D. L. PRICE, JR., J. LEHMANN & J. C. HEDREEN. 1985. Neuropathological, neurochemical, and behavioral studies of the aging nonhuman primate. In Behavior and Pathology of Aging in Rhesus Monkeys. R. T. Davis & C. W. Leathers, Eds. Alan R. Liss. New York. (In press.)

59. PRICE, D. L., J. W. GRIFFIN, P. N. HOFFMAN, L. C. CORK & P. S. SPENCER. 1984. The response of motor neurons to injury and disease. In Peripheral Neuropathy. P. J. Dyck, P. K. Thomas, E. H. Lambert & R. Bunge, Eds. 1: 732–759. W.B. Saunders. Philadelphia.

60. PRICE, D. L., P. J. WHITEHOUSE, R. G. STRUBLE, A. W. CLARK, J. T. COYLE, M. R. DELONG & J. C. HEDREEN. 1982. Basal forebrain cholinergic systems in Alzheimer's disease and related dementias. Neurosci. Comment. 1: 84–92.

61. PRICE, D. L., P. J. WHITEHOUSE, R. G. STRUBLE, J. T. COYLE, A. W. CLARK, M. R. DELONG, L. C. CORK & J. C. HEDREEN. 1982. Alzheimer's disease and Down's syndrome. Ann. N.Y. Acad. Sci. 396: 145–164.

62. PRICE, D. L., P. J. WHITEHOUSE, R. G. STRUBLE, D. L. PRICE, JR., L. C. CORK, J. C. HEDREEN & C. A. KITT. 1983. Basal forebrain cholinergic neurons and neuritic plaques in primate brain. Biological Aspects of Alzheimer's Disease. Banbury Rep. 15: 65–77.

63. RICHARDSON, R. T. & M. R. DELONG. 1984. Neuronal activity in nucleus basalis of Meynert during a delayed response task in monkey. Soc. Neurosci. Abstr. 10: 128.

64. ROLLS, E. T., M. K. SANGHERA & A. ROPER-HALL. 1979. The latency of activation of neurones in the lateral hypothalamus and substantia innominata during feeding in the monkey. Brain Res. 164: 121–135.

65. ROSSOR, M. N., N. J. GARRETT, A. L. JOHNSON, C. Q. MOUNTJOY, M. ROTH & L. L. IVERSEN. 1982. A post-mortem study of the cholinergic and GABA systems in senile dementia. Brain 105: 313–330.

66. RUBERG, M., A. PLOSKA, F. JAVOY-AGID & Y. AGID. 1982. Muscarinic binding and choline acetyltransferase activity in parkinsonian subjects with reference to dementia. Brain Res. 232: 129–139.

67. SIMS, N. R., D. M. BOWEN, S. J. ALLEN, C. C. T. SMITH, D. NEARY, D. J. THOMAS & A. N. DAVISON. 1983. Presynaptic cholinergic dysfunction in patients with dementia. J. Neurochem. **40:** 503–509.

68. STRUBLE, R. G., L. C. CORK, D. L. PRICE, JR., D. L. PRICE & R. T. DAVIS. 1983. Distribution of neuritic plaques in the cortex of aged rhesus monkeys. Soc. Neurosci. Abstr. **9:** 927.

69. STRUBLE, R. G., L. C. CORK, P. J. WHITEHOUSE & D. L. PRICE. 1982. Cholinergic innervation in neuritic plaques. Science **216:** 413–415.

70. STRUBLE, R. G., J. C. HEDREEN, L. C. CORK & D. L. PRICE. 1984. Acetylcholinesterase activity in senile plaques of aged macaques. Neurobiol. Aging. **5:** 191–198.

71. STRUBLE, R. G., M. MCKINNEY, P. R. SANBERG, C. A. KITT, M. R. DELONG, J. T. COYLE & D. L. PRICE. 1982. Ibotenic acid lesions of the primate nucleus basalis of Meynert result in decreased cortical choline acetyltransferase. Soc. Neurosci. Abstr. **8:** 211.

72. STRUBLE, R. G., K. A. KATT, L. C. WALKER, L. C. CORK & D. L. PRICE. 1984. Somatostatinergic neurites in senile plaques of aged non-human primates. Brain Res. **324:** 394–396.

73. STRUBLE, R. G., J. LEHMANN, S. J. MITCHELL, L. C. CORK, J. T. COYLE, D. L. PRICE, M. R. DELONG & P. G. ANTUONO. 1985. Cortical cholinergic innervation: distribution and source in monkeys. *In* Dynamics of Cholinergic Function. I. Hanin, Ed. Plenum Press. New York.

74. TAGLIAVINI, F. & G. PILLERI. 1983. Neuronal counts in basal nucleus of Meynert in Alzheimer disease and in simple senile dementia. Lancet **1:** 469–470.

75. TOMLINSON, B. E., G. BLESSED & M. ROTH. 1968. Observations on the brains of non-demented old people. J. Neurol. Sci. **7:** 331–356.

76. TOMLINSON, B. E., G. BLESSED & M. ROTH. 1970. Observations on the brains of demented old people. J. Neurol. Sci. **11:** 205–242.

77. UHL, G. R., D. C. HILT, J. C. HEDREEN, P. J. WHITEHOUSE & D. L. PRICE. 1983. Pick's disease (lobar sclerosis): depletion of neurons in the nucleus basalis of Meynert. Neurology **33:** 1470–1473.

78. UHL, G. R., M. MCKINNEY, J. C. HEDREEN, C. L. WHITE, III, J. T. COYLE, P. J. WHITEHOUSE & D. L. PRICE. 1982. Dementia pugilistica: loss of basal forebrain cholinergic neurons and cortical cholinergic markers. Ann. Neurol. **12:** 99.

79. WHITEHOUSE, P. J., J. C. HEDREEN, B. E. JONES & D. L. PRICE. 1983. A computer analysis of neuronal size in the nucleus basalis of Meynert in patients with Alzheimer's disease. Ann. Neurol. **14:** 149–150.

80. WHITEHOUSE, P. J., J. C. HEDREEN, C. L. WHITE, III & D. L. PRICE. 1983. Basal forebrain neurons in the dementia of Parkinson disease. Ann. Neurol. **13:** 243–248.

81. WHITEHOUSE, P. J., J. C. HEDREEN, C. L. WHITE, III, A. W. CLARK & D. L. PRICE. 1983. Neuronal loss in the basal forebrain cholinergic system is more marked in Alzheimer's disease than in senile dementia of the Alzheimer type. Ann. Neurol. **14:** 149.

82. WHITEHOUSE, P. J., D. L. PRICE, A. W. CLARK, J. T. COYLE & M. R. DELONG. 1981. Alzheimer disease: evidence for selective loss of cholinergic neurons in the nucleus basalis. Ann. Neurol. **10:** 122–126.

83. WHITEHOUSE, P. J., D. L. PRICE, R. G. STRUBLE, A. W. CLARK, J. T. COYLE & M. R. DELONG. 1982. Alzheimer's disease and senile dementia: loss of neurons in the basal forebrain. Science **215:** 1237–1239.

84. WHITEHOUSE, P. J., R. G. STRUBLE, A. W. CLARK & D. L. PRICE. 1982. Alzheimer disease: plaques, tangles, and the basal forebrain. Letter to the Editor. Ann. Neurol. **12:** 494.

85. WISNIEWSKI, H. M., B. GHETTI & R. D. TERRY. 1973. Neuritic (senile) plaques and filamentous changes in aged rhesus monkeys. J. Neuropathol. Exp. Neurol. **32:** 566–584.

86. YATES, C. M., J. SIMPSON, A. GORDON, A. F. J. MALONEY, Y. ALLISON, I. M. RITCHIE & A. URQUHART. 1983. Catecholamines and cholinergic enzymes in pre-senile and senile Alzheimer-type dementia and Down's syndrome. Brain Res. **280:** 119–126.

Electrophysiological Markers of Aging and Memory Loss in Rats[a]

LEYLA DE TOLEDO-MORRELL[b]

Departments of Neurological Sciences and Psychology
Rush Medical College
Chicago, Illinois 60612

AND

FRANK MORRELL

Department of Neurological Sciences
Rush Medical College
Chicago, Illinois 60612
and
Marine Biological Laboratory
Woods Hole, Massachusetts 02543

INTRODUCTION

Loss of recent memory is one of the cardinal signs of aging in man. A very similar impairment in recent memory occurs in the early stages of Senile Dementia of the Alzheimer Type (SDAT), well before there is any significant loss of general cognitive function. It is this selective failure to encode or to retain new information in the face of preserved retrieval for older experiences that renders the age-associated memory loss similar to those deficits produced by bilateral temporal lobectomy involving the hippocampal formation[1-3] (or bilateral hippocampal damage[4]) in humans. These kinds of amnesic syndromes are also quite similar in nature to the types of memory deficits seen in rats following bilateral damage to the hippocampal system.[5]

It is not surprising that the age-associated or disease-induced amnesias should resemble the effect of surgically produced lesions of the hippocampus in man and animal since this structure seems to be especially vulnerable to the aging process. For example, anatomical studies have shown significant age-related decreases in axodendritic and axosomatic synapses[6-9] as well as decreases in neuronal cell density[10,11] in the hippocampus of rats. The decreased synaptic density involving the entorhinal input to hippocampus via the perforant pathway reported in rodents[6-9] has recently been documented in patients with SDAT and such perforant pathway pathology has been suggested as playing a major role in the memory loss associated with the disease.[12] To some extent, these losses may be compensated for by increased synaptogenesis.[13-15] However, such anatomical compensation could lead to diminished synaptic specificity.[16-18] Furthermore, there is now substantial biochemical evidence demonstrating an age-dependent decrease in the number of muscarinic cholinergic binding sites in the

[a]Supported by grants AG 03410 and AG 03151 from the National Institute on Aging and the Hoechst-Roussel Pharmaceutical Co., which supplied pentoxifylline.
[b]Address correspondence to: Dr. Leyla de Toledo-Morrell, Department of Neurological Sciences, Rush Medical College, Chicago, IL 60612.

hippocampus of rats[19,20] in addition to a diminution in the responsiveness of hippocampal pyramidal cells to iontophoretically injected acetylcholine.[20,21] A reduction in muscarinic cholinergic receptors has also been reported for patients with SDAT, but only when hippocampal tissue was examined.[22,23] Loss of the presynaptic cholinergic marker, choline acetyltransferase (CAT), is one of the most consistent biochemical abnormalities in the brain of SDAT patients.[24] The loss is concentrated in frontal and temporal cortices and is thought to be a consequence of cell death in the major cholinergic projection to these areas, the nucleus basalis of Meynert.[25] Of greatest importance to the present argument is the fact that the cholinergic supply to hippocampus, either via the septum[26,27] or via some portions of the perforant path input,[12] is especially compromised. Perry and her colleagues[26,27] have particularly emphasized the close correlation between normal aging and senile dementia in terms of the biochemical pathology of the hippocampus, although in later stages of dementia (and unlike normal aging) the damage extends far beyond the hippocampus. Nevertheless, it is this strong correlation between hippocampal damage and memory dysfunction that has led us directly to our animal model for studying the neurobiology of age-related memory deficits and has determined the research strategy we employ.

In the search for electrophysiological markers of aging and memory loss, we felt it was crucial to utilize a readily quantifiable mnemonic behavior with a known anatomical substrate toward which we could direct our electrodes as well as biochemical and morphological probes. For our purposes, therefore, the one-trial passive avoidance task, although quick, convenient, and well established in aging research,[28,29] was not suitable since its anatomical substrate is not clear. Instead, we selected the eight-arm spatial maze task[30,31] to assess memory in our experiments. In one version of this task, every arm of the maze is baited with food. Since once consumed, food is not replaced, the optimal strategy for a hungry animal is to "remember" where he has been and not go back to an arm that has already been visited. (This type of memory for events within a given trial has been referred to as "working" memory.[5]) Accurate performance in this situation, which may be viewed as equivalent to remembering an eight-item list, has been shown to depend crucially on the integrity of the hippocampus and its afferent connections and to be relatively unaffected by neocortical or amygdala lesions.[5,32–36] In an elegant disconnection analysis, Olton et al.[37] utilized various combinations of unilateral or bilateral fornix and entorhinal lesions with or without commissure transection to show that for accurate radial maze performance, at least one pathway had to remain available through the hippocampus by which the fornix could relay information from subcortical cell stations to the entorhinal cortex (and thereby the neocortex). In short, the anatomical evidence is clear and extremely precise.

In the absence of experimenter-induced lesions, deficits in spatial working memory in the eight-arm maze have also been demonstrated in aged animals.[38–43] This is not surprising, since, as indicated above, hippocampal integrity seems to be severely compromised by the aging process. Furthermore, as will be described in detail below, results from our laboratory[40,41] and those of others[43,44] have shown that such age-related deficits in spatial memory are tightly related to hippocampal plasticity measured electrophysiologically, suggesting that the memory deficit may depend upon altered synaptic transmission in hippocampal cortex.

In summary, our strategy has been to seek out a quantifiable behavior in an animal model that had face validity as analogous to memory disturbances characteristic of human aging and had a known anatomical substrate. Lesion techniques as described above[37] are most useful in establishing the gross localization of a substrate for a behavior. Microscopic localization within the structure, i.e. pre- or postsynaptic, dendritic or somatic, and the beginnings of an insight into mechanism require the precision of local field or single unit recording. These techniques, when combined with the behavior on the one hand and with biochemical and morphological data on the other, have begun to yield insights into the underlying cellular mechanisms of memory and of memory loss. It is particularly crucial to stress the importance of the behavioral benchmark. For example, if a difference between young and aged animals were not found in electrophysiological studies, one would not know whether a memory deficit did not exist or whether the electrophysiological measures were inappropriate or taken from an uninvolved site. It is the correlation between the two that makes the strongest case, just as it was not the pathology alone but the correlation between the cholinergic deficit and dementia that allowed the breakthrough in the understanding of the pathophysiology in SDAT.

ELECTROPHYSIOLOGICAL MARKERS OF AGE-RELATED MEMORY LOSS

We first examined the relationship between spatial working memory as a behavior and electrophysiological indices of hippocampal plasticity in the same subjects.[40,41] Speed of hippocampal "kindling" via perforant path stimulation was used as a measure of neuronal plasticity.

In the kindling paradigm, first described by Goddard,[45] a subthreshold electrical stimulus is delivered to a local brain area once or twice a day for a duration of two seconds. When first applied, the electrical stimulation results in only brief afterdischarge (AD) and no behavior. Without any change in stimulation parameters, the AD gradually increases in duration and spreads from the stimulus site to increasingly distant, though synaptically related, brain regions. There also occurs a progressive alteration of stimulus-induced behavior beginning with momentary arrest of ongoing activity and proceeding through localized twitching to a major motor convulsion. It is important to note that once kindling has taken place, cessation of stimulation for many months does not result in loss of the newly established behavior. In the sense that kindling represents a durable modification of nerve function based on synaptic facilitation and brought about by the "experience" of repeated electrical stimulation, it may be considered a robust model of synaptic plasticity related to learning and memory.[46-48] There are further correspondences between behavioral learning, kindling, and other neuronal analogs of learning and memory such as long-term potentiation (LTP). Inhibition of protein synthesis, which interferes with the formation of long-term memory,[49-51] blocks hippocampal kindling,[48] as well as LTP.[52] Enhancement of synaptic responsiveness is characteristic of the kindled state[53] and has also been demonstrated in neurons that have specifically participated in a learned response.[54]

The apparatus used to test spatial memory was an eight-arm radial maze similar to that described by Olton and Samuelson[30] and is shown in FIGURE 1. During training, two 45-mg food pellets were placed at the end of every alley. After being deprived to 80% body weight, three ($N = 21$) and 26 ($N = 25$) month old Fischer 344 strain male rats were given one trial a day in the maze and trained to a criterion of three consecutive trials with no errors (i.e., no repeated entries into a given alley) or to a maximum of 30 trials. A trial consisted of placing the animal in the center of the maze, raising the guillotine doors and allowing 10 choices (eight if all were correct choices) or a maximum of 15 min, whichever came first. The results indicated that significantly more young animals (16/21) reached our very stringent criterion than did old ones (7/25). Furthermore, on the last three days of training, young animals made a greater number of correct choices (7.76) than the old ones (6.55). Since the task requirements in the eight-arm maze could be viewed as similar to the recall of an eight-item list (or an examination of "memory span"), it is useful to further inquire where in the sequence of choices errors occur. FIGURE 2 shows the probability of a correct response (corrected for chance and presented as a fraction of maximum performance) for choices 2–8 on days 11–15 of training. The first choice is by definition always correct. A score of 1.0 indicates errorless performance and a score of 0, chance performance. A comparison of young and old animals on this measure indicated that choice accuracy for the aged ones was markedly impaired after the fourth response. These data provide clear evidence of a decreased "memory span" in aged animals. It is important to note that the choice accuracy of aged rats that reached criterion was almost at the level of that of young ones. Thus the task seems to differentiate not only between young and old, but also between old but not "senescent" and "senescent" rats; i.e., between chronological and physiological age. As in the case of the human dementias, such

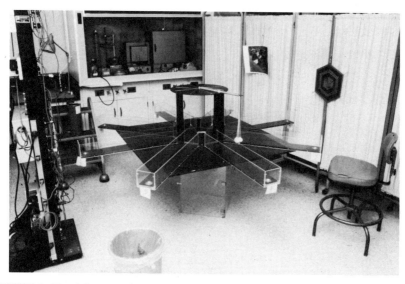

FIGURE 1. The eight-arm radial maze used to test spatial memory. The arms were separated from the central part by Plexiglas guillotine-type doors. The maze was located in an ordinary laboratory room with external cues placed close to each arm since the availability of extra-maze cues has been shown to control accurate performance and prevent simple strategies that do not involve memory, such as choosing arms in order.[55]

individual differences are important for establishing electrophysiological, biochemical, or anatomical markers of memory deficits.

Following these behavioral studies, the same animals were implanted with bipolar stainless steel stimulating electrodes in the perforant path on the right side and recording electrodes in the ipsilateral dentate gyrus and on the cortical surface bilaterally. After a two-week recovery period, they were stimulated twice a day (with 60 Hz, biphasic, 1 msec pulses for a duration of 2 sec) at current levels, which produced an AD duration of 10 sec or less. Young and old animals were compared on the number of stimulations necessary to reach a criterion of five generalized seizures. If a generalized seizure did not occur within 110 stimulations, kindling was stopped and a score of 115 assigned, since at least five more stimulations would have been required to reach criterion.

The electrophysiological results showed that kindling of the hippocampus via perforant path stimulation is much slower in aged rats. The mean number of trials to reach the kindling criterion was 95.9 for old animals and 59.6 for young ones. There was no difference among the two groups in the amount of current necessary to elicit an

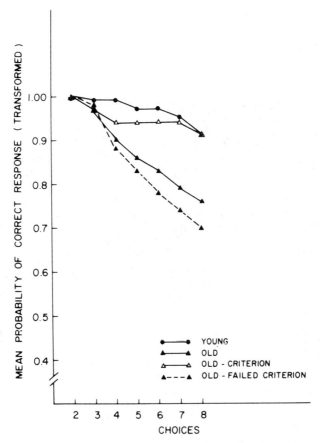

FIGURE 2. Probability of a correct response for choices 2–8 on days (trials) 11–15 of training. The first choice is not included, since it is always correct. The filled triangles with the solid line are based on the performance of the aged group as a whole. The unfilled triangles show the data for the aged animals that eventually reached criterion, whereas the filled triangles with the broken line depict the results for those that did not reach criterion. The score was derived from the following formula: (p[correct] observed − p[correct] expected)/(100 − p[correct] expected) × 100, where p[correct] observed = (number of correct choices/total number of choices) × 100, and p[correct] expected = (number of arms not chosen/8) × 100. For details, see Olton and Samuelson.[30]

AD of 10 sec or less. The most interesting and important finding in our experiment, however, was a striking relationship between performance in the eight-arm spatial maze (as determined by number of trials to reach criterion, with rats failing criterion being assigned a score of 33) and number of trials to reach the kindling criterion for both young and old rats ($r = 0.685$, $p < .001$). Aged animals that reached criterion in the spatial maze kindled as fast as young ones. Conversely, young animals that did not reach criterion in the maze kindled more slowly than those that did.

To our knowledge, the present study represents the first demonstration of a tight relationship between memory measured behaviorally and speed of kindling. It lends support to the notion that pathological features not withstanding, significant aspects of the kindling phenomenon may be shared with the neuronal mechanisms subserving learning and memory. Our findings concerning a tight relationship between deficits in spatial memory and in speed of kindling via perforant path stimulation are consistent with those of Barnes[43] who showed rapid decay of potentiation in aged, memory-deficient rats, especially since synaptic potentiation has been shown to play a role in the early development of kindling.[56,57] Furthermore, the lack of a difference in AD threshold is also consistent with the findings of Barnes and McNaughton[58] who showed that although granule cells in the dentate gyrus of aged rats lose a significant portion of their excitatory input from perforant path,[9] the remaining synapses are more effective than those of young animals.

What could be a possible mechanism responsible for both poor spatial memory and impaired hippocampal kindling via perforant path stimulation in aged animals? It is clear, for example, that the loss of synaptic contacts shown by Geinisman and his collaborators[6–9] involving the perforant path input to dentate gyrus would result in loss of incoming information. Furthermore, it has now been clearly demonstrated that reestablishment of a pathway by sprouting and synaptogenesis does not necessarily restore the original physiological function of the system. Wilson and colleagues,[16,17] for example, have shown impaired LTP in such a regenerated pathway. In addition, Barnes et al.[59] have demonstrated that "place" cells in the CA_1 region of aged rats have much more poorly defined receptive fields than is typical in young animals. Both findings reflect diminished precision in information transfer.

The kindling phenomenon, dependent as it is on sequential synaptic modification in a cascading neural system, would be expected to be especially vulnerable to age-related alterations in postsynaptic (e.g. a decrease in muscarinic cholinergic receptor sites[19,20]) as well as presynaptic mechanisms.[60,61] In fact, any degradation of synaptic transmission, whether consequent to loss of synapses, decreased number of muscarinic receptors, or a diminution of specificity, would be expected to result in impaired kindling as well as impaired performance in the spatial maze. Our results, therefore, support the notion that the spatial memory deficit associated with aging results from an age-dependent decline in the specificity, efficacy, and flexibility of synaptic transmission in hippocampal cortex.

EFFECTS OF PENTOXIFYLLINE ON SPATIAL MEMORY, KINDLING, AND LONG TERM POTENTIATION

As indicated above, there is now extensive evidence of loss of cholinergic fibers in aging and in SDAT, which is believed to compromise mnemonic function. Yet, exogenous choline administration has failed to reverse the age-related memory loss.[23] It has been suggested that this failure might reflect an inability of the energy-deficient aged brain to acetylate and thus utilize the excess choline. Therefore, a strategy in which exogenous choline is combined with agents thought to augment oxidative metabolism has been adopted and shown to improve memory in aged animals.[29]

In the first experiment to be described in this section,[62] we used a similar strategy with pentoxifylline, a phosphodiesterase inhibitor known to increase ATP production.[63] Our interest in the drug was stimulated by the results of an electron microscopic study of the brains of ischemic gerbils that demonstrated a remarkable enlargement of mitochondria, particularly evident in the hippocampus, and to a lesser extent, the neocortex of pentoxifylline-treated animals.[64] The enlargement did not seem to be associated with any disruption of structural integrity, i.e., it was not a consequence of swelling. Since these organelles are the site of oxidative energy production, the above observations suggested to us that the agent may affect energy metabolism *in vivo*. We therefore tested the effects of pentoxifylline alone and of pentoxifylline plus choline on the age-dependent decline in spatial memory.

The procedure used to test spatial memory was similar to that described above. Different groups of 3-month-old and 26-month-old Fischer 344 rats were treated daily, 30–40 min prior to testing in the eight-arm maze, with i.p. injections of saline, 20 mg/kg of pentoxifylline, 20 mg/kg of pentoxifylline plus 100 mg/kg of choline

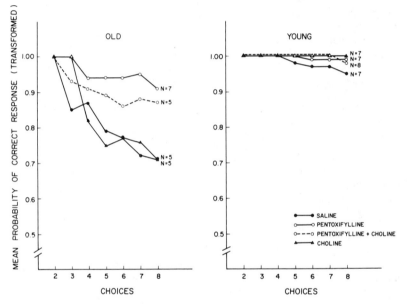

FIGURE 3. Probability of a correct response for choices 2–8 on the last three days (trials 16–18) of training. The performance of young and old animals treated with either saline, pentoxifylline, pentoxifylline and choline, or choline are plotted separately. The score was derived from the formula presented in FIGURE 2. (From de Toledo-Morrell *et al.*[62] With permission from *Behavioral and Neural Biology.*)

chloride, and 100 mg/kg of choline chloride. The dose of pentoxifylline was selected on the basis of advice from the manufacturer and was slightly higher than that (15 mg/kg) which resulted in mitochondrial enlargement.[64] The pentoxifylline plus choline group, like the piracetam plus choline groups in the experiment of Bartus *et al.*,[29] tests whether any effect shown by the drug might be mediated through facilitated use of neurotransmitter substrate. All animals were given one trial a day and trained to a criterion of three consecutive trials with no errors or to a maximum of 18 trials.

The probability of a correct response for choices 2–8 on the last three days of training are plotted separately for the various groups in FIGURE 3. As was the case in our previous experiment (FIGURE 2), a comparison of the 'young saline' and 'old saline' groups once again showed choice accuracy to be impaired for the aged animals after the third or fourth response. The most important finding, however, was the marked improvement in choice accuracy in the pentoxifylline-treated aged rats. Surprisingly, the addition of choline to pentoxifylline did not improve accuracy above that attributable to pentoxifylline alone. Thus, the effect, which is based on chronic administration of the drug, cannot be ascribed to pentoxifylline-induced increased capacity to utilize exogenously supplied neurotransmitter substrate; rather, a different and unanticipated action of the drug is implied. It is important to note that the pentoxifylline-treated young animals did not differ from the young saline controls either in choice accuracy or number of trials to reach criterion.

The effect of choline alone was opposite to that of pentoxifylline: it failed to improve choice accuracy in aged rats (a finding consonant with the bulk of previous research using both human and animal subjects), but it had a beneficial effect on young ones. Young rats treated with choline reached the criterion of three consecutive trials with no errors significantly faster than young saline controls.

As a first step in determining possible mechanisms of action of pentoxifylline, we examined alterations in both the number and affinity of muscarinic cholinergic receptor sites in the hippocampus of saline or pentoxifylline-treated young and old animals following behavioral testing in the eight-arm maze as described above. (This experiment is being carried out in collaboration with Dr. Ana Hitri from the Georgia Medical College who has performed the receptor binding assays.) Twenty-four hours after the last trial in the maze, each animal was given one last dose of either saline or pentoxifylline and sacrificed by decapitation 30 min later. The brain was quickly removed, rapidly frozen, and the right hippocampus dissected out at 4°C. Muscarinic cholinergic receptors were measured with a radioligand binding assay using tritium-labeled quinuclidinyl benzilate (QNB) according to the method of Yamamura and Snyder.[65] So far, based on five rats in each of the four groups, our results show a significant (36%) decrease in the number of QNB binding sites in the untreated (saline) aged animals compared to young ones. There is, however, no difference in affinity. These findings are in agreement with those of Lippa et al.[19,20] Pentoxifylline-treated aged animals exhibited a 14% increase in the number of QNB binding sites compared to aged saline controls. This difference missed statistical significance, possibly due to the small number of subjects involved. However, there was a highly significant correlation between performance in the eight-arm maze and number of QNB binding sites ($r = 0.745$, $p < .001$) irrespective of age or treatment, indicating that the animals that had good choice accuracy were the ones that showed a larger number of cholinergic receptor sites. This result further corroborates the importance of the cholinergic system in the mediation of accurate performance in the eight-arm maze. As a control, we also examined dopaminergic receptors in caudate using [^{3}H]spiroperidol as a ligand in the same animals. There was no relationship between the number (or affinity) of receptor sites and performance in the eight-arm maze.

We have also examined the effects of pentoxifylline on the two electrophysiological indices of hippocampal plasticity that have been shown to be intimately related to impairments in spatial memory, namely kindling and LTP.[41,43] Although both experiments are still in progress, the results are exciting enough to warrant mention. Let us first turn to kindling.

Following implantation of stimulating electrodes in the perforant path and recording electrodes in the dentate gyrus and on the cortical surface bilaterally, different groups of 4- and 27-month-old Fischer 344 strain rats were treated twice daily with either 20 mg/kg of pentoxifylline or saline 30 min prior to each of the two perforant path stimulations. The parameters and procedure were as described for the kindling experiment above. Pentoxifylline or saline treatment was started five days (i.e.

10 injections) prior to the first stimulation. Another difference between our previous experiment and this one is that kindling was not terminated after 110 stimulations, but was continued until the criterion of five generalized seizures was reached. Our preliminary results seem to indicate that pentoxifylline has a beneficial effect on speed of hippocampal kindling in aged animals. So far, the mean number of trials to criterion is 84 for pentoxifylline-treated aged rats compared to 124 for aged saline controls. As was the case for spatial memory, there seems to be no effect of pentoxifylline on speed of kindling in young animals.

The results of experiments that investigated LTP in the hippocampus of aged rats are somewhat controversial. Barnes,[43] for example, studied LTP in the perforant path-dentate synapse of aged and young rats and reported that although aged animals potentiated to the same extent as young ones, they lost the potentiated response much faster. The conclusion was based on an examination of the augmentation in the extracellularly recorded field potential (EPSP) following high frequency stimulation, rather than an examination of the population spike. Landfield and colleagues,[66,67] on the other hand, looked at the changes in the population spike using the Schaffer collateral input for stimulation and the CA_1 pyramidal cells for recording. They found impaired potentiation in aged animals compared to young controls both in *in vivo* and *in vitro* experiments. The difference between the two sets of results could be due to differences in stimulation site, stimulation parameters, or type of response examined (i.e. EPSP versus population spike).

In our study (carried out in collaboration with Dr. T. J. Hoeppner of Rush Medical College), following implantation of stimulating electrodes in the perforant path and recording electrodes in the dentate gyrus,[a] different groups of 4- and 27-month-old rats were treated once daily with either 20 mg/kg of pentoxifylline or with saline for two weeks before the beginning of the experiment as well as throughout the experiment. The procedure used for establishing LTP is similar to that described by Barnes.[43] For each animal, the intensity and duration of each stimulation pulse was set at a level that initially produced a minimal population spike. Baseline response levels were determined on each of two consecutive days by stimulating with single pulses once every 5 sec and averaging (with a Nicolet Med 80 computer) four sets of 10 responses. High frequency stimulation was carried out on each of four consecutive days and consisted of fifteen 20 msec bursts of 400 Hz delivered at 0.2 Hz. Four sets of 10 test responses were averaged (with pulses delivered every 5 sec) 2 min, 10 min, 1 hr, 6 hr, and 24 hr, following each of the four high frequency stimulations and 48 hr, 1 wk, 2 wk, and 3 wk after the fourth high frequency stimulation. In determining the amount of potentiation and its retention, both changes in the EPSP and population spike are taken into account.

So far, our results with respect to extent of potentiation seen in young and old animals seem to be in line with those of Barnes.[43] In addition, the most exciting finding is that pentoxifylline-treated aged animals lose the potentiation more slowly than aged saline controls. Baseline responses and test responses at various time intervals following the fourth high frequency stimulation are presented for an untreated (saline control) old animal in FIGURE 4 and a pentoxifylline-treated old one in FIGURE 5. As is shown in FIGURE 4, the amplitudes of both the EPSP and the population spike were back to baseline within a two-week period for the aged saline controls. On the other hand,

---

[a]In this and in the kindling experiments described above, depth electrode placement was accomplished using stereotaxic coordinates initially and then correcting until single pulse stimulation of the perforant path yielded a "population spike" of the dentate gyrus granule cells.[68]

pentoxifylline-treated aged rats still showed some potentiation, especially evident in the population spike even after three weeks (FIGURE 5). In fact, an examination of input-output functions (population spike divided by EPSP) revealed that one week following the last high frequency stimulation, pentoxifylline-treated aged animals still retained 69% of the change (from baseline) in input-output function, the young

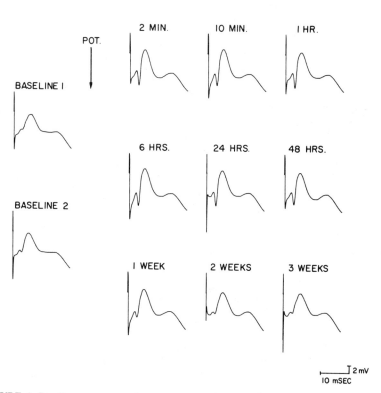

OPS-2

FIGURE 4. Baseline responses and test responses taken at various time intervals following the fourth high frequency stimulation for an aged rat treated with saline. Each tracing is based on an average of 10 responses (see text).

animals retained 33% of the change, and the aged saline rats only 19%. Once again, there seems to be no effect of pentoxifylline on the young.

CONCLUSIONS

In the experiments reported above, we have shown a tight relationship between impairments in electrophysiological measures of hippocampal synaptic plasticity and deficits in working memory in aged animals using the eight-arm spatial maze task. We have further demonstrated that pharmacologic interventions that improve memory also result in an augmentation of synaptic transmission.

It is important to note that the behavioral deficit we observed in aged rats cannot be explained on the basis of performance variables that do not involve memory. First of all, none of the animals that reached criterion in the maze did so by choosing arms in order. Secondly, although old animals moved around slightly more slowly than young

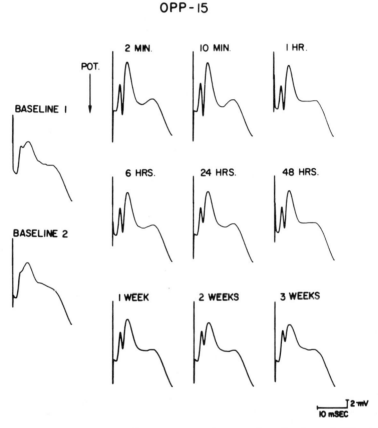

FIGURE 5. Baseline responses and test responses taken at various time intervals following the fourth high frequency stimulation for an aged rat chronically treated with pentoxifylline. Each tracing is based on an average of 10 responses.

ones, the 15 min time limit did not interfere with their completion of a trial. Thus, the deficit we report is based on the number of errors made on a given trial and where in the sequence of choices these errors occurred. Furthermore, the tight correlation between measures of hippocampal synaptic transmission and extent of memory loss argues against a "performance" explanation of the results.

What could be some of the possible mechanisms of action of pentoxifylline? Although our original hypothesis presupposed that pentoxifylline, by enhancing oxidative metabolism, might facilitate uptake and utilization of exogenously supplied choline, our results did not support that hypothesis. The failure of exogenous choline to contribute to the reversal of the age-dependent memory loss, however, does not necessarily rule out other possible interventions within the cholinergic system. For example, impaired oxidation of pyruvic acid has been shown to result in decreased synthesis of acetylcholine despite a more than adequate substrate supply.[69] Indeed, the provision of acetyl-Co A from pyruvate oxidation has been considered the rate-limiting step in ACh synthesis.[70] Furthermore, if one considers the evidence that pyruvate dehydrogenase (PDH) deficiency occurs in the senescent brain[26] and more specifically in SDAT,[71–73] and that the same protein (or at least its subunit) is actively phosphorylated during certain training procedures,[74] it seems not overly farfetched to suggest that pentoxifylline may stimulate phosphorylation in the PDH complex, thereby augmenting cholinergic function.

Other entirely different putative mechanisms that may have less to do with energy metabolism and transmitter availability than with regulation of the cytoskeletal architecture must also be considered. One method of augmenting the efficiency of synaptic transmission may be the "unmasking" of additional receptor sites on the cell membrane (or the synthesis of new ones); alteration of the shape of dendritic spines and synaptic complexes is another. Pentoxifylline has already been shown to alter the shape and deformability of red blood cells, at least in the presence of calcium.[75] Perhaps even more important is the finding that pentoxifylline increases levels of triphosphoinositide in leukocyte membrane in a dose-dependent fashion and markedly augments neutrophil chemotaxis.[76] In the leukocyte system, the effect is to destabilize the membrane and facilitate cell motility. In the central nervous system, it would seem reasonable to envisage an effect of pentoxifylline on membrane-bound protein (e.g., tubulin or fodrin; see Lynch & Baudry[77])—an effect that would be calcium dependent and would result in changes of just those structural elements (e.g., ionophores, synaptic surface configuration, receptor molecules, or microtubules) that control cellular flexibility and determine synaptic excitability and axonal transport.

Some constraints on these speculations will undoubtedly emerge when dose-response curves are carried out to delimit the range of drug effectiveness. However, the most interesting constraint may depend on the striking selectivity of drug action for the aged. It is possible that the memory enhancing effect of pentoxifylline results from potentiation of exactly those natural compensatory mechanisms by which the aging organism limits or mitigates the impact of age-related metabolic exhaustion and cell loss—mechanisms which the younger organism has not yet had to develop. In any event, an understanding of the mechanism of the action of pentoxifylline may provide important insights into the nature of those components of the memory process that decline with age.

ACKNOWLEDGMENTS

Dedicated to Benjamin R. Morrell who kept reminding us that we would be too late for him in our endeavors. We thank S. Fleming for experimental and B. Brown for histological assistance and Carolyn Kurt for typing the manuscript.

REFERENCES

1. SCOVILLE, W. B. & B. MILNER. 1957. Loss of recent memory after bilateral hippocampal lesions. J. Neurol. Neurosurg. Psychiatr. **20:** 11–21.

2. MILNER, B. 1978. Clues to the cerebral organization of memory. *In* Symposium on Cerebral Correlates of Conscious Experience. P. A. Buser & A. Rougel-Bouser, Eds. Elsevier. Amsterdam.

3. CORKIN, S. 1984. Lasting consequences of bilateral medial temporal lobectomy: Clinical course and experimental findings in H. M. Sem. Neurol. **4:** 249–259.

4. WOODS, B. T., W. SCHOENE & L. KNEISLEY. 1982. Are hippocampal lesions sufficient to cause lasting amnesia? J. Neurol. Neurosurg. Psychiatr. **45:** 243–247.

5. OLTON, D. S. 1983. Memory functions and the hippocampus. *In* Neurobiology of the Hippocampus. W. Seifert, Ed. Academic Press. London.

6. BONDAREFF, W. & Y. GEINISMAN. 1976. Loss of synapses in the dentate gyrus of the senescent rat. Am. J. Anat. **145:** 129–136.

7. GEINISMAN, Y. 1979. Loss of axosomatic synapses in the dentate gyrus of aged rats. Brain Res. **168:** 485–492.

8. GEINISMAN, Y. 1981. Loss of axon terminals contacting neuronal somata in the dentate gyrus of aged rats. Brain Res. **212:** 136–139.

9. GEINISMAN, Y. & W. BONDAREFF. 1976. Decrease in the number of synapses in the senescent brain: A quantitative electron microscopic analysis of the dentate gyrus molecular layer in the rat. Mech. Age. Dev. **5:** 11–23.

10. LANDFIELD, P. W., G. ROSE, L. SANDLES, T. C. WOHLSTADTER & G. LYNCH. 1977. Patterns of astroglial hypertrophy and neuronal degeneration in the hippocampus of aged, memory-deficient rats. J. Gerontol. **32:** 3–12.

11. LANDFIELD, P. W., L. D. BRAUN, T. A. PITLER, J. D. LINDSEY & G. LYNCH. 1981. Hippocampal aging in rats: A morphometric study of multiple variables in semithin sections. Neurobiol. Aging **2:** 265–275.

12. HYMAN, B. T., G. W. VAN HOESEN & A. R. DAMASIO. 1984. Perforant pathway pathology and the memory impairment of Alzheimer's Disease. Neurosci. Abstr. **10:** 384.

13. COTMAN, C. W. & S. W. SCHEFF. 1979. Compensatory synapse growth in aged animals after neuronal death. Mech. Age. Dev. **9:** 103–117.

14. HOFF, S. F., S. W. SCHEFF, L. S. BENARDO & C. W. COTMAN. 1982. Lesion induced synaptogenesis in the dentate gyrus of aged rats: I. Loss and reacquisition of normal synaptic density. J. Comp. Neurol. **205:** 246–252.

15. CURCIO, C. A. & J. W. HINDS. 1983. Stability of synaptic density and spine volume in dentate gyrus of aged rats. Neurobiol. Aging. **4:** 77–87.

16. WILSON, R. C. 1981. Changes in translation of synaptic excitation to dentate granule cell discharge accompanying long-term potentiation. I. Differences between normal and reinnervated dentate gyrus. J. Neurophysiol. **46:** 324–338.

17. WILSON, R. C., W. B. LEVY & O. STEWARD. 1981. Changes in translation of synaptic excitation to dentate granule cell discharge accompanying long-term potentiation. II. An evaluation of mechanisms utilizing dentate gyrus dually innervated by surviving ipsilateral and sprouted crossed temporodentate inputs. J. Neurophysiol. **46:** 339–355.

18. SHAPIRO, M. L., D. SIMON, D. S. OLTON, F. H. GAGE, A. BJORKLUND & U. STENEVI. 1984. Brain transplants can restore single unit activity in the hippocampus. Neurosci. Abstr. **10:** 125.

19. LIPPA, A. S., R. W. PELHAM, B. BEER, D. J. CRITCHETT, R. L. DEAN & R. T. BARTUS. 1980. Brain cholinergic dysfunction and memory in aged rats. Neurobiol. Aging. **1:** 13–19.

20. LIPPA, A. S., D. J. CRITCHETT, F. EHLERT, H. I. YAMAMURA, S. J. ENNA & R. T. BARTUS. 1981. Age-related alterations in neurotransmitter receptors: An electrophysiological and biochemical analysis. Neurobiol. Aging **2:** 3–8.

21. SEGAL M. 1982. Changes in neurotransmitter actions in aged rat hippocampus. Neurobiol. Aging **3:** 121–124.

22. RINNE, J. O., J. K. RINNE, K. LAAKSO, L. PALJARVI & U. K. RINNE. 1984. Reduction in muscarinic receptor binding in limbic areas of Alzheimer brain. J. Neurol. Neurosurg. Psychiatr. **47:** 651–653.

23. BARTUS, R. T., R. L. DEAN, B. BEER & A. S. LIPPA. 1982. The cholinergic hypothesis of geriatric memory dysfunction. Science **217:** 408–416.

24. TERRY, R. D. & P. DAVIES. 1980. Dementia of the Alzheimer type. Ann. Rev. Neurosci. **3:** 77–95.

25. COYLE, J. T., D. L. PRICE & M. R. DE LONG. 1983. Alzheimer's disease: A disorder of cortical cholinergic innervation. Science **219**: 1184–1189.
26. PERRY, E. K., R. H. PERRY, P. H. GIBSON, G. BLESSED & B. E. TOMLINSON. 1977. A cholinergic connection between normal aging and senile dementia in the hippocampus. Neurosci. Lett. **6**: 85–89.
27. PERRY E. K., G. BLESSED, B. E. TOMLINSON, R. H. PERRY, T. J. CROW, A. J. CROSS, G. J. DOCKRAY, R. DIMALINE & A. ARREGUI. 1981. Neurochemical activities in human temporal lobe related to aging and Alzheimer-type changes. Neurobiol. Aging **2**: 251–256.
28. BARTUS, R. T. & R. L. DEAN. 1981. Age-related memory loss and drug therapy: Possible directions based on animal models. *In* Aging. Brain Neurotransmitters and Receptors in Aging and Age-Related Disorders. S. J. Enna, T. Samarajski & B. Beer, Eds. Vol. 17. Raven Press. New York.
29. BARTUS, R. T., R. L. DEAN, K. A. SHERMAN, E. FRIEDMAN & B. BEER. 1981. Profound effects of combining choline and piracetam on memory enhancement and cholinergic function in aged rats. Neurobiol. Aging **2**: 105–111.
30. OLTON, D. S. & R. J. SAMUELSON. 1976. Remembrance of places passed: Spatial memory in rats. J. Exp. Psychol.: Anim. Behav. Proc. **2**: 97–116.
31. OLTON, D. S., C. COLLISON & M. A. WERZ. 1977. Spatial memory and radial arm maze performance in rats. Learn. Motiv. **8**: 289–314.
32. BECKER, J. T., J. A. WALKER & D. S. OLTON. 1980. Neuroanatomical bases of spatial memory. Brain Res. **200**: 307–320.
33. OLTON, D. S. 1978. The function of septo-hippocampal connections in spatially organized behavior. *In* Functions of the Septo-hippocampal System. Ciba Foundation Symposium 58. Elsevier. New York.
34. OLTON, D. S., J. A. WALKER & F. H. GAGE. 1978, Hippocampal connections and spatial discrimination. Brain Res. **139**: 295–308.
35. OLTON, D. S., J. T. BECKER & G. E. HANDELMANN. 1979. Hippocampus, space and memory. Behav. Brain Sci. **2**: 313–365.
36. WINOCUR, G. 1982. Radial-arm-maze behavior by rats with dorsal hippocampal lesions: Effects of cueing. J. Comp. Physiol. Psychol. **96**: 155–169.
37. OLTON, D. S., J. A. WALKER & W. A. WOLF. 1982. A disconnection analysis of hippocampal function. Brain Res. **233**: 241–253.
38. BARNES, C. A., L. NADEL & W. K. HONIG. 1980. Spatial memory deficits in senescent rats. Can. J. Psychol. **34**: 29–39.
39. DAVIS, H. P., A. IDOWU & G. E. GIBSON. 1983. Improvement of 8-arm maze performance in aged Fischer 344 rats with 3,4-diaminopyridine. Exp. Aging. Res. **9**: 211–214.
40. DE TOLEDO-MORRELL, L., F. MORRELL, E. KESSLER & S. FLEMING. 1981. Spatial memory and hippocampal kindling are impaired as a function of aging. Neurology **31**: 101.
41. DE TOLEDO-MORRELL, L., F. MORRELL & S. FLEMING. 1984. Age dependent deficits in spatial memory are related to impaired hippocampal kindling. Behav. Neurosci. **98**: 902–907.
42. WALLACE, J. E., E. E. KRAUTER & B. A. CAMPBELL. 1980. Animal models of declining memory in the aged: Short term and spatial memory in the aged rat. J. Geront. **35**: 355–363.
43. BARNES, C. A. 1979. Memory deficits associated with senescence: A neurophysiological and behavioral study in the rat. J. Comp. Physiol. Psychol. **93**: 74–104.
44. BARNES, C. A. 1983. The physiology of the senescent hippocampus. *In* Neurobiology of the Hippocampus. W. Seifert, Ed. Academic Press. London.
45. GODDARD, G. V. 1967. The development of epileptic seizures through brain stimulation at low intensity. Nature **214**: 1020–1021.
46. GODDARD, G. V. & R. M. DOUGLAS. 1975. Does the engram of kindling model the engram of normal long-term memory? Can. J. Neurol. Sci. **2**: 385–394.
47. GODDARD, G. V. 1981. Component properties of the memory machine: Hebb revisited. *In* The Nature of Thought: Essays in Honor of D. O. Hebb. P. W. Jusczyk & R. M. Klein, Eds. Lawrence Erlbaum. Hillsdale, NJ.
48. MORRELL, F., N. TSURU, T. J. HOEPPNER, D. MORGAN & W. H. HARRISON. 1975.

Secondary epileptogenesis in frog forebrain: Effect of inhibition of protein synthesis. Can. J. Neurol. Sci. **2:** 407–416.

49. AGRANOFF, B. W. 1972. Effects of antibiotics on long-term memory formation in the goldfish. *In* Animal Memory. W. K. Honig & P. H. R. James, Eds. Academic Press. New York.

50. BARONDES, S. H. 1975. Protein synthesis dependent and protein synthesis independent memory storage processes. *In* Short-Term Memory. J. A. Deutsch & D. Deutsch, Eds. Academic Press. New York.

51. SQUIRE, L. R. & S. H. BARONDES. 1973. Memory impairment during prolonged training in mice given inhibitors of cerebral protein synthesis. Brain Res. **56:** 215–225.

52. STEWARD, O. & S. BRASSEL. 1983. Intrahippocampal injections of cycloheximide reversibly block long-term potentiation. Neurosci. Abstr. **9:** 690.

53. RACINE, R., L. TUFF & J. ZAIDE. 1975. Kindling, unit discharge patterns and neural plasticity. Can. J. Neurol. Sci. **2:** 395–405.

54. WOODY, C. D., J. D. KNISPEL, T. J. CROW & P. A. BLACK-CLEWORTH. 1976. Activity and excitability to electrical current of cortical auditory receptive neurons of awake cats as affected by stimulus association. J. Neurophysiol. **39:** 1045–1060.

55. SUZUKI, S., G. AUGERINOS & A. H. BLACK. 1980. Stimulus control of spatial behavior on the eight arm maze in rats. Learn. Motiv. **11:** 1–18.

56. DOUGLAS, R. M. & G. V. GODDARD. 1974. Long-term potentiation of the perforant path granule cell synapses in the rat hippocampus. Brain Res. **86:** 205–215.

57. RACINE, R., E. KAIRISS & G. SMITH. 1981. Kindling mechanisms: The evolution of the burst response versus enhancement. *In* Kindling 2. J. A. Wada, Ed. Raven Press. New York.

58. BARNES, C. A. & B. L. MCNAUGHTON. 1980. Physiological compensation for loss of afferent synapses in rat hippocampal granule cells during senescence. J. Physiol. **309:** 473–485.

59. BARNES, C. A., B. L. MCNAUGHTON & J. O'KEEFE. 1983. Loss of place specificity in hippocampal complex spike cells of senescent rat. Neurobiol. Aging **4:** 113–119.

60. SHERMAN, K. A., J. A. KUSTER, R. L. DEAN, R. T. BARTUS & E. FRIEDMAN. 1981. Presynaptic cholinergic mechanisms in brain of aged rats with memory impairments. Neurobiol. Aging **2:** 99–104.

61. PETERSON, C. & G. E. GIBSON. 1983. Amelioration of age-related neurochemical and behavioral deficits by 3,4-diaminopyridine. Neurobiol. Aging **4:** 25–30.

62. DE TOLEDO-MORRELL, L., F. MORRELL, S. FLEMING & M. M. COHEN. 1984. Pentoxifylline reverses age related deficits in spatial memory. Behav. Neural Biol. **42:** 1–8.

63. STEFANOVICH, V. 1978. The biochemical mechanism of action of pentoxifylline. Pharmatherapeutica **2:** 5–16.

64. HARTMANN, J. F., R. S. BECKER & M. M. COHEN. 1977. Effects of pentoxifylline on cerebral ultrastructure of normal and ischemic gerbils. Neurology **27:** 77–84.

65. YAMAMURA, H. I. & S. H. SNYDER. 1974. Muscarinic cholinergic binding in rat brain. Proc. Natl. Acad. Sci. USA **71:** 1725–1730.

66. LANDFIELD, P. W., J. L. MCGAUGH & G. LYNCH. 1978. Impaired synaptic potentiation processes in the hippocampus of aged, memory-deficient rats. Brain Res. **150:** 85–101.

67. LANDFIELD, P. W. & G. LYNCH. 1977. Impaired monosynaptic potentiation in *in vitro* hippocampal slices from aged, memory-deficient rats. J. Gerontol. **32:** 525–533.

68. LØMO, T. 1971. Patterns of activation in a monosynaptic cortical pathway: The perforant path input to the dentate area of the hippocampal formation. Exp. Brain Res. **12:** 18–45.

69. GIBSON, G. E., R. JOPE & J. P. BLASS. 1975. Decreased synthesis of acetylcholine accompanying impaired oxidation of pyruvic acid in rat brain minces. J. Biochem. **148:** 17–23.

70. TUCEK, S. 1978. Acetylcholine Synthesis in Neurons. Chapman & Hall. London.

71. BLASS, J. P., G. E. GIBSON, M. SHIMADA, T. KIHARA, M. WATANABE & K. KURINIOTO. 1980. Brain carbohydrate metabolism and dementias. *In* Biochemistry of Dementia. P. J. Roberts, Ed. Wiley. New York.

72. PERRY, E. K., R. H. PERRY, B. E. TOMLINSON, G. BLESSED & P. H. GIBSON. 1980.

Coenzyme-A acetylating enzymes in Alzheimer's disease: Possible cholinergic 'compartment' of pyruvate dehydrogenase. Neurosci. Lett. **18:** 105–110.
73. SORBI, S., E. D. BIRD & J. P. BLASS. 1983. Decreased pyruvate dehydrogenase complex activity in Huntington and Alzheimer brain. Ann. Neurol. **13:** 72–78.
74. MORGAN, D. G. & A. ROUTTENBERG. 1981. Brain pyruvate dehydrogenase: Phosphorylation and enzyme activity altered by training experience. Science **214:** 470–471.
75. MULLER, R. 1979. Pentoxifylline—a biomedical profile. J. Med. **10:** 307–329.
76. SHEETZ, M. P., W.-P. WANG & D. L. KREUTZER. 1984. Polyphosphoinositides as regulators of membrane skeletal stability. *In* White Cell Mechanics: Basic Science and Clinical Aspects. J. Meiselman, Ed. Alan R. Liss. New York.
77. LYNCH, G. & M. BAUDRY. 1984. The biochemistry of memory: A new and specific hypothesis. Science **224:** 1057–1063.

Analysis of Age-Related Impairments in Learning and Memory in Rodent Models

DONALD K. INGRAM

Molecular Physiology and Genetics Section
Laboratory of Cellular and Molecular Biology
Gerontology Research Center[a]
National Institute on Aging
Francis Scott Key Medical Center
Baltimore, Maryland 21224

A sound demographic basis supports the increased need for animal models of memory dysfunction associated with human aging. Industrialized nations are experiencing a rapid growth in the aged segments of their populations. For example, over the last half of this century, the proportion of the U.S. population over 65 years of age will grow from 8% to over 12% with projected increases up to 17% by the year 2030.[1] This trend carries the potential for proportional and absolute increases in persons suffering from some type of memory impairment. These dysfunctions can range in severity from the subtle decrements observed among healthy, elderly individuals[2] to the marked deficits observed among individuals diagnosed as having senile dementia of the Alzheimer type.[3]

The development of animal models of age-related memory dysfunction addresses several issues pertaining to gerontology and geriatrics, including behavioral characterization of these impairments, analysis of neurobiological etiology, and identification of possible therapies. Animal models offer powerful practical advantages over human research. Most important from a gerontological perspective is the fact that typically the life spans of laboratory animals are much shorter than that of humans. Second, ethical considerations of human research prohibit the types of invasive analyses and treatments that can be accomplished with animal models. Finally, control of genetic and environmental factors in animal research presumably affords an advantage over human studies that can be affected by ample variation from these sources.

As evidenced in FIGURE 1, the number of animal studies of age-related performance differences in learning and memory tasks has grown exponentially over the last 20 years to meet the increased demand in this area. This is an impressive trend representing the influx of many new investigators into the field. Much of this research is focused on aging as the biological phenomenon and applies behavioral paradigms to gerontological investigations, while other efforts focus on behavior as the biological phenomenon and apply life span developmental paradigms to neurobiological investigations. Regardless of orientation, however, the evolution of this scientific endeavor must be guided by several methodological principles. These principles are not novel to neurobiological or gerontological research. They have been underscored in several excellent reviews of the literature.[4-6] The objective of the present paper is to reaffirm these principles. The emphasis will be on analysis of complex maze performance in rodent models; however, the strategy to be illustrated can be applied to most other paradigms and animal models and, in some cases, has been applied to other systems.[7]

[a]The Gerontology Research Center is fully accredited by the American Association for Accreditation of Laboratory Animal Care.

METHODOLOGICAL ISSUES

Sampling

Behavioral performance undergoes a wide range of alterations during senescence in laboratory rodents.[5–9] It should be emphasized, however, that the effects of aging are deduced typically from cross-sectional studies, that is, from the comparison of two or more age groups, presumably representative of the animal's life span. It is assumed that control of environmental and genetic factors afforded users of animal models permits this almost exclusive reliance on cross-sectional analysis. Such is not the luxury in human studies where confounds due to cohort and period effects can markedly influence results.[10]

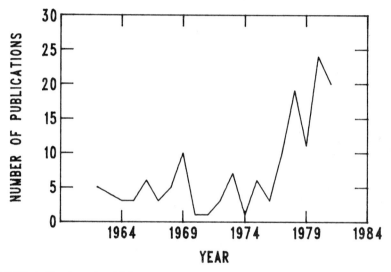

FIGURE 1. Number of published papers involving analysis of age-related impairments in learning/memory tasks in laboratory animals as a function of year. Data are from author's review of the literature.

At issue is whether the age samples selected are truly representative of the life span. First, there is the issue of a criterion for determining whether the oldest age group analyzed can be considered senescent. The conventional criterion is that the oldest group should be at least near or beyond the mean/median life span for the species/strain. Many reports do not specify the mean or median life span of the subjects used. As suggested previously, many past efforts clearly cannot be considered as studies of aging because their oldest age group did not even approach this criterion.[4–6]

In addition, the over-reliance on comparisons of just two age groups as being representative of the life span has been criticized.[4,5] This problem is most acute when the youngest age group is still clearly in a developmental stage of the life span, e.g., a 2-month-old mouse.[4] A finding of no significant difference between this group and an acceptably aged group may reflect the fact that both occupy relatively similar positions

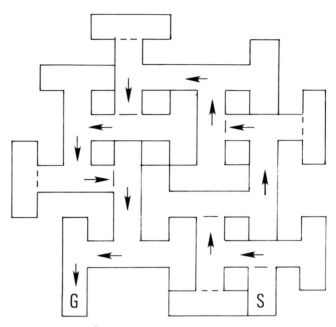

FIGURE 2. Configuration of 14-unit T-maze. Arrows denote correct pathway from start (S) to goal (G); solid lines denote guillotine doors used to prevent back-tracking; broken lines denote false doors.

on a quadratic performance curve (inverted U-shaped function) with the highest peak occurring somewhere in between, e.g., at 6 months in the mouse. This problem perhaps can be alleviated by analyzing additional age groups or at least a third group midpoint to the two extremes. Barring these options, comparison of older, mature groups, e.g., 6-month-old mice, to acceptably aged groups is a more satisfactory experimental design.

Confounding Variation

Investigators of memory impairments must be vigilant for confounding due to noncognitive performance factors, specifically variation due to sensory, motor, and motivational factors.[11] The nature of experimental design in this area of investigation requires that evidence of memory impairment be deduced from performance differences between experimental and control groups or, in the case of gerontological studies, between age groups. In studies where the objective is to induce memory impairments through experimental manipulation, e.g., pharmacological or surgical, the investigator must be cognizant of the possibility that treatment also may affect sensory or motor abilities or motivational levels that impinge on performance and thus may confound the comparison of performance differences due to memory impairment. In a gerontological study, it is presumed that these sources of extraneous variation exist[5-7]; therefore, the investigator should demonstrate that they do not impinge significantly on the comparison of interest. The following discussion describes our strategy for assessing whether these factors contribute to the age-related impairment observed in a complex maze task.

ANALYSIS OF COMPLEX MAZE PERFORMANCE

Goodrick's Studies

In a series of studies, Goodrick[12–17] demonstrated an age-related impairment in the performance of Wistar rats in a 14-unit T-maze. Stone[18] introduced this maze, the configuration of which is depicted in FIGURE 2. Stone observed no age differences in the performance of rats in this task, but Goodrick[17] attributed these negative findings to small sample sizes, incomplete statistical analysis, and severely reduced body weight among aged animals.

Goodrick's protocol involved food rewards, specifically a sweetened condensed milk solution. Initially, the animals were housed individually and received reduced access to food, both in amount and time, over a 3–5 week period. Target body weights were usually 75–80% of baseline. Prior to maze training, each animal received training in a straight runway for the food reward during 3–5 daily trials for 7–10 days. If the animals responded satisfactorily (no criterion given), then training began in the 14-unit T-maze. This phase involved 1–4 daily trials to a maximum of 28 trials, by which time performance appeared to plateau. FIGURE 3 depicts a typical pattern of error responses among young (6 mo) and aged groups (26 mo) of male Wistar rats.[13] The mean life span of this rat strain is about 22–24 mo. Clearly, the rate of learning, as measured by the reduction in errors as a function of trials, was faster among the young group, and the asymptotic level of error performance was higher among the aged group. Also noted is the learning curve of a subgroup of aged rats, whose error performance was comparable to that of young animals. This observation underscores the concept of examining individual differences within aged groups, a discussion of which is presented later.

Goodrick attributed the observed age difference to several factors.[17] He reported a

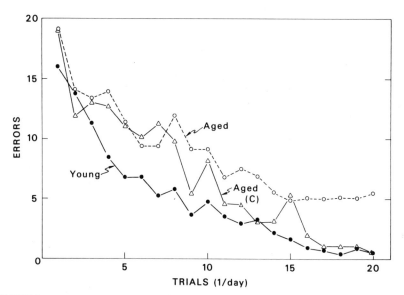

FIGURE 3. Age comparison ($N = 16$) of mean errors of male Wistar rats in 14-unit T-maze for food rewards. Difference between young and aged is significant at trials 16–20, $p < .01$. Group C represents 6/16 aged rats that learned the maze. (Data from Goodrick.[13])

higher frequency of perseverative errors among aged compared to young groups. Aged animals tended to repeat errors at particular choice-points. Moreover, Goodrick[16] demonstrated that this response bias probably represented a form of behavioral rigidity that could be utilized to enhance maze performance under certain conditions. Specifically, when all animals received early training trials that forced them to run the correct path by blocking off all incorrect turns, aged animals displayed superior maze performance compared to younger counterparts. Goodrick[17] also suggested that impaired short-term memory processing was an important factor in age-related decline in maze performance. Evidence for this factor was provided in an experiment comparing young and aged animals under conditions of massed (4 daily trials) and distributed (1 daily trial) practice.[15] Because the aged animals benefited differentially more from massed practice and performed worse under distributed practice compared to young animals, Goodrick[15] deduced that the age-related impairment was partly due to deficient short-term memory processing. A third factor that Goodrick identified was task complexity.[13] He observed no age-related impairment in simple maze tasks (i.e., less than five choice-points), thus, training in a task requiring learning and remembering more than five position discriminations was an important factor in producing age-related performance differences.

Because Goodrick observed this age-related impairment in maze performance across several experiments and because it has been observed by other investigators using similar protocols,[19,20] these findings would appear to represent a robust phenomenon. However, several questions remained to be answered about the robustness of these findings. Were age differences that he and others observed confounded by sensory, motor, or motivational factors?

Motivational Issues

Age differences in motivational levels are a potential source of confounding variation in learning/memory tasks. For appetitive tasks, it should be a requisite that the investigator demonstrate that the motivation to perform for rewards is equivalent across age groups. Alternatively, if there is an age-related decline in performance in a learning/memory task, the investigator may opt to demonstrate that aged animals have a higher level of motivation than younger animals yet still perform worse. Similarly for aversive tasks, it should be a requisite that the investigator demonstrate that the negative reinforcement does not affect age groups differentially. Unlike the situation with appetitive tasks, it is perhaps not accepted that the aged groups be more affected, since there is the risk that the greater response to negative reinforcement among aged animals may impair performance due to greater residual effects from the stress of the task.

Age differences in motivational response to food deprivation represent a possible source of confounding variation in Goodrick's studies. Typically, aged (24–26 mo) rats have higher body weights compared to young (6–8 mo) rats, and much of this extra body weight is in additional adipose tissue, represented as increased cell size.[21] The use of percentage body weight loss instead of absolute body weight loss has been recommended in gerontological studies using rodent models with differential weights across age.[9] However, even with equivalent percent body weight reductions, aged animals could have a greater proportion of adipose tissue as a source of energy reserves and, thus, have less physiological need for the food reinforcement. This reserve might translate into reduced motivation for food rewards. Although Goodrick did not conduct any systematic analysis of age differences in motivation for food rewards in the maze, he attempted to offset this possibility by imposing an even greater percentage of body weight loss among aged animals compared to young counterparts, e.g., 75% versus 80%, respectively, as standard procedure.[17]

The question remains, though, whether the procedure was effective in controlling possible motivational confounding. An alternative strategy can be applied to determine whether the age difference in maze performance remains intact when the assumption of motivational differences is clearly biased toward aged animals. This would be the case in applying fluid deprivation to motivate maze performance for water rewards. Water consumption generally increases with age in laboratory rodents, and it is thought to be related to age-related impairments in hydrostatic mechanisms.[9,22] Therefore, an equivalent period of water deprivation for young and aged rats should induce a greater physiological demand for water among the older group.

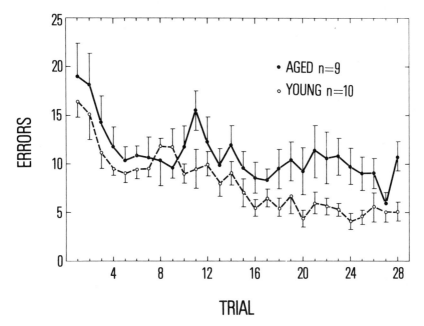

FIGURE 4. Age comparison of mean errors of female Wistar rats in 14-unit T-maze for water rewards ($p < .01$).

FIGURE 4 presents the results of an experiment from our laboratory in which young (6 mo) and aged (25 mo) female Wistar rats were trained in the 14-unit T-maze for water rewards. The protocol involved single housing during two weeks on a 22-hr fluid deprivation schedule. During the second week, all animals received three daily trials of training in a straight runway for brief exposure to a water tube, followed by 2-hr access to water in the home cage. Maze training was conducted during weeks 3–6, with one trial daily for 30-sec access to water in the goal box and 2-hr access in the home cage. Still obvious is the age difference that Goodrick observed using food rewards in male rats of the same strain.

This observation also extended to an age comparison of maze performance in another species. FIGURE 5 presents data on errors and run time of young (6–8 mo) and aged (26–27 mo) male C57BL/6J mice trained for water rewards in the 14-unit

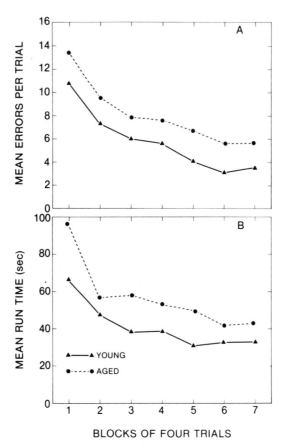

FIGURE 5. Age comparison (N = 10–12) of mean errors (A) and run time (B) of male C57BL/6J mice in 14-unit T-maze for water rewards (p < .01 for errors, and p < .01 for run time).

T-maze. Goodrick[23] estimated the mean life span of this mouse strain to be 26–27 mo. The maze training protocol was identical to that of the rat study, and the results also were very similar. The aged animals made on the average three more errors per trial and showed higher error performance at the asymptotic level compared to young animals (FIGURE 5A).

Aged animals are also slower in the maze compared to young animals (FIGURE 5B). This difference might be interpreted to reflect impaired motor performance or reduced motivation or both. Regarding the issue of impaired motor performance, it is difficult to assess this factor because run time is correlated with error performance, i.e., the more errors an animal makes, the longer it takes to run the maze. However, it should be clear that the animal is not handicapped by being slower. Actually it can proceed at its own pace. Therefore, the comparison of error performance is the most germane dependent variable. Regarding the issue of reduced motivation indicated by slower run times of aged animals, the question can be approached from another angle. FIGURE 6 provides the age comparison of water intake and body weight during the maze experiment with mice as subjects. Aged mice drink relatively more water when given the opportunity in their home cage (FIGURE 6A). Moreover, the relative body weight loss during 22 hr of deprivation is greater among aged mice (FIGURE 6B). These observations suggest a greater physiological deficit produced by water deprivation among aged mice compared to young counterparts.[9] Thus, it is more likely that the slower run times among aged animals reflect their higher error performance rather than reduced motivation or impaired motor performance.

Sensory Issues

Age differences in maze performance also could be confounded by age-related impairments in sensory abilities. Audition probably is not a factor because the maze location was usually planned to control for possible sound cues. In addition, there is not

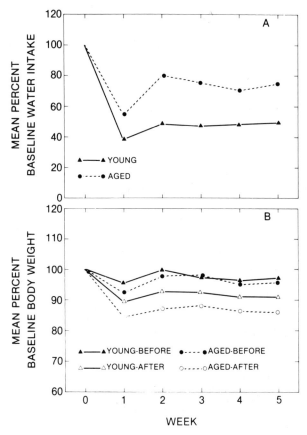

FIGURE 6. Age comparison of mean water intake (A) and mean body weight (B) as percent of baseline in male C57BL/6J mice during 22-hr fluid deprivation schedule (before and after rehydration).

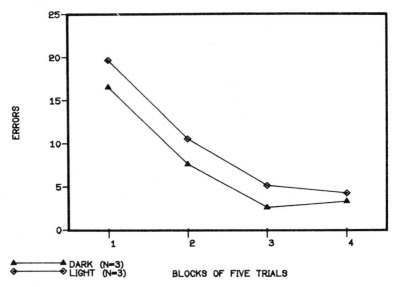

FIGURE 7. Mean errors of 8-mo-old male Wistar rats in 14-unit T-maze for water rewards under illuminated (N = 3) or dark conditions (N = 3).

an obvious source of such cues within the maze apparatus itself. Nonetheless, in current designs we provide white noise to mask auditory cues. Attempts have been made to eliminate olfactory cues by spraying or mopping the maze with a masking odor. Although the nocturnal nature of laboratory rats and mice makes them less dependent upon vision than upon other sensory systems, ample evidence exists to document their ability to use visual cues in learning tasks.[24]

Results of classic studies, using enclosed mazes similar to the 14-unit T-maze, suggest that intact vision is unnecessary for accurate performance in rats.[24] Enucleated animals performed as well as visually intact animals.[24] Results shown in FIGURES 7 and 8 demonstrate that vision is not necessary for accurate performance in the 14-unit T-maze. Data in FIGURE 7 represent young (8 mo) male Wistar rats trained for water rewards. One group was run under illuminated conditions, while the other was run in the dark, the only illumination in the room being a dim red light to provide vision for the experimenter but presumably not for the rat.[24] Error performance was scored through an automated system utilizing a series of infrared photocells, a microprocessor that could track and store data on the animal's movement through the maze, and a computer program that could score errors. Under visually blind conditions, young rats could learn the maze as rapidly as rats given the opportunity to use visual cues. FIGURE 8 reveals that young (8-mo) male C57BL/6J mice could also demonstrate learning under dark conditions.

Although we have not conducted a study to compare the maze performance of young and aged animals under dark conditions, these data indicate that the age difference observed under illuminated conditions is not likely due to the impaired vision of older animals, since even young animals can learn the maze in the dark. Further research is necessary to determine the involvement of other sensory factors, such as cutaneous and kinesthetic cues.

Response Biases and Strategies

If rats and mice do not require visual cues to learn the 14-unit T-maze, what cues do they use? An analysis of where errors occur in the maze indicates that one response strategy may involve the sequencing of turns rather than reliance on specific cues to discriminate among particular turns. FIGURE 9 presents the percent distribution of errors occurring in the maze across the 14 choice-points for the C57BL/6J mice whose performance was depicted in FIGURE 5. The top panel reveals the percent distribution of all errors, while the bottom panel provides the distribution of perseverative errors, or those response strings indicating an error at a particular choice-point occurred across five consecutive trials. Evidently the majority of errors occurred at only four choice-points. Choice-points 3, 5, 8, and 11 accounted for over 60% of all errors and 85% of the perseverative errors in both young and aged mice.

Why did these choice-points account for such an inordinate proportion of errors in this maze? A close examination of the error direction, as indicated along the x-axis, reveals that these choice-points represented the second in a string of two consecutive turns in the same direction. Choice-point 13 was the only other location where two consecutive turns in the same direction were required. This distribution of errors indicates that the mice were applying an alternation strategy for learning the maze. A strategy of alternating left-right turns would be very efficient except when consecutive turns in the same direction were required; hence, one observes the great frequency of errors at four of five of those choice-points having this requirement.

Are there age differences in this response strategy? It appears that both young and aged mice were exhibiting the alternation strategy as indicated by the distribution of

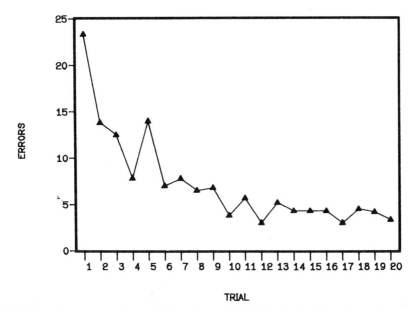

FIGURE 8. Mean errors of 8-mo-old ($N = 5$) male C57BL/6J mice in 14-unit T-maze for water rewards under dark conditions.

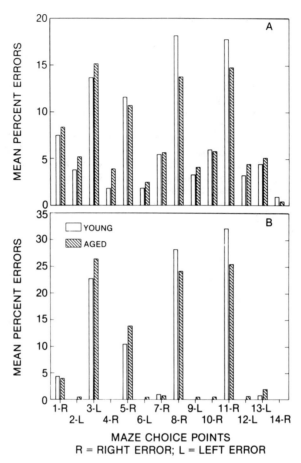

FIGURE 9. Age comparison of percent distribution of all errors (A) and perseverative errors (B) of male C57BL/6J mice in 14-unit T-maze under illuminated conditions.

errors in FIGURE 9. However, for aged compared to young mice, the relative frequency of perseverative errors was slightly higher at choice-points 3 and 5 and lower at choice-points 8 and 11. A further analysis indicated a significantly higher probability for aged animals to err to the left as compared with young mice.

Goodrick[17] suggested that the higher error rate among aged rats was due to their higher frequency of perseveration. In the mouse experiment depicted in FIGURE 5, a significant age difference in the frequency of perseverative errors was also noted (8.6 errors for young mice versus 11.1 for aged mice). However, this higher frequency of perseverative errors was correlated with a higher frequency of total errors, so that an analysis of covariance with total errors as the covariate revealed a nonsignificant age difference in perseverative errors. Thus, in this experiment both young and aged mice apparently applied an alternation strategy that resulted in a high frequency of perseverative errors, relatively the same in both. The age differential apparently reflected a lower overall error rate among young mice. Further analysis of response patterns are needed to elucidate age differences in learning strategies.

Another consideration of learning strategies used in the 14-unit T-maze further complicates the issue of sensory involvement. FIGURE 10 depicts the error distribution of young (8 mo) mice trained in the dark in the automated maze described above (FIGURE 8). The distribution of errors is clearly more random than observed in FIGURE 9. It is possible, then, that while mice do not require visual cues to learn the maze, they might utilize visual cues to facilitate learning strategies, such as alternation. Thus, unresolved is the issue of whether to consider response biases and strategies as important cognitive factors in learning/memory tasks or as sources of confounding variation related to sensory, motor, or motivational factors. As a further example, Rigter et al.[25] observed age differences in the performance of Wistar rats in an active avoidance task. However, when they placed the escape platform at the side rather than in the middle, the age difference disappeared because the aged animals had tended to run along the sides of the apparatus. This response bias is more clearly a noncognitive performance factor that could be controlled by changing the apparatus.

Shock-Motivated Maze Learning

Recently, we have expanded our studies of maze performance to another motivational manipulation.[26] We have trained rats to avoid shock in the 14-unit T-maze. The protocol involves pretraining in one-way active avoidance in a straight runway. The animals have 10 sec to move from the start box to a goal box one meter away to avoid

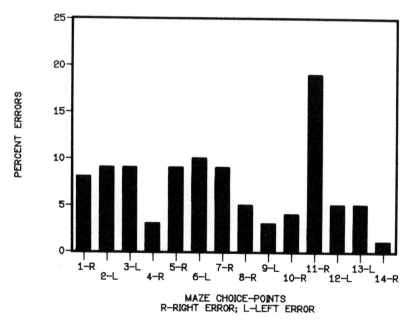

FIGURE 10. Percent distribution of all errors of 8-mo-old male C57BL/6J mice in 14-unit T-maze under dark conditions.

footshock (1.0 mA). Each animal is provided 10 daily trials to a criterion of eight out of ten successful avoidances across two consecutive days. When this criterion is met, the animal is trained in the 14-unit T-maze during 10-trial sessions across two consecutive days under illuminated conditions. The contingency is similar to that in the straight runway. The animal must negotiate each of five segments of the maze (with the correct path about 1–1.5 m in length) within 10 sec to avoid footshock (1.0 mA).

As observed in FIGURE 11, male Wistar rats demonstrate learning in this task. Moreover, the age-related decrement in error performance is still evident even with the addition of a middle-aged group. It is not likely that the age difference in performance was due to deficient acquisition of the shock avoidance contingency or to age differences in motivation or shock sensitivity, since prior to maze training, each animal was required to demonstrate accurate responding in the straight runway. The mean

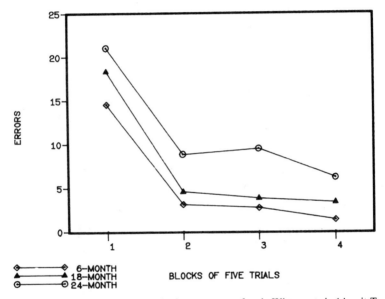

FIGURE 11. Age comparison ($N = 6–8$) of mean errors of male Wistar rats in 14-unit T-maze for shock avoidance/escape ($p < .05$).

trials to criterion in the runway for the animals shown in FIGURE 11 were 37, 38, and 31, for the 6, 18, and 24 mo groups, respectively; and these means were not significantly different. However, only in the aged group did we observe failure (6 of 15 animals tested) to meet criterion during pre-training.

Robustness

In summary, the age-related impairment observed in the 14-unit T-maze appears to represent a robust phenomenon. It has been observed in more than one strain, sex, and species of laboratory rodent under several motivational conditions. Sensorimotor factors do not appear to be significantly involved in accurate performance, but may be involved in response strategies. The task may be acquired through utilization of specific response strategies, such as alternation, but further research is required to better characterize them.

MEMORY PROCESSES

Thus far, the discussion of performance in the 14-unit T-maze has involved demonstration of learning. Two types of memory processing involved in acquisition of the task can be identified, however. First, the use of short-term, or working, memory[27] is probably important to within-trial performance. This type of memory processing would be required for learning the correct path by retaining instances of incorrect turns during that trial. Second, the probably more heavily taxed is long-term, or reference, memory.[27] The correct response required of the animal remains invariant across trials. Therefore, retention of both correct and incorrect responses across trials is beneficial for learning the correct path.

The final product is probably a response sequence that orders the correct turns in the maze. At this stage of research, we have no data to indicate that the animal forms a cognitive map.[28] The information, once learned, remains available for an extended period of time. Goodrick[12] observed substantial savings of learning over a 45-day interval in both young and aged Wistar rats. When corrected for differences in initial learning, the age difference in retention that Goodrick observed was not significant. Therefore, he suggested that long-term memory processing was relatively unimpaired in older animals. Impaired short-term memory processing was suggested to account for some portion of the age-related decrement because aged animals benefited differentially from massed practice.[15] However, differences in performance under massed versus distributed practice cannot be attributed solely to differences in short-term memory processing.[29] Further research will be required to determine the relative contribution of working versus reference memory to the age-related impairment observed in the 14-unit T-maze. Complicating this search, of course, will be possible age differences in response strategies. Barnes et al.[30] attributed much of the age difference they observed in maze performance to this source.

By assessing performance in other maze tasks, the issue of which components of memory processing are affected by aging can be further analyzed. For example, Ingram et al.[31] observed an age-related decrement in the performance of Wistar rats in a radial maze. Olton et al.[32] have suggested that this task heavily taxes working memory. With lesion studies they have linked accurate performance to the integrity of septo-hippocampal connections. If aged rats are impaired in this task, it is probable, as Goodrick suggested, that this impairment is also operational in the 14-unit T-maze. Other analyses of radial maze performance have not attributed the age difference to impaired short-term memory but instead have emphasized sensory involvement in the task.[33]

The capability of assessing both types of memory processing, working versus reference, in one task would be a very efficient design. Recently, Lowy et al.[34] attempted such a design. Male ACI rats were trained in a food-motivated T-maze task that required two different types of discriminations. In the stem of the maze, the rat was required to make a left-right discrimination to gain access to the arms. In the arm of the maze, an alternation response was required, the direction of which was contingent upon its response 5–10 sec previously. Thus, the discrimination in the stem required reference memory, while the discrimination in the arms required working memory. Olton et al.[39] have shown that these memory components can be dissociated in this task with specific brain lesions.

Analysis of data from two separate experiments revealed that the aged animals, compared to young counterparts, were equally impaired in both components of this task. Thus, it was suggested that age-related impairments existed in both working and reference memory processing. This indeed might be the case for the age-related impairment in the 14-unit T-maze. Further investigation of similar tasks that can dissociate memory processing will further elucidate whether aging differentially affects specific components of memory processing.[36]

INDIVIDUAL DIFFERENCES

Analysis of individual differences is an integral component of human gerontology.[37] Considerable interest exists in the large variability observed in the pattern of age-related decline in cognitive function. This variability can be ascribed to either genetic or environmental factors or to their interaction. While abundant research has been conducted to determine the role of these factors in cognitive performance among children and adults, a life span perspective on this issue has yet to emerge. Gerontological research in this area will accrue from the aging of relevant data sources, such as twin studies.

Genetic Factors

The dearth of gerontological studies addressing issues related to genetic effects in animal models is surprising. With few exceptions,[5,38] most investigators appear content to examine age differences in performance in only one species/strain. Differences in the pattern of aging among inbred strains in performance of learning/memory tasks has been demonstrated.[38] With further analysis, such genotype effects provide the potential for identifying biochemical pathways through which aging is expressed.[39]

In comparisons between inbred strains, there are marked differences in the pattern of age differences in neurotransmitter synthetic enzyme activities.[40] For example, striatal glutamic acid decarboxylase activity exhibits an age-related decline in A/J mice but an age-related increase in C57BL/6J mice.[40] Marked species and strain differences exist as well for choline acetyltransferase activity and muscarinic receptor binding in various brain regions.[41,42]

While at first glance these varied findings appear to complicate the search for general conclusions regarding the effects of aging on neurochemical correlates of memory loss, they underscore the fact that functional aging is expressed through complex processes heavily determined by genetic factors. Rather than complicate, further utilization of genetic analysis will help to elucidate the nature and magnitude of these factors.[39]

Environmental Factors

Individual differences also can be assessed within strains of animals. Goodrick emphasized the existence of individual variability in maze performance within aged groups of rats.[13] Further analysis has indicated that individual differences can be correlated to neuromorphological[43] and neurochemical[31] parameters. Such findings within random bred strains still represent sources of genetic variability; however, correlations between neurobiological and behavioral parameters within inbred strains represent presumably the influence of environmental factors. Such correlations have been demonstrated within the inbred C57BL/6J strain for motor and maze performance.[44,45]

What environmental factors may contribute to individual differences? The role of experiential factors in the pattern of behavioral aging has also received relatively little attention. One very important factor may be the variety of environmental stimulation. So-called environmental enrichment or the exposure of animals to continual variety of objects in their home cages has been demonstrated to affect both morphological and behavioral consequences even when begun in mature animals.[46,47] Cerebral cortical thickness was enhanced and performance in a learning task was improved by such environmental manipulations. Even handling has improved the performance of older rats in a learning task.[48] Despite these findings, the conventional cross-sectional study in gerontological research remains a comparison between young and aged animals that have spent all of their lives in standard laboratory cages with a few other cagemates but little variety in stimulation.

Similarly, it is likely that the conventional, cross-sectional study compares the performance of animals maintained on an *ad libitum* diet that maximizes growth. Numerous studies have documented that restricting dietary intake to levels less than *ad libitum* can have profound beneficial effects on survival in particular and other physiological and biochemical parameters in general.[49] Furthermore, Goodrick[50] demonstrated that the performance of 30-mo-old Wistar rats undergoing dietary restriction since weaning was indistinguishable from that of young (6 mo) rats in the 14-unit T-maze while the age-related impairment was evident among a group of 22-mo-old *ad libitum* fed rats. Because this study used Goodrick's food-motivated protocol, the involvement of motivational factors is undetermined. However, the results underscore nutrition as a potentially important environmental variable, one that should be considered as a source of intervening variation or that can be studied systematically as a manipulation of effects associated with aging.

Breeding history also may be an important source of experiential variation. It was reported in a recent review[51] that a notable proportion of studies in the gerontological literature used retired breeders as subjects without specifying a clear rationale, other than availability, for their use. In a number of these studies, the performance of young virgin animals was compared to older retired breeders. The extent to which this difference in experience intervened on the age comparison remains unknown, although there may be performance differences between aged virgin and retired breeder animals.[51] Investigators should be aware that breeding history may be a powerful variable contributing to individual differences.[5]

Circadian rhythmicity represents a more intrinsic source of variability possibly contributing to individual differences. Evidence is emerging that some aspects of circadian rhythmicity become altered with age in laboratory rodents.[52] Individual differences in circadian patterning of behavioral activity have been predictive of life span in mice.[53] Conventionally, gerontological studies of learning/memory performance are conducted during diurnal hours, which may differentially handicap aged animals.

A final source of variability in behavioral performance to be considered is pathology. The proper analysis of aging usually attempts to identify the existence of pathology and rule out its effects on the variable of interest.[4] While most behavioral researchers in this field probably screen their subjects for obvious, overt signs of morbidity, few attempt to confirm the health of their animals with any systematic pathological analysis. Some investigators[54] have taken the trouble to assess whether certain pathologies hinder the performance in which they are interested, but this approach is far from routine.

CONCLUSIONS

Despite the apparent demographic demand for greater research of geriatric memory impairment using animal models, one can argue that the use of aged animals provides a potentially contaminated resource. Control over noncognitive performance factors presents a very demanding challenge. Indeed, researchers might contend that the use of young animals with specific lesions is perhaps a better approach. Certainly this strategy should be fostered; however, even if it proves effective in identifying specific mechanisms and suggesting certain remedies, ultimately these remedies and therefore a test of the hypothesized mechanism will have to be attempted in aged animals. Therefore, we are stuck with aged animals as ultimate models.

Deficiencies in the analysis and control of possibly confounding variation and the lack of systematic investigation of potentially relevant individual variation no doubt stem from the short supply of aged animals to study. Recent large increases in these supplies by the National Institute of Aging and the beginnings of aging colonies within individual investigators' laboratories will reduce the problem of availability so that the issues can be addressed more fully in the future.

The intent of this presentation is to reemphasize that the study of aging is not merely the comparison of presumably young and aged groups, but is more deservedly the analysis of a complex biological phenomenon that requires specific methodological considerations and rigorous investigation to comprehend fully its impact on memory processes and to assess fully the utility of animal models thereof. The issues discussed here have their counterparts in human gerontological research; and their influence might have the potential of altering the direction of research similar to the impact of benchmark issues, such as interpretation of cross-sectional versus longitudinal studies, in the human literature.[10] Specifically, it was long assumed from the results of cross-sectional studies that human intelligence declined markedly as a function of age. Longitudinal studies helped to clarify that this decline was not as dramatic as previously indicated, that specific components of intelligence were more affected than others, and, most importantly, that environmental variables, evidenced as period and cohort effects, markedly affected the pattern of age-related change. Such a breakthrough in the methodological philosophy of investigators using animal models of geriatric memory dysfunction is currently in a formative stage of development.

ACKNOWLEDGMENTS

The author greatly appreciates the contributions of John Freeman and Edward Spangler for assistance in behavioral assessments; Richard Hiner, Maurice Zimmerman, Raymond Banner, and Gunther Baartz for design and construction of the maze apparatus; Mark Reynolds, Nancy Cider, and William Richards for help in analyzing the data; Rita Wolferman for clerical assistance; Edythe London, Edward Spangler, Mark Reynolds, and George Roth for constructive reviews of the manuscript; and finally the late Charles Goodrick for his continued inspiration.

REFERENCES

1. BUREAU OF THE CENSUS. 1976. Demographic aspects of aging and the older population. Current Population Reports. Series P-23, No. 59. U.S. Government Printing Office. Washington, DC.

2. ARENBERG, D. & E. A. ROBERTSON-TCHABO. 1980. Age differences and age changes in cognitive performance: New old perspectives. *In* Age, Learning Ability, and Intelligence. R. L. Sprott, Ed: 139–157. Van Nostrand Reinhold Co. New York.

3. CORKIN, S. 1983. Some relationships between global amnesias and the memory impairments in Alzheimer's disease. *In* Alzheimer's Disease: A Report of Progress. S. Corkin, K. L. Davis, J. H. Growdon, E. Usdin & R. J. Wurtman, Eds: 149–164. Raven Press. New York.

4. NATIONAL RESEARCH COUNCIL. 1981. Mammalian Models of Research on Aging. National Academy Press. Washington, DC.

5. ELIAS, M. F. 1979. Aging studies of behavior with Fischer-344, Sprague-Dawley, and Long-Evans rats. *In* Development of the Rodent as a Model System of Aging. D. C. Gibson, R. C. Adelman & C. Finch, Eds. DHEW Pub. No. (NIH) 79–161: 255–300. U.S. Government Printing Office. Washington, DC.

6. SPROTT, R. L. 1980. Senescence and learning behavior in mice. *In* Age, Learning Ability, and Intelligence. R. L. Sprott, Ed: 26–40. Van Nostrand Reinhold Co. New York.

7. BARTUS, R. T., C. FLICKER & R. L. DEAN. 1983. Logical principles for the development of animal models of age-related memory impairments. *In* Assessment in Geriatric Psychopharmacology. T. Crook, S. Ferris & R. Bartus, Eds: 263–299. Powly Associates. Hartford, CT.

8. INGRAM, D. K. 1983. Toward the behavioral assessment of biological aging in the laboratory mouse: Concepts, terminology and objectives. Exp. Aging Res. 9: 225–238.

9. ELIAS, M. F. & P. K. ELIAS. 1977. Motivation and activity. *In* Handbook of the Psychology of Aging. J. E. Birren & K. W. Schaie, Eds: 357–383. Van Nostrand Reinhold Co. New York.

10. SCHAIE, K. W. 1980. Age changes in intelligence. *In* Age, Learning Ability, and Intelligence. R. L. Sprott, Ed: 41–77. Van Nostrand Reinhold Co. New York.

11. OLTON, D. S., E. GAMZU & S. CORKIN. 1985. Memory dysfunctions: Theoretical descriptions, pathological bases, and therapeutic interventions from clinical and preclinical perspectives. Ann. N.Y. Acad. Sci. (This volume.)

12. GOODRICK, C. L. 1968. Learning, retention and extinction of a complex maze habit for mature-young and senescent Wistar albino rats. J. Gerontol. 23: 298–304.

13. GOODRICK, C. L. 1972. Learning by mature-young and aged Wistar rats as a function of test complexity. J. Gerontol. 27: 353–357.

14. GOODRICK, C. L. 1973. Error goal-gradients of mature-young and aged rats during training in a 14-unit spatial maze. Psychol. Reports 32: 359–362.

15. GOODRICK, C. L. 1973. Maze learning of mature-young and aged rats as a function of distribution of practice. J. Exp. Psychol. 98: 344–349.

16. GOODRICK, C. L. 1975. Behavioral rigidity as a mechanism for facilitation of problem solving for aged rats. J. Gerontol. 30: 181–184.

17. GOODRICK, C. L. 1980. Problem solving and age: A critique of rodent research. *In* Age, Learning Ability, and Intelligence. R. L. Sprott, Ed: 5–25. Van Nostrand Reinhold Co. New York.

18. STONE, C. 1929. The age factor in animal learning. I. Rats in the problem box and the maze. Genet. Psychol. Mono. 5: 1–130.

19. ALTMAN, H. J., R. D. CROSLAND, D. J. JENDEN & R. F. BERMAN. 1984. Comparison of the effects of nucleus basalis, diagonal band, and septal lesions on learning and memory in Sprague-Dawley rats. Neurosci. Abst. 10: 775.

20. MICHEL, M. E. & A. W. KLEIN. 1978. Performance differences in a complex maze between young and aged rats. Age 1: 13–16.

21. MASORO, E. J. 1979. Lean body mass and adipose tissue changes with age. *In* Development of the Rodent as a Model System of Aging. D. C. Gibson, R. C. Adelman & C. Finch, Eds. DHEW Pub. No. (NIH) 79–161: 241–244 U.S. Government Printing Office. Washington, DC.

22. JAKUBCZAK, L. F. 1970. Age differences in the effects of water deprivation on activity, water loss, and survival of rats. Life Sci. 9: 771–780.

23. GOODRICK, C. L. 1975. Life-span and inheritance of longevity of inbred mice. J. Gerontol. 30: 257–263.

24. MUNN, N.L. 1950. Handbook of Psychological Research on the Rat. Houghton Mifflin Co. Boston, MA.

25. RIGTER, H., J. L. MARTINEZ & J. C. CRABBE. 1980. Forgetting and other behavioral manifestations of aging. *In* The Psychobiology of Aging. D. Stein, Ed: 161–175. Elsevier-North Holland. New York.

26. INGRAM, D., E. SPANGLER, J. FREEMAN & W. RICHARDS. 1984. Age differences in performance of rats and mice in a 14-unit T-maze. Neurosci Abst. **10:** 452.

27. HONIG, W. K. 1978. Studies of working memory in the pigeon. *In* Cognitive Aspects of Animal Behavior. S. H. Hulse, H. F. Fowler & W. K. Honig, Eds: 211–248. Lawrence Erlbaum. Hillsdale, NJ.

28. MENZEL, E. W. 1978. Cognitive mapping in chimpanzees. *In* Cognitive Aspects of Animal Behavior. S. H. Hulse, H. F. Fowler & W. K. Honig, Eds: 375–422. Lawrence Erlbaum. Hillsdale, NJ.

29. WALLACE, J. E., E. E. KRAUTER & B. A. CAMPBELL. 1980. Animal models of declining memory in the aged: Short-term and spatial memory in aged rat. J. Gerontol. **35:** 355–363.

30. BARNES, C. A., L. NADEL & W. K. HONIG. 1980. Spatial memory deficit in senescent rats. Can. J. Psychol. **34:** 29–39.

31. INGRAM, D. K., E. D. LONDON & C. L. GOODRICK. 1981. Age and neurochemical correlates of radial maze performance in rats. Neurobiol. Aging **2:** 41–47.

32. OLTON, D. S., J. T. BECKER & G. E. HANDELMANN. 1980. Hippocampal function: Working memory or cognitive mapping? Physiol. Psychol. **8:** 239–246.

33. CAMPBELL, B. A., E. E. KRAUTER & J. W. WALLACE. 1980. Animal models of aging: Sensory-motor and cognitive function in the aged rat. *In* The Psychobiology of Aging. D. Stein, Ed: 201–226. Elsevier North Holland. New York.

34. LOWY, A. M., D. K. INGRAM, D. S. OLTON, S. B. WALLER, M. A. REYNOLDS & E. D. LONDON. 1985. Discrimination learning requiring different memory components in rats: Age and neurochemical comparisons. Behav. Neurosci. (In press.)

35. OLTON, D. S. 1985. Criteria for establishing and evaluating animal models. Ann. N.Y. Acad. Sci. (This volume.)

36. KESNER, R. P. 1984. Correspondence between humans and animals in coding of temporal attributes: Role of hippocampus and prefrontal cortex. Ann. N.Y. Acad. Sci. (This volume.)

37. BOTWINICK, J. 1977. Intellectual abilities. *In* Handbook of the Psychology of Aging. J. E. Birren & K. W. Schaie, Eds: 580–605. Van Nostrand Reinhold. New York.

38. SPROTT, R. L. 1980. An appraisal of the utility of genetic techniques for the study of neurobiology and aging in mice. *In* The Psychobiology of Aging. D. Stein, Ed: 22–33. Elsevier-North Holland. New York.

39. RUSSELL, E. S. & R. L. SPROTT. 1974. Genetics and the aging nervous system. *In* Survey Report on the Aging Nervous System. G. J. Maletta, Ed. USPHS Pub. No. 74–296. U.S. Government Printing Office. Washington, DC.

40. WALLER, S. B., D. K. INGRAM, M. A. REYNOLDS & E. D. LONDON. 1983. Age and strain comparisons of neurotransmitter synthetic enzyme activities in the mouse. J. Neurochem. **41:** 1421–1428.

41. BARTUS, R. T., R. L. DEAN, B. BEER & A. S. LIPPA. 1982. The cholinergic hypothesis of geriatric memory dysfunction. Science **217:** 408–417.

42. LONDON, E. D. & S. B. WALLER. 1984. Relations between choline acetyltransferase and muscarinic binding in aging rodent brain and in Alzheimer's disease. *In* Dynamics of Cholinergic Function. I. Hanin, Ed. Plenum Press. New York. (In press.)

43. KLEIN, A. W. & M. E. MICHEL. 1977. A morphological study of the neocortex of young adult and old maze-differentiated rats. Mech. Ageing Dev. **6:** 444–452.

44. BERNSTEIN, D. E., D. S. OLTON, D. K. INGRAM, S. B. WALLER, M. A. REYNOLDS & E. D. LONDON. 1985. Radial maze performance in young and aged mice: Neurochemical correlates. Pharmacol. Biochem. Behav. (In press.)

45. INGRAM, D. K., E. D. LONDON, S. B. WALLER & M. A. REYNOLDS. 1983. Age-dependent correlation of motor performance with neurotransmitter synthetic enzyme activities in mice. Behav. Neural. Biol. **39:** 284–298.

46. REIGE, W. H. 1971. Environmental influences on brain and behavior of year-old rats. Dev. Psychobiol. **4:** 157–167.
47. DOTY, B. A. 1972. The effects of cage environment upon avoidance responding of aged rats. J. Gerontol. **27:** 358–360.
48. DOTY, B. A. & K. M. O'HARE. 1966. Interaction of shock intensity, age, and handling effects on avoidance conditioning. Percept. Motor Skills. **23:** 1311–1314.
49. BARROWS, C. H. & G. C. KOKKONEN. 1978. Diet and life extension in animal model systems. Age **1:** 131–143.
50. GOODRICK, C. L. 1984. Effects of lifelong restricted feeding on complex maze performance in rats. Age **7:** 1–2.
51. INGRAM, D. K., E. L. SPANGLER & G. P. VINCENT. 1983. Behavioral comparison of aged virgin and retired breeder mice. Exp. Aging Res. **9:** 111–113.
52. INGRAM, D. K., E. D. LONDON & M. A. REYNOLDS. 1982. Circadian rhythmicity and sleep: Effects of aging in laboratory animals. Neurobiol. Aging **3:** 287–297.
53. WAX, T. M. & C. L. GOODRICK. 1978. Nearness to death and wheelrunning behavior in mice. Expl. Gerontol. **13:** 233–236.
54. STEIN, P. G. & E. J. MUFSON. 1979. Tumor induced brain damage in rats. Implications for behavioral and anatomical studies with aging animals. Exp. Aging Res. **6:** 537–546.

The Cholinergic Hypothesis: A Historical Overview, Current Perspective, and Future Directions

RAYMOND T. BARTUS, REGINALD L. DEAN,
MICHAEL J. PONTECORVO, AND CHARLES FLICKER

Department CNS Research
Lederle Laboratories
Medical Research Division of American Cyanamid
Pearl River, New York 10965
and
New York University Medical Center
New York University
New York, New York 10016

INTRODUCTION

When one considers that Alzheimer's disease was initially characterized in the first decade of this century,[1] it seems remarkable that the disease remains such a mystery. The relative etiologic roles played by various genetic, toxic, viral, and immunologic influences remain ill-defined, and the origin and direct functional implications of its most characteristic neuropathological markers, neurofibrillary tangles and amyloid plaques, likewise are unknown. Although it has been shown that inadequate blood supply to the brain does not provide a tenable explanation for the primary symptoms of Alzheimer's disease,[2] the final neurological pathways that are responsible remain obscure.

One possible exception to this is the recent accumulation of evidence suggesting that a breakdown of central cholinergic transmission plays an important role in the earliest and primary symptoms of the disease, manifested as a severe and progressive cognitive disturbance highlighted by an inability to remember recent events.[3–5] With normal aging, a similar, though less severe, memory loss has been documented[6,7] (sometimes referred to as benign senescent forgetfulness[8]) with similar evidence for a parallel role of cholinergic dysfunction.[6,7,9,10] The logic and empirical support for this line of thinking have collectively become known as the "cholinergic hypothesis of geriatric memory dysfunction."[3–7] Stated in its most simple and direct terms, the cholinergic hypothesis asserts that significant, functional disturbances in cholinergic activity occur in the brains of aged and especially demented patients, these disturbances play an important role in the memory loss and related cognitive problems associated with old age and dementia, and proper enhancement or restoration of cholinergic function may significantly reduce the severity of the cognitive loss.

One should note that the cholinergic hypothesis states nothing about etiological factors responsible for aging or dementia. Rather, it attempts to explain only the most direct, cause-effect relationship associated with the primary symptoms (i.e., memory loss). Likewise, the hypothesis does not address the additional roles that cholinergic dysfunction may play in other neurobehavioral disturbances of aging or dementia. Finally, no exclusive or solitary involvement of the cholinergic system in age-related

332

memory loss is implied, for it is commonly acknowledged that other neurotransmitter systems are also, most probably, involved. However, the hypothesis does imply that the existence of relationships between neurotransmitter dysfunction and age-related memory loss is most clearly established with respect to the cholinergic system. The testing and establishment of similar relationships for other neurotransmitter systems remain among the challenges of future research.

During the last four to five years, basic and clinical research efforts directly and indirectly related to the cholinergic hypothesis have accelerated rapidly. This increased interest presumably is related to a growing recognition of the enormous socio-economic problems confronting our society as our population continues to age. The additional emotional and financial burdens imposed by age-related cognitive decline, especially the severe decline associated with Alzheimer's disease, contributes further to this interest. From this perspective, the primary significance of research concerned with the cholinergic hypothesis is based upon the presumption that greater insight into the common neural pathways responsible for the cognitive disturbances may eventually lead to effective therapeutic treatment of the problem.

Because of the rapid development of thinking in this area, and the continuing intensive research activity and controversy it provokes, a cohesive overview of progress and issues might be useful. The present paper, therefore, will attempt to provide a brief historical overview of the research and ideas that gradually evolved into the current cholinergic hypothesis, offer some perspective upon current thinking and research efforts in the area, and finally, provide a loose conceptual framework and specific suggestions for future work.

HISTORICAL OVERVIEW AND CURRENT PERSPECTIVE UPON THE CHOLINERGIC HYPOTHESIS

Early Historical Foundation

What the cholinergic hypothesis may lack in definitive, quantitative evidence, it enjoys in the diversity and breadth of its support. The initial empirical foundation for the cholinergic hypothesis can be traced to at least four distinct areas of study: biochemical determinations of human brain tissue, particularly from Alzheimer's patients; animal psychopharmacological studies; clinical pharmacological observations; and (for lack of a better descriptor), basic neuroscience research. Starting from these four somewhat independent areas of investigation, thinking and research directives evolved relatively rapidly, converging into a mutually corroborated network of circumstantial support.

By the mid-1960s, seminal findings in all four areas generated sufficient evidence to support some of the initial integrative concepts of the cholinergic hypothesis. As shown in TABLE 1, early predescendent clinical teachings recognized that drugs blocking central cholinergic activity produced a dementia-like syndrome, with concomitant memory loss.[11-13] Indeed, one popular means of facilitating childbirth in the 1950s and 1960s involved giving a relatively light dose of a sedative or hypnotic simultaneously with a central anticholinergic, producing a state of consciousness defined as "twilight sleep."[14] An important and interesting characteristic of this condition was a marked reduction in the ability of patients to remember events occurring just prior to and during the operation.[15,16] Interestingly, this phenomenon and therapeutic application was described very early in this century,[14] coincidentally close in time to when Alzheimer published his classic case study characterizing the disease which now bears his name.[1]

TABLE 1. Abbreviated Conceptual/Empirical History of Cholinergic Hypothesis

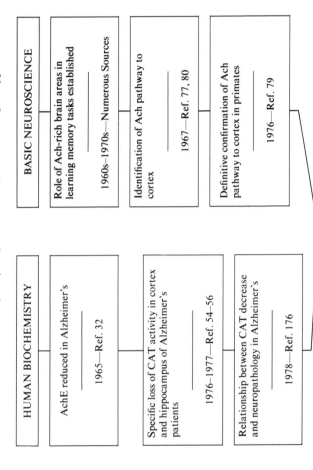

BASIC NEUROSCIENCE
Role of Ach-rich brain areas in learning memory tasks established
1960s–1970s—Numerous Sources
Identification of Ach pathway to cortex
1967—Ref. 77, 80
Definitive confirmation of Ach pathway to cortex in primates
1976—Ref. 79

HUMAN BIOCHEMISTRY
AchE reduced in Alzheimer's
1965—Ref. 32
Specific loss of CAT activity in cortex and hippocampus of Alzheimer's patients
1976–1977—Ref. 54–56
Relationship between CAT decrease and neuropathology in Alzheimer's
1978—Ref. 176

TABLE 1 *Continued*

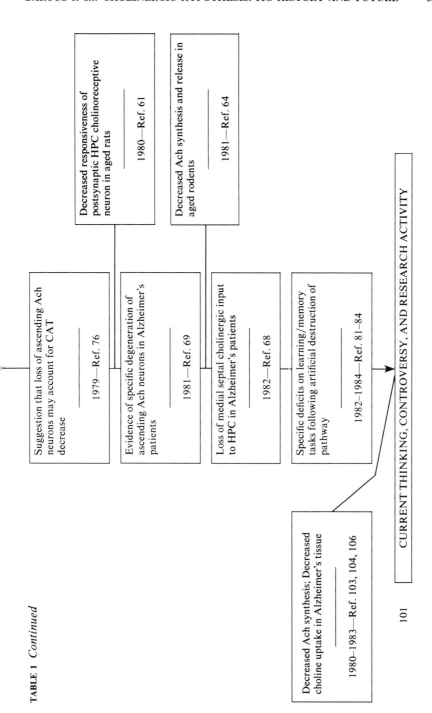

Suggestion that loss of ascending Ach neurons may account for CAT decrease

1979—Ref. 76

Decreased responsiveness of postsynaptic HPC cholinoreceptive neuron in aged rats

1980—Ref. 61

Decreased Ach synthesis and release in aged rodents

1981—Ref. 64

Evidence of specific degeneration of ascending Ach neurons in Alzheimer's patients

1981—Ref. 69

Loss of medial septal cholinergic input to HPC in Alzheimer's patients

1982—Ref. 68

Specific deficits on learning/memory tasks following artificial destruction of pathway

1982–1984—Ref. 81–84

Decreased Ach synthesis; Decreased choline uptake in Alzheimer's tissue

1980–1983—Ref. 103, 104, 106

101   CURRENT THINKING, CONTROVERSY, AND RESEARCH ACTIVITY

TABLE 1. Continued

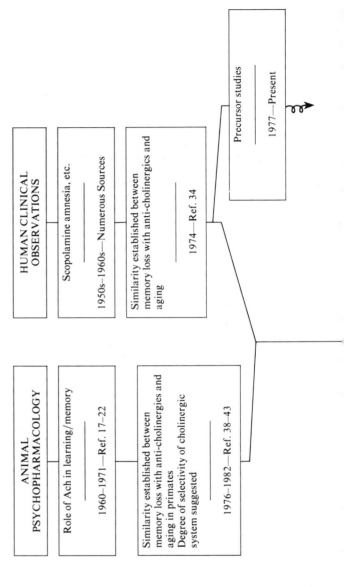

ANIMAL
PSYCHOPHARMACOLOGY

Role of Ach in learning/memory

1960–1971—Ref. 17–22

Similarity established between
memory loss with anti-cholinergics and
aging in primates
Degree of selectivity of cholinergic
system suggested

1976–1982—Ref. 38–43

HUMAN CLINICAL
OBSERVATIONS

Scopolamine amnesia, etc.

1950s–1960s—Numerous Sources

Similarity established between
memory loss with anti-cholinergics and
aging

1974—Ref. 34

Precursor studies

1977—Present

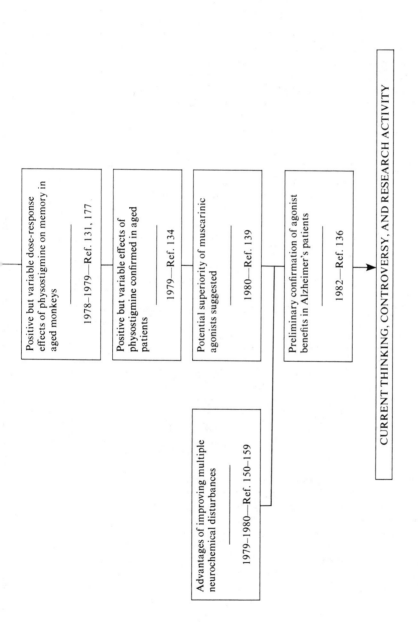

In the animal psychopharmocological literature, early work in the 1960s characterizing the behavioral effects of centrally acting drugs, began to generate support for an important role of cholinergic activity in learning and memory.[13,17-19] Most notably, Herz[20] and Meyers and Domino,[21,22] suggested specifically that one effect of blocking cholinergic function in the central nervous system may include an impairment of recent memory. The systematic studies of Deustch and colleagues[17,18] helped demonstrate a clear role for cholinergic-sensitive neurons in mediating learning and memory. Their publications played a key part in establishing general acceptance of this idea.

Simiiarly, the basic neuroscience research of the same era began to demonstrate that brain regions now known to be rich in cholinergic neuronal elements (e.g. hippocampus, septum, amygdala, and frontal cortex) seemed to play important roles in learning and memory phenomena.[23-27] Indeed, it is interesting to note that in one of the earlier studies of the effects of anticholinergics, it was speculated (on the basis of the nature of the behavioral results) that a hippocampal site of action may mediate the anticholinergic memory deficits observed.[22] The existence of dense fields of muscarinic receptors in the hippocampus was not confirmed neurochemically for another decade.[28-31]

Finally, attempts to characterize changes in the brains of Alzheimer's patients led to the observation of significantly reduced acetylcholinesterase (AChE) activity by Pope et al.[32] However, because of general controversy regarding the specificity of this marker and the lack of attention paid by the authors toward the reduced AChE activity, this paper remained relatively obscure until recently.

Later Pharmacological Studies

The first formal suggestion that the specific cognitive effects of age may be similar to the cognitive effects of anticholinergic drug treatment (in young subjects) was published by Drachman and Leavitt.[33,34] Interestingly, Crow and Grove-White[35] independently suggested a relationship between anticholinergic memory loss and Korsakoff's amnesia a year earlier. Drachman and Leavitt[34] demonstrated that young subjects given an acute dose of scopolamine performed various tasks of a cognitive test battery in a manner similar to normal elderly subjects. They concluded that the selective performance failures on certain memory tests that are observed in elderly subjects may therefore be related to a cholinergic deficiency in aged brains. Others have since drawn similar parallels between the memory loss of Alzheimer's patients and the effects of anticholinergic drugs in young subjects.[36,37]

Soon after the Drachman study, a series of papers was published showing similarly parallel memory deficits in aged monkeys and scopolamine-treated young monkeys.[38-40] In addition, scopolamine's age-mimicking effects upon memory were shown to be at least somewhat specific to its effects on central muscarinic receptors, since similar age-like effects on memory were not obtained with a number of other drug treatments, including dopaminergic and alpha-adrenergic blockers,[40,41] several nonspecific and catecholaminergic stimulants,[42] nicotinic receptor blockers,[43] and peripheral anticholinergics.[43] Although most researchers readily acknowledge that other neurochemical systems must also be involved in the mediation of recent memory, few non-cholinergic pharmacological agents have yet been identified that also produce specific, age-similar effects on memory performance. The two most notable exceptions, observed in both human and non-human primates, are diazepam and tetrahydrocannabinol.[43-48] Interestingly, both drugs show evidence of interacting directly or indirectly with cholinergic neurons.[49-53]

Determinations from Alzheimer's Brains

During the time these drug studies in humans and animals were being conducted, independent neurochemical assessments were being performed on postmortem tissue from brains of Alzheimer's patients. Bowen *et al.*[54] first published evidence that choline acetyltransferase (CAT) activity was reduced in Alzheimer's patients (relative to age-matched controls). Further, they observed that the reduction was widespread (involving several brain regions), that some degree of specificity existed (since markers from other neurotransmitter systems were not similarly reduced), and that the decrease in CAT activity may be correlated with loss of cognitive function and density of plaques and tangles. Very soon after, similar findings were published by Davies and Maloney[55] and Perry *et al.*[56] Thus, within a period of a few months, three British laboratories independently reported that the brains of patients with Alzheimer's disease exhibited a profound (and somewhat specific) loss of CAT activity upon postmortem examination. These initial observations were soon followed by a flood of papers confirming the basic findings.[3,4] Observations of decreases in CAT activity ranging from 50 to 80 percent are now quite common in brains from Alzheimer's patients.[3]

Although the loss of CAT activity gained widespread acceptance as an important characteristic of Alzheimer's disease, other mysteries emerged. For example, the neural mechanism through which the loss of CAT activity might play a causative role in the functional declines of Alzheimer's disease (especially the loss of cognitive ability) remained unclear. It has been known for some time that CAT is not a rate-limiting enzyme for acetylcholine synthesis,[57–59] for inhibition of greater than 90 percent of available CAT produces only nominal effects on acetylcholine synthesis *in vitro*. How then might one entertain that a loss of only 50 to 80 percent of CAT activity could be responsible for the devastating loss of cognitive capacity? Two mutually compatible explanations have emerged. The first was primarily logical and recognized that, in addition to the dementia-specific decrease in CAT activity, most Alzheimer's patients possess additional decreases in cholinergic function characteristic of normal aging.[3] Thus, it was deduced that the collective co-existence of certain age-related disturbances, such as reduced post-synaptic cholinergic responsivity[60–62] and impaired synthesizing capacity of ACh neurons,[63,64] may create a condition where the additional, profound loss of CAT activity produces substantial functional consequences. In other words, it was suggested that although the loss of CAT activity alone may not normally be sufficient to reduce overall cholinergic function, when the loss is added to an already impaired system, additive (or possibly synergistic) functional impairments should result.[3]

More recently, postmortem histological observations from Alzheimer's brains demonstrated that many demented patients may suffer a significant deterioration of neurons originating in the nucleus basalis of Meynert and the septum.[65–72] These brain regions are known to provide the primary cholinergic input to the hippocampus and cerebral cortex,[73–80] areas that suffer major loss of CAT activity in Alzheimer's brains.[3,4,54–56] Thus, it is possible that the loss of CAT activity reflects a degeneration of cholinergic neurons projecting to the cortex, as opposed to a proportional decrease of CAT activity within individual, functionally intact neurons. The consequences of such extensive neuro-degeneration would be expected to produce a profound disruption of central cholinergic function far beyond what would be predicted by the effects of inhibiting CAT activity *in vitro*.

Recent reports in rodents demonstrating that specific destruction of homologous cholinergic neurons in the basal forebrain produces specific impairments on memory tasks[81–84] add further support to the concept that cholinergic degeneration may be causally linked to cognitive dysfunction in elderly humans. However, as discussed later in this paper, certain caveats must be recognized before hypothesizing any simple, cause-effect relationship between cholinergic degeneration and memory loss.

More Recent Studies of Cholinergic Dysfunction

While many laboratories in the latter half of the 1970s focused on the pathological changes correlated with Alzheimer's disease, others concentrated on identifying and defining functional impairments in the cholinergic system that might be partly responsible for the cognitive impairments of age and dementia. Many of these studies are listed in TABLE 1, but some of the more noteworthy include evidence for specific decreased responsiveness to acetylcholine by hippocampal pyramidal cells of aged rats,[60-62] loss of acetylcholine-synthesizing capacity in brains of aged rodents *in vivo*,[63,64,102] and loss of acetylcholine-synthesizing capacity of biopsy tissue of Alzheimer's patients.[103,104]

Research directed toward other phenomena, such as changes in muscarinic receptor density and high affinity choline uptake,[103,105-111] remains controversial or inconclusive. Certainly, substantial work remains to be done before a sufficient understanding of the nature of the cholinergic dysfunction associated with aging and dementia (as well as differences between the two) is established. Nevertheless, a remarkable amount of information has been generated during the last six years, and little doubt can remain that there are significant reductions in numerous aspects of cholinergic transmission in the aged brain and that additional changes are associated with Alzheimer's disease.

Evidence for Interacting Non-Cholinergic Influences

It should be noted that changes in other neurotransmitter markers and degeneration of noncholinergic neurons have also been reported in brains of Alzheimer's patients. These include various changes in noradrenergic,[85-88] dopaminergic,[85,89,90] serotoninergic,[86,91] and somatostatin[92-95] markers, as well as evidence for profound degeneration of noradrenaline-containing neurons of the locus coeruleus.[96-99] However, the significance of these changes to the cognitive loss of Alzheimer's disease remains unclear and somewhat controversial. Some of the alterations (such as decreases in dopamine markers) have not been consistently reported,[55,86,97,100,101] while others (e.g. degeneration of locus coeruleus), appear to be present only in presumed subpopulations of patients lacking independent identification.[99] Further, it has been argued that many of these changes are due to improper patient screening procedures, resulting in the inclusion of patients with multiple diseases (such as concomitant Parkinson's disease or clinical depression), making any interpretations specific to Alzheimer's disease problematic.[5] Finally, additional problems of interpretation exist due to necessary focusing on the end-stage condition of the brains of Alzheimer's patients.

However, even if one accepts the accuracy and reliability of these changes, their contribution to the memory loss of Alzheimer's disease remains virtually untested. That is, simply demonstrating that significant changes in a particular neurotransmitter system occur in Alzheimer's disease or aging does not establish a relationship between those changes and loss of any behavioral functions, including memory. Considerably more multidisciplinary work is required to confirm and corroborate possible functional relationships before insight can be gained and conclusions drawn about a possible role in the cognitive loss of Alzheimer's disease.

Early Attempts to Improve Memory via Cholinomimetics

Although these functional studies of cholinergic dysfunction have contributed significantly to the idea of an important cholinergic role in age-related memory loss, the question of whether this line of thinking could serve as a starting point in the development of therapeutically significant effects remained in doubt. While skeptics criticized the cholinergic hypothesis as inherently simplistic, advocates pointed out the apparent analogy to the dopamine deficiency hypothesis of Parkinson's disease and the success of L-dopa in treating the symptoms of that disorder.[112,113]

Almost from the inception of the cholinergic hypothesis, clinicians were eager to test the corollary that cholinomimetics might be effective in the treatment of memory problems associated with Alzheimer's disease and aging. These attempts can be classified into one of three approaches: precursor therapy, anticholinesterase treatment, and muscarinic receptor agonist treatment. Because cholinergic precursors have a wide margin of safety, and relatively loose government regulations associated with their use, the vast majority of these studies adopted a precursor therapy approach. The impetus for this approach was derived from the observation that choline availability (unlike CAT activity) normally is rate-limiting for acetylcholine synthesis.[58,59] Cohen and Wurtman,[114] and Haubrich *et al.*[115] independently demonstrated that acute injections of choline chloride produced a significant, transient effect on brain acetylcholine levels in rats and guinea pigs. It was later shown that increasing dietary choline chloride[116] or lecithin[117] (a normal dietary source of choline) also significantly increased levels of brain acetylcholine. Thus, it was suggested that cholinergic function might be therapeutically enhanced by precursor treatment.[118,119] The rationale of these precursor studies was therefore straightforward and conceptually similar to that used to treat other neurobehavioral disturbances with precursor loading techniques.[119,120]

Nonetheless, scores of clinical trials have failed to demonstrate beneficial cognitive effects with either choline or lecithin in demented or nondemented aged patients.[3,122] In fact, it had been noted that certain assumptions inherent in this rationale, especially when applied to geriatric patients, had never been tested and may not be true.[3,121,122] These involve issues concerning the overall functional condition of the cholinergic system in aged brain and its ability to utilize extra exogenous choline in a functionally meaningful manner. Indeed, recent observations of decreased high affinity choline uptake in Alzheimer's brain,[103,106] reduced acetyl Co A production,[123] presynaptic neuronal degeneration,[65–72] and numerous other disturbances in normal aging and Alzheimer's disease provide empirical support for this caution. As we continue to generate data, perceptions gained from the benefit of hindsight make this approach seem less and less viable, although possible prophylactic benefits[121,124–126] remain primarily untested.

By contrast, the testing of cholinergic agonists and cholinesterase inhibitors as a means of improving geriatric memory has not been as extensive as precursor therapy, but has been somewhat more successful. To date the most popular cholinomimetic has been the anticholinesterase physostigmine. Early studies with young adults reported moderate improvement in cognitive tasks within a very restricted dose range.[127] Those doses outside this narrow range produced either no change in performance or marked impairment. Although initial attempts to demonstrate improvement with physostigmine in geriatric patients were not successful,[128–130] it is now generally accepted that physostigmine can improve geriatric memory. However, the effects are quite subtle, requiring strictly controlled test conditions and special attention to large individual variations in the most effective dose.[131,132] Furthermore, the most consistent effects have been obtained with intravenous injections of the drug.[132–136] Thus, despite the theoretical importance of these data, their direct therapeutic relevance remains in doubt.

More recently, preliminary evidence suggests that the oral form of physostigmine may not require as much attention to individual differences in most effective dose.[137] However, this suggestion requires confirmation[138] and there is no *a priori* reason to believe that the therapeutic effects of oral physostigmine should be more robust than those obtained with systemic injections.

The final class of cholinergics to be considered are those drugs that directly stimulate central muscarinic receptors. Recent reports that degeneration of cholinergic forebrain nuclei may account for the loss of CAT activity in Alzheimer's patients provides additional impetus for studies with cholinergic agonists. That is, if one assumes this degeneration plays a major role in the cognitive symptoms of the disease, then the most effective means available to treat the deficit would be to compensate for the loss of cholinergic input to the cortex and hippocampus by stimulating the surviving postsynaptic receptors with direct muscarinic agonists. Certainly drugs requiring functionally intact, presynaptic cholinergic terminals (such as cholinergic precursors and anticholinesterases) should be less capable of improving cholinergic tone or restoring the balance of the central nervous system than are drugs that interact with postsynaptic cholinergic receptors. Although relatively few studies with muscarinic agonists have been performed, the earlier tests have provided additional (albeit modest) support for using cholinergic stimulants to improve geriatric memory. When the direct muscarinic agonist arecoline was tested in aged monkeys, not only was significant improvement obtained in a delayed recall task,[139] but the dose response effects were also more consistent from monkey to monkey, as compared to physostigmine. Similar results have also been reported with Alzheimer's patients.[136] Clearly, additional clinical tests are required.

By way of contrast, other tests evaluating the dopamine receptor agonist apomorphine, GABA receptor agonist muscimol, and the alpha-adrenergic receptor agonist clonidine, have failed to produce any significant effects in aged monkeys.[140] Taken together, these initial tests in aged monkeys and Alzheimer's patients suggest that muscarinic agonists may provide a more effective means for treating the memory losses associated with aging and dementia than that provided by anticholinesterases, cholinergic precursors, and certain agonists acting upon other neurotransmitter receptors. However, none of these possibilities can be excluded conclusively at this time. Clearly the pharmacological studies supporting the superiority of cholinergic agonists remain sparse and tentative and require additional tests and comparisons.

At the same time, the degeneration of basal forebrain cholinergic neurons remains controversial and its implications are unclear. For example, recent studies have questioned the consistency and severity of the degeneration in Alzheimer's patients that was originally reported.[65,141,142] Moreover, others have reported significant loss of cells in the nucleus basalis of Meynert in several other clinical maladies, some of which are presumably unrelated to Alzheimer's disease.[65,66,143–145] Furthermore, the functional consequences of degeneration of these neurons have yet to be defined. Lesion studies in animals have only recently begun (see later section), and no detailed attempt to correlate degree of degeneration with cognitive loss in demented and non-demented subject populations has yet been reported. Finally, even assuming a significant and functional role of cholinergic cell death in age-related memory loss, the possibility still exists that increasing acetylcholine release from surviving neurons might provide an effective means of treating memory problems in aging and dementia. Recent preliminary reports support this possibility, with evidence of enhanced cholinergic function in rodents[146,147] and improved performance in aged rats[148] and Alzheimer's patients[149] treated with diaminopyridines (calcium uptake enhancers that promote acetylcholine release).

Current Status of Treatment Approaches

In sum, the available studies with cholinomimetic agents provide the optimist with a basis of hope for future drug development, but they admittedly offer no immediate promises of providing effective therapeutic intervention. However, it must be recognized that currently available cholinergic agents suffer clear deficiencies that may contribute to their lack of efficacy. For example, as briefly discussed above (and recently reviewed by Bartus *et al.*[122]), there now exist many reasons for questioning why precursors such as choline or lecithin should provide significant efficacy in impaired aged or demented patients. Moreover, the two classes of cholinomimetics for which some positive evidence does exist (i.e., anticholinesterases and muscarinic agonists) suffer serious pharmacokinetic limitations, including very short durations of action, lack of specificity for particular targets (i.e. particular muscarinic receptor subtypes within specific brain regions), and narrow therapeutic window (i.e., narrow range of effective doses).

Additionally, presuming that the cholinergic system is not the sole contributing factor to the memory disturbance, it has been suggested that in order to achieve substantial efficacy in aged subjects, it may be necessary to reduce multiple, interactive neurochemical dysfunctions in the aged and demented brain.[150,151] Drug combination studies in animals and humans have only recently begun to generate interest but it may be heuristically noteworthy that several tentatively positive findings with such combinations have begun to appear.[152–160] The future of this more complicated approach clearly awaits the test of time and will demand exceptionally rigorous evaluation of therapeutic efficacy and clinical relevance.

FUTURE DIRECTIONS

Basic Research on Interactive Cholinergic and Non-Cholinergic Variables

Given the intellectual and methodological status of research in this area, several compelling directions for future research efforts are readily apparent. One obvious need is to characterize more precisely the cholinergic defect in the brains of aged animals and humans, and humans suffering from Alzheimer's disease. Only in this way will we gain sufficient knowledge of the similarities and differences between various subject populations, and therefore understand when it is prudent to extrapolate from one to the other, and when it is dangerous. Of more fundamental importance, only through this information can the necessary insight be obtained for rationally designing or developing an effective treatment for geriatric cognitive loss. Of course, further knowledge regarding the intricacies of cholinergic function may be required before we can fully understand the changes that occur with age or dementia. Fundamental information about basic neurotransmitter mechanisms, such as second messengers, multiple receptor subtypes, receptor conformational changes, membrane fluidity, and other phospholipid events, as well as information regarding the interaction of multiple neurotransmitter systems should be invaluable in this regard.

Additionally, a more in-depth understanding of the relationship between the primary cholinergic marker of Alzheimer's disease (i.e., loss of CAT activity) and the primary neuropathological markers of the disease (plaques and tangles) should be developed. Although a definitive functional role has yet to be established for either of the classic neuropathological markers (in fact, they are known to exist in some degree in many completely normal, undemented aged people[161,162]), their importance in characterizing this disease has withstood the test of time. Further, they constitute a possible link between the etiology of the disease and the neurobiology of its primary symptoms.

Finally, systematic studies should be directed toward establishing a functional relationship between age-related changes in other neurotransmitter system(s), age-related memory loss, and the cholinergic dysfunctions documented. Surely, the identification and understanding of the roles played by other neurotransmitter systems in the memory loss of aging and dementia will require much work. To date, the majority of the arguments for the involvement of other systems has been based simply on the fact that changes in the markers of these systems have been observed in aged or demented brains. However, once substantiated, these observations merely satisfy the first of several steps required to demonstrate a functional role in the cognitive disturbances. They also presently fall far short of offering logical, empirically supported directions for drug development or pharmacotherapy.

Develop Characteristic-Specific Cholinergic Agents

Although admittedly simplistic, the cholinergic hypothesis nevertheless provides an important framework for directing pharmacological development and treatment. Few researchers in the area expect any cholinergic stimulant to reverse completely the cognitive dysfunction of Alzheimer's disease, let alone halt its insidious attack on the mind. Yet, epidemiological and sociological studies suggest that much human suffering could be reduced and billions of dollars saved annually simply by increasing the intellectual capacity of Alzheimer's patients to the point where self-care is possible and the need for expensive and dehumanizing institutionalization is therefore eliminated. It is from this perspective that the cholinergic hypothesis offers some hope and specific direction for attempting to find a solution.

Several shortcomings can be identified with currently available cholinergic agents, providing at least one approach for future drug development. Even accepting the potentially over-simplistic premise of the cholinergic hypothesis, it is difficult to imagine that any cholinergic agent will provide therapeutically significant effects unless it is improved in all or most of the following: greater selectivity and specificity for the end target; longer duration of action; wider therapeutic window; ready passage across blood-brain barrier; lack of peripheral side effects; no down-regulation of cholinergic activity; and extremely safe and non-toxic. How much might be gained by simply correcting these deficiencies of existing drugs remains an empirical issue that cannot yet be answered, but one that lies well within the scope of abilities to address.

Develop Reliable Animal Models of Primary Symptoms

The development and utilization of effective animal models can greatly facilitate discoveries to help understand and treat nearly any disease imaginable. Recognition of this, along with a growing concern for the consequences posed by Alzheimer's disease, has contributed to recent interest in developing animal models to study memory problems associated with that disease.[121,163,164] From the standpoint of the cholinergic hypothesis, the development of useful animal models would improve our ability to test and/or refine the hypothesis, provide an important and efficient means of evaluating newly developed cholinergic agents, and offer a convenient means of comparing the effects of cholinometics with alternative pharmacological approaches. However, work in this area is particularly difficult, in part because of problems inherent in accurately measuring memory in animals, and in part because Alzheimer's disease seems to be a human-specific disease. Although recent studies suggest it may be possible to gain some insight into treatment approaches from data derived from aged animals,[121,163,165-167] there is no question that greater predictability might be achieved with an animal model that shares more of the characteristic neuropathology and neurochemical deficiencies found in the brains of Alzheimer's patients. Earlier attempts to artificially induce neurofibrillary tangles in animals via aluminum[168,169] have been disappointing, neither providing greater insight into the nature of the disease nor leading to more effective means of testing drugs to treat its symptoms. Other attempts to produce an animal model through injection of presumed transmissible agents may continue to hold promise, but have so far been equally disappointing.[170,171]

More recently, however, the evidence implicating severe deterioration in the nucleus basalis in Alzheimer's patients has given new momentum to the development of potential animal models of the disease. Although destruction of this brain region would certainly not be expected to produce the plaques and tangles observed in Alzheimer's patients, it nevertheless would provide an animal model that shares other CNS deficiencies associated with that disease, such as loss of cortical CAT activity, reduced cortical high affinity choline uptake, and degeneration of basal forebrain cholinergic neurons. At a minimum, destruction of the homologous brain region in animals should help determine the functional consequences of such degeneration and provide an empirical test of its possible role in the cognitive loss of Alzheimer's disease and other degenerative disorders.

Although work in this area is very new, recent studies in rodents already have demonstrated interesting and selective behavioral effects following destruction of this brain region. For example, in one comprehensive assessment, no effects of the lesion were observed on four different psychomotor tasks (intended to measure muscle strength, stamina, and coordination), on tests of shock sensitivity, or on the initial latency to respond in a one-trial, passive avoidance task.[82] However, the nucleus basalis–lesioned rats were severely impaired on retention of the passive avoidance task; the same test that revealed the most robust behavioral disturbances in aged rats.[163] Similar retention deficits following nucleus basalis lesions have been reported by others as well.[83,84] It should be noted that the effects of the lesion in this study were more severe than those noted with aging, for the nucleus basalis–lesioned animals exhibited deficits at both one hour and twenty-four hour retention intervals. Because a clear temporally related decline was not observed, it remained uncertain whether the deficit reflected disturbances in learning, memory, or both. Further, the passive-avoidance procedure is recognized as a relatively crude behavioral paradigm and its results are often open to multiple alternative interpretations.

For these reasons a second rodent experiment was performed in a new group of rats.[81] These rats were first trained to obtain food reward by visiting each of eight arms of a radial arm maze only once. Repeat visits to an arm were never reinforced and were scored as errors. Following several months of training and establishment of near perfect performance, the rats received sham lesions or lesions of the nucleus basalis. Two weeks following surgery the rats were retested on the radial arm maze task. This retesting revealed that the animals with nucleus basalis lesions possessed normal post-operative retention of the learned task (FIGURE 1). Thus, the lesioned rats not only retained their ability to run on the eight-arm maze and earn food reinforcement, but were also unimpaired in accurately going to each of the eight arms only once during

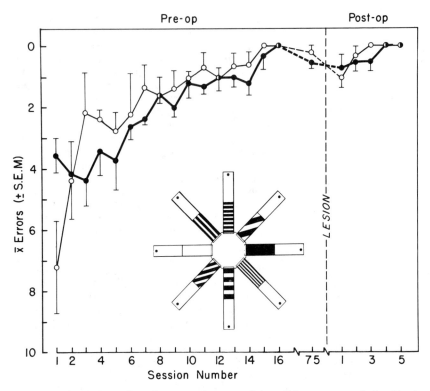

FIGURE 1. Acquisition and steady-state performance of the radial arm maze, as depicted by the mean number of errors to successfully complete all eight choices in the maze task. Repeat responses to any arm previously entered within the session are not reinforced and are treated as errors. Note no effect of nucleus basalis lesion on performance of task.

control test sessions. However, when a recent memory component was added to the task procedure, a profound deficit in the lesion group was revealed (FIGURE 2). In other words, when a retention interval was interposed between the selection of the first four arms and the remaining four arms a time-dependent decrement in performance occurred. This time-related deficit suggested that destruction of cholinergic neurons in the nucleus basalis of rats may create disturbances in recent memory analogous to those seen in aging and dementia. In addition to these lesioned young rats, aged rats, mice, monkeys, humans, and early Alzheimer's patients all exhibit memory losses that share a number of operational similarities.[121,163] Although certain quantitative differences may exist among these various conditions, members of each share a deficit in memory characterized by a somewhat preferential inability to remember brief, discrete events, with greatest deficits existing in situations where there is little or no repetition or opportunity to practice or rehearse the information to be remembered, and a time-related decline in retention, which occurs relatively rapidly (usually within minutes or hours).

The operational and conceptual similarities between the deficits produced by nucleus basalis lesions in rats and the early recent memory deficits of Alzheimer's patients were consistent with a role for this brain region in mediating memory loss of

Alzheimer's disease. However, further work with these animals revealed some of the limitations inherent in lesion procedures and cautioned that a more complex interpretation of the data was required. During the course of several months of training on the radial-arm maze task, the performance of the lesioned rats on the delay conditions gradually improved. By six months after surgery, retention was not different from the controls (FIGURE 2). Further, when trained and tested in the same passive avoidance task that earlier had revealed marked impairments from these lesions, these animals exhibited no retention deficit (FIGURE 3). Finally, following sacrifice, a series of neurochemical determinations revealed that neither cortical CAT activity nor high affinity choline uptake recovered measurably in the rats exhibiting the behavioral recovery, nor was there any hint of compensatory changes in the hippocampus or olfactory bulbs (terminal areas for parallel cholinergic pathways). Finally, no changes in muscarinic receptor density were observed in any brain region studied (TABLE 2). In summary, although severe and selective deficits in recent memory were observed following destruction of basal forebrain cholinergic neurons in young rats, complete recovery of the memory loss gradually occurred over the next several months. Further, no neurochemical correlate of this recovery could be identified.

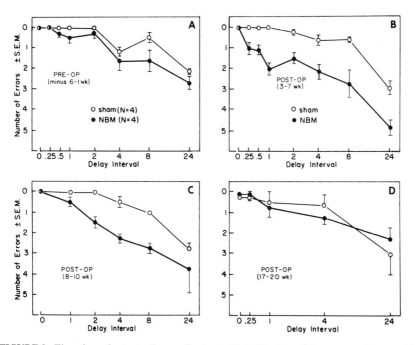

FIGURE 2. Time-dependent retention gradients established in the radial-arm maze by rats with nucleus basalis (shaded circles) and sham lesions (open circles). The gradients were established by allowing access to only four of the eight arms before the delay interval. Following variable delay intervals, all eight arms were available to assess the animals' ability to remember which arms had been visited earlier in the session. (A) Performance 1–6 weeks prior to surgery; (B) Performance 3–7 weeks following surgery; note significant effect of lesion when delay interposed between selection of first and last four arms; (C) Performance 8–10 weeks post-op, with persistence of deficit, but hint of recovery of function; (D) Performance 17–20 weeks post-op; note complete recovery of lesioned rats.

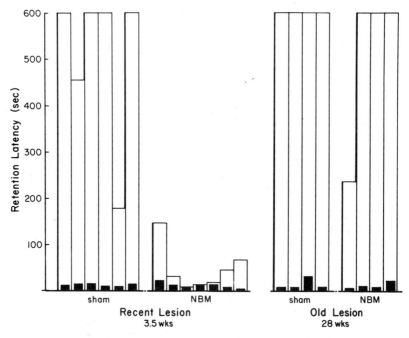

FIGURE 3. Retention of passive avoidance task within one month of NBM lesion or several months following surgery. The animals in the "old lesion" group (28 weeks post surgery) exhibited no deficit on the task and had been trained on the radial-arm maze task (as depicted in FIGURE 2) prior to training and testing on this procedure.

TABLE 2. Cholinergic Markers Determined Two Weeks (Recent) or Six Months (Long Term) Following Nucleus Basalis Lesions in Rats (Compared to Sham-Operated Controls)

		CAT Activity[a]	HACU	QNB
Frontal cortex	Recent Lesion	−46%	−32%	no change
	Long-term Lesion	−42%	−33%	no change
Parietal/temporal cortex	Recent Lesion	−36%	n.d.	no change
	Long-term Lesion	−26%	n.d.	no change
Hippocampus	Recent Lesion	no change	no change	no change
	Long-term Lesion	no change	no change	no change
Olfactory bulbs	Recent Lesion	no change	n.d.	no change
	Long-term Lesion	no change	n.d.	no change

[a]Abbreviations: CAT—choline acetyltransferase, HACU—high affinity choline uptake, QNB—specific binding of the ^{3}H-labeled, muscarinic antagonist, quinuclidinyl benzilate, and n.d.—not determined.

The data from this study leave unanswered the question of the functional role played by degenerated neurons in homologous brain regions in Alzheimer's patients. However, in our opinion, the data clearly support the idea that this group of neurons (and their extrinsic projections to the cortex) plays an important and potentially quantifiable role in mediating recent memory. Certainly the behavioral recovery observed after six months hardly outweighs the evidence supporting an important involvement of the region in mediating recent memory. Indeed, considerable empirical evidence exists for some to predict such complete recovery of function.[172–174] Rather, the specificity and severity of memory loss strongly implicates this nucleus and pathway in mediating memory. This evidence, coupled with the operational similarities of the deficit observed to the memory loss described for aged rodent, primates, humans, and Alzheimer's patients, makes the argument even more compelling. A major question that presents itself is whether similarly complete recovery would have occurred if the lesion had been performed in aged animals who may have a reduced capacity to recover lost function. From a different perspective, aged animals with basal forebrain degeneration may represent a more accurate analogue to Alzheimer's patients. Also of interest would be the effects of combining lesions of the basal forebrain with other areas also implicated in Alzheimer's disease (such as hippocampus or locus coeruleus). Finally, the question of the functional significance of the classic neuropathology of Alzheimer's disease (i.e., tangles and plaques) must be considered; perhaps both the neuropathology and neurodegeneration must exist to cause a severe and permanent loss of cognitive function.

The question of species suitability for these studies is another issue deserving some comment. Although the ventrolateral globus pallidus is commonly agreed to represent an area homologous to the primate nucleus basalis of Meynert,[73,75,76] the region is poorly defined in rodents and certain differences in topographical projections and cellular distribution may exist. Further, the nature of the specific memory loss impaired with age and dementia continues to present problems when studied in rodents. Alternatively, the similarity of structure and organization of the basal forebrain nuclei in human and non-human primates, combined with the relative similarity of behavioral repertoire and cognitive test capabilities in these species, greatly reduces the assumptions necessary to extrapolate from the effects of lesions in monkeys to the functional consequences of degeneration of the basal forebrain nuclei in aged, demented humans.

Recent accounts of the first studies with non-human primates have been equivocal. For example, using a delayed, non-matching task, Aiger *et al.*[175] reported that lesions of the nucleus basalis failed to significantly impair memory, but that reliable deficits in comparison to controls were observed when the subjects were given a normally low dose of anticholinergic. On the basis of these data, it has been concluded that destruction of that brain region alone is not sufficient to cause significant memory loss in primates. However, such a conclusion rests on the somewhat tenuous logic of accepting the null hypothesis based on a single behavioral paradigm that used few subjects, lesions without histological confirmation, and no independent demonstration of task validity. Clearly, additional systematic work is required before any gross generalizations can be made. Future experimental work in both primates and rodents, as well as with postmortem tissue from various demented and non-demented patient populations, should help clarify the role of this brain region in mediating behavior and its relationship to the cognitive loss associated with aging and dementia.

Although the development of a valid animal model of Alzheimer's disease could prove invaluable in helping to identify effective pharmacological treatments for the cognitive symptoms of this disorder, it is also likely that the answers to questions raised during the development of such animal models will prove to be equally useful. In addition to their more glamorous and optimistic intentions, it is in areas such as this, that the direction offered by concepts like the cholinergic hypothesis demonstrate their worth as viable scientific contributions.

REFERENCES

1. ALZHEIMER, A. 1907. Uber eine eigenartige erkrankung der hirnrinde. Allg. Z. Psychiatr. **64:** 146–148.
2. SIMARD, D, J. OLESEN, O. B. PAULSON, N. A. LASSEN & E. SKINHOJ. 1971. Regional cerebral blood flow and its regulation in dementia. Brain **94:** 273–288.
3. BARTUS, R. T., R. L. DEAN, B. BEER & A. S. LIPPA. 1982. The cholinergic hypothesis of geriatric memory dysfunction. Science **217:** 408–417.
4. COYLE, J. T., D. L. PRICE & M. R. DELONG. 1983. Alzheimer's disease: A disorder of cortical cholinergic innervation. Science **219:** 1184–1190.
5. DAVIES, P. 1981. Theoretical treatment possibilities for dementia of the Alzheimer's type: The cholinergic hypothesis. *In* Strategies for the Development of an Effective Treatment for Senile Dementia. T. Crook & S. Gershon, Eds.: Mark Powley Associates. New Canaan, CT.
6. DRACHMAN, D. A. 1977. Memory and the cholinergic system. *In* Neurotransmitter Function: Basic and Clinical Aspects. W. S. Fields, Ed. Stratton. New York.
7. DRACHMAN, D. A. 1983. How normal aging relates to dementia: A critique and classification. *In* Aging of the Brain. D. Samuel, S. Algeri, S. Gershon, V. E. Grimm & G. Toffano, Eds. Raven Press. New York.
8. KRAL, V. A. 1978. Benign senescent forgetfulness. *In* Alzheimer's Disease: Senile Dementia and Related Disorders. R. Katzman, R. D. Terry & K. L. Bick, Eds. Raven Press, New York.
9. MCGEER, P. L., E. G. MCGEER, J. SUZUKI, C. E. DOLMAN & T. NAGAI. 1984. Aging, Alzheimer's disease, and the cholinergic system of the basal forebrain. Neurology **34:** 741–745.
10. TERRY, R. D. 1978. Aging, senile dementia, and Alzheimer's disease. *In* Alzheimer's Disease: Senile Dementia and Related Disorders. R. Katzman, R. D. Terry & K. L. Bick, Eds. Raven Press. New York.
11. DUNDEE, J. W. & S. K. PANDIT. 1972. Anterograde amnesic effects of pethidine, hyoscine and diazepam in adults. Br. J. Pharmac. **44:** 140–144.
12. HOLLISTER, L. E. 1968. Chemical Psychoses. Charles Thomas. Springfield, IL.
13. LONGO, V. G. 1966. Behavioral and electroencephalographic effects of atropine and related compounds. Pharmacol. Rev. **18:** 965–996.
14. GAUSS, C. J. 1906. Geburten im Kunstlichem Dammerschlaf. Arch. Gynak. **78:** 579–631.
15. LAMBRECHTS, W. & J. PARKHOUSE. 1961. Postoperative amnesia. Br. J. Anesth. **33:** 397–404.
16. PANDIT, S. K. & J. W. DUNDEE. 1970. Preoperative amnesia: The incidence following the intramuscular injection of commonly used premedicants. Anesthesia **25:** 493–499.
17. DEUTSCH, J. A., M. D. HAMBURG & H. DAHL. 1966. Anticholinesterase-induced amnesia and its temporal aspects. Science **151:** 221–223.
18. DEUTSCH, J. A. 1971. The cholinergic synapse and the site of memory. Science **174:** 788–794.
19. WHITEHOUSE, J. M. 1964. Effects of atropine on discrimination learning in the rat. J. Comp. Physiol. Psychol. **57:** 13–15.
20. HERZ, A. 1960. Die Gedentung der Gahung fur die wirkung von scopolamin und ahnlichen substanzen auf Gedingte reaktionen. Z. Biol. **112:** 104–112.
21. MEYERS, B. & E. F. DOMINO. 1964. The effect of cholinergic blocking drugs on spontaneous alteration in rats. Arch. Int. Pharmacodyn. **150:** 3–4.
22. MEYERS, B., D. H. ROBERTS, R. H. RICIPUTI & E. F. DOMINO. 1964. Some effects of muscarinic cholinergic blocking drugs on behavior and the electrocorticogram. Psychopharmacology **5:** 289–300.
23. DOUGLAS, R. J. 1967. The hippocampus and behavior. Psychol. Bull. **67:** 416–442.

24. IVERSEN, S. D. 1973. Brain lesions and memory in animals. *In* The Physiological Basis of Memory. J. A. Deutsch, Ed. Academic Press. New York.

25. IVERSEN, S. D. 1976. Do hippocampal lesions produce amnesia in animals? Int. Rev. Neurobiol. **19:** 1–49.

26. STEPIEN, L. S., J. P. CORDEAU & T. RASMUSSEN. 1960. The effect of temporal lobe and hippocampal lesions on auditory and visual recent memory in monkeys. Brain **83:** 470–489.

27. J. M. WARREN & G. K. AKERT, Eds. 1964. The Frontal Granular Cortex and Behavior. McGraw Hill. New York.

28. YAMAMURA, H. I. & S. H. SNYDER. 1974. Postsynaptic localization of muscarinic cholinergic receptor binding in rat hippocampus. Brain Res. **78:** 320–326.

29. YAMAMURA, H. I., M. J. KUHAR & S. H. SNYDER. 1974. In vivo identification of muscarinic cholinergic receptor binding in rat brain. Brain Res. **80:** 170–176.

30. KUHAR, M. J. & H. I. YAMAMURA. 1975. Light autoradiographic localisation of cholinergic muscarinic receptors in rat brain by specific binding of a potent antagonist. Nature **253:** 560–561.

31. YAMAMURA, H. I., M. J. KUHAR, D. GREENBERG & S. H. SNYDER. 1974. Muscarinic cholinergic receptor binding: Regional distribution in monkey brain. Brain Res. **66:** 541–546.

32. POPE, A., H. H. HESS & E. LEWIN. 1965. Microchemical pathology of the cerebral cortex in pre-senile dementias. Trans. Am. Neurol. Assoc. **89:** 15–16.

33. DRACHMAN, D. A. 1977. Memory and cognitive function in man: Does the cholinergic system have a specific role? Neurology **27:** 783–790.

34. DRACHMAN, D. A. & J. LEAVITT. 1974. Human memory and the cholinergic system: A relationship to aging? Arch. Neurol. **30:** 113–121.

35. CROW, T. J. & I. G. GROVE-WHITE. 1971. A differential effect of atropine and hyoscine on human learning capacity. Br. J. Pharmac. **43:** 464.

36. DAVIS, K. L., R. C. MOHS, B. M. DAVIS, M. LEVY, G. S. ROSENBERG, T. B. HORRATH, Y. DENIGRIS, A. ROSS, P. DECKER & A. ROTHPEARL. 1981. Cholinominetic agents and human memory: Clinical studies in Alzheimer's disease and scopolamine dementia. *In* Strategies for the Development of an Effective Treatment for Senile Dementia. T. Crook & R. S. Gershon, Eds. Mark Powley Associates. New Canaan, CT.

37. SMITH, C. M. & M. SWASH. 1978. Possible biochemical basis of memory disorder in Alzheimer's disease. Ann. Neurol. **3:** 471–473.

38. BARTUS, R. T. & H. R. JOHNSON. 1976. Short term memory in the rhesus monkey: Disruption from the anticholinergic scopolamine. Pharmacol. Biochem. Behav. **5:** 39–46.

39. BARTUS, R. T., D. FLEMING & H. R. JOHNSON. 1978. Aging in the rhesus monkey: Debilitating effects on short term memory. Gerontology **33:** 858–871.

40. BARTUS, R. T. 1980. Cholinergic drug effects on memory and cognition in animals. *In* Aging in the 1980's: Psychological Issues. L. W. Poon, Ed. American Psychological Association. Washington, D.C.

41. BARTUS, R. T. 1978. Short-term memory in the rhesus monkey: Effects of dopamine blockade via acute haloperidol administration. Pharmacol. Biochem. Behav. **9:** 353–357.

42. BARTUS, R. T. 1979. Four stimulants of the central nervous system: Effects on short-term memory in young versus aged monkeys. J. Am. Ger. Soc. **27:** 289–297.

43. DEAN, R. L., B. BEER & R. T. BARTUS. 1982. Drug induced memory impairments in non-human primates. Neurosci. Abst. **8:** 322.

44. GHONEIM, M. M., J. V. HINRICHS & S. P. MEWALDT. 1984. Dose-response analysis of the behavioral effects of diazepam: I. Learning and memory. Psychopharmacology **82:** 291–295.

45. MCMILLAN, D. E. Behavioral pharmacology of the tetrahydrocannabinols. *In* Advances in Behavioral Pharmacology. T. Thompson & P. B. Dews, Eds. Academic Press. New York.

46. ROMNEY, D. M. & W. R. ANGUS. 1984. A brief review of the effects of diazepam on memory. Psychopharm. Bull. **20:** 313–316.

47. SULKOWSKI, A. 1980. Marihuana "high": A model of senile dementia? Perspect. Biol. Med. **23**: 209–214.
48. MARRIOTT, J. G., J. S. ABELSON & R. T. BARTUS. 1979. Diazepam impairment of delayed-response performance in young and old rhesus monkeys. Neurosci. Abst. **5**: 1053.
49. ASKEW, W. E., A. P. KIMBALL & B. T. HO. 1974. Effect of tetrahydrocannabinols on brain acetylcholine. Brain Res. **69**: 375–378.
50. CLEMMESEN, L., P. L. MIKKELSEN, H. LUND, T. G. BOLWIG & O. J. RAFAELSEN. 1984. Assessment of the anticholinergic effects of antidepressants in a single-dose cross-over study of salivation and plasma levels. Psychopharm. **82**: 348–354.
51. DOMINO, E. F. 1981. Cannabinoids and the cholinergic system. J. Clin. Pharmacol. **21**: 249S–255S.
52. JOHNSON, K. M. & W. L. DEWEY. 1978. Effects of −THC on the synaptosomal uptake of ^{3}H-Tryptophan and ^{3}H-Choline. Pharmacol., **17**: 83–87.
53. LADINSKY, H., S. CONSOLO, C. BELLANTUONO & S. GARATTINI. 1981. Interaction of benzodiazepines with known and putative neurotransmitters in the brain. *In* Handbook of Biological Psychiatry. H. M. Van Praag, M. H. Lader, O. J. Rafaelsen & E. J. Sachar, Eds. Vol. 4. Marcel Dekker. New York.
54. BOWEN, D. M., C. B. SMITH, P. WHITE & A. N. DAVISON. 1976. Neurotransmitter-related enzymes and indices of hypoxia in senile dementia and other abiotrophies. Brain **99**: 459–496.
55. DAVIES, P. & A. J. F. MALONEY. 1976. Selective loss of central cholinergic neurons in Alzheimer's disease. Lancet **2**: 1403.
56. PERRY, E. K., R. H. PERRY, G. BLESSED & B. E. TOMLINSON. 1977. Necropsy evidence of central cholinergic deficits in senile dementia. Lancet **1**: 189.
57. HAUBRICH, D. R. & T. J. CHIPPENDALE. 1977. Regulation of acetylcholine synthesis in nervous tissue. Life Sci. **20**: 1465–1478.
58. ATWEH, S., J. R. SIMON & M. J. KUHAR. 1975. Utilization of sodium–dependent high affinity choline uptake in vitro as a measure of the activity of cholinergic neurons in vivo. Life Sci. **17**: 1535–1544.
59. JENDEN, D. S., R. S. JOPE & M. H. WEILER, 1976. Regulation of acetylcholine synthesis: Does cytoplasmic acetylcholine control high affinity choline uptake? Science **194**: 635–637.
60. LIPPA, A. S., D. J. CRITCHETT, F. EHLERT, H. I. YAMAMURA, S. J. ENNA & R. T. BARTUS. 1981. Age-related alterations in neurotransmitter receptors: An electrophysiological and biochemical analysis. Neurobiol. Aging **2**: 3–8.
61. LIPPA, A. S., R. W. PELHAM, B. BEER, D. J. CRITCHETT, R. L. DEAN & R. T. BARTUS. 1980. Brain cholinergic dysfunction and memory in aged rats. Neurobiol. Aging **1**: 13–19.
62. SEGAL, M. 1982. Changes in neurotransmitter actions in the aged rat hippocampus. Neurobiol. Aging **3**: 121–124.
63. GIBSON G. E., C. PETERSON & J. SANSONE. 1981. Neurotransmitter and carbohydrate metabolism during aging and mild hypoxia. Neurobiol. Aging **2**: 165–172.
64. GIBSON, G. E., C. PETERSON & D. J. JENDEN. 1981. Brain acetylcholine synthesis declines with senescence. Science **213**: 674–676.
65. CANDY, J. M., R. H. PERRY, E. K. PERRY, D. IRVING, G. BLESSED, A. F. FAIRBAIRN & R. L. TOMLINSON. 1983. Pathological changes in the nucleus of Meynert in Alzheimer's and Parkinson's diseases. J. Neurosci. **54**: 277–289.
66. TAGLIAVINI, F. & G. PILLERI. 1983. Basal nucleus of Meynert: A neuropathological study in Alzheimer's disease, simple senile dementia, Pick's disease and Huntington's chorea. J. Neurol. Sci. **62**: 243-260.
67. TAGLIAVINI, F. & G. PILLERI. 1983. Neuronal counts in basal nucleus of Meynert in Alzheimer disease and in simple senile dementia. Lancet **1**: 469–470.
68. NAKANO, I. & A. HIRANO. 1982. Loss of large neurons of the medial septal nucleus in an autopsy case of Alzheimer's disease. J. Neuropath. Exp. Neurol. **41**: 341.
69. WHITEHOUSE, P. J., D. L. PRICE, A. W. CLARK, J. T. COYLE & M. R. DELONG. 1981.

Alzheimer's disease: Evidence for selective loss of cholinergic neurons in the nucleus basalis. Ann. Neurol. **10:** 122–126.
70. WHITEHOUSE, P. J., D. L. PRICE, R. G. STRUBLE, A. W. CLARK, J. T. COYLE & M. R. DELONG. 1981. Alzheimer's disease and senile dementia: Loss of neurons in the basal forebrain. Science **215:** 1237–1239.
71. WHITEHOUSE, P. J., R. G. STRUBLE, A. W. CLARK & D. L. PRICE. 1982. Alzheimer's disease: Plaques, tangles and the basal forebrain. Ann. Neurol. **12:** 494.
72. WILCOCK, G. K., M. M. ESIRI, D. M. BOWEN & C. C. T. SMITH. 1983. The nucleus basalis in Alzheimer's disease: Cell counts and cortical biochemistry. Neuropath. Appl. Neurobiol. **9:** 175–179.
73. DIVAC, I. 1975. Magnocellular nuclei of the basal forebrain project to neocortex, brainstem and olfactory bulb: Review of some functional correlates. Brain Res. **93:** 385–398.
74. FIBIGER, H. C. 1982. The organization and some projections of cholinergic neurons of the mammalian forebrain. Brain Res. Rev. **4:** 327–388.
75. GORRY, J. D. 1963. Studies on the comparative anatomy of the ganglion basali of Meynert. Acta Anatomica **55:** 51–104.
76. JOHNSTON, M. V., M. MCKINNEY & J. T. COYLE. 1979. Evidence for a cholinergic projection to neocortex from neurons in basal forebrain. Proc. Natl. Acad. Sci. USA **76:** 5392–5396.
77. LEWIS, P. R. & C. C. D. SHUTE. 1967. The cholinergic limbic system: Projections to hippocampal formation, medial cortex, nuclei of the ascending cholinergic reticular system, and the subfornical organ and supra-optic crest. Brain **90:** 521–542.
78. MESULAM, M. M., E. J. MUFSON, A. I. LEVEY & B. WAINER. 1983. Cholinergic innervation of cortex by the basal forebrain: Cytochemistry and cortical connections of the septal area, diagonal band nuclei, nucleus basalis (substantia innominata) and hypothalamus in the rhesus monkey. J. Comp. Neurol. **214:** 170–197.
79. MESULAM, M. M. & G. W. VAN HOSEN. 1976. Acetylcholinesterase rich projections from the basal forebrain of rhesus monkey to neocortex. Brain Res. **109:** 152–157.
80. SHUTE, C. C. D. & P. R. LEWIS. 1967. The ascending cholinergic reticular system: Neocortical, olfactory and subcortical projections. Brain **90:** 497–522.
81. BARTUS, R. T., R. L. DEAN, C. FLICKER, M. J. PONTECORVO, J. FIGIEURIDO & S. K. FISHER. 1985. Selective memory loss following nucleus basalis lesions: Long term behavioral recovery despite persistent neurochemical deficiencies. (Manuscript submitted for publication.)
82. FLICKER, C., R. L. DEAN, D. L. WATKINS, S. K. FISHER & R. T. BARTUS. 1983. Behavioral and neurochemical effects following neurotoxic lesions of a major cholinergic input to the cerebral cortex in the rat. Pharmacol. Biochem. Behav. **18:** 973–981.
83. FRIEDMAN, E., B. LERER & J. KUSTER. 1983. Loss of cholinergic neurons in rat neocortex produces deficits in passive avoidance learning. Pharmacol. Biochem. Behav. **19:** 309–312.
84. LOCONTE, G., L. BARTOLINI, F. CASAMENTI, I. MARCONCINI-PEPEU & G. PEPEU. 1982. Lesions of cholinergic forebrain nuclei: Changes in avoidance behavior and scopolamine actions. Pharmacol. Biochem. Behav. **17:** 933–937.
85. ADOLFFSON, R., C. G. GOTTFRIES, L. ORELAND, B. E. ROOS & B. WINBLAD. 1978. Reduced levels of catecholamines in the brain and increased activity of monoamine oxidase in platelets in Alzheimer's disease: Therapeutic implications. *In* Alzheimer's Disease: Senile Dementia and Related Disorders. R. Katzman, R. D. Terry & K. L. Bick, Eds. Raven Press. New York.
86. ARAI, H., K. KOSAKA & R. IIZUKA. 1984. Changes of biogenic amines and their metabolites in postmortem brains from patients with Alzheimer-type dementia. J. Neurochem. **43:** 388–393.
87. CROSS, A. J., T. J. CROW, J. A. JOHNSON, M. H. JOSEPH, E. K. PERRY, R. H. PERRY, G. BLESSED & B. E. TOMLINSON. 1983. Monoamine metabolism in senile dementia of Alzheimer type. J. Neurol. Sci. **60:** 383–392.
88. CROSS, A. J., T. J. CROW, E. K. PERRY, R. H. PERRY, G. BLESSED & B. E. TOMLINSON.

1981. Reduced dopamine-beta-hydroxylase activity in Alzheimer's disease. Br. Med. J. **282:** 93–94.

89. GOTTFRIES, C. G., I. GOTTFRIES & B. E. ROOS. 1969. The investigation of homovanillic acid in the human brain and its correlation to senile dementia. Br. J. Psychiatry **115:** 563–574.

90. SOININEN, H., E. MACDONALD, M. RÉKONEN & P. J. RIEKKINEN. 1981. Homovanillic acid and 5-hydroxyindoleacetic acid levels in cerebrospinal fluid of patients with senile dementia of Alzheimer type. Acta Neurol. Scandinav. **64:** 101–107.

91. BOWEN, D. M., S. S. ALLEN, J. S. BENTON, M. J. GOODHART, E. A. HAAN, A. M. PALMER, N. R. SIMS, C. C. T. SMITH, J. A. SPILLANE, M. M. ESIRI, D. NEARY, J. S. SNOWDON, G. K. NILCOCK & A. N. DAVISON. 1983. Biochemical assessment of gerontonergic and cholinergic dysfunction and cerebral atrophy in Alzeimer's disease. J. Neurochem. **41:** 266–272.

92. FERRIER, I. N., A. J. CROSS, J. A. JOHNSON, G. W. ROBERTS, T. J. CROW, J. A. N. CORSELLIS, Y. C. LEE, D. O'SHAUGHNESSY, T. E. ADRIAN, G. P. MCGREGOR, A. J. BARACESE-HAMILTON & S. R. BLOOM. 1983. Neuropeptides in Alzheimer type dementia. J. Neurol. Sci. **62:** 159–170.

93. DAVIES, P., R. KATZMAN & R. D. TERRY. 1980. Reduced somatostatin-like immunoreactivity in cerebral cortex from cases of Alzheimer's disease and Alzheimer senile dementia. Nature **228:** 279–280.

94. DAVIES, P. & R. D. TERRY. 1981. Cortical somatostatin-like immunoreactivity in cases of Alzheimer's disease and senile dementia of the Alzheimer type. Neurobiol. Aging **2:** 9–14.

95. ROSSOR, M. N., P. C. EMSON, C. Q. MOUNTJOY, M. ROTH & L. L. IVERSON. 1980. Reduced amounts of immunoreactive somatostatin in the temporal cortex in senile dementia of Alzheimer type. Neurosci. Lett. **20:** 373–377.

96. BONDAREFF, W., C. Q. MOUNTJOY & M. ROTH. 1982. Loss of neurons of origin of the adrenergic projection to cerebral cortex (nucleus locus ceruleus) in senile dementia. Neurology **32:** 164–168.

97. IVERSEN, L. L., M. N. ROSSOR, G. P. REYNOLDS, R. HILLS, M. ROTH, C. Q. MOUNTJOY, S. L. FOOTE, J. H. MORRISON & F. E. BLOOM. 1983. Loss of pigmented dopamine-β-hydroxylase positive cells from locus coeruleus in senile dementia of Alzheimer's type. Neurosci. Lett. **39:** 95–100.

98. MANN, D. M. A., P. O. YATES & B. MARCYNIUK. 1984. A comparison of changes in the nucleus basaslis and locus coeruleus in Alzheimer's disease. J. Neurol. Neurosurg. Psych. **47:** 201–203.

99. TOMLINSON, B. E., D. IRVING & G. BLESSED. 1981. Cell loss in the locus coeruleus in senile dementia of Alzheimer type. J. Neurol. Sci. **49:** 419–428.

100. MANN, J. J., M. STANLEY, A. NEOPHYTIDES, M. J. DE LEON, S. H. FERRIS & S. GERSHON. 1981. Central amine metabolism in Alzheimer's disease: In vivo relationship to cognitive deficit. Neurobiol. Aging **2:** 57–60.

101. YATES, L. M., Y. ALLISEN, J. SIMPSON, A. F. J. MALONEY & A. GORDEN. 1979. Dopamine in Alzheimer's disease and senile dementia. Lancet **2:** 851–852.

102. SASTRY, R., V. E. JANSON, N. JAISWAL & O. S. TAYEB. 1983. Changes in enzymes of the cholinergic system and acetylcholine release in the cerebra of aging male Fischer rats. Pharmacology **26:** 61–72.

103. SIMS, N. R., D. M. BOWEN, S. J. ALLEN, C. C. T. SMITH, D. NEARY, D. J. THOMAS & A. N. DAVISON. 1983. Presynaptic cholinergic dysfunction in patients with dementia. J. Neurochem. **40:** 503–509.

104. SIMS, N. R., D. M. BOWEN, C. C. T. SMITH, R. H. A. FLACK, A. N. DAVISON, J. S. SNOWDEN & D. NEARY. 1980. Glucose metabolism and acetylcholine synthesis in relation to neuronal activity in Alzheimer's disease. Lancet **1:** 333–335.

105. SHERMAN, K. A., J. E. KUSTER, R. L. DEAN, R. T. BARTUS & E. FRIEDMAN. 1981. Presynaptic cholinergic mechanisms in brain of aged rats with memory impairments. Neurobiol. Aging **2:** 99–104.

106. RYLETT, R. J., M. J. BALL & E. H. COLHOUN. 1983. Evidence for high affinity choline

transport in synaptosomes prepared from hippocampus and neocortex of patients with Alzheimer's disease. Brain Res. **289:** 169–175.

107. RINNE, J. O., J. K. RINNE, K. LAAKSO, L. PALJARVI & U. K. RINNE. 1984. Reduction in muscarinic receptor binding in limbic areas of Alzheimer brain. J. Neurol. Neurosurg. Psych. **47:** 651–653.

108. NORDBERG, AGNETA, C. LARSSON, R. ADOLFSSON, I. ALAFUSOFF & B. WINBLAD. 1983. Muscarinic receptor compensation in hippocampus of Alzheimer patients. J. Neural Trans. **56:** 13–19.

109. LANG, W. & H. HENKE. 1983. Cholinergic receptor binding and autoradiography in brains of non-neurological and senile dementia of Alzheimer-type patients. Brain Res. **267:** 271–280.

110. WALLER, S. B. & E. D. LONDON. 1983. Age-differences in choline acetyltransferase activities and muscarinic receptor binding in brain regions of C57Bl/6j mice. Exp. Gerontol. **18:** 419–425.

111. STRONG, R., P. HICKS, L. HSU, R. T. BARTUS & S. J. ENNA. 1980. Age related alterations in the rodent brain cholinergic system and behavior. Neurobiol. Aging **1:** 59–63.

112. BARBEAU, A. 1981. The use of L-DOPA in Parkinson's disease: A 20 year follow-up. Trends Pharm. Sci. **2:** 299–303.

113. COTZIAS, G. C., M. H. VAN WOERT & L. M. SCHIFFER. 1967. Aromatic amino acids and modification of Parkinsonism. N. Eng. J. Med. **276:** 374–379.

114. COHEN, E. L. & R. J. WURTMAN. 1975. Brain acetylcholine: Increases after systemic choline administration. Life Sci. **16:** 1095–1102.

115. HAUBRICH, D. R., P. F. L. WANG, D. E. CLODY & P. W. WEDEKING. 1975. Increase in rat brain acetylcholine induced by choline and deanol. Life Sci. **17:** 975–980.

116. WURTMAN, R. J. & J. D. FERNSTROM. 1976. Control of brain neurotransmitter synthesis by precursor availability and nutritional state. Biochem. Pharmacol. **25:** 1691–1696.

117. HIRSCH, M. J. & R. J. WURTMAN. 1978. Lecithin consumption increases acetylcholine concentrations in rat brain and adrenal gland. Science **202:** 223–224.

118. JENDEN, D. J. 1979. The neurochemical basis of acetylcholine precursor loading as a therapeutic strategy. *In* Brain Acetylcholine and Neuropsychiatric Disease. K. L. Davies & P. A. Berger, Eds. Plenum. New York.

119. WURTMAN, R. J. 1979. Precursor control of transmitter synthesis. *In* Nutrition and the Brain. Vol. 5: Choline and Lecithin in Brain Disorders. A. Barbeau, J. H. Growdon & R. J. Wurtman, Eds. Raven Press. New York.

120. GROWDON, J. H. 1979. Neurotransmitter precursors in the diet: Their use in the treatment of brain diseases. *In* Nutrition and the Brain, Vol. 3: Disorders of Eating: Nutrients in Treatment of Brain Diseases. R. J. Wurtman & J. J. Wurtman, Eds. Raven Press. New York.

121. BARTUS, R. T., R. L. DEAN, S. JONES & K. SCHILL. 1985. The relevance of animal models to clinical memory assessment and drug development. *In* The Handbook of Clinical Memory Assessment of Older Adults. L. W. Poon, Ed. American Psychological Association. Washington, D.C.

122. BARTUS, R. T., R. L. DEAN & B. BEER. 1984. Cholinergic precursor therapy for geriatric cognition: Its past, its present and a question of its future. *In* Nutrition in Gerontology. J. M. Ordy, D. Harman & R. Alfin-Slater, Eds. Raven Press. New York.

123. PERRY, E. K., R. H. PERRY, B. E. TOMLINSON, G. BLESSED & P. H. GIBSON. 1980. Coenzyme A-acetylating enzymes in Alzheimer's disease: Possible cholinergic "compartment" of pyruvate dehydrogenase. Neurosci. Lett. **18:** 105–110.

124. BARTUS, R. T., R. L. DEAN, J. A. GOAS & A. S. LIPPA. 1980. Age-related changes in passive avoidance retention: Modulation with dietary choline. Science **209:** 301–303.

125. CHRISTIE, J. E., I. M. BLACKBURN, A. I. M. GLEN, S. ZEISEL, A. SHERING & C. M. YATES. 1979. Effects of choline and lecithin on CSF choline levels and on cognitive function in patients with presenile dementia of the Alzheimer type. *In* Nutrition and the Brain. Vol. 5. Choline and Lecithin in Brain Disorders. A. Barbeau, J. H. Growdon & R. J. Wurtman, Eds. Raven Press. New York.

126. LEVY, R., A. LITTLE, P. CHUAQUI & M. REITH. 1983. Early results from double blind,

placebo controlled trial of high dose phosphatidylcholine in Alzheimer's Disease. Lancet **1:** 987–988.

127. DAVIS, K. L., R. C. MOHS, J. R. TINKLENBERG, A. PFEFFERBAUM, L. E. HOLLISTER & B. S. KOPELL. 1978. Physostigmine: Improvement of long-term memory processes in normal humans. Science **20:** 272–274.

128. DRACHMAN, D. A. 1978. Central cholinergic system and memory. *In* Psychopharmacology: A Generation of Progress. M. A. Lipton, A. DiMascio & K. F. Killan, Eds. Raven Press. New York.

129. DRACHMAN, D. A. & B. J. SAHAKIAN. 1980. Memory and cognitive function in the elderly: Preliminary trial of physostigmine. Arch. Neurol. **37:** 383–385.

130. SMITH, C. M. & M. SWASH. 1979. Physostigmine in Alzheimer's disease. Lancet **1:** 42.

131. BARTUS, R. T. 1979. Physostigmine and recent memory: Effects in young and aged nonhuman primates. Science **206:** 1087–1089.

132. GOODNICK, P. & S. GERSHON. 1984. Chemotherapy of cognitive disorders in geriatric subjects. J. Clin. Psychiatry **45:** 196–209.

133. DAVIS, K. L. & R. C. MOHS. 1982. Enhancement of memory processes in Alzheimer's disease with multiple-dose intravenous physostigmine. Am. J. Psychiatry **139:** 1421–1424.

134. DAVIS, K. L., R. C. MOHS & J. R. TINKLENBERG. 1979. Enhancement of memory by physostigmine. N. Engl. J. Med. **301:** 946.

135. CHRISTIE, J. E., A. SHERING, J. FERGUSON & A. I. M. GLEN. 1981. Physostigmine and arecholine: Effects of intravenous infusions in Alzheimer's presenile dementia. Br. J. Psychiatry **138:** 46–50.

136. CHRISTIE, J. E. 1982. Physostigmine and arecholine infusions in Alzheimer's disease. *In* Alzheimer's Disease: A Report of Progress in Research. S. Corkin, K. L. Davis, J. H. Growdon, E. Usdin & R. J. Wurtman, Eds. Raven Press. New York.

137. THAL, L. J. & P. A. FULD. 1983. Memory enhancement with oral physostigmine in Alzheimer's disease. N. Eng. J. Med. **308:** 720.

138. JOTKOWITZ, S. 1983. Lack of clinical efficacy of chronic oral physostigmine in Alzheimer's disease. Ann. Neurol. **14:** 690–691.

139. BARTUS, R. T., R. L. DEAN & B. BEER. 1980. Memory deficits in aged Cebus monkeys and facilitation with central cholinomimetics. Neurobiol. Aging **1:** 145–152.

140. BARTUS, R. T., R. L. DEAN & B. BEER. 1983. An evaluation of drugs for improving memory in aged monkeys: Implications for clinical trials in humans. Psychopharm. Bull. **19:** 168–184.

141. PERRY, R. H., J. M. CANDY, E. K. PERRY, D. IRVING, G. BLESSED, A. F. FAIRBAIRN & B. E. TOMLINSON. 1982. Extensive loss of choline acetyltransferase activity is not reflected by neuronal loss in the nucleus of Meynert in Alzheimer's disease. Neurosci. Lett. **33:** 311–315.

142. PEARSON, R. C. A., M. V. SOFRONIEW, A. C. CUELLO, T. P. S. POWELL, F. ECKENSTEIN, M. M. ESIRI & G. K. WILCOCK. 1983. Persistence of cholinergic neurons in the basal nucleus in a brain with senile dementia of the Alzheimer's type demonstrated by immunohistochemical staining for choline acetyltransferase. Brain Res. **289:** 375–379.

143. NAKANO, I. & A. HIRANO. 1984. Parkinson's disease: Neuron loss in the nucleus basalis without concomitant Alzheimer's disease. Ann. Neurol. **15:** 415–418.

144. UHL, G. R., D. C. HILT, J. C. HEDREEN, P. J. WHITEHOUSE & D. L. PRICE. 1983. Pick's disease (lobar sclerosis): Depletion of neurons in the nucleus basalis of Meynert. Neurology **33:** 1470–1473.

145. TAGLIAVINI, F., G. PILLERI, C. BOURAS & J. CONSTANTINIDIS. 1984. The basal nucleus of Meynert in patients with progressive supranuclear palsy. Neurosci. Lett. **44:** 37–42.

146. GIBSON, G. E. & C. PETERSON. 1983. Pharmacologic models of age-related deficits. *In* Assessment in Geriatric Psychopharmacology. Mark Powley Associates. New Canaan, CT. T. Crook, S. H. Ferris & R. T. Bartus, Eds.

147. PETERSON, C. & G. E. GIBSON. 1983. Amelioration of age-related neurochemical and behavioral deficits by 3,4-diaminopyridine. Neurobiol. Aging **4:** 25–30.

148. DAVIS, H. P., A. IDOWU & G. E. GIBSON. 1983. Improvement of 8-arm maze performance in aged Fischer 344 rats with 3,4-diaminopyridine. Exp. Aging Res. **9:** 211–214.

149. WESSLING, H., S. AGOSTON, G. B. P. VAN DAM, J. PASMA, D. J. DEWITT & H. HAVINGA. 1984. Effects of 4-aminopyridine in elderly patients with Alzheimer's disease. N. Eng. J. Med. **310:** 988–989.

150. BARTUS, R. T., R. L. DEAN, K. A. SHERMAN, E. FRIEDMAN & B. BEER. 1981. Profound effects of combining choline and piracetam on memory enhancement and cholinergic function in aged rats. Neurobiol. Aging **2:** 105–111.

151. FLOOD, J. F., G. E. SMITH & A. CHERKIN. 1982. Memory retention: Potentiation of cholinergic drug combinations in mice. Neurobiol. Aging **4:** 37–43.

152. POMARA, N., R. BLOCK, J. ABRAHAM, E. F. DOMINO & S. GERSHON. 1983. Combined cholinergic precursor treatment and dihydroergotoxine mesylate in Alzheimer's disease. IRCS Med. Sci. **11:** 1048–1049.

153. FERRIS, S. H., B. REISBERG, E. FRIEDMAN, M. K. SCHNECK, K. A. SHERMAN, P. MIR & R. T. BARTUS. 1982. Combination choline/piracetam treatment of senile dementia. Psychopharm. Bull. **18:** 94–98.

154. FRIEDMAN, E., K. A. SHERMAN, S. H. FERRIS, B. REISBERG, R. T. BARTUS & M. K. SCHNECK. 1981. Clinical response to choline plus piracetam in senile dementia: Relation to red cell choline levels. N. Eng. J. Med. **304:** 1490–1491.

155. SERBY, M., J. CORWIN, J. ROTROSEN, S. H. FERRIS, B. REISBERG, E. FRIEDMAN, K. A. SHERMAN, B. JORDAN & R. T. BARTUS. 1983. Lecithin and piracetam in Alzheimer's disease. Psychopharm. Bull. **19:** 126–129.

157. SMITH, R. C., G. VROULIS, R. JOHNSON & R. MORGAN. 1984. Comparison of therapeutic response to long-term treatment with lecithin versus piracetam plus lecithin in patients with Alzheimer's disease. Psychopharm. Bull. **20:** 542–545.

158. GROWDON, J., S. CORKIN & F. J. HUFF. 1984. Alzheimer's disease: Treatment with nootropic drugs. Proc. Third Meeting Int. Study Group on the Treatment of Memory Disorders Associated with Aging. R. J. Wurtman, S. Corkin & J. H. Growdon, Eds. Zurich.

159. PETERS, B. H. & H. S. LEVIN. 1979. Effects of physostigmine and lecithin on memory in Alzheimer's disease. Ann. Neurol. **6:** 219–221.

160. PETERS, B. J. & J. S. LEVIN. 1982. Chronic oral physostigmine and lecithin administration in memory disorders of aging. *In* Alzheimer's Disease: A Report of Progress. S. Corkin, K. L. Davis, J. H. Growdon, E. Usdin & R. J. Wurtman, Eds. Raven Press. New York.

161. BLESSED, G., B. E. TOMLINSON & M. ROTH. 1968. The association between quantitative measures of dementia and of senile change in the cerebral grey matter of elderly subjects. Br. J. Psychiat. **114:** 797–811.

162. BOWEN, D. M. 1981. Alzheimer's disease. *In* The Molecular Basis of Neuropathology. A. N. Davison & R. N. S. Thompson, Eds. Edward Arnold. London.

163. BARTUS, R. T., C. FLICKER & R. L. DEAN. 1983. Logical principles for the development of animal models of age-related memory impairments. *In* Assessment in Geriatric Psychopharmacology. T. Crook, S. Ferris & R. T. Bartus, Eds. Mark Powley Associates. New Canaan, CT.

164. OLTON, D. S. 1985. Criteria for establishing and evaluating animal models. Ann. N.Y. Acad. Sci. This volume.

165. BARTUS, R. T., R. L. DEAN, C. FLICKER & B. BEER. 1983. Behavioral and pharmacological studies using animal models of aging: Implications for studying and treating dementia of Alzheimer's type. Banbury Report. Vol. 15.

166. BARTUS, R. T. & R. L. DEAN. 1981. Age related memory loss and drug therapy: Possible directions based on animal models. *In* Brain Neurotransmitters and Receptors in Aging and Age-Related Disorders. S. J. Enna, T. Samorajski & B. Beer, Eds. Raven Press. New York.

167. BARTUS, R. T., R. L. DEAN & B. BEER. 1983. An evaluation of drugs for improving memory in aged monkeys: Implications for clinical trials in humans. Psychopharm. Bull. **19:** 168–184.

168. CRAPPER, D. R. & A. J. DALTON. 1972. Alterations in short-term retention, conditioned

avoidance response acquisition and motivation following aluminum induced neurofibrillary degeneration. Physiol. Behav. **10:** 925–932.

169. CRAPPER, D. R. & A. J. DALTON. 1973. Aluminum induced neurofibrillary degeneration, brain electrical activity and alteration in acquisition and retention. Physiol. Behav. **10:** 935–945.

170. KLATZO, I., H. WISNIEWSKI & E. STREICHER. 1965. Experimental production of neurofibrillary degeneration. J. Neuropath Exp. Neurol. **24:** 187–199.

171. WISHIEWSKI, H. M., M. E. BRUCE & H. FRASER. 1975. Infection etiology of neuritic (senile) plaques in mice. Science **190:** 1108–1110.

172. LASHLEY, K. S. 1929. Brain Mechanisms and Intelligence: A Quantitative Study of Injuries to the Brain. University of Chicago Press. Chicago, IL.

173. FINGER, S. & D. G. STEIN. 1982. Brain Damage and Recovery: Research and Clinical Perspectives. Academic Press. New York.

174. LEVERE, T. E. 1980. Recovery of function after brain damage: A theory of the behavioral deficit. Physiol. Psychol. **8:** 297–308.

175. AIGNER, T., J. AGGLETON, S. MITCHELL, D. PRICE, M. DELONG & M. MISKIN. 1983. Effects of scopolamine on recognition memory in monkeys after ibotenic and acid injections into the nucleus basalis of Meynert. Neurosci. Abst. **9:** 826.

176. PERRY, E. K., B. E. TOMLINSON, G. BLESSED, K. BERGMANN, P. H. GIBSON & R. H. PERRY. 1978. Correlation of cholinergic abnormalities with senile plaques and mental test scores in senile dementia. Br. Med. J. **2:** 1457–1459.

177. BARTUS, R. T. 1978. Aging in the Rhesus monkey: Specific behavioral impairments and effects of pharmacological intervention. *In* Recent Advances in Gerontology. H. Orimo, K. Shimada, M. Iriki & D. Maeda, Eds. Excerpta Medica. Amsterdam.

Models of Memory Dysfunctions

HERBERT WEINGARTNER

Cognitive Studies
National Institute of Mental Health
Bethesda, Maryland 20205

INTRODUCTION

The major theme of this paper is to explore and contrast different types of cognitive dysfunctions in humans. After summarizing the varieties of cognitive dysfunctions, which are apparent in man, examples of pharmacological and behavioral models of disordered cognition are presented. The major point that is made, in outline form, is that distinct psychobiological mechanisms may account for the different forms of memory dysfunctions. Such a position is supported not only on the bases of clinical studies, but cognitive experiments in unimpaired subjects, and from empirical studies of cognitive-like behaviors in lower animals which presumably model forms of memory failure. Defining a psychobiology of cognitive failure requires a research approach that would permit mapping of changes in distinct cognitive processes onto biological systems defined in terms of neuroanatomical and neurochemical features.[1]

Impairments in memory are associated with many psychiatric, neurological, and behavioral syndromes. Although differences in the expression of the cognitive changes in various disorders are apparent on clinical examination, experimental analyses of cognitive failures have often missed the major differentiating features of disturbances in higher mental functions.[2] This may be due to the fact that neuropsychological research is frequently driven more by methodology (cognitive assay) and a favored theoretical heurism, than an attempt to understand the differentiated nature of impaired cognition in some disease. For example, most experimental studies of cognitively impaired patients have been almost exclusively concerned with discerning the presence and severity of failures in recent memory and learning (episodic memory). This has also been the primary target response of interest in studies testing whether some treatment facilitates cognition. The most frequent question in such studies has been whether recently acquired information is remembered more accurately following some treatment. However, if we are to further our understanding of the psychobiological determinants of the varieties of memory pathologies, we must systematically ask questions about aspects of cognition that may not be reflected in the degree of success or failure in memory-learning performance. Assuming that all memory or cognitive failures are the same distorts both what we know about cognition and the specificity of the neuropathology of central nervous system disorders.

The paper begins with an outline of the varieties of cognitive dysfunctions that have resultant impairments in recent or episodic memory in common. Recent studies from several laboratories, as well as current National Institute of Mental Health research, suggest that different cognitive impairments, which may result in superficially similar disturbances in recent memory, are attributable to very different psychobiological mechanisms. Parallel findings are presented that describe how different drugs (and behavioral manipulations) can disrupt cognitive functions (memory) in distinct ways, thus modeling some of the memory impairments evident in a variety of clinical syndromes. All of these findings support the conclusion that memory and related mental functions are highly differentiated and are made up of distinct, identifiable, and specific psychobiological processes. This position is defined and reviewed in greater detail elsewhere.[1-3]

VARIETIES OF MEMORY-LEARNING FAILURES

Anterograde Memory Impairments

The most extensively and intensively studied type of memory dysfunction in humans, as well as in lower animals, is one that is most dramatically expressed as anterograde memory-learning.[4] Korsakoff's disease patients typify this form of memory impairment. The hippocampus, mammillary bodies, fornix, and medial dorsal nucleus of the thalamus are just some of the structures that may play a role in this type of memory impairment.[5-9] Generally, amnestic patients are relatively impaired under those conditions that are dependent upon episodic (recent) memory processes. Patients with this type of memory disturbance can, however, often learn and then "remember" skills without being able to appreciate the circumstances under which that learning had taken place.[10-12] Their ability to learn procedures but not "recall" having learned them may be because these patients demonstrate an ability to access and use previously acquired knowledge and skills despite profound impairments in recent memory.[3]

Episodic Memory Failures Linked to Impairments in the Use of Knowledge and Skills

The typical example of this type of memory impairment is seen in the progressive dementias, such as of an Alzheimer's type (SDAT). Patients with this form of memory impairment demonstrate a wide variety of other cognitive dysfunctions that become progressively more severe in close association with impairments in recent memory.[13] SDAT patients demonstrate cognitive loss in language functions, learning procedures, attention, encoding, processing information automatically, and use of previously acquired knowledge, including well-established skills (apraxies).[14,15] These cognitive dysfunctions are as profound as recent learning and memory impairments and these dysfunctions appear to vary together. Treatments that enhance recent memory functions appear to be mediated by changes in accessability of previously acquired knowledge and cognitive skills.[16,17]

Impairments in Effort (Cognitive Capacity) Demanding Processes

Some cognitive processes are more effort-demanding, requiring more control and cognitive capacity than other processes (automatic operations). The conceptual view of these processes has evolved from studies of unimpaired subjects.[18-20] Depressed patients and early stage Parkinson's disease patients demonstrate cognitive failures on tasks that demand effort and considerable cognitive capacity. A number of studies have shown that the degree to which effort-demanding cognitive functions are impaired is related to the intensity of disturbed mood[21] and the cognitive operations that are most disrupted in these patients are those that require "motivation," sustained effort, and cognitive capacity. Processes that require little cognitive capacity and can be accomplished equally well with or without "intention" (automatic tasks) are relatively unimpaired in depression.[22] A similar pattern of cognitive changes is seen in Parkinson's disease patients.[23] Selective impairments in effort or cognitive capacity-demanding processes have also been used to reconceptualize the nature of the cognitive impairment in schizophrenia.[24] Learned helplessness models of depressive behaviors serve to provide a behavioral framework that accounts for this pattern of cognitive dysfunctions.[25] The biological mechanisms that determine effort-demanding cognitive processes may involve the same brain systems that mediate brain self stimulation and reward.[26]

Encoding-Rehearsal Dysfunctions

Defining characteristics of episodic learning-memory functions in terms of a levels or elaborateness of processing approach has been a popular heuristic device first in the study of unimpaired subjects[27] and then later as an explanation for memory impairments in a variety of neuropsychiatric disorders.[28] The logic of this analysis of impairments in learning-memory processes is that they are linked to failures in encoding operations. Memory fails because of some type of defective encoding-rehearsal operation (non-specific cognitive function). Amnestic patients, depressed patients, learning disabled children, and schizophrenic patients, are some of the types of patients whose cognitive impairment has been described in this way. Critiques of this position have emphasized the circularity in design and explanation for encoding failure leading to memory failure.

Attentional Dysfunctions

A number of forms of learning-memory impairments in children have been attributed to disturbances in attention. Studies of the hyperactivity syndrome in children and other childhood disorders have attempted to link genetic, neurochemical, and electrophysiological changes with clinically relevant alterations in behavior. One of the more frequently studied behavioral consequences of these heterogeneous childhood disorders are cognitive impairments. Disorders of attention and attentional processes appear to play a prominent role in accounting for the cognitive changes seen in many of these children.[29] Attentional problems are, in fact, so prominent that in the most recent classification of psychiatric-neuropsychiatric and behavioral disorders, the designation of hyperactivity disorder has been renamed an attentional disorder.

Stimulus and Process Specific Cognitive Dysfunctions

Studies of patients with lateralized brain lesions have historically served as a basis for examining and dissociating lateralized cognitive operations. A variety of cognitive and sensory-perceptual processes appear to be lateralized, in some form, in the brain. Processing of language information, pattern information, emotion, sequential versus parallel processing, and "gestalt" versus analytic or detailed processing are but a few of the processes that have been considered to be mediated by somewhat distinct and lateralized brain systems. This type of analysis of cognitive failure has been used to describe not only cognitive failures associated with focal brain lesions but also the cognitive changes in a variety of more diffusely defined brain syndromes.

Cognitive Impairments Without Subjective Awareness

Some patients with non-dominant hemisphere lesions and some amnestic patients demonstrate cognitive impairments without an appreciation of their deficits. It would appear that these patients are unable to appreciate and perhaps encode the presence or expression of their deficit, which can involve sensory, perceptual-motor-memory, mood, or generalized cognitive dysfunctions. This lack of awareness of obvious deficits is often so pervasive and complete that it is not easily explained on the basis of a dynamic explanation involving a form of denial of illness. Dissociations of knowing how from knowing that, or stated another way, being able to perform some "learned" behavior but not remember having learned it may be another variation of this type of cognitive dysfunction.[30,31] Patients with non-dominant hemisphere lesions demonstrate a similar phenomenon. These patients are unable to link the fact of a cognitive dysfunction with the biographical and subjective experience of that dysfunction.

Failures in Memory Consolidation

Theories and models that rely on the concept of memory consolidation to account for aspects of memory-learning processes have been used almost exclusively in considering findings in animals other than humans.[32] The reasons for not using memory consolidation concepts in describing characteristics of human information processing have been that such research efforts were less concerned with biological phenomena and avoided concepts that are not easily defined operationally. Nevertheless, several types of changes in memory and learning in humans (e.g., following electroconvulsive therapy, acute effects of ethanol) appear to be best explained by emphasizing the role of post processing biological events in determining whether some event will be maintained (and elaborated) in memory.[33] One recently conceptualized function that may be part of memory consolidation processes is the continuous updating and cataloging of information represented in memory.[34] That is, memory consolidation processes may take place over an extended period of time long after an initial acquisition phase of learning is completed. A number of other types of memory failure, including amnestic syndromes, have also been described in terms of disruptions in memory consolidation.

Retrieval Failures

Some forms of memory failure appear to occur because retrieval strategies used to access memory are inconsistent with the encoding strategies used to organize information at the time of learning. When this occurs, memory representations for recent events may be available in memory but inaccessible. Providing subjects with appropriate retrieval schemas reverses this type of memory failure. State-specific encoding and retrieval operations and resultant memory failure have been associated with various drug states including ethanol, marijuana, and cholinergic drugs, as well as mood states.[35,36]

MODELS OF TYPES OF COGNITIVE DYSFUNCTIONS

Criterion of a model of a syndrome with prominent impairments in memory must include features that distinguish that form of cognitive failure from the pattern of memory impairments evident in other disorders. Distinctive features should include aspects of both cognitive and non-cognitive behaviors that are linked to that memory failure. This presumes measurement and scaling of different kinds of cognitive processes that are associated with test conditions that disrupt memory and presumably model a disorder. The heuristic value of a model of some cognitive impairment rests upon the critical and distinctive features of similarity and contrasting effects seen in different component cognitive domains.

The Benzodiazepine Receptor—Modeling Anterograde Amnesia

Numerous studies have demonstrated that benzodiazepines can disrupt aspects of cognition.[37-41] Generally, the choice of documentation of cognitive changes produced by this class of drugs tends to be based upon a psychometric tradition rather than methods of analysis derived from some cognitive theoretical framework.

In a recently completed experiment (Hommer, Wolkowitz, and Weingartner, in preparation), an attempt was made to map changes in specific cognitive domains, in response to a neuropharmacological treatment that would alter activity of the benzodiazephine receptor. The study was designed to provide a picture of the ways in which various aspects of cognition might be differentially disrupted with increasing doses of diazepam administered to ten young healthy normal volunteers. The drug was administered intravenously in increasing doses over a period of two hours. The methods used to define the cognitive response to this drug treatment had previously been tested and validated in a series of clinical and neuropharmacological studies of cognitive functions. The methods that were available allowed us to compare, contrast, and dissect the psychobiologically distinct aspects of the cognitive response to increasing doses of valium treatment. The resultant distinct pattern of cognitive changes would then be compared to different types of memory impairments seen in neurological disorders.

Subjects were first familiarized with and then practiced on all of the procedures used in the experiment. Only after learning to learn effects were eliminated were subjects administered placebo followed by increasing doses of diazepam. We were particularly interested in comparing the relative effects of diazepam, at different doses in terms of the following cognitive processes: attention and vigilance, episodic memory processes, automatic cognitive operations, and access to previously acquired knowledge.

Normal volunteers experienced numerous physiological and behavioral changes in response to diazepam treatment. Subjectively, they experienced and reported many changes in their behavior with increasing doses of drug treatment (e.g., mood and alertness), and these changes were confirmed by a variety of laboratory tests. The efficiency or effectiveness of much of their cognitive behavior was disrupted with increasing doses of diazepam. There was also a very close relationship ($r = .93$, $p < .001$) between changes in their rated subjective experience of the drug (assessed using standardized rating scales) and their ability to learn and remember new information.

Also apparent was the highly differentiated unfolding in impairment in components of cognition with increasing doses of diazepam. Not all aspects of cognition were equally disrupted or sensitive to the effects of diazepam. While attention-vigilance, memory for information that requires effort-demanding processing, and memory for information acquired automatically were all disrupted and were comparably sensitive to drug effects, access to knowledge memory remained relatively intact even at the highest doses of diazepam tested in this experiment.

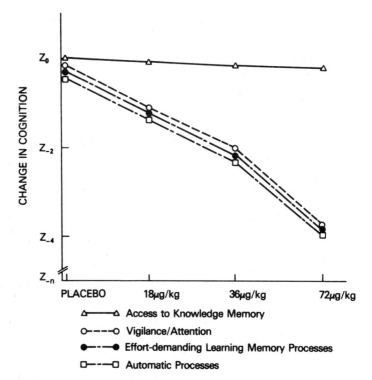

FIGURE 1. Models of cognitive failure (I). Benzodiazepine receptor blockade simulates antero-grade amnesia.

These findings are summarized in FIGURE 1, which displays contrasting changes from the mean baseline-placebo performance in terms of the same unit of analysis expressed as a change in each cognitive domain based upon standard errors of the mean. This pattern of data represents a close fit to the features of the cognitive impairment evident in many forms of anterograde amnesia.

Incomplete Encoding Operations and Consequent Memory Failures

A number of manipulations can produce encoding failures that then result in impaired learning and memory. This type of model of memory failure does require some evidence that information that has been poorly encoded has nevertheless been attended. It also assumes that it is possible to dissociate operations that define completeness of encoding and memory performance.

A great deal of experimental data is available in support of this type of model of memory failures. These experiments have demonstrated that when subjects superficially, rather than elaborately, process events they are less likely to remember them. These experimental findings have served as empirical bases for encoding or single-trace theories of memory in contrast to multiple-trace theories of memory.[27-42] The effectiveness of encoding can be manipulated not only on the bases of the types of operations subjects perform in attending to information but the time they have available to consider and rehearse information. Rapid processing conditions produce effects on memory performance that are similar to those that occur following the use of weak encoding operations. Rapid processing conditions also have particularly powerful effects in disrupting memory for difficult-to-encode events. That is, information that is inherently more difficult to encode, such as words that cannot easily be imaged, is more likely not to be recalled under rapid processing conditions than information that is more readily encodable, e.g., concrete, imageable words. Presenting items once rather than several times similarly alters the degree to which that item has been encoded in memory, and therefore, the likelihood with which it is recalled. In general, the cognitive consequences of incomplete encoding are most evident under more demanding memory test conditions such as free recall, rather than recognition memory, or in selecting between similar events that did and did not occur as opposed to tests of recognition memory requiring discrimination between old and new items which are very different.

A manipulation (disruption) of encoding processes in unimpaired subjects, such as when forcing them to process information very rapidly, produces impairments in memory that resemble many of the features of the cognitive dysfunctions associated with some types of neuropsychiatric disorders.[43,44] It is, however, not a good model for the types of cognitive-memory dysfunctions, such as Alzheimer's disease. These findings are presented in summary form in FIGURE 2.

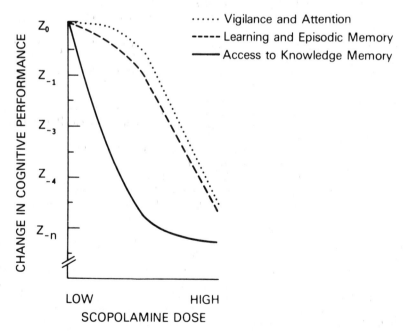

FIGURE 2. Models of cognitive failure (II). Cholinergic antagonist scopolamine models dementia-like memory disorder.

Cholinergic Neuron

It is well established that the cholinergic antagonists disrupt memory functions.[45-49] What is less clear are the unique or distinctive features of such changes in learning-memory functions and cognition.

In reviewing previous studies of changes in cognitive behavior that follow cholinergic antagonist treatment it would appear that access to previously acquired knowledge is compromised along with impairments in recent memory.[50] Preliminary findings from a study presently under way at the National Institute of Mental Health appear to confirm this pattern of cognitive changes in response to increasing doses of scopolamine. The design of the experiment was similar to that used in the study of the role of the diazepam receptor in cognition. In this experiment Sunderland, Tariot, Mueller, Murphy, Cohen, and Weingartner investigated the relative selective cognitively impairing effects of different doses of a cholinergic antagonist (scopolamine) in normal volunteers as well as in SDAT patients. The question posed was, when cognitive changes do appear, which aspects of cognition are likely to change the most and perhaps determine alterations and disruptions in other cognitive behaviors?

Subjects were tested under placebo and under several scopolamine conditions using a variety of cognitive measures. Different doses of scopolamine (0.1, 0.25, and 0.5 mg) were administered intravenously in a double-blind, placebo-controlled, random order crossover design with at least two no-test days occurring between treatment days. On each test day cognitive and behavioral changes were monitored at regular intervals starting before drug or placebo infusion and lasting for a period of hours after drug administration.

The observed impairments in cognitive behavior were not at all like the pattern of cognitive changes seen following diazepam treatment (described above). Access to knowledge memory was particularly sensitive to change in response to scopolamine treatment and change in that domain was linked to changes in episodic memory. This was particularly evident in SDAT patients tested. Even on gross clinical examination (as assessed by our rating scales) it was clear that scopolamine had a particularly powerful effect in disrupting access to previously acquired knowledge as measured by the speech production (in SDAT patients; $p < .001$). The expected physiological response to cholinergic antagonist treatment (e.g., dry mouth, drowsiness, pupil changes, $p < .05$) were also evident. These findings, along with those from previous studies are illustrated in FIGURE 3.

Despite heroic research efforts cognitivists still disagree on how to describe and account for aspects of cognition in humans and in lower animals. Not only do they disagree about the value of the many available theories and models but they also differ in their preference for methods of approach and the perceived relevance of different types of data. All kinds of processes have been proposed as useful descriptors of different aspects of human cognition. For example, dozens of conceptual schemas are currently used to account for only one aspect of cognition, episodic learning, and memory, (recent, context, and sequence dependent memory). Some of these conceptual models have considered episodic memory processes as made up of stages such as sensory processing, working memory, short term and long term memory, memory consolidation, retrieval, and so on. Other concepts have stressed the importance of types of processes or operations that are used in short or long term memory, attentional processes, retention, rehearsal, retrieval operations, working memory, effort (cognitive capacity-demanding processes and cognitive operations that can be performed automatically)—this represents only a partial list of concepts that have served to account for episodic memory. Each of these stages, processes, or operations may or may not have a psychobiological life of its own. Additional concepts have been used to describe and account for operations and processes associated with other cognitive domains, such as concept formation, maintenance of set and selective attention, learning of motor skills, pattern processing, language processing, the use of logic, and the use of previously acquired knowledge. Given the immensity and uncertainty associated with cognitive research it is not surprising that, historically, cognitivists have attempted to simplify and restrict the nature of research. This has meant narrowing research focus by ignoring whole domains of cognitive phenomena. For most cognitive psychologists this has meant either a complete dissociation from the study of clinical and neuropharmacological phenomena or an occasional excursion into the territory of clinical phenomena with the limited goal of obtaining furthering support for some favored

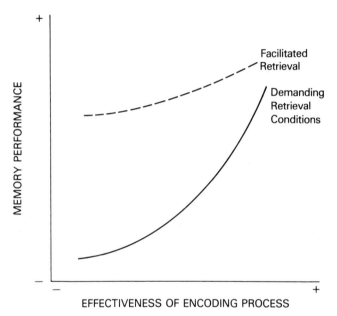

FIGURE 3. Models of cognitive failure (III). Encoding operations determine memory performance. Encoding dysfunctions produce weak, difficult-to-access memory traces.

information processing theory. This last position obviously severely limits what can be learned about cognition from the study of disorders of cognition.

In fact, it is quite clear that a systematic examination of cognitive changes associated with different neuropsychiatric disorders provides an important source of information about the differentiated nature of cognitive processes. Similar pictures emerge in the study of the kinds of cognitive responses that are evident following drug treatments that selectively alter the activity of differentiated aggregates of neurons. It is the mapping of different cognitive systems onto differentiated neurobiological systems upon which we will be able to base viable theories of a psychobiology of cognition. This, in turn will provide us with better diagnostic tools and new directions for treating cognitive disorders.

REFERENCES

1. WEINGARTNER, H. 1984. *In* Neuropsychology of Memory. 203–212. Gulford Press. New York.
2. WEINGARTNER, H. 1985. A psychobiological analysis of cognitive failures: structure and mechanisms. Arch. Gen. Psychiat. (In press.)
3. WEINGARTNER, H., J. GRAFMAN, W. BOUTELLE, W. KAYE & P. MARTIN. 1983. Forms of memory failure. Science 221(4610): 380–382.
4. WHITTY, C. W. M. & O. L. ZANGWILL, Eds. 1977. Amnesia. Butterworths. London.
5. MILNER, B. 1970. Memory and the medial temporal regions of the brain. *In* Biology of Memory. K. H. Pribram & D. E. Broadbent, Eds.: 29–50. Academic Press. New York.
6. MISHKIN, M. 1978. Memory in monkeys severely impaired by combined but not by separate removal of amygdala and hippocampus. Nature 273: 297–298.
7. VICTOR, M., R. D. ADAMS & G. H. COLLINS. 1971. The Wernicke-Korsakoff Syndrome. Blackwell. Oxford University Press. London.
8. WARRINGTON, E. K. & L. WEISKRANTZ. 1973. The Physiological Basis of Memory. L. A. Deutsch, Ed. Academic Press. New York.
9. WARRINGTON, E. K. & L. WEISKRANTZ. 1982. Neuropsychologia 20: 233–248.
10. COHEN, N. J. & L. R. SQUIRE. 1980. Preserved learning and retention of pattern-analyzing skill in amnesia: Dissociation of knowing how and knowing that. Science 210: 207–210.
11. CORKIN, S. 1968. Acquisition of motor skill after bilateral medial temporal-lobe excision. Neuropsychologica 6: 255–266.
12. HUPPERT, F. A. & M. PIERCY. 1978. Dissociation between learning and remembering in organic amnesia. Nature 275: 317–318.
13. CUMMINGS, J. L. & D. F. BENSON. 1983. Dementia: A Clinical Approach. Butterworths. Boston.
14. WEINGARTNER, H., W. KAYE, S. A. SMALLBERG, M. EBERT, J. C. GILLIN & N. SITARAM. 1981. Memory failures in progressive idiopathic dementia. J. Abnorm. Psychol. 90(3): 187–196.
15. WEINGARTNER, H. 1985. Automatic and effort demanding cognitive processes in depression: A model for distinguishing types of impairments in information processing. Larry Poon, Ed. In Edited Volume of George Talland Conference, 1984. Handbook for Clinical Memory Assessment of Older Adults. American Psychological Association.
16. WEINGARTNER, H., W. KAYE, P. GOLD, S. SMALLBERG, R. PETTERSON, J. C. GILLIN & M. EBERT. 1981. Vasopressin treatment of cognitive dysfunction in progressive dementia. Life Sci. 29: 2721–2726.
17. WEINGARTNER, H., P. W. GOLD, J. C. BALLENGER, S. A. SMALLBERG, R. M. POST & F. K. GOODWIN. 1981. Effects of vasopressin on memory. Science 211: 601–603.
18. ATKINSON, R. C. & R. M. SHIFFRIN. 1968. Human memory: A proposed system and its control processes. Adv. Theory Res. 211: 601–603.
19. HASHER, L. & R. T. ZACKS. 1979. Automatic and effortful processes in memory. J. Exp. Psychol. Gen. 108(3): 356–388.
20. ZACKS, R. T., L. HASHER & H. SANFT. 1982. Automatic encoding of event frequency: Further findings. J. Exp. Psychol. 8(2): 106–116.
21. COHEN, R. M., H. WEINGARTNER, S. SMALLBERG & D. L. MURPHY. 1982. Effort in cognitive processes in depression. Arch. Gen. Psychiat. 39: 593–597.
22. WEINGARTNER, H., W. KAYE, S. SMALLBERG, R. COHEN, M. H. EBERT, J. C. GILLIN & P. GOLD. 1985. Determinants of memory failures in dementia. *In* Alzheimer's Disease: A Review of Progress. S. Corkin, Ed. Vol. 19. Raven Press. New York.
23. WEINGARTNER, H., S. BURNS, R. DIEBEL & P. A. LEWITT. 1984. Cognitive impairments in Parkinson's Disease: Distinguishing between effort-demanding and automatic cognitive processes. Psychiatry Res. 11: 223–235.
24. GJERDE, P. F. 1983. Attentional capacity dysfunction and arousal in schizophrenia. Psychol. Bull. 93: 57–72.
25. WEINGARTNER, H. & E. SILBERMAN. 1984. *In* Neurobiology of Mood Disorders. B. Post & J. Ballenger, Eds. Williams and Wilkins. Baltimore, MD.
26. ESPOSOTO, R. U., E. S. PARKER & H. WEINGARTNER. 1985. Enkephalinergic-dopaminergic

reward pathways: A critical substrate for the stimulatory, euphoric and memory enhancing actions of alochol? Substance and Alcohol Actions and Misuses. (In press.)

27. CRAIK, F. I. M. & E. TULVING. 1975. Depth of processing and the retention of words in episodic memory. J. Exp. Psychol. Gen. 1: 268–294.

28. BUTTERS, N. & L. S. CERMAK. 1980. Alcoholic Korsakoff's Syndrome. Academic Press. New York.

29. ROSENTHAL, R. H. & T. W. ALLEN. 1978. An examination of attention, arousal, and learning dysfunctions of hyperkinetic children. Psychol. Bull. 85(4): 689–715.

30. JACOBY, L. C. & M. DALLAS. 1981. On the relationship between autobiographical memory and perceptual learning. J. Exp. Psychol. Gen. 110(3): 306–340.

31. JACOBY, L. L. & D. WITHERSPOON. 1982. Remembering without awareness. Can. J. Psychol. 36: 300–324.

32. MCGAUGH, J. C. & M. J. HERZ. 1972. Memory Consolidation. Albion. San Francisco, CA.

33. WEINGARTNER, H. & E. S. PARKER, Eds. 1985. Memory Consolidation. Lawrence Erlbaum Associates Press. Hillside, NJ. (In press.)

34. MILLER, R. R. & N. A. MARLIN. 1985. The physiology and semantics of consolidation. In Memory Consolidation. H. Weingartner & E. Parker, Eds. Lawrence Erlbaum Associates Press. Hillsdale, NJ. (In press.)

35. OVERTON, D. A. 1974. Experimental methods for the study of state-dependent learning. Fed. Proc. 33: 1800–1813.

36. WEINGARTNER, H. 1978. In Drug Discrimination and State Dependent Learning. D.W. Richards & D. C. Chute, Eds.: 361–382.

37. BROWN, J., M. BROWN & J. BOWES. 1983. Effects of lorazepam on rate of forgetting, on retrieval from semantic memory and on manual dexterity. Neuropsychologia 21(5): 501–512.

38. BROWN, J., V. LEWIS, M. BROWN, G. HORN & J. B. BOWES. 1982. A comparison between transient amnesias induced by two drugs (diazepam or lorazepam) and amnesia of organic origin. Neuropsychologia 20(1): 55–70.

39. FILE, S. E. & R. C. LISTER. 1982. Do Lorazepam-induced deficits in learning result from impaired rehearsal, reduced motivation or increased sedation? Br. J. Clin. Pharmac. 14: 545–550.

40. CLARK, E. O., M. GLANZER & H. TURNDORF. 1979. The pattern of memory loss resulting from intravenously administered diazepam. Arch. Neurol. 36: 296–300.

41. HINRICHS, J. V., S. P. MEWALDT, M. M. GHONHEIM & J. L. BERIE. 1982. Diazepam and learning: assessment of acquisition deficits. Pharmacol. Biochem. Behav. 17: 165–170.

42. TULVING, E. & M. J. WATKINS. 1975. Structure of memory traces. Psychol. Bull. 82: 261–275.

43. WEINGARTNER, H., E. D. CAINE & M. EBERT. 1979. Encoding processes, learning and recall in Huntington's Disease. Adv. Neurol. 23: 215–226.

44. WEINGARTNER, H., E. D. CAINE & M. H. EBERT. 1979. Imagery, encoding and the retrieval of information from memory: Some specific encoding-retrieval changes in Huntington's disease. J. Abnorm. Psychol. 8: 52–58.

45. DRACHMAN, D. A. & J. LEAVITT. 1974. Human memory and the cholinergic system. Arch. Neurol. 30: 113–121.

46. DUNN, A. J. 1980. Neurochemistry of learning and memory: An evaluation of recent data. Ann. Rev. Psychol. 18: 343–390.

47. BARTUS, R. T., R. L. DEAN, B. BEER & A. S. LIPPA. 1982. The cholinergic hypothesis of geriatric memory dysfunction. Science 217: 408–417.

48. DAVIS, K. L., R. C. MOHS, J. R. TINKLENBERG, A. PFEFFERBAUM, L. E. HOLLISTER & B. S. KOPELL. 1978. Science 201: 272.

49. SITARAM, N., H. WEINGARTNER & J. C. GILLIN. 1978. Science 201: 274.

50. CAINE, E. D., H. WEINGARTNER, C. L. LUDLOW & E. A. CUDAHY. 1981. Qualitative analysis of scopolamine-induced amnesia. Psychopharmacology 74: 74–80.

Animal Behavioral Models
in the Discovery of Compounds
To Treat Memory Dysfunction

ELKAN GAMZU[a]

Department of Pharmacology
Hoffmann-LaRoche, Inc.
Nutley, New Jersey 07110

This paper describes a pragmatic approach to the discovery of new chemical agents to treat memory dysfunctions that focuses on the use of animal behavioral tests to predict clinical utility. It is independent of any theoretical assumptions about disease states or specific pharmacological mechanisms of drug action. It is not in any way mutually exclusive of the more mechanistic approaches to the study of pharmacological alleviation of memory dysfunction that are described in other contributions to this volume. On the contrary, this approach is often applied in conjunction with one or more mechanistic approaches. Nevertheless, the pragmatic approach, based purely on animal behavior, can stand on its own as a legitimate strategy for the discovery of memory protective compounds.

First, it is necessary to define the goals of this approach. In most general terms, the application of memory-enhancing drugs has been targeted toward disease states that are most broadly described as cognitive disorders or dementias. It is important to note this terminology because although memory loss is the most prominent feature of dementias,[1] these disorders encompass impairments in many other processes as well. Furthermore, since the goal of such research is to develop drugs to treat clinical manifestations of certain disease states, it is not essential for a drug to have demonstrable effects on memory for it to be useful in a clinical setting. It is conceivable, for example, that a compound could have a salutary effect on attention or motivation, thereby ameliorating cognitive loss and so be a very useful compound. Thus, it is crucial to retain the perspective that clinical utility is the ultimate criterion of the success of preclinical prediction.

A list of some potential target diseases for drugs of this type (FIGURE 1) illustrates the point. Some of these result from specific lesions, but others are less clearly defined with respect to etiology. Three important points are immediately obvious from the figure. The first is that cognitive impairment is not restricted to any particular portion of the human life span. Secondly, it is quite obvious that there is no common etiology in this set of disorders. Indeed, in some cases there is no known etiology. Thirdly, the only common feature that these disease states share is a cognitive manifestation, characterized by a loss in learning and memory ability. Since these functional losses can only be studied in the intact animal, animal behavioral models are of paramount importance. On the other hand, a clear limitation of this approach to the development of pharmacological agents for the treatment of cognitive dysfunction is that it focuses on amelioration of symptoms rather than on the cause of the disease state. For example,

[a]Present address: Clinical Research Department, Warner Lambert Company, 2800 Plymouth Road, Ann Arbor, MI 48105.

prevention of the viral etiology of Jakob-Creutzfeld disease is clearly more important in treating and preventing that disease than is the amelioration of the cognitive symptoms. However, in the absence of well-defined etiology for the most common of these disease states (Alzheimer's, senile dementia, dyslexia, Multi-infarct dementia, and hyperkinesis), animal behavioral research is essential.

The prevalence of some of these disease states is shown in TABLE 1. Minimal brain dysfunction (also known as attention deficit disorder or hyperkinesis) is estimated to be a major problem for between three and ten percent of all young members of society, with the incidence being greater in males than females. Moreover, up to 30 percent of

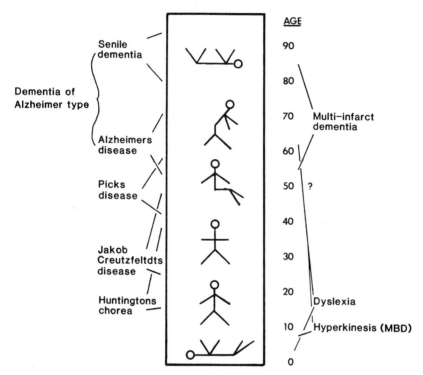

FIGURE 1. Cognitive disorders and dementias as a function of age (Adapted from Gottfries. *Trends in Neurosciences*. 1980. **3:** 55–77.)

these people will continue to have cognitive difficulties throughout life. Dyslexia is a disorder detectable in young children and characterized by problems with reading and writing. The theory that specific reading retardation (i.e., dyslexia not attributable to low intellectual or general ability) is related to deficits in working memory has been recently reviewed by Jorm.[2] According to the Department of Health, Education, and Welfare, 15 percent of all children have some form of dyslexia, and, according to the Dyslexia Society, 20 percent of all adults are dyslexic. Of disease states that usually occur later in life, the American Heart Association claims that there are over 500,000 new survivors of stroke per year, with the number of survivors being 1.8 million in 1979. Estimates of senile dementia and/or Alzheimer's dementia vary considerably.[3,4]

TABLE 1. Cognitive Disorders and Medical Needs[a]

	Young	Adult	Aged
Minimal brain dysfunction (attention-deficit hyperkinesis)	3–10% ♂ > ♀	15–30% of young MBD cases continue through life	
Dyslexia	15% of all children (HEW)	20% of all adults (Dyslexia Society)	
Stroke			169,000/year deaths 500,000 new survivors/ year 1.8 million survivors (1979) (AHA)
Senile dementia			1.5–4 million
Alzheimers			all dementias

[a]Incidence of selected cognitive disorders in the United States.
Note: The author thanks Sharon O'Neil of Roche Marketing Research for help in compiling these data.

The table lists a range that is probably quite conservative. Clearly, the need exists for agents to treat the symptoms of these disorders, while a better understanding of the etiology and prevention remain the ultimate goals.

With these facts in mind we can now turn to some of the principles that should guide the use of animal models in the area of memory dysfunction. These principles derive from the historically successful use of animal models in psychopharmacology in general. First of all, it is important to demonstrate pharmacological specificity of a given test. That is, those compounds that are clinically active in treating memory dysfunctions should be active in the behavioral tests, while compounds of other pharmacological classes (such as antidepressants, anxiolytics, etc.) should be inactive. A second important principle is to show behavioral specificity; active compounds should affect the target behavior (reflecting memory) but not other non-specific behaviors. Ideally, one should be able to measure at least two types of behavior concomitantly, one relevant and one irrelevant. An example of the type of animal testing that achieves this goal can be found in the conflict models for the discovery and study of anxiolytic agents.[5] These are procedures in which suppressed lever pressing alternates with unsuppressed lever pressing. Antianxiety agents, at selected doses, specifically release the suppressed behavior while having minimal or no effects on the unpunished behavior. In general, this degree of behavioral specificity is seldom obtained in most paradigms used in studies of learning and memory. Most investigators have used independent tests to demonstrate that compounds with claimed memory-enhancing properties do not affect other central nervous system functions. Tasks such as the repeated-acquisition procedure of Thompson and Moerschbaecher[6] and the delayed match-to-sample[7] come close to meeting this criterion by containing components to differentiate learning or memory from performance variables.

A major obstacle to rapid advancement in this field is the absence of any clinically defined standards. Thus, although we expect to see pharmacological specificity, it is not easy to agree on a clinically effective standard. In human studies, some compounds have been shown to enhance learning or memory. These include physostigmine,[8] vasopressin,[9,10] and some ACTH/MSH[11,12] peptides. However, these compounds are not practical as clinical agents because of their side-effect liability. In the United States, Hydergine (a mixture of ergot alkaloids) is the only compound that is available for treatment of "confusional states in the elderly."[13] The clinical efficacy of this compound has been reviewed a number of times, and while it does not appear to produce outstanding clinical benefits, there is sufficient evidence to warrant its continued use.[14] The other two compounds that are used in the U.S. to treat cognitive disorders are methylphenidate and pemoline, both psychostimulants and both used to treat minimal brain dysfunction in children.[13] In contrast, in other parts of the world a variety of other compounds are available.[15] Some of these are shown in FIGURE 2. Among these are centrophenoxine (also known as meclofenoxate), naftidrofuryl, vincamine (and a variety of related vinca alkaloids), and many compounds containing the 2-pyrrolidinone moiety, such as piracetam, aniracetam, etc. The compounds are often referred to as "nootropics," a term that was first coined by Cornel Giurgea in 1967.[16] It derives from the Greek words *noos* (meaning mind) and *tropein* (toward) and was originally applied to piracetam. Although used freely to describe the 2-pyrrolidinone-containing compounds, recent usage is much broader.[17] Giurgea and Salama[18] suggested that any compound that enhances learning, protects against learning impairment or brain insult, and has low toxicity qualifies as a nootropic. The 2-pyrrolidinones are particularly safe and can be given in gram quantities without any adverse effect.[15] Among their most reliable features is the ability to block the disruptive effects of hypoxia on a variety of different CNS functions including learning and memory in sub-human species.[18] However, a recent review of the clinical data on reversal of memory dysfunctions indicates that the effectiveness of the agents is equivocal.[19] Despite the difficulty in showing efficacy in Alzheimer's disease,[20,21] piracetam has been shown to improve performance in dyslexics[22-27] and in normal college students.[28] It is not entirely clear whether the absence of substantial clinical efficacy is due to the lack of a pharmacological effect or to the fact that careful and sensitive techniques of clinical measurement of improved cognitive function are still in

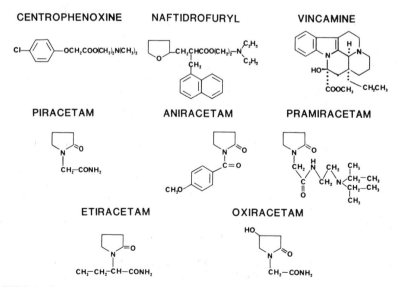

FIGURE 2. Selected nootropic compounds either in clinical investigation or in clinical use outside the USA.

the development stage. Regardless, since there is some clinical evidence of memory enhancement by nootropics, it is mandatory that any animal behavioral test that purports to measure learning or memory effects of drugs show sensitivity to at least some of the agents shown in FIGURE 2. Given the equivocal clinical findings, it seems unreasonable to require that the behavioral tests show activity with all of these agents.

In the clinical studies in which piracetam was effective, it was administered over a fairly prolonged treatment period prior to measurement of the clinical effect. Therefore, it is not unreasonable to assume that chronic treatment is necessary for an effect to be manifest. In contrast, most behavioral tests use either acute or rather short treatment periods to evaluate compounds. This is especially true in the search for new drugs, where it is often necessary to look at a large number of compounds in order to find the most promising agent. This problem of acute testing in animals versus chronic application for clinical efficacy is not unique to the area of learning and memory dysfunction. It also remains a major problem in the discovery and development of new antidepressant agents.

STRATEGIES

At this point we can now consider the two global strategies that have been employed to develop animal models for the discovery of compounds to treat memory dysfunctions (TABLE 2). The first major strategy is to study the effects of drugs in normal animals. In this most obvious approach, the goal is to find compounds that enhance an animal's rate of learning or its ability to remember a new response. There are two major assumptions to this type of research. The first is that the behavior of normal animals can be improved by pharmacological manipulation. Although this seems like a reasonable approach, in some sense it is asking if we can "improve upon evolution." The second, and more crucial assumption that is seldom explicitly stated, is that a compound useful in enhancing the learning and/or memory of a normal organism will also be beneficial to patients whose performance is less than optimal. Despite the absence of any verification of these two assumptions, the nootropic agents piracetam[16,29–31] and etiracetam[32,33] have been shown to improve the acquisition of water-maze and Y-maze escape/avoidance and retention of various responses in normal rodents. However, there have been failures to enhance the learning/memory of normal animals using these procedures,[34,35] although for obvious reasons only few are published. Overall, this strategy has not been very successful, but it has recently been employed in the discovery of 3-phenoxypyridine, CI-844,[36] a compound currently in clinical testing.

The more successful global strategy is depicted in the center and right hand columns of TABLE 2 and can be described as attempting to look at pharmacological effects on performance under deficit conditions. This particular approach more closely parallels the concept of designing an animal model of the disease state and trying to alleviate it. However, as pointed out above, the etiology of many cognitive disorders is unknown. From a practical perspective, there are many manipulations that will interfere with learning and/or memory. Consequently, a variety of different disruptors has been employed and has been successfully overcome by compounds of the pyrrolidinone class.

For convenience, the deficits can be considered to be in two different categories. The first is that of naturally occurring deficits. The most obvious of these are the changes in memory that accompany the aging process. This particular approach has been very adequately covered[8,37] and will only be touched on here. This tactic has the obvious advantage of face validity. Although there are similarities between deficits in memory in older animals and the deficits that are seen in Alzheimer's disease, it is less clear that such deficits in older animals necessarily parallel the types of memory loss in other dementias. Furthermore, Alzheimer's patients are qualitatively distinct from their age-matched cohorts in mnemonic ability. While aged rodents and primates have poorer mnemonic ability than younger members of their respective species, this is not universally the case.[38] In a recent study, we found that naive middle-aged rats were considerably poorer in learning and remembering a serial spatial discrimination reversal (SSDR) than young rats.[39] In one of our recent studies we compared experimentally naive and experimentally experienced middle-aged rats to young naive rats in the same test. We were able to confirm that 18-month-old naive rats did not do as well as 2-month-old naive rats in terms of number of errors and error elimination (FIGURE 3). However, 18-month-old animals with previous experience in the test at 12 months of age performed equivalently to naive younger animals. Not only does this show that the age deficit is not simply one of memory, but it also indicates that older rodents, while showing impairments in initial exposures to such a task, can retain the information learned in that task for over a six month period—a considerable time in the life span of this particular species. Moreover, the SSDR test has been shown to be sensitive to lesions of the magnocellular nuclei of the basal forebrain (the rodent equivalent to the nucleus basalis of Meynert).[40,41]

TABLE 2. Strategies for Studying Pharmacological Enhancement or Protection of Learning and/or Memory in Animals

	Deficits	
Normals	Naturally Occurring	Induced
Assume sub-optimal	Old animals	CNS specific lesions
Assume if compound is active in normals, can be useful in patients.	Genetic strain	Hypoxia/anoxia
	"Poor learners"	Electrical disruption
	Temporal (?)	Pharmacological
		Ischemia

Reservations about the use of older animals are not designed to impugn the research that has rather exquisitely shown age-related impairments. Certainly, pharmacological enhancement of such behavior has led to important theoretical developments.[42] Indeed, piracetam has been shown to improve slightly the retention of passive avoidance in aged rats[43] and was "remarkably more active in improving" the acquisition of two-way shuttle avoidance in aged mice as compared to its effects in young mice.[44] However, some caution is warranted in interpreting apparent "memory" effects in aged animals.

A second type of natural deficit can be seen in certain genetic strains. As an example we tested spontaneously hypertensive (SH) rats and their Wistar Kyoto (WK) normotensive genetic controls.[45] SH rats have been shown to have low levels of vitamin E in the central nervous system.[46] Since vitamin E is an important antioxidant, it was interesting to compare the two strains on a variety of different learning and memory procedures. The results obtained in training the rats to make ten nose-poke responses for each pellet of food (FR10) are shown in FIGURE 4. The SH rats were superior to their genetic controls. However, the values obtained from SH rats were similar to the values obtained from control Sprague-Dawley CD1 rats in other experiments. In contrast, the WK normotensive rats learned more slowly than CD1

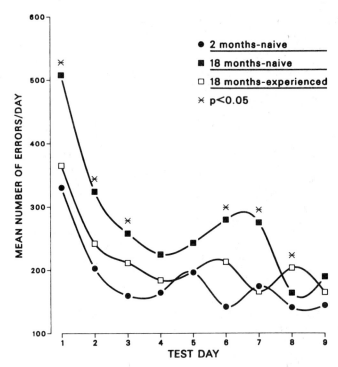

FIGURE 3. Acquisition of a serial spatial discrimination (SSDR) in Charles River CD rats of different ages. Each daily session consisted of 14 components and took place in a Coulbourn modular cage with two recessed food troughs. The rat had to break a photobeam in the food trough four times to receive a food pellet (FR4). Each component lasted until five reinforcements were obtained or 10 minutes had elapsed. The "correct" and "incorrect" responses (i.e., left or right) alternated between components without any stimulus. There were breaks in testing of 5 and 8 days between sessions 3 and 4 and between sessions 4 and 5, respectively. Statistical significance of the mean number of errors in the two 18-month-old groups for each day was compared to that of the 2-month-old rats by means of a Dunnett t-test for multiple comparsions.

control rats and may represent an interesting strain for pharmacological studies. Although the use of genetic strains has not yet been employed in the pharmacological discovery process, genetic manipulations have been used effectively and extensively by Quinn and his colleagues[47] to study memory in the blow-fly. The availability of genetic strains of rodents that appear to have specific learning disabilities[48,49] will no doubt have an effect on the discovery process.

A third naturally occurring deficit is one listed in TABLE 2 under the rubric of "poor learners." We have recently been making use of the finding that about 5 to 8 percent of mice fail to learn a basic response during preliminary avoidance training. A schematic of the equipment and procedure is shown in FIGURE 5. These "poor learners" fail to escape from shock on any of the five morning training trials. Compounds are administered immediately after the last trial of the afternoon training session. Testing occurs without any drug treatment 24 hours later. As can be seen in FIGURE 6, aniracetam dose-dependently facilitates consolidation in these mice. Moreover, a variety of control experiments[50] has indicated that this effect is only obtained in this subset of "poor learners." A number of additional points need to be made. The first is that the enhanced performance occurs some 24 hours after drug administration, but does not reach the mean level of "normal" mice. Secondly, piracetam was inactive in this test, as was physostigmine. Thirdly, while this subset of mice is clearly distinguishable from the rest of the population with respect to this specific behavioral task, we cannot make any statement about their general "learning ability" until additional characterizing studies have been completed. Given the history of the equipment-specific ability of the genetically selected Tryon maze-bright and maze-dull rats,[51] it seems prudent to be cautious in extrapolating these results.

The final category under naturally occurring deficits is entitled "temporal?" The reason for the question mark is not to indicate a doubt as to whether temporal manipulations do induce deficits. They clearly do and there are many examples of their use in this volume. Rather, the use of the question mark is to indicate some doubt as to whether the use of temporal manipulations to produce lower levels of memory performance should be considered a deficit or whether it should be under the category of study of normal animals. For some this may seem simply a semantic difference, but it depends on whether one's theory and philosophy of the memory process stress that the loss of information over time is a passive or active process. Without espousing a particular theory of memory loss over time, it is at least reasonable to subsume the use

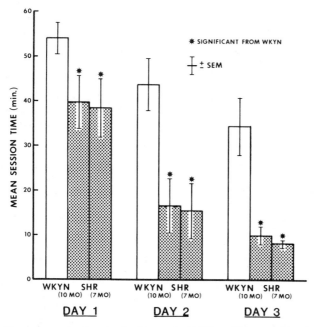

FIGURE 4. The mean session duration for 10-month-old Wistar-Kyoto normotensive (WKYN) rats, 10-month-old spontaneously hypertensive rats (SHR), and 7-month-old SH rats to acquire a nose-poke response into a single food trough as described for Figure 3. Rats could obtain a total of 50 reinforcements by an escalating schedule of a fixed number of responses (FR) for each food pellet. The last 10 reinforcements required an FR10. For each daily session (maximum duration 60 minutes), the mean time for the SH rats to complete the session was compared to the mean time of the WKYN rats using a Dunnett t-test for multiple comparisons with $p < 0.05$.

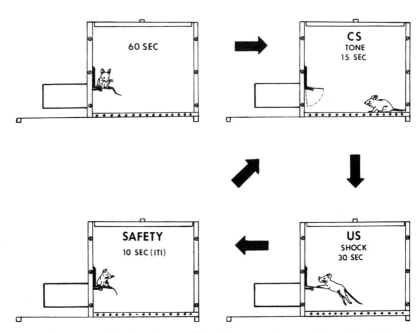

FIGURE 5. Automated platform-jump avoidance/escape equipment and procedure. Naive mice are placed on the platform for one minute prior to the initiation of a series of 5 or 10 trials. At the beginning of each trial, a tone (CS) is sounded and the platform retracted, dropping the mouse to the grid floor. The CS continues for 15 seconds and is followed by 1.3 mA footshock for 30 seconds. The mouse can avoid or escape the shock by jumping onto the platform. A 10-second safety period intervenes between shock termination and the onset of the next trial. Each mouse receives two 5-trial training sessions approximately 4 hours apart, one in the morning and one in the afternoon. Approximately 24 hours later, the mice receive a 10-trial testing session.

of temporal manipulations under the rubric of deficit conditions. The use of delayed recall has been in existence almost as long as memory has been studied[52] and will not be reviewed here. However, it is important to emphasize the utility of this manipulation in terms of studying pharmacological and physiological effects on performance. Because memory can be normal with a zero delay and show a significant disruption with a longer delay,[53,54] it is at least possible in some situations to indicate that an animal has in fact acquired information but simply cannot retain it over a longer period of time. This is not a trivial point since under certain circumstances, and this is especially true of the so-called amnesia produced by scopolamine, it is not always clear that the animals have actually learned the task in question, as opposed to having learned and then forgotten it.[55,56] An example of how the use of different temporal manipulations can prove fruitful in showing the memory-enhancing properties of pyrrolidinones is shown in FIGURE 7. In these studies[57] squirrel monkeys were trained on a delayed match-to-sample task. Having responded to a sample stimulus, the monkeys are required to match the memory of that sample stimulus to one of three test stimuli. A crucial element of the task is the amount of time elapsing from the initial presentation of the stimulus to be matched until the presentation of the three choice stimuli. As can be seen in FIGURE 7, an optimal dose of aniracetam can selectively improve performance at those long delays that by themselves result in a "memory deficit." The beneficial effects of aniracetam on delayed match-to-sample have been independently replicated in a second primate species.[58]

It is clear that naturally occurring deficits are a useful baseline on which to assess the potential of compounds that might alleviate memory dysfunction. In many of these procedures, nootropics improve performance only where a deficit occurs, but not in normal young adult animals performing under optimal conditions. These facts confirm the general impression that the strategy of trying to improve the learning and/or memory of normal animals may not be as fruitful as the use of animals under deficit conditions. One can draw an analogy to the effects of aspirin on temperature. In normal organisms it is difficult to show aspirin's hypothermic effect, which is easily obtainable in organisms with elevated temperature.

The second major category of deficits are those that are induced by the experimenter. The number and type of such induced deficits is limited only by the experimenter's ingenuity and theoretical breadth. We have chosen to focus on a few of these because of their relevance to nootropic drugs.

The first category is that of CNS-specific lesions. There are many examples in this volume of lesions to specific loci in the brain that produce clear deficits in learning and/or memory. However, to the best of my knowledge, there are no publications on the use of these procedures to discover or develop new therapeutic agents. One less specific model that has been used to verify activity is the use of methylazoxymethanol (MAM). When injected into pregnant female rats at the appropriate doses and gestational period, this antimitotic substance results in offspring that are microce-

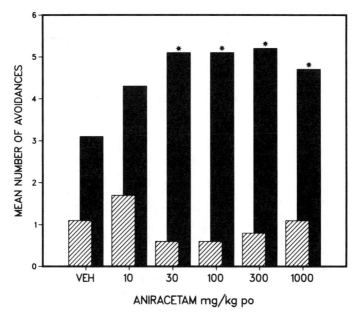

FIGURE 6. Aniracetam dose-dependently facilitates memory consolidation in "poor-learning" mice. The striped bars show the mean number of avoidance responses for the various groups during the afternoon 5-trial training session. Aniracetam or vehicle were administered *per os* immediately following this session. The solid bars show the mean number of avoidance responses for the various groups when tested approximately 24 hours later.

ANIRACETAM

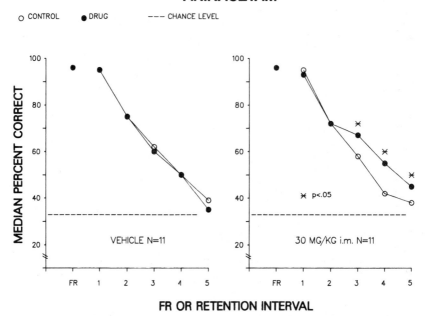

FIGURE 7. Effects of vehicle and 30 mg/kg i.m. aniracetam (corrected for vehicle) on three choice matching-to-sample in squirrel monkeys. Each trial of the procedure (100 trials/session) consisted of a simultaneous matching component (requiring two consecutive correct responses [FR2]) followed by a delay (i.e., retention) response component. Five different retention intervals (0–152 sec) were selected for each animal to generate control retention curves ranging from near perfect to chance (33%). The first retention interval was 0 seconds for all animals, with the absolute value of the longer retention intervals being a function of each individual animal's performance.

phalic. With judicious choice of dose, the animals appear relatively normal, both behaviorally (although they are more active) and in terms of growth. Nonetheless, they are not as proficient as normal offspring in learning certain responses.[59,60] Giurgea and colleagues demonstrated that treatment of such offspring with piracetam restored their ability to learn a passive avoidance to the level of offspring of vehicle-treated dams.[61]

Probably the most common technique for inducing disruption is hypoxia/anoxia. Although failures to replicate some of the piracetam effects have been reported,[30,34,35] there seems to be agreement that the most pronounced and reliable effect of nootropic compounds is their ability to protect against a variety of electrophysiological, behavioral, and other disruptions of the CNS that can be produced by exposure to low levels of oxygen.[18] Thus, from the early piracetam work of Giurgea and his colleagues using hypoxia to induce EEG changes[62] and to disrupt learning and memory,[16] to more recent usages to assess peptides[42,63] and new nootropics,[17,64] protection against hypoxic disruption of learning and memory continues to be a very useful procedure. This should not be terribly surprising since it has been known for some time that hypoxia severely disrupts the cognitive ability of humans.[65] Indeed, hypoxia produces biochemical effects that are similar to those seen in aging and there may well be a parallel between these effects and cognitive deficits.[66]

Another procedure that has been employed rather extensively is electrical stimulation, either of specific brain regions or more generally applied. It has, of course, been known for some time that electroconvulsive shock (ECS) produces a rather severe retrograde amnesia. This effect is well documented at the clinical level[67] and has been extensively studied on the animal level.[68] In his initial work, Giurgea employed reversal of amnesia to show the protective effect of piracetam. Although this phenomenon is not always replicated using piracetam,[30,64] variations have been employed to demonstrate efficacy of both aniracetam[64] and pramiracetam.[69]

Specific stimulation of the hippocampus was described by Poschel as a useful procedure in the discovery of compounds to treat memory dysfunction.[70] In this regard it is interesting to note that Olton and Wolf[71] have shown that hippocampal stimulation produces reversible deficits in radial arm maze performance that are equivalent to the irreversible deficits produced by lesions of various aspects of the hippocampus.[72]

Disruptions in retrieval seem to be the primary memory disorder in older patients[73] and are one of the two major sources of memory problems in Alzheimer's patients.[74] We have been employing a transcorneally administered non-convulsive electroshock to disrupt memory retrieval. In our initial work we used a one-way shuttle active avoidance procedure, in which mice were required to learn to move through a narrow aperture from a starting box into an identical chamber prior to the onset of a signalled shock.[75] On the following day, compounds were injected before a brief non-convulsant electrical brain-shock (EBS), which was administered five minutes prior to testing. This EBS resulted in a transient memory retrieval deficit. Control experiments indicated that it was not a motoric, analgesic, or global performance deficit, but relatively specific to memory retrieval since animals that were allowed to recover over a

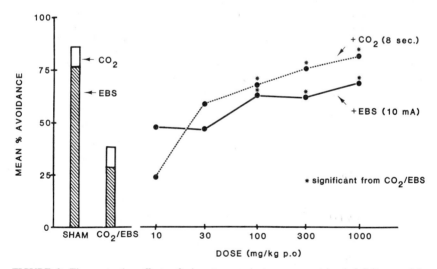

FIGURE 8. The protective effects of piracetam against memory-retrieval deficit caused by electrobrain-shock (EBS) or CO_2 hypoxia given five minutes prior to a 10-trial retention testing session of one-way shuttle avoidance in mice. All mice had received 10 trials of training the day before. Vehicle or piracetam were administered *per os* sixty minutes prior to testing. The bars represent the mean number of avoidances for the vehicle-treated groups that received either sham shock or normoxia, or EBS (200 msec train of 12 10-msec unipolar 10 mA pulses) or eight seconds of exposure to pure CO_2. All piracetam-treated groups received either EBS or CO_2.

period of half an hour would then perform normally. What was particularly exciting to us, at that time, was the fact that many of the standard nootropic agents could completely protect against this memory disruption, as is shown for piracetam in FIGURE 8. Also shown in FIGURE 8 is the ability of a brief period of hypoxia to produce an equivalent disruption of memory retrieval. Piracetam was equally effective in protecting against this hypoxic disruption. Furthermore, we found that other compounds with purported cognitive action including aniracetam, etiracetam, magnesium pemoline, naftidrofuryl, and vincamine were all effective to some extent in protecting against the EBS-disruption at one or more doses. Of the standard agents that we evaluated in that procedure, only Hydergine and oxiracetam were inactive. In contrast, compounds such as amphetamine, chlorpromazine, diazepam, and imipramine had no effect. Thus, the goal of pharmacologic specificity was achieved with this procedure.

We have subsequently developed an automated avoidance procedure that requires animals to jump onto a shelf in order to avoid or escape shock.[50,76] The equipment is the same as that shown in FIGURE 5 and the procedure is depicted in FIGURE 9. Since it has been designed to do so, this new automated procedure produced a baseline somewhat similar to the shuttle avoidance procedure. More important was the fact that the EBS produced similar deficits in both procedures, and the active compounds were equivalently effective in protecting against the effects of EBS in both procedures (FIGURE 10).

Thus, the nootropic agents can protect against memory retrieval deficits produced by either hypoxia or EBS and in procedures requiring different motor patterns, suggesting a fairly generalized effect of these compounds. FIGURE 10 also illustrates the inverted U-shaped dose-response function that is obtained in all preclinical demonstrations of pharmacologically improved learning or memory. This particular type of dose-response curve suggests that there should also be a "window" of activity at the clinical level, either side of which higher or lower doses will be ineffective. Consequently, choosing a dose of a compound to test at the clinical level can be a risky venture, especially in the absence of well-defined, broadly accepted clinical agents. Clearly a desirable feature of future agents will be a broader window of activity. We have now evaluated a large number of compounds in the automated procedure and continue to find overall activity of the standard agents as well as various peptides and other research compounds that have been shown to affect memory. As might be

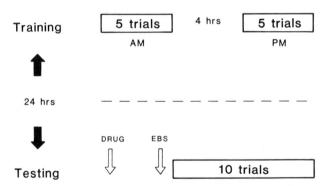

FIGURE 9. Procedure for producing EBS disruption of memory retrieval for a platform-jump avoidance response in mice. The equipment is as described in the FIGURE 2 legend. In this case, drug or vehicle is administered prior to the EBS manipulation that occurs 5 minutes before testing. EBS is administered transcorneally using the parameters described for FIGURE 7.

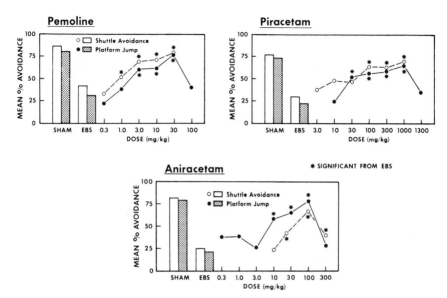

FIGURE 10. Aniracetam, piracetam, and pemoline protect against EBS disruption of memory retrieval for an avoidance response in mice. Mean number of avoidances out of a maximum of 10 in the one-way shuttle or platform-jump avoidance responses for control and drug-treated mice. See earlier figures and text for additional details.

expected, we have also found protective effects in a few compounds of non-nootropic pharmacological classes, but by and large, the nootropic agents are unique in their ability to consistently protect against this disruption in the absence of any general effects on behavior.

A further method that has been used to produce disruption in an effort to discover new agents is the injection of a variety of pharmacologically active drugs. The most commonly used of these is scopolamine because of its well-established history of producing memory deficits in animals and in human patients.[8] Protection against the disruptive effect of scopolamine on one-trial passive avoidance has been shown for aniracetam and piracetam,[64] as well as for newer compounds such as CAS 997 (a thienyl-piperazinone), HR 001 (a 1,5 benzodiazepine), and propentofylline.[17] The general use of a pharmacological disruption, however, is complicated by the fact that a variety of neurochemical systems have beem implicated in learning and memory. Thus, for example, in addition to the cholinergic hypothesis, this volume contains ample evidence of deficits of noradrenergic,[77,78] dopaminergic,[79] and serotonergic[80,81] systems being implicated in learning/memory. Thus, a wide variety of such manipulations is clearly available. The choice of a specific one seems to imply either a hypothesis about the disease state or the specific neurotransmitter that one is trying to effect. To the extent that the goal concerning the compound being developed is neurotransmitter-specific, then these procedures are useful. From the more pragmatic perspective taken in this paper, protection against as many pharmacological disruptors as possible is desirable.

The final category listed under deficit conditions is ischemia, presumably as a model for multi-infarct dementia. In some recent interesting experiments, Nicolaus[82] and Banfi et al.[83] have been able to demonstrate that treatment with oxiracetam prevented both the morphological and behavioral deficits seen in spontaneously hypertensive rats exposed to hypertonic saline over a pronounced period of time. In this case, the morphology can be described as being similar to that seen in multi-infarct dementia. Similarly, piracetam and CAS 997 partially reversed the deficit in passive avoidance produced by exposing gerbils to a short global ischemia.[17]

PERFORMANCE VARIABLES

In addition to the importance of strategy and tactics in the use of animal behavior to discover new agents, there are a number of important performance variables that have to be considered. In general, these represent confounding factors. A partial list of such general variables can be found in TABLE 3. A large number of authors have independently dealt with the necessity of ascertaining that the results one obtains when studying drugs is on the learning or memory process as opposed to a variety of alternate processes.[37,42,84] The problem was elegantly captured by Lynch and Baudry who stated that since "the integrated activity of primary, physiological, and behavioral processes is a necessary . . . condition for the occurrence of memory, any manipulation of these

TABLE 3. Potentially Confounding Performance Variables in Studies of Pharmacological Effects on Learning and/or Memory

Perception	Complexity
	Single trial/simple
Motivation	Choice
Positive (food etc.)	Strategies
Negative (shock etc.)	
Exploration	Process
	Acquisition
Required Behavior	Consolidation
Active	Retrieval
Passive	

processes will inevitably have an impact."[85] Thus, it is always desirable to rule out perceptual or motivational factors in interpreting drug effects. By and large, specific controls are not common in the literature of pharmacological enhancement of memory. Rather, the ability of a compound to affect a wide variety of cognitive behaviors in different procedures together with independent evidence of minimal effects on non-cognitive parameters has been taken as evidence that the compound affects underlying mnemonic processes.

Beyond the necessity of being aware of the possible mediation of performance effects through perceptual variables, it is immediately obvious that drug effects on motivation can alter peformance in ways that might be incorrectly attributed to effects on memory. Thus, it is desirable to show effects of a drug both on behavior that is mediated by positive reinforcement (e.g., the seeking out of food or water) as well on negative reinforcement (e.g., the avoidance of shock). Recently, Ivan Izquierdo has used habituation of exploratory behavior as one of the techniques for demonstrating the ability of opiate agonists and antagonists to interfere with and improve memory, respectively.[86] More important from the perspective of this paper is a series of experiments by Platel and Porsolt demonstrating that nootropic compounds enhance the habituation to a normal environment when administered immediately after the first exposure to that environment.[87]

To be considered as having memory-enhancing effects and to be eliminated as a "false positive" that merely affects locomotor activity, a compound must be active not only in behavioral tasks requiring that the animal perform an active response, but also in tasks requiring that the animal refrain from making a high probability response. An example of the latter, passive avoidance, is the most commonly used procedure for studying memory. The most common variation involves the brief exposure of an animal to a footshock. When tested sometime later (usually 24 hours), control animals tend to refrain from entering into the location in which the shock was administered. It is also possible to generate equivalent learning using a single-exposure to procedures employing appetitive motivation. However, these procedures are not equivalently sensitive to different amnesic treatments.[88,89] Moreover, the passive avoidance procedure is particularly sensitive to diurnal rhythms,[90] and any experimenter who has attempted to set up a passive avoidance procedure knows the difficulties of exactly replicating the findings of any published study. Nonetheless, by careful attention to parametric manipulations, studious use of limited time periods during the day, and use of appropriate control procedures,[91] a large number of investigators have employed the passive avoidance procedure to gain important insights into the pharmacological, as well as other neurobiological, aspects of learning and memory. It is intriguing that the well-known aphorism "once bitten, twice shy" captures the essence of the passive avoidance procedure. The very existence of such a saying suggests that the type of learning that occurs in the passive avoidance paradigm is in fact quite common in human experience. Moreover, the ease and rapidity with which one can conduct experiments using the passive avoidance technique guarantees its continued use for many years.

One can point out two limitations of the use of simple procedures employing active responding. TABLE 4 shows data collected in our laboratories on experiments in which a variety of different compounds were administered to rats prior to the acquisition of a simple lever press avoidance response.[92] It is immediately obvious that a variety of stimulants can induce an increase in avoidance responding. However, on the following day there is no residual evidence of this increase and more importantly, in all but one instance (CI-844, 3-phenoxypyridine), the dose at which the increase occurred was identical to the dose at which stimulation of motor behavior was obtained in an independent test. This type of erroneous "false positive" result can be avoided if one employs a choice procedure, such as an avoidance/escape requirement in a Y-maze. Using such procedures, it has been shown that stimulants, e.g., amphetamine, will dose-dependently increase avoidance, but have no effect on the accuracy of choice behavior.[93,94] In general, procedures that require an animal to make a choice are less likely to be affected by general CNS stimulation or depression. On the other hand, such procedures often require fairly extensive training and therefore are used in conjunction with procedures that employ simpler response requirements.

Certain procedures, such as the SSDR described earlier in this paper and the radial arm maze as described by Olton and Samuelson,[95] require that animals learn patterns of behavior that can be readily described by simple strategies (although the determination of whether the animals are actually using the strategies may require considerable additional experimentation). In the SSDR, the optimal strategy can be described as win-stick lost-shift, whereas in the radial arm maze, optimal strategy would be win-shift. Clearly, a compound's ability to enhance behavior requiring different types of strategies would suggest a more general utility in the clinical situation. In fact, it has been claimed that chronic treatment with pentoxifylline can improve learning of a spatial-maze[96] and that 3,4-diaminopyridine can improve working memory in the maze.[97] In both cases, this is only true for the lower levels of performance shown by aged rats. It has also been shown that naloxone can improve performance in the radial-arm maze, but only when the maze is placed in a novel environment.[98]

A parallel rodent model to the repeated acquisitions test in primates[6] has been developed.[99] However, compounds such as the ACTH analog Org 2766 and physostigmine that might have been expected to improve performance in this "learning to learn" task were either inactive or disrupted the behavior.[100]

Without espousing a particular theory, one can operationally define at least three processes necessary for learning and memory: acquisition, consolidation, and retrieval. Again, it is important for a compound to be active in procedures that reflect as many of

TABLE 4. The Effects of Various Compounds on Acquisition of a Lever-Press Avoidance Response in Male Charles River CDF Rats[a]

	Pretreatment (minutes)	Statistically Active Doses[b] (mg/kg)	Peak Effect % Change from Control	CMA SD200[c] (mg/kg) p.o.
d-amphetamine, p.o.	30	1,2	+336	1.0
Magnesium pemoline, p.o.	30	5,10,20	+233	10.3
Methylphenidate, p.o.	30	8	+173	3.8
Caffeine, p.o.	60	20,40,60	+147	19.4
Nicotine, p.o.	60	4	+170	55% increase at 2 and 4 mg/kg
Strychnine, p.o.	60	—	+22	—
3-Phenoxypyridine, i.p.	60	30	+362	48% decr. at 30 mg/kg
Vincamine, p.o.	60	sig. decrease	−78	38% decr. at 100 mg/kg
Naftidrofuryl, p.o.	60	—	+73	—
Centrophenoxine, p.o.	60	—	−62	—
Hydergine, p.o.	60	—	−22	—
Physostigmine, i.p.	5	—	−51	—
Carbamazepine, p.o.	60	—	+74	—
Piracetam, p.o.	120	—	+5	at 900 mg/kg: 119% increase at 15 min
Diphenylhydantoin, p.o.	60	—	−29	—
Aniracetam, p.o.	30–180	—	+53	—
MSH/ACTH 4–10, s.c.	30	—	−68	—

[a]Compounds were administered prior to a 60-trial session. Each trial began with the sounding of a tone (CS) for 15 seconds. This was followed by 15 seconds of 1.0 mA footshock applied to the grid. The rat could avoid or escape by pressing the lever which terminated both the CS and US. There was a 15-second intertrial interval. Rats were retested the following day without any drug administration.

[b]Confinement motor activity in CD-1 rats; stimulant dose required to increase activity by 200% above control levels.

[c]$p < 0.05$, one-tailed Dunnett t-test.

these processes as possible. Clearly, a number of the examples that have been cited are representative of one or more of these processes.

SUMMARY AND NEW DIRECTIONS

Although this review of the literature has been somewhat limited, it should be obvious to the reader by now that nootropics, especially the pyrrolidinone class of compounds (in particular, piracetam and aniracetam), are active in a wide variety of procedures. They improved the performance of normal animals or protected against a variety of disruptions of acquisition, consolidation, or retrieval processes. This is true in a number of species and for several motivational systems. Despite some disagreements in the literature, this represents a growing consensus, especially with respect to learning and memory under deficit conditions. This consensus is based on behavioral studies because the mechanism of action by which these compounds exert their beneficial effects on learning and memory is as yet unknown. There seems to be a general agreement that these compounds do not interact directly with any of the major neurotransmitter systems, although there has been some speculation about their indirect effects on both cholinergic[43,101–104] and GABAergic systems.[105,106] In the absence of a clear mechanism of action, the memory protective effects of these agents represent a major challenge to those neurobiologists and clinicians interested in dysfunctions of learning and memory. One can make an analogy to the early 1950s when chlorpromazine was shown to be an effective antipsychotic agent both clinically and ultimately preclinically. The existence of the compound had a major effect on both theories and treatment of schizophrenia. Similarly, in the 1960s the description of the pharmacology of benzodiazepines, both clinically and preclinically, stimulated research into the biological underpinnings of anxiety and its relief. In both cases, the importance of dopamine in schizophrenia and the very existence of a benzodiazepine receptor were not known. It does not seem unreasonable to speculate that the current situation might yield similarly fruitful insights. There does seem to exist a class of agents that have a protective effect against memory disruption without having any pronounced effects on other CNS functions or on primary neurotransmitter systems. A major effort to understand the mechanism by which this occurs should surely lead to greater insights into the integrative aspects of CNS function that underlie learning and memory.

At the same time, it is important to realize that the evidence for activity of this class of agents is primarily preclinical. An important future direction will entail a systematic evaluation of selected compounds in this class for their ability to protect against a variety of learning and memory dysfunctions as reflected in human disease states. The current emphasis on testing these compounds in Alzheimer's disease may result in an inappropriate evaluation of these compounds. While there can be no denying the social and economic importance of Alzheimer's disease, there is little in the preclinical literature to suggest that the compounds should be specifically targeted to that disease state. Rather, the compounds seem to have general effects on learning and memory function. As such, continued evaluation of other conditions characterized by cognitive disruption (e.g., dyslexia) may be just as fruitful. Another possibility would be the development of clinical models that parallel the animal models. Such a development would not necessarily be designed towards the introduction of a new clinical agent, but rather to ascertain whether the beneficial effects that are seen in the animal models generalize to the human situation and warrant continued study of the mechanism of action of these compounds.

The preclinical research done to data lacks any true analog of the common human disease states. This is a major limitation of the pragmatic approach described in this paper. Thus, while it is easy to criticize the emphasis on testing piracetam analogs in Alzheimer's disease, it is not so easy to point to the specific disease state in which those compounds should be evaluated. Clearly, the development of animal models that more accurately reflect human disease states is desirable. A major limitation in this regard is the absence of known etiologies for many of the disease states. However, the recent development of models such as the stroke-prone hypertensive rat and lesions of the nucleus basalis of Meynert do seem to be moving in that direction. Nonetheless, even in the area of lesions of the nucleus basalis, some caution is required. In our research, we have found that lesioned animals do in fact learn, albeit slowly, and other investigators have shown both behavioral recovery[91] and even biochemical recovery[107] over longer periods of time. The growing acceptance of multiple memory systems, which is a theme of many papers in this volume, is only recently being studied at the animal level. As progress is made along these lines, one can expect greater focus on pharmacological improvement of some, but not all, aspects of animal memory.

The research detailed herein indicates a growing interest and skill in testing strategies, tactics, and procedures for discovering and developing pharmacological agents that might treat memory dysfunction. To some extent this approach has been successful in delineating the pharmacological effects of nootropic compounds, especially the pyrrolidinones. Moreover, the existence of this behavioral pharmacological strategy can now be applied to more mechanistic approaches towards disease states. Parallel developments in the clinical assessment of memory dysfunction and its pharmacological alleviation, together with a close interaction between these two developing sciences, suggest that considerable progress in understanding the basic problems of memory dysfunctions and their treatment will occur in the years ahead.

ACKNOWLEDGMENT

A number of colleagues and collaborators have had major influences on the development of the ideas in this chapter, the conduct of the experiments, and the quality and clarity of the manuscript. I thank Ed Boff, Elias Schwam, Jerry Sepinwall, John Sullivan, Tony Verderese, and George Vincent. I thank Domenica Iannicelli for her excellent preparation of this paper and especially for her most important role in the organization of the conference.

REFERENCES

1. AMERICAN PSYCHIATRIC ASSOCIATION. 1980. Diagnostic and Statistical Manual of Mental Disorders. 3rd edit. American Psychiatric Association. Washington, D.C.
2. JORM, A. F. 1983. Specific reading retardation and working memory: A review. Br. J. Psychol. 74: 311–342.
3. REISBERG, B. 1981. Brain Failure: An Introduction to Current Concepts of Senility. Free Press. New York.
4. REISBERG, B. 1983. An overview of current concepts of Alzheimer's disease, senile dementia, and age-associated cognitive decline. In Alzheimer's Disease. B. Reisberg, Ed.: 3–20. Free Press. New York.
5. SEPINWALL, J. 1984. Behavioral effects of antianxiety agents: Possible mechanisms of action. In Behavioral Pharmacology of Psychotropic Agents. L. S. Seiden & R. L. Balster, Eds. Alan R. Liss, Inc. New York.
6. THOMPSON, D. M. & J. M. MOERSCHBAECHER. 1979. An experimental analysis of the effects of d-amphetamine and cocaine on the acquisition and performance of response chains in monkeys. J. Exp. Anal. Behav. 32: 433–444.
7. SCHWAM, E., A. KUEHN, L. RUMENNIK & J. SEPINWALL. 1984. Cholinergic mechanisms of short-term memory in the squirrel monkey. Fed. Proc. 43: 504.
8. BARTUS, R. T., R. L. DEAN, M. J. PONTECORVO & C. FLICKER. 1985. The cholinergic hypothesis: A historical overview, current perspective, and future directions. Ann. N.Y. Acad. Sci. (This volume.)
9. WEINGARTNER, H., P. GOLD, J. C. BALLENGER, S. A. SMALLBERG, R. SUMMERS, D. R. RUBIMOW, R. M. POST & F. K. GOODWIN. 1981. Effects of vasopressin on human memory functions. Science 211: 601–603.

10. FERRIS, S. H. 1983. Neuropeptides in the treatment of Alzheimer's disease. *In* Alzheimer's Disease. B. Reisberg, Ed.: 369–373. Free Press. New York.
11. FERRIS, S., B. REISBERG, & S. GERSHON. 1980. Neuropeptide modulation of cognition and memory in humans. *In* Aging in the 1980s: Selected Issues in the Psychology of Aging. L. W. Poon. Ed. American Psychological Association. Washington, D.C.
12. PIGACHE, R. M. & H. RIGTER. 1981. Effects of peptides related to ACTH on mood and vigilance in man. *In* Frontiers of Hormone Research. T. van Wimersma Greidanus & L. H. Rees, Eds. Vol. 8. S. Karger. Basel.
13. Physicians' Desk Reference. 1984. Medical Economics Company, Inc. Oradell, NJ.
14. REISBERG, B., S. FERRIS & S. GERSHON. 1981. An overview of pharmacologic treatment of cognitive decline in the aged. Am. J. Psychiatry **138**: 593–600.
15. Martindale The Extra Pharmacopoeia. 1982. Twenty-Eighth Edition. The Pharmaceutical Press. London.
16. GIURGEA, C. 1976. Piracetam: Nootropic pharmacology of neurointegrative activity. Curr. Dev. Psychopharmac. **3**: 221–273.
17. SCHINDLER, U., D. K. RUSH & S. FIELDING. 1984. Nootropic drugs: Animal models for studying effects on cognition. Drug Dev. Res. **4**: 567–576.
18. GIURGEA, C. & M. SALAMA. 1977. Nootropic drugs. Prog. Neuropsychopharmacol. **1**: 235–247.
19. GOODNICK, P. & S. GERSHON. 1984. Chemotherapy of cognitive disorders in geriatric subjects. J. Clin. Psychiatry **45**: 196–209.
20. SCHNECK, M. K. 1983. Nootropics. *In* Alzheimer's Disease. B. Reisberg, Ed. Free Press. New York.
21. CROOK, T. H. 1985. Clinical drug trials in Alzheimer's Disease. Ann. N.Y. Acad. Sci. (This volume.)
22. WILSHER, C. R., G. ATKINS & P. MANSFIELD. 1979. Piracetam as an aid to learning in dyslexia: Preliminary report. Psychopharmacologia **65**: 107–109.
23. SIMEON, J., B. WATERS & M. RESNICK. 1980. Effects of piracetam in children with learning disorders. Psychopharmacol. Bull. **16**: 65–66.
24. WILSHER, C. R. & J. MILEWSKI. 1983. Effects of piracetam on dyslextic's verbal conceptualizing ability. Psychopharmacol. Bull. **19**: 3–4.
25. CONNERS, C. K., A. G. BLOUIN, M. WINGLEE, L. LOUGEE, D. O'DONNELL & A. SMITH. 1984. Piracetam and event-related potentials in dyslexic children. Psychopharmacol. Bull. **20**: 667–673.
26. HELFGOTT, E., R. RUDEL & J. KRIEGER. 1984. Effect of piracetam on the single word and prose reading of dyslexic children. Psychopharmacol. Bull. **20**: 688–690.
27. CHASE, C. H., R. L. SCHMITT, G. RUSSELL & P. TALLAL. 1984. A new chemotherapeutic investigation. Piracetam effects on dyslexia. Ann. Dyslexia **34**: 29–48.
28. DIMOND, S. & E. Y. M. BROUWERS. 1976. Improvement of human memory through the use of drugs. Psychopharmacologia **49**: 307–309.
29. GIURGEA, C. & F. MOURAVIEFF-LESUISSE. 1971. Effet facilitateu du piracetam sur un apprentissage repetitif. J. Pharmacol. (Paris) **2**: 226–227.
30. WOLTHUIS, O. L. 1971. Experiments with UCB 6215, a drug which enhances acquisition in rats: Its effects compared with those of methamphetamine. Eur. J. Pharmacol. **16**: 283–297.
31. SARA, S. J. & M. DAVID-REMACLE. 1974. Recovery from electroconvulsive shock-induced amnesia by exposure to the training environment: Pharmacological enhancement by piracetam. Psychopharmacologia **36**: 59–66.
32. WOLTHUIS, O. L. 1981. Behavioral effects of etiracetam in rats. Pharmacol. Biochem. Behav. **15**: 247–255.
33. SARA, S. J. 1980. Memory retrieval deficits: Alleviation by etiracetam, a nootropic drug. Psychopharmacology **68**: 235–241.
34. BURESOVA, O. & J. BURES. 1982. Radial maze as a tool for assessing the effect of drugs on the working memory of rats. Psychopharmacology **77**: 268–271.
35. OGLESBY, M. M. & J. C. WINTER. 1974. Strychnine sulfate and piracetam; lack of effect on learning in the rat. Psychopharmacologia **36**: 163–173.
36. BUTLER, D. E., B. P. H. POSCHEL & J. G. MARRIOTT. 1981. Cognition-activating properties of 3-(Aryloxy) pyridines. J. Med. Chem. **24**: 346–356.

37. INGRAM, D. 1985. Analysis of age-related impairments in learning and memory in rodent models. Ann. N.Y. Acad. Sci. (This volume.)

38. BERNSTEIN, D., D. S. OLTON, D. K. INGRAM, S. B. WALLER, M. A. REYNOLDS & E. D. LONDON. 1985. Radial maze performance in young and aged mice: Neurochemical correlates. Pharmacol. Biochem. Behav. (In press.)

39. GAMZU, E., E. BOFF, M. ZOLCINSKI, G. VINCENT & T. VERDERESE. 1983. A rapidly acquired, appetitively motivated, serial spatial discrimination reversal in rats from evaluating manipulations of learning and memory. Soc. Neurosci. Abstr. 9: 824.

40. LERER, B. E., E. GAMZU, & E. FRIEDMAN. 1985. Cortical cholinergic hypofunction and behavioral impairment produced by basal forebrain lesions in the rat. In The Dynamics of Cholinergic Function. I. Hanin, Ed. Plenum Press. New York. (In press.)

41. LERER, B., J. WARNER, E. FRIEDMAN, M. ZOLCINSKI, G. VINCENT & E. GAMZU. 1985. Cortical hypocholinergic functioning resulting from lesions of the rat magnocellular forebrain correlates with impaired passive avoidance in serial discrimination reversal behavior. Behavioral Neuroscience. (In press.)

42. BARTUS, R. T., C. FLICKER. & R. L. DEAN. 1983. Logical principles for the development of animal models of age-related memory impairments. In Assessment in Geriatric Psychopharmacology. T. Crook, S. Ferris & R. Bartus, Eds. Mark Powley Associates. New Canaan, CT.

43. BARTUS, R. T., R. L. DEAN, K. A. SHERMAN, E. FRIEDMAN & B. BEER. 1981. Profound effect of combining choline and piracetam on memory enhancement and cholinergic function in aged rats. Neurobiol. Aging 2: 105–111.

44. VALZELLI, L., S. BERNASCONI & A. SALA. 1980. Piracetam activity may differ according to the age of the recipient mouse. Int. Pharmacopsychiatry 15: 150–156.

45. VINCENT, G., E. GAMZU, E. BOFF & M. ZOLCINSKI. 1983. SH rats, vitamin E levels, and performance on simple learning tasks. Fed. Proc. 42: 1347.

46. BENDICH, A., E. GABRIEL & L. J. MACHLIN. 1983. Differences in vitamin E levels in tissues of the spontaneously hypertensive and Wistar-Kyoto rats Proc. Soc. Exp. Biol. Med. 172: 297–300.

47. QUINN, W. G. & R. J. GREENSPAN. 1984. Learning and courtship in drosophila: 2 stories with mutants. Ann. Rev. Neurosci. 7: 67–94.

48. NANDY, K., H. LAL, M. BENNETT & D. BENNETT. 1983. Correlation between a learning disorder and elevated brain-reactive antibodies in aged C57BL/6 and young NZB mice. Life Sci. 33: 1499–1503.

49. HARRIS, C. M., M. J. FORSTER, K. C. RETZ, N. FRANTZ & H. LAL. 1984. Deficient retention of appetitive and aversive learning in New Zealand black mice. Soc. Neurosci. Abstr. 10: 125.

50. VINCENT, G., A. VERDERESE & E. GAMZU. 1984. The effects of aniracetam (Ro 13-5057) and piracetam on the enhancement of memory in mice. Soc. Neurosci. Abstr. 10: 258.

51. SEARLE, L. V. 1949. The organization of hereditary maze-brightness and maze-dullness. Genet. Psychol. Monogr. 39: 279–325.

52. EBBINGHAUS, H. 1964. Memory: A Contribution to Experimental Psychology. Dover. New York. Originally published in 1885.

53. AIGNER, T., S. MITCHELL, J. AGGLETON, M. DeLONG, R. STRUBLE, D. PRICE & M. MISHKIN. 1984. Effects of scopolamine and physostigmine on recognition memory in monkeys after ibotenic acid injections into the area of the nucleus baslalis of Meynert. In Alzheimer's Disease: Advances in Basic Research and Therapies. R. J. Wurtman, S. H. Corkin & J. H. Growdon, Eds. Center for Brain Sciences and Metabolism. Cambridge, MA.

54. LIPPA, A., R. W. PEXHAM, B. BEER, D. J. CRITCHETT, R. L. DEAN & R. T. BARTUS. 1980. Brain cholinergic dysfunction and memory in aged rats. Neurobiol. Aging 1: 13–19.

55. GAMZU, E., L. PERRONE, K. KEIM, T. SMART, A. B. DAVIDSON & L. COOK. 1982. A mouse passive-avoidance model of anterograde amnesia: Comparison of benzodiazepine and scopolamine induced amnesias and EEG effects. Fed. Proc. 41: 1067.

56. SPENCER, D. G., JR. & H. LAL. 1983. Effects of anticholinergic drugs on learning and memory. Drug Dev. Res. 3: 489–502.

57. SCHWAM, E., K. KEIM, R. CUMIN, E. GAMZU & J. SEPINWALL. 1985. The effects of aniracetam on primate behavior and EEG. Ann. N.Y. Acad. Sci. (This volume.)

58. PONTECORVO, M. J. & H. L. EVANS. 1985. Effects of aniracetam on delayed match-to-sample performance of monkeys and pigeons. Pharm. Biochem. Behav. (In press.)
59. HANADA, S., T. NAKATSUKA, I. HAYASAKA & T. FUJII. 1982. Effects of pre-natal treatment with methylazoxy methanol acetate on growth development, reproductive performance, learning ability, and behavior in rat offspring. J. Toxicol. Sci. 7: 93–110.
60. WEINBERG, J., R. HADDAD & R. DUMAS. 1983. Acquisition and extinction of a conditioned taste aversion in micrencephalic rats. Soc. Neurosci. Abstr. 9: 637.
61. GIURGEA, C., M. G. GREINDL, S. PREAT & J. PUIGDEVALL. 1981. Piracetam-compensation of MAM-induced behavioural deficits in rats. Abstract presented at the First Meeting of the International study group on the pharmacology of memory disorders associated with aging. Zurich.
62. GIURGEA, C. & F. MOYERSOONS. 1970. Differential pharmacological reactivity of three types of cortical evoked potentials. Arch. Int. Pharmacodyn. 188: 401–404.
63. DEAN, R. L., C. LOULLIS, D. L. WATKINS & R. T. BARTUS. 1981. Neuropeptides in animal models of aging. Soc. Neurosci. Abstr. 7: 380.
64. CUMIN, R., E. BANDLE, E. GAMZU & W. E. HAEFELY. 1982. Effects of Ro 13-5057, a new and potent cognition activating compound on impaired learning and memory. Psychopharmacology 78: 104–111.
65. SIESJO, B. K., H. JOHANNSSON, B. LJUNGGREN & K. NORBERG. 1974. Brain dysfunction in cerebral hypoxia and ischemia. Res. Proc. Assoc. Res. Nerv. Ment. Dis. 53: 75–112.
66. GIBSON, G. E., C. PETERSON & J. SANSONE. 1981. Neurotransmitter and carbohydrate metabolism during aging and mild hypoxia. Neurobiol. Aging 2: 165–172.
67. SQUIRE, L. R. 1984. ECT and memory dysfunction. In ECT: Basic Mechanisms. B. Lerer, R. D. Weiner & R. H. Belmaker, Eds. Libbey. London.
68. SQUIRE, L. R. 1981. The pharmacology of memory: A neurobiological perspective. Ann. Rev. Pharmacol. Toxicol. 21: 323–356.
69. POSCHEL, B. P. H., J. G. MARRIOTT & M. I. GLUCKMAN. 1983. Pharmacology of the cognition activator pramiracetam (CI-879). Drugs Exp. Clin. Res. IX:853–871.
70. POSCHEL, B. P. H. 1977. The hippocampally-stimulated rat as a model for Korsakoff-type amnesia. Lab. Anim. Sci. 27: 738–747.
71. OLTON, D. S. & W. A. WOLF. 1981. Hippocampal seizures produce retrograde amnesia without a temporal gradient when they reset working memory. Behav. Neural Biol. 33: 437–454.
72. OLTON, D. S., J. T. BECKER & G. E. HANDELMANN. 1979. Hippocampus, space, and memory. Behav. Brain Sci. 2: 313–365.
73. BRANCONNIER, R. J. & D. R. DeVITT. 1983. Early detection of incipient Alzheimer's disease: some methodological considerations on computerized diagnosis. In Alzheimer's Disease. B. Reisberg, Ed. Free Press. New York.
74. CORKIN, S., J. H. GROWDON, M. J. NISSEN, F. J. HUFF, D. M. FREED & H. J. SAGAR. 1984. Recent advances in the neuropsychological study of Alzheimer's disease. In Alzheimer's Disease: Advances in Basic Research and Therapies. R. J. Wurtman, S. H. Corkin & J. H. Growdon, Eds. Center for Brain Sciences and Metabolism. Cambridge, MA.
75. GAMZU, E. & L. PERRONE. 1981. Pharmacological protection against hypoxic and electro-brainshock disruption of avoidance retrieval in mice. Soc. Neurosci. Abstr. 7: 525.
76. VERDERESE, A., E. GAMZU & G. VINCENT. 1983. An automated avoidance procedure for rapid screening of compounds that pharmacologically protect against EBS-induced deficits in memory. Paper presented at the Eastern Psychological Association. Philadelphia, PA.
77. ZORNETZER, S. F. 1985. Catecholamine system involvement in age related memory dysfunction. Ann. N.Y. Acad. Sci. (This volume.)
78. McGAUGH, J. L. 1985. Peripheral and central adrenergic influences on brain systems involved in the modulation of memory storage. Ann. N.Y. Acad. Sci. (This volume.)
79. ARNSTEN, A. F. T. & P. S. GOLDMAN-RAKIC. 1985. Catecholamine loss and cognitive disorders in adult and aged rhesus monkeys. Ann. N.Y. Acad. Sci. (This volume.)
80. REYNOLDS, G. P., L. ARNOLD, M. N. ROSSOR, L. L. IVERSEN, C. Q. MOUNTJOY & M.

ROTH. 1984. Reduced binding of [^{3}H]Ketanserin to cortical 5-HT$_2$ receptors in senile dementia of the Alzheimer type. Neurosci. Lett. **44:** 47–51.

81. ALTMAN, H. 1985. Mediation of storage and retrieval with two drugs which selectively modulate serotonergic neurotransmission. Ann. N.Y. Acad. Sci. (This volume.)

82. NICOLAUS, B. J. R. 1982. Chemistry and pharmacology of nootropics. Drug Dev. Res. **2:** 463–474.

83. BANFI, S., W. FONIO, E. ALLIEVI, M. PINZA & L. DORIGOTTI. 1984. Cyclic gaba-gabob analogues. Il Farmaco. **39:** 16–22.

84. HEISE, G. A. 1984. Behavioral methods for measuring effects of drugs on learning and memory in animals. Med. Res. Rev. **4:** 535–558.

85. LYNCH, G. & M. BAUDRY. 1984. The biochemistry of memory: A new and specific hypothesis. Science **224:** 1057–1063.

86. IZQUIERDO, I. 1985. Role of β-endorphin in learning and memory and its interaction with other neurohumoral and hormonal systems. Ann. N.Y. Acad. Sci. (This volume.)

87. PLATEL, A. & R. PORSOLT. 1982. Habituation of exploratory activity in mice: A screening test for memory enhancing drugs. Psychopharmacology **78:** 346–352.

88. BOAST, C. A. & Y. ISLAMI. 1982. Differential amnestic effects of CO$_2$ and N$_2$ on aversive and appetitive tasks. Soc. Neurosci. Abstr. **8:** 319.

89. MURPHY, D. E. & C. A. BOAST. 1985. Searching for models of Alzheimer's disease: A comparison of four amnestic treatments in two behavioral tasks. Ann. N.Y. Acad. Sci. (This volume.)

90. COLBERN, D. L., D. A. GORELICK & E. G. ZIMMERMAN. 1981. Ethanol induced facilitation of passive avoidance behavior shows diurnal variation. Alcoholism: Clin. Exp. Res. **5:** 146.

91. BARTUS, R. T., R. L. DEAN, S. JONES & K. SCHILL. 1985. The relevance of animal models to clinical memory assessment and drug development. *In* The Handbook of Clinical Memory Assessment of Older Adults. American Psychological Association. Washington, D.C. (In press.)

92. BOFF, E., E. GAMZU, D. POONIAN & M. ZOLCINSKI. 1982. Effects of cognitive performance enhancement reference compounds in a rat avoidance acquisition procedure. Soc. Neurosci. Abstr. **8:** 320.

93. RAY, O. S. & R. J. BARRETT. 1975. Behavioral, pharmacological, and biochemical analysis of genetic differences in rats. Behav. Biol. **15:** 391–417.

94. TANG, A. H. & S. R. FRANKLIN. 1983. Acquisition of brightness discrimination in the rat is impaired by opiates with psychotomimetic properties. Pharmacol. Biochem. Behav. **18:** 873–878.

95. OLTON, D. S. & R. J. SAMUELSON. 1976. Remembrance of places past: Spatial memory in rats. J. Exp. Psychol.: Anim. Behav. Proc. **2:** 97–116.

96. DE TOLEDO-MORRELL, L. & F. MORRELL. 1985. Electrophysiological markers of aging and memory loss in rats. Ann. N.Y. Acad. Sci. (This volume.)

97. DAVIS, H. P., A. IDOWU & G. E. GIBSON. 1983. Improvement of 8-arm maze performance in aged Fischer 344 rats with 3,4-diaminopyridine. Exp. Aging Res. **9:** 211–214.

98. GALLAGHER, M., R. A. KING & N. B. YOUNG. 1983. Opiate antagonists improve spatial memory. Science. **221:** 975–976.

99. POLLARD, G. T., S. T. MCBENNETT, K. W. ROHRBACH & J. L. HOWARD. 1981. Repeated acquisition of 3 response chains for food reinforcement in the rat. Drug Dev. Res. **1:** 67–76.

100. HOWARD, J. L. & G. T. POLLARD. 1983. Effects of d-amphetamine, Org 2766, scopolamine, and physostigmine on repeated acquisition of four-response chains in rat. Drug Dev. Res. **3:** 37–48.

101. WURTMAN, P. J., S. G. MAGIL. & D. K. REINSTEIN. 1981. Piracetam diminishes hippocampal acetylcholine levels in rats. Life Sci. **28:** 1091–1093.

102. KUBOTA, A., T. HAYASHI, T. SAKAGAMI, A. WATANABE & K. NAKAMURA. 1982. Scopolamine model of retrograde amnesia: its prevention and relevant cerebral nuclei involved. Excerpta Med. Int. Congr. Ser. pp. 96–118.

103. SETHY, V. H. 1983. Effect of piracetam on high affinity choline uptake. Soc. Neurosci. Abstr. **9:** 429.

104. PLATEL, A., M. JALFRE, C. PAWELEC, S. ROUX & R. D. PORSOLT. 1984. Habituation of exploratory activity in mice: Effects of combinations of piracetam and choline on memory processes. Pharmacol. Biochem. Beh. 21: 209–212.
105. DLABAC, A., I. KREJCI & B. KUPKOVA. 1981. The interaction of nootropic drugs with anticonvulsants. Activ. Nerv. Sup. (Praha) 23: 218–219.
106. KOPELEVICH, V. M., I. A. SYTINSKY & V. I. GUNAR. 1981. Current approach to the design of nootropic agents on the basis of gamma-aminobutyric acid (review of literature). Khim. Farm. Zh. 15: 27–38.
107. WENK, G. L. & D. S. OLTON. 1984. Recovery of neocortical choline acetyltransferase activity following ibotenic acid injection into the nucleus basalis of Meynert in rats. Brain Res. 293: 184–186.

Locus Coeruleus as a Target for Psychogeriatric Agents

HANS-RUDOLF OLPE, MARTIN W. STEINMANN, AND
ROLAND S.G. JONES

Pharmaceuticals Division
Biological Research Laboratories
Ciba-Geigy Ltd.
4002 Basel, Switzerland

INTRODUCTION

Today the noradrenergic-containing nucleus locus coeruleus is probably one of the best documented neuronal systems in brain. The locus coeruleus is thought to be involved in various functions such as the control of attention,[1] central blood pressure,[2] anxiety,[3] and processes related to memory and learning.[4] No unifying concept is available to explain the relative contribution and exact role of this small nucleus in these diverse functions. The role of the locus coeruleus in processes related to memory and learning has gained a lot of attention and has been intensively investigated in the past fifteen years but the issue remains controversial. Whereas earlier behavioral studies strongly supported a role of locus coeruleus in these processes,[5-8] more recent investigations militate against this hypothesis.[9] However, although behavioral studies remain controversial, recent electrophysiological investigations give a more coherent picture pointing to a basic role of the locus coeruleus in information processing. Single-cell recording studies performed in freely moving mammals have demonstrated that neuronal activity in the locus coeruleus correlates with the level of vigilance.[10-13] Highest levels of neuronal activity are observed during wakefulness and lower firing rates occur when the animals are drowsy and in slow wave and paradoxical sleep. The neurons respond with transient, biphasic changes in discharge to auditory, visual, and somatosensory stimuli.[12,14] These findings suggest that the locus coeruleus affects target cell systems concerned with processing of external stimuli. In keeping with this notion, it has been shown that noradrenaline differentially affects the activity of auditory cortex neurons in the awake monkey.[15] Iontophoretically applied noradrenaline reduced both spontaneous and evoked (acoustic stimulus) firing but the latter was relatively less affected.[15] In line with these findings, it has been shown in various brain areas that noradrenaline enhances neuronal responsiveness to natural stimulation of afferent pathways[15] or to microiontophoretically applied GABA[16] and ACh[17] in various brain areas. In contrast we have shown that the amine can reduce cortical neuron sensitivity to substance P.[18] These electrophysiological findings point to a modulatory role of noradrenaline in central information processing.

A large consensus of data indicates that the central noradrenergic system displays a functional decline with advancing age. Both pre- and postsynaptic markers of noradrenergic activity show such changes. The spontaneous firing rate of locus coeruleus neurons declines[19] and the sensitivity of target neurons to noradrenaline attenuates in various brain areas with advancing age.[20,21] Endogenous noradrenaline levels[22] and the stimulation of adenylate cyclase[23] by noradrenaline were found to be reduced in aged mammals. The density of beta-adrenergic receptors is reduced in the aged cerebellum[24] but not in the cortex.[24]

In humans, the number of neurons in the locus coeruleus declines with advancing age.[25-28] Degeneration appears to advance slightly faster in male than in females.[29] The locus coeruleus is a brain area that, like the central cholinergic system, is particularly susceptible to neuronal degeneration in Alzheimer's disease. There is some evidence suggesting that Alzheimer patients can be divided into patients with moderately degenerated locus coeruleus and those with a strongly degenerated locus coeruleus. Patients with the latter type die earlier and suffer more severe dementia.[30]

Apposition of the postulated role of the noradrenergic system with its functional decline in senescence provided the rationale for the present study. The activity of locus coeruleus neurons appears to correlate with the state of vigilance of the mammalian brain. This group of neurons is activated by all kinds of sensory stimuli, which are also accompanied by changes of cortical activity. Considering the wide and quite dense noradrenergic innervation of the entire cortex arising from locus coeruleus, it is not unreasonable to assume that these neurons participate in the mediation or modulation of these cortical effects. The postulated role of locus coeruleus in cognitive processes and the fact that this system displays age-related functional impairments has prompted us to study the action of a number of drugs that are claimed to improve processes related to learning and memory by affecting neuronal activity in this nucleus. Thus we have investigated the effects of parenteral administration of these drugs on the firing rate of locus coeruleus neurons in the rat. These experiments were performed in anesthetized animals.

METHODS

A detailed description of the methodology has been presented elsewhere[31] and a brief account only is given here. Experiments were performed on male rats (RAI f (SPF)), 260–320 g), anesthetized with chloral hydrate (400 mg/kg i.p.), and mounted in a stereotaxic apparatus. Extracellular single cell recording was accomplished by means of single barrel glass electrodes (tip size, 2–5 μm) filled with NaCl (4 M) or NaCl (2 M) saturated with Fast Green for labeling the recording site. Locus coeruleus was approached stereotactically and noradrenergic neurons were identified using electrophysiological, pharmacological, and anatomical identification criteria.[31] Only one neuron was investigated per rat. When a noradrenergic neuron was found, its activity was recorded during a control period lasting 10–15 min. Following this period, drugs were administered intraperitoneally in cumulative doses at intervals of 30 min. Only one drug was administered per rat. All drugs were dissolved in physiological saline solution. Single cellular activity was recorded for one to four hours following drug administration. The effect of each dose of a drug was determined separately by comparing the mean firing rate recorded 25–30 min after injection with the mean firing rate observed during the entire period of control recording.

The effects of three agents on the firing rate of medial septal neurons were tested in a similar way to that described above. In these experiments the anesthetic was a urethane/chloralose mixture. Medial septal neurons were identified on the basis of their bursting pattern of firing and the fact that they responded with a pronounced and long lasting increase in firing to the intravenous administration of the cholinesterase inhibitor physostigmine. Deposition of Fast Green from the recording electrode was used to histologically verify recording sites in the medial septum.

Some drugs were also tested on the firing rate of neurons in layers III–VI of the anterior cingulate cortex of chloral hydrate anesthetized rats.

RESULTS

Effects on Locus Coeruleus Neurons

Psychogeriatric Agents

The most widely used compounds often used for comparative purposes are co-dergocrine, vincamine, and piracetam. All three of these drugs, given parenterally, resulted in an increase in firing rate of neurons in the locus coeruleus.[32] The dose-response curves for this effect are shown in FIGURE I. Piracetam was considerably less potent than the other two drugs in eliciting increases in neuronal firing rate. Although the action of piracetam was weak, several closely related derivatives of the compound also increased locus coeruleus neuronal activity (data not shown). Derivatives of vincamine generally displayed marked activating effects (not shown).

Dose-response curves for four other drugs used in the treatment of cognitive disturbances in aged patients are shown in FIGURE 2. Despite the chemical heterogeneity of this group, all the compounds also activated locus coeruleus cells. Nicergoline

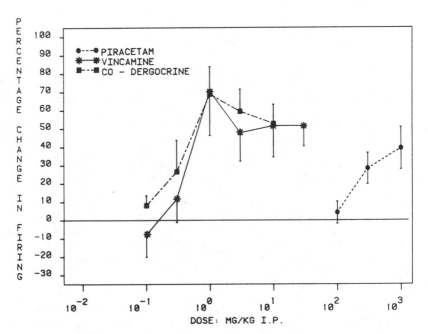

FIGURE 1. Dose-response curves of the action of vincamine, piracetam, and codergocrine on the firing rate of locus coeruleus neurons. (From Olpe and Steinmann.[19] By permission from *Brain Research*.)

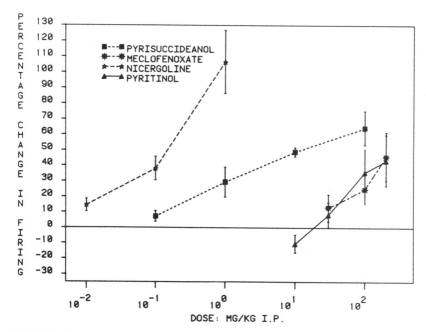

FIGURE 2. Dose-response curves of the action of pyrisuccideanol, nicergoline, meclofenoxate, and pyritinol on the firing rate of locus coeruleus neurons. X ± S.E.M.

was very potent in this respect. On a mg/kg basis pyrisuccideanol had a similar potency to vincamine and codergrine while meclofenoxate and pyritinol were more similar in potency to piracetam.

Psychostimulants

Four drugs that have central stimulating actions were tested for effects on locus coeruleus firing after parenteral administration. Amphetamine ($N = 6$) and methylphenidate ($N = 4$) both reduced the firing of locus coeruleus neurons. A rate-meter record showing reduction of firing after methylphenidate is shown in FIGURE 3. In contrast to the other three agents, caffeine, like the psychogeriatric agents, increased the firing rate of locus coeruleus neurons. The dose-response relationship for caffeine is shown in FIGURE 4.

Other Agents

The last group of drugs tested comprised three compounds that have been shown to have a beneficial effect in some learning paradigms in mammals. Of these, physostygmine and nicotine were very active in increasing locus coeruleus cell firing (FIGURE 5) but strychnine (1 mg/kg) was inactive (data not shown).

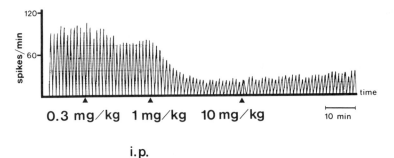

FIGURE 3. The inhibiting effect of intraperitoneally administered methylphenidate on the firing rate of a rat locus coeruleus neuron is depicted.

Effects on Medial Septal Neurons

Piracetam, vincamine, and codergocrine were tested for effects on septal neuron firing after parenteral administration. FIGURE 6 shows that none of the drugs at any of the doses tested caused any significant alteration in firing rate of medial septal neurons.

Effects on Cingulate Cortical Neurons

Vincamine (N = 9), codergocrine (N = 14), and piracetam (N = 12) all failed to significantly alter the firing rate of neurons in the anterior cingulate cortex. These results are summarized in FIGURE 7.

DISCUSSION

The primary drawback of any discussion of the possible mechanism of action of drugs that we term psychogeriatric agents lies with the fact that we are by no means sure as to the clinical efficacy of the compounds. Although these agents constitute a large proportion of the totally prescribed drugs in many countries, the question of clinical efficacy is still widely debated. In a recent review, Spagnoli and Tognoni[33] stated "The question is whether or not there is documented evidence of clinical benefit, and it could not be more open."

Accepting the above uncertainty but assuming for the moment that these drugs do elicit some clinical advantages, what is the likelihood that our currently observed effects in locus coeruleus may be linked to these clinical effects? FIGURE 8 shows the relationship between the daily therapeutic doses of psychogeriatric agents and the ED_{30} (i.e. dose producing a 30% increase) for activation of locus coeruleus neuron firing. There seems to be a reasonable correlation between these two parameters, so it is possible that the action of the drugs in the clinic may be related in some way to an effect in the locus coeruleus.

What then would be the relevance of locus coeruleus activation to improvement of cognitive function after treatment with psychogeriatric agents? As mentioned earlier the noradrenergic system projecting from locus coeruleus is almost certainly involved in processing of neuronal information transfer in the forebrain. Of particular relevance are studies indicating a role of this system in control of attention[1] and processes related to learning and memory.[5–8] The clear decrement in these processes that accompanies senescence in humans[25–28] would conceivably involve an age-related deficit in function of the noradrenergic system. The ability of the drugs to improve mental status may be connected with the activation of noradrenergic afferent pathways. Certainly there does seem to be a dysfunction of this system occurring with advancing age. The forebrain of aging animals displays a decrease in brain noradrenergic content,[22] catecholamine turnover,[34] number of noradrenergic receptors,[24] sensitivity of adenylate cyclase to NA,[23] and of target neurons to exogenously applied NA.[20,21] At the brainstem level a decline in firing rate of locus coeruleus neurons has been noted in rats[19] and degeneration and decline of locus coeruleus neuron number in humans[25] occurring with age. Overall there seems likely to be a decrement in the efficiency of this system in age that may be corrected at least partly by the activating effects of psychogeriatric agents. Clearly, all the drugs we have tested so far, which are reportedly effective as psychogeriatrics, are able to augment firing of locus coeruleus neurons.

As yet, we have no indications as to the basic mechanisms of the activating action in the locus coeruleus. Since we used a parenteral route of administration we are unable even to predict whether this action may be direct or indirect on the locus coeruleus or may be even peripheral in origin. It may be that the activating effects are linked to blockade of central alpha-receptors. It has been suggested that the firing of locus coeruleus neurons appears to be under the tonic influence of a collateral inhibitory input mediated by the action of noradrenaline on alpha-receptors located on their soma or dentrites.[35] Administration of alpha-antagonists results in blockade of the collateral inhibition and augmentation of neuronal firing.[36] The two most potent

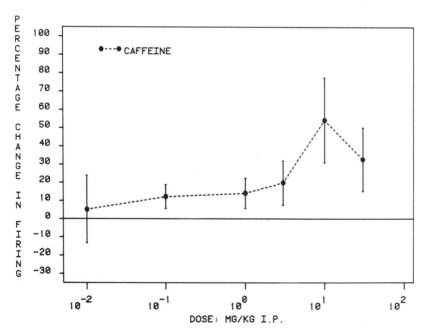

FIGURE 4. Dose-response curve of the effect of caffeine on the spontaneous cellular discharge in rat locus coeruleus. X ± S.E.M. (From Olpe *et al.*[31] By permission from *Experientia.*)

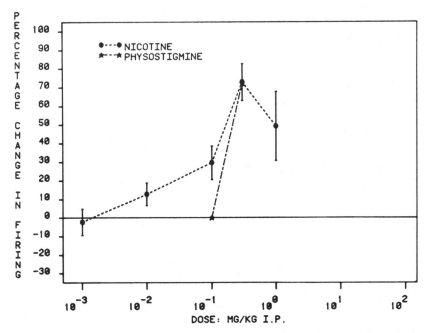

FIGURE 5. Dose-response curves of intraperitoneally administered nicotine and physostigmine on neuronal activity in locus coeruleus. X ± S.E.M. (From Olpe et al.[31] By permission from Experientia.)

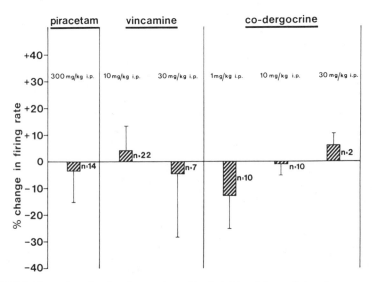

FIGURE 6. The action of various intraperitoneally administered doses of piracetam, vincamine, and codergocrine on the firing rate of spontaneously discharging neurons of the medial septal nucleus. X ± S.E.M.

drugs in our study, nicergoline[37] and codergocrine,[38] are potent alpha-blockers and it is possible that the activating effects of these is due to alpha-receptor antagonism. Pending further investigations, this interpretation remains speculative at present.

Whatever the ultimate mechanism of the activating action of the psychogeriatric compounds, a note of caution is necessary concerning the overall effect of these drugs on the central noradrenergic system. The inclination is to assume that the increased firing results in a net facilitation of noradrenergic transmission in terminal areas. This is by no means certain. For example, tricyclic antidepressant drugs are generally held to facilitate noradrenergic transmission by blocking the reuptake of the amine. However, nearly all these compounds decrease locus coeruleus neuron firing rates, probably by enhancement of noradrenaline-mediated feedback inhibition.[39,40] In this connection it is interesting that depression is very often accompanied by disturbances

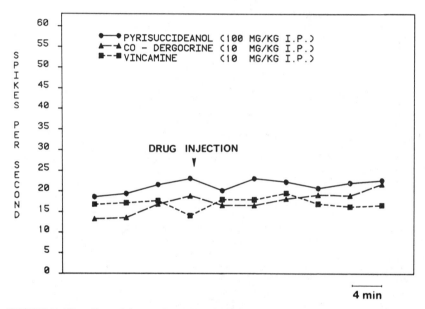

FIGURE 7. The effect of intraperitoneally administered pyrisuccideanol, codergocrine, and vincamine on the spontaneous discharge rate of three different cingulate cortical neurons.

in cognitive functions and that these disappear with antidepressant treatment.[41] On the other hand, there is anecdotal evidence[42-44] for mood-improving properties of some psychogeriatrics so that the relationship between drug-induced changes in locus coeruleus activity and mood, memory, etc. is by no means clear-cut. Another interesting observation with regard to the activating effects of psychogeriatrics concerns the recently postulated role of the noradrenergic nucleus in anxiety.[45] This hypothesis proposes that the locus coeruleus, as part of the sympathetic nervous system, is activated in fearful and stressful situations. Drugs such as minor tranquilizers and clonidine inhibit locus coeruleus firing and are anxiolytic.[45] On this basis one might expect drugs that accelerate locus coeruleus firing to be anxiogenic, but there are no indications from clinical studies of anxiety-producing properties of psychogeriatrics.

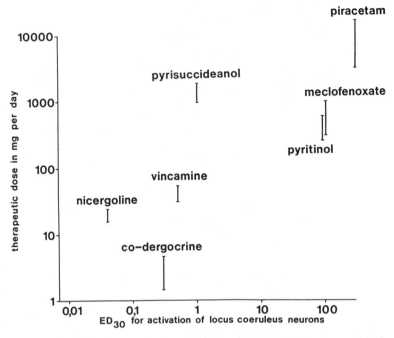

FIGURE 8. Mean daily therapeutic doses of various psychogeriatric drugs are plotted as a function of the mean dose of these drugs inducing a 30% increase in neuronal firing in rat locus coeruleus. This ED_{30} was determined by interpolation.

It is not the intention of this manuscript to postulate a cut and dried role for locus coeruleus as underlying cognitive deficits associated with senescence nor to propose the locus coeruleus as the primary target of psychogeriatric agents. Nevertheless, the "slowing down" of the noradrenergic system in aging brain may be a biologically meaningful and adaptive process secondary to other degenerative events occurring in the aged organism. There is no proof available yet for a correlation between decline in noradrenergic cell function during aging and the deficits in learning and memory that occur concurrently. However, it has certainly been speculated that the cellular degeneration of the locus coeruleus may be linked with the progressive cognitive impairments.[46] The electrophysiological literature on the pharmacology of the central noradrenergic systems—in particular on the locus coeruleus—is quite extensive. The question of selectivity of the drug effect reported for psychogeriatric compounds can therefore be discussed in detail. TABLE 1 gives a qualitative description of the effect of various types of psychotropic agents on locus coeruleus neuronal activity. All the drugs listed have been studied in anesthetized animals. Since there are no comparative investigations of this type in anesthetized versus unanesthetized animals, it remains unclear as to whether the reactivity of locus coeruleus neurons to psychotropic agents is affected by anesthesia. It is not unlikely that neurons are more sensitive to centrally active drugs in unanesthetized mammals. The majority of drugs tested so far exert a depressant action on locus coeruleus neuronal activity. This effect may be moderate, as in the case of minor tranquilizers,[47,48] or it may lead to a complete arrest of firing with increasing doses, as in the case of antidepressants,[39,40] amphetamine,[49] and clonidine.[50]

Locus coeruleus neurons are activated not only by the drugs mentioned above but also by α-receptor blocking compounds (piperoxane, yohimbine),[51] the neuroleptics haloperidol and chlorpromazine,[31] and by clozapine.[52] The latter three compounds may conceivably increase neuronal firing rate in the locus coeruleus as a result of their α-receptor blocking property. The majority of antiepileptics, with the exception of carbamazepine,[53] do not significantly alter neuronal activity in this brain area.

CONCLUSION

There is a limited drug specificity with regard to the psychogeriatrics' stimulating action on locus coeruleus.

The physiological processes underlying memory formation are still unknown. As we learn more about them rather more specific pharmacological studies can be performed. Many authors believe that the phenomenon of long-term potentiation is linked with memory processes. Recent studies have addressed the question of whether long-term potentiation is altered by drugs claimed to affect cognitive processes. Among the drugs tested in our study, two have been thus investigated—vincamine[56] and piracetam.[57] Piracetam was found to be without effect but vincamine unexpectedly blocked long-term potentiation. The significance of these results for the clinical actions of the drugs is obscure at present.

Electrophysiological studies perhaps have afforded a better understanding of the mode of action of psychogeriatric agents and have at least opened a new avenue of research into the possible mechanism of action of these drugs. For the future,

TABLE 1. The Action of Various Classes of Psychotropic Agents on Locus Coeruleus Neuronal Activity

Type of Drugs	Action on Locus Coeruleus		Comments	References
	Activation	Inhibition		
Antidepressants		+	Tricyclic antidepressants, monoamine oxidase blockers	39, 40, 47
Minor tranquilizers		+	Only a few drugs tested	47, 48
Neuroleptics	+		Only a few drugs tested	47
Antiepileptics	φ	φ	Exception: carbamazepine activates	53
Psychostimulants				
amphetamine		+		
methylphenidate		+		
caffeine	+			
amfonelic acid		+		54
Hallucinogens				
mescaline		+		55
LSD		+		55
Psychogeriatrics	+			
Others				
α-blockers	+			51
clonidine		+		50
nicotine	+			
physostigmine	+			
strychnine	φ	φ		

combination of these studies with neurochemical and behavioral investigations may significantly contribute to the development of more efficacious drugs that are urgently needed to treat the cognitive disorders of aging patients.

REFERENCES

1. MASON, S. T. & S. D. IVERSEN. 1978. Brain Res. **150:** 135–148.
2. WARD, D. G. & C. G. GUNN. 1976. Brain Res. **107:** 401–406.
3. REDMOND, D. E. & Y. H. HUANG. 1979. Life Sci. **25:** 2149–2162.
4. AMARAL, D. G. & J. A. FOSS. 1975. Science **188:** 377–379.
5. CROW, T. J. 1968. Nature **219:** 736–737.
6. KETY, S. S. 1970. In The Neurosciences: Second Study Program. F. O. Schmitt, Ed.: 324–336. Rockefeller University Press. New York.
7. CROW, T. J. & S. WENDLANDT. 1976. Nature **259:** 42–44.
8. VELLEY, L. & B. CARDO. 1982. Behav. Neural Biol. **35:** 395–407.
9. HAGAN, J. J., J. E. ALPERT, R. G. M. MORRIS & S. D. IVERSEN. 1983. Behav. Brain Res. **9:** 83–104.
10. CHU, N. & F. E. BLOOM. 1974. J. Neurobiol. **5:** 527–544.
11. HOBSON, J., R. MCCARTEY & P. WYZINSKI. 1975. Science **189:** 55–58.
12. FOOTE, S. L., G. ASTON-JONES & F. E. BLOOM. 1980. Proc. Natl. Acad. Sci. USA **77:** 3033–3037.
13. ASTON-JONES, G. & F. E. BLOOM. 1981. J. Neurosci. **8:** 876–886.
14. ASTON-JONES, G. & F. E. BLOOM. 1981. J. Neurosci. **1:** 887–900.
15. FOOTE, S., R. FREEDMANN & O. OLIVIER. 1975. Brain Res. **86:** 229–242.
16. WATERHOUSE, B. D. & D. J. WOODWARD. 1980. Exp. Neurol. **67:** 11–34.
17. WATERHOUSE, B. D., H. C. MOISES & D. J. WOODWARD. 1981. Neuropharmacology **20:** 907–920.
18. JONES, R. S. G. & H.-R. OLPE. 1984. Brain Res. (In press.)
19. OLPE, H.-R. & M. STEINMANN. 1982. Brain Res. **251:** 174–176.
20. MARWAHA, J., B. HOFFER, R. PITTMAN & R. FRIEDMAN. 1980. Brain Res. **201:** 85–97.
21. JONES, R. S. G. & H.-R. OLPE. 1983. Neurobiol. Aging **4:** 97–99.
22. GOLDMAN-RAKIC, P. S. & R. M. BROWN. 1981. Neuroscience **6:** 177–187.
23. SCHMIDT, M. J. & J. F. THORNBERRY. 1978. Brain Res. **139:** 169–177.
24. MAGGI, A. M., J. SCHMIDT, B. GHETTI & S. J. ENNA. 1978. Life Sci. **24:** 367–374.
25. VIJAYASHANKAR, N. & H. BRODY. 1979. J. Neuropath. Exp. Neurol. **38:** 490–497.
26. MANN, D. M. A., J. LINCOLN, P. O. YATES, J. E. STAMP & S. TOPER. 1980. Brit. J. Psychiat. **136:** 533–541.
27. PERRY, E. K., B. E. TOMLINSON, G. BLESSED, R. H. PERRY, A. J. CROSS & T. T. CROW. 1981. J. Neurol. Sci. **51:** 279–287.
28. IVERSEN, L. L., M. N. ROSSOR, G. P. REYNOLDS, R. HILLS, M. ROTH, C. Q. MOUNTJOY, S. L. FOOTE, J. H. MORRISON & F. E. BLOOM. 1983. Neurosci. Lett. **39:** 95–100.
29. WREE, A., H. BRAAK, A. SCHLEICHER & K. ZILLES. 1980. Anat. Embryol. **160:** 105–119.
30. BONDAREFF, W., C. Q. MONTJOY & M. ROTH. 1981. Lancet April **4:** 783–784.
31. OLPE, H.-R., R. S. G. JONES & M. W. STEINMANN. 1983. Experientia **39:** 242–249.
32. OLPE, H.-R. & M. W. STEINMANN. 1982. J. Neural. Trans. **55:** 101–109.
33. SPAGNOLI, A. & G. TOGNONI. 1983. Drugs **26:** 44–69.
34. GOLDMAN-RAKIC, P. S. & R. M. BROWN. 1981. Neuroscience **6:** 177–187.
35. AGHAJANIAN, G. K., J. M. CEDARBAUM & R. Y. WANG. 1977. Brain Res. **136:** 570–577.
36. CEDARBAUM, J. M. & G. K. AGHAJANIAN. 1976. Brain Res. **112:** 413–419.
37. ARCARI, G. L., L. BERNARDI, B. BOSISIO, S. CODA, G. B. FREGNAN & A. H. GLÄSSER. 1972. Experientia **28:** 819–820.
38. MARKSTEIN, R., C. CLOSSE & W. FRICK. 1983. Eur. J. Pharmacol. **93:** 159–168.
39. NYBÄCK, H. V., J. R. WALTERS, G. K. AGHAJANIAN & R. H. ROTH. 1975. Eur. J. Pharmacol. **32:** 302–312.
40. SCUVÉE-MOREAU, J. J. & A. E. DRESSE. 1979. Eur. J. Pharmacol. **57:** 219–225.
41. STERNBERG, D. E., M. D. MURRAY & E. JARVIK. 1976. Arch. Gen. Psychiat. **33:** 219–224.

42. DINGLI, D. & C. BLATRIX. 1973. Vie Méd. **14.**
43. CRISPI, G., R. S. DI LORENTO & A. GENTILE. 1975. Minerva Med. **66:** 3683–3685.
44. EINSPRUCH, B. C. Diseases Nerv. System **37:** 439–442.
45. REDMOND, D. E. & Y. H. HUANG. 1979. Life Sci. **25:** 2149–2162.
46. VAN DONGEN, P. A. M. 1981. Prog. Neurobiol. **17:** 97–139.
47. REDMOND, D. E. 1982. TIPS **3:** 477–480.
48. SANGHERA, M. K. & D. C. GERMAN. 1983. J. Neural. Trans. **57:** 267–269.
49. GRAHAM, A. & G. K. AGHAJANIAN. 1971. Nature **234:** 100–102.
50. SVENSSON, T. H., B. S. BUNNEY & G. K. AGHAJANIAN. 1975. Brain Res. **92:** 291–306.
51. CEDARBAUM, J. M. & G. K. AGHAJANIAN. 1977. Eur. J. Pharmacol. **44:** 375–385.
52. SONTO, M., J. M. MONTI & H. ALTIER. 1979. Pharmac. Biochem. Behav. **10:** 5–9.
53. OLPE, H.-R. & R. S. G. JONES. 1983. Eur. J. Pharmacol. **91:** 107–110.
54. GERMAN, D. C., M. S. SANGHERA, R. S. KISER, B. A. MCMILLEN & P. A. SHORE. 1979. Brain Res. **166:** 331–339.
55. AGHANJANIAN, G. K. 1980. Brain Res. **186:** 492–498.
56. OLPE, H.-R. & G. S. LYNCH. 1982. Eur. J. Pharmacol. **80:** 415–419.
57. OLPE, H.-R., G. BARRIONUEVO & G. LYNCH. 1982. Life Sci. **31:** 1947–1953.

Memory Dysfunction and Vigilance: Neurophysiological and Psychopharmacological Aspects

B. SALETU AND J. GRÜNBERGER

Department of Psychiatry
School of Medicine
University of Vienna
Währinger Cürtel 74-76
1090 Vienna, Austria

INTRODUCTION

Since Berger[1] assumed a relationship between "psychic energy" and brain physiology and hypothesized that the energy produced by metabolic processes of the brain may be measured as electricity, scientists have looked intensively for relationships between cognitive processes and human brain function. In the 1960s Thompson and Obrist[2] described that learning is associated with cortical activation. In an experimental group, recall of verbal material and nonsense syllables coincided with an increased number of beta waves and a decreased number of alpha waves in EEG scalp recordings, while a control group did not show any frequency changes. Moreover, the EEG alterations were most pronounced when the subjects gave correct answers. While these findings suggest that learning changes human brain activity, other studies indicate the reverse—that the state of the central nervous system influences learning ability. The latter was already postulated by Head[3] when he explained his concept of vigilance through which he describes the dynamic state of the total neuronal activity determining the availability and the grade of organization of man's adaptive behavior. Vigilance should not be mixed up with vigility or arousal although an inverse U-shaped relationship exists between the two. Indeed, Thompson and Wilson[4] noted that subjects with good learning abilities exhibited faster EEG background activity than those with low learning capacity who showed generally slower activities. This is consistent with psychological data of Berlyne and Lewis[5] with regard to the effect of arousal during acquisition of verbal material and immediate and delayed recall. Investigating the influence of different arousal states immediately preceding recall of 50 double-syllable words, Uehling and Sprinkle[6] observed that white noise increased recall 24 hours or one week after the acquisition. Thus, both neurophysiological and psychological literature suggests that learning influences brain activity and vice versa. The advent of computerized facilities enabled us to obtain more objective and quantitative information about the relationship between mental performance and human brain function in both normal and abnormal aging. The aim of this paper is to give a survey about neurophysiological findings in aging and dementia, to describe correlations between memory and vigilance, and to discuss quantitative EEG and psychometric changes after several representatives of antihypoxidotics/nootropics and the improvement of vigilance as therapeutic principle.

NEUROPHYSIOLOGICAL ASPECTS OF NORMAL AGING

The human EEG shows progressive slowing of the background activity with advancing age. While this can be seen by the unaided eye, it can be demonstrated more clearly by computer-assisted quantitative analysis of the EEG. Utilizing spectral analysis of 3-min V-EEG recording segments, obtained in 102 elderly subjects aged between 56–96 years (mean 76 years), we could find significant correlations between age and several quantitative EEG variables: the higher the age, the slower the dominant frequency of the alpha activity and the greater the relative power in the delta and theta activity (FIGURE 1). This is in agreement with the data of Surwillo,[7] Van Der Drift et al.,[8] Matejcek and Devos,[9] and Obrist,[10] who found the magnitude of the slowing of the dominant alpha activity related to health status, longevity, and intellectual functioning. While the young adults show on the average a dominant frequency between 10–10.5 Hz, the latter is significantly lower in people around the age of 70 (9–9.5 Hz) and even more so in people in the 80s (8.5–9.0 Hz). Regarding alpha activity, we observed with increasing age a trend towards a decrease of relative power in the faster alpha range (10.5–13 Hz) as was the case with total beta activity (13–40 Hz). Our results corroborate those of Matejcek and Devos,[9] who found the decrease of alpha activity at the level of statistical significance as they had a larger population, while their total beta activity (12–40 Hz) showed only a trend towards a slight decline. Interestingly, subdivision of the total beta activity resulted in opposite findings regarding the behavior of slow and fast beta activities: while the slow beta activity (12–25 Hz) decreased, faster beta activities (25–40 Hz) increased.

The above-described increase of delta and theta activity and decrease of alpha activity can be viewed as deterioration in vigilance and may be due to deficits in the vigilance-regulatory systems. The latter may be even documented in recording sessions lasting only a few minutes. As can be seen in FIGURE 2, the 76-year-old man is quite able to sustain his vigilance, which is reflected by the persistence of the alpha activity throughout the 6 min recording session, while a 96-year-old man showed a deterioration in vigilance indicated by an increase in delta and theta power and a decrease of alpha activity. Indeed, a diminished adaptability (as for instance to new situations) in old age has been known to clinicians for a long time.

A similar way to demonstrate vigilance changes over time has been described by Matejcek using chronospectrogram analysis, which shows the evolution in time of different EEG variables.[11]

There are many other neurophysiological variables changing with age. Focal alterations (theta and delta waves), amplitude asymmetries, sharp waves, and spikes first appear to a significant degree after the age 40—mostly so over the anterior temporal lobes with a prevalence over the left side. Busse and Obrist[12] found temporal slow waves in 20% of normals in the age between 40–60 years, in contrast to less than 5% under the age of 40 years, while the incidence rose to 35% after the age of 60. Despite the fact that temporal foci are frequently observed in cerebral vascular disorder (CVD) (exceeding 60% in acute stroke patients), they cannot be considered pathognomonic of a neurological or psychic deficit in the average old person. It seems rather likely that the anterior temporal lobe undergoes early pathological changes. Tomlinson and Henderson[13] described a relatively high incidence of neuronal loss, gliosis, and plaques in the anterior temporal lobe which, in demented patients, were usually widespread and gross.

With increasing age, fewer individuals show alpha blocking[14] and the response latency is prolonged.[15] The latencies of evoked potentials increase as well. Measuring

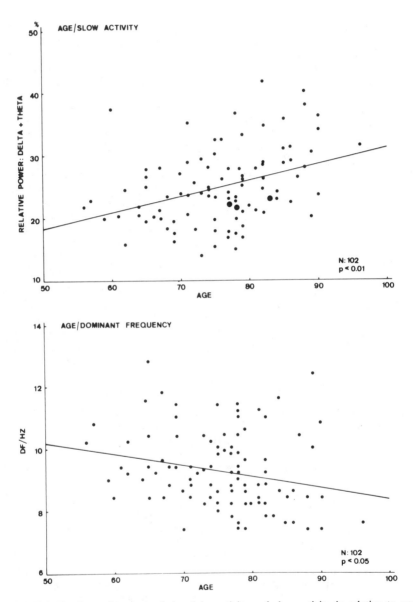

FIGURE 1. Dominant frequency of the alpha activity and slow activity in relation to age. Relations between EEG, age, SCAG, and memory. Age is shown in the abscissa, dominant frequency (in Hz) and relative power in the delta and theta bands are indicated in the ordinates. A slowing of the dominant frequency and an increase of delta and theta activity with increasing age can be seen.

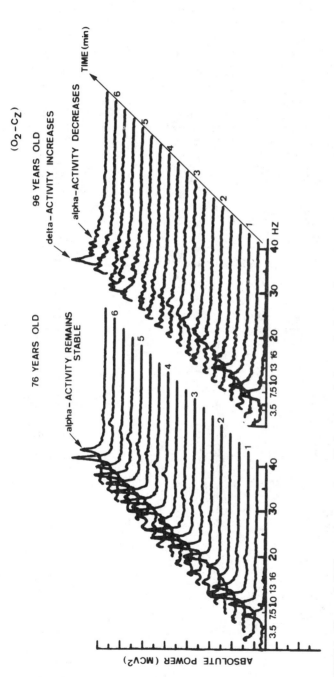

FIGURE 2. Changes in EEG power spectra of two elderly patients during one 7-min recording session. While the 76-year-old man exhibits quite a constant alpha activity over the 6 min recording time, the 96-year-old man shows a decline in alpha activity and increase of delta and theta activity reflecting a deterioration of vigilance.

the P_{300} component of acoustic-evoked potentials (AEP), Squires et al.[16] described an increase in the latency from 310 msec at the age of 15 at the rate of 1.69 msec per year ($p < 0.001$), reaching a latency of over 400 msec by the eighth decade. Photic driving responses and induction of slow waves by hyperventilation is significantly reduced in senescence.[14,15]

Not only the wake EEG, but also the all night sleep EEG changes significantly with increasing age (TABLE 1). As the awakenings increase in frequency and length, sleep becomes more fragmented. Sleep stage 4 and (slightly less) stage REM decrease, while stage 2 increases. The best known change, however, is the shortening of the total sleep time (TST), which has been noted in polygraphic and non-polygraphic studies in larger groups of subjects estimating their own sleep times.[17,18] In the laboratory studies a significant decline in the number of 12–14 Hz spindles was observed, which are replaced by lower frequency spindle-like rhythms.[19] Correlating performance scores on the Wechsler Adult Intelligence Scale (WAIS) with the nightly amount of REM sleep and stage 4, Prinz[20] found a positive correlation thereby confirming Feinberg's Sleep-Cognition Hypothesis, which held that EEG sleep changes reflect the physiologic capacity of the brain, particularly to acquire and process information.[21]

NEUROPHYSIOLOGICAL ASPECTS OF DEMENTIA

Dementia of Alzheimer Type

Generally, it can be said that the usual senile EEG features are accentuated in senile dementia, whereas the presenile cases show the most marked abnormalities (TABLE 2). It has been increasingly accepted that Alzheimer's disease and senile

TABLE 1. Differences in the All-Night Sleep ($\bar{x}$, s) between Younger and Elder Subjects ($N = 10,10$)

Sleep Variables	Younger ($\bar{x}$ 25a)	Elder ($\bar{x}$ 62a)	Differences U-Test
Latency 1 (min)	12(14)	7(6)	
Latency 2 (min)	16(15)	11(6)	
Total sleep time (min)	416(23)	348(62)	
Efficiency index	93(4)	86(14)	
Awakenings (f)	2,7(2,4)	8,4(3,1)	xxx
Awake$_{total sleep time}$ (min)	8(8)	37(52)	x
Stage 1%	6(4)	8(6)	
2%	49(12)	62(10)	x
3%	10(5)	7(4)	
4%	9(7)	4(6)	x
REM %	24(7)	17(3)	xx
REM (f)	4,0(1,0)	3,6(0,8)	
REM interval (min)	78(24)	75(21)	
REM latency (min)	83(47)	113(72)	
Stage-Shifts	92(31)	88(27)	
Movement time (min)	9(3)	6(3)	x
Wake threshold	56(19)	47(11)	

x = $p < 0.05$, xx = $p < 0.01$, and xxx = $p < 0.001$.

TABLE 2. Neurophysiological Findings in Dementia-Alzheimer Type

Senility < Senile Dementia < Presenile Dementia
Alpha – A ↓; DF (HZ) ↓; % ↓
Diffuse slow (delta & theta) activity ↑
Differences between areas ↓
Overall amplitude ↓   References 10, 22–28
Sharp waves spikes focal features rarely
K-complexes, sleep-spindles ↓
Reason for slowing: Atrophy[26]
Neurofibrillary tangles[27]
Senile plaque[28]
Asymmetry of slow activity common[29]
Alpha blocking ↓[14]
Photic driving ↓[15]
AEP-latency ↑[16]
Sleep S2, S4, REM ↓, W ↑[19]
EEG abnormalities relate poor[35] and well[29] to clinic

dementia differ only in their age of onset and thus the latter term is becoming obsolete.

Several authors, such as Mundy-Castle et al.,[22] Lairy,[23] Letemendia and Pampiglione,[24] Passouant et al.,[25] Gordon and Sim,[26] Constantinidis et al.,[27] Müller and Schwartz,[28] and Obrist[10] described that alpha activity decreases markedly in regard to amount, amplitude, persistence (% time), and dominant frequency in these patients. Diffuse slow delta and theta activity, usually of low amplitude, becomes more prominent so that the general appearance of the EEG is polymorphic. Differences between areas disappear although asymmetry of slow activity is not uncommon.[29] It was believed that the reduction of alpha and the increase of slow activity show only an approximate relation to the degree of dementia, but that in advanced cases no alpha or faster frequencies may be identifiable.[30] In this context it is of interest that by utilizing computer-assisted, spectral-analysis of the EEG we found a significant positive correlation between the relative power in the delta and theta bands and the SCAG score and a significantly negative correlation between the amount of slow activity and mnestic performance as measured by the Grünberger verbal memory test in 102 elderly subjects with a mean age of 76 years (FIGURE 3). Our results, obtained by means of computerized power spectral density analysis, are in agreement with those derived by manual analysis from Obrist,[31] who found that patients with an organic brain syndrome exhibited more delta and theta and less alpha activity than healthy controls.

The incidence of EEG abnormalities in presenile cases of Alzheimer's disease is high. In various studies described by Letemendia and Pampiglione,[24] Liddell,[32] Swain,[33] and Gordon and Sim,[26] all the patients had abnormal EEGs. The findings of Gordon and Sim[26] are especially of interest as all cases were confirmed by cerebral biopsy. Liddell[32] thought it characteristic of 18 cases of Alzheimer's disease that their EEGs showed alterations between theta or slow alpha rhythm and high voltage bilateral, often rhythmic, slow waves. As these changes tended to occur on stimulation and resembled those of sleep, Liddell hypothesized that they were "related to the lowered awareness which these patients show clinically" rather than to any specific pathological feature of the disease. On the other hand, Nevin[29] attributes such runs of random delta to amyloid degeneration of small vessels.

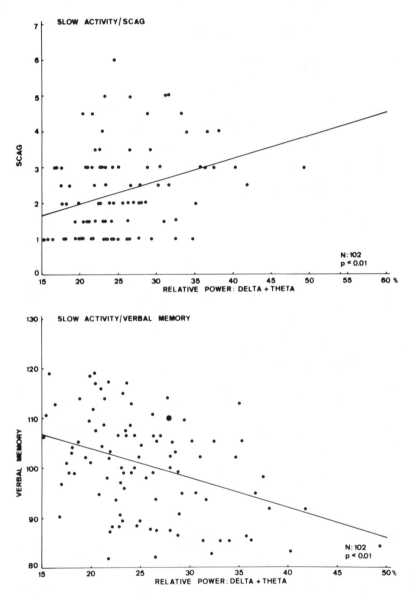

FIGURE 3. Relationship between SCAG score, mnestic performance, and slow EEG activity. The greater the relative power in the delta and theta band, the higher the SCAG score and the worse the mnestic performance as measured by the verbal memory test of Grünberger.

The question arises why some cases of presenile dementia show normal EEGs, while others show obvious abnormalities. Some of the normal EEGs may be due to the fact that premorbid records contain mostly faster rhythms, the slowing of which fails to transgress the lower limits of normality. Johannesson et al.[34] postulated that frontal delta activity may be related to degenerative changes in the brain stem, which they could verify by autopsy. In patients with no brain stem abnormalities EEGs were normal or only mildly abnormal even though there was marked atrophy of the frontal lobe cortex. A compatible observation would be the one by Stefoski et al.[35]—that EEG abnormalities correlate poorly with ventricular size as indicated by CAT scans.

Regarding the EEG reactivity, the threshold of the blocking response rises and this response might be lost altogether. Demented patients show a markedly prolonged AEP latency (P_{300}), exceeding the mean value of normal aging subjects by 3.61 standard deviation.[16]

Sleep patterns of demented patients undergo similar but more pronounced alterations than normal aging persons. Feinberg et al.[19] described longer and more numerous periods of wakefulness, greater reductions in stage 4 sleep and amount of spindle activity, and a striking decrease of REM sleep. Decrease of REM sleep was of particular interest since it is correlated with impairment in intelligence and memory tests.[21,22] EEG sleep measures may even be helpful in the differential diagnosis of dementia and depression in the elderly. Recently Reynolds et al.[36] demonstrated that patients with dementia showed significantly less sleep continuity disturbance, less REM activity, a different temporal distribution of REM density, and a longer REM latency than patients with depression. These differences may be related to defects in acetylcholine production in dementia, cholinergic mechanisms of REM sleep, and increased cholinergic induction of REM sleep in depression.

Findings in Pick's Disease

Passouant et al.[25] made no distinctions between cases of Pick's and Alzheimer's types and Lairy[23] states that they are electrically identical. On the other hand, Gordon and Sim[26] and Nevin[29] found the EEG in Pick's disease mostly normal, but even when they were abnormal, alpha activity could usually still be seen. Kiloh et al.[30] described changes as similar to those seen in Alzheimer's disease but less marked, while focal changes are not a feature of Pick's disease.

Multi-infarct Dementia

According to Gordon and Sim,[26] Constantinidis et al.,[27] and Müller and Schwartz,[28] multi-infarct dementia (MID) patients show usually a well-preserved slow alpha rhythm between 7 and 8 Hz. This observation is quite in contrast to Alzheimer's disease as is the case regarding the higher incidence of focal delta and theta activity in MID, which is due to cerebral infarction. In MID patients with episodes of delirium, regular bifrontal delta activity may appear. Van de Drift[37] attributes this to ischemia of the anterior region of the diencephalon.

VIGILANCE AND MEMORY

Regression and correlation analysis of spectral-analyzed EEG data and memory data in 102 elderly residents of an old people's home and a nursing home, whose

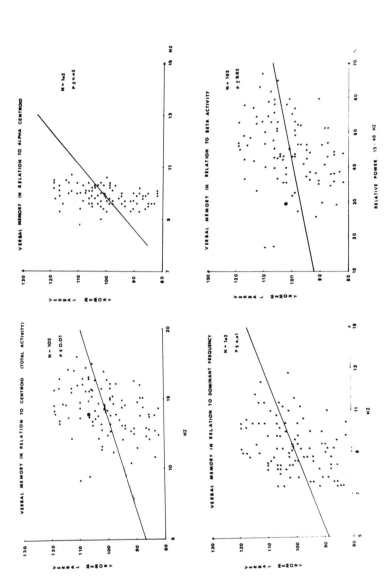

FIGURE 4. Relationship between verbal memory and several spectral and analyzed EEG variables. The faster the centroid of the total activity and of the alpha activity, the higher the dominant frequency and the more beta activity, the better is the performance in the Grünberger Verbal Memory Test.

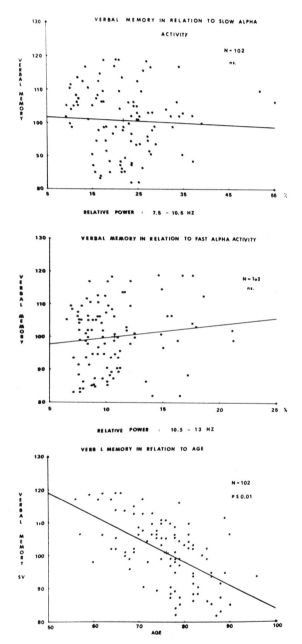

FIGURE 5. Relationship between verbal memory, slow alpha and fast alpha, and age. While verbal memory tends to improve with the amount of fast alpha activity and shows the reverse relationship to slow alpha activity, it clearly decreases with increasing age.

psychopathology was characterized by slight mnestic and intellectual dysfunctions, slight lack of drive and disturbed affect (thus showing a mild organic brain syndrome (OBS)) demonstrated the following findings: the less slow delta and theta activity ($p < 0.01$), the more beta activity (13–40 Hz) ($p < 0.05$), the higher the dominant frequency ($p < 0.01$), the faster the centroid of the alpha activity ($p < 0.05$) and of the total activity ($p < 0.01$); the better the mnestic performance (total standardized score including all three subtests of the Grünberger Verbal Memory Test[38]: general memory, associative memory, and numerical memory) (FIGURES 3 and 4). Concerning alpha activity, we could not determine any significant findings, since fast and slow alpha activity showed oppositional trends: while fast alpha activity (10.5–13 Hz) tended to be positively correlated with mnestic performance, slow alpha activity (7.5–10.5 Hz) showed the oppositional trend (FIGURE 5). Although our findings suggested that elderly subjects with a better neurophysiologically defined vigilance performed better in the memory test, one has to correct for age, as age itself plays an important role both in regard to brain activity (FIGURE 1) and mnestic performance (FIGURE 5). Therefore, we were interested in detecting neurophysiological differences between subjects with good and bad mnestic performance who were matched according to age. As can be seen in FIGURE 6 we could still find that subjects with good performance in three memory tests[38] (general memory, associative memory, and numerical memory) had less slow and more fast activity, a faster centroid of the alpha, and total activity than subjects with bad performance in these tests. Following up on the question whether these mnestic differences may be due to differences in vigilance at the time of the acquisition or at the time of recall, we found that in both instances vigilance was better in the good

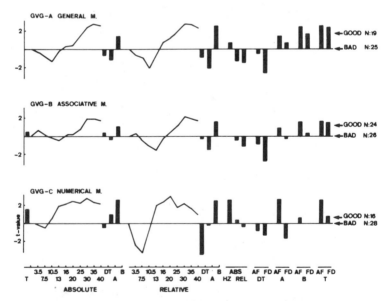

FIGURE 6. Differences in spectral-analyzed R-EEG between elderly subjects with good and bad memory (age-corrected data). 38 spectral-analyzed EEG variables are shown in the abscissa, differences between elderly subjects with good and bad memory are shown in the ordinates. Data were obtained regarding general memory, associative memory, and numerical memory. As can be seen in all three instances, subjects with good memory do have fewer slow and more beta activities.

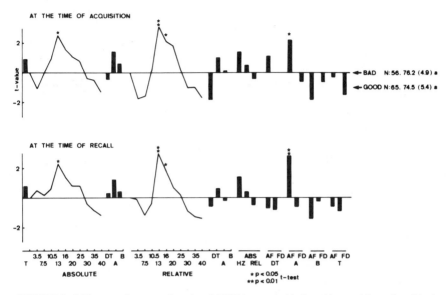

FIGURE 7. Differences in spectral-analyzed EEG between elderly subjects with good and bad memories at the time of acquisition and at the time of recall. Age-matched subjects with good memories exhibit both at the time of acquisition and at the time of recall less slow activity but significantly more alpha and slow beta activity than subjects with bad memory. Moreover, the alpha centroid of the former is significantly faster than in the latter.

than in the bad performers (FIGURE 7). Good performers exhibit both at the time of acquisition and recall less relative power in the low frequency bands, significantly more power in the fast alpha and slow beta bands, and a faster centroid of the alpha activity than bad performers.

PHARMACO-EEG PROFILES OF ANTIHYPOXIDOTIC/NOOTROPICS

Based on the aforementioned neurophysiological findings in normal and pathological aging, one may hypothesize that any procedure inducing an improvement in vigilance as reflected in the EEG should necessarily lead to an improvement in human behavior. Indeed, we have discovered in the last years that several antihypoxidotic/ nootropic drugs do produce changes in the EEG, which are characterized by a decrease of slow activity and an increase of alpha and slow beta activity, thereby inducing CNS changes oppositional to age-related alterations described previously in this paper (FIGURE 8). Such drugs include representatives of different chemical subclasses (FIGURE 9), such as dihydroergotoxine and nicergoline of the ergotalkaloids,[39–41] vincamine, vinconate, SL76100, and SL 76188 of the vincamine alkaloids and analogues,[43–45] ifenprodil, tinofedrine, suloctidile of the phenylethanolamines,[46] piracetam, etiracetam, and aniracetam of the pyrrolidine derivatives structurally related to GABA,[47–51] ethophylline of the xanthine derivatives,[47] buflomedil,[52] ouabaine (g-strophantine) of the cardiac glycosides, acrihelline of the cardiac steroids, and CRL 40028 (a benzhydrylsulfinyl-acetonehydroxamid acid) and its main metabolite CRL 40476 (a benzohydrysulfinylacetamid). Further drugs inducing such CNS changes were piridoxilate (a glyoxilic acid-substituted pyridoxine),[83] Actovegin® (a standard-ized deproteinized hemoderivate), hexobendine and its combination with ethophylline and ethamivan, Instenon forte®,[54,57] and the calcium antagonist cinnarizine.[54] Not only are the aforementioned drugs of different chemical provenance, but they do belong also to different subclasses regarding their mode of action. Metabolically active antihypoxi-dotics include dihydroergotoxine, nicergoline, vincamine, vinconate, buflomedil, pira-cetam, etiracetam, aniracetam, piridoxilate, Actovegin®, and suloctidil. Nicergoline, buflomedil, cinnarizine, and suloctidil have an additional antithrombotic effect,

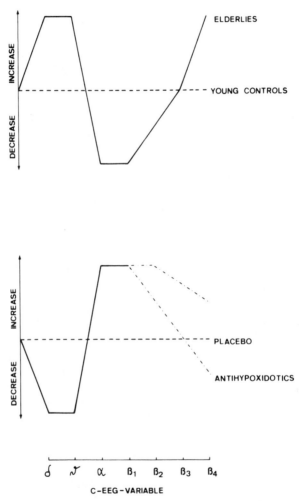

FIGURE 8. Schematic quantitative EEG changes in the elderly and after antihypoxidotics/nootropics. Certain antihypoxidotics induce EEG alterations characterized by decrease of delta and theta and increase of alpha and slow beta activity. These alterations are interestingly oppositional to age-related changes and indicative of vigilance-improving properties of the drugs.

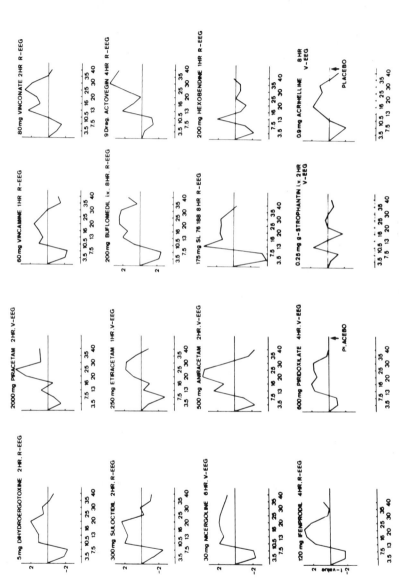

FIGURE 9. Pharmaco-EEG profiles of several antihypoxidotic/nootropics as compared with placebo ($N = 10$). A common decrease in delta and theta activity and an increase in alpha and/or beta activity can be seen as compared with placebo.

suloctidil and buflomedil are also rheologically active. To the vasoactive compounds one may add nicergoline, vincamine, hexobendine, Instenon forte®, buflomedil, cinnarizine, ifenprodil, suloctidil, and ethophylline. Indirect antihypoxidotics are the cardiac steroids and glycosides as they are providing more blood to the brain, although a direct mode of action is discussed.[56]

RELATIONSHIP BETWEEN NEUROPHYSIOLOGICAL AND BEHAVIORAL CHANGES AFTER ANTIHYPOXIDOTIC/NOOTROPICS

In an effort to show a more direct relationship between neurophysiological and behavioral changes after administration of antihypoxidotic drugs, we investigated correlations between etiracetam-induced changes in delta activity in the EEG and "wakefulness" as evaluated by means of a semantic differential polarity profile in elderly subjects. As can be seen in FIGURE 10, the greater a decrease of relative power in the delta band, the greater an increase in wakefulness was experienced by the subjects themselves.

However, since vigilance as defined by Head[3] reflects much more than just "wakefulness" or "vigility," one would expect that changes in brain activity are related to changes in other psychometric variables. Examining, for instance, neurophysiological and behavioral alterations after aniracetam in elderly subjects,[50] we found that increase in dominant frequency, decrease in delta activity, and increase in slow beta activity (16–20 Hz) was associated with an improvement in motor activity, complex reaction, reaction time, mood, affectivity, attention variability, tapping, and an increase in CFF (FIGURE 11). This association was not only found in acute studies, but also after chronic administration of antihypoxidotics (such as nicergoline)[41] in the elderly, which supports the idea that improvement of vigilance is linked to improvement in adaptive behavior in man.

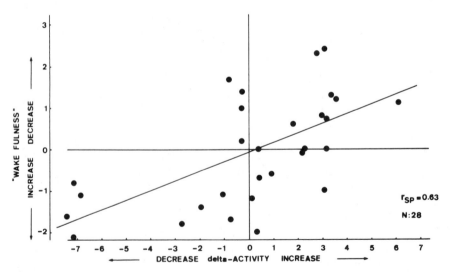

FIGURE 10. Relationships between etiracetam-induced changes in delta activity (relative power, V-EEG) and subjectively experienced "wakefulness."

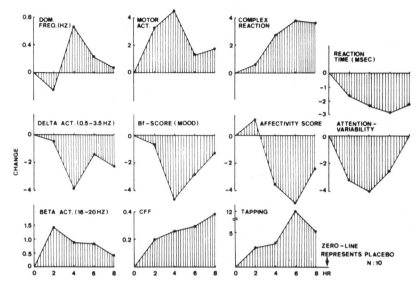

FIGURE 11. Relation between changes in the spectral-analyzed EEG and psychometric variables after single oral doses of 1,000 mg aniracetam (RO 13-5057) in the elderly $N = 10$. An acceleration of dominant frequency, decrease of delta activity, and increase of beta activity in the EEG is linked to improvement in motor activity, complex reaction, reaction time, mood, affectivity, attention variability, critical flicker frequency, and tapping.

NEUROPHYSIOLOGICAL ASPECTS IN PROVING THERAPEUTIC EFFICACY OF ANTIHYPOXIDOTICS IN HUMANS

While the pharmaco-EEG method has been shown to be of great help in the early screenings of antihypoxidotics/nootropic drugs in humans as it was possible to assess objectively and quantitatively the encephalotropic effects of new compounds at the target organ, the human central nervous system,[47–49] we were looking also for human models to prove more directly the therapeutic efficacy of antihypoxidotics apart from the usual double-blind trials in patients with primary degenerative or vascular dementia.

One such an approach was to investigate the protective properties of antihypoxidotics against cerebral hypoxic hypoxidosis.[57,58] Hypoxic hypoxidosis was induced by a fixed gas combination of 11.3% oxygen and 88.7% nitrogen, which was inhaled under normobaric conditions by healthy volunteers for a period of 23 minutes. The attainment of hypoxemia was controlled by blood-gas analysis of the arterialized capillary blood from the ear lobes. Under this condition, oxygen tension decreased significantly from initial values of around 98 mm Hg to approximately 40 mm Hg within 14 minutes and remained stable thereafter. Spectral analysis of the EEG demonstrated under hypoxia a marked and significant change in brain function characterized by an increase in delta activity, a decrease in alpha and slow beta activity as well as an increase in fast beta activity, while under normoxia only minimal alterations occurred. Antihypoxidotic drugs, for instance aniracetam, attenuated the hypoxia-induced augmentation of slow activities and decrease of alpha activity, thus exhibiting protective properties against hypoxia in humans (FIGURE 12). These protective qualities could also be substantiated at the behavioral level, as psychometric changes during hypoxia were mitigated by the drug (FIGURE 13). The hypoxia-induced behavioral deterioration was characterized by a decrease in psychomotor activity, attention and mood, as well as by a slightly less pronounced decrease in attention variability, mnestic performance, and increase of errors in a reaction time task.

Another clinical approach lies in the utilization of the organic brain syndrome (OBS) of the alcoholic patient. The alcoholic organic brain syndrome is a reversible OBS, whose time-course may be studied under much better conditions than in elderly patients, as the latter are usually on different drugs for various ailments resulting in interaction problems, while the alcoholic OBS patients are treated mainly by psychotherapy and group and occupational therapy. As we have done already some years ago,[59] we recently studied the spontaneous remission of the OBS in abstaining alcoholic patients by clinical, psychometric, and quantitative EEG analyses and investigated further the question of whether or not this remission could be accelerated by the antihypoxidotic drug piridoxilate.[60] This drug, a reciprocal salt between two stereoisomers of the glyoxylic acid-substituted pyridoxine, has been predicted by us in a double-blind, placebo-controlled pharmaco-EEG experiment to have encephalotropic

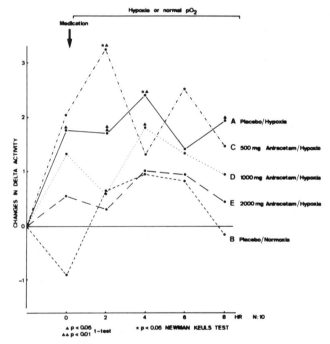

FIGURE 12. Changes in relative power of the delta activity during hypoxia after placebo and aniracetam. Time is shown in the abscissa, changes in delta activity as compared with baseline (00) are indicated in the ordinate. While under normoxia only small changes or even a decrease in delta activity occurs, hypoxia induces a significant augmentation of delta activity, which is attenuated by higher doses of aniracetam.

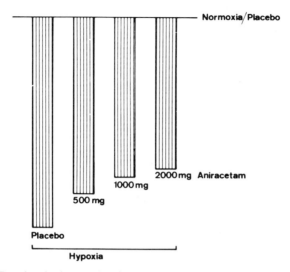

FIGURE 13. Deterioration in mental performance during hypoxic hypoxidosis and the protective properties of aniracetam shown by means of Euclid's distances based on discriminant analysis of changes in eight psychometric variables.

and psychotropic properties.[53] Similar to other antihypoxidotics/nootropics, its pharmaco-EEG profile was characterized by a decrease of slow activities as well as by an increase of alpha and beta activities and an acceleration of the dominant frequency as compared with placebo. These neurophysiological changes were associated behaviorally by an improvement in concentration, attention variability, complex reaction, affectivity, and by an increase in CFF as compared with placebo. In the present OBS study assessments were carried out before as well as at the end of the second, fourth, and sixth week of therapy and included clinical ratings, psychometric tests, blood tests, and quantitative EEG investigations. Statistical analysis of the psychopathological data demonstrated that the patients on piridoxilate showed a statistically significant greater improvement of their OBS than patients on placebo (FIGURE 14). This was paralleled in the quantitatively analyzed EEG by a significantly greater decrease in delta activity in the piridoxilate-treated patients than in the placebo-treated ones. The correlation coefficient between the OBS score and the delta activity was +0.686. Thus the study could demonstrate that an antihypoxidotic/nootropic drug, identified as such by the pharmaco-EEG, may improve the organic brain syndrome.

SUMMARY

Human brain function as measured by the computer-assisted spectral analyzed electroencephalogram (EEG) shows significant alterations in normal and pathological aging characterized by an increase of delta and theta activity and by a decrease of alpha and alpha-adjacent beta activity as well as by a slowing of the dominant frequency. These changes are indicative of deficits in the vigilance-regulatory systems. By the term vigilance we understand the availability and grade of organization of man's adaptive behavior, which in turn is dependent of the dynamic state of the total neural activity. An impairment of vigilance was found to be significantly correlated with the clinical symptomatology of the organic brain syndrome (OBS) as well as with mnestic performance deficits. Elderly subjects with bad memory exhibit slower activity and less alpha and alpha-adjacent beta activity than those with good memory. This was found to be true for both the time of acquisition and recall. Antihypoxidotic/nootropic drugs, such as the ergotalkaloids dihydroergotoxine and nicergoline, vincamine-alkaloids, piracetam, aniracetam, etiracetam, piridoxilate and others, induce interestingly just oppositional changes in human brain function, thereby improving vigilance.

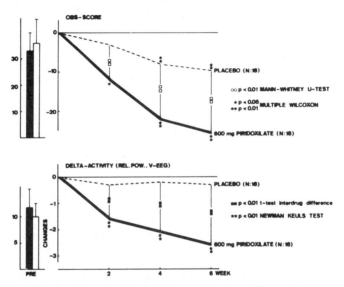

FIGURE 14. Clinical and neurophysiological changes of patients with an alcoholic organic brain syndrome during treatment with either piridoxilate (3 × 200 mg) or placebo. Changes in the OBS score at different time periods are shown in the upper part of the figure, changes in the spectral-analyzed delta activity of the R-EEG are demonstrated in the lower part of the figure. As can be seen, a significantly more pronounced decrease in the organic brain syndrome of piridoxilate patients than in placebo-treated patients is paralleled by a significantly greater decrease in delta activity.

Other methods for proving therapeutic efficacy in man, like experimentally induced hypoxic hypoxidosis and the reversible alcoholic OBS, are discussed.

REFERENCES

1. BERGER, H. 1921. Psychophysiologie in 12 Vorlesungen. Fischer. Jena, Germany.
2. THOMPSON, L. W. & W. D. OBRIST. 1964. EEG-correlates of verbal learning and overlearning. Electroencephalogr. Clin. Neurophysiol. **17:** 332–343.
3. HEAD, H. 1923.

4. THOMPSON, L. W. & WILSON. 1966. Electocortical reactivity and learning in the elderly. J. Gerontol. **21:** 45–51.

5. BERLYNE, D. E. & J. L. LEWIS. 1963. Effects of heightened arousal on human exploratory behavior. Can. J. Psychol. **17:** 398–410.

6. UEHLING, B. & R. SRINKLE. 1968. Recall of a serial list as a function of arousal and retention interval. J. Exp. Psychol. **74:** 289–293.

7. SURWILLO, W. 1968. Timing of behavior in senescence and the role of the central nervous system. In Human Aging and Behavior. E. Talland, Ed.: 1–33. Academic Press. New York.

8. VAN DER DRIFT, J. H. A., N. K. D. KOK, E. NIEDERMEYER, R. NAGUET & R. S. VIGOUROUX. 1972. The EEG in relation to pathology in simple cerebral ischaemia. In Handbook of Electroencephalography and Clinical Neurophysiology. A. Remond, Ed. Vol. 14A. Amsterdam. Elsevier.

9. MATEJCEK, M. & J. E. DEVOS. 1976. Selected methods of quantitative EEG analysis and their application in psychotropic drug research. In Quantitative Analytic Studies in Elipepsy. P. Kellaway & I. Peterson, Eds.: 183–205. Raven Press, New York.

10. OBRIST, W. D. 1980. Cerebral blood flow and EEG changes associated with aging and dementia. In Handbook of Geriatric Psychiatry. E. W. Busse & D. G. Blazer, Eds. Van Nostrand Reinhold Company, New York.

11. MATEJCEK, J. 1979. Chronospectrogram analysis in the assessment of spontaneous and drug-induced changes in vigilance. In Neuro-Psychopharmacology. B. Saletu, P. Berner & L. Hollister, Eds.: 409–416. Pergamon Press. Oxford.

12. BUSSE, E. W. & W. D. OBRIST. 1965. Pre-senescent electroencephalographic changes in normal subjects. J. Geront. **20:** 315–320.

13. TOMLINSON, B. E. & G. HENDERSON. 1976. Some quantitative cerebral findings in normal and demented old people. In Neurobiology of Aging. R. D. Terry & S. Gershon, Eds.: 183–204, Raven Press. New York.

14. OTOMO, E. & R. TSUBAKI. 1966. Electroencephalography in subjects sixty years and over. Electroenceph. Clin. Neurophysiol. **20:** 77–82.

15. MANKOVSKY, N. B. & R. P. BELONO. 1971. Aging of the human nervous system in the electroencephalographic aspect. Geriatrics **26:** 100–116.

16. SQUIRES, K., T. CHIPPENDALE, K. WREGE, D. GOODIN & A. STARR. 1980. Electrophysiological assessment of mental function in aging and dementia. In Determining the Effects of Aging on the Central Nervous System. G. E. Gurski, Ed.: 93–104. Free University of Berlin/Schering AG. Berlin.

17. FREEMON, F. R. 1972. Sleep Research: A Critical Review. C. C. Thomas. Springfield, IL.

18. TUNE, G. S. 1969. Sleep and wakefulness in 509 normal adults. Brit. J. Med. Psychol. **42:** 75–80.

19. FEINBERG, I., R. L. KORESKO & N. HELLER. 1967. EEG sleep patterns as a function of normal and pathological aging in man. J. Psychiat. Res. **5:** 107–144.

20. PRINZ, P. N. 1977. Sleep patterns in the healthy aged: Relationship with intellectual function. J. Geront. **32:** 179–186.

21. FEINBERG, I. 1976. Functional implications of changes in sleep physiology with age. In Neurobiology of Aging. R. D. Terry & S. Gershon, Eds.: 23–41. Raven Press. New York.

22. MUNDY-CASTLE, A. C., L. A. HURST, D. M. BEERSTECHER & T. PRINSLOO. 1954. The electroencephalogram in the senile psychoses. Electroenceph. Clin. Neurophysiol. **6:** 245.

23. LAIRY, G. C. 1956. Organization de l'electroencephalogramme normal et pathologique. Rev. Neurol. **94:** 749.

24. LETEMENDIA, F. & G. PAMPIGLIONE. 1958. Clinical and electroencephalographic observations in Alzhemier's disease. J. Neurol. Neurosurg. Psychiat. **21:** 167.

25. PASSOUANT, P., J. CADILHAC, M. WALTER & E. MORETTI. 1956. Les indications assportées par l'E.E.G. au cours des encephaloses. Rev. Neurol. **95:** 573.

26. GORDON, E. B. & M. SIM. 1967. The EEG in presenile dementia. J. Neurol. Neurosurg. Psychiat. **30:** 285–291.

27. CONSTANTINIDIS, J., M. KRASSOIEVITCH & R. TISSOT. 1969. Correlations entre les perturbations electroencephalographiques et les lesions anatomohistologiques dans les demences. L'Encéphale **58:** 19–52.
28. MÜLLER, H. F. & G. SCHWARTZ. 1978. Electroencephalograms and autopsy findings in geropsychiatry. J. Geront. **33:** 504–513.
29. NEVIN, S. 1967. On some aspects of cerebral degeneration in later life. Proc. R. Soc. Med. **60:** 517.
30. KIHOH, L. G., A. J. MCKOMAS, J. W. OSSELTON & A. R. M. UPTON. 1981. Clinical Electroencephalography. Butterworths. London.
31. OBRIST, W. D. 1976. Problems of aging. In Handbook of Electroencephalography and Clinical Neurophysiology. A. Remond, Ed. 6(Part A): 275–292. Elsevier Publishing Co. Amsterdam.
32. LIDDELL, D. W. 1958. Investigation of EEG findings in presenile dementia. J. Neurol. Neurosurg. Psychiat. **21:** 173.
33. SWAIN, I. M. 1959. Electroencephalographic abnormalities in presenile atrophy. Neurology **9:** 722.
34. JOHANNESSON, G., A. BRUN, I. GUSTAFSON & D. H. INGVAR. 1977. EEG in presenile dementia related to cerebral blood flow and autopsy findings. Acta Neurol. Scand. **56:** 89.
35. STEFOSKI, D., D. BERGEN, J. FOX, R. MORRELL, M. HUCKMAN & R. TAMSEY. 1976. Correlation between diffuse EEG abnormalities and cerebral atrophy in senile dementia. J. Neurol. Neurosurg. Psychiat. **39:** 751.
36. REYNOLDS, C. F., D. G. SPIKER, I. HANIN & D. J. KUPFER. 1983. Electroencephalographic sleep, aging and psychopathology: New data and the state of art. Biol. Psychiatry **18:** 139–155.
37. VAN DER DRIFRT, J. H. A. 1961. Ischaemie cerebral lesions. Angiology **12:** 401.
38. GRÜNBERGER, J. 1977. Psychodiagnostik des Aldoholkranken. Ein methodischer Beitrag zur Bestimmung der Organizität in der Psychiatrie. Maudrich. Vienna.
39. SALETU, B., J. GRÜNBERGER & L. LINZMAYER. 1977. Classification and determination of cerebral bioavailability of psychotropic drugs by quantitative "pharmaco-EEG" and psychometric investigations (studies with AX-A-411-BS). Int. J. Clin. Pharmacol. **15:** 449–459.
40. SALETU, B., J. GRÜNBERGER & L. LINZMAYER. 1979. Bestimmung der encephalotropen, psychotropen und pharmakodynamische Eigenschaften von Nicergolin mittels quantitativer Pharmako-elektroenzephalographie und psychometrischer Analysen. Arzneim.-Forsch. Drug. Res. **29:** 1251–1261.
41. SALETU, B., J. GRÜNBERGER, L. LINZMAYER & P. ANDERER. 1979. Proof of CNS efficacy and pharmacodynamics of nicergoline in the elderly by acute and psychometric studies. In Drug Treatment in Chronic Cerebrovascular Disorders. G. Tognoni & S. Garattini, Eds.: 245–272. Biomedical Press. Elsevier/North Holland. Amsterdam.
42. BENTE, D., G. GLATTHARR, G. ULRICH & M. LEWINSKY. 1979. Quantitative EEG-Untersuchungen zur vigilanzfördernden Wirking von Nicergolin. Ergebnisse einer Doppelblindstudie bei gerontopsychiatrischen Patienten. Arzneimittel-Forsch. **29:** 1804–1808.
43. SALETU, B. & J. GRÜNBERGER. 1982. Zur Pharmakocynamik von Vicamin: Pharmako-EEG und psychometrische Studien bei Alternden. In Fortschritte in Pathophysiologie, Diagnostik und Therapie cerebraler Gefäßkrankheiten. H. Lechner, Ed.: 154–177. Excerpta Medica. Amsterdam.
44. SALETU, B., J. GRÜNBERGER, L. LINZMAYER & R. WITTEK. 1984. Classification and determination of pharmacodynamics of a new antihypoxidotic drug, vinconate, by pharmaco-EEG and psychometry. Arch Gerontol. Geriatr. **3:** 127–146.
45. SALETU, B., J. GRÜNBERGER, L. LINZMAYER & H. STÖHR. 1982. Objective measures in determining the central effectiveness of a new anti-hypoxidotic SL 76188: Pharmaco-EEG, psychometric and pharmacokinetic analyses in the elderly. Arch. Gerontol. Geriatr. **1:** 261–285.
46. SALETU, B. & P. ANDERER. 1980. Double-blind placebo-controlled quantitative pharmaco-EEG investigations after tinofedrine i.v. in geriatric patients. Curr. Ther. Res. **28:** 1–15.

47. SALETU, B. 1981. Application of quantitative EEG in measuring encephalotropic and pharmacodynamic properties of antihypoxidotic/nootropic drugs. *In* Scientific International Research. Drugs and Methods in C.V.D. Proc. Int. Cerebrovascular Diseases. pp. 79–115. Pergamon Press. France.

48. SALETU, B. 1981. Nootropic drugs and human brain function. *In* Stress and the Heart. D. Wheatley, Ed.: 327–359. Raven Press. New York.

49. SALETU, B. & J. GRÜNBERGER. 1980. Antihypoxidotic and nootropic drugs: Proof of their encephalotropic and pharmacodynamic properties by quantitative EEG investigations. Prog. Neuro-Psychopharmacol. **4:** 469–489.

50. SALETU, B., J. GRÜNBERGER & L. LINZMAYER. 1980. Quantitative EEG and psychometric analyses in assessing CNS-activity of RO13-5057—a cerebral insufficiency improver. Meth. Find. Exptl. Clin. Pharmacol. **2:** 269–285.

51. BENTE, D. 1977. Vigilanz: Psychophysiologische Aspekte. Verh. dtsch. Ges. Med. **83:** 945–952.

52. SALETU, B., J GRÜNBERGER, L. LINZMAYER & H. STÖHR. 1984. Encephalotropic and psychotropic effects of intravenous buflomedil in the elderly: Double blind, placebo-controlled pharmaco-EEG and psychometric studies. Int. J. Clin. Pharm. Res. **4:** 95–107.

53. SALETU, B., J. GRÜNBERGER, P. RAJNA & H. STÖHR. 1982. Vigilanz-verbesserung bei alternden Menschen. Doppelblinde, placebokontrollierte neurophysiologische und psychometrische Studien mit Piridoxilat. Therapiewoche **32:** 5590–5603.

54. SALETU, B. & J. GRÜNBERGER. 1978. Antihypoxidotic and nootropic drugs: Proof of their encephalotropic and pharmacodynamic properties by quantitative EEG investigations. Prog. Neuro-Psychopharmacol. **2:** 543–551.

55. SALETU, B. 1976. Psychopharmaka, Gehirntätigkeit und Schlaf. Karger. Basel.

56. HEISS, W. D. & K. ZEILER. 1978. Medikamentöse Beeinflussung der Hirndurchblutung. Pharmakotherapie **1:** 137–144.

57. SALETU, B. & J. GRÜNBERGER. Cerebral hypoxic hypoxidosis: Neurophysiological, psychometric and pharmacotherapeutic aspects. Adv. Biol. Psychiat. **13:** 146–164.

58. SALETU, B. & J. GRÜNBERGER. 1984. The hypoxia model in human psychopharmacology: neurophysiological and psychometric studies with aniracetam i.v. Human Neurobiol. **3:** 171–181.

59. SALETU, B., J. GRÜNBERGER, M. SALETU, R. MADER & J. VOLAVKA. 1978. Treatment of the alcoholic organic brain syndrom with EMD 21657—a derivative of a pyritinol-metabolite: Double-blind clinical, quantitative EEG and psychometric studies. Int. Pharmacopsychiat. **13:** 177–192.

60. SALETU, B., M. SALETU, J. GRÜNBERGER & R. MADER. 1983. Spontaneous and drug induced remission of alcoholic organic brain syndrome: clinical psychometric, and quantitative EEG studies. Psychiatry Res. **10:** 59–75.

Clinical Drug Trials
in Alzheimer's Disease

THOMAS CROOK

Center for Studies of the Mental Health of the Aging
National Institute of Mental Health
Rockville, Maryland 20857

Alzheimer's disease (AD) may be the most tragic and dehumanizing disorder of late life. In AD one literally "loses one's mind," being reduced from the unique product of decades of personal experience to a drifting, vegetative state in which the children and spouse to whom a lifetime was devoted become unrecognizable and, eventually, even the abilities to move about and utter interpretable sounds are lost. Nearly one and one-half million Americans are now incapacitated as a result of AD and that number will double within the next fifty years as the rapid and unprecedented growth of the elderly population continues.

The search for effective pharmacologic treatments for the symptoms of AD and other age-related disorders was underway well before the journey of Ponce de Leon to the new world in 1513. Only in recent years, however, have attempts to treat late-life dementing disorders been based on sound empirical data rather than on assumptions about disease processes. It is noteworthy that in the late 1700s Benjamin Rush, the first American psychiatrist and signer of the Declaration of Independence, reasoned that mental disorders were caused by sludging of the blood within the brain and developed the "gyrating chair" in which patients were spun in a circular motion to improve blood flow and, hence, facilitate mental function. Until scarcely more than a decade ago, some two hundred years after Dr. Rush's experiments, most treatment strategies for AD and related disorders were still based on a presumed vascular etiology. Although the gyrating chair had been replaced by vasodilators, anticoagulants, and other drugs, as well as such creative techniques as hyperbaric oxygenation, assumptions about the etiology of dementia remained virtually unchanged. Of course the causes of AD are still unknown but, as described in many of the excellent foregoing papers in this volume, several rational treatment strategies have emerged during recent years based on specific neurochemical deficits demonstrated in AD or on behavioral drug effects discovered in animal models relevant to the disorder.

This paper will review the drugs currently prescribed in the United States for the treatment of AD and consider a broad range of investigational drugs recently studied or currently under study in AD. Particular emphasis will be placed on recent trials with cholinergic compounds, neuropeptides, and nootropic drugs.

CURRENT PHARMACOLOGIC TREATMENTS

The drugs currently marketed for the treatment of age-related cognitive symptoms such as those seen in AD are listed in TABLE 1. Of these, by far the most widely prescribed is dihydroergotoxine. This compound is a combination of three ergot alkaloids in their dihydrogenated forms. Dihydroergotoxine has been studied in more than 33 double-blind, clinical trials in aged patients with complaints of memory impairment. Most of the trials were undertaken prior to the development of current diagnostic criteria and samples were probably composed of both AD and multi-infarct dementia (MID) patients as well as patients with other specific organic disorders and with depression. In such studies, dihydroergotoxine has consistently been shown to exert a quite modest but statistically significant effect on a broad range of clinical symptoms assessed through patient report and clinical observation.[1,2] However, where patient performance has been measured directly, using psychological tests or mental status exams, drug effects have generally not been apparent.[3] It thus appears that the drug exerts a mild activating or mood-elevating effect rather than a direct effect on memory or cognitive processes.[4] Nevertheless, dihydroergotoxine may produce overall clinical improvement in some AD and MID patients and, given the absence of reasonable alternatives, a trial of the drug in individual patients may be warranted. Two recent studies[5,6] suggest that a daily dose of 6 mg rather than the standard 3 mg dose may be more efficacious. Also, it has been argued that an extended trial of six months is warranted.[2]

Aside from the question of diminishing established symptoms, it has been argued that dihydroergotoxine is effective in preventing cognitive deterioration in normal or mildly impaired elderly persons.[7,8] Of course, a great deal more evidence will be required to establish any such prophylactic effect.

TABLE 1. Drugs Currently Prescribed in the United States to Treat Cognitive Impairments in the Elderly

dihydroergotoxine
Vasodilators
papaverine
isoxsuprine
cyclandelate
"Stimulants"
methylphenidate
pentylenetetrazol
procaine GH3 (in Nevada)

Evidence of clinical efficacy for the three vasodilators listed in TABLE 1 is extremely limited in either AD or MID.[1] In the case of papaverine, for example, five direct comparisons with dihydroergotoxine favor the latter drug despite its quite modest therapeutic effects. Clinical studies recently undertaken with these "desi" drugs are currently being examined by the Federal Food and Drug Administration and their future in the marketplace is uncertain.

The two stimulants listed in TABLE 1 are currently approved for multiple indications, including the treatment of selected symptoms associated with senile dementia. In general, the utility of stimulants in AD or MID is extremely limited.[9,10] Methylphenidate does not appear to directly improve memory or other cognitive processes,[11] but the drug may be of some limited value in treating secondary symptoms of dementia seen in some patients such as fatigue, motor retardation, or depressed mood.[12] In the case of pentylenetetrazol, or the many compounds containing pentylene-tetrazol and nicotinic acid, there appears to be no sound evidence of efficacy.

The last drug listed in TABLE 1, a procaine formulation marketed as Gerovital or GH3 is not approved by the Federal Food and Drug Administration for the treatment of primary or secondary symptoms of dementia but is sold within the state of Nevada. The drug appears to have no direct effect on cognition but it is a relatively weak monoamine oxidase inhibitor and may have mild mood-elevating effects.[13,14]

In addition to the drugs listed in TABLE 1, compounds marketed for other indications, such as anticoagulants, have been studied in AD but no satisfactory evidence of efficacy has emerged.

Thus, it would appear that compounds currently available to the clinician for treating the primary symptoms of senile dementia are of quite limited utility. It is important to emphasize, however, that, in a sense, many major psychotropic agents on the market could be described as antidementia drugs. For example, neuroleptics are used to treat a broad range of dyssocial and psychotic symptoms that may accompany the disorder; antidepressants are widely used to treat affective symptoms that accompany, and may even mimic, senile dementia; and sedative-hypnotics are used to treat the sleep disorders that predictably occur in dementia patients.

The place of neuroleptics in the treatment of dementia patients is particularly important. Despite the widespread use of these drugs in severely impaired dementia patients, remarkably little is known about their optimal use in that population. It is clear that many generalizations from research in young adult schizophrenics are hazardous. For example, neuroleptic dosage requirements in demented elderly patients are frequently far lower than in younger psychotic patients.[15] Although a great deal more clinical research with neuroleptics in elderly dementia patients is needed, and it is clear that these drugs will not cure senile dementia, they remain extremely important management tools that may delay, and in some cases prevent, institutionalization.

INVESTIGATIONAL DRUGS

Cholinomimetic Compounds

A number of strategies have been employed in the search for an effective treatment for AD.[16] Clearly, the most systematic research has followed the cholinergic hypothesis of geriatric memory dysfunction described so elegantly in the foregoing papers of Drs. Davies, Price, and Bartus. Because cholinergic drug trials were discussed in earlier papers, only a brief review of clinical trials will be presented here.

The principal cholinomimetic drugs or drug combinations studied to date are identified in TABLE 2. The most thoroughly studied of these compounds are the acetylcholine precursors choline and lecithin. More than 20 controlled clinical trials have been conducted with these compounds in patients with presumed AD. As a result

TABLE 2. Cholinomimetics

Acetylcholine precursors
choline chloride
lecithin (phosphatidylcholine)
Acetycholinesterase inhibitors
physostigmine
tetrahydroaminoacridine (THA)
Agonists
arecoline
RS-86
bethanecol
Combination treatments
lecithin plus piracetam
lecithin plus physostigmine

TABLE 3. Neuropeptides

ACTH 4–10
ORG 2766 (ACTH 4–9 analog)
vasopressin
lysine vasopressin (LVP)
l-desamino-8-d-arginine vasopression (DDAVP)
desglycinamide-arginine vasopression (DGAVP)
naloxone, naltrexone

---

of these trials it now appears reasonable to conclude that precursor therapy is not an effective treatment in AD.[17] There is one recent study[18] arguing that long term lecithin administration exerts a therapeutic effect in a subgroup of AD patients, but the study is clearly open to methodologic criticism.

Trials with acetylcholinesterase inhibitors, physostigmine, and tetrahydroamino-acridine (THA), and with muscarinic agonists such as arecoline and RS86 are somewhat more encouraging. Briefly, studies with physostigmine, alone[19] and in combination with lecithin,[20,21] have shown clinically modest but quite clear drug effects on selected cognitive measures in some AD patients. Similar changes have also been reported with another cholinesterase inhibitor, tetrahydroaminoacridine,[22] and with the muscarinic agonist arecoline.[23] Preliminary reports of subjective improvement in confirmed AD patients have also come from Dr. Robert Harbaugh and colleagues at Dartmouth University where the muscarinic agonist bethanecol has been administered by intracranial infusion delivered through an implantable pump.

Studies have also been conducted in both humans and animals in which lecithin was combined with the much-studied "nootropic" compound piracetam. The combination treatment was found more effective than treatment with either compound alone in facilitating retention in aged rats[24] and preliminary analyses of ongoing controlled studies in humans suggest that modest improvement may occur in some AD patients on specific measures.[25,26] These studies are discussed in detail by Dr. Growdon in the following chapter.

In general, the cholinergic agents studied to date have clearly not been established as clinically effective therapeutic agents in AD. However, studies with cholinesterase inhibitors, muscarinic agonists, and combined therapies demonstrate that small but reliable changes can be produced in a disease previously thought to be marked by inexorable deterioration.

Neuropeptides

As described in earlier papers by Dr. Koob and others, several neuropeptides have been shown to exert significant effects on learning and memory in animal models. On the basis of these findings, clinical trials with neuropeptides related to adrenocortico-trophic hormone (ACTH) and vasopressin (VP) have been undertaken in patients with presumed AD, as well as in normals and persons suffering from other forms of cognitive impairment. The principal ACTH and VP compounds studies are listed in TABLE 3 together with the opiate antagonist naloxone, a compound also recently studied in AD.

In general, clinical studies with ACTH and VP peptides have been disappointing, although clinical effects have been reported and the search continues for more effective compounds.[27,28] It appears that the principal effects of the ACTH peptides are on mood and attention, rather than on learning and memory, and, thus, drug effects may

TABLE 4. Vascular and Rheologic Agents

nylidrin
pentoxifylline
suloctodil
naftidrofuryl
vincamine, apovincamine, vinconate
calcium channel blockers (nimodipine)

resemble those seen with dihydroergotoxine and other "geriatric drugs."[19] Similarly, VP peptides appear to produce non-specific CNS stimulation, rather than direct improvement of memory or other cognitive functions impaired in AD.[28] Whatever the mechanism, the magnitude of clinical change observed in clinical studies of ACTH and VP peptides in AD has been generally quite modest.

A recent study that generated considerable interest[30] suggested that the narcotic antagonist naloxone may be of clinical value in treating AD. Other evidence[31] questions the utility of the drug and, at present, several well-controlled studies are underway to determine whether the drug, or the oral analog naltrexone, is clinically effective in AD. Evidence from animal studies suggests that, like the ACTH and VP peptides, the primary effects of the drug may be on attentional processes rather than learning and memory.[32]

Vascular and Rheologic Agents

As discussed in the previous section on marketed drugs, the evidence to support use of the established vasodilators in AD is, at best, tenuous.[1] The use of these compounds grew out of the hypothesis that dementia results from cerebral arteriosclerosis, reduced blood flow, and consequent cerebral ischemia. Of course, it is now clear that this is not the cause of AD and even in the case of vascular dementias, vasodilator therapy may be problematic since it may actually reduce blood flow to ischemic areas.[33] Thus, there is little current research interest in vasodilator therapy in AD.

In contrast to the direct-acting vasodilators, the compounds listed in TABLE 4 have more complex metabolic or rheologic effects and have been studied, or are under study, in patients with presumed AD or in samples that include AD patients. In general, these drugs may produce quite modest effects in some patients on psychiatric ratings of alertness, depression, and confusion, but there is no sound evidence of objective changes in memory or other cognitive variables. Of primary research interest at present are selected calcium channel blockers, particularly nimodopine, which have diverse metabolic effects and have not yet been adequately tested in either vascular dementias or AD.

TABLE 5. Other Investigational Drugs of Interest

piracetam and analogs (aniracetam, oxiracetam, pramiracetam)
CI-911
4-amino-pyridine, 3,4-diaminepyridine
Active lipid
centrophenoxine
aluminum chelators
alapractolate

Other Investigational Drugs of Interest

Several of the many other investigational drugs of interest are listed in TABLE 5. Among the compounds listed, those that have received by far the most attention are the so-called nootropic agents, piracetam and its analogs and CI-911. These drugs have clear behavioral effects in animal learning paradigms but do not produce the side effects seen with other psychoactive drugs. Piracetam, the prototype nootropic compound, is an analog of gamma aminobutyric acid (GABA) that has clear effects on brain metabolism, facilitates performance on measures of learning and retention in rats, and protects against hypoxia-induced memory impairment in animals.[34] Controlled clinical studies in AD and other age-related cognitive disorders have been equivocal and suggest no clear pattern of cognitive improvement.[25] As noted previously, a combination treatment of piracetam plus lecithin was found more effective than either drug alone in facilitating retention in aged rats[35] and preliminary analyses of ongoing clinical studies[26,36] suggest that some patients with AD may also show response to this treatment. However, any effects are likely to be quite subtle.

Positive reports have appeared concerning the efficacy of the newer piracetam analogs in AD[37,38] and multi-center studies with several of these drugs, as well as with CI-911, are currently underway. Any conclusion as to whether these drugs represent significant improvements over the extremely modest effects of piracetam must await the outcome of these studies. A dramatic therapeutic advance appears unlikely.

Among other experimental drugs of interest in AD are 4-amino-pyridine and 3,4-diaminepyridine, compounds with multiple pharmacologic effects that facilitate oxidative metabolism;[39] Active lipid, a compound designed to fluidize cell membranes;[40] centrophenoxine, a stimulant also thought to deplete age-related lipofuscin accumulation;[41] aluminum chelators, such as desferrioxamine;[42] and alaproclate, a 5-HT reuptake inhibitor.[43]

In view of the emerging neurochemical evidence that AD involves multiple neurotransmitter systems,[44,45] it may be that therapeutic strategies involving combination treatments or even an individualized "cocktail" approach[43] will be necessary to develop effective treatments for what may be the most tragic and dehumanizing of all mental disorders.

Although clearly effective drugs have not yet been developed for treating the primary symptoms of AD, dramatic progress has been made in recent years in uncovering the neurochemical deficits in the disorder and, hence, in developing rational treatment strategies. If the pace of this progress continues, we may see the development of a truly effective compound for treating AD. Such a drug would be of inestimable personal and social value.

REFERENCES

1. YESAVAGE, J. A., J. R. TINKLENBERG, L. E. HOLLISTER & P. A. BERGER. 1979. Vasodilators in senile dementia: A review of the literature. Arch. Gen. Psychiatry **36:** 220–223.

2. HOLLISTER, L. E. & J. A. YESAVAGE. 1985. Co-dergocrine for senile dementias: After thirty years many unanswered questions. Ann. Intern. Med. (In press.)

3. MCDONALD, R. J. 1982. Drug treatment of senile dementia. In Psychopharmacology of Old Age. D. Wheatly, Ed. Oxford University Press. London.

4. CROOK, T. Hydergine and the vasodilators: Are they useful in geriatric psychiatry. Paper presented at the annual Brookdale Symposium on Geriatric Medicine, December 1983. Mt. Sinai School of Medicine. New York.

5. YESAVAGE, J. A., L. E. HOLLISTER & E. BURIAN. 1979. Dihydroergotoxine: 6-mg versus

3-mg dosage in the treatment of senile dementia. Preliminary report. J. Am. Geriatr. Soc. **27:** 80–82.

6. YOSHIKAWA, M., S. HIRAI, T. AIZAWA, Y. KUROIWA, F. GOTO, I. SOFUE, Y. TOYOKURA, H. YAMAMURA & Y. IWASAKI. 1983. A dose-response study with dihydroergotoxine mesylate in cerebrovascular disturbances. J. Am. Geriatr. Soc. **31:** 1–7.

7. KUGLER, J., W. D. OSWALD, U. HERZFELD, R. SEUD, J. PINGEL & D. WELZEL. 1978. Long-term treatment of the symptoms of senile cerebral insufficiency: A prospective study of hydergine. Dtsch. Med. Wochenschr. **103:** 456–462.

8. SPIEGEL, R., F. HUBER & S. LOBULE. 1985. A controlled long-term study with ergoloid mesylates (Hydergine) in healthy, elderly volunteers: Results after 3 years. J. Am. Geriatr. Soc. (In press.)

9. CROOK, T. 1979. Central-nervous-system stimulants: Appraisal of use in geropsychiatric patients. J. Am. Geriatr. Soc. **27:** 476–477.

10. LOEW, D. M. & J. M. SINGER. 1983. Stimulants and senility. *In* Stimulants: Neurochemical, Behavioral, and Clinical Perspectives. I. Creese, Ed. Raven Press. New York.

11. CROOK, T., S. FERRIS, G. SATHANANTHAN, A. RASKIN & S. GERSHON. 1977. The effect of methyphenidate on test performance in the cognitively impaired aged. Psychopharmacology **52:** 251–255.

12. BRANCONNIER, R. J. & J. O. COLE. 1980. The therapeutic role of methylphenidate in senile organic brain syndrome. *In* Psychopathology in the Aged. J. O. Cole & J. E. Barrett, Eds.: 183–194. Raven Press. New York.

13. JARVIK, L. F. & J. F. MILNE. 1975. Gerovital-H3: A review of the literature. *In* Genesis and Treatment of Psychologic Disorders in the Elderly. S. Gershon & A. Raskin, Eds.: 203–227. Raven Press. New York.

14. OSTFELD, A., C. M. SMITH & B. A. STOTSKY. 1977. The systemic use of procaine in the treatment of the elderly: A review. J. Am. Geriatr. Soc. **25:** 1–19.

15. DAVIS, J. M. 1981. Antipsychotic drugs. *In* Physicians Handbook on Psychotherapeutic Drug Use in the Aged. T. Crook & G. Cohen, Eds.: 12–25. Mark Powley Associates. New Cannaan, CT.

16. CROOK, T. & S. GERSHON, Eds. 1981. Strategies for the Development of an Effective Treatment for Senile Dementia. Mark Powley Associates. New Canaan, CT.

17. ROSENBERG, G. S., B. GREENWALD & K. DAVIS. 1983. Pharmacologic treatment of Alzheimer's disease: An overview. *In* Alzheimer's Disease: The Standard Reference. B. Reisberg, Ed. The Free Press. New York.

18. LITTLE, A., P. CHUAQUI-KIDD & R. LEVY. 1984. Early results from a double-blind, placebo-controlled trial of high dose lecithin in Alzheimer's disease: Psychometric test performance, plasma choline levels and the effects of drug compliance. *In* Alzheimer's Disease: Advances in Basic Research and Therapies. R. J. Wurtman, S. H. Corkin & J. H. Growdon, Eds.: 313–331. Center for Brain Sciences and Metabolism Charitable Trust. Cambridge, MA.

19. DAVIS, K. L., R. C. MOHS, W. G. ROSEN, B. S. GREENWALD, M. I. LEVY & T. B. HORVATH. 1983. Memory enhancement with oral physostigmine in Alzheimer's disease. N. Engl. J. Med. **308:** 721–723.

20. THAL, L. J., P. A. FULD, D. M. MASUR & N. S. SHARPLESS. 1983. Oral physostigmine and lecithin improve memory in Alzheimer's disease. Ann. Neurol. **13:** 491–496.

21. THAL, L. J., D. M. MASUR, N. S. SHARPLESS, P. A. FULD & P. DAVIES. 1984. Acute and chronic effects of oral physostigmine and lecithin in Alzheimer's disease. *In* Alzheimer's Disease: Advances in Basic Research and Therapies. R. J. Wurtman, S. H. Corkin, J. H. Growdon, Eds.: 333–347. Center for Brain Sciences and Metabolism Charitable Trust. Cambridge, MA.

22. SUMMERS, W. K., J. O. VIESSELMAN & G. M. MARSH. 1981. Use of THA in treatment of Alzheimer-like dementia: Pilot study in twelve patients. Biol. Psychiatry **16:** 145–153.

23. CHRISTIE, J. E., A. SHERING, J. FERGUSON & A. I. M. GLENN. 1981. Physostigmine and arecoline: Effects of intravenous infusions in Alzheimer presenile dementia. Br. J. Psychiatry **138:** 46–50.

24. BARTUS, R. T., R. L. DEAN, K. A. SHERMAN, E. FRIEDMAN & B. BAER. 1981. Profound effects of combining choline and piracetam on memory. Neurobiol. Aging **2:** 105–111.

25. FERRIS, S. H., B. REISBERG, T. CROOK, E. FRIEDMAN, M. SCHNECK, P. MIR, K. A. SHERMAN, J. CORWIN, S. GERSHON & R. T. BARTUS. 1982. Pharmacologic treatment of senile dementia: Choline, L-DOPA, piracetam, and choline plus piracetam. *In* Alzheimer's Disease: A Report of Progress. S. Corkin, K. L. Davis, J. H. Growdon, E. Usdin & R. J. Wurtman, Eds.: 475–481. Raven Press. New York.

26. GROWDON, J. H., S. CORKIN & F. J. HUFF. 1984. Alzheimer's disease: Treatment with nootropic drugs. *In* Alzheimer's Disease: Advances in Basic Research and Therapies. R. J. Wurtman, S. H. Corkin & J. H. Growdon, Eds.: 375–389. Center for Brain Sciences and Metabolism Charitable Trust. Cambridge, MA.

27. BERGER, P. A. & J. R. TINKLENBERG. 1981. Neuropeptides and senile dementia. *In* Strategies for the Development of an Effective Treatment for Senile Dementia. T. Crook & S. Gershon, Eds.: 155–171. Mark Powley Associates. New Cannan, CT.

28. TINKLENBERG, J. R., J. E. THORNTON & J. A. YESAVAGE. 1985. Clin. Geriatric Psychopharmacol. Neuropeptides. (In press.)

29. PIGACHE, R. M. 1985. The human psychopharmacology of peptides related to ACTH and alpha-MSH. *In* Clinical Pharmacology and Psychiatry. L. Gram, E. Usdin, S. Dahl & P. Kragh-Sorensen, Eds. McMillan. New York. (In press.)

30. REISBERG, B., S. H. FERRIS, R. ANAND, P. MIR, V. GEIBER, M. J. DE LEON & E. ROBERTS. 1983. Effects of naloxone in senile dementia: A double-blind trial. N. Engl. J. Med. **208:** 721–722.

31. BLASS, J., M. J. REDING, D. DRACHMAN, A. MITCHELL, G. GLOSSER, R. KATZMAN, L. J. THAL, S. GRENELL, J. E. SPAR, A. LARUE & E. LISTON. 1983. Cholinesterase inhibitors and opiate antagonists in patients with Alzheimer's disease. N. Engl. J. Med. **309:** 555–556.

32. ARNSTEN, A. F. T. 1984. Behavioral effects of naloxone in animals and humans: Potential for treatment of aging disorders. *In* Alzheimer's Disease: Advances in Basic Research and Therapies. R. J. Wurtman, S. H. Corkin & J. H. Growdon, Eds.: 407–426. Center for Brain Sciences and Metabolism Charitable Trust. Cambridge, MA.

33. COOK, P. & I. JAMES. 1981. Cerebral vasodilators. N. Engl. J. Med. **305:** 1508–1513.

34. GIURGEA, C. 1976. Nootropic pharmacology of neurointegrative activity. Curr. Dev. Psychopharmacol. **3:** 221–276.

35. BARTUS, R. T., R. L. DEAN, K. A. SHERMAN, E. FRIEDMAN & B. BAER. 1981. Profound effects of combining choline and piracetam on memory. Neurobiol. Aging **2:** 105–111.

36. FERRIS, S. H. 1981. Empirical studies in senile dementia with central nervous system stimulants and metabolic enhancers. *In* Strategies for the Development of an Effective Treatment for Senile Dementia. T. Crook & S. Gershon, Eds.: 173–187. Mark Powley Associates. New Cannan, CT.

37. BRANCONNIER, R. J., J. O. COLE, E. C. DESSAIM, K. F. SPERA, S. GHAZRINIAN & D. DE VITT. 1983. The therapeutic efficacy of pramiracetam in Alzheimer's disease: Preliminary observations. Psychopharmacol. Bull. **19:** 726–730.

38. ITIL, T. M., G. N. MENON, M. BOZAK & A. SONGAR. 1982. The effects of oxiracetam (ISF 2522) in patients with organic brain syndrome (a double-blind controlled study with piracetam). Drug Dev. Res. **2:** 447–461.

39. GIBSON, G. E. & C. PETERSON. 1983. Pharmacologic models of age-related cognitive impairments. *In* Assessment in Geriatric Psychopharmacology. T. Crook. S. Ferris & R. Bartus, Eds.: 323–343. Mark Powley Associates. New Cannan, CT.

40. LYTE, M. & M. SHINITSKY. 1984. Possible reversal of tissue aging by a lipid diet. *In* Alzheimer's Disease: Advances in Basic Research and Therapies. R. J. Wurtman, S. H. Corkin & J. H. Growdon, Eds.: 295–312. Center for Brain Sciences and Metabolism Charitable Trust. Cambridge, MA.

41. NANDY, K. 1981. Lipofuscin pigment and immunological factors in the pathogenesis and treatment of senile dementia. *In* Strategies for the Development of an Effective Treatment for Senile Dementia. T. Crook & S. Gershon, Eds.: 231–245. Mark Powley Associates. New Canaan, CT.

42. DE BONI, V. & D. R. C. MCLACHLAN. 1981. Biochemical aspects of SDAT and aluminum as a neurotoxic agent. *In* Strategies for the Development of an Effective Treatment for

Senile Dementia. T. Crook & S. Gershon, Eds.: 215–228. Mark Powley Associates. New Canaan, CT.

43. CARLSSON, A. 1981. Aging and brain neurotransmitters. *In* Strategies for the Development of an Effective Treatment for Senile Dementia. T. Crook & S. Gershon, Eds.: 93–104. Mark Powley Associates. New Canaan, CT.

44. BONDAREFF, W., L. Q. MOUNTJOY & M. ROTH. 1982. Loss of neurons of origin of the adrenergic projection to cerebral cortex (nucleus locus coeruleus) in senile dementia. Neurology **32:** 164–168.

45. BOWEN, D. 1983. Biochemical assessment of neurotransmitter and metabolic dysfunction and cerebral atrophy in Alzheimer's disease. *In* Biological Aspects of Alzheimer's Disease. R. Katzman, Ed.: 219–231. Banbury Report 15. Cold Spring Harbor, NY.

Clinical Evaluation of Compounds for the Treatment of Memory Dysfunction

J. H. GROWDON,[a] S. CORKIN,[b] AND F. J. HUFF[a,b]

[a]Department of Neurology
Massachusetts General Hospital
Boston, Massachusetts 02114

[b]Department of Psychology
The Clinical Research Center
Massachusetts Institute of Technology
Cambridge, Massachusetts 02139

The quest for an effective treatment for Alzheimer's disease (AD) has gained high priority in scientific, medical, and public health sectors of our society. Although a wide variety of treatments have been tested over the years,[1] none has been sufficiently effective that physicians are satisfied with available pharmacotherapy. Recent advances in identifying the neurochemical abnormalities that accompany AD raise expectations that drug therapies can be developed that will correct or bypass the neurochemical lesions in AD and thereby restore normal cognitive function.[2] Investigators around the world have adopted principals of modern neuropharmacology and initiated a new series of drug trials in AD.[3] These efforts have, in turn, led to increased sophistication in the design of methods for testing memory-enhancing drugs. The purpose of this paper is to highlight critical issues in protocol design that are specific to AD and to illustrate these points with a report on a current drug trial using phosphatidylcholine (PC) in combination with the nootropic drug, piracetam.

PROTOCOL DESIGN

Protocol design varies depending upon the stage of drug development. Early clinical trials in normal subjects (Phase 1) test new compounds in order to study the pharmacokinetics of the drug, determine tolerance, and detect possible side effects. In Phase 2 studies, one or two selected doses of the drug are administered to small numbers of subjects in the target population. In Phase 3 studies, the drug is administered to a large number of subjects in multiple trials in order to obtain data on safety and efficacy required by the federal Food and Drug Administration (FDA) prior to releasing the drug for widespread use. Drug surveillance studies to monitor side effects and efficacy once the drug has been released constitute the final phase of drug testing (Phase 4). Most drug studies currently being conducted in patients with AD are in the early phases of testing and share the principal features of drug trial protocols listed in TABLE 1.

Objective

The goal of the study should be clearly stated. In AD, the aim is either to reverse impairments of memory and other cognitive functions or to retard their progression.

437

TABLE 1. Principal Features of Drug Trial Protocols

Objective of the study
Drug phase
Protocol goal
Design and duration
Open label
Double blind
Subject selection
Symptom vs. disease
Inclusion and exclusion criteria
Number of subjects
Informed consent
Variables to be measured
Neurological and psychiatric examinations
Neuropsychological tests
Behavioral rating scales
Laboratory tests
Protocol conduct
Data collection
Data analysis

The protocol should reflect these goals. A short-term study with a rapid acting drug would be appropriate for the first aim, whereas a protocol using a long-acting drug administered for years would be necessary in order to prove efficacy in slowing the course of dementia. The same compound is often tested under both conditions: PC given acutely has been ineffective in reversing memory loss[4] but may show promise when administered chronically.[5]

Design and Duration

In the early stages of a drug's development, open-label or single-blind studies to determine the optimal drug dose for the desired effect are often conducted in patients with AD. These studies can also provide information regarding tolerance and side effects in the target population. Since most drugs are first tested in normal young subjects, it is important to establish a drug's effect in older patients whose disease or other medical conditions may affect its acceptability. These early Phase 2 studies often guide the choice of drug dose and variables to be measured in subsequent larger studies.

Drugs are tested in double-blind protocols before they are accepted as effective. There are two principal designs: double-blind crossover and double-blind parallel studies. In a crossover design, each patient receives both the test drug and its placebo (or comparison drug). In parallel design studies, separate groups of patients receive either the test drug or its placebo (or comparison drug). To date, most studies in AD have employed a crossover design. Reasons for this choice include ease of recruiting patients, since all patients will receive active drug. Other advantages of the crossover design include the fact that each subject is his or her own control, and fewer subjects are required than in a parallel design. Investigators testing drugs according to this design must be careful to counterbalance the order of drug administration and make certain that the washout period between different treatments is sufficient for the drug to be eliminated from the body but not so long that the patient's clinical condition deteriorates. Most pharmacologists favor a parallel design, because these studies are free from potential confounding effects of prior treatment, and statistical analysis is cleaner than in the crossover design. Disadvantages of the parallel design include a larger number of subjects required than in the crossover design, and potential difficulty in recruiting subjects because some of them will receive placebo rather than active drug. Furthermore, care must be taken in selecting the patient groups; careful randomization is necessary but does not insure comparability in treatment groups.

Subject Selection

Care in selecting the target population is critical to the success of any drug study. In some diseases, subjects are selected on the basis of subjective symptoms. For example, subjects recruited to test a new antidepressant drug are commonly selected on the basis of a dysphoric mood (sadness), and perhaps associated vegetative symptoms, such as disordered sleep and appetite. Drug trials in which patients with signs and symptoms of dementia are lumped together would make sense if dementia were a single disorder. It isn't: Physicians now consider more than 50 causes of dementia whenever confronted with a patient with acquired cognitive deficits. Since the anatomical and biochemical substrates of memory loss often differ according to the etiology of the disease, it is unlikely that effective treatments for one condition would be useful in all dementias. Thus, antidepressant medication may help patients with the dementia of depression,[6] but will have little benefit in patients with Korsakoff's amnesia. Thyroid replacement will benefit patients with cognitive impairments associated with hypothyroidism, but will not improve memory in patients with AD. Every attempt should be made, therefore, to establish the presumed etiology of dementia in order to identify patients with conditions that are responsive to standard treatments and to exclude these patients from experimental drug studies directed toward AD. Most investigational drugs being tested are selected for their potential ability to correct the presumed biochemical deficits in brains of patients with AD. Since many of these deficits, such as decreased choline acetyltransferase (CAT) activity and decreased somatostatin levels, are relatively specific to AD,[7] there is no

TABLE 2. Criteria for the Diagnosis of Alzheimer's Disease

History of progressive impairments in
  memory
  attention
  language
  praxis
  visual perception
  activities of daily living

Characteristic neurological examination
  no focal motor, sensory, or coordination deficits
  no primary psychiatric disorder
  high Blessed Dementia Scale score

Laboratory test results that exclude other causes of dementia
  blood tests
  special neurological examinations, including
    lumbar puncture
    electroencephalography
    computerized tomographic brain scan
    Hachinski Ischemic Scale

rational basis for including in drug studies patients with other disorders such as multi-infarct dementia. As a general rule, the more homogeneous the target group, the more convincing the results of drug trials. In order to improve antemortem diagnosis, rigorous criteria for the diagnosis of AD have been proposed.[8,9] The recent diagnostic guidelines suggested by an ad hoc National Institute on Neurological and Communicate Disease and Stroke committee[10] are similar to those we employ in our studies (TABLE 2).

Not all patients with AD are suitable for participation in trials using experimental drugs and most investigators establish inclusion and exclusion criteria. Examples of inclusion criteria are willingness to participate indicated by signing an informed consent form; having general good health; stable living conditions with a responsible spouse, caretaker, or observer; a specified age range; minimum eighth grade education or satisfactory work history; and English as the primary language. Subjects are generally required to meet minimal levels of test performance in order to assure that improvements or deteriorations occurring during treatment can be detected. The Folstein Mini-Mental State,[11] Blessed Dementia Scale,[12] Hamilton Depression Scale,[13] and the Hachinski Ischemic Scale[14] are screening measures that are commonly used. For example, subjects selected for inclusion generally have mild to moderate dementia, and a confident clinical diagnosis of AD. Typical inclusion requirements are: a Mini-Mental State score greater than 12 but less than 23, a Blessed Dementia Scale score greater than 5 but less than 20, a Hamilton score less than 17, and a Hachinski score less than 6.

Criteria for exclusion are equally important and subjects with serious underlying medical conditions, such as cancer, unstable heart conditions, or organ failure should be excluded. Similarly, patients with suspected AD but who have a history of significant head trauma, alcohol abuse, or history of electroconvulsive therapy should be excluded because these factors may influence neuropsychological test performance. Finally, subjects who require psychoactive medications, such as anxiolytics, hypnotics, sedatives, analeptics, and neuroleptics should be excluded as well as those who require drugs prescribed for medical conditions that can affect cognitive function, such as reserpine, cimetadine, long-acting nitrates, and anticholinergics.

The number of subjects tested depends upon the goal of the study. In an exploratory study, substantial improvement in a single patient may be an important scientific observation and guide further drug development. In order to establish the efficacy of a medication as a prelude to commercial development, however, it is usually necessary to conduct several studies at different sites using 100 or more patients. The exact number of patients is usually established according to the number of variables being measured and the level of statistical significance being sought in order to show an effect. Subjects enrolled in drug studies are often stratified at the onset according to the degree of dementia, i.e., a group with a Mini-Mental Status score of 13 to 17 and another group with a score of 18 to 22. Stratification increases the homogeneity of treatment groups but also increases the number of subjects required.

Variables To Be Measured

The FDA has established clear guidelines for determining efficacy in some drug areas, but none exists in the field of psychogeriatrics. This situation reflects the fact that there is no consensus regarding the variables to be measured in studies testing drugs for AD, and there are no prototypic compounds with demonstrated efficacy that provide a standard of comparison. Ideally, drug studies should incorporate neurological and psychiatric examinations, neuropsychological testing, behavioral observations, and laboratory tests, all administered at specified intervals during the study.

Physical examinations, including the neurological examination, are conducted in order to elicit data regarding a drug's effect and to insure its safety. Psychiatric examinations are performed in order to detect mood changes or disturbances in thought that may occur during treatment. Standardized rating scales, such as the Hamilton Depression Scale,[13] the Psychiatric Status Schedule,[15] and Profile of Mood States,[16] are preferred since they are widely tested and can be scored by a computer.

A wide range of neuropsychological tests have been proposed,[17] but no single test has been universally accepted and incorporated into drug trials. A comprehensive neuropsychological assessment should include tests of verbal and nonverbal short-term and long-term memory using multiple but equivalent forms of each test whenever possible.[18] Similar arrays of tests have been developed in order to assess language performance and visuospatial abilities.[19] Practical considerations often dictate the number of neuropsychological tests chosen for monitoring a drug's effect, but tests selected should always be within the capabilities of the patients being tested and relevant to their disabilities.

Behavioral observations regarding a patient's capacity for self-care, employment, work at home, communication skills, and social relationships are an integral part of assessing a drug's effect in patients with AD. Impairment in these activities of daily living constitutes a major deficit in AD and contributes to its diagnosis. For a drug to be useful clinically, as opposed to simply showing a statistically significant effect on neuropsychological testing, improvement should be detected on these activities of daily living measures. A few of them have been incorporated into the Blessed Dementia Scale;[12] we use a modification of the Lawton scale[20] in our studies. Rating scales should offer multiple choice responses for each area of concern in a format suitable for computer entry and analysis. Scales can be adapted for patients at home (form filled out by spouse or caretaker) or for hospitalized patients (form filled out by ward staff or physician).

Laboratory tests are usually obtained during the course of a study in order to document expected physiological effects or to detect unsuspected toxic side-effects. In some instances, changes in electrophysiological or biochemical variables related to dementia that occur during treatment provide evidence of the drug's biological activity and possible mode of action. Thus, Canter *et al.*[21] reported a positive correlation between the extent of dementia as measured by the Blessed Dementia Scale score and the amount of delta activity on the EEG, and that short-term administration of an ineffective treatment (lecithin) did not alter this pattern. Conversely, Thal *et al.*[22] found a positive correlation between the degree of acetylcholinesterase activity inhibition in the cerebrospinal fluid of patients with AD and their improvement on selected memory tests. As additional biological markers of AD are discovered, their change during drug administration should be incorporated into experimental protocols.

ADMINISTRATION OF PHOSPHATIDYLCHOLINE AND PIRACETAM TO PATIENTS WITH AD: A PRELIMINARY REPORT

In order to illustrate some of the practical issues in clinical investigation, the results of an ongoing trial testing the combination of phosphatidylcholine (PC) and piracetam are presented. Piracetam (2-pyrrolidone acetamide) is the lead compound in a new class of drugs described as nootropic, a term (*noos* = mind; *tropein* = toward) first proposed by Corneliu Giurgea in 1972.[23] The nootropic concept is best defined operationally: Nootropic compounds have physiological and behavioral effects in experimental animals without the side effects commonly observed following administration of other psychoactive drugs, such as the hypnotics, sedatives, neuroleptics, or analeptics. Nootropics are believed to activate mental functions, especially in experimental situations in which they are impaired. Many new compounds are being developed as nootropics even though there is still little evidence that they improve mental function in a clinically useful way. The nootropic concept has enormous appeal. The multiple cognitive deficits in patients with AD are believed to stem from diffuse dysfunction of the cerebral hemispheres. Neuropathological changes occur in many cortical areas,[24] and there is generalized decrease in neuronal metabolism throughout the cortex.[25] If compounds were available that acted diffusely to combat such abnormalities and thereby improve cognitive functions, these drugs would have widespread application. This approach gains additional strength inasmuch as clinical trials with cholinergic agonists thus far have had limited success in the treatment of AD[3] and it now appears that the cholinergic hypothesis must be re-examined because multiple neurotransmitter deficits, in addition to the acetylcholine one, have been reported in this disorder.[26–30] Proponents of the nootropic concept could argue that replenishing function in one of many damaged neurotransmitter systems is not likely to reverse the symptoms of AD, whereas a compound that improved neuronal efficiency globally or restored neuronal function in all neuron transmitter systems would be very useful. To date however, the nootropic concept has gained limited scientific acceptance because the rationale for memory enhancement remains obscure, and the mechanisms whereby such improvement could occur is unknown. With the possible exception of piracetam, nootropics have not been tested extensively in human subjects and none has been reported to improve memory or other cognitive functions in patients with AD. It is therefore apparent that the nootropic promise is much greater than its performance. Nonetheless, interest in nootropics continues to build, fueled by the high prevalence of benign senescent forgetfulness in elderly people and by the increased recognition of Alzheimer-type dementia.

Nootropic compounds gain access to the central nervous system. Some, such as piracetam, are not metabolized and are excreted intact by the kidney. Others, such as aniracetam, are transformed within the body to an active metabolite. Although differences in potency among these compounds have been reported,[31] they all show activity in behavioral tests believed to involve learning and memory. It is an article of faith, however, that performance on such tests by rats predicts beneficial effects in memory-impaired humans. In one preliminary study, piracetam in combination with lecithin was reported to improve behavior but not memory in some patients with AD.[32] In another study, pramiracetam was reported to improve mood in Alzheimer patients without improving their test performance.[33] Other nootropic drugs, such as aniracetam and CI-911, have just entered Phase 2 studies in the United States and there are no reports regarding efficacy.

Two independent sets of observations prompted us to initiate drug studies giving piracetam alone and in combination with phosphatidylcholine to patients with AD. Wurtman et al.[34] found that piracetam decreased levels of acetylcholine in the hippocampus of rats and postulated this was consistent with increased acetylcholine release. In separate experiments, Bartus et al.[35] found that the combination of choline and piracetam improved performance of aged rats in a passive avoidance task significantly more than either drug alone.

Fifteen patients with a diagnosis of AD established according to strict research criteria participated in these studies according to the provisions of protocols approved by the MIT Subcommittee on the Use of Humans as Experimental Subjects (TABLE

TABLE 3. Clinical Characteristics of AD Patients Treated with Piracetam

Patient	Age	Sex	Severity of Dementia[a]	Blessed Score	Piracetam Dose (g/day)
Protocol 1					
1	56	M	Moderate	18	6.6
2	64	M	Severe	35	6.6
3	70	F	Mild	28	6.6
4	63	F	Severe	43	6.6
Protocol 2					
5	67	M	Mild	7	6.6
6	63	F	Moderate	38	6.6
7	61	F	Mild	14	2.4
8	60	M	Mild	17	9.9
9	72	F	Mild	28	6.6
10	57	M	Mild	23	6.6
11	56	F	Mild	20	6.6
Protocol 3					
5	67	M	Mild	9	4.8 and 7.2
6	63	F	Moderate	38	4.8 and 7.2
12	75	F	Moderate	19	7.2
13	72	F	Mild	13	4.8 and 7.2
14	60	F	Moderate	23	4.8 and 7.2
15	58	F	Mild	13	4.8 and 7.2

[a]Classified according to the following criteria. Mild: Functions independently at home and can take all neuropsychological tests. Moderate: Activities restricted at home and can take some but not all of the neuropsychological tests. Severe: Does nothing independently at home and cannot take any of the neuropsychological tests.

3). The diagnosis of AD was based on a history of slowly progressive cognitive impairments, a careful neurological examination to exclude focal abnormalities suggesting other causes of dementia, and extensive laboratory testing, including electroencephalograms and CT brain scans (TABLE 2). Fourteen neuropsychological tests of memory and attention tailored to the energies and capacities of patients with

TABLE 4. Neuropsychological Tests Administered to Patients with Alzheimer's Disease

Brown-Peterson Distractor Task
Verbal Recognition Memory
Verbal Paired-Associate Learning—Immediate
Verbal Paired-Associate Learning—Delayed
Nonverbal Paired-Associate
        Learning—Immediate
Nonverbal Paired-Associate
        Learning—Delayed
Selective Attention (Median RT)
Selective Attention (Unexpected-Expected)
Digit Span (Forward)
Digit Span (Backward)
Block Span (Forward)
Block Span (Backward)
NYU Story (Immediate)
NYU Story (Delayed)

AD were specifically developed for these drug studies (TABLE 4). Piracetam was kindly supplied by Dr. Ernst Wulfert of the UCB Pharmaceutical Division.

Experiment 1. Piracetam Versus Placebo

Four patients with AD took 3.3 grams of piracetam twice a day (6.6 grams/day) as a single drug for three weeks according to a double-blind crossover protocol. During piracetam administration three of the four patients improved according to family reports. They were described as being more alert, interested in their surroundings, and sociable at home. Compared to baseline scores on neuropsychological tests, piracetam administration substantially improved performance by all four subjects on the verbal paired associate learning task. This finding may be due to a practice effect from first to subsequent sessions. A better comparison is between drug and placebo conditions where practice effects are balanced. When this analysis was done, piracetam superiority was recorded in only two of the four patients; the drug and placebo test scores were identical in one patient and placebo was superior in the other. Piracetam administration did not affect performance on any of the other neuropsychological tests.

Comment

This initial study was conducted in order to determine the safety of piracetam and how well it was accepted by patients with AD. All patients tolerated the dose of 6.6 g/day without developing clinical side effects or laboratory signs of toxicity. The slight improvement in a single memory test and the reports of benefit at home during piracetam administration (by blind observers) encouraged us to continue these studies.

Experiment 2. Piracetam (2.4–9.9 grams/day) in Combination with PC Versus Placebo in Combination with PC

Seven subjects with AD took piracetam and PC for one month and placebo and PC for one month according to a double-blind crossover protocol. Piracetam and placebo tablets were administered orally three times a day. PC was incorporated into the noodles in chicken noodle soup (courtesy of Dr. Harold Graham, Thomas J. Lipton Company) and packaged in the instant cup-of-soup format. Each packet of soup contained 9 grams of 80% PC; subjects took two packets of soup per day for a total dose of 18 grams of 80% PC.

The data were analyzed by comparing the patients' mean scores on the neuropsychological tests while taking piracetam plus PC to their scores while taking placebo plus PC. Performance on eight tests was superior during piracetam administration; performance on six tests was superior during placebo administration. Neither piracetam nor placebo exerted a statistically significant effect on any of the 14 tests. This finding might have been due to the fact that some patients could have improved during piracetam and others not, and that individual improvements might have been lost in the mean group scores. The data were therefore analyzed for individual patients on a test-by-test basis, by measuring each individual's performance in relation to the mean scores for the group. Performance was judged improved if the change during piracetam administration was greater than the mean change of the group as a whole. These data

TABLE 5. Tests Reflecting Improvement during Ingestion of Lecithin Plus Piracetam

Subject Number	Brown-Peterson Distractor Task	Verbal Recognition Memory	Verbal Paired-Associate Learning (Delayed)	Nonverbal Paired-Associate Learning (Immediate)	Nonverbal Paired-Associate Learning (Delayed)	Digit Span (Forward)	Digit Span (Backward)	Block Span (Forward)	No. of Tests Reflecting Improvement (of 8)
5	X	X			X			X	4
6					X		X	X	3
7			X			X		X	3
8		X	X	X					3
9			X		X				2
10		X	X				X		3
11	X			X	X	X	X	X	6

for the eight psychological tests in which the group as a whole showed a superior performance during piracetam administration are displayed in TABLE 5. Most of the subjects improved on two to four of the eight tests, whereas one subject improved on six of the eight tests. The observation by blind observers that she improved in activities of daily living during active drug but not placebo ingestion supports the treatment's efficacy.

Experiment 3. Piracetam (4.8 grams and 7.2 grams/day) in Combination with PC Versus Placebo in Combination with Placebo Soup

Six subjects with AD took piracetam plus PC according to a revised double-blind crossover protocol. There were two important changes in method: First, piracetam placebo was administered with PC placebo rather than PC-enriched soup, as in the previously described protocol. Although PC administered by itself for one month did not produce significant improvement in patients with AD,[4] PC is not really a placebo and might have blurred the piracetam results. Second, two dose levels of piracetam

TABLE 6. Piracetam and Phosphatidylcholine Administration to Patients with Alzheimer's Disease: Results of a Replication Study

Patient	Age	Sex	Severity	Outcome
5	67	M	Mild	No improvement
6	63	F	Moderate	No improvement
8	60	M	Mild	No improvement
9	72	F	Mild	No improvement
11	56	F	Mild	Consistent improvement long-term drug
12	75	F	Moderate	Consistent improvement long-term drug

were tested, 4.8 and 7.2 g/day, for three weeks each. Thus, there were three drug periods: two with piracetam plus PC and one with complete placebo conditions. The orders of drug administration were counterbalanced within the group of six patients.

Preliminary analysis of these data comparing high doses of piracetam (7.2 g/day) to placebo indicates that there was superior performance during piracetam administration on eight of the 14 tests, including paired associate learning and block span. This study is still in progress; there are too few patients yet to conduct meaningful statistical analyses.

Experiment 4. Replication Study

Seven patients with Alzheimer's disease who showed improvement on at least one memory test repeated the double-blind protocol (TABLE 6). Accordingly, patients 8, 9, and 11 repeated the protocol described in experiment 2; patients 5, 6, and 12 repeated the protocol described in experiment 3. Piracetam and PC were administered in the same order and dose during the second drug trial as in the original trial.

Patient 11 is a 56-year-old woman with mild dementia. Her scores on the

Brown-Peterson distractor task were higher during piracetam than during placebo administration (indicating superior performance) both times: Comparing drug to placebo conditions, her scores were 50 vs. 26 in the first trial and 57 vs. 29 in the second. Patient 12 is a 72-year-old woman with moderate dementia. She improved both times during piracetam administration on the Brown-Peterson task (49 vs. 28; 42 vs. 37) and on forward digit span (7 vs. 6; 8 vs. 7). Observers who were blind to the order of drug administration reported both times that there was improved mood, general level of interest, and increased performance of activities of daily living during the active drug conditions. Both patients now receive piracetam chronically as an open-label drug. Improvements were not reproduced in patients 5, 6, 8, and 9. Although some test scores were better during the active drug condition than during placebo administration, there was little correspondence to the pattern observed during the first trial. There were no obvious features on neurological examinations or in laboratory test results that distinguish the two patients who improved from those who did not.

Comment

The results of the piracetam plus PC drug trial illustrate some of the hazards that confront clinical drug studies in Alzheimer's disease. Had we limited neuropsychological test variables and conducted only a single drug trial, we might have concluded that the combination of piracetam plus PC improved memory on objective tests in 6 of 11 patients. It is possible that these results were due to chance: The magnitude of the effects were modest and the extent of improvement did not reach statistical significance. A replication study was performed in order to avoid citing an effect if none were there and to replicate the improvement that was apparent in the first trial. In four of six patients, scores during the second trial were scattered and incongruent with initial performance. In two subjects, however, there was good concordance between test scores on both drug trials, suggesting a true beneficial drug effect. Additional studies with larger numbers of subjects are necessary in order to determine the clinical importance of these observations.

REFERENCES

1. CROOK, T. J. 1985. Clinical drug trials in Alzheimer's disease. Ann. N.Y. Acad. Sci. (This volume.)
2. GROWDON, J. H. 1983. Neuropharmacology of degenerative diseases associated with aging. Med. Res. Rev. **3**: 237–257.
3. CORKIN, S., K. DAVIS, J. GROWDON, E. USDIN & R. WURTMAN. 1982. Alzheimer's Disease: A Report of Progress in Research. Raven Press. New York.
4. SULLIVAN, E. V., K. J. SHEDLACK, S. CORKIN & J. H. GROWDON. 1982. Physostigmine and lecithin in Alzheimer's disease. *In* Alzheimer's Disease: A Report of Progress in Research. S. Corkin, K. Davis, J. H. Growdon, E. Usdin & R. J. Wurtman, Eds.: 361–367. Raven Press. New York.
5. LEVY, R., A. LITTLE, P. CHUAQUI & M. REITH. 1983. Early results from double blind, placebo controlled trial of high dose phosphatidylcholine in Alzheimer's disease. Lancet **i**: 987–988.
6. FOLSTEIN, M. F. & P. R. MCHUGH. 1978. Dementia syndrome of depression. *In* Alzheimer's Disease: Senile Dementia and Related Disorders. R. Katzman, R. D. Terry & K. L. Bick, Eds.: 87–93. Raven Press. New York.
7. TERRY, R. D. & P. DAVIES. 1980. Dementia of the Alzheimer Type. Ann. Rev. Neurosci. **3**: 77–95.

8. AMERICAN PSYCHIATRIC ASSOCIATION. 1980. Diagnostic and Statistical Manual of Mental Disorders, 3rd edit. Washington, D.C.
9. CORKIN, S., J. H. GROWDON & S. RASMUSSEN. 1983. Parental age as a risk factor in Alzheimer's disease. Ann. Neurol. **13:** 674–676.
10. STADLIN, E. M. 1985. Clinical diagnosis of Alzheimer's Disease: A report of NINCDS-ADRDA Work Group. Neurology. (In press.)
11. FOLSTEIN, M. F., S. E. FOLSTEIN & P. R. McHUGH. 1975. Mini-mental state: A practical method for grading the cognitive state of patients. J. Psychiatric Res. **12:** 189–198.
12. BLESSED, G., B. E. TOMLINSON & M. ROTH. 1968. The association between quantitative measures of dementia and of senile changes in the cerebral grey matter of elderly subjects. Br. J. Psychiatry **114:** 797–811.
13. HAMILTON, M. 1960. A rating scale for depression. J. Neurol. Neurosurg. Psychiatry. **23:** 56–62.
14. HACHINSKI, V. C., L. D. ILLIFF & E. AILHA. 1975. Cerebral blood flow in dementia. Arch. Neurol. **32:** 632–637.
15. SPITZER, R. L., J. ENDICOTT, J. FLEISS, et al: 1970. Psychiatric status schedule: a technique for evaluating psychopathology and impairment in role functioning. Arch. Gen. Psychiatry **23:** 41–55.
16. BASS, A. H. & A. DURKEE. 1957. An inventory for assessing different kinds of hostility. J. Consultation Psychol. **21:** 343–349.
17. POON, L. 1985. Handbook for Clinical Assessment of Older Adults. American Psychological Association. Washington, D.C. (In press.)
18. CORKIN, S., J. H. GROWDON, E. V. SULLIVAN & K. SHEDLACK. 1981. Lecithin and cognitive function in aging and dementia. *In* New Approaches to Nerve and Muscular Disorders. A. D. Kidman, J. K. Tomkins & R. A. Westerman, Eds.: 229–249. Excerpta Medica. Amsterdam.
19. CORKIN, S., J. H. GROWDON, E. V. SULLIVAN, M. J. NISSEN & F. J. HUFF. 1985. Assessing treatment effects from a neuropsychological perspective. *In* Handbook for Clinical Assessment of Older Adults. L. Poon, Ed. American Psychological Association. Washington, D.C. (In press.)
20. LAWTON, M. P. & E. C. BRODY. 1969. Assessment of old people: Self maintaining and instrumental activities of daily living. Gerontologist **9:** 179–186.
21. CANTER, N. L., M. HALLETT & J. H. GROWDON. 1982. Lecithin does not affect EEG spectral analysis or P300 in Alzheimer disease. Neurology **32:** 1260–1266.
22. THAL, L. J., P. A. FULD, D. M. MASUR & N. S. SHARPLESS. 1983. Oral physostigmine and lecithin improve memory in Alzheimer's disease. Ann. Neurol. **13:** 491–496.
23. GIURGEA, C. E. 1980. Fundamentals to a Pharmacology of the Mind. Charles C. Thomas. Springfield, IL.
24. CORSELLIS, J. A. N. 1976. Aging and the dementias. *In* Greenfield's Neuropathology. W. Blackwood & J. A. N. Corsellis, Eds. Edward Arnold. London.
25. BENSON, D. F., D. E. KUHL, R. A. HAWKINS, M. E. PHELPS, J. L. CUMMINGS & S. Y. TSAI. 1983. The fluorodeoxyglucose 18F scan in Alzheimer's disease and multi-infarct dementia. Arch. Neurol. **40:** 711–714.
26. MANN, D. M. A., J. LINCOLN & P. O. YATES *et al.* 1980. Changes in monoamine containing neurones of the human CNS in senile dementia. Brit. J. Psychiat. **136:** 533–541.
27. BONDAREFF, W., L. O. MOUNTJOY & M. ROTH. 1982. Loss of neurons of origin of the adrenergic projection to cerebral cortex (nucleus locus coeruleus) in senile dementia. Neurology **32:** 164–168.
28. ADOLFSSON, R., C. G. GOTTFRIES, B. E. ROOS & B. WINBLAD. 1979. Changes in the brain catecholamines in patients with dementia of Alzheimer type. Brit. J. Psychiat. **135:** 216–221.
29. DAVIES, P., R. KATZMAN & R. D. TERRY. 1980. Reduced somatostatin-like immunoreactivity in cerebral cortex from cases of Alzheimer's disease and Alzheimer senile dementia. Nature **288:** 279–280.
30. BOWEN, D. 1983. Biochemical assessment of neurotransmitter and metabolic dysfunction and cerebral atrophy in Alzheimer's disease. *In* Biological Aspects of Alzheimer's Disease. R. Katzman, Ed.: 219–231. Banbury Report 15. Cold Spring Harbor. NY.

31. PUGSLEY, T. A., B. P. H. POSCHEL, D. A. DOWNS, Y. H. SHIH & M. I. GLUCKMAN. 1983. Some pharmacological and neurochemical properties of a new cognition activator agent, pramiracetam. Psychopharm. Bull. **19**: 721–726.
32. FRIEDMAN, E., K. A. SHERMAN, S. H. FERRIS, B. REISBERG, R. T. BARTUS & M. K. SHNECT. 1981. Clinical response to choline plus piracetam in senile dementia: Relation to red-cell choline levels. N. Engl. J. Med. **304**: 1490–1491.
33. BRANCONNIER, R. J., J. O. COLE, E. C. DESSAIN, K. F. SPERA, S. GHAZRINIAN & D. DEVITT. 1983. The therapeutic efficacy of pramiracetam in Alzheimer's disease: Preliminary observations. Psychopharm. Bull. **19**: 726–730.
34. WURTMAN, R. J., S. G. MAGILL & D. K. REINSTEIN. 1981. Piracetam diminishes hippocampal ACh levels in rats. Life Sci. **28**: 1091–1093.
35. BARTUS, R. T., R. L. DEAN, K. A. SHERMAN, E. FRIEDMAN & B. BAER. 1981. Profound effects of combining choline and piracetam on memory. Neurobiol. Aging **2**: 105–111.

Searching for Models of Alzheimer's Disease: A Comparison of Four Amnestic Treatments in Two Behavioral Tasks

D. E. MURPHY AND C. A. BOAST

Neuroscience Research
Pharmaceuticals Division
CIBA-GEIGY Corporation
Summit, New Jersey 07901

The hallmark of Alzheimer's disease is a deficit in time-dependent memory processes. In animals, the brief acquisition period of single-trial learning tasks allows for the evaluation of amnestic treatments on these time-dependent memory processes. For example, the aversively motivated inhibitory avoidance task has been shown to be sensitive to amnesia induced by a variety of manipulations including: pentylenetetrazol (PTZ) seizures,[1] scopolamine (SCOP) antagonism of acetylcholine,[2] nucleus basalis (NB) lesions,[3] and aging.[4,5] These treatments have been proposed as models for Alzheimer's disease.

We have developed and used an appetitively motivated single-trial maze task to investigate memory disruptions due to hypoxia.[6] The effects of PTZ (40 mg/kg i.p.), SCOP (1.5 mg/kg s.c.), and ibotenic acid (5 μg in 1 μl) lesions of the NB (coordinates: AP $-.5$, ML ± 2.8, DV -7.7) and aging (24–26 mo-old) on acquisition and retention in rats were compared in this new appetitive maze (AM) and in the inhibitory avoidance (IA) task. A viable model of the memory deficits associated with Alzheimer's disease should result in retention deficits in both tasks.

Pre-trial administration of PTZ and SCOP altered acquisition in the AM, but did not affect retention (FIGURE 1). These pre-trial treatments selectively impaired IA retention. Post-trial PTZ impaired retention in the AM when given immediately after training. In IA, post-trial PTZ administration impaired retention when given up to 15 min after training. Post-trial SCOP had no effect in either task. In general, ibotenic acid lesions of the NB did not produce memory deficits in either task (TABLE 1). Aged rats exhibited a selective memory impairment in the AM only (TABLE 1).

The present effects of PTZ and SCOP on acquisition and retention in IA are in agreement with previously published reports.[1,2] The impairment of acquisition induced by SCOP in the new AM is also consistent with a previous report.[7] The reports in the literature of selective memory deficits in IA in NB lesioned[2,3] and in aged rats[4,5] were not confirmed in our study. Some methodological differences, of course, might account for these discrepancies (e.g. our aged rats were tested repeatedly in IA). We consider our NB lesions (verified by AChE and Nissl histochemistry) more discrete and thus less prone to additive effects of tissue damage to other brain areas (globus pallidus, amygdala, etc.), than others. In general, the four treatments used do not appear to be viable models of the memory deficits associated with Alzheimer's disease.

REFERENCES

1. PALFAI, T. & P. KURTZ. 1973. Pharmacol. Biochem. Behav. **1**: 55–59.
2. LOCONTE, G., L. BARTOLINI, F. CASAMENTI, I. MARCONCINI-PEPEU & G. PEPEU. 1982. Pharmacol. Biochem. Behav. **17**: 933–937.

A. Appetitive Task

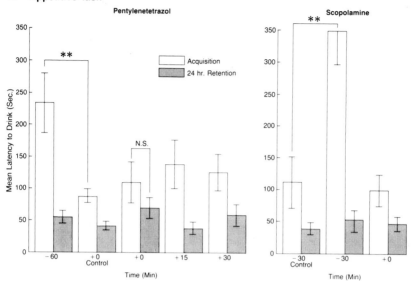

B. Inhibitory Avoidance

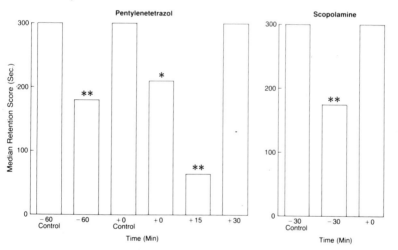

FIGURE 1. In panels A and B, the horizontal axis refers to the time of drug administration in minutes relative to acquisition training (time 0). Thus, time is preceded by a minus or a plus sign, indicating whether the drug injection was given prior to or following acquisition training. $*p < .05$, $**p < .002$. (Panel A) Appetitive task: The apparatus was a square (75 cm^2) open field with a water tube concealed in a blind alley located in one corner of the maze. For acquisition training, water-deprived rats (52 hr) were placed diagonally opposite the blind alley, and the latency to drink at the water tube was recorded. Subjects were retested 24 hr later, and the latency to drink was recorded (maximum latency = 600 sec). Data were analyzed using the t-test. (Panel B) Inhibitory avoidance: Rats were placed in the lighted, front chamber of a shuttlebox, and the latency to enter the darkened, rear chamber was recorded. A 1 mA footshock was delivered to the animal after entering the rear chamber, and escape was accomplished by returning to the front chamber. If the rat re-entered the shocked compartment within 60 sec it was excluded from the experiment. The subject was re-tested 24 hr later and the step-through latency was recorded (maximum = 300 sec). The non-parametric Mann-Whitney U-test was used to analyze the data.

TABLE 1. The Effects of Nucleus Basalis Lesions and Age in Two Behavioral Tasks

APPETITIVE TASK

| | | Mean Latency to Drink (sec) ± S.E. | | |
	(N)	Acquisition	24 hr Retention	p Value
Control	(14)	203 ± 34	32 ± 8	<.002
Nucleus basalis	(14)	252 ± 33	100 ± 27	<.002
Aged	(12)	134 ± 15	103 ± 25	n.s.

INHIBITORY AVOIDANCE

| | | Median Retention Score | | | | |
| | | Days Following Training | | | | |
	(N)	1	7	14	21	28
Young	(11)	300	300	300	300	300
Aged	(7)	300	300	300	300	300

	(N)	Median 24 Hr. Retention	Percent Reaching Maximum Retention
Sham	(18)	300	100
Nucleus basalis	(16)	300	63

3. FLICKER, C., R. L. DEAN, D. L. WATKINS, S. K. FISHER & R. T. BARTUS. 1983. Pharmacol. Biochem. Behav. **18:** 973–981.
4. SHERMAN, K. A., J. E. KUSTER, R. L. DEAN, R. T. BARTUS & E. FRIEDMAN. 1981. Neurobiol. Aging **2:** 99–104.
5. MARTINEZ, J. L. & H. RIGTER. 1983. Behav. Neural Biol. **39:** 181–191.
6. BOAST, C. A. & Y. ISLAMI. 1982. Soc. Neurosci. Abstr. **8:** 319.
7. FLOOD, J. F., D. W. LANDRY & M. E. JARVIK. 1981. Brain Res. **215:** 177–185.

Arginine Vasopressin Inoculates Against Age-Related Changes in Temporal Memory[a]

WARREN H. MECK AND RUSSELL M. CHURCH

Walter S. Hunter Laboratory of Psychology
Brown University
Providence, Rhode Island 02912

The purpose was to describe age-related changes in temporal memory of rats and to determine whether vasopressin (AVP) administered when the animals were mature (10–13 months of age) would prevent or reduce these changes when the rats became old (27–30 months of age).

The subjects were 20 male Charles River COBS CD rats. The apparatus consisted of 10 standard lever boxes. A 20-sec peak procedure was used.[6-8] After an intertrial interval (130 sec), a white noise signal occurred and, on a random half of the trials, food was primed after 20 sec and the rat's next lever press was reinforced; on the other trials, no food was available and the trial lasted for 130 sec. Sessions lasted three hours.

The rats were randomly partitioned into two groups of 10 each: The AVP group and the saline control group. Starting when they were 10 months old, the AVP group received an i.p. injection of 0.08 pressor units/kg of arginine vasopressin (AVP) 20 min prior to each of 30 sessions of peak training; the control group received similar treatment with physiological saline. Each rat was tested on the average of every third day according to a random selection process, so this treatment lasted until the rats were approximately 13 months old. Both the AVP and saline control groups were then trained on the 20-sec peak procedure intermittently (every other month) until 30 months of age.

On the sessions during which it was administered, when the rats were 10–13 months old, AVP had two main effects on performance in the peak procedure: It decreased the variability of the temporal discrimination and it shifted the peak time significantly earlier than 20 sec (FIGURE 1).

After AVP was no longer administered, the variability of the temporal discrimination and the peak time of the two groups became indistinguishable (FIGURE 1).

As the age of rats in the saline control group (27–30 months) increased, the variability of the temporal discrimination increased and the peak time shifted significantly later than 20 sec. In contrast, the rats in the group that had received AVP at 10–13 months of age did not have an increase in the peak time when they were 27–30 months old (FIGURE 1).

The smooth curve near the points is from a fit of scalar timing theory. The theory accounts for 99% of the variance of the mean functions and accounts for a median of 95% of the variance of the functions for individual rats. The parameters were estimated

[a]The research reported in this paper was supported in part by Research Grant MH 37049 from the National Institute of Mental Health.

453

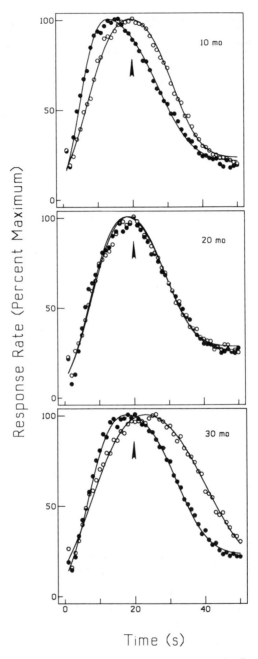

FIGURE 1. Open circles indicate rats trained under saline at 10 months of age and closed circles indicate rats trained under AVP at 10 months of age. Top panel shows performance on peak trials when the rats were 10–13 months old. Middle panel shows performance when the rats were 17–20 months old. Bottom panel shows performance when the rats were 27–30 months old.

from a hill-climbing procedure. The parameter K^*, the memory storage constant, was used as a measure of peak time. There was a significant interaction between treatment (AVP versus control) and age ($F = 8.8$, df $= 2,34, p < .001$). A Tukey HSD test found that the AVP rats at 10–13 months of age had a peak time significantly shorter than all other groups and that the control rats at 27–30 months of age had a peak time significantly longer than all other groups.

Previous research has found that physostigmine, an anticholinesterase that readily crosses the blood-brain barrier, and dietary lecithin (phosphatidylcholine), a source of choline that crosses the blood-brain barrier and is a precursor of acetylcholine synthesis, both decrease the variability and the time of the peak.[5] Atropine, an acetylcholine receptor blocker, increases the variability and the time of the peak.[4] Thus, the peak time may serve as a behavioral measure of the effective level of acetylcholine. An increase in the effective level of acetylcholine may decrease peak time and a decrease in the effective level of acetylcholine may increase peak time. The increase in peak times of aged control rats may reflect a decrease in the effective level of acetylcholine.

Disorders of cholinergic function have been related to cognitive impairments, particularly of memory processes. They have been implicated in some geriatric memory dysfunctions,[1] some psychiatric problems,[10] and in some disease processes.[2]

In the present experiment, AVP treatment of mature rats appears to prevent some age-related behavioral changes, perhaps through a mechanism that maintains the effective level of acetylcholine. Previous work has indicated that the administration of certain pituitary hormones (e.g., ACTH, MSH, and ADH) to neonatal rats can improve learning and memory when the same rats are later tested as adults.[11] The physiological mechanisms responsible for these long-term changes are uncertain but may involve changes at receptors sensitive to neuropeptides such as AVP.

The conclusion was that AVP treatment of mature rats prevents some changes in temporal memory when the animals become old. It remains to be determined whether the long-term effects of AVP can be related to changes in the cholinergic nervous system.

REFERENCES

1. BARTUS, R. T., R. L. DEAN, B. BEER & A. S. LIPPA. 1982. The cholinergic hypothesis of geriatric memory dysfunction. Science **217**: 408–417.
2. COYLE, J. T., D. J. PRICE & M. R. DeLONG. 1983. Alzheimer's disease: A disorder of cortical cholinergic innervation. Science **219**: 1184–1190.
3. GIBBON, J., R. M. CHURCH & W. H. MECK. 1984. Scalar timing in memory. Ann. N.Y. Acad. Sci. **423**: 52–77.
4. MECK, W. H. 1983. Selective adjustment of the speed of internal clock and memory processes. J. Exp. Psychol.: Anim. Behav. Proc. **9**: 171–201.
5. MECK, W. H. & R. M. CHURCH. 1983. The cholinergic nervous system and temporal memory in rats. Soc. Neurosci. Abstr. **9**: 478.
6. MECK, W. H. & R. M. CHURCH. 1984. Simultaneous temporal processing. J. Exp. Psychol.: Anim. Beh. Proc. **10**: 1–20.
7. MECK, W. H., R. M. CHURCH & D. S. OLTON. 1984. Hippocampus, time, and memory. Behav. Neurosci. **98**: 3–22.
8. MECK, W. H., F. N. KOMEILY-ZADEH & R. M. CHURCH. 1984. Two-step acquisition: Modification of an internal clock's criterion. J. Exp. Psychol.: Anim. Behav. Proc. **10**: 297–306.
9. MECK, W. H. & R. M. CHURCH. 1985. Nutrients that modify the speed of internal clock and memory storage processes. Behav. Neurosci. (In press.)

10. MELGES, F. T. 1982. Time and the Inner Future: A Temporal Approach to Psychiatric Disorders. Wiley. New York.
11. SANDMAN, C. A., A. J. KASTIN & L. G. MILLER. 1977. Central nervous system actions of MSH and related pituitary peptides. *In* Clinical Neuroendocrinology. L. Martini & G. M. Besser, Eds. Academic Press. New York.

The Influence of Sex Steroids on Human Nonverbal Memory Processes

J. D. E. GABRIELI AND S. CORKIN

Department of Psychology and Clinical Research Center
Massachusetts Institute of Technology
Cambridge, Massachusetts 02139

J. D. CRAWFORD

Endocrine Metabolic Unit
Massachusetts General Hospital
Boston, Massachusetts 02114

Little is known about specific biological influences upon the development of either human memory capacities or the brain structures supporting them. Patients with Turner's syndrome are phenotypic females with X chromosome monosomy or partial monosomy due to a structurally abnormal second sex chromosome. These patients are gonadally dysgenic, have nonfunctional ovaries, and cannot produce normal levels of sex steroids from about the fourth month in utero. The study of patients with Turner's syndrome may present an opportunity to learn about hormonal constraints governing the growth of mnemonic abilities.

SUBJECTS

Subjects included 15 patients with Turner's syndrome (mean age 13.0 years, range 8–18 years). The normal control subjects were 15 siblings of these patients (11 female, 4 male); their mean age was 13.4 years (range 9–25 years).

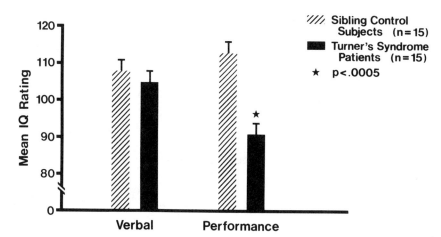

FIGURE 1. Reduction of Wechsler Performance IQ rating but not Wechsler Verbal IQ rating in Turner's syndrome (bar = 1 S.E.M.).

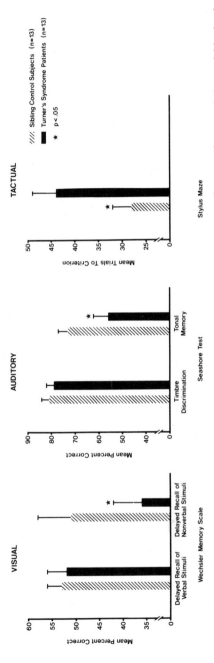

FIGURE 2. Contrasting performance on patients with Turner's syndrome and control subjects on tests of memory for nonverbal material in the visual, auditory, and tactual modalities (bar = 1 S.E.M.).

METHODS

All subjects received neurological examinations and underwent detailed neuropsychological evaluations. Results from four tests are reported here.

RESULTS

Patients with Turner's syndrome scored as well as their siblings on the Wechsler Verbal Scale (FIGURE 1). This finding supports other results showing that most cognitive capacities are normal in Turner's syndrome. The patients in our study did score significantly lower than did their siblings on the Wechsler Performance Scale, consistent with our finding that patients with Turner's syndrome are poor at mental rotation, right-left orientation, and discovering figures embedded in more complex figures.

Patients with Turner's syndrome also have an impairment of memory for nonverbal material presented in three modalities (FIGURE 2). They had normal delayed recall for verbal material on the Wechsler Memory Scale, but an impaired recall for nonverbal material. Although the patients were as good as their siblings at discriminating tonal quality on the Seashore Test, they performed poorly when the task demanded memory for the tonal quality. Further, patients with Turner's syndrome required significantly more trials than did their siblings to learn a tactual stylus maze to criterion. It is of interest to note that patients with lesions in the right temporoparietal area have been reported to show deficits on the same three tests as did the patients with Turner's syndrome.

CONCLUSIONS

Patients with Turner's syndrome have a deficit in nonverbal cognition and an impairment in memory for nonverbal materials in three perceptual modalities. This sort of memory impairment appears to be related to a deficit in processing the material to be remembered, in contrast to the disorder in chronic global amnesia, which may occur in the absence of deficits in non-mnemonic stimulus processing.

Normal exposure to sex steriods may be necessary for the normal development of nonverbal cognitive and mnemonic capacities. Normal exposure is, at least in this population, not necessary for the development of normal verbal abilities.

Normal exposure to gonadal hormones may be required for the full expression of some cognitive functions dependent upon the right temporoparietal, but not any other, area of the brain.

An Automatic Encoding Deficit in the Amnesia of Korsakoff's Syndrome

DEBORAH KOHL AND JASON BRANDT

Department of Psychology
The Johns Hopkins University
Baltimore, Maryland 21288

Several investigators have proposed that the key feature of chronic organic amnesia is a failure to discriminate among past events on the basis of environmental context.[1,2] This research was undertaken to determine whether patients with the chronic organic

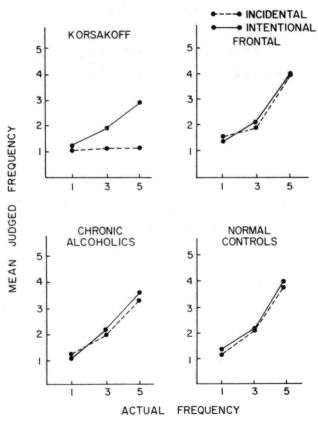

FIGURE 1. Frequency judgments of all four groups under both incidental and intentional instruction conditions.

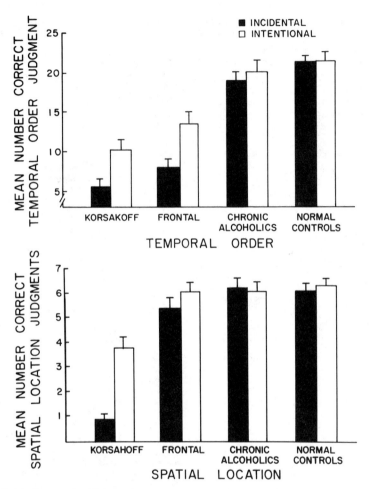

FIGURE 2. Temporal order judgments (top) and spatial location judgments (bottom) of all four groups under both instruction conditions.

amnesia of Korsakoff's syndrome are capable of encoding frequency of occurrence, temporal order, and spatial location, elements of context that neurologically intact individuals encode automatically.[3]

Six patients with the amnesia of alcoholic Korsakoff's syndrome, eleven patients with circumscribed damage to the frontal lobes, fifteen chronic alcoholics, and fifteen normal controls were tested on their ability to recognize words and to encode frequency of occurrence (how often), temporal order (when), and spatial location (where) information under both incidental and intentional instructions.

The groups did not differ significantly on recognition memory performance, an indication that Korsakoff amnesics and patients with frontal lobe damage are quite capable of encoding item information.

Results for context judgment performance are presented in FIGURES 1 and 2.

Under incidental instructions, the frequency judgment ($F_{3,43} = 17.50$, $p = .001$) and the spatial location judgment ($F_{3,43} = 19.75$, $p = .001$) performance of Korsakoff amnesics was significantly worse than that of the other subject groups. Their performance was also significantly worse than the two control groups on the temporal order task, but they did not differ from the frontally damaged subjects on this task.

Under intentional learning instructions, Korsakoff amnesics showed significant improvement in contextual judgment performance for all three tasks. However, this improved performance resulted in a significant impairment in their recognition memory performance.

Both the frontally damaged group and the two control groups were equally good at judging frequency and spatial location under both instruction conditions. However, the frontal group was impaired on temporal order judgments under incidental instructions. Analysis of the errors made by this group suggests that they failed the task due to perseverative tendencies rather than due to a failure of automatic encoding.

The severely impaired performance of the Korsakoff amnesics on context judgment tests under incidental instructions suggests a distinct impairment in their ability to automatically encode elements of context that are essential for normal memory performance. The improvement in context judgments under intentional instructions suggests that the deficit is one of automatic encoding and is not peculiar to the type of information itself. This improvement, coupled with the suppression of recognition memory performance under intentional instructions, also suggests that effortful processing may be intact in these subjects.

The results of this study suggest that the context encoding deficit of Korsakoff amnesics is due to a failure of automatic encoding. This deficit is central to their amnesia and is not attributable to their purported frontal lobe damage.

REFERENCES

1. HUPPERT, F. A. & M. PIERCY. 1982. In search of the functional locus of the amnesic syndrome. *In* Human Memory and Amnesia. L. S. Cermak, Ed. Erlbaum. Hillsdale, NJ.
2. KINSBOURNE, M. & F. WOOD. 1982. Theoretical considerations regarding the episodic-semantic memory distinction. *In* Human Memory and Amnesia. L. S. Cermak, Ed. Erlbaum. Hillsdale, NJ.
3. HASHER, L. & R. T. ZACKS. 1979. Automatic and effortful processes in memory. J. Exp. Psychol. Gen. **80:** 356–388.

Auditory Emotional Memories: Establishment by Projections from the Medial Geniculate Nucleus to the Posterior Neostriatum and/or Dorsal Amygdala

JOSEPH E. LeDOUX, AKIRA SAKAGUCHI, JIRO IWATA,
AND DONALD J. REIS

Laboratory of Neurobiology
Cornell University Medical College
New York, New York 10021

It has long been known that sensory receiving and association areas of the neocortex are not required for the expression of conditioned or unconditioned emotional responses evoked by sensory stimuli.[1-4] Such responses must therefore be mediated by brain areas receiving sensory information that has diverged from the primary afferent pathway at some subcortical site. To identify the pathway we sought to determine whether: auditory emotional conditioning is disrupted by lesions of the medial geniculate nucleus (MG), the primary thalamic station of the auditory pathway; MG sends projections to subcortical targets; and interruption of projections from MG to subcortical targets disrupts conditioning.

Male Sprague-Dawley rats were subjected to stereotaxic lesions of various brain regions, allowed to recover for two weeks, and implanted with a catheter for recording mean arterial pressure (MAP) and heart rate (HR) while freely moving. The animals were then either classically conditioned by pairing a pure tone conditioned stimulus (CS) with a brief delivery of electric footshock or pseudoconditioned by presenting footshock in a random relation to the CS. The next-day changes in MAP and HR and the suppression of exploratory activity evoked by the CS were measured as indices of conditioned fear.

Presentation of the CS to normal unoperated rats elicited increases in MAP and HR and suppressed exploratory activity and drinking (TABLE 1). Animals subjected to pseudoconditioning control procedures exhibited smaller changes in MAP and less suppression of somatomotor behavior than conditioned animals, but similar increases in HR. While MAP increases and somatomotor suppression reflect associative conditioning, HR changes elicited by the CS are non-associative in origin.

Lesions of the auditory cortex did not affect the changes in MAP, HR, or somatic activity elicited by the CS. In contrast, bilateral lesions of MG disrupted the conditioning of MAP and somatic responses, but did not block the expression of tachycardia during the CS. Lesions of the inferior colliculus (IC), the primary source of afferent input to MG, exactly reproduced the effects of MG lesions. The associative conditioning of MAP and somatic responses thus appears to depend on auditory input diverging from the auditory pathway in MG. Findings concerning the effects of cortical, MG, and IC lesions have been published previously.[5]

Wheat germ agglutinin conjugated horseradish peroxidase (WGA-HRP) was microinjected into MG to determine possible subcortical projections. Anterograde transport was seen in the caudal neostriatum, dorsal amygdala, ventromedial hypothalamus, and subparafascicular thalamus. Injections of the caudal neostriatum and dorsal amygdala resulted in retrograde labeling of cells in the medial and suprageniculate aspects of MG. Injections of other areas did not label MG cells. Thus, the medial and suprageniculate divisions of MG send projections to subcortical targets.

Connections between MG and subcortical targets were interrupted by placing unilateral lesions in MG. Contralaterally, the target area was lesioned. Such lesions involving either the amygdala or neostriatal areas disrupted MAP and somatic conditioning, but did not affect the tachycardia. Lesions of MG and the contralateral ventromedial hypothalamus or subparafascicular thalamus did not affect any of the responses.

We conclude that auditory emotional memories established through classical conditioning are mediated by sensory input ascending in the auditory pathway through IC to MG. From there the signal is relayed to a striatal field involving the caudal neostriatum and the immediately underlying aspects of the archistriatum (central and lateral nuclei of the amygdala).

TABLE 1. Mean Arterial Pressure, Heart Rate, and Freezing Responses Elicited by Acoustic CS[b]

	(N)	Peak Change in		Duration of Freezing (sec)
		MAP (mm Hg)	HR (bpm)	
Unoperated				
Conditioned	(5)	16 ± 3	18 ± 4	95 ± 12
Pseudoconditioned	(4)	7 ± 3[a]	13 ± 4	40 ± 15[a]
Lesioned				
Auditory cortex	(10)	20 ± 4	14 ± 5	95 ± 12
Medial geniculate	(10)	4 ± 3[a]	12 ± 4	39 ± 15[a]
MG and contralateral:				
Posterior neostriatum	(4)	5 ± 5[a]	19 ± 4	36 ± 18[a]
Dorsal amygdala	(5)	8 ± 4[a]	16 ± 5	49 ± 15[a]
Ventromedial hypothalamus	(5)	14 ± 3	25 ± 6	99 ± 8
Subparafascicular thalamus	(4)	13 ± 2	15 ± 4	90 ± 12

[a] = $p < 0.01$; significance indicated relative to unoperated conditioned setup. [b]Values represent mean ± S.E.

REFERENCES

1. CANNON, W. B. & S. W. BRITTON. 1925. Psuedo-affective medulliadrenal secretion. Am. J. Physiol. **72:** 283–294.
2. BARD, P. & D. M. RIOCH. 1937. A study of four cats deprived of neocortex and additional portions of the forebrain. Bull. Johns Hopkins Hosp. **60:** 73–125.
3. KELLY, J. B. & S. J. GALZIER. 1978. Auditory cortex lesions and discrimination of spatial location by the rat. Brain Res. **80:** 317–327.
4. OAKLEY, D. A. & I. S. RUSSELL. 1975. Role of cortex in Pavlovian discrimination learning. Physiol. Behav. **15:** 315–321.
5. LeDOUX, J. E., A. SAKAGUCHI & D. J. REIS. 1984. Subcortical efferent projections of the medial geniculate nucleus mediate emotional responses conditioned to acoustic stimuli. J. Neurosci. **4:** 683–698.

The Inaccessible, But Intact Engram: A Challenge for Animal Models of Memory Dysfunction

CHARLES F. MACTUTUS[a] AND NANCY M. WISE

Laboratory of Behavioral and Neurological Toxicology
National Institute of Environmental Health Sciences
Research Triangle Park, North Carolina 27709

INTRODUCTION

The expression of learned behavior that is otherwise forgotten has been shown to follow brief exposure to one of several components of the original training environment.[5,6] This phenomenon of cue-induced memory reactivation is now well-established and has been demonstrated in a variety of paradigms.[1,2,7] However, the mechanism(s) by which cuing facilitates retention performance has received much less attention.

We used a recently developed multiple measure passive avoidance task[4] in a re-examination of cue-induced memory reactivation. Our aims were to replicate the finding that passive avoidance behavior is composed of two response dimensions and that these dimensions are differentially affected by length of retention interval and prior training experience, and to determine whether reactivation treatment might differentially affect inhibition and vacillation.

METHODS

The offspring of Fischer-344 rats were maintained under standard laboratory conditions. At 18 days of age one half of the pups were trained, using a 1-sec 0.8 mA footshock, in a one-trial passive avoidance (PA) paradigm. The remaining animals received sham training (ST), i.e., no footshock was administered upon crossing into the dark compartment. However, 1 hr later, these latter pups received a comparable, but noncontingent footshock (NCFS) in a neutral compartment. Retention tests (no footshock) were given 24 or 168 hr after training. Seven dependent measures were recorded during each test session.[3] The initial latency and total number of head poke (head including ears), half cross (head and two forepaws), and full cross (all four paws) responses into the darkened compartment as well as the total time spent in the illuminated "safe" side were recorded during a 300.0 sec test session.

A reactivation treatment was given to all animals eight days after original training. A single NCFS (1-sec 0.8 mA) was administered within a neutral compartment. The effect of the reactivation treatment on PA behavior was evaluated after 24 hr with the test procedure as stated above.

[a]Address correspondence to: Charles F. Mactutus, Ph.D., Laboratory of Behavioral and Neurological Toxicology, NIH-NIEHS, P.O. Box 12233, Research Triangle Park, NC 27709.

TABLE 1. Rotated Factor Loadings: Independent Groups of Rats Received Contingent or Noncontingent Footshock during Training and Were Tested after a 24- or 168-hr Retention Interval

Variables	Factor 1	Factor 2
Full cross latency	0.910	−0.319
Half cross latency	0.903	−0.315
Total time on "safe" side	0.894	0.000
Head poke latency	0.773	0.000
Number of full crosses	−0.407	0.831
Number of half crosses	−0.263	0.942
Number of head pokes	0.000	0.932
Percent of total variance		
Explained	46.8%	38.7%/85.5%
"Label"	Inhibition	Vacillation

Factor loadings less than 0.250 have been replaced by zeroes.

RESULTS

The mean (± SEM) training response latencies ranged from 14.8 ± 1.9 to 25.0 ± 6.2 sec and did not differentiate the treatment groups. The seven dependent variables were subjected to principle components analysis to remove redundancy among the measures and identify the dimensions underlying the test behavior.

Newly Acquired Memory

Two response dimensions characterized retention performance (TABLE 1). Factor one had the highest loadings on "inhibitory" behavior, whereas factor two described the "vacillatory" behavior of the animals. As seen in FIGURE 1, a clear loss of inhibition was apparent across the 24 hr to 168 hr retention intervals [$F(1, 76) = 11.9$, $p <$

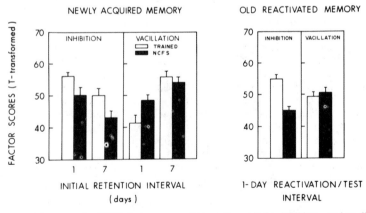

FIGURE 1. The mean (± SEM) factor scores (T-transformed) for inhibitory and vacillatory components of both newly acquired and old reactivated memories are shown, respectively, in the left and right panel.

0.001]. However, a robust contingency effect $[F(1, 76) = 10.8, p < 0.001]$ without a significant interaction indicated that despite this decrease in inhibition, those animals that received PA training displayed greater inhibition than ST/NCFS controls through seven days after training. In contrast, a marked increase in vacillatory behavior was observed with increasing retention interval $[F(1, 76) = 26.2, p < 0.001)$, but was clearly more pronounced for PA trained than for ST/NCFS controls $[F(1, 76) = 5.3, p < 0.024]$.

Old Reactivated Memory

As is also shown in FIGURE 1, inhibition was significantly greater for those animals that had originally received PA training rather than the ST/NCFS treatment $[F(1, 76) = 25.9, p < 0.001]$. The vacillatory behavior of the PA trained animals, however, was not significantly altered relative to that of ST/NCFS controls $[F(1, 76) < 1.0]$.

Newly Acquired Versus Old Reactivated Memory

Comparison of the response dimensions characterizing newly acquired and old reactivated memories indicated that the inhibition displayed following reactivation was similar to that observed 24 hr after training $[F(1, 76) < 1.0]$ and greater than that noted 168 hr after training $[F(1, 76) = 4.1, p < 0.046]$. The reactivation treatment did not affect the inhibition displayed by the ST/NCFS controls; i.e., inhibition was significantly less than that observed 24 hr after training $[F(1, 76) = 5.1, p < 0.027]$ and was not any greater than at 168 hr after training $[F(1, 76) < 1.0]$. Vacillatory behavior following the NCFS reactivation treatment was less than that observed 168 hr after training $[F(1, 76) = 7.6, p < 0.007]$, but was also greater than that detected 24 hr after original training $[F(1, 76) = 11.0, p < 0.001]$. In other words, the increase of inhibition following reactivation treatment was not directly attributable to NCFS-induced "freezing." Moreover, the reactivation treatment did not appreciably alter the vacillatory behavior of the ST/NCFS controls relative to that noted 24 hr or 168 hr after original training $[Fs(1, 76) = 2.1, \text{ and } <1.0, \text{ respectively}]$.

DISCUSSION

As previously suggested,[4] a multivariate passive avoidance paradigm indicated that test behavior is composed of two response dimensions, inhibition and vacillation. Moreover, these dimensions appeared empirically independent; i.e., they were differentially affected by length of retention interval and by whether contingent or noncontingent footshock was administered during training.

Following a noncontingent footshock reactivation treatment, inhibitory behavior was restored to a level approximating that observed at a comparable interval after original learning. While vacillatory behavior after reactivation treatment was also restored towards that noted 24 hr after original training, vacillation remained significantly greater than that observed for a newly acquired memory. The inclusion of sham-trained/noncontingent footshock controls, which also received the noncontingent footshock reactivation treatment, indicated these observed changes were not an artifact of alterations in behavioral activation per se. Collectively, these findings are consistent with the tenor of many reports on cue-induced facilitation of retention performance and imply that memory dysfunction in infrahumans may often be more appropriately viewed as a loss of access to, rather than a loss of, the "engram."

REFERENCES

1. GORDON, W. C. 1981. Mechanisms of cue-induced retention enhancement. *In* Information Processing in Animals: Memory Mechanisms. N. E. Spear & R. R. Miller, Eds.: 319–339. Lawrence Erlbaum Associates. Hillsdale, NJ.
2. LEWIS, D. J. 1979. Psychobiology of active and inactive memory. Psychol. Bull. **86:** 1054–1083.
3. MACTUTUS, C. F., K. L. UNGER & H. A. TILSON. 1982. Neonatal chlordecone impairs early learning and memory in the rat on a multiple measure passive avoidance task. Neurotoxicol. **3:** 27–44.
4. MACTUTUS, C. F. & N. M. WISE. 1984. Multiple response dimensions in passive avoidance responding: Behavioral and pharmacological dissociation. Paper presented at the Eastern Psychological Association. Baltimore, MD.
5. QUARTERMAIN, D., B. S. MCEWEN & E. C. AZMITIA, JR. 1970. Amnesia produced by ECS or Cycloheximide: Conditions for recovery. Science **169:** 554–555.
6. ROHRBAUGH, M. & D. C. RICCIO. 1970. Paradoxical enhancement of learned fear. J. Abnor. Psychol. **75:** 210–216.
7. SPEAR, N. E. 1978. The Processing of Memories: Forgetting and Retention. Lawrence Erlbaum Associates. Hillsdale, NJ.

Neurobehavioral Effects of Chronic Choline-Containing Diets on the Adult and Aging C57BL/6NNIA Mouse Brain[a]

RONALD MERVIS,[b] LLOYD HORROCKS,[b]
PAUL DEMEDIUK,[b] LANE WALLACE,[c]
DONALD R. MEYER,[d] SUSAN BEALL,[d]
KIMBERLY CARIS,[e] AND EDWARD NABER[f]

*The Brain and Aging and Neuronal Plasticity Research Group
Departments of [b]Pathology, [c]Physiological Chemistry,
[d]Pharmacology, [e]Psychology, and [f]Poultry Science
Ohio State University
Columbus, Ohio 43210*

Choline-containing diets were chronically fed to male C57BL/6NNIA mice for either 5 or 11 months: from 8–13 months or 13–24 months, respectively. The choline in the chow was supplied in one of three ways: as free choline (choline chloride) or as bound choline as found in a 95% purified preparation of phosphatidylcholine (PC) and in an oil-free granular lecithin formulation (centrolex). The choline in these diets (either free or bound forms) was enriched at low, medium, or high levels (containing 2.4, 4.8, or 10.8 mg/g of chow, respectively). Two low choline diets contained 0.9 and 1.5 mg/g of choline, respectively, but were regarded as choline-adequate since the minimal nutritional requirement for choline is thought to be 0.6 mg/g of chow. All these diets were isocaloric and isonitrogenous. A standard rodent laboratory chow (Purina) contained 2.3 mg/g of choline.

One-trial passive-avoidance testing for retention of learning indicated that mice of the C57BL/6NNIA strain show little normal age-related memory loss between 8–24 months old. As such, dietary enrichments did not significantly improve performance in comparison to the mice on the standard lab chow containing abundant choline. Learning was improved, however, in relation to mice on lower choline control diets, by supplementation with choline, PC, or lecithin. Whereas the younger mice tended to respond better at higher levels of enrichment, the older (24 months old) mice showed superior retention of learning following low enrichment levels of PC and lecithin. This suggests that there may be an age-related shift in the optimal, potentially prophylactic, dietary "window."

Additional studies are evaluating some parameters reflecting potential membrane changes as a consequence of the various dietary regimens. Analysis of membrane phospholipids in a plasma membrane fraction from mouse forebrain indicated that membrane composition remains remarkably constant; however, diet-modulated enhanced membrane fluidity is suggested by a reduced cholesterol-to-phospholipid ratio in the older mice on low levels of chronic dietary enrichment. Receptor-binding studies from the neocortex (muscarinic, α- and β-adrenergic), hippocampus (musca-

[a]Supported by a grant from Central Soya Company.

rinic, GABAnergic), and striatum (muscarinic) of 8–13-month-old mice have indicated no clear-cut dose-response trends for any of these receptors.

Preliminary findings from quantitative morphometric studies of Golgi-impregnated neocortical pyramidal neurons in 8–13-month-old mice suggest that supplementation with the choline-containing diets not only results in a higher spine density, but in addition, there is a higher proportion of dendritic spines with a configuration regarded as optimal for efficient transfer of information.

Simple Delayed Discrimination in the Rat: A Behavioral Baseline

DEBORAH A. OLIN AND ANTHONY L. RILEY

Psychopharmacology Laboratory
The American University
Washington, D.C. 20016

Short-term memory in the rat has been studied extensively under a variety of procedures during the past 25 years.[1,2] Most of this work, however, has been carried out in various maze designs, e.g., radial-arm, parallel-arm, Hebb-Williams, and T-maze. Although such procedures do allow an assessment of memory capacity, their very design precludes comparisons across species for which the maze has never been used to assess memory. The design most used with other species is the delayed discrimination procedure, e.g., the delayed simple and delayed conditional discrimination tasks.[3] To allow for a more direct comparison of memory in the rat with that of other species, it is necessary to examine species under similar training and testing conditions.[4,5] To provide such a baseline, the memory capacity of the rat was examined in the present experiment using a simple delayed discrimination procedure.

Following response shaping to lick a dry tube, rats were trained to discriminate between two tastes, i.e., licking (20 licks within an 8-sec limited hold period) following the presentation of sodium saccharin (SD) was reinforced with access to water, while licking following the presentation of sodium chloride was not reinforced (SΔ). Once this discrimination was acquired and maintained above 80% correct, a delayed discrimination procedure was initiated. In this procedure, various delays were imposed between the presentation of the taste and the opportunity to respond. To control for aftertastes that might have lingered during the delay, a saccharin or sodium chloride taste was randomly delivered immediately following presentation of the initial SD or SΔ taste. The only stimuli relevant to the discrimination, therefore, were the initial saccharin or sodium chloride tastes.

FIGURE 1 presents the overall percent correct performance of the taste discrimination at various delay intervals. As illustrated, all subjects were able to perform the taste discrimination when a delay was imposed between delivery of the taste and the opportunity to respond (discrimination was noted as occurring when responding followed presentation of saccharin (SD), but did not follow presentation of sodium chloride (SΔ)). Although performance fell below 80% correct at different delays for individual subjects, all rats were able to maintain the discrimination at delays longer than 34 sec, with several subjects demonstrating discrimination at delays of up to 54 sec. FIGURE 2 illustrates performance in the individual SD and SΔ components for each subject across the various delays. As illustrated, for three of the four subjects performance was more accurate following presentation of saccharin (SD) than following presentation of sodium chloride (SΔ). For these three subjects, an overall decrease in performance at longer delays was primarily due to incorrect performance following SΔ, i.e., subjects responded following the presentation of sodium chloride. At longer delays, the fourth subject simply failed to respond following either SD or SΔ.

It is clear from these data that rats can perform in a delayed discrimination procedure. Furthermore, because this design is similar to procedures for assessment of memory in other species, more direct comparison can be made of memory capacities

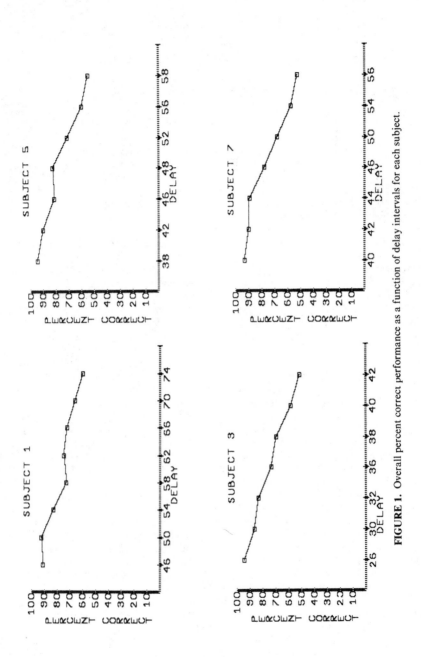

FIGURE 1. Overall percent correct performance as a function of delay intervals for each subject.

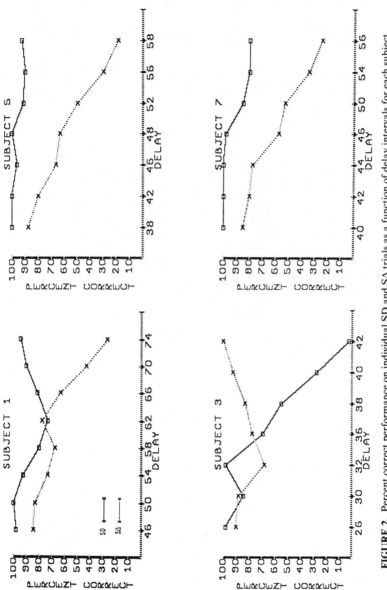

FIGURE 2. Percent correct performance on individual SD and SΔ trials as a function of delay intervals for each subject.

with the rat. Also, because much of the assessments of memory processing in other species has been examined within this same design, the use of the delayed discrimination procedure with the rat should allow for an assessment and comparison of the mechanisms underlying memory in the rat.

ACKNOWLEDGMENT

The authors are greatly indebted to Robert Colnes for his capable assistance in the research for this report.

REFERENCES

1. KONORSKI, J. 1959. A new method of physiological investigation of recent memory in animals. Bull. Acad. Pol. Sci. Ser. Sci. Biol. 7: 115–117.
2. OLTON, D. & R. SAMUELSON. 1976. Remembrances of places past: Spatial memory in rats. J. Exp. Psychol. Anim. Behav. Proc. 2: 97–116.
3. HONIG, W. 1978. Studies of working memory in the pigeon. In Cognitive Processes in Animal Behavior. S. H. Hulse, H. Fowler & W. K. Honig, Eds. Lawrence Erlbaum Associates. Hillsdale, NJ.
4. WALLACE, J., P. STEINHART, S. SCOBIE & N. SPEAR. 1980. Stimulus modality and short-term memory in rats. Anim. Learn. Behav. 8: 10–16.
5. PONTECORVO, M. J. 1983. Effects of proactive interference on rats' continuous nonmatching-to-sample performance. Anim. Learn. Behav. 11: 356–366.

Spatial Aspects of Memory Implicated in Face Drawings of Alcoholic Men

ANNELIESE A. PONTIUS

Department of Psychiatry
Harvard Medical School
Boston, Massachusetts 02115

Spatial representation has empirically been found useful in mnemonic devices since antiquity,[1] apparently facilitating spatially ordered encoding. A subtle spatial-relational misrepresentation was hypothesized to exist in chronic skid row alcoholic men, who are known as a group to have deficits in recent memory, which in turn implicate a deficient encoding process.[2] A novel test shown in FIGURE 1, was used: Draw-A-Person-With-Face-In-Frontal-View (DAPF).[3–5] Note the simple determination (which in future could be quantified): A ruler was used (involving no qualitative

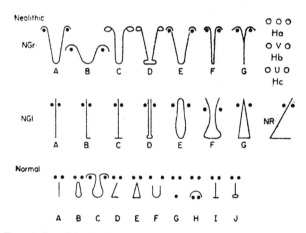

FIGURE 1. Frontal view of forehead-nose-eyes sector of face patterns, measured with a ruler. "Neolithic face" patterns "NGr" and "NG1": continuation of forehead into nose without any indication of a narrowing, indentation, or discontinuity at the bridge (root) of the nose, i.e., at the area between the eyes. Thus, a ruler placed at the upper and lower borders of the eyes measures the presence or absence of a neolithic face configuration. Subtype NGr is present if at least at the lower border of the eyes (if not even above it) the nose is as wide there as it is at its tip (NGr: A—Ha, b, c), discounting a bulbous enlargement of the cartilaginous parts around the tip of the nose (NGr:D). Note that patterns Ha, b, c depict the same principle of obliteration of the bridge of the nose area: even at the *upper* border of the eyes, the nose is at least as wide here as it is at its "tip" area. Subtype NG1 is present if the nose extends above the upper border of the eyes into the forehead (NG1: A—G). A half-profile type "NR" is not rated, as it is intermediate between "neolithic" and normal faces. Normal face patterns (A—J) are characterized by the indication of a discontinuity between forehead and nose at the bridge of the nose area through (a) narrowing or (b) indentation, or (c) a beginning of the nose design only below the lower border of the eyes. In all face patterns dots and circles can be interchanged without affecting the rating. (From Pontius.[4] With permission from *Experientia*.)

judgement) to rate patterns of the face (even of stick figures) as accurate ("normal," showing signs of interruption, indentation, or narrowing at the bridge of the nose area) or as inaccurate ("neolithic," showing continuity between forehead and nose, as was characteristic worldwide of art during the "neolithic period," by definition a preliterate one). The configuration of the human face is here used for its subtle spatial relations, ratios, and directions.[6] Face perception or recognition are reasonably ruled out as playing a role in that the human face is typically drawn without looking at it, rather by resorting to a mental representation of the face pattern.

The DAPF is sensitive to detect subtle spatial-relational misrepresentation of a graphic and implied mental kind. Thus, it has previously delineated certain proportions of diverse populations and periods, detecting a close correspondence between depiction of "neolithic faces" in the DAPF and the officially reported illiteracy rates,[4] both dysfunctions lacking refined spatial-relational representational skills.

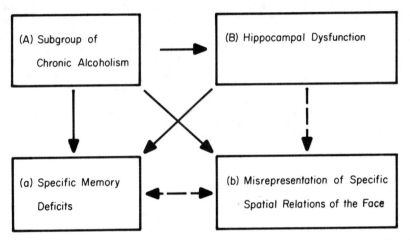

FIGURE 2. Schema of new testable hypotheses (‒‒‒) generated by the present data, considered in conjunction with other neuropathological data already known (——). (From Pontius.[5] With permission from Percept. Mot. Skills.)

In this context it is reasonable to interpret the specific spatial-relational misrepresentation of the pattern of the face by 22% of chronic skid row alcoholic men (as against 12% of controls) as being indicative of a subtly deficient spatial-relational encoding. This interpretation appears to be the more reasonable as chronic alcoholism not only implicates the hippocampal system, mediating certain aspects of spatial representation,[7] but is also known to be associated with deficient recent memory, implicating poor encoding[2] (FIGURE 2).

REFERENCES

1. YATES, F. 1965. The art of memory. University of Chicago Press. Chicago, IL.
2. PRIBRAM, K. H. 1969. The amnestic syndromes: disturbances in coding? In The Pathology of Memory. G. A. Talland & N. C. Waugh, Eds.: 127–157. Academic Press. New York.
3. PONTIUS, A. A. 1981. Geometric figure-rotation task and face representation in dyslexia: role of spatial relations and orientation. Percept. Mot. Skills **53:** 607–614.

4. PONTIUS, A. A. 1982. Face representation linked with literacy level in colonial American tombstone engravings and Third World pre-literates' drawings—Toward a cultural-evolutional neurology. Experientia **38**: 577–581.
5. PONTIUS, A. A. 1983. Pictorial misrepresentation of spatial relations of the face by certain chronic alcoholic men: An interpretation implicating spatial aspects of memory. Percept. Mot. Skills **57**: 895–910.
6. CAREY, S. & R. DIAMOND. 1977. From piecemeal to configurational representation of faces. Science **195**: 312–314.
7. HANDELMANN, G. E. & D. S. OLTON. 1981. Spatial memory following damage to hippocampal CA3 pyramidal cells with kainic acid: impairment and recovery with preoperative training. Brain Res. **217**: 41–58.

Piracetam Plus Lecithin Trials in Senile Dementia of the Alzheimer Type

T. SAMORAJSKI, G. A. VROULIS, AND R. C. SMITH

Texas Research Institute of Mental Sciences
1300 Moursund
Houston, Texas 77030

Although deficits in brain cholinergic neurons are known to contribute to the symptoms associated with senile dementia of the Alzheimer type (SDAT), efforts to restore cholinergic function with high doses of choline or lecithin (precursor-loading strategy) have been unsuccessful. Recent studies suggest, however, that the combined administration of lecithin (L) and piracetam (Pr), a metabolic enhancer, is significantly more effective than treatment with either agent alone in restoring memory deficits in old rodents[1] and human beings who have SDAT.[3,4] This report summarizes the neuropsychological results of long-term treatment with a combination of lecithin and piracetam in patients who have SDAT.

Eleven patients (mean age 67.1 ± 8.3 yrs.) with an SDAT diagnosis participated in a six-month double-blind, placebo-controlled cross-over study (three months drug, three months placebo). Active medication consisted of 35 g lecithin/day plus 4.8 g piracetam/day (FIGURE 1). Patients were evaluated during a drug-free baseline period and at monthly intervals during medication or placebo treatment with the following neuropsychological tests: Buschke Total Recall,[2] Halstead-Wepman Aphasia Screening Test,[5] and Pfeiffer Mental States Exam.[6]

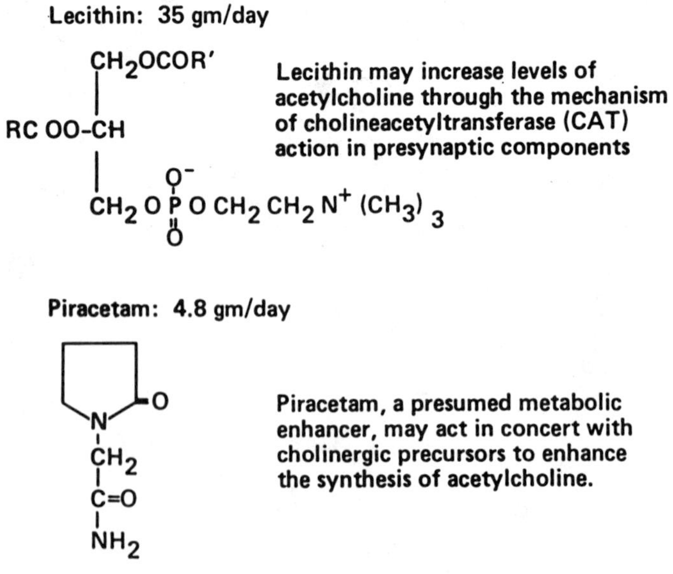

Lecithin: 35 gm/day

Lecithin may increase levels of acetylcholine through the mechanism of cholineacetyltransferase (CAT) action in presynaptic components

Piracetam: 4.8 gm/day

Piracetam, a presumed metabolic enhancer, may act in concert with cholinergic precursors to enhance the synthesis of acetylcholine.

FIGURE 1. Drug dosage and action information.

478

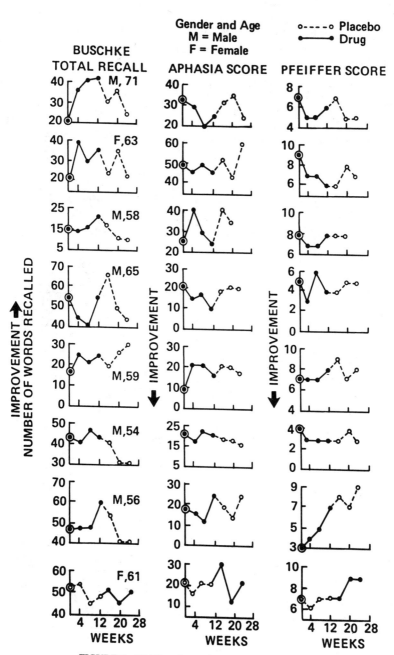

FIGURE 2. SDAT patients with high aphasia scores.

Preliminary results indicate that 8 of 11 patients showed various degrees of improvement (mainly in memory performance) during the medication phase compared to the placebo phase (FIGURE 2). The remaining three patients either did not improve or worsened during the active phase, and they improved during the placebo or washout phase that followed (FIGURE 3). All three patients had little or no aphasia compared to the significantly higher dysphasia scores of those who responded.

From these limited results it appears that treatment with piracetam plus lecithin may substantially ameliorate selective memory deficits in some patients with SDAT. Since brain cholinergic deficits have been correlated with the extent of cognitive deficits in dementia, the fact that the 11 patients' memory scores improved more than did their aphasia or general mental status (PMS) scores is consistent with the

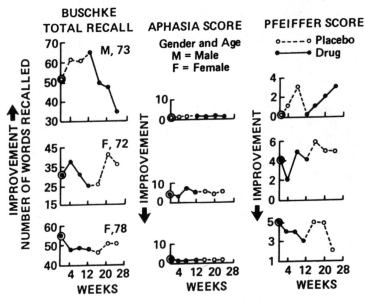

FIGURE 3. SDAT patients with low aphasia scores.

suggestion that the combination of PR + L enhances brain cholinergic function. The negative effects of Pr + L in three patients may be the result of misdiagnosis or differences in stage or progression of the disease. Although the nonresponders had moderate levels of memory deficits, they had a slightly lower degree of memory impairment compared to the responders. More important, the nonresponders were characterized by lower aphasia symptoms than were the responders. One previous open-design study of piracetam also suggested that this drug has a greater therapeutic effect in more severely demented patients.[3] Taken together, these preliminary studies suggest that there may be a subgroup of SDAT patients who will respond to combined lecithin and piracetam treatment. Evaluation of more patients and more precise clinical procedures may provide better validation of these results.

REFERENCES

1. BARTUS, R. T., R. L. DEAN & K. A. SHERMAN. 1981. Profound effects of combining choline and piracetam on memory enhancement and cholinergic function in aged rats. Neurobiol. Aging **2:** 105–111.
2. BUSCHKE, H. 1973. Selective reminding analysis of memory and learning. J. Verb. Learn. Verb. Behav. **12:** 543–550.
3. FERRIS, S. H., B. REISBERG & T. CROOK. 1982. Pharmacologic treatment of senile dementia: Choline, L-DOPA, piracetam, and choline plus piracetam. Aging **19:** 475–481.
4. FRIEDMAN, E., K. A. SHERMAN & S. H. FERRIS. 1981. Clinical response to choline plus piracetam in senile dementia: Relationship to red-cell choline levels. N. Eng. Med. **304:** 1490–1491.
5. LEZAK, M. D. 1976. Neuropsychological Assessment. pp. 260–261. Oxford University Press. New York.
6. PFEIFFER, E. 1975. A short portable mental status questionnaire for the assessment of organic brain's deficit in elderly patients. J. Am. Geriatr. Soc. **23:** 433–440.

The Effects of Aniracetam on Primate Behavior and EEG

ELIAS SCHWAM,[a] KEVIN KEIM,[a] RUDI CUMIN,[b]
ELKAN GAMZU,[a] AND JERRY SEPINWALL[a]

[a]Department of Pharmacology I,
Hoffmann-La Roche Inc.
Nutley, New Jersey 07110

[b]Pharmaceutical Research Department 1
F. Hoffmann-La Roche & Co.
CH-4002 Basel, Switzerland

Aniracetam (1-anisoyl-2-pyrrolidinone), a compound used in clinical trials as a cognitive performance enhancer, protects against a variety of induced behavioral deficits in rodents[1] and enhances consolidation in mice exhibiting spontaneously poor learning.[2] The present studies evaluated the effects of aniracetam on the behavior and electrocortical activity (ECoG) of squirrel monkeys under deficit and non-deficit conditions.

In each trial of a delayed matching-to-sample (DMTS) procedure, a simultaneous matching component (requiring two consecutive correct matches [FR2]) was followed by a delay (i.e., retention) response component. Five different retention intervals (0 to 152 sec) were selected for each animal to generate baseline retention curves ranging from near perfect (90 to 100%) to chance (33%); simultaneous matching accuracy was 90 to 100%. As shown in TABLE 1, i.m. administration of aniracetam enhanced retention at doses of 30 to 300 mg/kg. Doses of 100, 200, and 300 mg/kg administered i.g. were inactive.

When a single, brief delay interval (3 to 5 sec) variant of the procedure was used to engender high levels of retention (80 to 100%), scopolamine (0.01 to 0.04 mg/kg i.m.) dose-dependently decreased retention. A dose of scopolamine (0.02 to 0.03 mg/kg) was selected for each animal to produce a decrease of delay performance to 60 to 70% of

TABLE 1. Median Percent Change from Control DMTS Performance[a] Produced by Aniracetam

Dose (mg/kg i.m.)	Simultaneous Matching (FR) or Retention After Intervals 1–5[b]					
	FR	1	2	3	4	5
Vehicle	1	2	4	− 3	0	−11
30	0	−2	9	19[c]	31[c]	20[c]
50	0	0	−10	26[c]	10	33[c]
100	−1	−2[c]	2	− 1	10	29[c]
150	−1	−2[c]	− 1	20[c]	10	12
300	−1	−2	− 8	20[c]	−11	12[c]

[a]Median of [(Drug − Control)/Control · 100] adjusted for vehicle.
[b]Intervals range from 0 (interval 1 for all animals) to 152 sec (interval 5 range = 77–152 sec).
[c]$p \leq .05$, one-tailed Wilcoxon test.

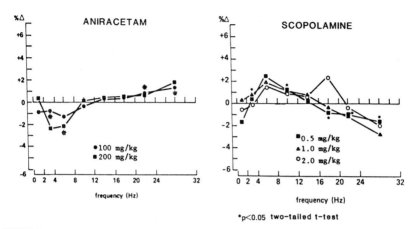

FIGURE 1. Effects of aniracetam and scopolamine on ECoG. The difference in percent of total area under ECoG spectrum between drug day and preceding vehicle day is plotted as a function of frequency.

control. Unlike physostigmine and arecoline which, respectively, produced strong (78% peak effect at 0.16 mg/kg i.m.) and weak (28% peak effect at 0.04 mg/kg i.m.) attenuation of scopolamine-induced disruption, aniracetam was inactive at doses of 30, 100, and 300 mg/kg i.m. However, in macaque monkeys 25 mg/kg p.o. has been reported to attenuate scopolamine-induced deficits (0.02 mg/kg i.m.), as well as enhance performance when administered alone in a variable retention interval DMTS procedure.[3] Furthermore, aniracetam protected against scopolamine-induced amnesia for passive avoidance in rodents.[1]

We also studied the ECoG from an implanted monopolar electrode touching the dura over the frontal cortex of the squirrel monkey brain during a VI60 sec food-reinforced operant schedule. A computerized spectral analysis of the 0–32 Hz frequency spectrum indicated that, consistent with reports in geriatric patients,[4] aniracetam (100 and 200 mg/kg i.g.) attenuated 2–8 Hz and enhanced 16–32 Hz activity (FIGURE 1); VI response rate was unaffected. Scopolamine (0.5–2 mg/kg i.g.), in contrast, increased 2–12 Hz, decreased 16–32 Hz ECoG activity, and dose-dependently decreased VI response rate. Aniracetam (100 mg/kg i.g.) failed to prevent the electrocortical or behavioral changes induced by coadministered scopolamine (2 mg/kg i.g.).

In a two-lever continuous avoidance procedure monkeys could avoid (40 sec response-shock interval) or escape (20 sec shock-shock interval) a 5-sec footshock (1 mA). Administration of haloperidol (1 mg/kg i.g.) immediately prior to the three-hour session markedly disrupted behavior as characterized by a virtual cessation of responding approximately 45 min after drug administration. In an interaction study, the onset of haloperidol-induced disruption was delayed by aniracetam (0.1 to 100 mg/kg, i.g. or i.p.) administered as long as 24 hr prior to haloperidol. The delay of disruption was dose-dependent, with 30 mg/kg i.p. completely preventing the disruption. Aniracetam alone, up to 1000 mg/kg i.g., had no effect on behavior.

These results extend to non-human primates the cognitive performance-enhancing effects of aniracetam reported in rodents.

ANNALS NEW YORK ACADEMY OF SCIENCES

REFERENCES

1. CUMIN, R., E. F. BANDLE, E. GAMZU & W. E. HAEFELY. 1982. Psychopharm. **78:** 104–111.
2. VINCENT, G., A. VERDERESE & E. GAMZU. 1983. Neurosci. Abstr. **9:** 824.
3. PONTECORVO, M. J. & H. L. EVANS. 1985. Ann. N.Y. Acad. Sci. (This volume.)
4. SALETU, B., J. GRUNBERGER & L. LINZMAYER. 1980. Meth. Find. Exp. Clin. Pharm. **2:** 269–285.

Family Member Reports in Geriatric Psychopharmacology

GERRI E. SCHWARTZ

Department of Psychiatry
College of Physicians and Surgeons
Columbia University
New York, New York 10032

Nootropic agents and other interventions may produce subtle changes in behavior that can go unnoticed in the context of the clinical interview. To assess changes in outpatients living in their own social evnironments, there are several distinct advantages in having observations made by family members. Because of their unique perspective, significant others can report on relevant changes in patient behavior such as memory functioning, activities of daily living, and personal care and grooming.

On the other hand, there may be other response biases to consider when evaluating data collected by untrained observers. For example, value judgements and expectations on the part of the untrained observer may produce a bias in behavioral reporting. Moreover, personal involvement of the family member may distort reports on the patient's behavior. The information may be biased depending on the relationship between the informant and the patient. Furthermore, the issues of social desirability and burden may lead to response biases in reporting. All of these warrant careful consideration for clinicians who will use untrained observers as informants.

The Geriatric Evaluation by Relative's Rating Instrument (GERRI) is a new rating scale specifically designed to assess the functioning of geriatric outpatients over the age of 55 years who show varying degrees of mental decline. This scale covers the areas of cognitive functioning, social functioning, and mood. The 49 items in the GERRI are short sentences designed to assess the frequency of typical behavioral disturbances and complaints. Inter-rater reliability, the internal consistency of the scale, and validity of the scale have been reported elsewhere.[1] Because the individual "clusters" of cognitive functioning, social functioning, and mood were preserved in the scale, this will permit greater flexibility in its use. For example, researchers who are interested in evaluating anti-depressant drug effects in the elderly can use the mood cluster of the GERRI, which contains a set of reliable items.

Reports by significant others can contribute valuable additional information concerning the functioning of geriatric patients. The Geriatric Evaluation by Relative's Rating Instrument meets acceptable standards of reliability and validity. As with any other research tool, data generated by the GERRI scale should be interpreted cautiously.

REFERENCE

1. SCHWARTZ, G. E. 1983. Development and validation of the Geriatric Evaluation by Relative's Rating Instrument (GERRI). Psychol. Rep. **53:** 479–488.

Classical Conditioning of the Nictitating Membrane Response in Aged Rabbits

PAUL R. SOLOMON AND CYNTHIA A. GRAVES

Department of Psychology
Williams College
Williamstown, Massachusetts 02167

The rabbit's classically conditioned nictitating membrane response (NMR) has rapidly become the most widely used model system for studies of associative learning in mammals and may be especially well suited for studies of learning deficits that can accompany aging.[1] Using this relatively simple form of learning it is possible to rule out performance variables, such as sensorimotor deficits or fatigue, that may affect the learned response.

The purpose of the present experiments was to examine the effects of aging on acquisition of the conditioned response in both delay and trace conditioning. In delay conditioning, the CS and UCS occur contiguously in time. In trace conditioning, there is a stimulus free (trace) period between CS offset and UCS onset.

METHODS

Eight young (6 months) and eight old (36–60 months) white rabbits (*Oryctolagus cuniculus*) were conditioned (5 days, 100 trials per day) in a delay paradigm in which

CR ACQUISITION

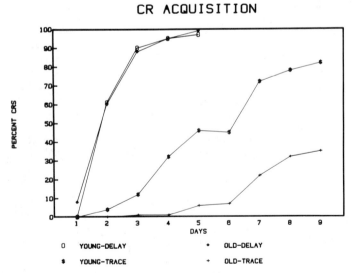

	YOUNG–DELAY		OLD–DELAY
	YOUNG–TRACE		OLD–TRACE

FIGURE 1. Percent conditioned responses for old and young rabbits in the delay and trace conditioning paradigms.

486

TABLE 1. Mean Tone and Shock Sensitivity for Old and Young Animals

	Tone Sensitivity (dB)	Shock Sensitivity (mA)
Old	59.5	.375
Young	59.5	.440

the tone CS (85 dB, 1,000 Hz) lasted 500 msec with the shock UCS (2 mA infraorbital eye shock) overlapping the final 50 msec of the CS. Following acquisition of the CR, all animals underwent generalization testing to the tone. This was followed by threshold testing to the tone CS and shock UCS.

Eight young and seven old rabbits were conditioned (9 days, 100 trials per day) in the trace paradigm in which the tone CS lasted 450 msec followed by a 500 msec stimulus free (trace) period followed by 50 msec shock UCS.

RESULTS

FIGURE 1 shows acquisition of the conditioned response over days of conditioning. In the delay paradigm, old and young animals acquired the response at about the same rate. In the trace paradigm, however, young animals acquired the CR significantly faster ($p < .01$).

TABLE 1 shows the mean tone and shock sensitivity for old and young rabbits. There were no differences between old and young animals on either measure. Similarly, there were no differences in either absolute or relative generalization gradients for old and young animals.

SUMMARY AND CONCLUSIONS

There was no difference between old and young animals in acquisition of the conditioned response in the delay conditioning paradigm, nor were there any age-related differences in generalization to the tone CS or in sensitivity to the tone CS or eye shock UCS. In the trace conditioning paradigm, however, old animals acquired the conditioned response significantly slower than young animals. Because the same stimulus parameters and the same responses were used in both paradigms, it is unlikely that the age-related differences in trace conditioning were due to differences in stimulus sensitivity, motor deficits, motivation, or fatigue. Rather, the differences appear due to associative factors. The increased demands of the trace paradigm, which includes a within trial memory component, may be a critical factor in the age related disruption. Moreover, recent data suggest that trace and delay conditioning may involve different neuronal systems (e.g., hippocampus appears necessary for trace but not delay conditioning)[2,3] and these systems may be differentially effected by the aging process.

REFERENCES

1. GRAVES, C. A. & P. R. SOLOMON. 1985. Age related disruption of trace but not delay classical conditioning of the rabbit's nictitating membrane response. Behav. Neuro. 99: 88–96.

2. SOLOMON, P. R., S. D. SOLOMON, E. R. VANDERSCHAAF & H. E. PERRY. 1983. Altered activity in hippocampus is more detrimental to classical conditioning than removing the structure. Science 220: 329–331.
3. SOLOMON, P. R., E. R. VANDERSCHAAF, A. C. NOBRE, D. J. WEISZ & R. F. THOMPSON. Hippocampus and trace conditioning of the rabbit's nictitating membrane response. Soc. Neuro. Sci. Abs. 9.

The Effects of Aniracetam (Ro 13-5057) on the Enhancement and Protection of Memory

GEORGE VINCENT, ANTHONY VERDERESE,
AND ELKAN GAMZU

Department of Pharmacology I
Hoffmann-La Roche Inc.
Nutley, New Jersey 07110

Aniracetam, 1-anisoyl-2-pyrrolidinone, is a novel compound in a class of CNS-active substances known as nootropics or cognitive activators.[1] Compounds in this class have been reported to attenuate deficits in learning and memory in some clinical situations.[2,3]

Previous reports have indicated that aniracetam protected against a variety of induced memory deficits in rodents including non-convulsant electrobrain shock (EBS)–induced disruption of retrieval in a one-way shuttle avoidance procedure.[4,5]

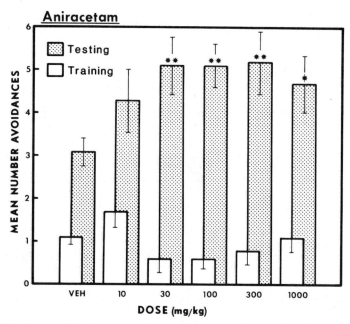

FIGURE 1. Mean (±SEM) of the number of avoidances for mice during the five-trial training session (open bars) and for the 10-trial testing session (stipled bars). Vehicle or aniracetam was administered orally immediately after the second training session. Statistical comparisons were based on the testing performance of the vehicle-treated animals with that of mice in each of the aniracetam treatments (*$p < .05$, **$p < .01$).

Using non-deficit procedures with primates, aniracetam improved memory and increased EEG vigilance.[6] The results from the studies presented here indicate that aniracetam is also beneficial in situations involving the consolidation and retrieval of newly acquired information in mice tested in an automated platform-jump avoidance procedure.

Mice were trained to avoid shock by jumping up onto a platform in two five-trial sessions, separated by four hours. Testing was conducted 24 hours later using a 10-trial avoidance session.

Aniracetam improved the memory consolidation process in mice that failed to successfully escape shock during the first training session (i.e., "poor learners"). Poor learning mice given aniracetam one hour before (100 mg/kg) or immediately after the

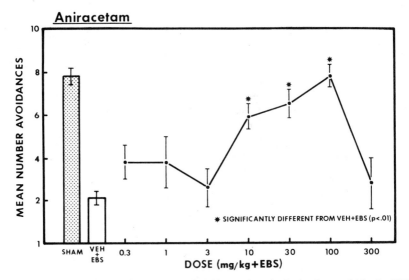

FIGURE 2. Mean (±SEM) of the number of avoidances for mice in the sham, vehicle plus EBS, and each of the aniracetam plus EBS treatment conditions. Vehicle or aniracetam was administered orally one hour prior to the 10-trial testing session. EBS occurred five minutes before testing.

second training session (30 to 1000 mg/kg) exhibited a significant improvement in avoidance performance during testing 24 hr later compared to the performance of vehicle-treated mice (FIGURE 1). However, administration of the compound (10 to 100 mg/kg) to "normal" mice (i.e. those that exhibited one or more escape or avoidance responses during the five-trial training session) immediately after a single training session failed to improve memory consolidation.

Aniracetam, administered 1 hr prior to testing, also protected against retrieval disruption (10, 30, and 100 mg/kg) in mice that had been subjected to non-convulsive EBS (FIGURE 2). The EBS (200 msec train of square wave unipolar D/C pulses, 10 msec duration, 60 Hz, 10 mA constant current) was delivered transcorneally five minutes before testing. These results corroborate previously reported findings[4,5] using a different avoidance task, indicating that aniracetam protects against a memory retrieval deficit induced by EBS.

These findings, therefore, confirm and extend the memory-protective effects seen with aniracetam in situations involving impairment of learning and memory function.

REFERENCES

1. GIURGEA, C. 1976. Piracetam: Nootropic pharmacology in neurointegrative activity of the brain. Curr. Dev. Psychopharmacol. **3:** 223–273.
2. WILSHER, C. R., G. ATKINS & P. MANSFIELD. 1979. Piracetam as an aid to learning in dyslexia: Preliminary report. Psychopharmacologia **65:** 107–109.
3. SCHNECK, M. K. 1983. Nootropics. *In* Alzheimer's Disease: The Standard Reference. B. Reisberg, Ed. The Free Press. New York.
4. CUMIN, R., E. F. BANDLE, E. GAMZU & W. F. HAEFELY. 1982. Effects of the novel compound aniracetam (Ro 13-5057) upon impaired learning and memory in rodents. Psychopharmacology **78:** 104–111.
5. GAMZU, E. & L. PERRONE. 1981. Pharmacological protection against hypoxia and electro-brainshock disruption of avoidance retrieval in mice. Neurosci. Abstr. **7:** 424.
6. SCHWAM, E., K. KEIM, R. CUMIN, E. GAMZU & J. SEPINWALL. 1985. Ann. N.Y. Acad. Sci. (This volume.)

Amnesia in Humans and Animals After Ischemic Cerebral Injury

BRUCE T. VOLPE AND WILLIAM A. PULSINELLI

Department of Neurology
Cornell University Medical College
New York, New York 10021

HASKER P. DAVIS

Department of Psychology
St. John's University
New York, New York 11439

Advances in medical care have increased the number of patients surviving global cerebral injury after cardiac arrest. Survivors of cardiac arrest may have variable degrees of brain injury manifested as sensorimotor deficits in some, and intellectual deficits in others.[1] Cognitive impairments are increasingly being recognized as the major cause of permanent disability.[1–3] Investigators have described some survivors of cardiac arrest with an amnestic syndrome, which may be permanent, characterized by impaired learning and memory.[4–7] Similar to patients with amnesia from other types of pathophysiologic injury, post cardiac arrest patients who are amnestic retain their general intelligence and learn and remember tasks that are highly practiced.[7,8]

The cerebral locus of damage may be difficult to identify ante mortem in post cardiac arrest amnestic patients since X-ray CT scans are often normal, or show "watershed" infarcts in arterial boundary zones.[6,7] However positron emission tomography (PET) scanning, which permits *in vivo* analysis of regional cerebral oxygen metabolism and blood flow, has demonstrated focal abnormalities in oxygen metabolites confined to the medial temporal lobes bilaterally.[9–11] The rare neuropathologic post mortem analysis of amnestic patients who survived the primary cardiac arrest shows damage to specific populations of neurons thought to be highly vulnerable to global ischemic injury.[4,6] Neurons that are "selectively vulnerable" include, among others, neocortical neurons in layers 3, 5, and 6, medium-sized striatal neurons, Purkinje cells in the cerebellum and, most significantly, pyramidal cells in the hippocampal CA regions of the medial temporal lobes.[12,13] We attempted to assess whether ischemic damage to these neurons in the rat, and in particular damage to hippocampal neurons, would result in deficits of learning and memory analogous to those seen in humans.

Severe forebrain ischemia, produced by temporary occlusion of the four major blood vessels (4VO) that supply the brain in rats,[14] results in reproducible and quantifiable morphologic brain injury.[15] The most severe damage occurs in the CA-1 zone of the hippocampus, with additional but less extensive damage in the dorsolateral striatum, neocortical layers 3, 5, and 6, and the Purkinje cells in the cerebellum. Rats subjected to 4VO and then trained on a radial eight-arm maze in which five of eight arms were baited, demonstrated "working"[16] performance impaired out of proportion to "reference" performance, when compared to unoperated controls during 65 acquisition trials.[17] Alterations in sensorimotor activity could not account for the performance difference since controls and 4VO rats demonstrated equivalent choice time per maze arm.[17]

In recent experiments, rats were trained for 70 trials prior to 4VO on an eight-arm maze in which five arms were baited. Half the rats were subjected to 4VO and then returned to the maze. Results show no difference between 4VO (N = 9) and control rats (N = 15) in performing the reference task [$F(1,22)$ = 3.07, $p > .05$]; both groups showed learning over trials [$F(49,1078)$ = 3.7, $p < .001$]; and there was no interaction between group and trials [$F(49,1078)$ = 1.34, $p > .05$]. However 4VO rats made more working errors than controls [$F(1,22)$ = 12.3, $p < .01$]; again both groups showed learning over trials [$F(49,1078)$ = 3.9, $p < .001$]; but there was a significant interaction between group and trials [$F(49,1078)$ = 1.96, $p < .001$]. These results suggest that global transient ischemia in rats damages networks of selectively vulnerable neurons that may be required for learning and memory. Furthermore the lesion causes a significantly greater impairment of learning and memory for information that varies from trial to trial, as 4VO rats are able to learn and remember information that is invariant and repetitive over trials. Rats with damage to networks of selectively vulnerable neurons, particularly CA-1 hippocampus, appear to have an isolated memory deficit and therefore present a model for studying post ischemic amnesia that may provide insight into humans with post cardiac arrest amnesia.

REFERENCES

1. LONGSTRETH, W. T., L. INUI, A. COBB & M. COPASS. 1983. Neurologic recovery after out of hospital cardiac arrest. Ann. Int. Med. **95**: 580–92.
2. BEDELL, S. E., T. L. DELBANCO, E. F. COOK & F. H. EPSTEIN. 1983. Survival after cardio-pulmonary resuscitation in the hospital. N Engl. J. Med. **309**: 569–576.
3. BELL, J. A. & H. J. F. HODGSON. 1974. Coma after cardiac arrest. Brain **97**: 361–372.
4. BRIERLEY, J. & E. COOPER. 1962. Cerebral complications of hypotensive anesthesia in a healthy adult. J. Neur. Neurosurg. Psych. **25**: 24–30.
5. MCNEILL, D. L., D. TIDMARSH & M. L. ROSTALL. 1965. A case of dysmnesia syndrome following cardiac arrest. Br. J. Psych. **111**: 697–699.
6. CUMMINGS, J. L., U. TOMIYASU, S. READ & D. F. BENSON. 1984. Amnesia with hippocampal lesions after cardiopulmonary arrest. Neurol. **34**: 679–681.
7. VOLPE, B. T. & W. HIRST. 1983. The characterization of an amnesic syndrome following hypoxic ischemic injury. Arch. Neurol. **40**: 436–440.
8. HIRST, W. & B. T. VOLPE. 1984. Cognitive processes in the neurologic patient—Automatic and effortful encoding with amnesia. M. S. Gazzaniga, Ed.: 369–386. Handbook of Cognitive Neuroscience. Plenum. New York.
9. VOLPE, B. T., P. HERSCOVITCH, M. E. RAICHLE, M. S. GAZZANIGA, W. HIRST & D. C. DERRINGTON. 1983. Cerebral blood flow and metabolism in patients with amnesia. J. Cereb. Blood Flow Metab. 3 (Suppl.): 5–6.
10. VOLPE, B. T., P. HERSCOVITCH & M. E. RAICHLE. 1984. PET evaluation of patients with amnesia after cardiac arrest. Stroke **15**: 16a.
11. VOLPE, B. T., P. HERSCOVITCH & M. E. RAICHLE. 1985. PET defines metabolic abnormalities in transient and chronic amnesia. Neurology. (Submitted for publication.)
12. BRIERLEY, J. B. 1973. Pathology of cerebral ischemia. *In* Cerebral Vascular Disease Eight Conference. F. H. McDowell & R. W. Brennan, Eds.: 59–75. Grune & Stratton. New York.
13. SIESJO, B. K. 1981. Cell damage in the brain. J Cereb. Blood Flow Metab. **1**: 155–185.
14. PULSINELLI, W. P. & J. BRIERLEY. 1979. A new model of bilateral hemispheric ischemia in the unanesthetized rat. Stroke **10**: 267–272.
15. PULSINELLI, W. P., J. B. BRIERLEY & F. PLUM. 1982. Temporal profile of neuronal damage in a model of transient forebrain ischemia. Ann. Neurol. **11**: 491–498.
16. OLTON, D. S., J. T. BECKER & G. E. HANDELMANN. 1979. Hippocampus, space and memory. Behav. Brain Sci. **2**: 313–365.
17. VOLPE, B. T., W. A. PULSINELLI, J. TRIBUNA & H. P. DAVIS. 1984. Behavioral performance of rats following transient forebrain ischemia. Stroke **15**: 558–562.

An Electrophysiological Method for Examining the Effects of Potential Therapeutic Agents on Memory Function

CYNTHIA G. WIBLE, SHARON CRANE,
AND DAVID S. OLTON

Department of Psychology
The Johns Hopkins University
Baltimore, Maryland 21218

Anticholinergic drugs such as scopolamine have been shown to disrupt hippocampal function and performance on memory tasks. Hippocampal ablation in humans and animals can also impair certain types of memory. Single unit activity in the hippocampus of the rat was examined during performance of a working memory task to delineate the role of the hippocampus in memory and to determine how memory is processed in the hippocampus at the level of the single unit.

Rats were trained to perform a cued delayed-match-to-sample task (DMTS) in which the two discriminative stimuli used were black and white. The stimuli were located in two goal compartments that were side by side, but were not fixed in space. The rat chose a stimulus by entering a compartment. At the beginning of a trial the rat was forced to enter one of the compartments and was rewarded. The rat was then removed from the compartment and allowed to choose which compartment to enter. Entering the same colored compartment that was entered on the forced run was rewarded. The left-right position of the stimuli were switched pseudorandomly so that rats would not be able to perform the discrimination on the basis of spatial location.

A ten pin electrode was chronically implanted over the CA1 layer of the hippocampus. Activity was examined during performance of the task until a complex spike unit could be isolated. Once a unit was isolated, information about stimulus conditions and cell firing was fed on-line into a microcomputer while the rat performed the DMTS task.

If the hippocampus is required for the task, the unit activity should be differentially correlated with whether the rat was in the forced or choice run of the task (either in registration or recall). Furthermore, the rate of unit activity should be differentially correlated with the color of the stimulus to be remembered (black or white).

The majority of units responded differentially to a certain color; some only when that colored goal box was in one spatial position. Other units responded differentially to a certain color and the firing rate changed more when the rat was in either the forced run (during registration of the stimulus information) or the choice run (during recall of the stimulus information).

These correlates of unit activity are consistent with a memory interpretation of hippocampal function. The results, along with those from lesion experiments, suggest that the hippocampus processes working memory information. The rate of unit activity during a DMTS task is differentially correlated with a highly integrated combination of spatial and nonspatial cues, and with registration and recall of stimulus information. By determining a profile of unit activity during memory processing, drug effects on activity can be assessed to determine their relationship to memory processing. Drugs can be given during performance of the task and unit activity in the hippocampus can be examined to delineate the relationship between unit activity, drug action, and memory. Thus, this study provides a potential electrophysiological method for assessing drug effects on hippocampal function.

Mediation of Storage and Retrieval with Two Drugs that Selectively Modulate Serotonergic Neurotransmission

HARVEY JAY ALTMAN

Lafayette Clinic
951 East Lafayette Avenue
Detroit, Michigan 48207

The effects of blocking the high affinity serotonergic (5-HT) reuptake system with alaproclate (ALAP) or blocking postsynaptic receptors with the 5-HT antagonist pirenperone (PIREN) on memory were examined in mice using a modification of the standard one-trial inhibitory avoidance paradigm.[1] Briefly, thirsty mice were given an opportunity to drink from a tube in the lick suppression apparatus (Adaptation: Day 1) and 24 hr later (Training: Day 2), following an initial period of drinking (5 sec), were shocked (2.0 mA/7 shock max.) each time they made contact with the drinking tube. Immediately after training, half of the animals were injected with either saline (SAL), ALAP (60 mg/kg), or PIREN (1.0 mg/kg) and tested 7, 14, 21, 28, 42, or 56 days later by again measuring each animal's latency to complete 5 sec of drinking. The other half of the animals were trained as described above, injected with SAL immediately after training, and beginning with the 21-day retention test, groups of 30 animals each were randomly selected out and injected with either SAL, ALAP, or PIREN 30 min prior to the retention test.

The results of the experiments are depicted in FIGURES 1 and 2. As can be seen, both drugs had a facilitory effect on memory in this task. In addition, the facilitation was exhibited regardless of whether the compounds were injected immediately after training or shortly before the retention test (possibly suggesting an action by these compounds on a common process). Since the behavioral response indicative of memory in this task is a suppression of responding (i.e. long latencies), it is possible that the longer test latencies exhibited by the animals injected with ALAP or PIREN 30 min prior to the retention test were due to effects of the drugs on behavior in general (e.g. activity, thirst, or illness). Therefore, an additional group of animals originally not punished for drinking in the lick suppression chamber and shocked elsewhere were also included (non-contingently shocked = NCS). These animals, like those originally trained in the lick suppression task, were also injected with either ALAP or PIREN 30 min prior to testing. As can be seen from an inspection of both figures, neither NCS group exhibited long test latencies, suggesting that the elevated latencies of the CS group were probably due to the effect(s) of these drugs on memory.

These data offer strong support for the hypothesis that serotonin may play an important role in memory.[1,3–5] In addition, these data further the hypotheses that serotonin may exert an inhibitory influence on the processes mediating memory of an aversive habit. Finally, the results of the present series of experiments suggest that serotonin's role in memory is not simply restricted to processes occurring on or about the time of training, but can also extend to processes underlying retrieval.

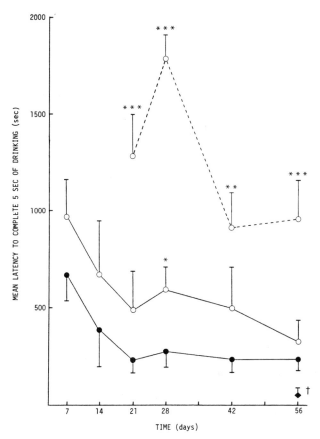

FIGURE 1. Effects of ALAP on memory as a function of the training to test interval. SAL or ALAP (60 mg/kg) were injected either immediately after training or 30 min prior to the retention test. (●——●) CS-SAL-SAL, (○——○) CS-ALAP-SAL, (○---○) CS-SAL-ALAP, and (♦) NCS-SAL-ALAP. NCS = non-contingently shocked, CS = contingently shocked. Each point represents the mean latency to complete 5 sec of drinking ± SEM. Comparisons between specific pairs of means were evaluated by the Newman-Keuls Procedure (*$p < 0.05$, **$p < 0.01$, and ***$p < 0.001$). †$p < 0.001$ NCS-SAL-ALAP vs. CS-SAL-ALAP.

REFERENCES

1. ALTMAN, H. J., D. A. NORDY & S. O. ÖGREN. 1984. Role of serotonin in memory: Facilitation by alaproclate and zimeldine. Psychopharm. **84:** 496–502.
2. QUARTERMAIN, D. & H. J. ALTMAN. 1982. Facilitation of retrieval by d-amphetamine following anisomycin-induced amnesia. Physiol. Psych. **10**(3): 283–292.
3. ÖGREN, S. O. 1982. Forebrain serotonin and avoidance learning: Behavioral and biochemical studies on the acute effects of p-chloroamphetamine on one-way active avoidance learning in the male rat. Pharmacol. Biochem. Behav. (In press.)
4. ARCHER, T., S. O. ÖGREN & C. JOHENSSEN. 1981. The acute effect of p-chloroamphetamine

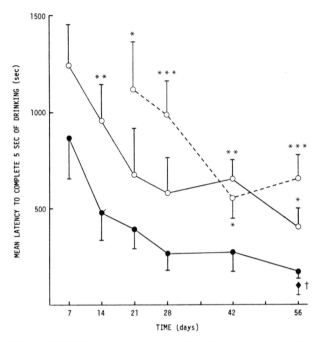

FIGURE 2. Effects of PIREN on memory as a function of the training to test interval. SAL or PIREN (1.0 mg/kg) were injected either immediately after training or 30 min prior to the retention test. (●——●) CS-SAL-SAL, (O——O) CS-PIREN-SAL, (O---O) CS-SAL-PIREN, and (♦) NCS-SAL-PIREN. NCS = non-contingently shocked, CS = contingently shocked. Each point represents the mean latency to complete 5 sec of drinking ± SEM. Comparisons between specific pairs of means were evaluated by the Newman-Keuls Procedure (*$p < 0.05$, ** $p < 0.01$, and ***$p < 0.001$). †$p < 0.001$ NCS-SAL-PIREN vs. CS-SAL-PIREN.

on retention of fear conditioning in the rat: Evidence for a role of serotonin in memory consolidation. Neurosci. Lett. **25**: 75–81.

5.   LORENS, S. S. 1978. Some behavioral effects of serotonin depletion depend on method: A comparison of 5,7-dihydroxytryptamine, p-chlorophenylalanine, p-chloroamphetamine and electrolytic raphe lesions. Ann. N.Y. Acad. Sci. **305**: 532–555.

6.   FIBIGER, H. C., F. G. LEPIANE & A. G. PHILLIPS. 1978. Disruption of memory produced by stimulation of the dorsal raphe nucleus: Mediation by serotonin. Brain Res. **155**: 380–386.

The Effect of Aging on Learning Curves[a]

M. L. BLEECKER, K. BOLLA-WILSON, AND J. R. HELLER

Department of Neurology
John Hopkins School of Medicine
Baltimore City Hospitals
Baltimore, Maryland 21224

Critical examination of aging on simple learning was studied. We asked the question: Is there a differential effect on the acquisition of new material when tasks of free, serial, and cued recall are employed? Twenty healthy males, 25–83 years old with 14–21 years of education, were given a comprehensive neuropsychological test battery as part of an ongoing longitudinal study on the cognitive changes that occur in normal aging. All subjects had comparable scores on WAIS-R Vocabulary and Similarities subtests. Performance was compared between the 10 men (YM) under the age of 50 (median age 40 range 25–47) with 10 men (OM) over the age of 50 (median age 60 range 54–83).

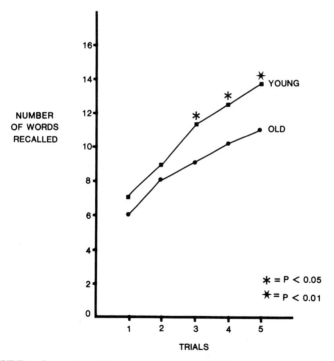

FIGURE 1. Comparison of learning curves on the AVLT in young and old subjects.

[a]Supported by NIA Teaching Nursing Home Award (1P01 AG04403–01).

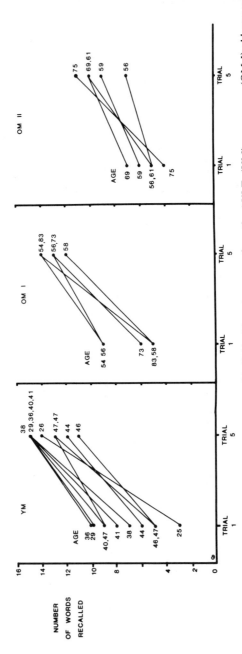

FIGURE 2. A differential aging effect found by examination of individual learning curves from the AVLT. (YM) young men, (OM I) old men with minimum scores of 12 on AVLT-V, and (OM II) old men with scores below 12 on AVLT-V.

Tasks of verbal memory and learning were measured by the Auditory Verbal Learning Test (AVLT),[1] Verbal-Verbal Associates (V-V)[2] (10 hard pairs), and Serial Digit Learning (SDL).[3] Free recall of words from a 15-word list repeated over five trials (AVLT) was similar in the YM and OM groups on the first two trials suggesting that immediate memory under a stimulus overload condition was not affected by age. However, significantly lower recall was found in the OM group on trials three through five (FIGURE 1). Simple learning defined as the amount retained on trial V was examined using the criteria of 12 words (Lezak) as within normal limits. No subject in the YM group had a maximum word recall of less than 12/15. Within group examination of the OM group revealed two subgroups OM I (ages 54, 56, 58, 73, and 83) who recalled 12 or more words on trial 5 and OM II (ages 57, 59, 61, 69, and 75) with a maximum word recall on trial 5 below 12. FIGURE 2 shows the individual learning curves for the three groups with OM I and YM having similar slopes with a relative plateau effect in the OM II group. Closer examination of strategies revealed all 20 subjects to have a recency effect with the greatest number of words recalled from the end of the list (last five words), followed by the beginning (first five words), and then the middle (middle five words). OM I and YM were similar when frequency of words recalled grouped by order of presentation were examined. OM I and OM II had no group differences in recall of the last five words, but the OM II group recalled significantly fewer words from the beginning of the list ($p < .01$) and even fewer from the middle of the list ($p < .001$).

Recall of a supraspan of nine digits (SDL) produced significantly higher scores in the YM group 21 ± 3.8 versus the OM group with 12 ± 8.9 ($p < .01$). If the OM group was again examined under the OM I and OM II criteria previously established, no difference was found on this task of serial recall (OM I = 12.6 ± 9.3; OM II = 12.2 ± 9.09) indicating within subject task specifically for aging effects. Another task of learning over repeated trials, V-V (10 hard pairs), did not discern any differences in the learning curves of the YM and OM groups, suggesting cued recall of unrelated word pairs was preserved in the OM group.

Learning of a supraspan task is dependent upon organizational skills that have previously been shown to deteriorate with age.[4] Difficulties in this area were most apparent on the AVLT. After the recency effect, a limited organizational ability was seen in the OM II group. V-V may be considered a more difficult task than AVLT or SDL, which employs the formation of associates, visual imagery, and other complex strategies. Minimal organizational skills are required for this task of cued recall, which may account for the absence of an aging effect.

REFERENCES

1. LEZAK, M. D. 1983. Neuropsychological Assessment. 2nd Edit. Oxford University Press, Inc. New York.
2. BUTTERS, N. & L. S. CERMAK, Eds. 1980. Alcoholic Korsakoffs Syndrome: An information processing approach to amnesia. Academic Press. New York.
3. BENTON, A. L., K. D. HAMSHER, N. R. VARNEY & O. SPREEN. 1983. Contributions to Neuropsychological Assessment. Oxford University Press, Inc. New York.
4. DRACHMAN, D. A. & J. ARBIT. 1966. Memory and hippocampal complex. II. Is memory a multiple process? Arch. Neurol. **15:** 52–61.

Uncovering Malingered Amnesia

JASON BRANDT, ELIZABETH RUBINSKY,[a] AND
GEORGE LASSEN[b]

Department of Psychology
The Johns Hopkins University
Baltimore, Maryland

[a]*University of Maryland School of Law*
[b]*University of Baltimore*

One approach to the discovery of malingered amnesia is to exploit the fact that true amnesics can learn and remember under some conditions and can display their knowledge when appropriately tested. In particular, patients with organic amnesia of several etiologies can recognize previously presented but unrecalled words at much higher than chance rates.[1,2] Recognition better than free recall is also characteristic of posthypnotic amnesia[3] and normal memory degraded by long delays.[4] Thus, these phenomena appear to be general characteristics of memory loss and are not restricted to brain-damaged populations. The naive malingerer is presumed not to know this and so "overplays" the role, performing worse than true amnesics. To test the presumption, four groups of subjects (normal college students, college students instructed to malinger amnesia, and memory-disordered patients with Huntington's disease, and head trauma) were asked to freely recall a 20-item word list and then to attempt two-alternative, forced-choice recognition of each of the 20 words.

As seen in FIGURE 1, the four groups differed significantly in recall performance. The normals differed from each of the other groups. The malingerers performed most poorly and were not significantly different from either of the patient groups.

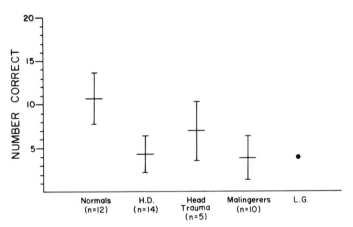

FIGURE 1. Free recall of 20-item word list by normals, normals feigning amnesia, patients with Huntington's disease, patients with head trauma, and patient L.G. (Means ± 1 standard deviation.)

RECOGNITION

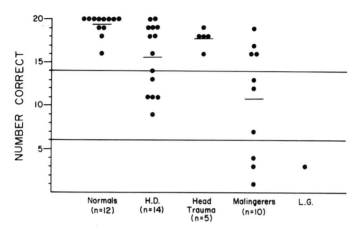

FIGURE 2. Number of target words correctly recognized on 20-item, two-alternative recognition test. (Individual scores and group means). Chance performance is 6 to 14 correct (binomial test; $\alpha = .05$).

The four groups also differed significantly in recognition performance, as seen in FIGURE 2. All normals and head trauma patients performed better than chance. Eight of the 14 Huntington's disease patients had better than chance recognition; the remaining six performed at chance levels. As a group, the malingerers' recognition was not above chance. A subgroup (three out of 10) had recognition scores below chance.

Patient L.G. is a 64-year-old man charged with the murder of his wife. He claims total amnesia for the event. L.G. freely recalled four target words, a performance comparable to the memory-disordered patients. However, on forced-choice recognition, he correctly selected only three of the target words. This performance is worse than chance, indicating that, at some level, L.G. knew most of the 20 words. It is suggested that he was feigning his anterograde memory deficit and it would be reasonable to conjecture that his retrograde memory deficit was similarly malingered.

These results suggest that malingered amnesia may be characterized by recognition performance worse than that in organic amnesia. Some naive individuals, of normal intelligence and purposely feigning amnesia, fail to appreciate laws of probability that predict that no knowledge at all should yield between 6 and 14 correct selections on a 20-item, two-choice recognition test.

REFERENCES

1. HUPPERT, F. A. & M. PIERCY. 1976. Recognition memory in amnesic patients: Effects of temporal context and familiarity of material. Cortex **12**: 3–20.
2. VOLPE, B. T. & W. HIRST. 1983. Amnesia following the rupture and repair of an anterior communicating aneurysm. J. Neurol. Neurosurg. Psychiatry **46**: 704–709.
3. WILLIAMSEN, J. A., H. J. JOHNSON & C. W. ERIKSEN. 1965. Some characteristics of post-hypnotic amnesia. J. Abnorm. Psychol. **70**: 123–131.
4. SHEPARD, R. N. 1967. Recognition memory for words, sentences, and pictures. J. Verbal Learn. Verbal Behav. **6**: 156–163.

Pharmacological Effect of Phosphatidylserine on Age-Dependent Memory Dysfunction

G. CALDERINI, F. APORTI, F. BELLINI, A.C. BONETTI,
S. TEOLATO, A. ZANOTTI, AND G. TOFFANO

Fidia Research Laboratories
Department of Biochemistry
Via Ponte della Fabbrica 3/A
35031 Abano Terme, Italy

Among cerebral functions, memory seems to be extremely sensitive to the aging process, particularly in the pathological condition. In this case memory decline is one of the first and more consistent symptoms observed.

The similarities between the memory deficit induced by anticholinergic drugs and by elderly people have been the origin of the cholinergic hypothesis of geriatric memory.[1] Cholinomimetics and/or acetylcholine precursors have been tentatively used in geriatric patients to facilitate and improve memory function. Unfortunately the results obtained with this therapeutical approach have not been consistent. We now report the pharmacological effect of a natural compound, phosphatidylserine, on the

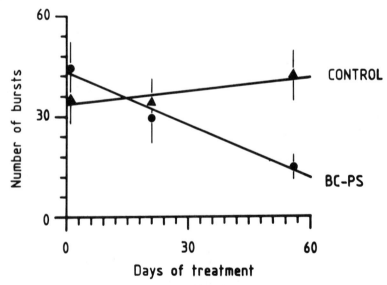

FIGURE 1. Effect of chronic treatment of BC-PS on EEG abnormalities in middle-aged rats. Rat chronically implanted with EEG electrodes were recorded for 30 minutes after 10 minutes of adaptation. EEG analyses were performed by computer.

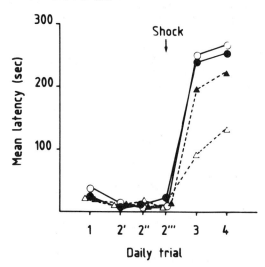

○ Normal rats treated with TRIS (5)
● Normal rats treated with BC-PS (5)
△ Rats with epileptiform spikes treated with TRIS (11)
▲ Rats with epileptiform spikes treated with BC-PS (12)

FIGURE 2. Effect of BC-PS on passive avoidance performance of aged rats (17 months) with and without epileptiform spikes.

age-dependent decline in memory function in aged rats. Phosphatidylserine (BC-PS) is a naturally occurring acidic phospholipid extracted and purified from bovine brain, which exhibits pharmacological activity in the central nervous system.[2] In young rats BC-PS stimulates ACh release from cerebral cortex[3] and antagonizes the effect of scopolamine on spontaneous alternation in a Y maze and on the electroencephalographic activity.[4]

Based on this experimental evidence, we have investigated whether a chronic treatment with this phospholipid could modify the age-dependent decline of memory function observed in aged Sprague-Dawley rats. In these animals, aging significantly reduces their capability to remember an aversive experience as assayed in a passive avoidance test. The decreased memory function seems to correlate with the appearance of abnormal spontaneous asymptomatic spike-wave discharges at cortical level. The abnormal EEG activity occurs in about 15% of the animals already at 10–12 months of age and in about 90% of the animals at 20–24 months. The correlation between EEG alterations and memory dysfunction seems to be particularly true in middle-aged animals (17–18 months) where the poor performance on the passive avoidance test is present only in those animals with abnormal EEG pattern.

In this group of animals, the effect of a long-term treatment with BC-PS has been tested. The animals were divided into two groups according to the presence or absence of abnormal EEG discharges. The two subpopulations were treated with vehicle or 15 mg/kg i.p. BC-PS for about two months. EEG was recorded before, during, and at the end of the treatment while memory test was applied only at the end of the treatment. As reported in FIGURE 1, long-term treatment with BC-PS consistently reduces the occurrence of EEG abnormalities. The effect is due to a reduction of both the number and duration of spike-wave discharges. In addition, the reduction of abnormal EEG discharges is associated with an improvement of behavioral response in the passive avoidance test, suggesting a recovery of memory function (FIGURE 2). Interestingly, BC-PS seems to be active only in those animals that concomitantly presented memory impairment and EEG abormalities. No effect has been detected in very old rats (30 months).

It can be speculated that a particular period of life exists in which the alterations of cerebral function are still pharmacologically reversible, while this does not occur during the last period of life. Data presented suggest a possible use of BC-PS as a new therapeutical agent for memory dysfunction, one of the most common inconveniences observed in elderly people.

REFERENCES

1. BARTUS, R. T., R. L. DEAN III, B. BEER & A. S. LIPPA. 1982. The cholinergic hypothesis of geriatric memory dysfunction. Science **217:** 408–417.
2. TOFFANO, G. & A. BRUNI. 1980. Pharmacological properties of phospholipid liposomes. Pharmac. Res. Commun. **12:** 829–845.
3. CASAMENTI, F., P. MANTOVANI, L. AMADUCCI & G. PEPEU. 1979. Effect of phosphatidylserine on acetylcholine output from the cerebral cortex of the rat. J. Neurochem. **32:** 529–533.
4. MANTOVANI, P., F. APORTI, A. C. BONETTI & G. PEPEU. 1982. Effects of phosphatidylserine on brain cholinergic mechanisms. In Phospholipids in the Nervous System. Vol. 1: Metabolism. L.A. Horrocks, G.B. Ansell & G. Porcellati, Eds.: 165–172. Raven Press. New York.

Alleviation of Forgetting by Pretest Contextual Cueing in Rats

BERNARD DEWEER AND SUSAN J. SARA

Centre National de la Recherche Scientifique
Laboratoire de Physiologie Nerveuse
Psychophysiology Department
91190 Gif-sur-Yvette, France

With a relatively complex maze, reliable forgetting is observed when the training-to-test interval is 25 days. In this case, forgetting is a lapse, not a loss, since performance attains the last training trial level at a subsequent test. Furthermore, a reminder treatment (a 90-sec exposure to background stimuli in the experimental room, just prior to the test trials), which does not in itself contain sufficient information to facilitate performance of naive animals, significantly improves maze performance in rats that have "forgotten," even on the first test trial.[1]

Two experiments[2] were aimed at assessing the role of duration of cueing and cueing-test interval. In the first one, the animals were presented with the reminder (90 sec in duration) at different times before the test trial (0, 1, or 24 hr). This treatment alleviated forgetting when given immediately prior to testing, but had only marginal effects when the cueing-test interval was 1 hr or 24 hr. In the second experiment, contextual cues were presented just prior to the test in all experimental groups, but varied in duration. The results showed that animals given the reminder for only 10 sec performed at the same level as non-reminded controls, cueing for 30 sec or 90 sec alleviated forgetting, and a longer exposure to background stimuli (300 sec) led to intermediate performance levels, perhaps due to a partial extinction of the cue value of these stimuli.

In the next experiment, we evaluated the importance of similarity between training and testing context for effective cueing as well as for effective retrieval in this paradigm. Contextual conditions at testing were manipulated by varying the spatial relationships between the maze and extra-maze stimuli available in the experimental room, and the place where animals were given pretest cueing in that room. Our data confirmed that, when training and testing are given in the same conditions, pretest exposure to background stimuli alleviates the forgetting observed in control animals. However, the place where animals were cued was of crucial importance. This treatment was effective in alleviating forgetting only when given next to the startbox of the maze, and had no effect when given next to the goalbox. On the other hand, when the maze was rotated 180 degrees relative to the room for testing, animals made fewer errors when cued next to the goalbox (i.e. at the start point of the maze during original training). The interaction between the orientation of the maze and the place of cueing was significant. These data confirmed that the degree of contextual similarity between training and testing influences the effectiveness of memory retrieval: during original learning, the general relationships between the maze and extra-maze stimuli and, more specifically, the spatial configuration of those stimuli from the start point of the maze, were stored as attributes of memory. The presence or the absence of these particular cues at testing determined the extent to which the target memory could be retrieved.

In a last series of experiments, we compared the effectiveness of two reminder treatments, given alone or in combination, on the maze performance after a long

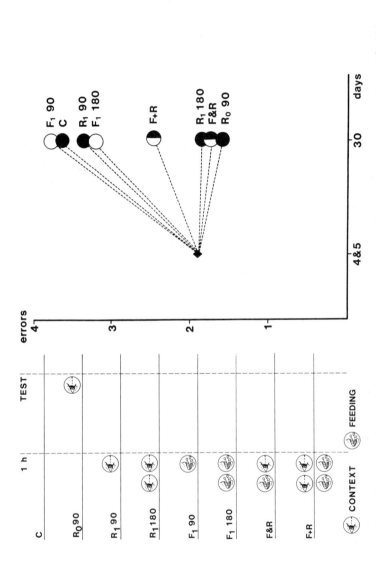

FIGURE 1. Comparison of the effectiveness of two pretest treatments, given alone or in combination (see experimental design, left side) on the maze performance after a long-retention interval (right side). Note that the successive (group F & R) or simultaneous (group F + R) exposure to two treatments which, when given alone (groups R_1 90 and F_1 90 or F_1 180), have no effect on performance, leads to prevention of forgetting (compare to group C).

training-to-test interval. The first step consisted of examining the effects of pretest access to the reinforcer (distinctive food pellets) in the colony room, adjacent to the experimental room. Surprisingly, this treatment (given immediately or 1 hr before testing) had no facilitating effect on subsequent performance. In a second experiment (FIGURE 1), rats in five groups were submitted to the following pretest treatments: 90-sec or 180-sec exposure to background stimuli in the experimental room and 90-sec or 180-sec access to the reinforcer, in the colony room. These treatments were administered 1 hr before testing, except for one group which was exposed to contextual stimuli for 90 sec just before testing. Two additional groups were submitted to the two "reminders," 1 hr before testing, either successively (90-sec feeding on pellets in the colony room, then 90-sec exposure to the experimental room) or simultaneously (180-sec feeding in the experimental room). Test performances were compared to that of a control, non-reminded group.

Our results showed that the 90-sec exposure to contextual stimuli alleviated forgetting when administered immediately, but not 1 hr before testing;[2] (b) the same treatment, administered for 180 sec, 1 hr before testing, was efficient in alleviating forgetting; pretest access to the reinforcer (for either 90 sec or 180 sec) in the colony room had no effect on test performances; and the exposure to two treatments which, when given alone, had no effect on performance (90-sec feeding in the colony room, or 90-sec exposure to contextual stimuli, 1 hr before testing), led to alleviation of forgetting.

The fact that the simultaneous or successive activation of two attributes of memory leads to a perfect retention performance, one hour later, reaffirms the lability of the retrieval process. More generally, these data, showing that the reactivation of a "forgotten" memory can be modulated by varying the duration or the number of pretest cues, fit well with the notion that "a memory is stored as a collection of separate attributes, corresponding to separate events that constitute an episode registered by the organism."[3]

REFERENCES

1. DEWEER, B., S. J. SARA & B. HARS. 1980. Contextual cues and memory retrieval in rats: alleviation of forgetting by a pretest exposure to background stimuli. Anim. Learn. Behav. **8:** 265–272.
2. DEWEER, B. & S. J. SARA. 1984. Background stimuli as a reminder after spontaneous forgetting: role of duration of cueing and cueing-test interval. Anim. Learn. Behav. **12:** 238–247.
3. SPEAR N. E. 1978. The Processing of Memories: Forgetting and Retention. Erlbaum. Hillsdale, NJ.

Normal Learning Set and Facilitation of Reversal Learning in Rats with Combined Fornix-Amygdala Lesions: Implications for Preserved Learning Abilities in Amnesia[a]

A. FAGAN, H. EICHENBAUM, AND N. COHEN

Department of Biology
Wellesley College
Wellesley, Massachusetts 02181

Department of Psychology
Massachusetts Institute of Technology
Cambridge, Massachusetts 02139

Recent evidence of preserved skill learning in patients suffering from "global" amnesia has led to postulation of a qualitative distinction between the learning of declarative knowledge, i.e. facts and associations, and the learning of procedural knowledge, i.e. rules or procedures that permit the expression of skilled performance not dependent on particular facts or associations. For example, the well-known patient H.M. has successfully acquired a variety of skills despite his otherwise profound memory impairment.[1] In a further development of our rodent model of temporal-lobe amnesia,[2] we examined the effects of combined experimental lesions of the fornix and amygdala (F-A) on learning performance on a series of odor discriminations and a reversal and on delayed spatial alternation.

OLFACTORY DISCRIMINATION AND REVERSAL

The performance of normal rats on discrimination problems improves dramatically across successive problems, i.e. they develop a learning set that is generalizable across particular associations. This improvement is thought to be largely dependent on the acquisition of discrimination procedures. Both normal rats and F-A rats showed rapid improvement in solving two-odor discriminations, developing the set within three problems (FIGURE 1). Subsequent presentation of a reversal of the third discrimination elicited a marked dissociation between F-A and control groups. The performance of normal rats was severely affected by the reversal, presumably because they remembered the associations of the previous stimuli. In contrast, F-A animals were relatively insensitive to the reversal, possibly because they forgot the previous stimulus associations and perceived the odors of novel. Analysis of response patterns (FIGURE 2) indicated that normal rats treated the reversal much as the initial discrimination rather

[a]Supported by Public Health Service grant NS18744 and Office of Naval Research contract N00014-83-K0337.

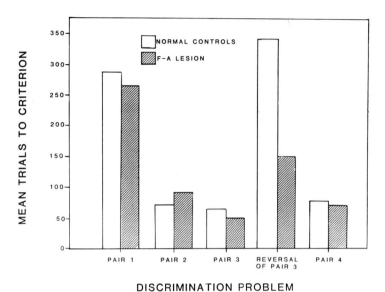

FIGURE 1. Performance on olfactory tasks.

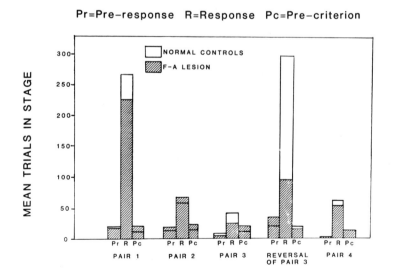

FIGURE 2. Performance during problem stages.

than as a new discrimination; their learning in both the reversal and the initial problem was characterized by a prolonged partially rewarding response-strategy stage preceding a stage of consistently correct response to each cue. In contrast, F-A animals had a short response-strategy stage during reversal, as is characteristic of new discriminations acquired after development of the learning set.

DELAYED SPATIAL ALTERNATION

The same experimental subjects were also trained to alternate the choice of arms in a Y-maze in trials given at 60-second delay intervals. Normal rats typically acquired the task in one to two daily 50-trial intervals. In contrast, F-A rats either required twice as many trials as normal rats to reach criterion or failed to reach criterion.

CONCLUSION

Recently, a number of studies have been successful in modeling the human amnesic syndrome in monkeys with combined hippocampus and amygdala damage (H-A).[3] Our results suggest that cross-species similarities in the effects of medial temporal-lobe damage can be extended to rodents. Thus F-A rats, like H-A monkeys, are normal in learning single sensory discriminations, but impaired in delayed spatial alternation. Furthermore F-A rats, like monkeys with fornix lesions, are better than normal animals at discrimination reversal.[4] Other studies have shown that primates with medial temporal-lobe damage, like human amnesics, have a preserved domain of skill learning despite impairment in memory for sensory associations.[5] In their normal capacity for learning set, F-A rats also demonstrate preserved acquisition of a skill in contrast to their deficient memory for specific olfactory and spatial associations.

REFERENCES

1. COHEN, N. & S. J. CORKIN. 1981. Neurosci. Abst. **7**: 235.
2. KAT et al. 1983. Neurosci. Abstr. **9**: 638.
3. MISHKIN. 1978. Nature **273**: 297–298.
4. ZOLA & MAHUT. 1973. Neuropsych. **11**: 271–284.
5. ZOLA-MORGAN & N. SQUIRE. 1983. Neurosci. Abstr. **9**: 27.

Animal Models of Environmentally Induced Memory Impairment[a]

H. L. EVANS, P. J. BUSHNELL, M. J. PONTECORVO,[b]
AND J. D. TAYLOR

Institute of Environmental Medicine
New York University Medical Center
New York, New York 10016

Cognitive dysfunction has been reported as a consequence of occupational exposure to chemicals such as metals and solvents.[1,2] It is difficult to identify the causative agent in these clinical cases because of ethical restrictions on performing experiments with humans and because of numerous confounding variables in occupationally exposed populations (e.g., alcohol and drug use, health status, and exposure to a wide variety of industrial chemicals).

In spite of the obvious impact of industrial products upon the nervous system, toxicologists have only begun to measure and interpret cognitive function in animals. Pharmacologists, on the other hand, have relied heavily upon single-response, one-trial tests (e.g. passive avoidance), which are not effective in separating the non-specific effects of drugs and toxicants measured as rate and speed from specific effects upon cognition. More suitable are operant, multiple-choice measures of accuracy, a less ambiguous index of cognitive function than speed. These issues were reviewed more fully by Evans and Daniel.[3] We therefore developed experimental models of cognitive dysfunction with the macaque monkey, which closely resembles the human in both cognitive function and in response to drugs and toxicants.[4,5] Also, pigeons were used as an alternative model because they are economical and yet capable of complex cognitive behavior.[6,10]

A three-choice, variable-delay matching-to-sample (DMS) procedure provided an objective and challenging test of short-term memory. Both monkeys and pigeons were trained to perform the DMS for positive reinforcement before exposure to toxicants and drugs began. The retention interval (delay between the presentation of the sample stimulus and the choice stimuli) was manipulated to provide psychophysical evidence of specificity of any changes in matching performance. Animals were tested in a three-choice appetitive procedure, an improvement over two-choice procedures in that a wider range of baselines can be obtained and evidence of non-specific effects such as position bias is more easily documented. Performance tests of this type circumvent the cultural bias of many human tests and may thus provide an important thread of continuity between the clinic and the laboratory. We now summarize preliminary results to be published in detail elsewhere.

Delayed matching of previously trained pigeons was evaluated following daily inhalation of toluene or *n*-hexane. Inhalation of 3,000 ppm toluene reduced matching

[a]Animal care conformed to the National Institutes of Health Guide. Supported by National Institutes of Health Grant OH-00973, ES-03461, Training Grant ES-07065, and Center Grant ES-00260.
[b]Present address: Department of CNS Research, Bldg. 56, Lederle Labs., Pearl River, NY 10965.

accuracy after one to two weeks of daily exposure; recovery occurred within two weeks after the exposure stopped. The effect of toluene was greater at longer retention intervals. Inhalation of *n*-hexane at concentrations up to 3,000 ppm did not affect DMS of pigeons or monkeys. Monkeys showed no observable effects of toluene up to 1,000 ppm.

Acute inhalation of toluene by monkeys during performance of the DMS task produced a different type of impairment. Unlike the gradually emerging deficit observed in animals tested following each repeated exposure, testing during acute exposure to toluene produced immediate decrements in both accuracy and reaction time. These deficits were constant across retention intervals, suggesting disruption of attention and/or motivation, rather than short-term memory.[7]

Alkyltins represent another occupational health hazard that may involve impaired cognition. A decrement in DMS occurred in monkeys and pigeons 5–7 days after acute oral exposure to trimethyltin. Monkeys were affected by 0.5 mg/kg trimethyltin, while the minimum effective dose for pigeons was 2.0 mg/kg. Impaired DMS in monkeys occurred in the absence of other toxic signs, suggesting that the monkey may provide a more specific model of trimethyltin-induced memory impairment than does the pigeon.[8]

These early findings, and work currently in progress, confirm our ability to measure cognitive behavior in experimental animal models. Such models provide a means to assess the impact of occupational health hazards on cognition, as well as an experimental paradigm for evaluating potential therapeutic compounds.[9,10]

REFERENCES

1. ELOFSSON, S.-A., F. GAMBERALE, T. HINDMARSH, A. IREGREN, A. ISAKSSON, I. JOHNSSON, B. KNAVE, E. LYDAHL, P. MINDUS, H. E. PERSSON, B. PHILIPSON, M. STEBY, G. STRUWE, E. SODERMAN, A. WENNBERG & L. WIDEN. 1980. Exposure to organic solvents. A cross-sectional epidemiological investigation on occupationally exposed car and industrial spray painters with special reference to the nervous system. Scan. J. Work Environ. Health **6**: 239–273.

2. FORTEMPS, E., G. AMAND, A. BOMBOIR, R. LAUWERYS & E. C. LATERRE. 1978. Trimethyltin poisoning: A report of two cases. Int. Arch. Occup. Environ. Health **41**: 1–6.

3. EVANS, H. L. & S. A. DANIEL. 1984. Discriminative behavior as an index of toxicity. Adv. Behav. Pharmacol. **4**: 257–283.

4. EVANS, H. L. & B. WEISS. 1978. Behavioral toxicology. *In* Contemporary Research in Behavioral Pharmacology. D. E. Blackman & D. J. Sanger, Eds.: 449–487. Plenum Publishing Corp. New York.

5. EVANS, H. L. 1982. Assessment of vision in behavioral toxicology. *In* Nervous System Toxicology. C. L. Mitchell, Ed.: 81–107. Raven Press. New York.

6. TEAL, J. J. & H. L. EVANS. 1982. Effects of DDAVP, a vasopressin analog on delayed matching behavior in the pigeon. Pharmacol. Biochem. Behav. **17**: 1123–1127.

7. TAYLOR, J. D. 1984. Thesis for M.S. degree. N.Y.U. Medical Center.

8. BUSHNELL, P. J. & H. L. EVANS. 1984. Trimethyltin-induced memory impairment in nonhuman primates. Fed. Proc. **43**: 763.

9. PONTECORVO, M. J. & H. L. EVANS. 1985. Effects of antiracetam upon the delayed matching-to-sample performance of monkeys and pigeons. Ann. N.Y. Acad. Sci. (This volume.)

10. PONTECORVO, M. J. & H. L. EVANS. 1985. Effects of aniracetam on delayed matching-to-sample performance of monkeys and pigeons. Pharmacol. Biochem. Behav. **22**.

Animal and Human Memory Dysfunctions Associated with Aging, Cholinergic Lesions, and Senile Dementia

CHARLES FLICKER,[a,b,d] REGINALD DEAN,[a]
RAYMOND T. BARTUS,[a,b] STEVEN H. FERRIS,[b]
AND THOMAS CROOK[c]

[a]Department of CNS Research
Lederle Laboratories
Pearl River, New York 10965

[b]Department of Psychiatry
New York University Medical Center
New York, New York 10016

[c]Center for Study of Aging
National Institute of Mental Health
Rockville, Maryland 20857

In an effort to develop animal models of age-related mental impairment in humans, we have investigated the cognitive abilities of the aged in several species. Although not all behavioral paradigms reveal age-specific deficits, significant impairments have been identified on a number of behavioral tasks, the most consistent of which involve tests of recent spatial memory. Aged nonhuman primates have been previously found to exhibit deficient recall of spatial location in a delayed response task. More recently in a structurally similar paradigm, we found aged humans exhibited similar impaired spatial recall and that the impairment of subjects with senile dementia of the Alzheimer type (SDAT) was even more severe (FIGURE 1).

Other studies suggest that certain neurobehavioral disturbances of aged human and nonhuman primates may be shared by aged rodents as well. For example, deficient retention by aged rats and mice has been repeatedly demonstrated in a single-trial, step-through passive avoidance task. As with the human and monkey deficits described above, this rodent deficit: (1) can be shown to be independent of numerous non-mnemonic variables that could alter performance in the task; (2) involves a rapid decline in unrehearsed recall of a discrete, visuospatial stimulus event; and (3) is among the most severe of many behaviors tested. These common characteristics suggest common underlying factors may be involved and raise the possibility of using animals as models for future studies of age-related memory loss.

In the past, one problem with using animals as models for studying Alzheimer's disease was that the neuropathological and neurochemical profile of brains from Alzheimer's patients differed markedly from that of animals. However, recent suggestions that the decline in cortical choline acetyltransferase and the correlated loss of cognitive function observed in Alzheimer's patients may be related to specific

[d]Address correspondence to Charles Flicker, Department of Psychiatry HN 314, New York University Medical Center, 550 First Avenue, New York, NY 10016.

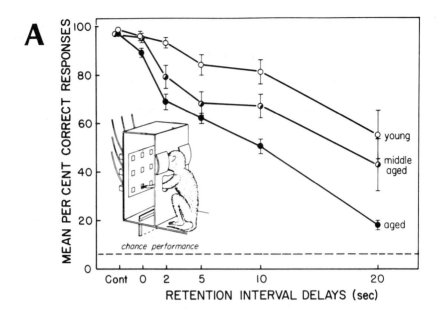

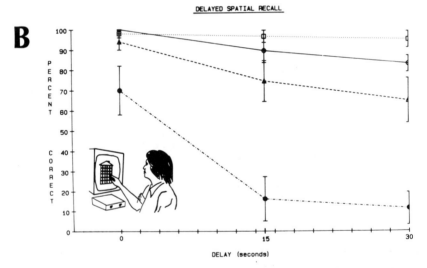

FIGURE 1. (A) Differences in performance of young, middle-aged, and aged Cebus monkeys on an automated, delayed response procedure. During the continuous information condition, the stimuli remained on during the opportunity to respond. Note progressively greater differences between age groups as duration of retention interval is increased. Inset: drawing of the Automated General Experimental Device (AGED) used to collect these data. (Modified by permission from Bartus *et al., Neurobiology of Aging* **1:** 145–152, 1980.)

(B) Effects of delays of between 0 and 30 seconds upon visuospatial recall of young normal (□), elderly normal (O), mildly-to-moderately demented (△), and moderately-to-severely demented (●) subjects. Subjects were asked to remember which room of a 25-room house, presented on a video monitor, had a light on in the window. During the delay interval they performed a reaction time task. Ordinate is percentage correct responses. At the 0-second delay, only the performance of the moderately-to-severely impaired subjects significantly differed from that of the other three groups. By 30 seconds post-stimulus, performance level was significantly different among all four groups. Inset: subject responding to the 5 × 5 matrix of rooms presented on the CRT screen. (Modified by permission from Flicker *et al., Neurobiology of Aging* **5:** 275–283, 1984.)

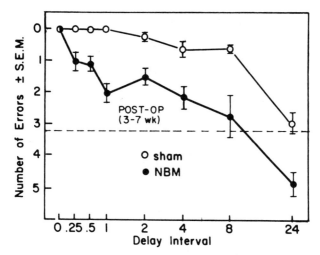

FIGURE 2. Performance of NBM-lesioned rats on a radial-arm maze memory task. The animals were trained to enter the eight arms of a radial-arm maze without repetition. In an extension of this procedure, animals were allowed to enter four of the eight arms and then were removed from the maze for a period of 15 minutes, 30 minutes, 1 hour, 2 hours, 4 hours, 8 hours, or 24 hours. When the rat was returned to the maze, food reinforcement was available in the four unentered arms. Half of the rats were administered sham lesions and half were administered bilateral ibotenic acid lesions of the NBM which reduced frontal cortical CAT by 48%. After recovery from surgery, both groups exhibited pre-surgery levels of performance under the no-delay condition. After the delay intervals, however, NBM-lesioned rats (●) exhibited a time-dependent increase in errors (reentered arms) relative to the sham-operated controls (○). These results suggest that NBM lesions induce a recent spatial memory deficit.

neuronal degeneration in the nucleus basalis of Meynert (NBM) offer a clear direction for further research. That is, similar neurochemical disturbances can be artificially induced in the rat via neurotoxic lesions in the homologous brain area, providing a convenient means of evaluating the behavioral consequences of such degeneration. We found that in comparison to sham-lesioned control rats, lesioned rats (like aged rats) exhibit deficient retention of a passive avoidance task, as well as poorer memory when overtrained to perform a radial-arm maze task (FIGURE 2).

The presence of comparable biochemical, neurodegenerative, and behavioral changes in humans with SDAT and rats with NBM lesions is consistent with the hypothesis that the degeneration of cortically projecting cholinergic neurons in the NBM is partly responsible for the cognitive loss associated with SDAT. These results support the usefulness of aged animals and the applicability of brain lesion techniques to the development of animal models of age-related cognitive dysfunction.

Lesions in Nucleus Basalis Magnocellularis and Medial Septal Area of Rats Produce Similar Memory Impairments in Appetitive and Non-appetitive Behavioral Tasks[a]

D. HEPLER, G. WENK, AND D. OLTON

Department of Psychology
The Johns Hopkins University
Baltimore, Maryland 21218

J. COYLE

Department of Psychiatry and Behavioral Science
The Johns Hopkins School of Medicine
Baltimore, Maryland 21205

The basal forebrain acetylcholinergic (CH) system innervates cortical brain regions. Within the basal forebrain are two regions of particular interest because they may be involved in memory: the nucleus basalis magnocellularis (NBM), the source of a major CH projection of neocortex, and the medial septal area (MSA), the source of a major projection to hippocampus. The present investigation evaluates the importance of the CH inputs for memory.

Rats received lesions produced by ibotenic acid in the NBM or the MSA. Control rats received sham operations. Three behavioral tasks, which placed different demands on memory, were used to assess changes in memory.

In the first task, rats received surgery and were then trained in a discrimination in which all eight arms of a radial maze were baited. The optimal strategy was to visit each arm only once. To successfully use this strategy, the rat had to remember a list of the places it had visited.

In the second task, rats were trained in a discrimination in which four of the eight arms were baited. After reaching a criterion level of performance, the rats received surgery and were then retested. Optimal performance in this discrimination required the rat to remember which arms were always baited as well as those arms visited within the trial.

Rats in the third task received surgery and were trained to avoid shock in a standard two-way shuttle box. During the first day of training the rats were placed in the shuttle box for 30 minutes with no CS or UCS. During the second day the rats were trained until they reached a criterion level of performance. During the third day, the rats were again trained to criterion in order to measure savings.

In the performance of all three tasks, rats with NBM and MSA lesions showed qualitatively similar changes in behavior relative to the performance of controls ($p < 0.05$). Choice accuracy was impaired in the radial arm maze discriminations, but

[a]Supported by grant NS18414 from National Institute of NCDS and by grant DAMD 17-82-C-2225.

was facilitated in the acquisition of two-way active avoidance. Thus, damage to CH neurons in both the NBM and MSA produced behavioral changes similar to those seen with damage to the hippocampus.

Choline acetyltransferase (ChAT) activity was decreased by approximately 40% in the medial frontal cortex of rats with NBM lesions, but was not significantly affected in the hippocampus. ChAT activity was decreased by approximately 45% in the hippocampus of rats with MSA lesions, but was not significantly affected in the frontal cortex. Lesion size and location were assessed in Nissl-stained histological material.

Taken collectively, the results of these experiments support the notion that abnormal CH functioning in neocortex and hippocampus can substantially impair cognition. Specifically, lesions in the NBM and MSA can produce considerable deficits in memory. These findings are consistent with the CH hypothesis of Alzheimer's disease and further our understanding of this disorder.

Intracerebral Injections of AF64A: An Animal Model of Alzheimer's Disease?

LEONARD E. JARRARD,[a] AHARON LEVY,[b]
JAMES L. MEYERHOFF,[c] AND G. JEAN KANT[c]

[a]Department of Psychology
Washington and Lee University
Lexington, Virginia 24450

[b]Israel Institute for Biological Research
Ness Ziona, Israel

[c]Department of Medical Neurosciences
Walter Reed Army Institute of Research
Washington D.C. 20307

Ethylcholine aziridinium ion (AF64A) is reported to result in a specific cholinergic hypofunction, both *in vitro* and *in vivo*.[1,2] Thus, it has been suggested that the compound may be used to generate an animal model of cholinergic dysfunction, especially senile dementia of Alzheimer's type.[3] The reported research was designed to test the animal model hypothesis and to study the specificity of the effects of AF64A on cholinergic systems of the brain in the rat.

EXPERIMENT 1

Separate experiments were carried out to determine the effects of intracerebroventricular (ICV) injections of AF64A on motivation (activity, eating, drinking), memory (working and reference memory), and several neurochemical transmitters (ACh, NE, DA).[4] AF64A was freshly prepared from acetyl AF64 following the procedure described by Fisher *et al.*[1] Following bilateral injections of 3 or 6 nmoles of AF64A into the lateral ventricles at the level of the fimbria-fornix, drinking and eating were depressed but returned to normal levels after several days; increased activity in the 6 nmole group persisted throughout the 21 days of observations. Performance on the complex place and cue memory tasks indicated that injected animals were impaired in reference memory only on the place task, but working memory was impaired on both tasks. Neurochemical measurements in a separate group of animals one week after AF64A injections resulted in large depletions of acetylcholine in hippocampus and corpus striatum, but not depletions of norepinephrine (hippocampus) or dopamine (striatum). Histological examination of the injection site revealed extensive damage to the fimbria-fornix (FIGURE 1, top). The above behavioral and neurochemical results are similar to those reported following electrolytic lesions of fimbria-fornix.

EXPERIMENT 2

Since we were not sure whether the results obtained in Experiment 1 were due to the specific effects of AF64A on cholinergic systems or non-specific damage at the site

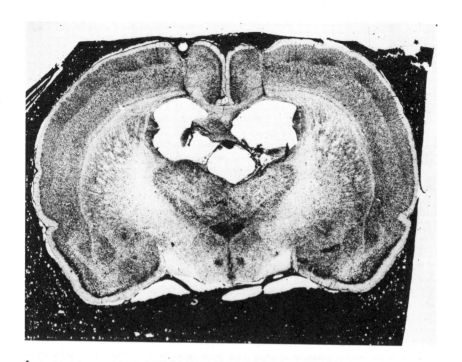

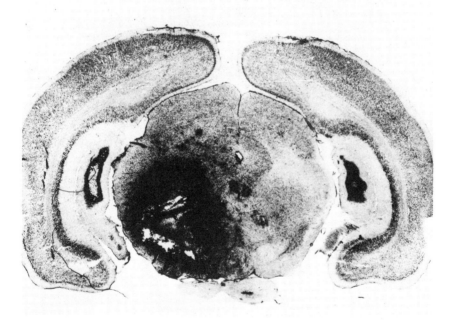

FIGURE 1. Photomicrographs of cell stained coronal sections at the site of injection showing the resulting brain damage following bilateral injection of AF64A into the ventricles in Experiment 1 (top; 1.5 nmoles each side, 13 week survival) and injections in Experiment 2 of AF64A into substantia nigra on the left side and vehicle on the right (bottom; 3.0 nmole, 2 week survival).

of injection, it was decided to examine the effects of injecting the neurotoxin into a predominantly non-cholinergic brain area (e.g., substantia nigra). After unilateral injections of 3 nmole of AF64A into substantia nigra there was spontaneous ipsilateral turning one day postinjection followed by contralateral circling after two days. When rats were challenged after 7 days with apomorphine there was ipsilateral circling. After 14 days the animals were sacrificed and corpus striatum and combined nucleus accumbens plus olfactory tubercle were assayed for dopamine. Striatal dopamine levels were depleted by approximately 50% ipsilateral to the AF64A injection site (112% ipsilateral/contralateral in vehicle as compared to 53% in AF64A injected rats). Histological examination showed that AF64A caused extensive damage at the site of injection (FIGURE 1, bottom).

In conclusion, the similarity in the effects of ICV injections of AF64A (Experiment 1) to the effects of electrolytic lesions of fimbria-fornix, and the similarity in effects of injecting the neurotoxin into the substantia nigra (Experiment 2) to those found following electrolytic and 6-OH-DA lesions, strongly suggest that our results are due to the non-specific lesion effects of AF64A rather than a specific effect on cholinergic systems. In view of these findings, it would appear that researchers using AF64A should be careful to determine that observed behavioral and/or neurochemical changes cannot be attributed to non-specific effects of the compound.

REFERENCES

1. FISHER, A., C. R. MANTIONE, D. J. ABRAHAM & I. HANIN. 1982. Long-term central cholinergic hypo-function induced in mice by ethylcholine aziridinium ion (AF64A) in vivo. J. Pharmacol. Exp. Ther. 222: 140–145.
2. TYLETT, B. J. & E. H. CALHOUN. 1980. Kinetic data on the inhibition of high-affinity choline transport into rat forebrain synaptosomes by choline-like compounds and nitrogen mustard analogues. J. Neurochem. 34: 713–719.
3. FISHER, A., C. R. MANTIONE, E. GRAUER, A. LEVY & I. HANIN. 1983. Manipulation of brain cholinergic mechanisms by ethylcholine aziridinium ion (AF64A), a promising animal model for Alzheimer's disease. In Behavioral Models and the Analysis of Drug Action. M. Y. Spiegelstein & A. Levy, Eds.: 333–342. Elsevier Press. Amsterdam.
4. JARRARD, L. E., G. J. KANT, J. L. MEYERHOFF & A. LEVY. 1984. Behavioral and neurochemical effects of intraventricular AF64A administration in rats. Pharmacol. Biochem. Behav. 21: 273–280.
5. LEVY, A., G. J. KANT, J. L. MEYERHOFF & L. E. JARRARD. 1984. Non-cholinergic neurotoxic effects of AF64A in the substantia nigra. Brain Res. 305: 169–172.

The Avoidance of Age Differences in Single-Trial Free Recall

LARS BÄCKMAN AND LARS GÖRAN NILSSON

Department of Psychology
University of Umeå
Umeå, Sweden

One of the most reliable findings in the literature on aging and memory is that of a pronounced age effect in favor of young adults in single-trial free recall.[6,7] Typically, the studies reporting age effects in free recall also report reduced or eliminated age differences in another task in which various types of contextual support are provided. For example, when the experimenter supplies the subjects with organizational strategies, imagery instructions, or verbal mediators at encoding, an attenuation of the age effect can be observed. Similarly, guidance provided at retrieval by means of copy cues (recognition) or category cues (cued recall) reduces or eliminates age differences in memory. This state of affairs actualizes the concept of compensation, i.e. the elderly are apparently capable of compensating for deficits in episodic remembering via different environmental aids. The aim of the four studies to be presented in this paper was to investigate if such compensatory capabilities among the aged could be demonstrated as a function of properties inherent in the to-be-remembered (TBR) materials. This was accomplished by employing a new memory task introduced by Cohen,[5] memory for so-called subject-performed tasks (SPTs). In SPTs, the subjects are instructed to perform series of acts for a subsequent free recall test. Some SPTs require the presence of real-life objects (e.g., bounce the ball, smell the perfume, eat the raisin) while some do not (e.g., stand up, nod in agreement, clap your hands). SPTs differ from standard verbal memory tasks in the sense that they allow a multimodal encoding (all five sensory systems could in principle be involved) and each modality possesses a variety of aspects on which encoding may be based (verbal aspects, color, shape, sounds, texture, motor aspects, gustatory aspects, olfactory aspects). Thus, it was hypothesized that the multimodal and rich properties of SPTs might constitute contextual support that older adults can utilize in order to maximize free recall performance, with the result that age differences in free recall could be attenuated.

In the first study,[2] young, middle-aged, and elderly adults were tested on the immediate and delayed free recall (IFR and DFR) of words, sentences, and SPTs. Typical age effects were obtained for the two former tasks but not for the SPTs. In the second study[3] the lack of age differences on IFR and DFR of SPTs was replicated. Furthermore, a hypothesis about visual imagery as a critical factor for the elderly's high performance in SPTs gained no support.

The multimodal and rich properties of SPTs are brought about by the fact that real-life objects are used as the TBR information, and that the subjects are instructed to act motorically. The third study[1] investigated the relative importance of the use of real life objects and motor action with respect to the activation of compensatory capabilities in the aged. For the third time, no age differences were observed on IFR and DFR of SPTs. However, in another task wherein the presence of real life objects remained, but the subjects did not physically interact with the objects, typical age differences in favor of the young adults were obtained. It thus appears that activity of the tactual mode and assimilation of motor aspects during encoding constitute important prerequisites for the absence of age differences on free recall of SPTs. The SPT paradigm was used in a fourth study[4] testing free and cued recall of SPTs and verbal items in four groups: 73 year olds, 82 year olds, mildly and moderately impaired subjects suffering from Alzheimer's disease. Preliminary data suggest that the improvement from verbal recall to SPT recall is even more accentuated for the two impaired groups than it is for the intact aged. Hence, it is concluded that old adults have the ability to utilize rich information from different modalities in order to optimize memory performance. By employing a memory task that possesses these properties, age differences in free recall can be avoided.

REFERENCES

1. BÄCKMAN, L. 1985. Further evidence for the lack of adult age differences on free recall of subject-performed tasks: The importance of motor action. Human Learn. (In press.)
2. BÄCKMAN, L. & L.-G. NILSSON. 1984. Aging effects in free recall: An exception to the rule. Human Learn. 3: 53–69.
3. BÄCKMAN, L. & L.-G. NILSSON. 1985. Prerequisites for the lack of age differences in memory performance. Exp. Aging Res. (In press.)
4. BÄCKMAN, L., T. KARLSSON, A. HERLITZ & L.-G. NILSSON. 1985. How to improve free recall performance in patients suffering from Alzheimer's disease. (Manuscript submitted for publication.)
5. COHEN, R. L. 1981. On the generality of some memory laws. Scand. J. Psychol. 22: 267–282.
6. KAUSLER, D. H. 1982. Experimental Psychology and Human Aging. John Wiley. New York.
7. SALTHOUSE, T. A. 1982. Adult Cognition. Springer Verlag. New York.

Morphine-Induced Disruption of Behavioral but not Hippocampal Conditioned Responses During Appetitive Classical Conditioning

CELIA G. OLIVER AND STEPHEN D. BERRY

Psychology Department
Miami University
Oxford, Ohio 45056

Mauk *et al.*[1] using the rabbit nictitating membrane (NM) paradigm, have shown that morphine produces a naloxone-reversible block of hippocampal and behavioral conditioned responses (CRs) while unconditioned responses (URs) remain unaffected. In an effort to assess the generality of such findings, we administered morphine immediately after acquisition of a classically conditioned appetitive jaw movement (CJM) response

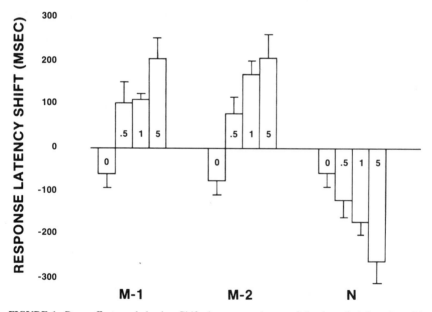

FIGURE 1. Drug effects on behavior. Shifts in response latency following administration of 0, 0.5, 1.0, 5.0 mg/kg of morphine and subsequent recovery after 0.1 mg/kg of naloxone (error bars = standard error). Latencies in the two morphine blocks are displayed as difference scores from the median pre-drug response latency. Naloxone latencies are expressed as differences from the median latency in the morphine blocks. (B = baseline; M-1 and M-2 = first and second blocks after morphine, respectively; N = first block after naloxone.)

in rabbits, and observed its effects on behavior and hippocampal multiple unit activity.

Rabbits were chronically implanted with bilateral stainless steel electrodes in area CA1 of the dorsal hippocampus and allowed one week to recover. Animals were then placed on a 22-hour water deprivation schedule and adapted to the apparatus and restraint. The next day, they were conditioned using a tone conditioned stimulus (CS: 1 kHz, 85 dB, 350 msec) followed by a saccharin unconditioned stimulus (US: 1 ml, 0.02%, 100 msec). The interstimulus interval was 250 msec and the intertrial interval averaged 60 sec. The behavioral responses were cyclic jaw movements in response to the saccharin solution and learning was assessed by the response latency to the tone onset.

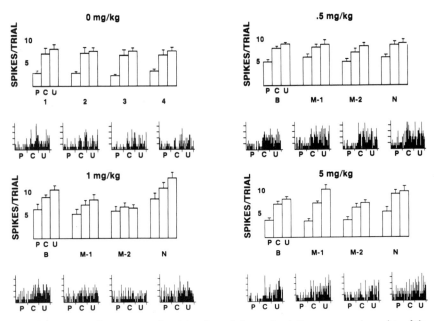

FIGURE 2. Drug effects on neural activity. At each dosage level, the upper graph consists of the group mean and standard errors of neural responses in the preCS (P), the CS (C), and the UCS (U) periods for each of the four blocks of trials. Below each group's data are representative neural response histograms in 10 msec bins, averaged across eight trials. (B = baseline; M-1 and M-2 = first and second blocks after morphine, respectively; N = first block after naloxone.)

Four blocks of nine trials were given (8 paired and 1 tone-alone trial per block). The first block was a no drug baseline condition, during which acquisition was observed. Prior to blocks 2 and 3, animals were given a single intravenous (i.v.) injection of 0.5, 1.0, or 5.0 mg/kg of morphine sulfate. Prior to block 4, all morphine-treated animals received 0.1 mg/kg i.v. of naloxone. A control group of animals received four blocks of training without any drug treatment. Behavioral and neural responses to the CS and the US were recorded on tape for later comparison to background activity (PreCS).

Behaviorally, morphine produced a dose-dependent increase in response latency, matching or exceeding reflex latencies typically seen in untrained rabbits, which averaged 280 msec. At higher doses (5.0 mg/kg), the UR as well as the CR was blocked. As indicated in FIGURE 1, the morphine-induced shifts in response latencies were very stable across both blocks, while naloxone immediately reversed these behavioral effects. Further, the amount of recovery after naloxone was directly proportional to the degree of impairment during the morphine blocks.

FIGURE 2 illustrates the effects of morphine and naloxone on conditioned neural responses at each dose level. Analyses of variance showed that, in general, conditioned neural responses were not prevented by morphine, with all groups showing significant neural CRs ($F(2, 48) = 85.7, p < .0001$). A small, but significant, naloxone-reversible attenuation was observed in later trials at 1.0 and 5.0 mg/kg. It is important to note, however, that these neural changes did not occur until the second block after morphine, in contrast to the behavioral effects, which were evident immediately. Further, behavioral impairments were a monotonic function of dose level, while the relation of dose to neural responses was more complex. Thus, there was a clear dissociation between the neural and behavioral effects of morphine during appetitive conditioning.

During aversive NM conditioning, morphine blocks both the behavioral and neural CRs.[1] In appetitive CJM training, however, only the behavioral conditioning was impaired by morphine, while neural CRs remained essentially intact. Our results, although different, are not necessarily inconsistent with Mauk et al.'s[1] interpretation of morphine as affecting motivation, in their case fear, in our case thirst. Thus, at some doses of morphine we were able to obtain the same behavioral results as in NM conditioning, but the neural results were quite different. These differences in the effect of morphine on hippocampal conditioned responses suggest that the role of the hippocampus in conditioning may vary as a function of the motivational state during training.

REFERENCES

1. MAUK, M. D., J. T. WARREN & R. F. THOMPSON. 1982. Selective, naloxone-reversible morphine depression of learned behavioral and hippocampal responses. Science **216:** 434–436.

Memory Complaints in Depressed Geriatric Inpatients

HELEN M. PETTINATI,[a,b] MARIE BROWN,[a] AND
KENNETH S. MATHISEN[a,b]

[a]Carrier Foundation
Belle Mead, New Jersey

[b]UMDNJ–Rutgers Medical School
Piscataway, New Jersey

Kahn[1] has reported that depressed geriatric patients complained about their memory, while non-depressed, organically impaired patients who performed poorly on memory performance tasks rarely complained about their memory. Memory complaints can be general: "I have trouble with my memory," or specific: "I can't remember where I put my eyeglasses." Differential memory components, such as short- versus long-term, verbal versus nonverbal, recall versus recognition, have been delineated and discussed in light of objective memory performance.[2] However, little is known about the dimensions of subjective memory.

The present study explored the quality of memory complaints and the potential relationship of several variables to memory complaints in elderly psychiatric patients. The variables chosen were age, sex, extent of dementia, objective memory performance, and depression.

SUBJECTS

The sample consisted of 52 elderly Caucasian individuals (age range: 64–84 yr) of mixed socioeconomic status. Thirty (8 male/22 female) were consecutive admissions to the inpatient geriatric unit of the Carrier Foundation, a private non–profit psychiatric hospital. DSM-III admitting diagnosis varied (47% Affective Disorder: $N = 14$). Age-matched volunteers ($N = 22$) from a local senior center were also evaluated. Exclusion criteria were: history of stroke, observable memory impairment, and depression.

PROCEDURE

Evaluation of cognition, mood, and subjective memory was completed in two sessions, 24 hours apart. Patient testing occurred 3–7 days after admission. The performance tasks were the Mini Mental State Exam[3] and two subtests from the Randt Memory Test[4] (Paired Words and Short Story, 10-minute delay). The Hamilton Rating Scale for Depression for patients and the Beck Depression Inventory for normals assessed mood. A modified version of the Metamemory Questionnaire[5] assessed subjective memory.

TABLE 1. Performance, Mood, and Subjective Memory for Depressed Patients at Admission Compared to Age-Matched Normal Volunteers

	Major Affective Disorder N = 14	Non-patient Controls N = 22	p <
Performance tasks			
Mini Mental Exam	24.2	27.4	.01
Short-Term Memory:			
Paired Words	10.3	13.1	.05
Delayed Story	6.8	8.1	n.s.
Mood evaluation			
Hamilton Depression Scale	20.4	–	–
Beck Depression Scale	–	7.9	–
Subjective memory			
Global Rating:			
Minor → Major Problems	21%	45%	n.s.
Examples of Specific Complaints:			
New Names	65%	82%	n.s.
Familiar Names	21%	18%	n.s.
Where You Put Things	50%	77%	n.s.
Words	0%	86%	.01

RESULTS

In the patient group, depression but not age, sex, extent of dementia, or objective memory performance correlated significantly with subjective memory ratings ($r = -.38$, $p < .05$): more severely depressed patients rated their memory as poorer than less depressed patients. Patients with major affective disorder performed more poorly than normal controls on the Mini Mental and Paired Words (TABLE 1). However, the incidence of memory complaints tends to be higher for control subjects than for patients. While depressed patients complained less frequently than controls, when they did report memory problems they typically described their problems as "more serious" than did normal controls (TABLE 2).

In conclusion, memory complaints in elderly psychiatric patients are correlated with severity of depression. Depressed patients however, complained less on general and specific memory problems than non-depressed controls. Depressed patients described some of their memory complaints as more serious compared to controls. Severity rather than frequency may prove to be an important dimension for

TABLE 2. "Seriousness" of Specific Memory Complaints of Sample

Complaints	"Serious"	"Not Serious"	N
New names			
Major affective disorder	56%	44%	9
Non-patient control	11%	89%	18
p = .023			
Where you put things			
Major affective disorder	71%	29%	7
Non-patient control	24%	76%	17
p = .042			

distinguishing between memory complaints made by depressed versus normal individuals.

REFERENCES

1. KAHN, R. L., S. H. ZARIT, N. M. HILBERT & G. NIEDEREHE. 1975. Arch. Gen. Psychiat. **32:** 1569–1573.
2. BADDELEY, A. D. 1976. The Psychology of Memory. Basic Books. New York.
3. FOLSTEIN, M. F., S. E. FOLSTEIN & P. R. MCHUGH. 1975. J. Psychiat. Res. **12:** 189–198.
4. RANDT, C. T., E. R. BROWN & D. P. OSBORNE. 1980. Clin. Neuropsych. **2:** 184–194.
5. ZELINSKI, E. M., M. J. GILEWSKI & L. W. THOMPSON. 1980. *In* New Directions in Memory and Aging. L. W. Poon, J. L. Fozard, L. S. Cermak, D. Arenberg & L. W. Thompson, Eds.: 519–544. Erlbaum. Hillsdale, NJ.

Effects of Aniracetam upon the Delayed Matching-to-Sample Performance of Monkeys and Pigeons[a]

M. J. PONTECORVO[b] AND H. L. EVANS

Institute of Environmental Medicine
New York University Medical Center
New York, New York 10016

Cumin et al.[1] have described a new compound, aniracetam (RO13-5057) that protected learning and retention of avoidance tasks by rodents against disruption by several experimental treatments. We report below that aniracetam also facilitates appetitively motivated delayed-matching-to-sample (DMS) short-term memory performance by normal and scopolamine-impaired monkeys and pigeons.

In Experiment I, six female cynomolgus macaques performed a three-choice DMS task with retention intervals of 0, 6, or 12 sec. Oral doses of 25 or 50 mg/kg aniracetam, given 1 hr prior to the DMS session improved matching accuracy at all delays, with no dose by delay interaction. A follow-up study with 12.5 mg/kg aniracetam produced no significant effects. No dose of aniracetam altered response probability or choice reaction time.

In Experiment II, 12 white Carneaux pigeons were tested in a similar (0, 4, and 8 sec delay) DMS task, 50 min following i.m. doses of 0, 12.5, 25, and 50 mg/kg aniracetam (in saline and 10% Tween 80). Aniracetam produced a modest facilitation of matching in pigeons. The effects approached but did not achieve significance.

In Experiment III, five monkeys received 0 or 25 mg/kg aniracetam as in Experiment I, and 0, 20, or 30 μg/kg scopolamine (i.m. in saline) 20 min prior to the session. Aniracetam pretreatment significantly reversed the moderate impairment produced by 20 μg/kg scopolamine, but was ineffective against the more severe effects of 30 μg/kg scopolamine.

The following conclusions emerge from these data, which are being reported elsewhere in greater detail.[2] (1) Aniracetam produced a modest enhancement of DMS accuracy in two species not previously studied, using two routes of administration, and (for monkeys) in normal and scopolamine-impaired subjects. (2) Aniracetam enhances appetitively, as well as aversively motivated behavior, and aniracetam enhances accuracy without altering response probability or reaction time. Thus, aniracetam appears to act directly upon cognitive processing and not on motivation, arousal, or motor behavior. (3) That aniracetam did not enhance performance by normal subjects selectively at the long retention intervals suggests that aniracetam alters processes like attention or encoding, which are independent of retention interval duration. Note however, that aniracetam did partially antagonize the selective retention deficits produced by 20 μg/kg scopolamine. (4) Since the effects of scopolamine on short term retention have also been a subject of controversy,[3,4] further research is needed to

[a]Supported by Grant OH-00973 from NIOSH and by Training Grant ES-07065 and Center Grant ES-00260, both awarded by NIEHS.
[b]Address correspondence to Dr. M. J. Pontecorvo, Dept. of CNS Research, Bldg. 56-Room 119, Lederle Laboratories, Pearl River, NY 10965.

elucidate the factors that determine whether drugs like scopolamine and aniracetam will alter the time course of retention. We suggest that factors such as the baseline level of stimulus control, which has been shown to affect the magnitude of drug response in a discrimination task, may also influence the magnitude and nature of effects seen in short term memory tasks.

REFERENCES

1. CUMIN, R., E. F. BANDLE, E. GAMZU & W. E. HAEFELY. 1982. Effects of the novel compound aniracetam (RO 13-5057) upon impaired learning and memory in rodents. Psychopharmacology **78**: 104–111.
2. PONTECORVO, M. J. & H. L. EVANS. 1985. Effects of aniracetam on delayed matching-to-sample performance of monkeys annd pigeons. Pharmacol. Biochem. Behav. **22.**
3. SPENCER, D. G., M. J. PONTECORVO & G. A. HEISE. 1985. Central cholinergic involvement in working memory: Effects of scopolamine on rats continuous non-matching and discrimination performance. Behav. Neurosci.
4. TEAL, J. J. & H. L. EVANS. 1982. Effects of DDAVP, a vasopressin analog, on delayed matching behavior in the pigeon. Pharmacol. Biochem. Behav. **17**: 1123–1127.

Dissociations Among Processes in Remote Memory

H. J. SAGAR,[a,b,c] N. J. COHEN,[a,b] S. CORKIN,[a,b] AND
J. H. GROWDON[b,c]

[a]*Department of Psychology*
[b]*Clinical Research Center*
Massachusetts Institute of Technology
Cambridge, Massachusetts 02139

[c]*Department of Neurology*
Massachusetts General Hospital
Boston, Massachusetts

Studies of learning in patients with focal cerebral lesions have demonstrated that component memory processes are dissociable. Patients with global amnesia due to bilateral medial temporal-lobe or bilateral diencephalic lesions show normal acquisition of motor, perceptual, and cognitive skills despite severe deficits in learning declarative (i.e., factual) information. Patients with unilateral frontal-lobe pathology have deficits in remembering the temporospatial context of new learning episodes, but not the content of these episodes. Dissociations among component memory processes related to the etiology of amnesia have begun to emerge in studies of remote memory function: Bilateral medial temporal-lobe lesions produce a retrograde amnesia that is temporally limited; in contrast, Korsakoff's syndrome and dementia, involving bilateral diencephalic lesions and widespread cerebral pathology, respectively, produce remote memory deficits that are temporally extensive. Our study addressed the selectivity of deficit in remote memory processes with respect to the age of the memory, the nature of the declarative information (personal versus public, content versus date), and the type of memory test (recall versus recognition). Subjects included patients with Alzheimer's disease (AD), Parkinson's disease (PD), long-standing focal brain trauma, the patient H.M., who underwent bilateral medial temporal-lobe resection, and healthy control subjects.

Remote memory for personal events was assessed using Crovitz's test. Subjects were asked to relate a personally experienced event incorporating each of 10 nouns, from any period of their life, and to say when the events occurred. After 24 hours, subjects had to reproduce the episodes recalled the previous day. When subjects had difficulty responding, they were cued with examples of specific episodes on Day 1, and components of Day 1 memories on Day 2. Responses were scored according to temporospatial specificity on a three-point scale. Remote memory for famous public events from five decades was evaluated using Squire's four-choice verbal recognition test, and a pictorial task, the Famous Scenes Test. In the recall version of the latter, subjects related the events represented in the picture and estimated the date when it was taken. The recognition version had a three-choice verbal format; the two foils represented real-life events that had occurred about 5 and 15 years before or after the event depicted in the picture. Recognition of content and date for these events was assessed separately but simultaneously.

Patients with AD were the most impaired in recalling autobiographical episodes even when cued, but did not differ from control subjects in the age of the episodes

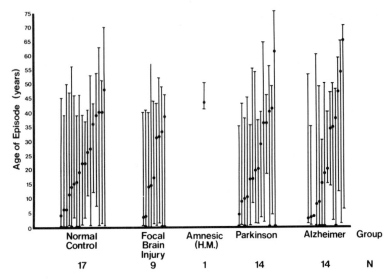

FIGURE 1. Age of episodes (median and range) recalled by individual subjects in the Modified Crovitz Test. H.M.'s memories were drawn entirely from the period more than 41 years ago when he was less than 17 years old, 11 years preoperatively. No other subject in any group recalled episodes of such restricted age distribution. Patients with Alzheimer's disease whose ability to recall episodes was impaired did not differ from control subjects in the age of those episodes that were recalled successfully.

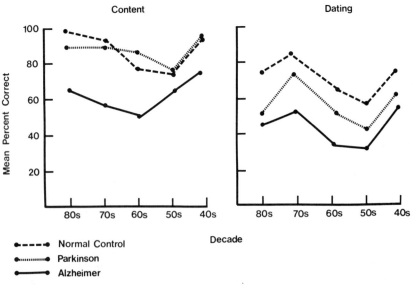

FIGURE 2. Correlation between recognition of content and date in the Famous Scenes Recognition Test in Alzheimer's disease and Parkinson's disease. Recognition of content and date were strongly correlated in both groups (Parkinson $r = 0.87$; Alzheimer $r = 0.78$), but patients with Parkinson's disease showed inferior dating recognition at all levels of content recognition.

recalled; in both groups, memories were drawn from the subject's entire life span (FIGURE 1). The amnesic patient H.M. was able to recall personal episodes, but they were restricted to the period more than 41 years ago when he was less than 17 years old, 11 years preoperatively. Patients with AD and H.M. reproduced the fewest Day 1 memories on Day 2; the deficit with or without specific cues was greater in AD. For public events, patients with AD and H.M. showed deficits on both content and date (AD p = .0005). In PD, by contrast, impairment in remote memory capacity disproportionately affected dating information (for content, p = .64; for date, p < .002). Content and dating recognition were correlated in both AD (r = .78) and PD (r = .87), but in PD patients, dating recognition was inferior to that of AD patients at all levels of content recognition. In AD and PD, the deficits extended to all time periods tested (FIGURE 2). H.M., by contrast, showed normal performance for events from the 1940s, but impaired performance for the 1950s–1980s. These data demonstrate dissociations between remote memory processes for content and temporal context in PD, and for encoding, storage, or retrieval of memories from different time periods in AD and H.M., but no dissociation between memory functions for personal and public events or between recall and recognition deficits.

Brain Transplants: Can They Restore Single Unit Activity in the Hippocampus?

M. L. SHAPIRO, D. SIMON, AND D. S. OLTON

Department of Psychology
The Johns Hopkins University
Baltimore, Maryland 21218

F. H. GAGE, A. BJORKLUND, AND U. STENEVI

Department of Histology
University of Lund
Lund, Sweden

Transplants of embryonic septal tissue in rats given fimbria-fornix (Ffx) lesions can either restore maze performance or lead to greater impairments than lesions alone.[1] The patterns of innervation produced in these two cases are not now distinguishable histologically. The present study investigated the effects of transplants of embryonic septal tissue upon single unit activity in the hippocampus of four groups of rats: normal rats, those given Ffx lesions, those given Ffx lesions and transplants that improved performance on spatial memory tests (trans/smart), and those given Ffx lesions and transplants that impaired maze performance (trans/impaired).

Rats were given either sham operations, aspiration lesions of the Ffx, or Ffx lesions and transplants (solid grafts) of embryonic septal tissue into the lesion cavity. Three months after surgery the rats were tested on a water maze that required spatial memory.[2] Performance on this task distinguished between trans/smart and trans/impaired rats. Electrodes for single unit recording were implanted surgically after behavioral testing, and recording began one week after surgery.

Theta unit activity was recorded from the CA-1 layer of the dorsal hippocampus during two behaviors: an appetitive behavior in which rats walked on an elevated track during recording and a consummatory behavior in which rats drank chocolate milk from a drinking tube.

Theta unit activity is characterized by changes in firing frequency and periodicity that vary with behavioral class. In normal rats, high frequency theta unit activity was organized into 7 Hz spike trains during walking, whereas low frequency activity was not organized into periodic spike trains during drinking. In rats given Ffx lesions, firing frequency increased during walking relative to drinking, whereas theta unit activity was never organized into periodic spike trains. In trans/smart rats, overall firing frequency increased during walking relative to drinking, and theta unit activity was somewhat organized into periodic spike trains. In trans/impaired rats, high frequency firing appeared during both behaviors, and theta unit activity did not appear to be organized normally during either behavior.

The modulation of theta unit activity was correlated with recovery of performance on the water maze. Unit activity recorded from trans/smart rats resembled that from normal rats, since both frequency and periodicity of theta units were correlated with behavioral class. Only one component of unit activity recorded from Ffx rats were correlated with behavior, since firing frequency, but not periodicity, increased during appetitive behavior. Unit activity recorded from trans/impaired rats was not correlated with behavioral class at all.

These results suggest that transplants modulate the activity of hippocampal neurons, the type of modulation may be critical to recovery of function brought about by transplants, and restoration of behavior may occur to the extent that patterns of modulation resemble those found in normal rats.

REFERENCES

1. GAGE, F. H., A. BJORKLUND & U. STENEVI. 1985.
2. MORRIS, GARRUD, RAWLINS & O'KEEFE. 1982. Nature **297**: 681–683.

AF64A Produces Long-Term Cognitive Impairments Following Infusion into the Lateral Cerebral Ventricles or the Dorsal Hippocampus: Involvement of Hippocampal Cholinergic Processes in Learning and Memory

THOMAS J. WALSH, JAMES J. CHROBAK,
AND HUGH A. TILSON

Laboratory of Behavioral and Neurological Toxicology
National Institute of Enviromental Health Sciences
Research Triangle Park, North Carolina 27709

DIANE L. DEHAVEN

University of North Carolina School of Medicine
Biological Sciences Research Center,
Chapel Hill, North Carolina 27514

ISRAEL HANIN

University of Pittsburgh
Medical Center, Department of Psychiatry
Pittsburgh, Pennsylvania 15261

INTRODUCTION

Manipulation of cholinergic tone predictably alters cognitive behavior in laboratory animals and man. Drugs that inhibit the uptake of choline, the synthesis of acetylcholine (ACh), or the activation of cholinergic receptors impair learning and retention of both food and shock-motivated responses.[1] In contrast, drugs that prevent the breakdown of endogenous ACh or activate muscarinic receptors directly facilitate memory processes. Recent studies suggest that the basal forebrain cholinergic system is an important substrate for learning and memory processes. Basal forebrain lesions impair the acquisition and/or retention of a variety of tasks.[2,4,5] Furthermore, clinical evidence indicates that the cognitive and mnemonic deficits associated with Alzheimer's disease result from a degeneration of cholinergic neurons in the basal forebrain.[3] These observations suggest that cholinergic mechanisms play an essential role in cognitive behavior. However, other studies suggest that central and/or peripheral catecholamine-mediated processes contribute to learning and memory.[9,10]

In the following studies ethylcholine mustard aziridinium ion (AF64A), a selective cholinotoxin,[6,7] was used to examine the role of hippocampal cholinergic processes in learning and memory. Secondly, the noradrenergic neurotoxins 6-hydroxydopamine (6-OHDA) and N-2-chlorethyl-N-ethyl-2-bromobenzylamine (DSP-4) were used to examine noradrenergic involvement in cognitive behavior.

538

TABLE 1. Effects of AF64A and 6-Hydroxydopamine on Retention of a Step-through Passive Avoidance Task

Treatment	24 Hr Retention Latencies	Number of Partial Entries
Intraventricular AF64A		
Artificial CSF	600	1.7 ± 0.5
AF64A (15 nmols)	410 ± 50[a]	14.1 ± 2.5[a]
AF64A (30 nmols)	350 ± 40[b]	12.0 ± 3.5[a]
Intrahippocampal AF64A		
Artificial CSF	600	1.0 ± 1.0
AF64A (8 nmols)	350 ± 40[b]	10.2 ± 2.9[a]
Dorsal noradrenergic bundle lesions		
Artificial CSF	550 ± 45	1.2 ± 0.2
6-OHDA (8 μg)	600	1.5 ± 0.5

Animals were trained 35 days following treatment. Step-through latencies on the training day were similar for all groups.
[a] $p < 0.05$, [b] $p < 0.01$ versus appropriate controls (Fisher's LSD Test).

METHODS AND RESULTS

Effects of AF64A and 6-OHDA on Cognitive Behavior

Adult male Fisher rats were bilaterally injected with: (1) artificial CSF (CSF) or AF64A (7.5 or 15 nmols/2.5 μl/side) into the lateral ventricles, (2) AF64A (4 nmols/0.5 μl/side) or CSF into the dorsal hippocampus (HPC) or (3) 6-OHDA (4 μg base +0.5% ascorbic acid, 1 μl/side) or CSF into the dorsal noradrenergic bundle.

Retention of a step-through passive avoidance task (0.8 mA, 1 sec, footshock),

TABLE 2. Effects of AF64A and DSP-4 on Performance in a Radial-Arm Maze

Treatment	Mean Number of Correct Arm Entries in First 8 Choices Trials			
	1–5	6–10	11–15	16–20
ICV AF64A				
CSF	5.7 ± .25	6.6 ± .20	7.4 ± .13	
AF64A (15 nmols)	3.9 ± .20	4.2 ± .21	4.8 ± .18	
AF64A (30 nmols)	3.7 ± .28	5.5 ± .40	5.5 ± .31	
Intrahippocampal AF64A				
CSF	6.0 ± .40	6.3 ± .30	6.9 ± .28	7.4 ± .25
AF64A (8 nmols)	4.5 ± .45	3.5 ± .50	3.4 ± .40	4.0 ± .50
DSP-4 acquisition group[a]				
Saline	6.0 ± .20	6.9 ± .16	7.2 ± .18	7.3 ± .10
DSP-4 (50 mg/kg)	6.3 ± .30	7.2 ± .16	7.3 ± .10	7.3 ± .11
DSP-4 reacquisition group[b]				
Saline	5.8 ± .46	6.6 ± .31	7.0 ± .29	7.0 ± .11
DSP-4	5.9 ± .32	7.0 ± .24	7.3 ± .17	7.5 ± .16

All animals were trained in a free choice eight-arm radial-maze task.
[a] Rats were injected with DSP-4 28 days prior to initial training in the maze.
[b] Rats were trained for 20 trials prior to injection with DSP-4 (data not shown). Twenty eight days following injection they were reintroduced into the maze for another 20 trials.

assessed 35 days after surgery, was impaired following AF64A administration into either the lateral ventricles or dorsal HPC (TABLE 1). These groups exhibited shorter retention latencies and more vacillatory responding during the 24-hour retest. 6-OHDA lesions of the DNB had no effect upon retention of the avoidance response.

Radial-arm maze (RAM) performance, measured 60–90 days after surgery, was also impaired in the AF64A groups (TABLE 2). The AF64A groups made fewer correct responses in their first eight choices and required more total selections to complete the task.

The neurochemical changes produced by AF64A, determined 120 days after treatment, consisted of decreases of ACh (50–65%) in both the HPC (15 and 30 nmol) and frontal cortex (30 nmol). Intrahippocampal AF64A reduced choline acetyltransferase activity 45% in the HPC. The regional concentrations of catecholamines, indoleamines and their metabolites, and choline were not affected by AF64A, regardless of site of injection.[8]

Effects of DSP-4 on Acquisition and Reacquisition of a Radial-Arm Maze Task

Rats injected with DSP-4 (50 mg/kg, i.p.) 28 days prior to RAM training (Acquisition group) learned the task as rapidly and efficiently as saline-injected controls. A second group (Reacquisition group) was trained for 20 sessions in the RAM and then injected with DSP-4. These rats exhibited good performance when they were reintroduced into the maze 28 days after injection. Neurochemical analysis performed either 60 (Reacquisition) or 90 days (Acquisition) after injection revealed a region-wide decrease of norepinephrine (45–80%) in the DSP-4 groups. Regional concentrations of serotonin and dopamine were not affected by DSP-4.

SUMMARY

In summary, the data presented here suggest that depleting ACh in the HPC has long term consequences on cognitive behavior. It is suggested that HPC cholinergic processes are an important neurobiological substrate of cognitive behavior. Finally, AF64A seems a useful tool for elucidating the cholinergic mechanisms underlying the modulation of behavior.

REFERENCES

1. BARTUS, R. T., R. L. DEAN, B. BEER & A. S. LIPPA. 1982. Science 217: 408–417.
2. BEATTY, W. W. & C. P. CARBONE. 1980. Physiol. Behav. 24: 675–678.
3. COYLE, J. T., D. L. PRICE & M. R. DELONG. 1983. Science 219: 1184–1190.
4. FLICKER, C., R. L. DEAN, D. L. WATKINS, S. K. FISHER & R. T. BARTUS. 1983. Pharmacol. Biochem. Behav. 18: 973–981.
5. GRAY, J. A. & N. MCNAUGHTON. 1983. Neurosci. Biobehav. Rev. 7: 119–188.
6. MANTIONE, C. R., A. FISHER & I. HANIN. 1981. Science 213: 579–580.
7. MANTIONE, C. R., M. J. ZIGMOND, A. FISHER & I. HANIN. 1983. J. Neurochem. 41: 251–255.
8. WALSH, T. J., H. A. TILSON, D. L. DEHAVEN, R. B. MAILMAN, A. FISHER & I. HANIN. 1984. Brain Res. 321: 91–102.
9. WALSH, T. J. & T. PALFAI. 1979. Pharmacol. Biochem. Behav. 11: 449–452.
10. WALSH, T. J. & T. PALFAI. 1981. Pharmacol. Biochem. Behav. 14: 713–718.

Pharmacological Manipulation of the Substantia Innominata–Cortical Cholinergic Pathway[a]

G. L. WENK

Department of Psychology
The Johns Hopkins University
Baltimore, Maryland 21218

The primary source of cholinergic (Ch) innervation to the cerebral cortex is from the large neurons in the substantia innominata (SI), they are located ventral to the globus pallidus[2] and stain for acetylcholinesterase. Pathological changes in the SI are associated with Alzheimer's disease.[3] The design of effective pharmacotherapies in the treatment of Alzheimer's disease can be assisted by a thorough knowledge of systems that regulate activity of the Ch neurons in the SI. The present study examined the

TABLE 1. The Effects of Various Pharmacological Agents upon Cholinergic Activity in the Substantia Innominata

Agent(N)	Pharmacological Effect	Amount Injected[a]	Percent Change in SDHACU
Decreases SDHACU			
Muscimol (8)	GABAergic agonist	44 nmole	-25^b
Muscimol (5)	GABAergic agonist	88	-50^b
Enkephalin (6)	Opiate agonist	40	-40^b
Imipramine (4)	Reuptake inhibitor[c]	100	-47^b
Increases SDHACU			
Glutamate (6)	Excitatory A.A.	20	$+25^b$
Does Not Affect SDHACU			
Saline (10)	Isotonic, pH 7.4		+10
LSD (4)	Serotonergic agonist	10	+1
Serotonin (4)	Serotonergic agonist	1000	+2
Clonidine (4)	α-Adrenergic agonist	10	+2
Isoproterenol (6)	β-Adrenergic agonist	100	+14
Muscimol (4)	GABAergic agonist	11	+5
ADTN (4)	Dopaminergic agonist	100	+9
Enkephalin and Naloxone[d] (4)	Agonist + antagonist	40	+14
Muscimol and Picrotoxin[e] (4)	Agonist + antagonist	44	+3

[a]Total injection volume was 1.0 μl.
[b]p < 0.05 by t-test.
[c]Imipramine is a norepinephrine and GABA re-uptake inhibitor.
[d]Given 10 min prior to enkephalin infusion (5 mg/kg, i.p.).
[e]Given 5 min prior to muscimol infusion (4.4 mg/kg, i.p.).

[a]Supported by US Army MRDC DAMD 17-18-C-2225.

effects of various pharmacological agents on Ch activity in the SI. Sodium-dependent high affinity choline uptake (SDHACU) was used as a measure of Ch neuronal activity.[1]

Rats (250–300 g) were implanted chronically with a guide cannula for local unilateral microinjection (1.0 μl) into the SI. Controls received buffered saline injections.

Fifty minutes after the infusion the rats were quickly sacrificed by decapitation. Right and left frontolateral cerebral cortex were removed and homogenized in 20 vol of ice-cold 0.32 M sucrose; SDHACU was determined.[1]

Muscimol, enkephalin, or imipramine decreased cortical SDHACU. Glutamate increased cortical SDHACU (TABLE 1). The effects of these local microinfusions into the SI reflect the possible interaction of afferents to the SI with Ch neurons. Although direct action of agonists on receptors located on Ch neurons may be likely, transynaptic modulation can not be excluded.

The present study identifies some of the afferent systems that synapse on cells in the SI. GABAergic and enkephalinergic systems have an inhibitory influence, glutamatergic systems have an excitatory input, while adrenergic, dopaminergic, and serotonergic neurotransmitter systems apparently have no influence. The physiological importance of these inputs remains to be determined.

REFERENCES

1. ATWEH, S., J. R. SIMON & M. J. KUHAR. 1976. Utilization of sodiumdependent high affinity choline uptake *in vitro* as a measure of the activity of cholinergic neurons *in vivo*. Life Sci. **17:** 1535–1544.
2. LEHMANN, J., J. I. NAGY, S. ATMADJA & H. C. FIBIGER. 1980. The nucleus basalis magnocellularis: The origin of a cholinergic projection to the neocortex of the rat. Neurosci. **5:** 1161–1174.
3. WHITEHOUSE, P. J., D. L. PRICE, R. G. STRUBLE, J. T. COYLE & M. R. DELONG. 1981. Evidence for selective loss of cholinergic neurons in the nucleus basalis. Ann. Neurol. **10:** 122–126.

GABA Effect on Conditioned Reflex Responses in Teleost

J. IVANUŠ, A. OROSZ, M. OROSZ, AND LJ. RAKIĆ

Brain Research Laboratory
P. O. Box 80
81330 Kotor, Yugoslavia

INTRODUCTION

The effect of GABA upon the nervous system in general, and especially upon isolated structures (i.e. cell body, axon, dendrite, receptors etc.) has been intensely studied. Topical GABA application leads to an increase in the threshold of evoked potential responses of nervous cells and receptors, while it does not affect axonal conduction.[1] The main site of action is believed to be at the cell body and dendrite. The CNS GABA level is determined by the balance between formation (decarboxylation of glutamic acid) and utilization (transamination). During the latter, GABA is introduced into the Krebs cycle. An increase in GABA level leads to decreased CNS excitability with an increase in the convulsion-inducing threshold. On the other hand, decreased GABA level induces convulsions due to a lowered convulsion-inducing threshold.[2] The protective effect of GABA has been demonstrated in a number of experimental and clinical convulsive states.

GABA effects upon processes of higher nervous activity have been studied to a lesser extent. This is probably due to the impossibility of maintaining an increased or decreased GABA level in CNS long enough without affecting other CNS functions and because of the toxicity per se of substances that affect the GABA level.

The majority of researchers believes that GABA effects are a result of its generalized hyperpolarizing action and not its specific inhibitory action.[3] Iontophoretic application of GABA into the spinal and higher neural structure neurons supports this view, although a number of electrographical observations implicates marked inhibitory action.[4]

Consideration of influence of GABA on higher nervous activities is studied in the performance of conditioned reflex behaviors in teleosts.

MATERIAL AND METHODS

Experiments were carried out with 8–15 cm long teleost fish (*Serranus scriba*, CUV) from Kotor Bay. After being caught, fish were kept in a common fresh sea-water aquarium for 15 days prior to the experiments. The fish were fasted during the experiments. Prior to daily tests, the fish were transferred in plastic containers to a dark chamber where they received aeration through an aquarium vibrator. Experiments were carried out with relation to the observed diurnal rhythm in the active part of the day, i.e. from 5 PM to 11 PM in dark chamber. Tests were performed in a shuttle-box that was simplified and adapted according to the method applied by Bitterman in his gold fish laboratory,[5] and which was later modified by Agranoff.[7] This training box (FIGURE 1) was made of thin metal sheets painted with insulational

543

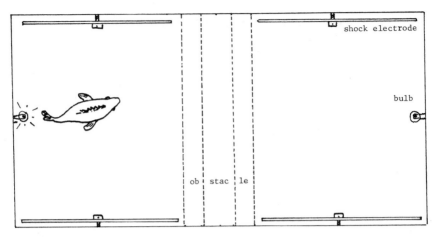

FIGURE 1. Avoidance shuttle box for fish.

enamel paint (dimensions: 18 cm wide, 36 cm long, and 18 cm deep). Across the middle the box were 6 cm high obstacles (6 cm wide at its base and 3 cm at its top). Thus the box was partitioned into two equally functional spaces that could be both illuminated with 15 W light bulbs situated outside the box at its opposite sides. Illumination was planned to be effected through the circular windows with 4 cm diameters situated in the middle of the wall at 0.5 cm height from the bottom. Each space had a pair of stainless steel electrodes fixed by the corresponding insulated screws, placed at the horizontal sides inside the box, thus covering the whole surface of 18 × 8 cm. The box was filled with sea-water such that the water level was 3–4 cm over the upper surface of the obstacle. Oxygen was supplied by means of an aquarium vibrator situated at the side of the obstacle upper surface in order to provide even aeration of both spaces.

One trial consisted of the following: a 20 sec long illumination being prolonged by a 20 sec paired illumination with electric shock and then followed by a 20 sec duration of

TABLE 1. Probability of GABA Effect on CR in Teleost

Group \ Treatment	Mean Number of Correct Response in 20 Trials ± SE		Difference Between Control and Experimental Group
	Control (Saline)	Experiment (GABA)	
I. Before injection	9 ± 2.00	11.66 ± 1.3	$p > 0.05$
II. After injection	7.00 ± 0.8	1.02 ± 0.6	$p < 0.01$
III. 24 hr after injection	9.37 ± 1.7	10.64 ± 1.7	$p > 0.05$
	48-HOUR PAUSE		
IV. Before injection	12.14 ± 1.0	12.43 ± 1.1	$p > 0.05$
V. After injection	7.15 ± 2.0	0.41 ± 1.1	$p < 0.01$
VI. 24 hr after injection	12.00 ± 1.2	9.66 ± 1.0	$p > 0.05$
Difference Between Control (Saline) and Experimental (GABA) Group	I–II	$p > 0.05$	$p < 0.01$
	I–III	$p < 0.05$	$p > 0.05$
	IV–V	$0.02 < p < 0.05$	$p < 0.01$
	IV–VI	$p > 0.05$	$p < 0.05$

$N = 40/2$. CR = conditioned defensive reflex.

darkness. After five such consecutive trials, a 3-min pause in the darkness was allowed. The shock was effected by means of AC current of 3 sequences, 4 V, 0.1 mA, 50 Hz with a duration of 20 sec. The whole cycle lasted five minutes and was repeated after three minutes for up to 20 trials. The fish were subjected to 20 daily trials and the reaction of an individual fish scored. To escape the shock, fish had to swim over the obstacle to the opposite compartment, which was kept dark.

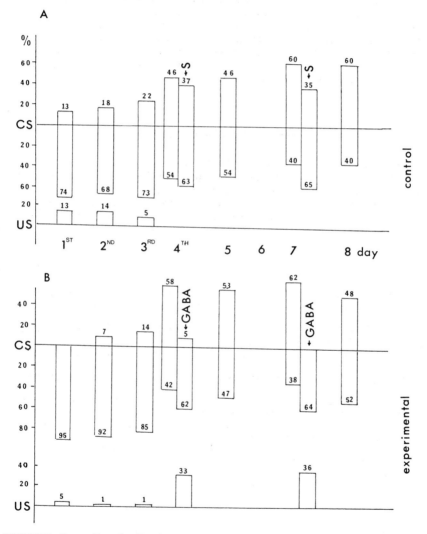

FIGURE 2. Score of learning (20 trials a day) in the course of eight days in teleost. (A) Response to CS (conditioned-light) and US (unconditioned-electric shock-stimuli) with repeated intracranial injection of 10 μl saline solution. $N = 20$. (B) Same procedure with 100 μg GABA (gamma-amino-butyric acid) in 10 μl saline solution. Graphs show significant depression effect on learning immediately after the injection, lasting over 24 hours. $N = 20$.

The first experimental group of fish were injected intracranially with 10 μl of 0.15 M NaCl solution containing 100 μg of GABA, while the other control group received the same volume of 0.15 M NaCl solution intracranially. The solution was injected using a Hamilton syringe and a No. 30 needle as follows: the fish were removed from the plastic pool and wrapped in gauze for easier handling. A trepan (hole) of 1 mm^2 at the level of saggital suture and posterior eye margin was performed by a dental drill. The syringe-needle was conducted through this opening under a 45° angle to a depth of 2 mm under the skull surface. Thus, a brain surface application was obtained in the region where the forebrain joins the optic tectum at the midline. After administration, the skull opening was closed by bone wax (W-30, Ethicon Inc.). The advantage of this method is in a secure closing by trepanation-made communication between outer medial line and intracranial space, and in the possibility of its easy removal in case a new injection is necessary. Two experimental groups of fish (in the course of three days) underwent 20 trials daily starting immediately after intracranial injection procedure.

RESULTS AND DISCUSSION

The results obtained (TABLES 1 and FIGURE 2) demonstrate that GABA suppresses positive conditioned reflex behavior in fish. Its application is followed by a decrease in the percentage of correct responses of shuttle-box–trained fish. The short duration of this suppressive effect is most likely related to its hyperpolarizing effect, which leads to decrease of nerve cell responsivenes to external stimuli and their consequent behavioral reaction.

REFERENCES

1. ROBERTS, E. 1962. Gamma-amino-butyric acid and neuronal function in ultrastructure and metabolism of the nervous system. Ass. Res. Nerv. Ment. Dis. **40:** 288–299.
2. EIDELBERG, E., C. F. BAXTER, E. ROBERTS, C. A. SALIDAS & J. D. FRENCH. 1959. Anticonvulsant properties of hydroxylamine and elevation of cerebral gamma-amino-butyric acid in cat. Proc. Soc. Exp. Biol. Med. **101:** 815–817.
3. KUFFLER, S. W. & C. EDWARDS. 1958. Physiology and pharmacology of the crayfish "stretch receptor." J. Neurophysiol. **21:** 589.
4. KRNJEVIC, K. 1964. Micro-iontophoretic studies on cortical neurons. Int. Rev. Neurobiol. **7:** 41–98.
5. HORNER, J. L., N. LONGO & M. E. BITTERMAN. 1961. A shuttle-box for fish and a cortical circuit of general applicability. Am. J. Psychol. **74:** 114–120.
6. DAVIS, R. E., P. J. BRIGHT & B. W. AGRANOFF. 1965. Effect of ESC and puromycin on memory in goldfish. J. Comp. Physiol. Psychol. **60:** 162–166.
7. AGRANOFF, B. W. & P. D. KLINGER. 1964. Puromycin effect on memory fixation in the goldfish. Science **146:** 952–953.

Index of Contributors

Subject Index